Drew Heywood's Windows® 2000 Network Services

Drew Heywood

201 West 103rd St., Indianapolis, Indiana, 46290 USA

Drew Heywood's Windows® 2000 Network Services

International Standard Book Number: 0-672-31741-9

Library of Congress Catalog Card Number: 99-63534

Printed in the United States of America

First Printing: February 2001

04   03   02   01   4   3   2   1

Trademarks

Warning and Disclaimer

ASSOCIATE PUBLISHER
Jeff Koch

EXECUTIVE EDITOR
Patrick Terrance Neal

ACQUISITIONS EDITOR
Gretchen Ganser

DEVELOPMENT EDITOR
Songlin Qiu

MANAGING EDITOR
Matt Purcell

PROJECT EDITOR
George E. Nedeff

COPY EDITOR
Kim Cofer

INDEXER
Sandra Henselmeier

PROOFREADER
Matt Wynalda

TECHNICAL EDITOR
Thomas Hielsberg

TEAM COORDINATOR
Vicki Harding

MEDIA DEVELOPER
J.G. Moore

INTERIOR DESIGNER
Gary Adair

COVER DESIGNER
Aren Howell

Overview

Contents

About the Author

Drew wanted to be a glamorous movie star, and but for a paucity of good looks and talent he might have succeeded. In 1979, informed during a late-night party that Hollywood talent scouts often frequented Bloomington, Indiana, Drew went to graduate school at Indiana University, meanwhile buying an Apple II so that he could write his Best Actor acceptance speech. Unaccountably, the talent scouts missed him, but the computer remained, and he had to go to work to pay for it. Misunderstanding what the entertainment business means by "networking," Drew started stringing wires between computers and the rest is history. For the past fifteen years or so, he's spent most of his time making computers communicate using NetWare and Windows. In the early nineties, he started writing books about networking topics. Dozens and dozens of Drew's fans will recognize him as the author of *Inside Windows NT Server 4* and *Networking with Microsoft TCP/IP*.

While not frustrating himself as an author, Drew enjoys brushing his cats, playing the piano (badly), watching films that unaccountably don't star himself, and enjoying the company of his family. He lives with his wife Blythe (who hasn't left him yet despite the limitless excuses afforded an author's spouse), their two-year old daughter Camille (who just figured out how to get into the pantry for cookies), and a sixteen year old son (about whom anything humorous Drew might say would probably be taken as the truth.) But he'd give it all up if the right film offer came along.

Drew Heywood (MCSE) is the best-selling author of a variety of networking books including *Inside Windows NT Server* and *Networking with Microsoft TCP/IP* from New Riders Publishing. Drew's extensive networking experience, his clear writing, and his strong teaching skills make him uniquely qualified to explain the intricacies of Windows 2000 network services.

About the Guest Author

Zubair Ahmad (MCSE, MCT, MCP+I, CNA, A+, CTT) works as a trainer and consultant in Seattle, Washington and has written extensively on Microsoft products for several years. He reviews technical books and articles for various publishers. He is known worldwide for his articles on Windows NT/2000, and has written as a contributing editor and online columnist for Windows 2000 Magazine. Zubair is a Microsoft EST endorsed trainer. In addition to writing monthly columns for Microsoft TechNet, he has been involved in writing Windows 2000 exam questions for Microsoft.

Zubair holds a degree in Computer Information Systems. He also holds a Bachelor of Science (B.S.) in Aeronautics and Astronautics Engineering, and a B.S. in Mathematics. He specializes in design, implementation, and engineering of enterprise network services. He speaks publicly at technical seminars and conferences.

About the Technical Editor

Thomas Hielsberg is currently a Senior Network Consultant for a small consulting company, Netropy Inc., which is based in Minneapolis, Minnesota. He has been working in the information technology field for over a decade and maintains several certifications, including MCSE, MCDBA, MCNE, CCNA, and CCDA. Thomas specializes in providing directory server, network management, network security, and network performance assessment services for his clients.

Dedication

For Camille. I get less work done now that you're around, but it's worth the distraction.

—Drew Heywood

Acknowledgments

Given that I am forced to work within my all too limiting limitations, I need a lot of help to turn an outline into a book. Insofar as this tome arrives in your hands with its i's dotted and its t's crossed, I owe a considerable debt to the following people:

- To Chris Denny, for having the faith in me that got the project started, to Gretchen Ganser for keeping things going, and to Terry Neal for wrapping things up.

- To Songlin Qiu, whose keen eyes and tenacity intercepted more errors than I would care to mention and who was, I am grateful to say, able to work with me for the duration of the project.

- To Elizabeth Finney, Katie Robinson, Kim Cofer, and George Nedeff (in no particular order—you were all great to work with) for doing all that you did to keep the work flowing and the results polished.

- To Thomas Hielsberg for an attentive technical edit and for many excellent suggestions.

- And finally, to my wife Blythe, for putting up with the way I get whenever a book is in progress.

—Drew Heywood

Tell Us What You Think!

As the reader of this book, *you* are our most important critic and commentator. We value your opinion and want to know what we're doing right, what we could do better, what areas you'd like to see us publish in, and any other words of wisdom you're willing to pass our way.

As an Associate Publisher for Sams Publishing, I welcome your comments. You can fax, email, or write me directly to let me know what you did or didn't like about this book—as well as what we can do to make our books stronger.

Please note that I cannot help you with technical problems related to the topic of this book, and that due to the high volume of mail I receive, I might not be able to reply to every message.

When you write, please be sure to include this book's title and author as well as your name and phone or fax number. I will carefully review your comments and share them with the author and editors who worked on the book.

Fax: 317-581-4770

Email: feedback@samspublishing.com

Mail: Jeff Koch
Associate Publisher
Sams Publishing
201 West 103rd Street
Indianapolis, IN 46290 USA

Introduction

Windows 2000 is not so much the next generation of Windows NT as it is an entirely new operating system that happens to be backward-compatible with earlier Windows versions. As I prepared this book, I was amazed at the amount of material I was unable to carry over from my books on Windows NT Server. It isn't simply that the dialog boxes have changed, or that MMC is now the management interface for most services. Enhancements, both subtle and profound, are everywhere. Old features have been enhanced, and new capabilities practically leap out of the dialog boxes.

If you've come to Windows 2000 from a Windows NT background, your learning experience is a mixed bag. Because Windows 2000 supports almost every feature that's offered by Windows NT 4, and because most services interoperate with their predecessors, very little of the theory and knowledge you have accumulated has become obsolete. You will have to deal with a lot of new features and ways of doing things, however.

Active Directory is at the heart of many of the changes you will encounter. At its core, Active Directory is a hierarchical database that has places to describe nearly everything that has network-wide impact. Because every domain controller has a copy of the Active Directory database for its domain, the simple act of storing something in Active Directory ensures that it will be available wherever it is needed, a capability with profound implications. Microsoft rethought many processes to take advantage of Active Directory, and you will see several examples in this book, such as the introduction of Active Directory–integrated zones in DNS, which we'll discuss in Chapter 3.

Another fundamental change in Windows 2000 is a total migration of native network services to TCP/IP. Windows 2000 network communication is based almost entirely on protocols that are standardized for use on the Internet. Designed from the beginning for use on wide area networks, TCP/IP protocols provide excellent functionality, performance, and robustness and are without peers in wide-area distributed computing. And, because Internet protocols are publicly standardized, license free, and widely supported, Windows 2000 interoperates quite effectively with non-Microsoft products.

There is a downside to this TCP/IP-everywhere approach. You can't do much of anything with Windows 2000 Server unless you know how to plan, configure, and manage a TCP/IP network. But that (May I have a drum roll, please?) is where this book comes to the rescue. (That sound you hear is a cheesy little Windows "Ta da!") This book is your guide to the art of Windows 2000 networking.

Did I Do Anything Different with This Book?

"Drew," you say, "There are lots of books on Windows 2000. What, if anything, makes yours special?" To begin with, I try very hard not only to cover the right topics but also to cover those topics in considerable depth, augmented with procedures for every task that needs to be performed. While doing so, I try to keep a broad spectrum of administrators in mind, providing basic information that ensures beginners won't get lost without neglecting the more advanced concerns of experienced administrators.

When I was writing my books on Windows NT Server 4, I felt I could do a pretty good job of covering the most important administrative tasks in a single volume, although I did need a separate volume to thoroughly cover TCP/IP. But when I began to work on an outline for a book on Windows 2000 Server administration, I reached the conclusion that any all-in-one book that I could be satisfied with would be far too big to fit between two covers. It gets really expensive to bind books that have more than about 1600 pages, and unless you are happy to read lots of itty-bitty type on very thin paper, 1600 pages isn't enough to do Windows 2000 Server justice. Windows 2000 is simply too vast for one-volume coverage, unless you're satisfied with superficial discussion.

I've encountered many Windows 2000 books that mention a topic but provide limited or no procedural guidance. As you try to learn something you run into gaping holes: tasks that you have to perform but are missed, answers to questions you will almost certainly ask, discussion of other topics that you must know about in order to tackle the subject at hand. I have tried to locate and fill as many of those holes as I can.

On the other hand, it's easy for authors to slip off into discussions that are of great interest to developers of network software and analysts but have little practical value to most network administrators. Almost every chapter in this book has a theory section, but I try not to wander deeper or further afield than a practical network administrator requires. If I get wrapped up in theory it is usually because the discussion is related to configuration options that you'll be encountering in the procedures. Take IPsec, for example. In Chapter 11, there's a lot of discussion about the Internet Key Exchange (IKE), which issues and renews keys used to implement IP security. You might think that IKE is a rather arcane topic, but if you don't understand how IKE manages keys, there are several configuration settings you won't have a clue about. There's a lot I could have added to the discussion about IKE, but it wouldn't have made you a better administrator of IPSec on Windows 2000. I've tried to cover things in a spirit of aggressive moderation. (Besides, saying too much provides me with the perfect opportunity to make a fool of myself. Oh, I have already? Oops.)

Is This Book for You?

"OK," you say, "Your book is the best thing since the invention of the Salad Shooter. But should I plunk down my hard-earned money for this thing?" Of course you should! (Hey, I've gotta eat!) But seriously, folks. Of course you should. Wait, I just said that, and you're not buying it, are you? OK, let's try a little persuasion.

My target audience is, of course, Windows 2000 network administrators, (Duh!) whom I, after much thought, have divided into the clever categories of beginners and non-beginners. (I'm omitting a third level: god-like extreme non-beginners. But hey! If you're that good, I'll be the one reading *your* book.)

When I use the term "beginner" in terms of this book, I am emphatically not saying that this book is written for a complete Windows newbie. I have to make some assumptions or the book would need to be an encyclopedia. My assumptions for beginners are

- You aren't a Windows novice so that I don't need to tell you to press the Next key at every step in a wizard and you can distinguish between the left and right buttons on a mouse. I'm going to assume that I can leave some things out of my discussion that anyone with some solid experience on a recent version of Windows will already understand.

- You have another source for learning Windows 2000 administration. For example, I don't tell you how to create user accounts or groups, share files and printers, or assign rights and permissions. You'll need to know that stuff to perform some of the tasks I discuss, but I expect the information to come from elsewhere.

When a network-related topic goes beyond basics, however, I do get involved. For example, in Chapter 4, I discuss sites in some depth because sites only become important when a network grows to significant scale. In the same chapter, I discuss Active Directory tree design because it is so intimately entwined with the Domain Name System. I've done my best to anticipate the kinds of skills that you won't get enough of in an all-in-one Windows 2000 Server administration book so that I can fill in the gaps here.

Almost every chapter consists of two parts: theory and practice. The theory section explains how a service works and how to plan an implementation of the service. The practice section consists of explicit procedures for doing all the important tasks that an administrator must perform. These procedures are broken up into individual sections so that you can easily locate the procedure you need in the table of contents.

For administrators with more advanced networking skills, I've tried to make it easy for you to find the material you need at the moment. Discussion is oriented around tasks to be performed, and everything is extensively cross-referenced. I have tried very hard to make it possible for advanced readers to find the information they need as efficiently as possible.

In summary, I've tried to make this book relevant to a broad spectrum of network administrators, making it easy for beginners to progress while making it easy for experienced administrators to skip to material that targets their particular concerns.

What Do You Need to Perform the Tasks in This Book?

I urge you to experiment on a test network before you apply anything to a production environment. Some mistakes can really screw things up, so make your mistakes where they cost time but little money.

You can learn a lot with just two computers: One to use as a server and one to use as a client. There are lots of functions you can't test without two servers, though. If one of the computers has the drive space to dual-boot Windows 2000 Professional and Windows 2000 Server, your capabilities are greatly expanded. It is possible with care to install both Windows 2000 versions with room to spare on a one gig hard drive. If you're short on space, I recommend you put Windows 2000 Server on both machines. If it isn't configured as a domain controller, Windows 2000 Server functions very much like Windows 2000 Professional from a network client standpoint.

A few functions require three or more servers to implement. If you want to set up a VPN as described in Chapter 11, you can either use two Internet connections addressed from different address ranges (which probably requires connections through two ISPs), or you need to simulate the presence of the Internet using a server that has two interfaces addressed from different address ranges and is configured to route traffic between the two "remote" networks.

For my testbed, I have three Windows 2000 servers, each equipped with two network adapters. One of these lab computers can be dual-booted to Windows 2000 Professional. I also have my production servers along with all the computers in my house networked so that I can call on them as clients. All this enables me to experiment with scenarios such as the one depicted in Figures 7.8–7.10. I'd love to have a lot more lab servers, but who wants all those fans in one's office? Besides, three servers along with a couple of client computers appears to be the "most bang for the buck" configuration. I've written a dozen networking books with the setup I've described.

I can hear you now. "Five computers? Just to experiment? My boss would hit the ceiling if I asked him for that." Fortunately, they don't have to be state-of-the-art or even high-performance boxes. When I upgraded my lab for Windows 2000, I settled on 350MHz Pentium III processors (which at the time had the best performance/price ratio) with 128 MB of RAM. By the standards of late in the year 2000, these computers are abysmally slow. But you know what? If I don't try to run everything on them at one time they do just fine. I'll add memory and faster hard drives before I touch the CPUs. It isn't until you start loading the servers up with lots of clients and network traffic that Windows 2000 begins to lust uncontrollably for expensive server hardware.

You'll probably get the best deal if you build the computers yourself. Servers don't need fast processors or frills. You can live without sound cards, and SVGA video is quite adequate. Any modem that can handle, say, 28.8Kbps will do when testing dial-up networking. Hard drives as small as 600 MB or so are adequate for experimentation, and EIDE drives are quite adequate unless you want to experiment with server clustering, which is not a major topic in the book. Lots of vendors offer inexpensive motherboards that work fine with Windows 2000. At a minimum I recommend 300MHz CPUs with 128 MB minimum RAM, but slower CPUs will serve.

For video, you can, in a pinch, get by with 800×600 pixel resolution, although you'll do a lot of scrolling unless resolution is at least 1024×768 or better. The best way to work with multiple computers is to hook them to a console switch so that they can share a monitor, keyboard, and mouse.

Do you need to use computer hardware from the Windows 2000 Hardware Compatibility List? In a production environment where servers are under stress, I'd say, "Yes." Molehills that may not matter in a lab become mountains when traffic hits production levels. Your first line of offense is to select tested hardware. In a lab, however, you'd be surprised what you can get away with.

Of course, you also need network adapters, hubs, and cables, but $40 five-port hubs from an office supply store are more than adequate. You can probably work with $20 Ethernet adapters, but you'll hate it if they aren't Plug-and-Play compatible. Of course, you need to have Windows 2000 drivers for whatever cards you use. Test one card before you break the shrink-wrap on all the boxes. Then, because some cheap network cards don't work well with routers, install two cards and test routing support. Obtain at least two hubs and, preferably, three or four. A good source for affordable Ethernet cables and other network components is Micro Warehouse (warehouse.com).

The bottom line? If you're experimenting at home, two computers and a hub let you perform many of the processes we'll examine. More, bigger, and faster is nicer, of course, but don't let a tight budget stop you from getting started.

You need at least one Windows 2000 Server license, of course, which unfortunately isn't cheap. Almost everything in the book can be done with Windows 2000 Server. The Windows 2000 Advanced and Datacenter Server releases are required for server clustering, but that topic is addressed only at the end of Chapter 5. As I write, the Microsoft Web site offers a 120-day evaluation version of Windows 2000 Advanced Server. See `www.microsoft.com/windows2000` to see what's available.

One way to get a multi-server license is to subscribe to Microsoft DeveloperNet. At $2,000 and up, it's not cheap, but it does set you up with copies of almost every bit of software Microsoft offers with a license that permits you to install it on multiple computers for development purposes. The license emphatically does not permit production use.

Conventions in the Book

I've used several typesetting conventions in this book:

- **Bold** text is used for field and button names. The use of bold type makes it easier to see where a long field name ends and regular text resumes.
- **Bold** is also used to identify commands that are entered by the user, particularly when showing the results of a command-line dialog.
- `Monospace` is used for data that you might enter or select. An example of text that might be entered in a dialog box field will be shown in monospace type, as will a selection that might be made from a pull-down menu.
- `Monospace` is also used to typeset dialogs that are generated at the command prompt.

What's on the Web Site?

Finally, let me mention that I've put the Network Monitor capture files that I worked with in Chapter 2 on the Web. You can visit `www.samspublishing.com` and search for the *Drew Heywood's Windows 2000 Network Services* page by ISBN, title, or author or you can go directly to the page by entering the following URL: `http://www.mcp.com/sams/detail_sams.cfm?item=0672317419`.

You will also find a Bonus Chapter on Microsoft's Internet Security and Acceleration Server. This firewall product is the Windows 2000 replacement for the Windows NT 4 Proxy Server. It's an interesting and valuable product and I think you'll find the Bonus Chapter to be a useful extension of this book.

Finally, you will find a handy-dandy table for converting decimal, binary, and hexadicamal numbers as well as an extensive glossary for the terms included in this book.

Thanks

If I haven't scared you away with bad humor, and by some miracle you're still with me, thanks for hanging in. I've tried to write the book I would have liked to buy when I started to work with Windows 2000 Server, and I sincerely hope it meets your needs as well.

The tour's at an end. Now buy the book, already! My cat needs orthodontry work, and you wouldn't want to be cruel to animals, would you? (Feeling guilty yet?)

Installation: Planning and Execution

IN THIS CHAPTER

Compared to Windows NT, Windows 2000 Server neatly inverts the relationship between planning for installation and the installation procedure itself. The mechanics of installing Windows 2000 Server are practically child's play. Most of the decisions are automated and most of those that remain are often self-explanatory.

Part of the reason software installation is so easy is that most of the configuration procedures are performed after the server software is running. Active Directory is utterly dependent on TCP/IP, and unless you are not planning to implement Active Directory, which is the single most important reason for deploying Windows 2000 Server, you will need to configure a TCP/IP network during the first stages of network configuration. Consequently, you will need to plan a TCP/IP infrastructure—including addressing, naming, and possibly routing—before you even start the Windows 2000 Server setup process. Procedures that could often be deferred with Windows NT now become up-front concerns.

Consequently, you need to learn a lot about both TCP/IP and Active Directory before you boot the installation CD-ROM and begin to configure your first server. You will find all the information you need to implement a TCP/IP network in this book. We'll start with basic skills, including planning concerns and a road map that will enable you to become an able Windows 2000 network administrator.

Then we'll look at some of the tools you'll use throughout this book to install network components, configure network connections, and use the many tools that are required to administer the network components of Windows 2000 Server.

> **NOTE**
>
> As I mentioned in the introduction, Windows 2000 is a vast product that resists being discussed in a single volume. I am forced to assume, therefore, that some of the skills required for this book will be learned through other means. To name just a few abilities, I assume you know how to manage user and group accounts, how to grant and revoke permissions to perform tasks or manipulate files and directories, and how to manage disk storage. These capabilities can be learned from a general-purpose Windows 2000 administration text or from the Help materials included with the product.

Planning for Installation

From a network management standpoint, there are two things you need to plan before installing Windows 2000 Server:

- The network's TCP/IP infrastructure
- Your plan for implementing Active Directory

Unless your network is very simple, don't try to wing it. There are some aspects of Active Directory that once established can be altered only with difficulty. A TCP/IP infrastructure can be redesigned down to the last detail, but Active Directory has to be done right from the beginning.

Because Active Directory depends on TCP/IP, we'll start by listing TCP/IP planning decisions first.

Planning TCP/IP

Very little happens automatically on a TCP/IP network. Everything, from computer addressing and names to routing, requires knowledgeable planning and execution. Here we'll develop a road map that will get you from a bunch of wires and network cards to a working TCP/IP network.

Addressing

If you've never set up a TCP/IP network, addressing will be your biggest hurdle. TCP/IP has its own scheme for identifying computers using so-called *IP addresses*. The method for addressing computers must be designed by an administrator, and considerable attention should be given to this topic before the first operating system is installed on the first computer.

IP addresses must be assigned to some computers manually, a practice that is referred to as *static addressing*. Most servers, for example, should have static addresses and for many server types static addressing is required.

For clients and some servers, however, there is a method for automatically assigning IP addresses, along with a variety of configuration parameters, called the Dynamic Host Configuration Protocol, or DHCP.

Naming

Naming doesn't happen automatically on TCP/IP networks either. You can't just assign a computer a NetBIOS name and have the name show up on the network. A service called the Domain Name System, or DNS, must be installed and configured with computer names; again, initially at least, a substantially manual process.

The names used by DNS, called *domain names*, are created in a hierarchical database called the *domain namespace*. The design of your network's domain namespace requires some forethought, particularly because it will be intimately associated with the structure of your Active Directory database.

Routing

If your network is extensive, particularly if it spans multiple buildings or sites, it will probably be subdivided into several smaller networks often called *subnets* by TCP/IP administrators. Communication between subnets is performed using *routers*, which are yet another thing that an administrator must configure manually. Networks with routers complicate IP addressing and consequently increase the need for pre-installation planning.

Planning the Directory

Active Directory is a distributed database that stores information about domains, computers, users, groups, and services. All this information is organized in a large tree, and part or all of that tree is stored on every Windows 2000 Server domain controller. In fact, that's the definition of a Windows 2000 domain controller: It stores a copy of Active Directory.

Because Active Directory comprehends the entire organization of your organization's Windows 2000 network, it is a lot more complex than the domain model that you may be familiar with from Windows NT. Every part of your network relates in some way to every other part through Active Directory.

That can make for a huge database, and surely you won't be surprised by the observation that huge databases don't just happen—they have to be designed. And before you can begin to deploy Windows 2000 Server and Active Directory, you need to have a pretty good idea how the database is going to be structured.

Active Directory works intimately with the Domain Name System. In fact, DNS is used to store all the computer names and service descriptions on which Windows 2000 servers and clients and servers depend. Gone is the Windows dependence on NetBIOS. Although NetBIOS is supported by Windows 2000 for the sake of supporting older versions of Windows, it isn't required. Eventually, when all of your computers have been upgraded to Windows 2000, you can turn off NetBIOS entirely.

From the beginning, however, you have to design a domain hierarchy that will meet your organization's needs for a long time. While the process will certainly grow simpler with time, at present it is very difficult to reorganize an Active Directory domain hierarchy once it is established.

Again, that means study and planning. You need to learn how Active Directory works and how it works with DNS. And you need to design a naming system that is flexible enough to meet your organization's needs now and reasonably far into the future.

A Learning and Planning Roadmap

Particularly if you are new to TCP/IP administration, you can't swallow all of the above topics in one gulp, so let's break the process down into small steps, which, not surprisingly, correspond to the next few chapters:

1. First learn how to use the essential tools discussed later in this chapter. You will return to them in nearly every chapter.

2. Then learn some basic TCP/IP theory by reading Chapter 2, "TCP/IP Protocol Concepts." You'll learn enough about how TCP/IP works to manage the services discussed in later chapters, and you'll learn a lot about IP addressing. Don't even think about moving on until you're fairly comfortable with the addressing material in this chapter.

3. Next, study Chapter 3, "The Domain Name System." Active Directory can't operate without DNS, so you can't postpone DNS implementation. At first, concentrate on the theory of designing a DNS namespace. Later, when you actually need to manage a DNS server, return to the second half of the chapter to learn the management procedures.

4. Now you are ready to examine Chapter 4, "Active Directory Concepts," where you will learn some of the theory of Active Directory operation and see how Active Directory and DNS interrelate. The single most important thing to be concerned with here is the design of the DNS namespace to support Active Directory. Take the time to plan your Active Directory domain structure and to design the domain or domains you will deploy in DNS.

5. At this point, you can begin to install Windows 2000 Server. Start simply and by all means don't try to upgrade a working Windows NT network until you have quite a bit of experience in a test network environment. If your organization can't set aside three or four computers as test servers and clients, don't even think about deploying Windows 2000 Server. There are lots of subtleties that can only be learned by experimentation.

6. If you are upgrading an existing network, I suggest you copy at least some of the servers to a separate test network. Don't do your first upgrades on production servers.

7. Now you can investigate network enhancements. For example:

   - Study Chapter 5, "Dynamic Host Configuration Protocol," and learn how to automate address assignment and computer configuration.

   - Study Chapter 7, "Routing with Routing and Remote Access Service," to learn how to extend your network.

If you get to the end of the above road map, you can consider yourself a qualified, if novice, Windows 2000 Server network administrator. There's lots of advanced material in the remaining chapters, such as dial-up communication and network security, but get through the basics before you worry about any of that stuff.

Identifying a Windows 2000 Computer

A networked Windows 2000 computer is identified by two names:

- A **computer name** uniquely identifies an individual computer.
- A **domain name** is the name of the domain that the computer has joined.

In most cases, Windows 2000 computers will be members of Active Directory domains. The organization for Active Directory domains is hierarchical, based on the hierarchical structure of domains in DNS. In fact, an Active Directory domain will always have a corresponding domain in DNS that has the same name. Thus, Active Directory domain names often look like domain names used on the Internet, such as PSEUDO-CORP.COM, which corresponds to a DNS domain named pseudo-corp.com. (Neither Active Directory nor DNS names are case sensitive, but my convention in this book is to express DNS names in lowercase to distinguish them from Active Directory names, which I display in uppercase.)

NOTE

Windows 2000 computers can function in two Windows name environments. The domain-based Active Directory recognizes domain boundaries and requires only that computer names be unique within their own domains.

NetBIOS, however, does not recognize domains. NetBIOS constitutes a "flat" database in that all NetBIOS names operating on the network are stored in the same container. Consequently, NetBIOS names, when used, must be globally unique. That is, the same NetBIOS name cannot be used to identify two computers even if the computers occupy different domains.

If a network consists entirely of Windows 2000 computers, it is possible to disable support for NetBIOS names entirely. This reduces network traffic and reduces name restrictions.

A computer that is a member of an Active Directory domain has a *qualified* name that consists of its computer name appended to its domain name. For example, the computer DREW in the domain PSEUDO-CORP.COM has the qualified name DREW.PSEUDO-CORP.COM.

A computer name is always specified when Windows 2000 is installed on a computer. In some cases, a computer will join a domain during installation and will have a domain name from the beginning. Both names can be modified after installation.

To display a computer's name and domain, open the System applet in the Control Panel and open the **Network Identification** tab, shown in Figure 1.1.

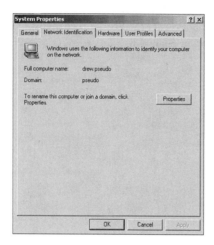

FIGURE 1.1

The Network Identification tab in the System applet displays the computer's name and domain name.

To change the computer name or domain membership, click **Properties** to open the **Identification Changes** dialog box shown in Figure 1.2. The dialog box has the following fields:

- **Computer name.** The computer name can usually be changed, although this should be done with caution, particularly on computers that are sharing files and printers. Shared files and printers are identified by the name of the computer that is sharing the resource, and changing the name will invalidate mappings established by clients. If the name is changed while clients are actively using shared resources, sharing will be interrupted.

- **Domain.** Select this radio button if the computer will be a member of a domain. Enter a domain name to join a domain, or edit the domain name to change domains. When joining an existing domain, you will need to specify the name and password for a user account that has administrator permissions in the target domain. To remove a computer from all domains, change its membership to **Workgroup**. The computer must be able to communicate with at least one Windows 2000 domain controller for the domain it will be joining.

- **Workgroup.** Select this radio button if the computer will be a member of a Windows workgroup. Enter a workgroup name to join a workgroup, or edit the name to change names.

You must be an administrator on the local computer to modify names or memberships. The computer must be restarted whenever its membership changes. (This is one of the very few instances in which a configuration change requires restarting a Windows 2000 computer.)

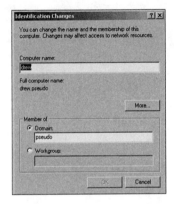

FIGURE 1.2
Computer names, as well as domain and workgroup memberships, can usually be changed.

In some situations, a computer's name and/or membership cannot be changed. For example:

- If a computer is a domain controller for an Active Directory domain, its membership cannot be modified unless it is first demoted to a server. See Chapter 4 for the procedures used to promote servers to domain controllers and to demote domain controllers to servers.
- Neither the name nor the membership can be changed for a server that is running the Certification Services (discussed in Chapter 10) unless the service is uninstalled.

Windows 2000 Installation and Network Services

As I mentioned earlier, we won't do a walkthrough of the Windows 2000 installation process because it's pretty self-explanatory. A complete discussion of the options, which involves concerns such as hard disks and storage volumes, is more properly the subject of a general Windows 2000 administration course. I'm only mentioning the subject here because network configuration is so critical to the installation process.

During installation, Windows 2000 attempts to detect any network adapters that are installed in the computer. These adapters are automatically configured to use TCP/IP with automatic IP address assignment. You can override the defaults, however, and in most cases will want to do so. When the **Networking Settings** dialog box is displayed during installation, you have two choices for each adapter:

- **Typical.** The adapter will be configured to use DHCP to obtain an IP address and configuration settings. If a DHCP server is already in operation on the network, that choice is appropriate for clients, but it is seldom the appropriate choice for a server. In nearly all cases, servers should be configured with fixed IP addresses. If this option is chosen and a DHCP server is unavailable, the computer is assigned IP addresses using Automatic Private IP Addressing. The addresses that are assigned are seldom usable on anything but a very simple network.

- **Custom.** If you select this option, you can configure all properties of the interface using dialog boxes very similar to the dialog boxes discussed in the section "Configuring Local Area Network Connections," which appears next in this chapter. Use this option to configure servers and other devices that require static IP addresses.

When you install Windows 2000, each of the adapters in your computer is detected and assigned an initial configuration. On computers with multiple network adapters, dialog boxes will be presented that enable you to configure each adapter in turn. Unfortunately, it is nearly impossible to determine which dialog boxes are configuring a particular adapter until after installation is complete and Windows 2000 is restarted. Be prepared to test the adapters and ensure that you have assigned the desired properties to each adapter.

Unlike Windows NT, Windows 2000 Server domain controllers are configured after installation of the operating system. If a server is to be a domain controller, you must use the DCPROMO utility to install Active Directory and add the new domain controller to the domain. The procedures for using DCPROMO are covered in Chapter 4.

After network communication is established and, if desired, the server has been upgraded to a domain controller, you will need to configure the network services that the server will support. These network services constitute the bulk of the material in this book. We'll get to them soon, but before we do, I want to spend some time on utilities and support resources that should be understood by every Windows 2000 administrator.

Configuring Local Area Network Connections

A server, by definition, needs to communicate with the clients that use its services. And a Windows 2000 Server that can't communicate without TCP/IP is a lobotomized Windows 2000 Server.

Windows NT and other versions of Windows make a distinction between dial-up and network communication, configuring each communication method through a different utility. Windows 2000, however, does not distinguish between dial-up and network communication. In Windows 2000 terminology, a *connection* is any channel through which the computer communicates. A connection may extend through a network card or a modem. But whatever the physical nature of the communication channel, it is a connection.

Because a connection is a connection, both network and dial-up connections are configured in one place: the new Network and Dial-Up Connections applet in the Control Panel. You will be using this applet throughout the book to configure and reconfigure connections, so I want to discuss it here, in the first chapter.

We'll be examining the configuration of dial-up connections in Chapter 8, "Supporting Dial-Up Connections with Routing and Remote Access Service." Here, we're going to focus on the configuration of connections to local area networks.

Using Network and Dial-Up Connections

Figure 1.3 shows the **Network and Dial-up Connections** window, which is opened from the Control Panel. Each network card is represented by an icon which is initially named **Local Area Connection** with a number added to distinguish icons for additional adapters. In the figure, the connection named **Local Area Connection 2** has failed, and its icon is marked with a red X.

FIGURE 1.3
The Network and Dial-Up Connections window with icons for two network cards.

TIP

The names of the icons in **Network and Dial-up Connections** have no functional significance and aren't particularly useful. These names pop up in several utilities, and it's useful to edit them so that they are a bit more meaningful. I like to change the icon names to the IP addresses of the connections. Then each interface has a unique name that clearly distinguishes it when it is referenced elsewhere.

If you are using network cards that Windows 2000 can detect, a Local Network Connection icon is created automatically for each installed adapter, either during Windows 2000 installation or during the Plug and Play setup process when the system is started. Frankly, considering the low cost of Plug and Play network adapters, I don't recommend that you mess around with any adapter that Windows 2000 can't detect and configure.

Connection Status

A nice improvement in Windows 2000 is the way it reports the status of each connection. As mentioned, each adapter that is detected by Windows 2000 is represented by an icon in **Network and Dial-Up Connections**. Each active connection has a **Status** dialog box, which can be displayed by double-clicking the icon. Figure 1.4 shows an example of a **Status** dialog box.

FIGURE 1.4

The Status dialog box for a network connection.

A connection that is enabled and is communicating with a network has a status of `Connected`. If the connection is inoperative for any reason, such as a disconnected cable, the **Status** dialog box cannot be opened.

In the properties for a connection, a **Show icon in taskbar when connected** option enables a highly desirable feature that causes an icon for each active connection to be displayed at the right end of the toolbar. This icon has several useful functions:

- It pops up a balloon that notifies you when the connection is broken. After the balloon is cleared, a red X on the icon reminds you of the connection's non-functional status.
- If you hover the mouse over the icon for a working connection, a balloon reports the numbers of bytes sent and received.
- If you double-click the icon, the connection's **Status** dialog box is displayed.

- You can disable or enable the connection by right-clicking the icon and choosing **Disable** or **Enable** from the context menu.
- You can open **Network and Dial-Up Connections** by right-clicking the icon and choosing the **Open** command from the context menu.

Connection Properties

You can modify the properties for any connection by opening the connection **Properties** dialog boxes using one of these techniques:

- Click the **Properties** button in the **Status** dialog box.
- Right-click the connection's icon to open a context menu and choose **Properties** in the context menu.

Figure 1.5 shows the **Connection Properties** dialog box, which has only two tabs. The **General** tab shown has the following properties:

- **Connect Using.** This field describes the network adapter that is associated with the connection. Click **Configure** to review or change the adapter configuration. See the next section, "Configuring the Network Adapter," for more information.
- **Components.** This box lists network components that are installed on the computer. See the section "Managing Connection Components" later in the chapter for more information.
- **Show icon in taskbar when connected.** This feature is discussed in the previous section, "Connection Status."

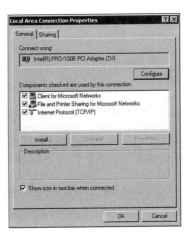

FIGURE 1.5

Properties for a connection.

NOTE

The **Sharing** tab is used to set up Internet Connection Sharing, a quick method of sharing a computer's network connection with other computers on a local network. See Chapter 8 for more information.

Configuring the Network Adapter

The **Network Adapter Properties** dialog box (see Figure 1.6) is accessed by clicking the **Configure** button in the **Connection Properties** dialog box (Figure 1.5). **Network Adapter Properties** reports the status of a network adapter, aids in troubleshooting, and supports adapter reconfiguration.

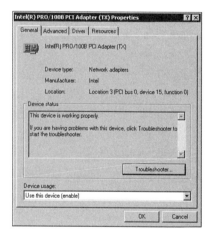

FIGURE 1.6
Network Adapter Properties: The General tab.

Network Adapter Properties: The General Tab

The primary function of the **General** tab, shown in Figure 1.6, is to report the status of the device and its driver. Two functions are available:

- Click **Troubleshooter** to open Help with a checklist for troubleshooting network adapters.

- Enable or disable the adapter by changing the setting in the **Device usage** field.

Network Adapter Properties: The Advanced Tab

The **Advanced** tab, shown in Figure 1.7, lists hardware characteristics of the adapter that can be configured. To change a setting, select an entry in the **Property** list and enter the new setting in the **Value** field. It is seldom necessary to modify these settings.

FIGURE 1.7

Network Adapter Properties: The Advanced tab.

Network Adapter Properties: The Driver Tab

The **Driver** tab, shown in Figure 1.8, has three buttons:

- **Driver Details.** This button opens the **Driver File Details** dialog box, which identifies the driver file that is being used along with the provider of the file and the version number.

- **Uninstall.** This button uninstalls the driver file. This might be done in preparation for removing a network adapter or in some troubleshooting procedures when a driver problem is suspected.

- **Update Driver.** This button starts the **Upgrade Device Driver Wizard**, which is used to install an updated version of the driver file.

Network Adapter Properties: The Resources Tab

The **Resources** tab, shown in Figure 1.9, reports the memory, interrupt, and other resources that are reserved for the adapter. Conflicts rarely occur with Plug and Play devices, but it may be necessary to intervene when older devices are in the configuration. Often, as in the case of the example, the entries on this tab cannot be modified.

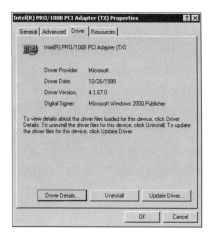

FIGURE 1.8

Network Adapter Properties: The Driver tab.

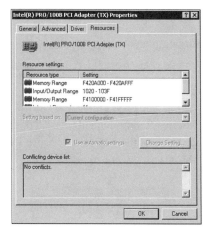

FIGURE 1.9

Network Adapter Properties: The Resources tab.

Managing Connection Components

Returning to the **Connection Properties** dialog box (Figure 1.5), we still need to discuss the **Components** list. Three components are installed by default in Windows 2000:

- **Client for Microsoft Networks.** This component enables the computer to authenticate and connect to Windows computers that are sharing resources. It should be enabled on connections that communicate with Windows networks, but can be disabled on connections that communicate only with non-Windows servers such as Web servers on the Internet.

- **File and Printer Sharing for Microsoft Networks.** This component enables Windows computers to share file and printer resources. In general, it should be enabled only on connections for which **Client for Microsoft Networks** is enabled, although it can be disabled on connections that are not used to share files or printers.

- **Internet Protocol (TCP/IP).** This is the Windows 2000 TCP/IP protocol stack, described in Chapter 2. It must be enabled on all Windows 2000 computers that are members of Active Directory domains.

A variety of network components can be added, removed, and configured from this list. After we discuss the method of adding components, we'll look at the procedures for configuring component properties.

Installing Connection Components

Click the **Install** button on the **General** tab to open the **Select Network Component Type** dialog box shown in Figure 1.10. To add a component, open the appropriate category. You then have two choices:

- Select a component category and click **Add**. Then select a component from the list and click **OK** to install a component that is included with Windows 2000. Some components are listed only if particular components have been installed previously.

- Click **Have Disk** and supply a vendor-provided disk to install a component that is not included with Windows 2000.

Of particular interest is the **Protocol** category. This is the category you choose to install support for AppleTalk, NWLink (Microsoft's implementation of IPX/SPX), and NetBEUI. There are also a few specialized drivers such as the Network Monitor Driver, which will be discussed in Chapter 12, "Managing and Monitoring Connections."

FIGURE 1.10

Network components are added from this dialog box.

Network components that are installed on a computer are added to the components lists of all local area network and dial-up connections. However, they are enabled individually on each connection. It is extremely common to enable different components on different connections.

For example, suppose a computer has a LAN connection to a Windows network and a WAN connection to the Internet. We would certainly want to enable the Microsoft client component on the LAN interface and possibly file and printer sharing as well, because those components enable the computer to communicate with other Windows computers.

But we would not want to enable the Microsoft client or file and printer sharing on the WAN connection. The Microsoft client is unnecessary on the WAN connection, and enabling file sharing on the WAN connection actually poses a security risk, creating an opening that might enable an intruder to gain access to the computer.

Configuring Component Properties

Many connection components are configurable through property pages. To open the property pages for a component, double-click the component, or select the component and click **Properties**. In the next few sections, we will look into the properties of three network components: **Internet Protocol (TCP/IP)**, **File and Print Sharing**, and **NWLink**.

Configuring the Internet Protocol Component

Of all the network components, the one we will be working with most closely in this book is Internet Protocol (TCP/IP). In fact, we'll be modifying properties of this component in nearly every chapter. So, before we get too far, let's look at this component in some detail.

You don't need to configure all the options to have a working TCP/IP connection. Some of the options are advanced, and you'll want to read the associated chapter before you worry about them. The minimum requirements for a TCP/IP connection on a Windows 2000 computer that uses Active Directory are an IP address, a subnet mask, and the address of at least one DNS server. Other properties are required only on a case-by-case basis.

The **Internet Protocol (TCP/IP) Properties** page is shown in Figure 1.11. The following properties are configured individually for each connection:

- **Obtain an IP address automatically.** Select this option if this connection will obtain an IP address and other configuration settings from a DHCP server, as described in Chapter 5.

- **Use the following IP address.** Select this option if this connection will be configured with static address properties. The following properties must be defined:

  - **IP address.** Enter the IP address (discussed in Chapter 2) for the connection in dotted-decimal form. This property is required for all statically configured connections.

  - **Subnet mask.** Enter the subnet mask in dotted-decimal form. An initial subnet mask is selected based on the class of the IP address that is entered. (Again, see Chapter 2.) This property is required for all statically configured connections.

- **Default gateway.** Enter the IP address of the default gateway (usually called a *router*) to be used by the connection. On computers with multiple LAN connections, specify a default gateway only on the connection that communicates directly with the subnet to which the router is connected. Leave the field blank on other LAN connections. (See Chapter 7 for information on default gateways.) This property is optional.

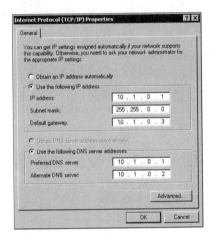

FIGURE 1.11

Internet Protocol Properties: The General dialog box.

Every Windows 2000 computer that is a member of an Active Directory domain must be configured with the IP address of a DNS server that can look up names in the domain. (See Chapter 3 for information about DNS.) This address can be specified in two ways:

- **Obtain DNS server address automatically.** This option can be selected only if **Obtain an IP address automatically** is enabled. When this option is selected, the client will attempt to obtain addresses of DNS servers from the DHCP server that issues an IP address to the connection.

- **Use the following DNS servers.** Select this option if DNS servers will be identified by static IP addresses. Two DNS servers can be specified:

  - **Preferred DNS server.** Enter the IP address, in dotted-decimal form, of the computer's primary DNS server. While this field is not required, many TCP/IP functions will fail if an available DNS server is not identified.

  - **Alternate DNS server.** Because DNS is so vital to the operation of Windows 2000 clients, a secondary DNS server should be configured and identified in this field.

All connections use the same list of DNS servers, and it is enough to specify DNS servers for one interface. When DNS server addresses are specified statically, the client does not accept DNS server addresses from DHCP. Suppose, for example, that a computer has two LAN connections: one is configured with static addresses, another obtains its IP address from DHCP. If the connection having a static IP address is configured with the addresses of DNS servers, those addresses will prevail over addresses that might be obtained from DHCP by the other connection.

Advanced TCP/IP Settings: The IP Settings Tab

Quite a few additional properties can be specified for a TCP/IP connection. Click the **Advanced** button in the **General** dialog box to open the **Advanced TCP/IP Settings** dialog box shown in Figure 1.12.

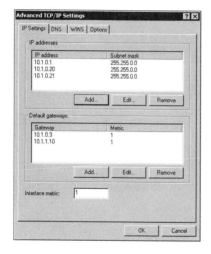

FIGURE 1.12
Advanced TCP/IP Settings: The IP Settings tab.

A TCP/IP connection can be configured with multiple IP addresses, a practice that is called *multi-homing*. These IP addresses can be added to the **IP Addresses** list on the **IP Settings** tab. Each entry is specified with an IP address and a subnet mask, both expressed in dotted-decimal form. The order in which IP addresses appear is not significant.

A TCP/IP computer can also be configured with multiple default gateways (routers), which may be used if the primary default gateway fails. Backup gateways can be added to the **Default gateways** list. Each entry includes a *metric* that defines the priority of that gateway. If a new default gateway must be selected, the gateway with the lowest metric is selected. (See Chapter 7 for more information about default gateways.)

The **Interface metric** specifies the cost of routing traffic through this interface. The metric is used to calculate the costs of routes, which are used to determine the most efficient route to a particular destination. The default interface metric is 1. See Chapter 7 for information about metrics and how they are used in routing tables.

Advanced TCP/IP Settings: The DNS Tab

The **DNS** tab is shown in Figure 1.13. Properties on this tab identify additional DNS servers the client may use, as well as the client's behavior with regard to DNS. See Chapter 3 for more information about DNS client and server behavior.

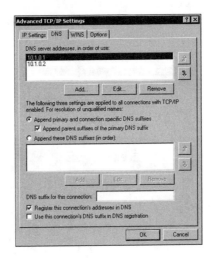

FIGURE 1.13

Advanced TCP/IP Settings: The DNS tab.

DNS Server Addresses

A client can be configured with the IP addresses of several DNS servers that are used as back-ups if the primary or secondary servers, specified on the **General** tab, are unavailable. These IP addresses are added to the **DNS server addresses, in order of use** list. The order in which addresses appear determines the order in which the client will attempt to use those DNS servers. To adjust the order, select an IP address and use the arrow buttons to move it up or down in the list.

Computer Names and Suffixes

I'm not going to discuss the remaining settings in the order in which they appear. Let's start by explaining the field **DNS suffix for this connection**. DNS names consist of two parts: a computer (also called a *host*) name, and a suffix, which is the name of the domain in which the computer's name is recorded. Consider a computer named drew.pseudo-corp.com. drew is the computer name and pseudo-corp.com is the suffix.

The computer name is the name that is assigned when Windows 2000 is installed. The computer's DNS suffix is the name of the Active Directory domain of which the computer is a member. The computer's name and domain membership can be modified on the **Network Identification** tab of the **System** applet in the Control Panel.

When a Windows 2000 computer joins an Active Directory domain, the computer's full name (more often called its *qualified name*) consists of its computer name appended to the domain name. If a computer named DREW is installed in an Active Directory domain named PSEUDO-CORP.COM, the computer is assigned the DNS name drew.pseudo-corp.com.

Each Windows 2000 computer is assigned a *primary DNS suffix* when it joins an Active Directory domain. This primary suffix is the same as the name of the Active Directory domain the computer has joined, and applies to all LAN connections. It is also the name of the DNS domain in which the computer's name is registered.

While all LAN connections on a computer share a primary name suffix, each connection can also have a *secondary DNS suffix*. This secondary DNS suffix is specified in the field **DNS suffix for this connection**.

Resolving Unqualified Names

An *unqualified name* is a DNS name that does not include the domain name suffix. For example, drew is an unqualified name. drew.pseudo-corp.com is a qualified name (also called a *fully qualified domain name* or an FQDN in DNS terminology).

Clients send queries to DNS when they wish to determine the address that is assigned to a computer having a particular name. This process of matching a name to an address is called *name resolution.* To query DNS, the client must send a qualified name so that DNS knows the domain it is to search for records pertaining to the computer name. If a process or user queries DNS without providing a fully qualified name, the client has several ways to construct candidate names.

One approach is to append the computer's primary DNS suffix to the computer name. For example, suppose the computer drew.pseudo-corp.com is asked to resolve the computer name blythe. It could start by constructing a qualified name by appending blythe to its primary DNS name, sending the name blythe.pseudo-corp.com to DNS.

Another approach is to use any secondary DNS suffixes that may be configured on the computer to construct qualified domain names.

A third approach is to consult a list of suffixes, constructing DNS queries for each suffix until DNS returns a positive response. Potentially, therefore, a query for the name blythe could be tried with many suffixes in the hope that the name will be found in one of the domains identified by the suffixes.

DNS name resolution behavior for unqualified names is configured by these settings on the **DNS** tab:

- **Append primary and connection specific DNS names.** If this setting is enabled, the client attempts to resolve unqualified names by using the primary DNS suffix as well as any secondary DNS suffixes defined on the computer's connections. When this option is selected, the following sub-option can be enabled.

  - **Append parent suffixes of the primary DNS suffixes.** Parent suffixes are the names of domains that are parents of this computer's primary domain. Suppose that the computer's primary DNS suffix is widgets.pseudo-corp.com. With this option enabled, a query for the unqualified name blythe would be conducted using the qualified names blythe.widgets.pseudo-corp.com, blythe.pseudo-corp.com, and blythe.com.

- **Append these DNS suffixes.** When this option is selected, only the suffixes included in the list will be used to resolve unqualified names. Add the desired suffixes to the list and use the arrow buttons to adjust their positions and determine the order in which each suffix should be tried.

Registering Connection Names in DNS

Windows 2000 network clients can automatically register themselves in the DNS database, a capability known as *dynamic DNS*. This is particularly useful for DHCP clients, whose IP addresses may change from time to time. Two settings determine whether and how the connection will be registered in DNS:

- **Register this connection's addresses in DNS.** If this option is enabled, the connection will register all IP addresses assigned to it using the computer's name and its primary name suffix (the domain name entered on the **Network Identification** tab of the **System** applet in the Control Panel). If this option is not enabled the computer is not registered using its primary DNS suffix.

- **Use this connection's DNS suffix in DNS registration.** If this option is enabled, the connection will register all IP addresses assigned to this connection using the computer's name and its secondary name suffix (as defined in the field **DNS suffix for this connection**). If this option is not enabled the computer is not registered using its secondary DNS suffix.

Advanced TCP/IP Settings: The WINS Tab

The **WINS** tab is shown in Figure 1.14. Windows computers that use NetBIOS names rely on the Windows Internet Name Service (WINS) to support naming on networks that incorporate routers. WINS is described in detail in Chapter 6.

Properties on this tab determine if and how the computer looks up NetBIOS names. These settings are available:

- **WINS addresses, in order of use.** To use WINS, a computer must be configured with the IP addresses of one or more WINS servers. After adding addresses to the list, use the arrow buttons to adjust the order in which the servers will be queried. All connections on the computer use the same list of WINS servers.

- **Enable LMHOSTS lookup.** LMHOSTS is a static text file that can be used to match NetBIOS names to IP addresses. On occasion, LMHOSTS files are used as a backup for WINS. If this option is enabled, the computer will consult a local LMHOSTS file to resolve names that cannot be found using other methods. If desired, an LMHOSTS file can be imported from a file located in local disk storage or in a drive that is mapped to a shared directory on another computer. This setting applies to all LAN connections that are configured to use TCP/IP. See Chapter 6 for information about LMHOSTS files.

- **Enable NetBIOS over TCP/IP.** Select this option to enable NetBIOS use on this connection.

- **Disable NetBIOS over TCP/IP.** Select this option to disable NetBIOS use on this connection.

- **Use NetBIOS setting from DHCP server.** Select this option if NetBIOS support for this connection is determined by settings obtained from DHCP. Use this option only for connections that are configured by DHCP.

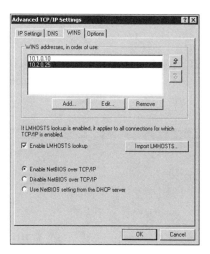

FIGURE 1.14
Advanced TCP/IP Settings: The WINS tab.

Advanced TCP/IP Settings: The Options Tab

The **Options** tab is shown in Figure 1.15. At first, only two options are present:

- **IP security.** This option is used to select a policy for using secure IP communication on this connection. See Chapter 11 for information about IP security.
- **TCP/IP filtering.** This option is used to configure filtering of TCP/IP protocols.

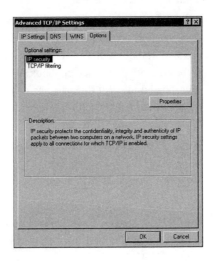

FIGURE 1.15

Advanced TCP/IP Settings: The Options tab.

Configuring TCP/IP Filtering

To configure filtering, select **TCP/IP filtering** and click **Properties** to open the **TCP/IP Filtering** dialog box, shown in Figure 1.16. Filters can be defined for the TCP, UDP, and IP protocols. See Chapter 2 for information about these protocols.

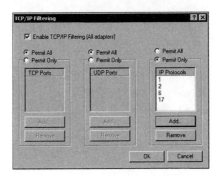

FIGURE 1.16

Configuring filtering for a connection.

Filtering can be used to permit all or select types of packets to be received or sent through this connection. TCP/IP filtering does not support filtering of packets in one direction only, nor does it support blocking of single protocols. For a more versatile filtering tool, examine the Internet Security and Acceleration Server, discussed in the Bonus Chapter available on the book's Web site.

For each category there are two options:

- **Permit All.** No packets are blocked for this category.
- **Permit Only.** All packets for this category are blocked unless they are specifically permitted.

When **Permit Only** is chosen, you must specify any packet types that are permitted. Packet types for TCP and UDP are identified by *port numbers*. Each process or application that uses TCP is identified by a unique port number. To allow packets for a process or application to cross the connection, the appropriate port number must be added to the list.

Packet types for IP are defined by protocol numbers. Like TCP and UDP ports, if **Permit Only** is enabled for IP, packets will be forwarded only if the appropriate protocol numbers are added to the list.

The **Permit Only** option is a bit dangerous. If it is enabled and no protocol numbers are specified, all TCP/IP activity on the connection ceases. On Windows 2000, that has almost the same effect as disabling the connection entirely. In most cases, the following protocol numbers should be included:

- 1 for the ICMP protocol
- 2 for the IGMP protocol (discussed in Chapter 7)
- 6 for the TCP protocol
- 17 for the UDP protocol

All of these protocols, as well as the use of protocol and port numbers, are described in Chapter 2.

Configuring the NWLink (IPX/SPX) Protocol Component

NWLink is often the easiest protocol to deploy on a Windows NT network. Windows 2000 provides NWLink, primarily to support interoperation with NetWare networks, but Active Directory cannot operate on a network that supports only NWLink. Consequently, NWLink will nearly always be configured as a secondary protocol on Windows 2000 computers.

NWLink has the virtue of being easily configured, particularly because it does not require manually assigned computer addresses. Figure 1.17 shows the settings dialog box for NWLink. Only two settings require configuration, but both require a bit of explanation.

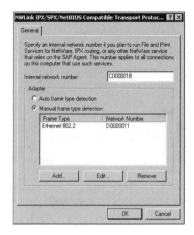

FIGURE 1.17

Configuring settings for NWLink.

Every IPX server is identified by a unique *internal network number*. As Chapter 7 explains, all routing on IPX networks involves routing to networks, and packets destined for a particular server are sent to the internal network that operates in that server. IPX identifies networks with a 32-bit number that is usually expressed as eight hexadecimal digits.

An IPX network number must be specified for all computers that run the Windows 2000 File and Print Services for NetWare, which is described in Chapter 13. On these computers, enter the network number in the **Internal network number** field.

NetWare supports several types of networks, each of which is distinguished by a NetWare *frame type*. The frame types for Ethernet networks are:

- **Ethernet 802.2.** This frame type adheres to the 802 standards as defined by the IEEE (the Institute of Electrical and Electronics Engineers). This is the most common standard for IPX/SPX and for other non-TCP/IP protocols.

- **Ethernet 802.3.** This frame type was defined before the IEEE 802 standards were completed. It uses non-standard packet formats and is no longer recommended for use.

- **Ethernet II.** This frame type was defined prior to the creation of the IEEE 802 protocols. It is the most common frame type for TCP/IP networks but is seldom used for IPX/SPX.

- **Ethernet SNAP.** This frame is an extension of the IEEE 802 standards that enables TCP/IP to function on IEEE 802 ethernets. It is seldom used for TCP/IP and is inefficient when used for IPX/SPX.

The Ethernet 802.2 frame type is overwhelmingly preferred for IPX/SPX networks and may be the only one you encounter.

Nevertheless, NWLink supports *automatic frame type detection*, which enables a computer to discover which frame type is being used on a given connection. It sounds like a solution to the problem of having multiple frame types, but it isn't. Automatic frame type selection generates extra network traffic and may not select the optimal frame type.

So don't be lazy. The best thing is to select **Manual frame type detection** and then to add only supported frame types to the list. When you add a frame type, you must select the frame type and specify the network number that is used for that frame type on the network that connects to the interface. As mentioned, on most networks, only the Ethernet 802.2 frame type is required.

Installing Windows 2000 Components

Most optional Windows 2000 components are installed using the Add/Remove Programs applet in the Control Panel. When you run the applet and select **Add/Remove Windows Components**, the **Windows Components Wizard** is started (see Figure 1.18). The **Components** scroll box lists categories of components.

Most components have subcomponents that can be installed individually. If some but not all subcomponents are installed, the box is checked and colored gray. If all subcomponents are installed, the box is checked and colored white.

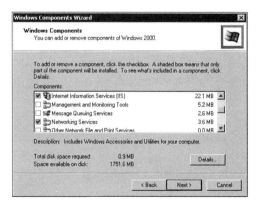

FIGURE 1.18

The Windows Components dialog box lists installed and uninstalled Windows components.

To install or uninstall components along with all their subcomponents:

1. Check components that are to be installed. Multiple components can be installed in a single operation.

2. Remove check marks from components that are to be uninstalled. Multiple components can be uninstalled in a single operation.

3. Click **Next** and follow the prompts.

To install or uninstall selected subcomponents:

1. Select the component entry and click **Details** to open a subcomponents list. Figure 1.19 shows the subcomponents list for the **Networking Services** component.

2. Check subcomponents that are to be installed. Multiple subcomponents can be installed in a single operation.

3. Remove the check marks from any subcomponents that are to be uninstalled. Multiple subcomponents can be uninstalled in a single operation.

4. Click **OK** to return to the **Windows Components** dialog box.

5. When all required changes are made, click **Next** and follow the prompts.

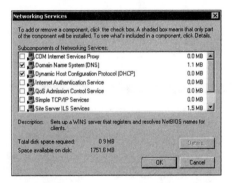

FIGURE 1.19

Networking Services subcomponents.

Some components require you to complete installation dialogs or wizards or to verify your intention to install or uninstall.

In many cases, when a component is installed shortcuts to management utilities are added to the Start menu. Most such shortcuts are added to the **Start→Programs→Administrative Tools** folder.

This folder is also reachable from the **Administrative Tools** icon in the Control Panel. If you would like to have a link to **Administrative Tools** on your desktop, create a shortcut. Shortcuts to all Control Panel applets can be created by right-clicking the appropriate icon and choosing **Create Shortcut** in the context menu.

Using the Microsoft Management Console

Many Windows 2000 components are managed using the Microsoft Management Console or MMC, an extensible console shell that accepts "snap-ins" that manage specific functions. There are two chief advantages to the shell-and-snap-in approach:

- The user interface tends to be more standardized between different utilities.
- Administrators can build custom consoles that contain the snap-ins they require.

Figure 1.20 shows the console identified as **Computer Management** in the **Administrative Tools** menu. This console illustrates several important features of the MMC.

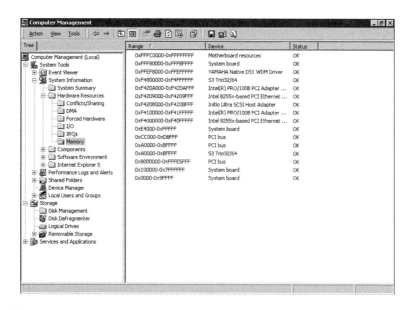

FIGURE 1.20

The Computer Management console.

The Console Tree

In the left-hand pane of the MMC is the *console tree*. To say that it is a tree is to say that it is a hierarchy of objects. With any hierarchy, it is useful to conceptualize the objects in two categories:

- *Leaf objects* cannot contain other objects. The purpose of a hierarchy is to store data in an organized, searchable form. Leaf objects are the data storage objects in a hierarchy. In a file system, files are leaf objects.

- *Container objects* can contain other objects, including other container objects and leaf objects. Directories in a hierarchical file system are container objects. Container objects are seldom used to store data.

Both container and leaf objects can have properties or attributes that determine their capabilities and how they may be used. A file system folder, for example, can be assigned properties such as Hidden or Read-Only. Not all types of objects have configurable properties, however.

In the MMC, the properties of objects are usually displayed by right-clicking on the object and choosing **Properties** from the context menu. Some properties can be modified by a user, while some are defined by the system or are hard-coded into the definition of the object. You will see many examples of object properties throughout this book.

Because containers can hold containers, it is possible to construct trees or hierarchies. Some MMC snap-ins include multi-level object trees. It is useful to think of the relationships between containers in a hierarchy as follows:

- The container that contains all other objects in a tree, usually drawn at the top of a vertically organized tree or at the left of a horizontally organized tree is the *root container*. In most cases, the root container is no different from other containers except for the fact that it is not contained by any other object.

- A container that contains other objects is the *parent container* for those objects.

- An object that is contained is a *child* of the parent container. Leaf objects can only be child objects. Container objects can be both child and parent objects, depending on the perspective from which they are viewed.

Even when displayed horizontally, tree organization is usually described in a top-down fashion, as though the trunk of the tree (the root container, probably identified as such because it is closest to the roots of an actual tree) is suspended upside-down at the top of the drawing, its branches extended downward. Containers that are closer to the root container are described as "higher" than containers and leaf objects that are closer to the tips of the branches, which are described as "lower" in the tree. Weird? You bet, but it's a convention that's been used for centuries, very likely starting with family trees. Look at the family tree for one of the European royal families (sorry, but I don't know how they're drawn in other cultures) and you'll probably see it organized in this inverted fashion with the oldest ancestors, who form the root of the family tree, at the top of the drawing.

The objects in the console tree are all containers. The parent object for the tree is a container for the snap-ins that are added to the console. The Computer Management console includes three snap-ins: **System Tools**, **Storage**, and **Services and Applications**.

When a container object is selected in the console tree, the right-hand *Details pane* displays the contents of the object.

When container objects contains child container objects, the child containers can be displayed by expanding the parent container in the console tree. Objects in the console tree are tagged in one of three ways:

- Any container object that is tagged with a + contains other containers. The child containers are listed in the right-hand pane. They can be revealed in the console tree by double-clicking the parent container.

- Containers that are fully expanded, that is to say, objects whose child containers are revealed in the console tree, are tagged with a – (minus) character. To hide the child objects, double-click the parent container. In the figure, I have fully expanded the tree under **Hardware Resources**. Notice that all of the containers in this branch are marked by – characters.

- Containers that have no child containers are not tagged. When they are selected, the Details pane displays any leaf objects that are stored in the containers. **Device Management** is an example of a container that has no child containers.

It is somewhat rare for a container in the MMC to be the parent to both container and leaf objects. Typically, only the last container in a branch contains leaf objects. Higher-level containers are usually parents only for other container objects.

The Details Pane

The Details pane has some rather useful capabilities. In most cases, you can reorganize the columns, hide or expose details, and sort the objects according to any of the columns.

Figure 1.21 shows the **Services** console. When the **Services** object is selected, all the service leaf objects are listed in the Details pane.

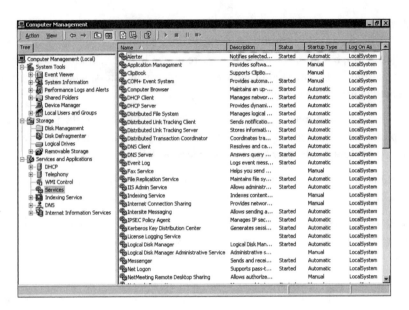

FIGURE 1.21
The Services console, with services listed in the Details pane.

In many cases, objects in the Details pane can be treated like files in Windows Explorer. They can be displayed as large or small icons and with or without details. To change the display, right-click any empty area in the Details pane and choose one of the following commands from the context menu:

- **View→Choose Columns.** This choice opens the **Modify Columns** dialog box (see Figure 1.22), which enables you to determine which columns will be displayed in Details view. Columns listed in the **Displayed Columns** list will appear in the Details pane. Adjust the order in which columns are shown by using the **Move Up** and **Move Down** buttons.

- **View→Large Icons.** Objects are identified by large icons arranged in rows and are displayed without further information. Icons are automatically positioned and cannot be positioned manually.

- **View→Small Icons.** Objects are identified by small icons arranged in rows and are displayed without further information. Icons are automatically positioned and cannot be positioned manually.

- **View→List.** Objects are identified by small icons arranged in alphabetical lists. They are displayed without further information.

- **View→Details.** Objects are displayed in columnar lists that include the detailed columns that are enabled in the **Modify Columns** dialog box.

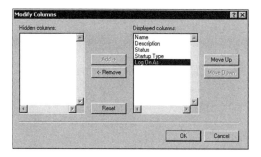

FIGURE 1.22
The Modify Columns dialog box determines which columns will be displayed in the Details pane.

Details view, as shown in Figure 1.20, is almost always the most useful view, particularly because the lists can be sorted, a great help when dealing with long lists of objects. When you select a column by clicking the header, a faint triangle appears beside the column name. (The triangle is probably too faint to reproduce in a book figure. In Figure 1.21, it's in the **Name** column pointing up.)

These triangles enable you to sort the lists according to any column, in ascending or descending order. Simply click a header to determine the column by which the list is sorted. Click the header again to reverse the order of the sort.

Creating Custom MMC Consoles

Windows 2000 comes with many pre-defined consoles, and an appropriate console is usually installed with a new component. In most cases, shortcuts to these consoles are created in the Administrative Tools menu.

Nevertheless, you will need to create custom MMC consoles from time to time, either to meet your personal administrative needs or because a required snap-in is not included in a pre-defined console.

To define a new MMC console, proceed as follows:

1. At the **Start→Run** prompt enter the command `mmc` to open a blank console.
2. Choose the command **Console→Add/Remove Snap-in** in the menu bar to open the **Add/Remove Snap-in** dialog box, shown in Figure 1.23 after some snap-ins have been added.
3. To add a snap-in, click **Add** to open the **Add Standalone Snap-in** dialog box shown in Figure 1.24.

   Select a snap-in to be added and click **Add**. Some snap-ins require configuration before they can be successfully added.

   After adding all desired snap-ins, click **Close**.

FIGURE 1.23

Any available snap-in can be added to a custom MMC.

FIGURE 1.24

The Add Standalone Snap-in dialog box.

4. To remove a snap-in, select it in the **Add Standalone Snap-in** dialog box and click **Remove**.

5. Click **OK** when all desired changes have been made. New snap-ins will appear in the console tree.

> **NOTE**
>
> There does not appear to be any way to change the order in which installed snap-ins are listed in the console tree. The only control you have is the order in which you add the snap-ins.

Some snap-ins can be configured to manage different types of objects, or objects in different locations. For example, the **Computer Management** snap-in can manage resources on the local computer or, for a user with proper permissions, on another computer. When such a snap-in is installed, you must specify the default object the snap-in will manage.

In some cases, the target object can be changed. To retarget a snap-in, right-click the icon in the MMC, choose **Connect to another computer** and select the computer.

Saving Custom Consoles

Consoles are saved in files with .msc filename extensions. When you save a console you first need to identify the console and decide the mode you want the console to start in. To configure the console mode, choose **Console→Options** to open the **Options** dialog box shown in Figure 1.25.

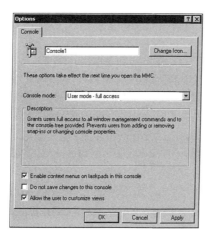

FIGURE 1.25

Options for an MMC console.

The name field to the right of the icon in the **Options** dialog box determines the name that will appear in the title bar of the console window.

To select the icon that will identify the console file in directories, click **Change Icon**. You can select one of the icons that is displayed, or browse for a different one. This procedure does not determine the icon that will be displayed for any shortcuts that are defined for this console.

The **Console mode** setting has four options:

- **Author mode.** When restarted, the console can be freely modified.
- **User mode—full access.** Users have full access rights to console management options but cannot add or remove snap-ins.
- **User mode—limited access, multiple window.** Users can access only areas of the console tree that are visible when the console is saved. Users can create new windows but cannot close existing ones.
- **User mode—full access, single window.** Users can access only areas of the console tree that are visible when the console is saved. Users cannot create new windows or close existing ones. This is the mode used to save built-in consoles.

If any of the User modes is selected, these three options are active:

- **Enable context menus on taskpads in this console.** When this option is enabled, context menus are displayed when users right-click objects.
- **Do not save changes to this console.** If this option is enabled, the user is not given the opportunity to save changes made to the console.
- **Allow the user to customize views.** If this option is enabled, the user can select and configure custom views.

Besides the mode, you also need to determine where the .msc file will be stored. Built-in consoles are saved in %SystemRoot%\system32. You can add the .msc files for custom consoles in the system32 folder, but remember that these files will be erased if you ever perform a new installation (as opposed to an upgrade) in the same system directory.

You may prefer to store the files in a separate folder that is under administrative control. Be sure that users of these consoles have Read permissions for the directory.

Starting Consoles

Consoles saved in .msc files can be started in several ways. Here are three:

- Browse Windows Explorer for the .msc file and double-click the file entry.
- At the **Start→Run** prompt execute the command mmc *path**filename*, where *path* is the folder containing the .msc file and *filename* is the name of the .msc file.
- Create a shortcut for the console. We'll discuss shortcuts in the next section.

Creating Shortcuts for Consoles

You will probably want to create desktop or menu shortcuts to the consoles you create. Before creating menu shortcuts, decide whether the console will be available to all users or to a specific user.

To make the shortcut available to all users, place the shortcut in the folder C:\Documents and Settings\All Users.WINNT\Start Menu\Programs\Administrative Tools. This is the location for the shortcuts to the built-in consoles. (If Windows 2000 is installed in a different system directory, change WINNT to the name of the system directory.)

To make the shortcut available to a specific user, place the shortcut in the folder C:\Documents and Settings*username*\Start Menu\Programs\Administrative Tools. For *username* enter the name of the user's personal directory in Documents and Settings.

One way to create a shortcut in a directory is as follows:

1. Open the directory in Windows Explorer.
2. Right-click any open space in the Details pane.
3. Click **New→Shortcut** to start the **Create Shortcut** wizard.
4. Specify the full pathname to the .msc file. Click the **Browse** button to browse for the file. Then click **Next**.
5. Enter the name for the shortcut that will appear in the menu and click **Finish**.

To create a shortcut on the desktop, right-click an open space on the desktop and choose **New→Shortcut** from the context menu. Then follow steps 4 and 5 in the above procedure.

To change the properties for the shortcut, display the shortcut in Windows Explorer or on the desktop, right-click the icon, and choose **Properties** in the context menu. The **Shortcut Properties** dialog box has three tabs.

On the **General** tab you can edit the display name for the shortcut and specify whether the shortcut is Read-Only or Hidden.

The **Shortcut** tab is shown in Figure 1.26. Properties on this tab are

- **Target.** Specifies the pathname for the target .msc file. Modify only if the filename or directory is changed.
- **Run in separate memory space.** This option applies only to Windows 3.1 applications.
- **Run as different user.** Check if the console requires permissions that are assigned to a different user account. You might need to use this option if you are creating a console that delegates select operations to a user who does not have the required permissions.

- **Start in.** In most cases, all resource files required by an application are found in the file with the application file. Change the pathname if required resources are located in another folder.

- **Shortcut key.** If desired, define a shortcut key that will open the console.

- **Run.** The console can be started in a **Normal**, **Minimized**, or **Maximized** window.

- **Comment.** Enter any required descriptive information.

FIGURE 1.26
Shortcut Properties: The Shortcut tab.

Modifying Consoles Saved in User Mode

Consoles saved in user mode cannot be modified when they are opened. To open a console file in author mode do one of the following:

- In Windows Explorer, browse for the .msc file. Right-click the file entry and choose **Author** in the context menu.

- At the **Start→Run** prompt start the console with the command mmc *path**filename* /a where *path* is the folder containing the .msc file and *filename* is the name of the .msc file. The /a option specifies that the console is to be opened in author mode.

Installing the Windows Support Tools

There are two Windows 2000 resources I want you to know about. The first is the Windows Support Tools, a freebie that is included on every Windows 2000 Server CD-ROM. To install the Windows Support Tools, execute the command `\support\tools\setup` on the Windows 2000 CD-ROM.

The Windows Support Tools include a variety of utilities that are handy additions to the ones installed with Windows 2000.

Also included are three Help files that include some really valuable documentation:

- The **Windows 2000 Deployment and Planning Guide** provides assistance that is particularly valuable if you are planning a large-scale migration to or a new installation of Windows 2000.

- While not complete, **Events and Error Messages** does provide descriptions of many commonly encountered entries that appear in Windows 2000 logs.

- **Tools Help** describes the capabilities and usage of the tools.

The Windows 2000 Server Resource Kit

Every organization should own at least one copy of the *Windows 2000 Server Resource Kit* and the *Windows 2000 Professional Resource Kit*. These kits include several useful utilities, but more importantly they include far more conceptual and planning information than you will find in the Help files.

I prefer the online versions of the Resource Kits. You will seldom read long sections of the Resource Kits, but you will often need to search for topics. Searching is difficult when you have five volumes and several thousand pages, but it's easy when everything is electronic.

The online Resource Kits are included on the CD-ROM that accompanies the hard-copy resource kits, but they can be obtained from other locations as well. If you are a subscriber to Microsoft's *TechNet* subscription CD service, your disks should include electronic copies of both Resource Kits. Subscribers to *Microsoft DeveloperNet* should also receive Resource Kit CD-ROMs with their subscriptions.

Microsoft Knowledge Base

The Microsoft Knowledge Base is a searchable database that documents problems and fixes for most Microsoft products. It is included in the *TechNet* CDs, but it can also be accessed and queried at Microsoft's Web site. The advantages of the Web site are that it doesn't have to be installed every month and it is always up-to-date.

Look for the Knowledge Base at `support.Microsoft.com`.

Now On with the Show

The next chapter is a sort of TCP/IP boot camp. If you're new to TCP/IP administration, it may be the most important chapter in the book for you, because you can't manage TCP/IP unless you have a good idea of the TCP/IP architecture and how the TCP/IP protocols work. If you have some experience at TCP/IP, I nevertheless urge you to skim the chapter to see if there is anything you need to brush up on. We'll be using the information found in Chapter 2 in every chapter of the book, so make sure you have the basics down before you move on to Chapter 3.

TCP/IP Protocol Concepts

IN THIS CHAPTER

Like Windows NT, Windows 2000 supports several popular LAN protocols, retaining support for the legacy NetBEUI protocol and for Microsoft's NWLink implementation of Novell's IPX/SPX protocol stack. But there is no question that with Windows 2000 TCP/IP has moved to the forefront. The ascendancy of TCP/IP makes perfect sense, given the trends of wide-area communication and of nearly universal connectivity to the Internet. NetBEUI was never intended to be a WAN protocol. IPX/SPX started out as a LAN protocol stack and despite improvements has never been the protocol of choice where WANs are concerned. But TCP/IP is first and foremost a WAN protocol stack, efficient and highly reliable, suitable for networks of any scale.

One thing that has endeared TCP/IP to network professionals is the open Internet standards process. All Internet protocol standards are public, as well as the debate that shapes them. Consequently, although isolated protocols such as Sun's Network File System are standardized by individual vendors, the TCP/IP protocol suite as a whole is incredibly open. This openness has in turn fueled the public discourse that has continually enhanced TCP/IP functionality over the past 30 years.

Although you can network Windows 2000 using NetBEUI or NWLink, if you really want to take advantage of everything Windows 2000 Server has to offer, you have to set up TCP/IP from the get go. Most of the features that make Windows 2000 Server such an improvement over its NT predecessor depend on Active Directory and Active Directory won't function without TCP/IP.

> **NOTE**
>
> For coverage of NetBEUI and NWLink, see these other chapters:
>
> - Chapter 1, "Installation: Planning and Execution," explained how to enable Microsoft's NWLink implementation of the IPX protocols as well as NetBEUI.
> - Chapter 6, "NetBIOS Name Support: LMHOSTS and WINS," explains characteristics of NetBIOS names on NetBEUI, IPX, and TCP/IP.
> - Chapter 7, "Routing with Routing and Remote Access Service," explains how to enable IPX routing support in the Routing and Remote Access service.

If you already understand TCP/IP concepts, you will be able to skip much or all of this chapter and probably most of the next as well. You will want to examine the material in Chapter 3, "The Domain Name System," which covers the configuration of the Windows 2000 Server DNS service. If you have avoided working with TCP/IP until now, prepare to experience a bit of a learning curve. Some of the new concepts you will encounter, particularly subnet masking, can be a bit tricky. Just hang in there. Things will start to fall into place when you get some practice.

> **NOTE**
>
> We'll be talking a lot about bits and binary numbers in this chapter, so at the risk of stating the obvious, I'll give you some definitions to be sure we are working with common terminology:
>
> - **Bit.** A binary digit. Always has a value of 1 or 0.
> - **Octet.** Always a group of eight contiguous bits. Used more often than byte when talking about networks.
> - **Byte.** Almost always a group of eight contiguous bits (with some exceptions on old system architectures).
> - **All 0s.** A sequence of bits that consists entirely of 0s.
> - **All 1s.** A sequence of bits that consists entirely of 1s.
> - **High-order digits (or bits).** Digits (or bits) starting with the left-most, highest-value digits in a number.
> - **Low-order digits (or bits).** Digits (or bits) starting with the right-most, lowest-value digits in a number.

Obtaining TCP/IP Documentation

This chapter contains only a brief discussion of the TCP/IP protocols. If you want to learn more detail (and there is a *lot* more to be learned), you can obtain copies of the protocol specifications, known as Request for Comments documents (RFCs). RFCs are identified by number and by title. For example, RFC 793 describes the transmission control protocol (TCP).

You can retrieve RFCs through the Web at `http://www.ietf.org`, a site maintained by the Internet Engineering Task Force, the body that oversees Internet protocol research and standardization. You can browse the IETF Web site to search for and download RFCs and other Internet documents. To obtain a specific document directly, use the URL `http://www.ietf.org/rfc/rfcnnnn.txt`, where *nnnn* is the number of the desired RFC *including* leading zeros, for example, `rfc0793.txt`.

FTP access is available at `ftp.ietf.org`. Log in with the username `anonymous` and use your email name as a password. RFCs are stored in the `/rfc` subdirectory. These files are stored on UNIX systems, and consequently filenames are case-dependent.

> **NOTE**
>
> To obtain a complete, current set of RFCs, download the file `RFC-all.zip`, an archive file, which is updated weekly. Look on the RFC Editor's Web Pages at `http://www.ietf.org` for a link to download the file. (The current URL for the Web page is `http://www.rfc-editor.org/rfc.html`.) The archive is also available in a tarred and compressed UNIX format.

Don't be put off by the fact that these documents contain technical specifications. RFCs often contain quite accessible discussions of their topics, although some of the technologies, such as those that incorporate encryption, are quite complex in nature. I suggest you keep a complete set of RFCs handy on your hard drive so that you can refer to them easily and often.

The TCP/IP Protocol Stack

TCP/IP is the collective name for a suite consisting of hundreds of network protocols that have been developed during the past 30 years to support the global Internet. Although there are a great many protocols in the TCP/IP suite, you don't need to understand all the protocols to understand how TCP/IP operates. You will, however, find it useful to have an overall understanding of the protocol architecture and of certain specific protocols.

The Internet Protocol Model

TCP/IP is organized around the four-layer model, shown in Figure 2.1. This model is often referred to as the DoD model because, for many years, an agency of the United States Department of Defense funded the research to develop the Internet protocols. In this book, the model will be referred to as the Internet protocol model, reflecting the new, privatized nature of the Internet.

The Internet protocol model is admirably simple, organizing the tasks of network communication into four distinct subfunctions, referred to as *layers*. You don't need to be intimately familiar with the layers to perform basic TCP/IP management tasks, but neither is ignorance bliss. As you administer the network, you will encounter layer-specific concepts such as the port numbers that are used to identify individual processes running at the process/application layer. So the next few sections contain simplified descriptions of the protocols that are implemented at each layer. Here is a summary of the layers, their functions, and their relationships:

- **Network Access Layer.** This layer represents electrical and software protocols used to deliver data through a physical network, such as Ethernet and token ring. Network Access protocols deliver data received from protocols functioning at the Internet protocol layer.

- **Internet Layer.** The Internet layer delivers data that it receives from the Host-to-Host protocols. The primary protocol at this layer is the internet protocol (IP), which is concerned with delivering data between local nodes and with forwarding data through routed networks.

- **Host-to-Host Layer.** Host-to-Host layer protocols receive data from upper-layer processes and take responsibility for delivering the data to the destination node. Protocols at this layer are concerned with the "big picture," controlling delivery of data between the source and destination nodes, ignoring the characteristics of the intervening network. This layer has two primary protocols, transmission control protocol (TCP) and user datagram protocol (UDP), which support different modes of data transport.

- **Process/Application Layer.** This layer encompasses all software that uses the network for data delivery. When a process or application needs to deliver data through the network, it passes the data to an appropriate Host-to-Host protocol. Common protocols at this level include file transfer protocol (FTP), simple mail transfer protocol (SMTP), and hypertext transfer protocol (HTTP).

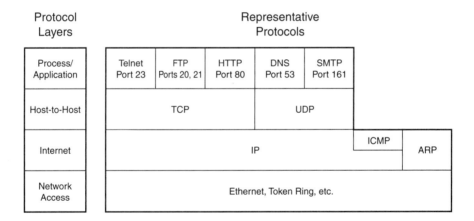

FIGURE 2.1

The Internet protocol model organizes protocols in four layers.

The primary purpose of this discussion is to illustrate the processes that occur as data flow up and down the protocol stack to the network. As data move down the protocol stack, each protocol has control information that it must add to the packet being built. The protocol constructs a *header* containing the protocol's control information and attaches the header to the beginning of the data that the protocol receives from the next higher layer. This combination of the protocol's header with data received from the upper layer is the *protocol data unit* (PDU) for that protocol. For example, when TCP receives data from an application, TCP builds a TCP header and appends it to the application data, constructing a TCP protocol data unit.

Figure 2.2 illustrates the process of constructing a PDU. We can think of the process as one of placing data from the upper layer into a sort of envelope that is labeled with the control information for the lower layer. Constructing a PDU by appending a header to data received from the next higher protocol layer is called *encapsulation*.

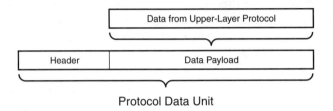

FIGURE 2.2

Constructing a protocol data unit by encapsulating upper-layer data.

Encapsulation takes place at each layer as data travel down the protocol stack from the application to the network. The progress of data as they are encapsulated by various protocols is illustrated in the left-hand column of Figure 2.3.

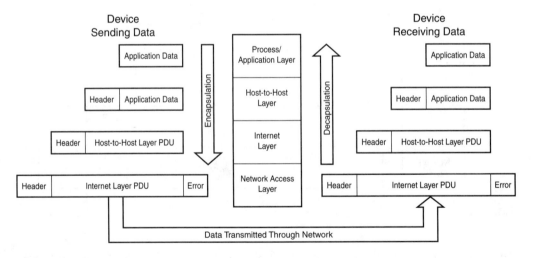

FIGURE 2.3

Encapsulation and decapsulation.

When the packet is received by the destination host, it must be transferred up the protocol stack until the data reach their target application. At each layer, the appropriate network protocol strips off its header to recover the control information that it requires, thus exposing the PDU for the next higher layer. The data portion of the packet is then passed up to the next protocol layer. In this way, the headers are removed one-by-one until the application data unit is revealed, and the data can be manipulated by the upper-layer process. *Decapsulation*, the complementary process to encapsulation, is illustrated in the right-hand column of Figure 2.3.

Encapsulation and decapsulation are key concepts used when performing protocol analysis, one of the topics running through this book and illustrated using the Network Monitor utility included with Windows 2000 Server. Protocol analysis enables you to capture and analyze packets that are transmitted on a network segment, providing information that is useful both for tuning network performance and for troubleshooting. You will learn how to use Network Monitor in Chapter 12, "Managing and Monitoring Connections," but we can start using it to examine network traffic without understanding the details of capturing packets. As we examine the Internet protocol model in the next few sections, we will look at some packets captured by Network Monitor, enabling you to connect theory with practice.

The Network Access Layer

This layer represents the physical network, such as Ethernet, token ring, or frame relay. Although the Internet protocol model includes a layer that comprehends physical networks, no network technologies were explicitly defined for use with TCP/IP. Rather, the Internet protocols were intended to interoperate with existing types of local- and wide-area networks. Over the years, network developers have adapted TCP/IP to nearly all types of physical networks. Some network types are more often associated with TCP/IP than others, however.

The Ethernet II Packet Structure

At the Network Access layer, the protocol data unit is usually called a *packet*, although with some protocols such as token ring the term *frame* is used. Occasionally, packets are referred to as *datagrams* because they are usually sent using a connectionless, "best-effort" mode of delivery that is referred to as *datagram delivery*. We will use the term *packet* in this book to refer to PDUs at the Network Access layer.

On LANs, TCP/IP is most often deployed over Ethernet II networks, and there is a close historical association between TCP/IP and Ethernet II that affects implementations of TCP/IP on different networks. When the Berkeley Standard Distribution (BSD) implementation of UNIX was being developed, network support was a design criterion. The BSD developers settled on Ethernet II as the LAN technology and on TCP/IP as the network protocol stack.

> **NOTE**
>
> Ethernet II is sometimes referred to as DIX Ethernet, reflecting the cooperation of Digital Equipment, Intel, and Xerox in developing the standard.

The Ethernet II packet structure is, in most ways, typical but, in one way, unique. Let's look at how it is organized. The structure of an Ethernet II packet is shown in Figure 2.4 and has the following fields:

- **Preamble.** A distinctive series of bits that signals the beginning of a packet, giving the receiving node fair warning that a packet is on the way.
- **Destination Address.** A 48-bit address that identifies the node that sent the packet.
- **Source Address.** A 48-bit address that identifies the node that is intended to receive the packet.
- **Ethernet Type.** Also known as the Ethertype, this field contains a number that identifies the upper layer protocol that is associated with the packet.
- **Data Payload.** The message to be delivered by the packet, consisting of the data handed to the Ethernet by the Internet layer.
- **Frame Check Sequence (FCS).** Contains information that is used by the receiving node to determine whether errors were introduced while the packet traversed the network.

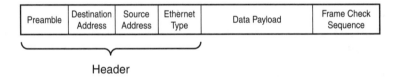

FIGURE 2.4

Structure of an Ethernet II frame.

> **NOTE**
>
> A *network node* is a network device that is assigned an address, and has the capability of sending and receiving packets. To function as a network node, a device must implement the Network Access layer, but it might not necessarily implement higher layers in the protocol stack. A bridge, for example, forwards packets based on the node addresses that are encoded in the Destination Address fields, but a bridge does not necessarily implement any TCP/IP protocols at the Internet protocol layer and higher.

A unique feature of the Ethernet II packet is a field identified as the *Ethernet type*, or *Ethertype*, which contains a number that specifies which upper-layer protocol should be used to process the packet. For example, IP is designated by the Ethertype 0x800. (The 0x prefix is a conventional method of indicating that the number is 800, expressed in hexadecimal notation. Ethertypes are seldom expressed in decimal form.) Another Ethertype you will encounter is 0x806, which identifies packets for the address resolution protocol (ARP) and the reverse address resolution protocol (RARP).

NOTE

ARP and RARP are described in the discussion about the Internet protocol layer later in this chapter.

2

TCP/IP PROTOCOL CONCEPTS

Figure 2.5 shows a sample Ethernet II frame that was captured by Network Monitor. I expanded the packet details under the Ethernet header to show you how the packet is structured and how it is represented in Network Monitor. The Detail pane helpfully decodes many of the fields it presents. For example, in the decode of the Ethernet Type field, Network Monitor reports the raw contents of the field (0800), as well as the protocol associated with the Ethertype (IP).

NOTE

Figure 2.5 illustrates how Network Monitor is used to view packets that have been captured from the network. When viewing packets, the Network Monitor has three panes, which can be individually sized by sliding the dividers:

- The top **Summary** pane provides a one-line summary of each packet in the order that they were captured, describing the source and destination nodes and the upper-layer protocol. These summaries enable you to quickly scan the list and select individual packets for detailed examination. You can slide the dividers between column headers to show more or less of each column or to obscure columns entirely.

- The middle **Details** pane decodes the packet that is selected in the Summary pane. Each protocol layer in the packet is represented by a heading along the left margin. Double-click the plus (+) symbol in the left-hand column to expand a layer and drill down to individual fields or even to details within fields. A heading that has been fully expanded is tagged with a minus sign (–). To collapse a layer that has been expanded, double-click the – to the left of the layer heading.

- The bottom **Hex** pane displays the raw bytes in the packet in both hexadecimal and ASCII representation. If you highlight a field in the Details pane, the bytes associated with that field will be highlighted in the Hex pane as well.

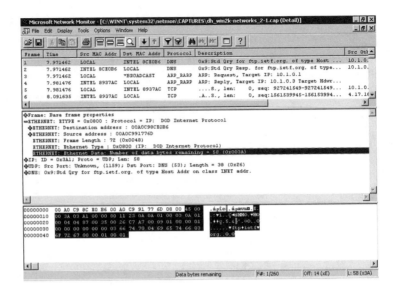

FIGURE 2.5

The Ethernet header has been expanded in the Details pane.

Hardware Addresses

Network and node addressing are critical considerations when packets are being delivered through the network. Many different addressing schemes are employed. For example, each Ethernet II node is identified by a unique 48-bit address that is permanently assigned to the interface, usually by burning the address into read-only memory on the node hardware. You can see examples of these 48-bit addresses (represented in hexadecimal notation) in Figure 2.5, where they appear in the Ethernet Destination Address and Source Address fields.

The Institute of Electrical and Electronics Engineers (IEEE), a professional organization that oversees many network standards, retained the Ethernet II node addressing scheme with only minor modifications when developing the IEEE 802 standards. (The 802.3 standard is derived from Ethernet II, and the 802.5 standard is derived from the IBM Token Ring technology.) These node addresses are often referred to as *hardware addresses,* or *MAC addresses*, a term derived from the media access control sublayer in the design of the IEEE LAN standards.

NOTE

The IEEE LAN standards subdivide the functionality of the Network Access layer into two sublayers: media access control (MAC) and logical link control (LLC). The MAC sublayer corresponds to the physical network and incorporates physical addresses. The LLC sublayer is concerned with identifying upper-layer protocols using numbers called *service access points*.

IEEE MAC addresses have two parts. The first 24 bits, assigned to vendors by the IEEE, comprise a vendor ID. The remaining 24 bits are assigned by vendors to individual network interface devices. As a result, every piece of Ethernet, token ring, or other IEEE-standardized equipment has a unique address.

> **NOTE**
>
> Many protocol analyzers, such as Network Monitor, translate the vendor portion of the MAC address to display the vendor's name. I am using Intel Ethernet adapters, which have a vendor ID of 0x009027. Network Monitor displays INTEL in the MAC address columns of the Summary pane.
>
> Network Monitor also identifies the interface on the machine that is collecting packets as LOCAL. These translations make it easier to scan the Summary pane for patterns.

In Figure 2.5, I selected the Ethernet Data field under the Ethernet header. This field consists of the data payload of the packet. When you select any field in the Details pane, Network Monitor selects the corresponding bytes in the Hex pane. As you will see, the data payload of the Ethernet packet is the protocol data unit prepared at the Internet layer. This is true at each protocol layer: The data payload of a layer corresponds to the entire PDU for the next higher layer.

> **NOTE**
>
> This would be an excellent time to obtain the file that contains the packet captures I used in this chapter. Download file dh_win2k-networks_2-1.cap from http://www.mcp.com/sams/detail_sams.cfm?item=0672317419.
>
> Also at that location, look for the file dh_win2k-networks_2-2.cap, which contains the Ethernet SNAP packets I discuss in the next section.
>
> Open the file in Network Monitor and browse through the packets to get a feel for the way things relate. Expand some lines in the Details pane. Then use the mouse to select various entries. Pay attention to the fields that are highlighted when you select entries in the Summary and Details panes.

SNAP Encapsulation

As mentioned previously, TCP/IP depends on the Ethertype field in the Ethernet II packet header. Only the Ethernet II header incorporates the Ethertype field, and a special mechanism called the Sub-Network Access Protocol (SNAP; RFC 1042) is required to provide Ethertype information on other types of networks. You are most likely to encounter SNAP encapsulation if your LAN is based on token ring. Before we leave our discussion about packet formats, I wanted to take a look at a SNAP header, in this case, in an IEEE 802.3 Ethernet packet, shown in Figure 2.6.

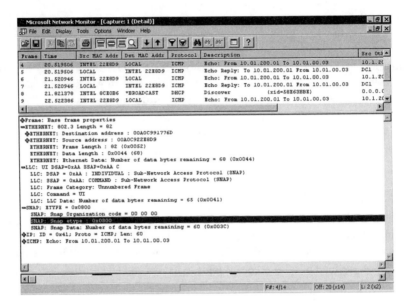

FIGURE 2.6

This Ethernet 802.3 frame includes a SNAP header.

Essentially, SNAP imposes a new protocol layer between the Internet layer and the Network Access layer. SNAP encapsulation is indicated by a value of 0xAA (decimal 170) in the Destination Service Access Point (DSAP) and Source Service Access Point (SSAP) fields in the LLC sublayer. The Service Access Point fields in the LLC header are used in IEEE LAN protocols to identify the upper-layer protocol targeted by the packet.

The Ethertype (etype) is encoded under the SNAP header.

Unless you require Windows 2000 to be compatible with an existing network that uses Ethernet SNAP encoding, it is difficult to think of a reason not to use Ethernet II. You can select the Ethernet frame type by creating the value ArpUseEtherSNAP in the following Registry key:

```
HKEY_LOCAL_MACHINE\
  SYSTEM\
  CurrentControlSet\
```

```
Services\
  Tcpip\
    Parameters
```

The `ArpUseEtherSNAP` value entry is not created by default, and, by default, Windows 2000 uses a value of `0x0`, configuring TCP/IP to use Ethernet II encoding. Create the value with type `REG_DWORD` and assign a value of `0x1` to configure TCP/IP to use Ethernet SNAP encoding.

SNAP encapsulation is automatically enabled when TCP/IP is bound on token ring and other networks that do not provide an Ethertype field.

Packet Delivery

As mentioned previously, each node on the network is identified by a unique numeric address. This is usually called a *hardware* address—because it is burned into a chip on the network interface board—or a *MAC* address. In order for a node that receives a packet to reply to the packet's originator, the hardware addresses of both the source and destination nodes are usually included in a packet that is to be transmitted. Exceptions to this rule are broadcast and multicast packets, which have special destination addresses.

In some cases, a node might need to send a packet to all nodes on the network, a technique called *broadcasting*. To do so, a special address is placed in the destination address. On most types of networks, the broadcast address consists entirely of 1 bits. TCP/IP broadcast addressing is covered in the section on IP addresses later in this chapter.

> **NOTE**
>
> Some types of networks require nodes to communicate through one-to-one connections called *virtual circuits*. Because these networks do not support one-to-many communication, they do not support broadcast message delivery. On non-broadcast networks, special procedures must be put in place to compensate for the networks' inability to support essential TCP/IP protocols that are dependent on broadcast or multicast messaging. For example, static tables can be substituted for the dynamic IP address resolution service that is provided by ARP.

Some processes need to send packets to limited groups of nodes. A technique called *multicasting* uses special types of addresses to define groups. A node that needs to receive a particular type of message joins the group associated with the message type and begins to accept messages destined for a particular multicast address. Special multicast routers ensure that multicast messages are forwarded to all network segments supporting nodes that are members of the multicast group.

A packet that is intended to be received by exactly one recipient is called a *unicast* packet. The MAC address for the intended recipient is inserted in the Destination Address field of the packet, and only the node with the matching MAC address should process the packet. All other nodes should ignore the packet. (No two nodes should ever have the same MAC address.)

> **NOTE**
>
> Some types of networks enforce unicast mode in the network interface. On a token ring, for example, the network interface permits the node to receive only packets that are specifically addressed to it. To enable software such as a protocol analyzer to examine all packets that traverse a token ring network, you must use a special network interface that can receive all packets. This capability is called *promiscuous mode*. All Ethernet cards can operate in promiscuous mode, so you don't need special hardware to connect a protocol analyzer to the network.

Figure 2.7 illustrates an example of unicast packet delivery. When A needs to send a packet to C, it must learn C's hardware address. (The methods for learning destination hardware addresses vary depending on the network type.) Then A can construct a packet with the source and destination hardware addresses and transmit the packet on the network. C examines the packets that stream by and retrieves a packet when it recognizes its own hardware address in the destination field. Other nodes, such as B in Figure 2.7, simply ignore packets that are not tagged with their hardware addresses in the Destination Address field.

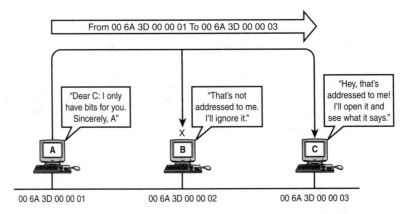

FIGURE 2.7

Delivering a message on a simple network.

The whole process is a lot like picking up your luggage at the airport. The baggage handlers simply put everyone's bags on the conveyer belt. Everyone examines each item, but ignores any bags that do not match the numbers on their claim stubs. You identify your suitcases by examining the tags and keep only the bags that are yours.

Protocols at the Network Access layer are only concerned with delivering packets between nodes that are connected to the same network segment. But networks don't always consist of a single media segment. It is often necessary to configure networks with multiple segments to accommodate large numbers of nodes or to enable the network to span distances beyond the limits of a single LAN. When networks are segmented, something must facilitate delivery of packets between segments. That job is usually performed by devices called *routers* using a technique called *routing*. Routing on TCP/IP networks is performed by the internet protocol (IP). To discuss the internet protocol, we need to move up a layer in the Internet protocol stack to the Internet layer.

The Internet Layer

The internet protocol is the workhorse protocol of the Internet protocol stack, used to perform message delivery but all but a very few TCP/IP protocols. IP is a connectionless protocol that performs nonreliable data delivery. *Nonreliable* means that IP does not attempt to detect or correct errors in delivery. Typically, when reliable service is required, a process or application is written to use the connection-oriented capabilities of TCP at the Host-to-Host layer. Because IP performs nonreliable data delivery, the IP protocol data unit is called a *datagram*.

NOTE

A *datagram* is a protocol data unit that is sent independently of other PDUs, without a logical connection between the sender and receiver, and without any error detection mechanisms at the protocol layer that generated it.

A *connection* is a formal agreement between two nodes to exchange data. Connections are established when it is essential to detect missing packets and request their retransmission.

IP is responsible for delivering datagrams and for routing, if the destination node is on a remote network. When IP receives data from the Host-to-Host layer, IP must determine the nitty-gritty details of constructing a datagram and delivering the datagram to its destination. There are two different scenarios with which IP must contend:

- *The source node and the destination node are connected to the same networks.* In this case, IP can transmit the datagram directly to the destination.

- *The source node and the destination node are connected to different networks that are separated by routers.* In this case, IP must transmit the datagram to a router, which then forwards the packet to the destination network.

Routers expect each network in the internetwork to be identified by a unique *network number.* They also expect a network number to be present in every datagram to be forwarded. Each router maintains a routing table that lists each network number on the internetwork and indicates the most appropriate interface to use when forwarding the datagram. For routing to work, a mechanism must exist for defining network numbers and encoding them in the datagrams. On TCP/IP networks, network numbers are defined in IP addresses.

Internet protocol gives its name to the distinctive method of addressing TCP/IP hosts. An *IP address* is a 32-bit number that encodes both the network to which a node is attached and the node's unique identification on that network. IP addresses are typically written in *dotted-decimal* form, consisting of four decimal fields (each with a value of 0 through 255) separated by periods, for example, 192.168.1.25.

IP addressing will be examined in greater detail later in this chapter. For now, it is sufficient to recognize that an IP address encodes two types of information identifying a TCP/IP network node:

- A *network identifier,* or *netid,* that identifies the node's network
- A *host identifier,* or *hostid,* that uniquely identifies each node on a local network

> **NOTE**
>
> This is the first time in our discussion that we have been forced to use the term *host,* which the non-TCP/IP world tends to associate only with multiuser mainframe computers, not with the personal nodes that now constitute the bulk of network nodes configured to communicate with TCP/IP. TCP/IP is very old as network protocols go, and early implementations were made on mainframe computers. These mainframes were also called *hosts* because they served as processing hosts for relatively unintelligent terminals. The term *host* remains in use as the name for any network node that is running TCP/IP protocols. That said, I will now feel free to use the term *host* interchangeably with *node.*

IP addresses enable the internet protocol to operate on a uniform type of host address, regardless of the network to which the host is connected. But, at the level of the physical network, all data are delivered using the network's native address scheme, such as the 48-bit hardware addresses used with Ethernet.

Hardware Address Discovery

Because network delivery of data uses network addressing rather than IP addressing, when IP needs to transmit a packet, IP must have a means of learning the hardware address of the destination node. The *address resolution protocol* (ARP) provides that means. The operation of ARP is illustrated in Figure 2.8 and works like this:

1. When host A needs to learn the hardware address of C, it broadcasts an *ARP request packet* that contains C's IP address.

2. Host B ignores the ARP request packet because it does not contain B's IP address.

3. Host C receives the ARP request packet because it contains C's IP address. C replies to A by unicasting an *ARP reply packet* that contains C's hardware address.

4. Host A uses the hardware address in the ARP reply to construct a packet that can be delivered to C by the network.

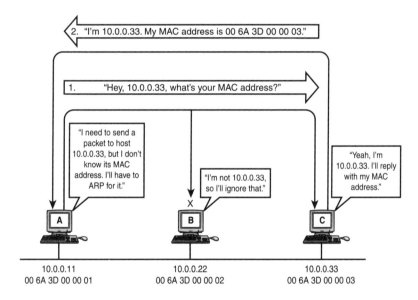

FIGURE 2.8

ARP is used to discover host C's hardware address.

NOTE

ARP is an acronym that has been turned into a verb. We often say, for example, that a host is "ARPing for an address."

To the best of my knowledge, few other TCP/IP protocol acronyms have metamorphosed into verbs. Certainly, IPing isn't a very appealing concept, and TCPing is even less so.

> **NOTE**
>
> Two techniques are used to reduce the number of ARP packets. The ARP request packet includes the hardware address of the source node, enabling the destination node to reply without generating an ARP request of its own. Also, on the assumption that the address information will be used again in the near future, the source and destination hosts cache the hardware addresses they learn for a period of time, enabling them to send subsequent packets without having to make an ARP request for each packet.
>
> There is a reverse ARP protocol (RARP) that is sometimes required when a host knows another host's hardware address and needs to learn its IP address.

Figure 2.9 shows an ARP request decoded in Network Monitor.

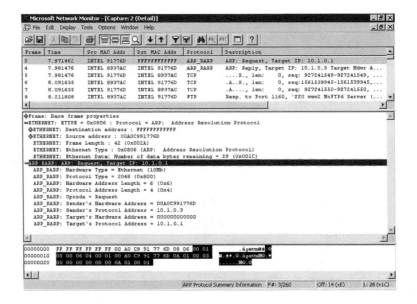

FIGURE 2.9

An ARP request packet.

There are several things you should take note of as you examine Figure 2.9:

- The ARP request packet is followed by a single ARP reply packet. Only the host that matches the MAC address in the ARP request responds.

- The Destination Address is FFFFFFFFFFFF, which is the Ethernet broadcast address. The client has no choice but to send the ARP request as a broadcast message because it does not yet know the MAC address of the destination host. Notice that the **Src Other Address** and **Dst Other Address** columns are empty in the Details pane.

- The ARP Request and ARP Reply are encapsulated directly in an Ethernet II packet with the Ethertype 0x806. ARP is unique among the TCP/IP protocols in that ARP messages are not encapsulated in IP. This makes sense because IP cannot send a datagram unless it knows the MAC address of the destination, and ARP must be used precisely because the destination MAC address is not known.

The trace shows a nice, normal ARP dialog consisting of a single ARP request followed by a single ARP reply. If you see repeated ARP requests that do not generate ARP replies, check the host issuing the ARP requests to determine why it is so persistently searching for a host that just isn't there. If you see a host frequently ARPing for another host, you might need to configure the host's ARP cache to extend the amount of time the host retains addresses from successful ARP requests.

NOTE

IP does all routing. ARP doesn't use IP. Therefore ARP messages cannot be routed. The fact that ARP messages are encapsulated directly in Ethernet packets is another confirmation that ARP messages cannot be routed. ARP is purely a local protocol. If you see a host ARPing for an IP address on a remote subnet, there is an error in the host's configuration. Incorrect subnet masks are among the causes of bad ARP behavior. Subnet masks are discussed in detail in the section "IP Addressing," later in this chapter.

Routing

When networks grow past certain limits, it becomes impossible to connect all the nodes to the same cable segment. For example, Ethernet is unsuitable for transmitting data long distances. If Ethernets at separate sites must exchange data, it is necessary to interconnect them through a wide-area network, as in Figure 2.10. When multiple networks are interconnected, the combined network is called an *internetwork,* or *internet* (small "i" to distinguish it from *the* Internet).

There are a variety of reasons for creating internetworks, including the following:

- To accommodate more hosts than can be supported on a media segment for a given topology

- To enhance traffic management, perhaps by configuring filters that limit the types of packets permitted to be transferred between networks

- To communicate between different types of networks, such as Ethernet and token ring, or between a LAN and a WAN, such as the Internet

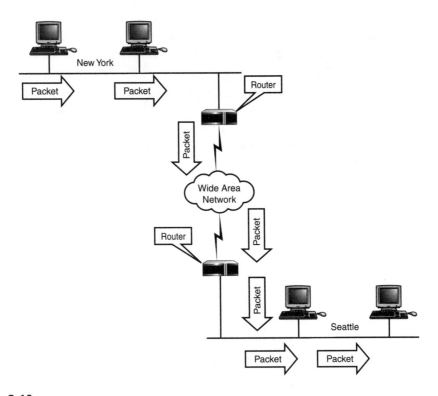

FIGURE 2.10
Routers enable packets to be forwarded between networks.

On an internetwork, a node might need to deliver a packet to another node that is not connected to the local network segment. Such delivery can't be performed directly. Delivery must be facilitated by forwarding the packet through the nodes that interconnect the various networks of the internetwork. Typically, that means using *routing*, a packet forwarding technique that is performed at the Internet layer of the Internet protocol stack. So let's leave the Network Access layer and meet the internet protocol, the heart of the Internet protocol suite.

> **NOTE**
>
> Two nodes that are on the same subnet and can communicate without going through routers are said to be *local* to one another.
>
> Two nodes that must communicate through a router are said to be *remote* from one another.

NOTE

There are other techniques besides routing for facilitating the transfer of packets across internetworks.

Bridging operates at the Network Access layer, using devices that maintain tables of all the MAC addresses on the network. Bridging is seldom used these days, except in the form of bridging switches.

Switching expedites the forwarding of packets by sending the packet on its way as soon as the required address information is encountered, without waiting for the entire packet to be buffered and processed. Because switches begin to forward the packet before they receive the error control information at the end of the packet, switches might forward damaged packets. This is seldom a problem on a properly functioning LAN, however. Switches traditionally forward packets based on MAC addresses (level 2 switches), functioning like fast bridges. Newer level 3 switches use network addresses to make packet-forwarding decisions and function like fast routers. Level 2 and level 3 reference layers in the 7-layer OSI protocol model where the bottom layers are the physical and data link layers (OSI layers 1 and 2, together corresponding to the Internet network access layer) and the network layer (OSI layer 3, corresponding to the internetwork layer in the Internet protocol model).

When a node sends a packet to a remote node, routers between the nodes must have sufficient information to enable them to forward the packet to the network where the destination node is connected. The information used to route packets is stored in *routing tables*, which are configured in either of two ways:

- *Static routes* are added manually to the routing table by network administrators and do not change as network conditions change.

- *Dynamic routes* are added to routing tables by routing protocols that enable routers to communicate with one another and to adjust their routing table entries as the network configuration alters.

Figure 2.11 shows an internetwork that consists of three LANs that communicate through routers. To enable packets to be delivered to the correct network, each network is identified by a unique network number (also called a *network ID*). Nodes consult network numbers to determine whether packets must be routed and, if multiple routes are available, which is the most efficient routing path to use.

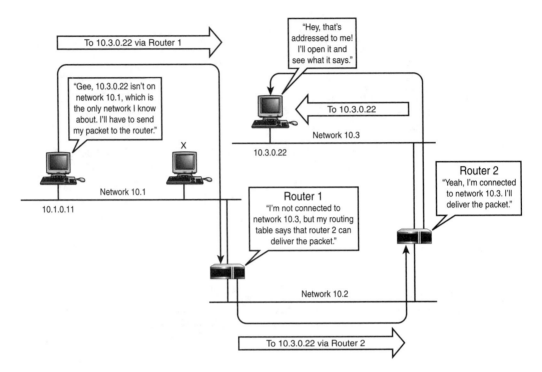

FIGURE 2.11

Routing data through an internetwork.

In some cases, non-routers run routing protocols so that they learn routes for nodes on remote networks. You might run routing software on a server, for example, so that it can transmit packets more intelligently. Routing protocols can require considerable processing power, however, so it is more common to leave the task of calculating network routes to dedicated routers. In such cases, the routing decisions for non-routers are simplified into two cases:

- If the destination network number is the same as the network number of the node originating the packet, the packet can simply be sent out on the local network.

- If the destination network number is different from the network number of the node originating the packet, the packet must be routed. The node checks its configuration for the address of a router and sends the packet to the router with the expectation that the router will facilitate delivery of the packet to the destination network.

If you examine the Ethernet II packet shown in Figure 2.4, you will notice that it contains fields for node IDs but not for network IDs. Network IDs are stored in the data payload of the packet and are read by higher-layer protocols that process that data payload. In other words, the physical network does not get involved with routing. Physical networks are only concerned with delivering packets between two nodes that are connected to the same subnet. Routing between networks is the responsibility of protocols operating above the Network Access level.

TCP/IP has its own protocols that support routing. In particular, routing is the responsibility of the internet protocol.

TCP/IP routing is a complex topic that requires its own chapter. See Chapter 7 for a description of the routing protocols supported by Windows 2000 Server and for the procedures used to configure and manage Windows 2000 routing.

This discussion about network communication has been extremely general and simplistic. Different protocols communicate quite differently, and it is time to get down to the specific methods used by TCP/IP protocols.

> **NOTE**
>
> *Source routing* is another way packets can be delivered through internetworks. A source-routed packet contains all required routing information in the packet header. As a result, no routing decisions need be made by intervening routers. This places an additional burden on the node originating a packet, requiring the node to have some means of determining an appropriate route to the destination.
>
> Source routing data can be defined manually, or it can be discovered by transmitting route discovery packets. Each time a source route discovery packet crosses a router, the router adds its address to the route information in the packet, enabling the packet to collect routing information as it traverses the internetwork to the destination. By the time a source route discovery packet reaches its destination, it might have spawned several packets that offer multiple routes. One of these routes will be selected for inclusion in all future packets that are sent between the source and destination nodes. Hence, each packet contains its own routing information, and the routers do not have to make any decisions.
>
> For source routing to work, routers on the network must have the programming required to enable them to annotate the route and to prevent routes from including loops. Many routers do not have these capabilities, and source routing is not commonly used on TCP/IP networks. However, source routing is an optional TCP/IP technique.
>
> We won't discuss source routing in this book except to mention that it is sometimes used by intruders, who want to bypass some types of network security barriers. For example, a source route might be inserted into a packet so that the packet gives the appearance of having originated on local, trusted networks, instead of on the intruder's remote system.
>
> Expect to encounter source routing on token ring networks, where token ring bridges support source routing based on MAC addresses. In some cases, source routing support must be manually enabled on nodes operating on token rings where source routing is employed.

IP subdivides the task of routing data into bite-sized pieces, delivering data one network at a time. Take the network shown in Figure 2.11. Here, the hosts are identified by their IP addresses. The first half of the IP address identifies the network to which the host is connected. There are three networks, 10.1, 10.2, and 10.3.

The remainder of the IP address provides each host with a unique ID on its local network. Thus the host with IP address 10.1.0.11 is host 0.11 on network 10.1. (Those of you who have worked with IP addresses know that the division between the network ID and the host ID is determined by a subnet mask. Subnet masks will be explained in detail later in the chapter in the section on IP addressing.)

Data sent from host 10.1.0.11 to host 10.3.0.22 must cross two routers. IP breaks down the entire process like this:

1. Host 10.1.0.11 discovers that the destination host is on a different network. Consequently 10.1.0.11 knows that the destination host is *remote*, that is to say, 10.3.0.22 is not on its local network. Therefore the data must be routed. 10.1.0.11 is configured to send a packet to Router 1 whenever it cannot deliver the packet to a local network.

2. IP on Router 1 examines the netid of the packet and discovers that the destination host is not on either of the networks attached directly to Router 1. So Router 1 consults a routing table that contains routes to various network destinations and determines that Router 2 is on the way to network 10.3. Router 1 then forwards the packet to Router 2.

3. IP on Router 2 examines the netid and discovers that the destination host is on a network that connects directly to Router 2, and therefore the destination host is *local* to Router 2. Router 2 prepares a packet that is addressed to 10.3.0.22 and sends the packet out on the network.

4. IP on 10.3.0.22 realizes that it is the recipient for the packet and accepts the packet from the network.

To avoid obscuring the big picture, that sequence of events ignores some of the details required to route packets. At each decision point, it is the responsibility of IP to determine whether the packet should be forwarded or received, and, if forwarded, what is the packet's best next destination. TCP and UPD are oblivious to all this hop-by-hop stuff, but IP gets its nose rubbed in the details, and is forced to deal with the hop-to-hop process of communicating between two hosts that are not connected to the same network segment.

IP makes routing decisions based on information in a local table of routing information called a *routing table*. As mentioned earlier, routing table entries can be either static or dynamic. Most IP hosts are configured with a single static routing table entry consisting of the IP address of the router to be used to deliver any IP datagrams not addressed to a host on a local network. This entry is referred to as a *default router*, or a *default gateway*, which is an older term that harkens back to the early days of TCP/IP when routers were called gateways.

Dynamic routing table entries are generated by a routing protocol that enables routers to exchange route information. Two primary routing protocols are used on TCP/IP LANs, the Routing Information Protocol (RIP) and the Open Shortest Path First protocol (OSPF).

NOTE

Much more will be said about routing in Chapter 7.

2

TCP/IP
PROTOCOL
CONCEPTS

IP on the Wire

In the trace in Figure 2.12, I expanded the IP portion of a packet to show the details of the IP header. Now that we are working with IP, we are concerned with IP addresses instead of MAC addresses. I adjusted the column headers in the Summary pane, hiding the MAC address columns and making room to display the IP addresses.

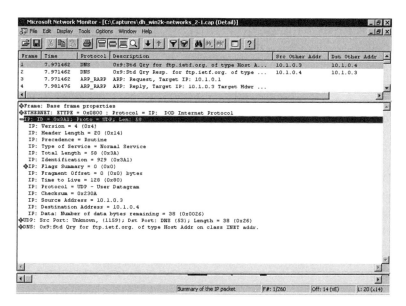

FIGURE 2.12

Contents of a typical IP header.

Exploring the details of the IP header, it comes as no surprise that the Source Address and Destination Address fields contain IP addresses. MAC addresses don't appear at all at this layer. Unless you get deeply involved with network analysis, only a few of the IP header fields are likely to interest you.

The Time to Live field is there to prevent undelivered IP datagrams from circulating endlessly through an internetwork. Every router that forwards an IP datagram is required to decrement the Time to Live value by at least 1. If a router encounters an IP datagram with a Time to Live of zero, it is required to discard the datagram.

The Data field is the payload of the IP message unit. This field usually will contain either a TCP or a UDP protocol data unit that IP receives from the Host-to-Host layer, although a few upper-layer protocols such as OSPF communicate directly with IP. The IP header includes a Protocol field that identifies the host-to-host protocol associated with this data, usually either TCP (0x06) or UDP (0x11). (As with many values, Network Monitor translates the numeric values that appear in the packets into a textual description. In Figure 2.12, the Protocol field has the value UDP — User Datagram (Protocol). If the Hex pane were shown, you would see a byte with the value 0x11 in the corresponding position.)

The remaining details of the IP header are beyond the scope of this book. You can learn more about them in RFC 791.

The Internet Control Message Protocol

The Internet Control Message Protocol (ICMP; RFC 792, extended by various other RFCs) is one of the protocols that distinguishes TCP/IP. ICMP is a versatile protocol that is used to deliver all sorts of network housekeeping messages. For example, if a destination cannot be found, perhaps because of a network failure, a router might return a Destination Unreachable message via ICMP. The ping utility, which is used to establish whether you can communicate with a desired host, relies on the Echo Request and Echo Reply messages offered by ICMP.

Although I am discussing protocol analysis in this book, this is not a book about protocol analysis, so I can't devote to ICMP the chapter-long discussion that it deserves. But if you are going to troubleshoot TCP/IP networks, you owe it to yourself to spend some time reading RFC 792. Then fire up Network Monitor and look for ICMP packets. You can always issue a ping command to generate some sample ICMP packets. In terms of understanding TCP/IP troubleshooting, few things will pay you dividends comparable to becoming intimately familiar with ICMP.

NOTE

Because ICMP must be included in all implementations of IP, it is a common entry point for network vandals. By sending lots (and I mean lots!) of ICMP Echo Request packets, it is possible to overwhelm a target system that simply cannot flush out the requests fast enough.

A look at traffic in a protocol analyzer will immediately expose one of these *ICMP flood attacks* in progress. Unfortunately, it is easy to "spoof" the source address of a packet, that is, to load an outgoing packet with an erroneous source IP address. Consequently, knowing the source IP address will not necessarily enable you to deal with the perpetrator.

A popular technique is to involve several innocent hosts in the attack, greatly increasing the number of packets that can be sent, making it more difficult to shut down the offending systems, and further concealing the attacker. Occasionally, a virus will be distributed that recruits computers into the attack. Attacks from the innocent "zombie" hosts often use source address spoofing to make it more difficult for the target organization to identify the sources of the attack. To reduce the likelihood that your hosts can be used to attack outside systems, you should enable filters on the routers that connect your organization to the Internet, blocking outbound packets that do not show a local IP address as the source of the packet.

To reduce their vulnerability to attacks, some organizations filter out some types of ICMP packets from the Internet, either with firewalls or the packet filtering capability of their routers. Chapter 7 explains how to configure filters for the Windows 2000 router.

Prior to version 4.0, Windows NT was vulnerable to another ICMP-based attack, sometimes called the Ping of Death. It involves sending an ICMP packet that is longer than allowed, causing vulnerable systems to crash.

2

TCP/IP
PROTOCOL
CONCEPTS

The Host-to-Host Layer

Network data delivery is a complex process. If every application had to contain all the intelligence required to communicate on the network, applications would be large and hard to develop. Worse, it is likely that each application would solve the problem of network communication in an individual way, making it difficult or impossible for different applications or systems to exchange data.

The Host-to-Host layer provides processes and applications with a uniform interface to the network. Essentially, a process supplies the Host-to-Host layer with some data and the IP address of a destination host. Then the Host-to-Host layer protocols assume the responsibility of delivering the data to its destination. The process itself knows almost nothing about the network or how the data are delivered.

The Host-to-Host layer gets its name because it bears end-to-end responsibility for delivering data from the source host to the destination host. When performing their tasks, host-to-host protocols are fairly oblivious to the sort of network that lies between the hosts. Whether the packet is crossing a local LAN or is going around the world through the Internet, it's all the same to host-to-host protocols. IP is responsible for the hop-to-hop details.

TCP/IP offers two host-to-host protocols: the transmission control protocol (TCP) and the user datagram protocol (UDP). These protocols have different capabilities, suitable to different types of applications.

Transmission Control Protocol

A tremendous amount could be said about TCP, but I am going to focus on two features that clearly distinguish TCP from UDP:

- TCP provides reliable delivery, performing error checking on each data unit that it sends. When hosts exchange data using TCP, they start by establishing a connection, essentially saying "Hello" to one another and setting up communication processes such as error detection and recovery. When a packet is garbled or lost on the network, the connection enables the receiving host to notify the sender of the error so that a replacement packet can be sent. Consequently, TCP is a very robust protocol, which is often required when data integrity must be guaranteed.

- TCP accepts any amount of data from upper-layer processes. In fact, TCP will accept data in a continuous stream if that is required by the application. But, although processes and applications often must send megabytes or gigabytes of data, networks always have a maximum packet size that they will support. Ethernet, for example, limits packet sizes to 1518 bytes, leaving at most 1500 bytes available to carry data. TCP has the capability to fragment large messages into packet-sized fragments, send each fragment through the network, and reassemble the fragments in order on the receiving host, while checking each fragment for error and retransmitting fragments that are lost or damaged. Applications are oblivious to the fragmentation and reassembly. The sending application simply sends a stream of data to TCP, and the receiving application receives a stream of identical data.

Because TCP can fragment large messages into chunks that can fit in network packets and reassemble the chunks in proper order at their destination, the protocol data unit for TCP is called a *segment.*

There are a few things you should know about the way TCP communicates. TCP is a common target of system attacks, such as so-called SYN and denial of service attacks. If you keep a protocol analyzer running on the network segment going into your organization and know what to look for, you can easily spot these attacks.

Connection-Oriented Delivery

The type of delivery provided by TCP is often referred to as *connection-oriented* or *reliable.* In connection-oriented communication, hosts establish a logical connection between themselves each time they begin to communicate. A connection enables hosts agree to communicate before they exchange any data and establishes communication parameters. Connection-oriented protocols are desirable for several reasons, most particularly for their capability to detect and correct transmission errors including lost or damaged segments in a large message. In this sense, *reliable* means that any errors that occur will be detected and corrected. That is exactly the capability that applications such as FTP require to transfer multimegabyte files or that HTTP needs to transfer graphics and large amounts of data on the World Wide Web. In fact, the majority of upper-layer processes rely on TCP.

The history of a connection has three phases:

- Establishing the connection
- Transfer of data with acknowledgment
- Closing (or "tearing down") the connection

TCP is reliable because every message segment it sends must be acknowledged by TCP on the receiving host. Each byte in the message is counted, enabling the receiver to acknowledge segments that have been transferred successfully and to identify message segments that have been lost or damaged so that retransmission can be requested.

Because it can be the target of some types of network attacks, the procedure for establishing a connection deserves some examination. Three fields in the TCP header are associated with connection establishment and maintenance.

The Sequence Number and Acknowledgment Number fields track the bytes that are sent and received, enabling the hosts to determine whether message segments were lost. Every byte in a message is assigned a sequence number, enabling every byte to be acknowledged. The TCP header specifies the sequence number for the first byte in the Data field along with a unique acknowledgment number. If a segment is not acknowledged by the recipient, the sending TCP retransmits the segment from a copy that was stored in cache. It isn't terribly important to understand how these fields are used, but it is important to understand that the Acknowledgment field is only significant when a connection is established.

Connection establishment and maintenance make use of two flags in the Control field of the TCP header:

- The SYN (S) bit is set to initiate the synchronization of the sequencing counters that control communication. In all other situations, the S flag is cleared.
- The ACK (A) bit is set to signal that the value of the Acknowledgment field is significant—that is, the connection is established, and communication is underway.

Several TCP/IP packets make use of flag fields to efficiently store information that can be expressed in the state of a single bit. Network Monitor displays the value and meaning of each bit when the Flags field is expanded.

A flag is said to be "set" if it has a value of 1, indicating that the feature is enabled.

A flag is said to be "cleared" if it has a value of 0, indicating that the feature is disabled.

The trace in Figure 2.13 highlights four packets that follow the establishment of a TCP connection from 10.1.0.3 to the FTP server on 4.17.168.6. The trace includes details for packet 7 and headers for packets 5, 6, 7, and 8.

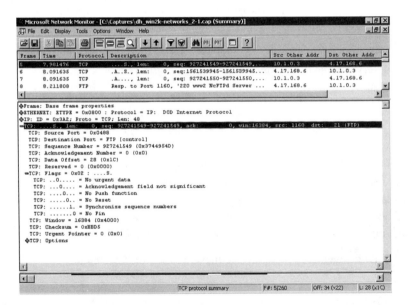

FIGURE 2.13

Packets 5, 6, 7, and 8 illustrate the establishment of a TCP connection.

Because the Control bits indicate so much about the operation of TCP, they (along with the sequence numbers) are displayed in the Description column of the Summary pane for each packet that has a TCP payload. The packets and their roles are as follows:

<table>
<tr><td>Packet 5</td><td>10.1.0.3 initiates the connection by sending a SYN message to the FTP service on 4.17.168.6. In a SYN message, the SYN (S) control bit is set, and the ACK (A) bit is cleared.</td></tr>
</table>

Packet 5   10.1.0.3 initiates the connection by sending a SYN message to the FTP service on 4.17.168.6. In a SYN message, the SYN (S) control bit is set, and the ACK (A) bit is cleared.

Packet 6   4.17.168.6 receives the SYN message and offers a connection by returning a SYN-ACK message that acknowledges the connection request and initializes the value of the acknowledgment field for that host. Both the SYN and ACK control bits are set.

Packet 7   10.1.0.3 responds with an ACK message that initializes the value of its Acknowledgment field. The ACK bit is set, and the SYN bit is cleared.

Packet 8   Now that the connection is established, FTP communication can commence. In this packet, FTP sends the system greeting from ftp.ietf.org ("220 optimus FTP server"). The message text is included in the Description column of the Summary pane and is visible both in the FTP decodes and in the ASCII display in the Hex pane (not shown in the figure).

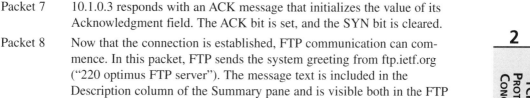

2

TCP/IP
PROTOCOL
CONCEPTS

FTP requires two ports to actually transfer a file. A connection to port 21 is used to exchange FTP control data. A second connection to port 20 (the default data port) is used to actually transfer file data. These ports are reserved for FTP among the "well-known ports" standardized by IANA. In the protocol capture, the client SYN request to open a connection with FTP port 20 is found in packet 27.

At the client end, the port to be used isn't prespecified. The client software can select any port that isn't in use on the client computer. In Figure 2.13, the client opened port 488 to communicate with the server's FTP control port (21) and port 489 to communicate with the servers FTP data port (20). The client's port information is included in the SYN packet so that the server can communicate with the proper port on the client.

After logging in to the FTP server, I transferred a file so that you could track the beginning, middle, and end of a TCP connection. If you step through the packets for the ensuing session, you will see the values increase in the Sequence Number and Acknowledgment fields, as TCP successfully delivers data. Figure 2.14 illustrates how the file transfer is completed. The sequence starts in packet 255; I entered the command Bye, which sent an FTP Goodbye message to the server, initiating a shutdown of the connection.

A connection cannot be closed abruptly because TCP needs to ensure that all data have been sent and acknowledged. There is a ritual dialog to close the session, in which one of the hosts sends a packet with the FIN (F) bit set, indicating that it is finished sending data. When all the data sent by the host at the other end of the connection has been acknowledged, that host sends a packet with the FIN and ACK flags set, completing closure of the connection.

As mentioned previously, FTP requires two connections to transfer a file. Both of these connections must be closed at the end of the session. That's why you see two FIN/FIN-ACK closing dialogs, in packets 256 and 257.

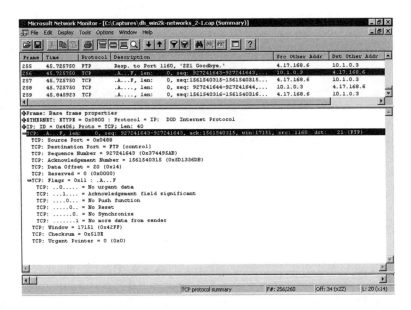

FIGURE 2.14

Packets 255 through 259 illustrate the procedure for closing a TCP connection.

Why am I telling you all this? For one thing, you can use this information to determine whether a service is active because now you know how a service will respond to a SYN request. For another thing, connection synchronization provides one opening that can be used to attack your servers.

Attacks That Target the TCP Connection Process

Two common attacks target the TCP connection synchronization dialog. In one attack, the intruder constructs a SYN packet and inserts the target server's own IP address in both the Source and Destination Address fields. A vulnerable server then attempts to open a connection with itself! In the worst case, this results in a locked-up server.

This sort of SYN request is never valid, and there is no reason why a server should treat it as valid. Many servers are designed to simply discard these packets, but Windows NT 4.0 was vulnerable to this sort of attack, which caused the server to hang. The problem was corrected in Windows NT 4.0 Service Pack 3, which included a new TCP/IP protocol stack.

Another type of attack is the *SYN flood*, which works like this:

1. The attacker sends a SYN packet to the server. In the packet the source IP address is spoofed, replaced with the address of a different system.

2. The server allocates resources for the connection and begins to transmit SYN ACK packets to the spoofed IP address. Typically, the server sends several SYN ACK replies, increasing the time-out with each attempt.

3. There is no response to the SYN ACK replies.

Until the server times out the last SYN ACK reply, the resources allocated for the connection remain unavailable for use. If a great many SYN requests are sent to the server, the server can run out of connection resources and be prevented from accepting legitimate connection requests.

> **NOTE**
>
> For more information about SYN flooding, see the article "Internet Server Unavailable Because of Malicious SYN Attacks" on Microsoft's Web site at the following URL: http://support.microsoft.com/support/kb/articles/Q142/6/41.asp.

User Datagram Protocol

TCP guarantees high data integrity but at a cost. It takes time to open a connection and to close it in an orderly manner when communication is completed. This connection overhead is easy to justify when large amounts of data are being transferred, but can be undesirable when messages are small and are not particularly critical.

UDP works in a very different manner than TCP. When UDP sends a message, it makes no attempt to warn the host to which the message is addressed that a packet is on its way. UDP simply sends out the packet and assumes that it will be received.

A mail analogy can help illustrate some of the distinctions between UDP and TCP. When you send a regular letter through the postal service, the recipient might be unaware that the letter is on its way. There is no mechanism to track the letter while it is in transit, and there is no means by which the sender can know whether the letter arrives, unless the recipient happens to reply. It is cheap to send the letter, but delivery is unreliable. The letter will usually arrive, but delivery is not guaranteed.

TCP, on the other hand, resembles the shipment of a registered letter. The letter is tagged with a number, so that it can be tracked and its delivery status can be determined. You can learn from the registration number if the letter has not been delivered in a certain amount of time. If it has not arrived, you can send a new one. If we add the idea that the sender notifies the recipient that a letter is on the way, we have a pretty good analogy to TCP. Notice that TCP is formal and has communication overhead that UDP does not have. TCP requires tracking of each message, for example, and it requires the sender and receiver to communicate with each other before the first bit of data can be sent.

UDP is often chosen to transport data for processes that communicate informally. The Simple Network Management Protocol (SNMP), for example, enables network nodes to send alert messages to network management consoles. Formal communication is unnecessary for SNMP. A node can simply send an alert several times if necessary until the condition inspiring the alert is attended to.

The Process/Application Layer

In the top layer of the Internet protocol model are all the programs, processes, services, applications, and what-have-you that make use of network services. Some of these programs can directly interface with the user, such as the File Transfer Protocol (FTP). Other processes underlie user activities. The Hypertext Transfer Protocol (HTTP), for example, underlies many of the functions that we perform with a World Wide Web browser. So don't get the notion that this layer of the Internet model itself consists of a single, monolithic layer. The Process/Application layer can encompass any number of layers, as required to support a given application or service. It is simply a catch-all layer where we can conceptually place everything that happens above the Host-to-Host layer.

As an administrator, you need to be aware of two features of the Process/Application layer. The first is the manner in which processes are identified using port numbers. The second is the method for providing users with "friendly" names for hosts using the Domain Name System (DNS).

Ports

The TCP/IP protocol model in Figure 2.1 contains boxes for several of the processes associated with the Process/Application layer. At any given time, several of these processes can be running on a given computer, which gives rise to the question, "How does the computer identify processes so that packets can be delivered to the right process?" It would make no sense to deliver a packet from an FTP server to an email program, for example.

Each process running above the Host-to-Host layer is identified by a unique *port* number that serves as a sort of address for delivering data to processes. In some cases, port numbers can be specified manually by the system administrator, in which case the administrator must take pains to ensure that a given port number is not assigned to more than one process. To reduce the opportunity for confusion, many processes are assigned particular ports for their exclusive use, a task that is overseen by the Internet Assigned Numbers Authority (IANA).

Many port assignments are described in RFC 1700, "Assigned Numbers," but the RFC update process is too cumbersome to keep up with new port assignments. For the latest information about port numbers and several other critical parameters, visit the IANA Web site at `http://www.iana.org`.

There are three categories of port numbers:

- **Well-known ports.** Ranging from 0 through 1023, these port numbers are assigned to particularly prominent Internet protocols.
- **Registered ports.** Ranging from 1024 through 49151, these port numbers are assigned to vendors and other organizations, reserving a port number for a particular application.
- **Dynamic or private ports.** Ranging from 49152 through 65535, these port numbers are not assigned to particular applications. They can be used by organizations that need to specify ports for internal use and can be used dynamically by applications.

An example of a well-known port is port 80, which is reserved for the Hypertext Transfer Protocol (HTTP). It is possible, however, to build a Web server using a different port, one that is not reserved for another protocol. Indeed, this is commonly done to conceal Web sites for privacy. These sites will not be accessible unless the user knows and enters the nonstandard port number in the URL. In such situations, an organization might elect to use one of the dynamic or private ports.

Because ports provide access to services, it is common for an intruder to make scans of network nodes to attempt to identify active ports. Suppose that a port scan notifies an intruder that a server is running a Telnet remote terminal server. (Port 23 will be active.) The intruder might attempt to log on to the system using Telnet as one method of breaking into the system.

Consequently, good network security involves closing down any ports that you don't want accessed. The Windows 2000 Routing and Remote Access Service, for example, can be configured with filters so that it will not allow packets destined for a particular port to enter your organization.

NOTE

Chapter 7 explains how to configure port and other types of filters on the Routing and Remote Access Service.

Name Resolution

As you know, we seldom interact with TCP/IP hosts by using their IP addresses. Instead we use their "friendly" domain names that are provided by the Domain Name System (DNS). In the dialog captured in the trace file used for this chapter, I accessed `ftp.ietf.org` by name.

IP, however, can transmit a datagram only if it knows the IP address of the destination host. The process of matching a host's name to an address is called *name resolution*. On TCP/IP networks, name resolution support is provided by the Domain Name System (DNS).

DNS takes on particular importance with Windows 2000 because DNS is the data store for Active Directory service information. Before a client can access a service, it must be able to identify a server that provides the service, a process that is called *service location*. A new Service Location DNS record type enables Active Directory to store service location information in DNS where it can be accessed by clients using standard DNS queries.

Without Active Directory, Windows naming and service locations are supported by NetBIOS. Every Windows device is assigned a NetBIOS name up to 15 characters in length. A 16th byte in the NetBIOS name is used to identify the services offered by a particular device. Because NetBIOS names encode both hostnames and service names, it has been necessary to support NetBIOS naming on TCP/IP networks. Until Windows 2000, DNS could not provide service location information. NetBIOS is cumbersome to support on TCP/IP because NetBIOS names are propagated using broadcast messages. As discussed earlier in the chapter, broadcast messages aren't allowed to cross TCP/IP routers. That is why Microsoft had to design the NetBIOS Name Service (RFC 1001, 1002), which was implemented as the Windows Internet Name Service (WINS). Whenever you include routers in a Windows NT network, you need to configure at least one WINS server to provide naming support. Unfortunately, WINS is a bit quirky, requiring careful configuration for the best results. Furthermore, Microsoft is the only network vendor offering an RFC 1001/1002 NetBIOS Name Server. These days, TCP/IP administrators prefer to rely on network standards that are implemented by more than one vendor. With Windows 2000, it becomes possible for the first time to provide name resolution services without relying on NetBIOS. If your network includes only Windows 2000 Server and Windows 2000 Professional systems, you can turn off NetBIOS support and get all that nasty broadcast traffic off your network.

That means, however, that you can't run a Windows 2000 Server network without managing a DNS service, so I have provided DNS coverage early in this book—in the next chapter, in fact. But before jumping into DNS, there is one more topic I need to cover: IP addressing. If you don't understand IP addressing you will be flat out of luck when it comes to setting up Windows 2000 Server.

> **NOTE**
>
> DNS is discussed in detail in Chapter 3.

IP Addressing

As you have learned, TCP/IP protocols identify nodes using IP addresses. Unlike MAC addresses, which are burned into the circuitry of network interface cards and are guaranteed to be unique, IP addresses are assigned via software, requiring a network administrator to see to it that each host is assigned a distinctive and correct IP address. Because of the manual configuration and bookkeeping that are required, errors in IP address assignments are among the most common causes of problems on TCP/IP networks.

IP addressing is an involved topic and is probably the aspect of TCP/IP that causes the most difficulty for new TCP/IP administrators. You must be conversant with IP addressing before you can even install Windows 2000, so, if you are new to TCP/IP management, take the time to study this section carefully.

IP Address Representation

IP addresses have 32 bits. Here is an example, presented in binary form:

10101100000100000011010011001011

Raw binary numbers aren't very easy for us to scan, so we need a way to make them easier for our non-computerized brains to process. The first step in translating the address into a form that is suitable for human consumption is to divide the address into 8-bit fields, sometimes called *octets*, like this:

10101100 00010000 00110100 11001011

Then, to make the addresses easier to scan and remember, each group of 8 bits is converted to a decimal number in the range of 0 through 255. The decimals are strung together but separated by periods to obtain the familiar *dotted-decimal* form most often used to represent IP addresses. Here is the address in dotted-decimal form:

172.16.55.203

You will often need to view IP addresses in binary form. An easy way to convert between decimal and binary representation is to use the Calculator applet included with Windows. If you select the **Scientific** option in the **View** menu, Calculator displays buttons that enable you to convert numbers between binary and decimal form.

> **NOTE**
>
> A binary-decimal conversion table is in Appendix B.

IP Address Classes

As shown in Figure 2.15, IP addresses are divided into two fields:

- A *network ID,* or *netid,* identifies the local network to which the host is attached. On internetworks, each network must be assigned a unique netid.

• A *host ID,* or *hostid,* identifies a particular host on a given network. Each host on a network must have a unique hostid.

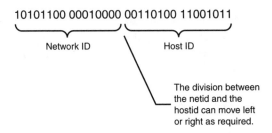

10101100 00010000 00110100 11001011

Network ID   Host ID

The division between the netid and the hostid can move left or right as required.

FIGURE 2.15

An IP address is subdivided into netid and hostid fields.

The dividing line between the netid and the hostid is not a fixed one. Rather, the division can be moved depending on the sizes and numbers of networks that are required. Originally, the location of the division was determined according to address classes, so we will look at class-based IP addressing first.

There are five IP address classes:

• **Class A** addresses begin with a 0 (zero) bit. The netid is specified in the first 8 bits and the hostid is specified in the remaining 24 bits. There are only 126 possible Class A networks, and each network can hold about 16 million hosts.

• **Class B** addresses begin with the bits 10. The first 16 bits are allocated to the netid, and the second 16 bits make up the hostid. There are 16,384 Class B networks possible, each of which supports up to 56,534 hosts.

• **Class C** addresses begin with the bits 110. The netid consists of the first 24 bits, and the hostid field contains the remaining 8 bits. There are more than 16 million possible Class C networks, but each network can support only 254 hosts.

• **Class D** addresses begin with the bits 1110. Class D addresses are used to address messages to members of multicast groups and are never assigned to individual hosts.

• **Class E** addresses begin with the bits 11110 and are used only for experimental purposes.

The A, B, and C classes were defined so that IP address ranges could be allocated to organizations of different sizes. Few organizations have 16 million hosts and need a Class A address allocation, but there are many organizations with 254 or fewer hosts that can work with a Class C address space. Table 2.1 summarizes the characteristics of these address classes.

TABLE 2.1   Characteristics of A, B, and C Address Classes

Class	From Netid	To Netid	From Hostid	To Hostid	Available Networks	Available Hosts/Network
A	1	126	0.0.1	255.255.254	126	16,777,214
B	128.0	191.255	0.1	255.254	16,384	16,384
C	192.0.0	223.255.255	1	254	2,097.152	254

If you pay close attention to Table 2.1 you will notice that there are some gaps in the numbers. For example, there is no Class A network with a netid of 0 or 127. Neither is there a Class C host with a hostid of 255. These and other missing values are excluded from the ranges of possible IP addresses because special uses are assigned to certain types of netids and hostids.

Special IP Addresses

There are several types of IP addresses that have special uses and are therefore unavailable for identifying hosts. Some are used to identify networks or as broadcast addresses. One, the "loopback" address, is useful for testing the protocol stack.

Network Addresses

It is useful to have IP addresses that identify entire networks. When the hostid of an IP address consists entirely of 0 bits (usually referred to as "all-0s"), the IP address refers to the network itself. For example, 172.16.0.0 refers to the Class B network with the netid 172.16.

The IP address 0.0.0.0 is interpreted as "this network." In Chapter 5, "Dynamic Host Configuration Protocol," you will encounter the address 0.0.0.0 in routing tables where it is used to identify a default route.

According to the rules for defining IP addresses, you cannot have a netid that is all-0s. Consequently, we cannot define a Class A network with a netid of 0. There cannot be a host with the IP address 0.45.33.215, for example.

Broadcast Addresses

On TCP/IP networks, broadcast messages are directed to every host on a particular network. A broadcast IP address consists entirely of 1 bits in either the hostid or the entire IP address.

The broadcast address you will see most often consists entirely of 1s and is written as 255.255.255.255 in dotted-decimal form. This is the address used to direct a broadcast message to the local network. Recall that earlier in the chapter you examined ARP packets addressed to the all-1s address. A packet with the destination address 255.255.255.255 will be received by all hosts on the local network but will not be forwarded to other networks by routers.

In some instances you will see broadcast addresses that identify a specific network. For example, to broadcast a message to every host on the Class C network 192.168.40.0, you would use 192.168.40.255 as the destination address. This form of IP address is seldom encountered, however.

Loopback Addresses

All addresses in the range 127.0.0.1 through 127.255.255.255 are *loopback* addresses. (Address 127.0.0.0 refers to the network and cannot be used for loopback testing.) When a packet is sent to a loopback address, the data travel down the protocol stack to the network interface and then bounce back up the protocol stack. The loopback address is used primarily for testing a protocol stack to determine whether it is installed and is functioning properly.

A common procedure is to use the ping command to send an ICMP Echo Request message to the loopback address. Figure 2.16 shows what happens when the protocol stack is fully functional. By default on Windows, ping sends four ICMP Echo Request messages, resulting in the return of four ICMP Echo Reply messages.

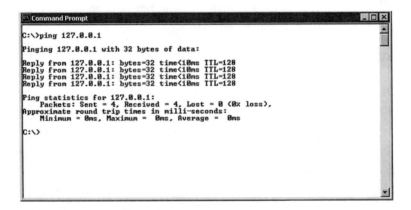

FIGURE 2.16
Pinging the loopback address is a quick way to test the protocol stack.

Because of the way the loopback address is defined, an entire Class A address range is unavailable for use as host IP addresses. That's a lot of address space to waste, but no one envisioned the current state of the Internet when the rules for IP addressing were originally defined.

Non-Routable IP Addresses

Three IP address ranges have been reserved for use on private networks. These IP addresses cannot be used to communicate with the Internet because packets that use them are not forwarded by Internet routers. There is one range of non-routable IP addresses for each IP address class:

- Class A: 10.0.0.0 through 10.255.255.255
- Class B: 172.16.0.0 through 172.31.255.255
- Class C: 192.168.1.0 through 192.168.255.255

Nearly all the IP addressing examples in this book make use of these non-routable addresses so that they don't conflict with IP addresses reserved for a particular organization. You can feel free to use these addresses on your own network, but remember that hosts configured with these addresses cannot directly communicate with hosts on the Internet.

Non-routable IP addresses can be used on a local network that is connected to the Internet if a network address translating (NAT) firewall is used to make the connection. Figure 2.17 shows an example. Notice that all the local hosts are configured with IP addresses on network 10.0.0.0. (This address is often used for private IP addressing and is often referred to as "10 net.") The NAT firewall has one interface on the local network and one on the Internet. (The IP addresses 209.51.67.zz and 132.151.1.zz are used to indicate IP addresses that are legitimately assigned for use on the Internet.)

2

TCP/IP
PROTOCOL
CONCEPTS

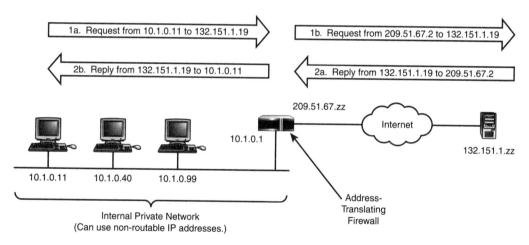

FIGURE 2.17

A network address-translating firewall can enhance network security by concealing hosts on the private network.

A NAT firewall does not simply forward packets from the local network to the Internet. When the NAT receives a packet from a local host (1a in Figure 2.17), it modifies the packet, entering its own IP address in the Source IP Address field (1b). Consequently, all communication with the outside world appears to come from the firewall. When a remote host returns a response (2a), the firewall consults tables in which it keeps records of the packets it sends. The router determines the IP address of the inside host that originated the conversation, inserts the IP address in the response, and sends the packet to the inside host (2b).

Address translation (usually called *network address translation* with the acronym NAT) is a powerful technique for securing a network from outside security threats. Because all communication appears to emanate from the firewall, hosts inside the firewall are hidden from outside inspection, making it more difficult (one never says "impossible" with regard to security) for an intruder to probe your computers from the outside.

> **NOTE**
>
> The Windows 2000 Server Routing and Remote Access Service includes a NAT firewall. See Chapter 7 for a description.

> **NOTE**
>
> Proxy servers use another technology that conceals hosts by having a single host masquerade for an entire network. But whereas proxy servers can support only specific protocols (such as HTTP, FTP, and SMTP), NAT firewalls are protocol-independent.

Summary of IP Addressing Rules

Let's summarize the rules presented in the previous sections:

- There are only three bit patterns that can appear at the beginning of a host IP address:

  0 appears at the beginning of a Class A address, for example, 10.35.18.2. The netid consists of the first 8 bits. The hostid consists of the last 24 bits.

  10 appears at the beginning of a Class B address, for example, 172.20.133.55. The netid consists of the first 16 bits. The hostid consists of the last 16 bits.

  110 appears at the beginning of a Class C address, for example, 192.168.4.18. The netid consists of the first 24 bits. The hostid consists of the last 8 bits.

- If a hostid is all 1s, the address is a broadcast to the network specified by the netid.
- If the entire IP address is 1s (255.255.255.255), the address is a broadcast to the local network.
- If the hostid is all 0s, the IP address identifies the network specified by the netid.
- If the entire IP address is 0s (0.0.0.0), the IP address refers to "this network," that is, to the network to which the host is attached.

Examples of Class-Based Addressing

Two things must be kept in mind when planning the IP addressing scheme for a network:

- The netid for a host must be identical to the netids of other hosts on the network segment. Otherwise, the hosts will be unable to communicate (except through a router).

- A given netid must not be used on more than one network segment in an internetwork (unless the netid is divided into subnets as described in a few pages).

- The hostid for a host must be unique among all hosts that share the same netid.

When these rules are followed, each host on an internetwork will be assigned a unique IP address. Let's look at some examples of correct IP address assignment.

Figure 2.18 shows an internetwork of three networks connected by routers. All three are addressed with Class C IP address ranges: 192.168.1.0, 192.168.2.0, and 192.168.3.0. The network works because a different netid is used on each cable segment. Notice that each router is assigned an IP address for each interface.

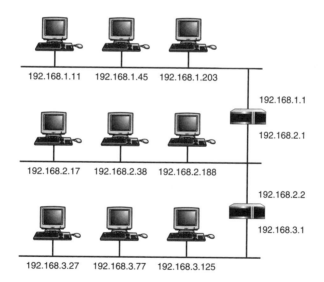

FIGURE 2.18

Each network segment on this internetwork is addressed with a Class C IP address range.

Figure 2.19 shows another internetwork. One network segment uses the Class A network 10.0.0.0. Two network segments use the Class B networks 172.16.0.0 and 172.17.0.0. Notice that it is unnecessary to use the same network class on different networks of an internetwork.

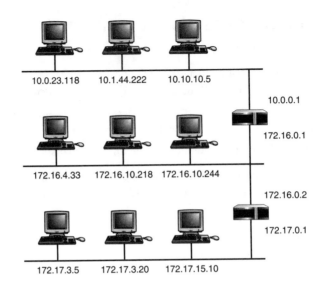

FIGURE 2.19
Addressing on this network uses one Class A address range and two Class B address ranges.

The Problem with IP Address Classes

Early in the history of the Internet, it became evident that pure class-based addressing would quickly become unworkable. Suppose that your organization is assigned a Class B address range that should theoretically support 65,534 hosts. You have two problems. Firstly, you have only 1150 hosts at your main site. Furthermore, your organization has several sites, whose networks are connected by routers. Given what we know so far, not only are you wasting more than 64,000 IP addresses, but also you would need a separate IP address range for each site.

To solve problems such as this one, what was needed was a way of subdividing an IP address range so that portions could be used on several networks. This would enable an organization to take a single IP address range and distribute it to several networks. The solution that was developed is called "subnetting," which is our next topic. After we've looked at subnetting, we'll peruse a related technique called "supernetting."

Subnetting

Ordinarily, it is assumed that the division between the netid and the hostid comes at a fixed point in each class of IP address. Suppose, however, that we could move the dividing point. For example, with a Class B network, we might move the division so that there are 20 bits allocated to the netid and 12 bits allocated to the hostid. Because we have more bits in the netid, we can have more networks, but the cost is that there are fewer bits from which we can make hostids, and there must be fewer hosts on each network.

Subnetting is this technique of subdividing a class address range into two or more subnetworks. The idea is fairly intuitive, but nothing causes more trouble for TCP/IP newbies than subnetting, so let's take things one step at a time.

> **NOTE**
>
> As you are learning about subnet masks, you will learn the most by doing the calculations manually. Nevertheless, it is useful to have a tool that can be used to double-check your results. An excellent, free subnet calculator is available at http://www.net3group.com.

The Subnet Mask

To determine where the netid is divided from the hostid, we define a *subnet mask* that specifies the way the bits in the IP address will be interpreted. A subnet mask has 32 bits, with one bit corresponding to each bit in the IP address. Subnet masking works like this:

- Where a 1 bit appears in a host's subnet mask, the corresponding bit in the IP address is part of the netid.
- Where a 0 bit appears in the host's subnet mask, the corresponding bit in the IP address is part of the hostid.

To see how subnet masks work in practice, let's look at some examples.

> **NOTE**
>
> You will often see the term *subnetid* used to describe the bits that are borrowed from the hostid portion of the IP address for the purposes of extending the bits available for the netid. In practice, however, we can simply consider the netid as consisting of all the bits that correspond to 1s in the subnet mask.

Subnetting a Class B Network

Figure 2.20 illustrates the IP address 172.20.45.103, along with a subnet mask.

Subnet masks are usually written in the same dotted-decimal form as IP addresses. The third portion of the subnet mask used in Figure 2.20 is 11110000 in binary, which is 224 in decimal. Consequently, the subnet mask would be represented as 255.255.224.0 in dotted-decimal form.

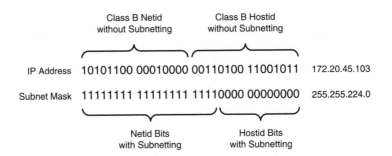

FIGURE 2.20
Subnetting a Class B address with a mask of 255.255.224.0.

NOTE

Terminology gets a bit muddy when TCP/IP administrators talk about networks. For some, any network segment is a subnet, even when the netid is assigned strictly according to address classes, and the terms network and subnetwork are pretty much interchangeable. For others, a subnet is a network segment that is addressed using a subnet IP address range, whereas a network is addressed using an entire class-based IP address range.

As you will see, however, every IP address is associated with a subnet mask. In practice, address classes don't matter much. What matters is the netid that is defined by the subnet mask.

With four bits added to the netid, we can define 16 new networks based on the original network of 172.20.0.0. These *subnetworks,* or *subnets,* can be used to segment the network for traffic control, to create separate network segments for different departments, or to support networks at several different locations.

Table 2.2 summarizes the subnets that are made possible with a subnet mask of 255.255.224.0 and a netid of 172.20.

TABLE 2.2 Subnets Available for Network 172.20.0.0 with a Subnet Mask of 255.255.224.0

From (Binary)	To (Binary)	From (Decimal)	To (Decimal)
10101100 00010100 **00000**000 00000001	10101100 00010100 **00000**111 11111110	172.20.0.1	172.20.15.254
10101100 00010100 **00010**000 00000001	10101100 00010100 **00001**111 11111110	172.20.16.1	172.20.31.254
10101100 00010100 **00100**000 00000001	10101100 00010100 **00010**111 11111110	172.20.32.1	172.20.47.254
10101100 00010100 **00110**000 00000001	10101100 00010100 **00111**111 11111110	172.20.48.1	172.20.63.254
10101100 00010100 **01000**000 00000001	10101100 00010100 **01001**111 11111110	172.20.64.1	172.20.79.254
10101100 00010100 **01010**000 00000001	10101100 00010100 **01011**111 11111110	172.20.80.1	172.20.95.254
10101100 00010100 **01100**000 00000001	10101100 00010100 **01101**111 11111110	172.20.96.1	172.20.111.254
10101100 00010100 **01110**000 00000001	10101100 00010100 **01111**111 11111110	172.20.112.1	172.20.127.254
10101100 00010100 **10000**000 00000001	10101100 00010100 **1000**1111 11111110	172.20.128.1	172.20.143.254
10101100 00010100 **10010**000 00000001	10101100 00010100 **1001**1111 11111110	172.20.144.1	172.20.159.254
10101100 00010100 **10100**000 00000001	10101100 00010100 **1010**1111 11111110	172.20.160.1	172.20.175.254
10101100 00010100 **10110**000 00000001	10101100 00010100 **1011**1111 11111110	172.20.176.1	172.20.191.254
10101100 00010100 **11000**000 00000001	10101100 00010100 **1100**1111 11111110	172.20.192.1	172.20.207.254
10101100 00010100 **11010**000 00000001	10101100 00010100 **1101**1111 11111110	172.20.208.1	172.20.223.254
10101100 00010100 **11100**000 00000001	10101100 00010100 **1110**1111 11111110	172.20.224.1	172.20.239.254
10101100 00010100 **11110**000 00000001	10101100 00010100 **11111**111 11111110	172.20.240.1	172.20.255.254

Examine Table 2.2 closely paying particular attention to third octet and the bits set in boldface type. See what happens to the four high-order (leftmost) bits in the third octet and note how they count upward in binary starting with 0000, 0001, and 0010 and proceeding up to 1110 and 1111. Looking only at these four bits, it is pretty clear in which subnet a particular IP address belongs.

Table 2.2 lists only legal host IP addresses. Consequently, two IP addresses must be omitted from each subnet: the IP addresses with hostids that are either all 0s or all 1s. That explains why 172.20.32.0 and 172.20.127.255 do not appear in the table. 172.20.32.0 has a hostid that is all 0s, and 172.20.127.255 has a hostid that is all 1s.

Now look at the dotted-decimal equivalents to the binary addresses. With Table 2.2 before you, it is pretty easy to tell which subnet is associated with a particular address. But cover the chart and try to determine whether the following IP addresses are in the same or different subnets: 172.20.203.88, 172.20.211.208, and 172.20.208.14. Also tell me whether 172.20.211.255 is a valid host IP address. Unless you are very good at making mental decimal-to-binary conversions, it isn't all that easy to tell, is it? (The answers are that the first three IP addresses are on two different subnets, and 172.20.211.255 is valid because, although the last octet is all-1s, taken as a whole, the hostid does contain 0 bits.)

Subnet addressing is responsible for more network problems than any other aspect TCP/IP configuration. Problems arise because administrators attempt to define subnets using dotted-decimal addresses and forget to look at the binary patterns. When you work with subnet addressing, you have to look at the bits!

NOTE

That point is so important that I'll state it again. When you work with subnet addressing, you have to look at the bits! Most addressing problems that are difficult to spot in dotted-decimal addresses practically leap off the page when you look at the addresses and masks in binary.

When defining the address scheme, keep in mind that hosts must communicate through a router unless the following conditions apply:

- They must have the same netid (consisting of all the bits that correspond to 1s in the subnet mask).
- The hosts must not be physically separated by a router. A router can forward packets between networks with different netids, but it is an error to place hosts that share a common netid on different sides of a router.

The All-0s and All-1s Subnets

If we go strictly according to the rules, two subnets must be left out of Table 2.2. RFC 950, which defines subnet addressing, has two rules that restrict the availability of subnets:

- The subnet portion of the address (the portion of the netid that is borrowed from the hostid) cannot be all 0s because an all-0s subnetid identifies "this subnet" just as an all-0s netid identifies "this network."

- The subnet portion of the address cannot be all 1s because an all-1s subnetid is a limited broadcast address for messages broadcast to a specific subnet.

If these rules are observed, the first and last subnets appearing in Table 2.2 should not be deployed.

In practice, however, little or no use has been made of the all-0s and all-1s subnets, resulting in the loss of potential subnet addresses without a corresponding gain in functionality. It has been suggested (see RFCs 1812 and 1878) that the restrictions in RFC 950 should be eliminated. Consequently, most TCP/IP protocol stacks now being deployed permit you to use the all-0s and all-1s subnets, including the protocol stacks for Windows NT and Windows 2000.

> **NOTE**
>
> This book will assume that the all-0s and all-1s subnets are valid. This assumption is safe with most recent TCP/IP implementations such as Windows NT and Windows 2000, but there remain a variety of protocol stacks that strictly observes RFC 950. Before you employ the all-0s or all-1s subnets on your network you should run tests to ensure that all your equipment, particularly older routers, can support their use.

Subnetting in Practice: Example 1

Let's take the IP addresses in Table 2.2 and apply them to a network. Figure 2.21 shows a typical internetwork addressed using subnets of a Class B address range. If you compare the IP addresses on each network segment to the ranges in Table 2.2, you will notice that all the hosts on a given network segment are assigned IP addresses from the same subnet range.

Because subnet masks cause so much trouble, I like to include subnet masks in the IP address notation. I append a slash to the IP address followed by a number that indicates the number of bits in the netid. I borrowed this convention from classless IP addressing (CIDR), discussed later in the chapter. A subnet mask of 255.255.224.0 specifies that the netid is 20 bits in length, so the IP address 172.20.0.18 with a subnet mask of 255.255.224.0 can be written as 172.20.0.18/20. This approach to indicating subnet masks is used with increasing frequency, and I suggest that you form the habit of including subnet masks as you document the IP addresses on your network. This notation is convenient and eliminates a lot of potential confusion.

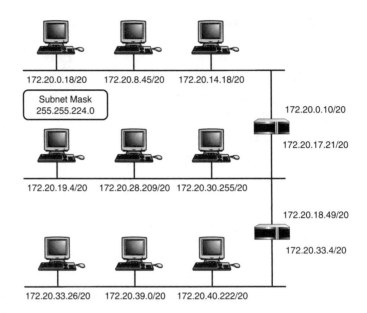

FIGURE 2.21

This network is addressed by subnetting a Class B address range.

Subnetting in Practice: Example 2

Class A and B addresses are scarce commodities these days, and you are more likely to be working with Class C IP address ranges. Because Class C address ranges are small, it is important to make the most of the address space you have. Let's look at what happens when we subnet a Class C address range, and then look at the limitations you will encounter.

Table 2.3 lists the subnets obtained when the Class C network 192.16.32.0 is subnetted with the subnet mask 255.255.255.224 (11111111 11111111 11111111 11100000). With three 1 bits in the subnet mask, it is possible to create eight subnets (assuming use of the all-0s and all-1s subnets).

The subnet mask extends the netid by three bits, enabling us to define eight subnets if we use the all-0s and all-1s subnets. Notice that because the all-0s and all-1s hostids cannot be used on each subnet, a total of 16 hostids are unavailable out of potential hostids of 0 through 255. If we were subnetting a Class B address range, the loss of 16 hostids wouldn't concern us. On a Class C network, however, creating 8 subnets costs us 6% of the potential IP addresses.

Table 2.4 summarizes the characteristics of the eight possible subnet masks that can be applied to a Class C address, concentrating on the fourth octet. Even assuming that the all-0s and all-1s subnets will be used, a lot of hostids are lost when the subnet mask is extended more than four bits. Sixteen subnets is probably the most you will want to create out of a Class C address range.

TABLE 2.3   Subnetting a Class C Address with the Subnet Mask 255.255.255.224

From (Binary)	To (Binary)	From (Decimal)	To (Decimal)
11000000 00010000 00100000 **000**00001	11000000 00010000 00100000 **000**11110	192.16.32.1	192.16.32.30
11000000 00010000 00100000 **001**00001	11000000 00010000 00100000 **001**11110	192.16.32.33	192.16.32.62
11000000 00010000 00100000 **010**00001	11000000 00010000 00100000 **010**11110	192.16.32.65	192.16.32.94
11000000 00010000 00100000 **011**00001	11000000 00010000 00100000 **011**11110	192.16.32.97	192.16.32.126
11000000 00010000 00100000 **100**00001	11000000 00010000 00100000 **100**11110	192.16.32.129	192.16.32.158
11000000 00010000 00100000 **101**00001	11000000 00010000 00100000 **101**11110	192.16.32.161	192.16.32.190
11000000 00010000 00100000 **110**00001	11000000 00010000 00100000 **110**11110	192.16.32.193	192.16.32.222
11000000 00010000 00100000 **111**00001	11000000 00010000 00100000 **111**11110	192.16.32.225	192.16.32.254

TABLE 2.4   Effects of Possible Class C Subnet Masks

Mask (Binary)	Mask (Decimal)	Subnets Available	Hosts per Subnet	Total Hosts Available
10000000	128	2	126	252
11000000	192	4	62	248
11100000	224	8	30	240
11110000	240	16	14	224
11111000	248	32	6	192
11111100	252	64	2	128
11111110	254	128	0	0

2

**TCP/IP
PROTOCOL
CONCEPTS**

NOTE

Although the rules don't require it, only insanity would adequately excuse an administrator who defines subnet masks with gaps between the 1s. Consequently, it is a mere walk in the park to convert between decimal and binary subnet masks. Just memorize these eight equivalencies, and you can convert masks in your head:

Binary	Decimal
00000000	0
10000000	128
11000000	192
11100000	224
11110000	240
11111000	248
11111100	252
11111110	254
11111111	255

Default Subnet Masks

A subnet mask is defined for every IP address on every host. If the address scheme being employed is strictly based on standard IP address classes, a default subnet mask is specified. The default subnet masks for the three IP address classes are as follows:

- Class A: 255.0.0.0 (8-bit netid)
- Class B: 255.255.0.0 (16-bit netid)
- Class C: 255.255.255.0 (24-bit netid)

In many cases, Windows data entry windows will supply a default subnet mask when you enter an IP address. You can then modify the default subnet mask if required to configure the host for your network address scheme.

Supernetting

Subnetting enables us to subdivide a large IP address range into subranges. There's another scenario being encountered with greater frequency on the Internet. Suppose that your organization has 1252 hosts. You're not going to be assigned a Class B address for such a small number of hosts, but you might be assigned three Class C address ranges. Wouldn't it be nice if you could consolidate several Class C address ranges so they could be handled as a single large range? That is exactly what supernetting does.

With subnetting, the subnet mask is used to extend the netid portion of an IP address, subdividing the address range into two or more subnetworks.

With *supernetting*, the subnet mask shortens the netid portion of the IP address. If supernetting is used with properly selected IP address ranges, the result is to consolidate the address ranges into fewer networks that support larger numbers of hosts per network. Let's see how supernetting enables us to consolidate four Class C address ranges.

Suppose that you are assigned the Class C address ranges 192.168.64.0, 192.168.65.0, 192.168.66.0, and 192.168.67.0.

Suppose further that your address scheme uses the subnet mask 255.255.252.0, which specifies a netid length of 22 bits rather than the default netid length of 24 bits for a Class C address.

Here are the four Class C address ranges expressed in binary. With a 22-bit subnet mask, the netids are shown in bold type:

```
11000000 10101000 01000000 00000000
11000000 10101000 01000001 00000000
11000000 10101000 01000010 00000000
11000000 10101000 01000011 00000000
```

Notice that the netid portions of these four addresses are identical. With these IP addresses and a 22-bit subnet mask, the result is a single address range that supports 1022 hosts. (Remember the all-0s and all-1s hostids cannot be used.)

Classless IP Addresses

These days, few organizations are assigned exactly a class-based IP address range. It is well known that the growth of the Internet has resulted in a scarcity of IP addresses, but it is less well known that much of the scarcity is because of simple inefficient use of the available IP addresses. For example, few of the organizations that were assigned Class B address ranges actually use all, or even most of, their 65,534 possible IP addresses. Even a Class C address range is too large for many organizations. If the IP address space were used with 100% efficiency, it could supply nearly three trillion IP addresses. Unfortunately, current practices result in the waste of a large fraction of those addresses.

Now that IP addresses are assigned by ISPs, the normal practice is to allocate a block of addresses that is adequate for an organization's needs with as little waste as possible. If your organization has 50 users, it would be inefficient to assign you an entire Class C address range when you could function adequately with, say, 62 IP addresses. In this case, your ISP would most likely assign you a Class C address range with a subnet mask of 255.255.255.192. And, as the previous section shows, supernetting enables an ISP to support moderately-sized organizations by allocating multiple Class C address ranges that are consolidated through supernetting.

When viewed in this manner, IP classes are irrelevant. An organization simply receives an IP address range that is adequate for its needs and configures all its hosts with an appropriate subnet mask. That is the idea behind Classless Interdomain Routing (CIDR; RFC 1518). Classes are ignored, and network masks are used to select an address range that matches the needs of the organization.

CIDR assignments are classified in terms of the number of 1s that appear in the subnet mask. The subnet mask 255.255.255.192 has 26 1-bits, and a CIDR address range with a 26-bit subnet mask is referred to as a /26 ("slash 26") address range.

> **NOTE**
>
> If you locate your organization behind a network address-translating firewall, as described earlier in the chapter, you can service all your hosts with a single Internet IP address! Of course, large organizations can deploy multiple firewalls, but the cost is just one Internet IP address per firewall.

You can further subdivide your assigned CIDR address range by extending the subnet mask appropriately. If you are assigned the address range 192.16.45.0 with a 26-bit subnet mask, you can use a 27-bit subnet mask to divide the range in half, enabling you to configure two subnets within your organization, with each subnet having 30 IP addresses.

Obtaining IP Addresses

Until the last few years, IP address ranges were assigned to organizations by a central Internet authority called the InterNIC. When the Internet began to experience its current growth and pressure escalated for globalization of Internet management, however, it was no longer realistic for one agency to handle the entire job of IP address assignment, so the task was distributed. Now three agencies oversee IP address assignment:

- APNIC (Asia-Pacific Network Information Center) has authority for Asia and other nearby regions. http://www.apnic.net
- ARIN (American Registry for Internet Numbers) has responsibility for North America and South America. http://www.arin.net
- RIPE (Reseau IP Europeens) assigns IP addresses in Europe. http://www.ripe.net

Unless your organization is very large (greater than about a half million hosts in one location), however, you will obtain your IP addresses from the Internet service provider (ISP) that provides your connection to the Internet. ISPs are assigned large blocks of IP addresses that they, in turn, offer to their customers.

In the area managed by ARIN, ISPs are empowered to grant IP address ranges up to /20. Only organizations that require an address space that is /19 or larger are assigned addresses directly by ARIN and you can bet that those organizations need to provide lots of justification for their request.

The Dynamic Host Configuration Protocol

You have probably decided that IP address administration can be a big pain in the patella, and you would be right. A lot of bookkeeping is required to track the IP addresses in use on each subnet. If Bob moves to a new department, you can't simply move his computer. You need to reconfigure it with an IP address, subnet mask, and default router address that are right for his new location. There's plenty of room for error.

The Dynamic Host Configuration Protocol (DHCP; RFC 2131) is a wonderful thing that can greatly reduce the difficulty of managing IP addresses. With DHCP, a host can query a DHCP server to request an IP address that is right for the host's subnet. With the IP address and subnet mask, the client can receive a variety of configuration parameters, such as the addresses of its default router or its DNS server. It can also receive a variety of configuration parameters that you would otherwise have to enter manually into the machine's configuration. If a setting changes for a subnet, then you make one change on the DHCP server, and all clients receive the new information when they renew their addresses.

For a long time, there was a problem with DHCP. Although a host could receive a dynamic IP address assignment from a DHCP server, there was no way to automatically update the host's name entry in DNS. The introduction of Dynamic DNS (DDNS; RFC 2136), which is incorporated into Windows 2000, finally enables DHCP to update hostname records in DNS. Consequently, it is now practical to manage nearly all the IP address assignments on your network using DHCP.

2

TCP/IP
PROTOCOL
CONCEPTS

> **NOTE**
>
> Chapter 5 shows you how to configure DHCP servers and clients.

Those Are the Basics

You now know enough about TCP/IP to configure a basic network that doesn't include any routers. Routing is a big topic that takes up a significant part of Chapter 7. But you can get Windows 2000 running without understanding routing, so I'm deferring that topic until later.

However, you can't set up even one Windows 2000 domain without understanding the Domain Name System and how it works with Active Directory. So we have two big topics to cover in the next two chapters: DNS and Active Directory. Let's start with DNS.

The Domain Name System

IN THIS CHAPTER

Even if you have never administered a Domain Name System (DNS) server, you are familiar with the way DNS enables you to use names to identify hosts on the Internet. DNS is simply a hierarchical database that can be used to store a variety of different kinds of information, such as hostnames and the names of mail servers. A new DNS record type introduced by Microsoft, the Service record, stores information about the locations of services. With the Service record type, Windows 2000 can use DNS for naming and service location, enabling a pure Windows 2000 network configured with Active Directory to operate independently of NetBIOS names.

If you have managed earlier Microsoft network operating systems, you know all too well the drawbacks of NetBIOS names. They are particularly problematic on TCP/IP networks because NetBIOS devices request information about services by sending broadcast messages, and broadcast messages aren't permitted to cross TCP/IP routers. To enable NetBIOS naming to work over TCP/IP, Microsoft devised the NetBIOS Name System, more familiar by the name of WINS, the Windows Internet Name System. WINS is used with Windows NT to support NetBIOS naming over routers. WINS works (usually), but, despite being documented as an Internet standard (RFC 1001/1002), the NetBIOS Name System remains a technology that is principally supported by Microsoft. DNS, on the other hand, is a universally accepted technology. The use of DNS as the name and service database is one of the most significant new features of Windows 2000.

Given the way Active Directory gets involved with almost every aspect of Windows 2000, it should come as no surprise that Microsoft has added some Active Directory twists to the Windows 2000 DNS service. Active Directory uses Dynamic DNS (DDNS) to store hostname records in DNS and also to update Service records in the DNS database. In turn, Microsoft has enabled the Windows 2000 DNS service to use Active Directory as its database store. Active Directory remains an optional feature of Windows 2000. You can configure Windows 2000 Servers and clients to support NetBIOS naming. But even if you don't activate Active Directory, you will probably find yourself configuring a DNS service to enable your clients to use DNS domain names to identify TCP/IP hosts.

That raises concern in many data centers because they already have a DNS service in operation, probably a UNIX system running the Berkeley Internet Name Domain (BIND) DNS implementation, which provides nearly all the DNS services on the Internet. Although I have not tested it, Microsoft states that BIND versions 8.1.2 and later have the features required to support Active Directory. If you are integrating Active Directory into a network with an existing DNS service, you will need to determine whether you will migrate to the Windows 2000 DNS service, run Active Directory with a foreign DNS service, or run both the foreign DNS service and Windows 2000 DNS. The advantages, disadvantages, and practices for each approach will be discussed later in the chapter.

> **NOTE**
>
> It's worth quoting Microsoft's statement about Windows 2000 DNS compatibility:
>
> "Windows® 2000 DNS is RFC-compliant and interoperates with other DNS implementations. It has been tested to work with Windows® NT® 4.0, BIND 8.2, BIND 8.1.2, and BIND 4.9.7. However, Windows® 2000 supports some features that other implementations of DNS do not support."
>
> I mention one of those feature distinctions later in the chapter. Windows 2000 DNS servers permit names to include Unicode characters that are not allowed by the RFCs. You must, of course, avoid these features in environments that have mixed types of DNS servers.
>
> I haven't encountered any tests that independently investigate DNS service interoperability issues, so you should mix DNS services with caution. Certainly, if you deploy Active Directory, all your DNS servers must support the required features. If you base your DNS services on BIND 8.1.2 or later, I suggest that you make your own tests before you deploy Active Directory on a large scale.

But first, for new DNS administrators, I need to go over some DNS essentials. You need to know how DNS domains work, and how servers cooperate to implement a large-scale DNS name service. After looking at general DNS configuration issues, we'll see how DNS integrates with Active Directory. Finally, we'll see how to implement DNS in an environment that contains non–Windows 2000 DNS servers.

> **NOTE**
>
> Before DNS, hostname resolution was performed using static HOSTS files that were stored on the local host. A HOSTS file is simply a text file in which each line maps a single IP address to one or more hostnames. A HOSTS file contains entries like the following:
>
> ```
> 127.0.0.1    loopback
> 10.1.1.122   blythe
> 10.1.0.50    drew drew.pseudo-corp.com
> ```
>
> A single entry can define one or more aliases, which are separated by spaces.
>
> On UNIX hosts, the HOSTS file is stored in a special directory named /etc. On Windows NT and 2000, the standard directory for HOSTS and other TCP/IP configuration files is %systemroot%\system32\drivers\etc.

HOSTS files work, but aren't of much value on a changing network. Because Active Directory dynamically modifies the name database, HOSTS files have little or no value on Windows 2000 networks. The same can be said for LMHOSTS files, static database files that provided a method of matching NetBIOS names to IP addresses before the introduction of the NetBIOS Name System.

DNS Architecture

DNS maintains a database that is often called a *namespace*, because its primary use is to store records about hostnames. The database is structured as a hierarchy of containers called *domains*. Each domain can store two sorts of information:

- The names of additional domains that fall at the next lower layer in the hierarchy, along with the information required to access information in those domains
- Various types of data, such as hostnames, that are stored in *resource records*

The Domain Hierarchy

Because domains can contain other domains, we can construct a hierarchy of domains. A domain that contains a subdomain is called a *parent domain*, and the subdomain is called a *child domain*. Figure 3.1 illustrates a small part of the domain name hierarchy that is found on the Internet. Like every hierarchy, the entire database originates from a single domain, typically placed at the top when the hierarchy is drawn. This "top" domain is the only domain that doesn't have a name. It is known as the *root domain*.

NOTE

It is worth stating up front that DNS domains and Windows domains are not the same thing. Both function as containers, but DNS domains are simply containers for data in a database. Windows domains establish administrative and security boundaries for Windows services and objects.

DNS and Windows domain concepts get a bit confused with Windows 2000 because an Active Directory Windows domain is always represented by a domain in a DNS database where the naming and service data for an Active Directory domain are stored. Thus there will always be a hierarchy of DNS domains that corresponds to the hierarchy of Active Directory domains.

I won't go into great detail about the organization of the Internet name space except to introduce a bit of terminology. The Internet root domain contains quite a few *first-level domains* such as the familiar COM, NET, EDU, ORG, and GOV domains, shown in Figure 3.1. Additionally, there is a first-level domain for each country, such as US for the United States or IT for Italy. It is up to each country to determine how its national domain will be structured.

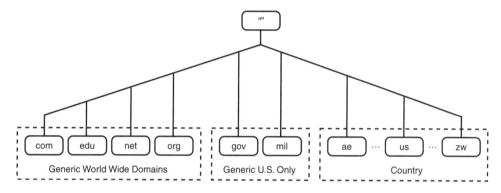

FIGURE 3.1

A portion of the Internet namespace.

3

> **NOTE**
>
> You can learn more about the generic and country-code top-level domains at
> http://www.iana.org/domain-names.html and in RFC 1591.

> **NOTE**
>
> The COM domain particularly is getting so crowded that it is becoming difficult to
> reserve a new domain name that isn't either obscure or awkward to type. To capital-
> ize on this shortage, many small countries have begun to sell space in their national
> domains. My favorite is the small country of Tuvalu, which owns the first-level
> domain name TV. Practically everyone in the TV business wants a place in that
> domain, so the registrars for the TV domain have been able to charge above-market
> rates to register domains. As other first-level domain names begin to catch on, it
> won't be a "Dot.COM" world for much longer.

Below the first-level domains are second-, third-, and fourth-level domains that are often referred to as *subdomains*. The RFCs do not specify a limit to the number of levels of subdomains that can be defined, but all DNS server implementations set some sort of limit. You don't want names to grow too long, however, and five or six levels seems to be a practical limit, at least for information that is accessed by users. In practice, you will seldom see domains that are deeper than the fourth level.

> **NOTE**
>
> If you don't want to be tied in to the Internet domain namespace, you can configure your DNS servers so that you have a private root domain. As we'll see in the next chapter, a private root domain might actually be the preferred way to set things up if you are running Active Directory.

Domain Names

A host's complete domain name is constructed by concatenating its hostname to the name of every domain between it and the root, separating the names with periods. This produces names in the familiar domain name form such as

```
www.pseudo-corp.com
```

or

```
ftp.ietf.org
```

In the first example, the name identifies a host named www that is in the pseudo-corp subdomain of the com top-level domain. Expressed in this way, the complete name of a domain is called a *fully qualified domain name*, usually referred to as an FQDN.

I deliberately placed the above names on separate lines so that punctuation wouldn't get in the way. Remember that there is a root domain at the top of the DNS name hierarchy. Where is the root domain in the previously mentioned names? The answer is that the root domain is implicit. Technically, because the root domain name is indicated with a period, it should be specified by adding a period to the end of the name like this:

```
www.pseudo-corp.com.
```

But that is almost never done in practice, and the root domain is usually implicit. You will see the trailing period in some DNS files, however, where it is used to indicate clearly that the name is a FQDN that starts at the root domain.

3

THE DOMAIN
NAME SYSTEM

> **NOTE**
>
> The RFCs limit the length of an FQDN to 255 characters, although you will seldom if ever want to define domain names this long. Although the RFCs don't limit the number of domain levels that can be defined, the FQDN length limitation ensures that any mad desire to keep adding levels to the domain hierarchy must eventually be curbed.
>
> Domain name requirements are standardized in RFCs 952 and 1123. Domain names can contain only characters a–z, 0–9, and the hyphen character (-). Names can be up to 63 characters in length. Periods can appear only as separators between domain names that appear in a relative or fully qualified domain name.
>
> The Windows 2000 DNS service optionally permits DNS names to contain other ASCII characters as well, such as Unicode characters. Be aware that these extended domain names are not supported by all DNS servers. See the section "Advanced Properties" later in this chapter for the procedure used to specify the characters that the DNS service will accept in domain names.

Making DNS Queries

A single DNS server could not possibly handle naming for the entire Internet. Two problems would arise if we tried to centralize naming: Demand would quickly outstrip any possible amount of processing power, and a huge, centralized bureaucracy would be required to keep current with changes. The designers of DNS realized that these problems could only be prevented if the database was distributed. Consequently, the Internet uses a great many computers, each running DNS-compliant name servers, each administered independently, and each responsible for but a small part of the entire Internet namespace.

A given name server can store the database for one domain or for many related or unrelated domains. Your ISP, for example, almost certainly hosts the domains of many of its clients, which share the same set of DNS servers. A DNS server that stores the records for a domain is said to be *authoritative* for that domain.

> **NOTE**
>
> A DNS name server manages the data for one or more *zones*, where a zone stores the DNS database for one or more domains. Thus it is common to refer to a DNS database as a *zone database*.

The most important function of a DNS server is to look up the IP address that matches a particular host's domain name. The process of looking up the IP address that corresponds to a domain name is called *resolving a name query*. Because no single DNS server has a copy of the entire Internet namespace, resolution of most name queries typically requires the involvement of two or more DNS servers.

Figure 3.2 illustrates the process of a typical query. In this case, the user on host `lauren.pseudo-corp.com` wants to connect to `www.microsoft.com`. Her name query would be answered something like this:

1. Her computer first sends queries to the name server that is listed in its TCP/IP configuration. This name server must provide one of the following responses:

   - Return the IP address of the host that is specified in the query, or
   - Return a message stating that no records can be found for the hostname specified

2. The local name server cannot resolve names in the `Microsoft.com` domain, so it must search for a name server that is authoritative for the target domain. When starting from scratch, a DNS server usually starts at the top of the domain hierarchy by querying a name server that is authoritative for the root domain.

3. The Internet root domain servers are authoritative for the root and `com` domains, but they are not authoritative for the `microsoft.com` domain. The root domain server responds with a referral to the IP address of a name server that is authoritative for `microsoft.com`.

4. The local name server queries the name server it learned about from the root domain servers.

5. This name server is authoritative for `microsoft.com` and can resolve `www.microsoft.com` to its IP address. This IP address is returned to the local name server.

6. The local name server returns the results of the query to the user's computer, completing the query.

There are several opportunities to shorten this process because name servers retain copies of searches they have recently conducted in a local cache. Suppose that the local name server has recently resolved `www.microsoft.com` for another user. It can resolve the query locally without the need to search outside name servers. On busy name servers, the local name cache results in significant improvements in resource usage. Caching is such a powerful technique for reducing WAN traffic that many organizations deploy cache-only name servers, also known as *forwarders*, a technique that is described later in the chapter.

Iterative and Recursive Queries

There are two types of DNS queries: iterative and recursive, both of which figure into the search process depicted in Figure 3.2. You will need to have some familiarity with these types of queries when you configure the DNS server.

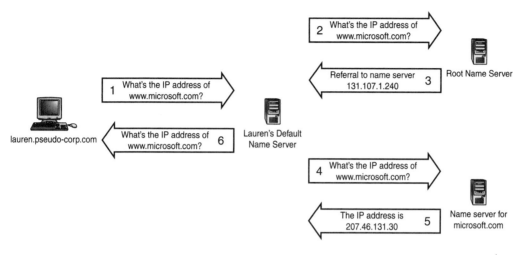

FIGURE 3.2

Resolving a name query for a remote domain.

Client software must be able to initiate a DNS query because it must know the IP address of a target host in order to instruct the Host-to-Host layer on the destination of a message. But it would be wasteful to build all the intelligence required to conduct a DNS search into each application. Typically, the developer of an application wants to generate a query that says to a DNS server, "Here's the name. It's your responsibility to succeed or fail in a name search. Let me know when you're done."

That type of query is called a *recursive query*. A DNS server that receives a recursive query must do one of two things:

- Resolve the name, consulting other DNS servers if necessary, or
- Report that the name cannot be resolved

In other words, a DNS server that receives a recursive query can't respond, "I don't know the answer, but you might try looking over there."

In theory, if your local name server can't resolve one of your recursive queries, it could send a recursive query to a root name server, requiring it to resolve the query or report failure. The root name server could then send a recursive query to a DNS server in microsoft.com. The DNS server in microsoft.com would send the result to the root name server, which would send the result to your local name server, which would finally send the result to you. Clearly, your local name server would get a break because it has to do a lot less work. But the root name servers would bear considerably more responsibility because they would have to keep track of every outstanding query and where it came from so that they could pass the response

3

THE DOMAIN
NAME SYSTEM

back to the correct name server. Chaining recursive queries to recursive queries saves work for the local name server but increases the burden on remote name servers that become involved in the query.

It is more common, therefore, for name servers to send iterative queries to other name servers. A DNS server can respond to an iterative query in several ways:

- It can provide the desired result.
- It can provide the IP address of another name server that is closer to the domain containing the requested information.
- It can report that, although it is authoritative for the target domain, it cannot find the requested information.

After a DNS server has provided any of these responses, it is done with an iterative query. Iterative queries make responding easier for the root name servers, but they require the local name server to be more intelligent about conducting its search. It must keep track of each unresolved query as it queries domains that successively enable it to locate and query name servers for the target domain.

Root Name Servers

Because most name searches start at the root of the namespace, it should come as no surprise that the Internet root name servers are very, very busy. Currently, 13 *root name servers* in various locations support the Internet root domain. The names and IP addresses of the root name servers are entered into the DNS server's configuration by an administrator (or, in the case of the Windows 2000 Server, by the software that installs and configures the DNS service). Microsoft calls these pointers to the root name servers *root name server hints*.

> **NOTE**
>
> *Delegation* is the capability whereby the manager of a parent domain can permit a child domain to be managed by a different organization or hosted by another DNS server.

OK, we've found name servers that support the root of the DNS naming tree. How do we search down to find a name server for microsoft.com? When a subdomain is configured, the parent domain is configured with hints that enable it to point to name servers in its child domains. Now it so happens that the Internet root name servers also service the com subdomain, so they can get us that far. Within the com subdomain are hints that point to name servers for the microsoft.com subdomain.

If your organization has a domain on the Internet, there must be at least one name server that is authoritative for the domain. (Although you must declare at least two name servers when you register a domain.) If you have two or more name servers, each will have a copy of the zone database so that queries can be resolved when one of the name servers is down. When you register a domain, the authority that completes your registration ensures that the parent domain for your domain is configured with the records that identify the name servers for your subdomain. After that, it is your responsibility to maintain the database within your subdomain.

In summary, name resolution on the Internet depends on the following characteristics of DNS:

- The root domain is managed centrally by Internet authorities.

- Some Internet top-level domains (com, org, and net) are hosted on the root domain name servers. Management of other top-level domains has been delegated to the entity responsible for the domain.

- Authority for second- and lower-level domains is delegated to the organization that registers the domain. That organization must ensure that suitable name servers are configured to support the domain.

- DNS servers are capable of accepting referrals to other DNS servers, enabling them to search for name servers that are authoritative for a target domain. Consequently, the search process is transparent to the user and to the user's software.

Many organizations, particularly small ones, let their ISPs host and manage their domains, eliminating the need to maintain two local name servers and to learn how to manage a DNS service. Most ISPs provide name services using BIND running over UNIX. Although BIND version 8.1.2 has the features required to support Active Directory, I would question whether it is a good idea to outsource DNS support when DNS is so crucial to Active Directory. If the WAN link fails, Active Directory would be unable to contact its requisite name servers and could not function. Fortunately, the Windows 2000 DNS service isn't all that difficult to manage, so it's not that big a deal to keep the service in house.

Resource Records

The primary purpose of DNS is to provide a database that matches hostnames to IP addresses, but DNS supplies other information as well. For example, DNS can be used to determine the addresses of mail servers that support a domain. The information in the DNS database is stored in the form of *resource records* (RRs). Each RR has a name and an abbreviation. Only a few types of RRs are essential to our purposes in this book. These are summarized in Table 3.1. We will discuss how these RRs are configured later in the chapter.

TABLE 3.1   Common Resource Records and Their Functions

Abbreviation	Name	Purpose
A	Address	Maps a domain name to an IP address
CNAME	Canonical Name	Maps an alias to a host domain name
MX	Mail Exchanger	Identifies a mail server for a domain
NS	Name Server	Identifies a name server for a domain
PTR	Pointer	Matches an IP address to a host domain name (the reverse of an A RR)
SOA	Start of Authority	Identifies the domain administrative contact and configures several operational parameters
SRV	Service Location	Provides the location of a service

We will look at these resource records more closely later in the chapter when we discuss how to manage zones and resource records.

Deploying DNS Servers

DNS is exceptionally scalable, as it has to be to handle name services on the Internet. This scalability is possible because the workload can be distributed across many DNS servers. There are several ways to combine DNS servers to enhance DNS service capabilities:

- Two or more name servers can serve as redundant authorities for the same domain. Clients can query any authoritative name server to retrieve records for the domain.
- Authority for subdomains can be delegated.
- Cache-only name servers can reduce query traffic by consolidating the results of recent queries.

You have already seen how DNS enables us to establish subdomains with their own name servers. Let's take a look at the theory behind the other two scalability techniques, redundant name servers and cache-only name servers.

Servicing a Zone with Multiple Name Servers

There are two excellent reasons for having at least two name servers with authority for a zone:

- **Fault tolerance.** The zone can advertise all the available name servers, so that clients have an alternative if one name server fails.
- **Scaling.** Clients can distribute their queries across all available name servers, enhancing the responsiveness of queries to the zone.

The Windows 2000 DNS service provides two means of supporting a domain with more than one name server. There is the traditional method with statically defined primary and secondary servers, but the Windows 2000 DNS service can also create zones that are integrated with the Active Directory. Let's discuss the merits of both approaches.

Primary and Secondary Zones

With most DNS servers, such as BIND and Windows NT 4, a master copy of a domain database is placed in a *primary zone*. All changes to the domain database must be made in the primary zone.

Under this approach, you can configure additional name servers with *secondary zones* that store copies of the zone data obtained from either the primary zone or another secondary zone. The source of the zone data is called a *DNS master*, and the process of transferring zone data from a DNS master to a secondary zone is called a *zone transfer*. Figure 3.3 illustrates the relationships that are possible among primary and secondary DNS zones.

FIGURE 3.3

Secondary zones can obtain zone data from the primary zone or from other secondary zones.

DNS servers supporting secondary zones retain copies of the zone data in case the server for the primary zone becomes unavailable. However, the zone data can only be updated in the primary zone, after which secondary zones are updated through zone transfers.

The databases for primary and secondary zones are usually stored in text files. The default location for the DNS database files on Windows 2000 is the folder `%SystemRoot%\System32\Dns`. These files are formatted to be compatible with BIND DNS servers, enabling you to import or export zones from BIND configuration files. (Windows NT 4 can read and write BIND-format data files but stores its working copy of DNS zone data in the Registry.)

Windows 2000 DNS supports primary and secondary zones so that it can interoperate with BIND and other standard DNS servers. A Windows 2000 DNS server can host a secondary zone that is transferred from an outside name server. Alternatively, you configure a BIND server with a secondary zone that is copied from a Windows 2000 Server system. A secondary zone doesn't have to accept dynamic updates, but it does need to support the SRV resource record if you are running Active Directory.

Active Directory–Integrated Zones

If you are running your primary name servers on Windows 2000 Server and have set up Active Directory, you can avoid many of the limitations of conventional primary and secondary zones by taking advantage of zones that are integrated with Active Directory.

The data for Active Directory–integrated zones are stored in Active Directory, extending to DNS data the advantages of Active Directory such as multimaster replication and enhanced security. Zone data are replicated to Domain Controllers (DCs) through normal Active Directory replication, and there is no need to explicitly configure zone transfers. Transfer of zone data is made more efficient because Active Directory replicates only properties that change, whereas a zone transfer requires replication of the entire zone database. Because each DC has a copy of the Active Directory database for the domain, any DC can become a DNS server for an Active Directory–integrated zone simply by adding the zone to its DNS server configuration. All DNS servers that are authoritative for an Active Directory–integrated zone are peers, and there is no distinction between primary and secondary zones. Consequently, it is not necessary to manage zone data only on the DNS server that supports the primary copy of the zone.

Active Directory–integrated zones support *secure dynamic updating*. When you integrate a zone into Active Directory, Access Control Lists are enabled that determine the users and groups that can update the zone or specific resource records. Windows 2000 DNS clients can update the zone directly, whereas legacy clients update the zone using DHCP as a proxy.

Delegating Authority

If you have a small organization, you will probably be quite happy with a single DNS domain. Management is simplified, and short names are better for users. When was the last time you typed a DNS name with more than three levels in addition to the hostname?

But there are at least two good reasons for creating subdomains and delegating their authority to additional name servers:

- **Scaling.** If your domain has grown too large, or the demand on your servers has become too great, delegation provides a method of scaling by hosting several smaller domains on multiple DNS servers.
- **Delegation of Control.** If your organization has multiple sites or departments, it might be necessary to delegate control of some of your DNS namespace. This can only be done by creating subdomains.

Let's look at two scenarios for Pseudo Corp, with sites in Chicago, Paris, and Tokyo. There are several questions to answer:

- Do we want to create subdomains for locations, for example, `tokyo.pseudo-corp.com`?

- Do we want to create subdomains for departments, for example, `sales.pseudo-corp.com` or `sales.chicago.pseudo-corp.com`?

Remember that there is no fixed relationship between a host's domain name and its physical location or the department in which it is used. `www.pseudo-corp.com` doesn't have to be in a `tokyo.pseudo-corp.com` domain, even if it is located in Tokyo. A given host can even be known by two names. You might call a host `www.tokyo.pseudo-corp.com` for administrative purposes, so that you make it clear where the machine is located. You could also give it the name `www.pseudo-corp.com` because that's what the public expects your Web server to be called. DNS is very flexible.

So let's investigate two scenarios, one a simplified approach with central administration of the entire DNS database, and one, more elaborate, with delegated control of subdomains.

Centralized DNS

First, let's assume that the DNS database will be centrally controlled. A name server in Chicago will host the primary zone database, and we will locate a DNS server at each site to host secondary copies of the zone. To keep things simple, we won't create zones for locations. All the resource records will be stored in the pseudo-corp.com domain.

Figure 3.4 illustrates this simplified approach. Each site has a DNS server that can respond to local queries. Once a day, zone transfers are scheduled to copy changes made to the primary zone database in Chicago to the DNS servers in Tokyo and Paris.

3

THE DOMAIN NAME SYSTEM

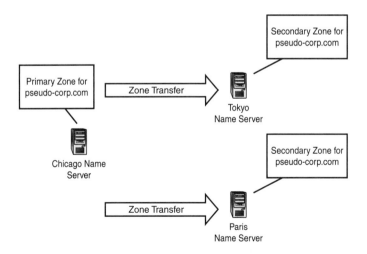

FIGURE 3.4

The DNS server in Chicago maintains all DNS data in a primary zone. Secondary copies of the zone are transferred to DNS servers in Tokyo and Paris.

An advantage of this approach is that all DNS administration is centralized. Secondary zones are essentially maintenance free, so the staff in Tokyo and Paris don't require a lot of DNS expertise.

Strictly speaking, it is not necessary to place DNS servers at Tokyo and Paris. Users there could easily configure their systems to use the DNS servers in Chicago. But local servers reduce WAN traffic, and WAN bandwidth is expensive. Also, local DNS servers provide added fault tolerance.

Tokyo and Paris might not be too happy with this approach. When a name change is needed at one of those locations, they must send the change request to Chicago and wait while staff in Chicago make the change, and a zone transfer takes place. Either because of the delay involved, or because Tokyo and Paris demand control of their local namespace, it might be necessary to establish location subdomains and delegate control of those subdomains to local administrators.

Decentralized DNS

You can't delegate control for part of a domain. The only way to give Tokyo control of its local domain names is to give Tokyo its own domain. So let's set up `chicago.pseudo-corp.com`, `tokyo.pseudo-corp.com`, and `paris.pseudo-corp.com` domains along with a suitable array of primary and secondary zones. The result looks like Figure 3.5.

Why doesn't Figure 3.5 include a zone for `chicago.pseudo-corp.com`? A separate zone isn't necessary. Chicago is a subdomain of `pseudo-corp.com`. Because the Chicago name servers will have the primary copies of data for the parent and child domains, `chicago` can be placed in the zone for `pseudo-corp.com`. A single zone takes care of both the parent and the child.

This approach doesn't require more hardware than the centrally managed approach in Figure 3.4. It does require that administrators in Paris and Tokyo understand DNS, and it does add another level to the organization's DNS names. The decision to centralize or distribute DNS authority within an organization requires careful consideration.

NOTE

As you will see later in the chapter, these concerns are less prominent when DNS is integrated with Active Directory. The distinction between primary and secondary zones disappears, and it becomes possible to administer DNS from any location.

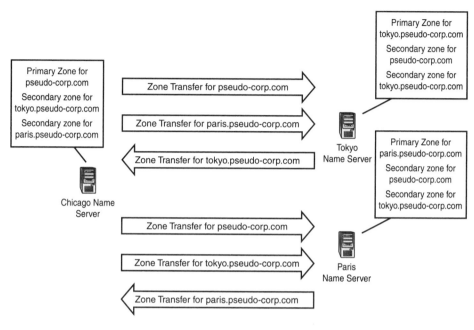

FIGURE 3.5

DNS authority has been distributed so that each site has control of its local database.

Reducing WAN Traffic with Forwarding DNS Servers

The value of a forwarding DNS server is a bit difficult to comprehend unless you picture a large enterprise network that has multiple DNS servers, such as the organization shown in Figure 3.6. A DNS server maintains a cache of recently resolved names. If a client requests resolution of a name, the DNS server first looks for the name in its cache. Thus, if many clients are making the same request, the DNS server can respond using the data in its cache after making a single outside lookup request.

It is particularly desirable to cache name lookups made through WANs such as the Internet because WAN connections have bandwidth limitations, and it is a waste of WAN capacity to repeatedly look up the same names. But, what happens if a large enterprise has many DNS servers independently making DNS queries to the Internet? There is a good chance that information on one DNS server might satisfy a lookup request that is received by another DNS server. However, knowing what we know now, there is no way for the DNS servers to consolidate the data in their caches. In Figure 3.6, suppose that several clients are requesting DNS to resolve the name www.microsoft.com. Because the DNS servers operate independently, each must process the query.

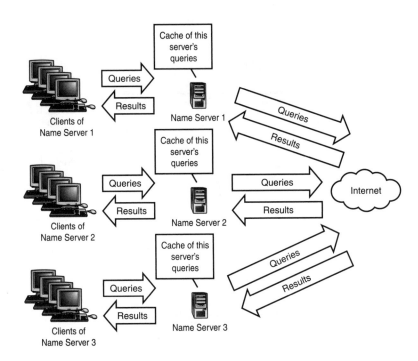

FIGURE 3.6

This organization has multiple DNS servers that function independently.

That's where a forwarding DNS server, also referred to as a *forwarder,* or a *cache-only name server,* comes in. Typically, the forwarder is not used directly by DNS clients and is not authoritative for any domains. Rather, as shown in Figure 3.7, local DNS servers send to the forwarding DNS server all queries that they cannot resolve using data in their cache or in zones for which they have copies. Consequently, the forwarding server has in its cache the results of every outside DNS query generated by the enterprise. This makes it much more likely that a DNS request can be satisfied locally without generating traffic on the WAN.

Reverse Lookup Zones

Until now, we have been looking only at the way DNS resolves a hostname to an IP address. Occasionally, it is necessary to take a known IP address and match it to a domain name. Resolving an IP address to a domain name is called a *reverse lookup.*

There is an entire naming hierarchy on the Internet just for reverse lookups. Reverse-naming zones are also called in-addr.arpa zones because the top two levels of the reverse-naming tree are named arpa (top level) and in-addr (second level). (Welcome to one of the fossils that will, perhaps forever, remind us of the days before the ARPAnet became known as the Internet.)

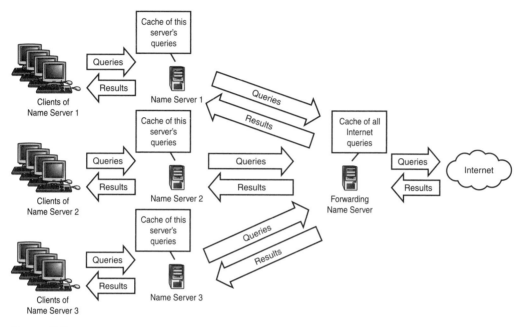

FIGURE 3.7

A forwarding DNS server stores all outside lookups in its cache and can provide them to any internal DNS server.

Figure 3.8 shows how the `in-addr.arpa` hierarchy is structured and the procedure for resolving the IP address 172.25.133.110 to a resource record that identifies the domain name of the host with that IP address. In this case, the name is `drew.pseudo-corp.com`. Layers three through six in the hierarchy correspond to octets in the available IP addresses, beginning with the first octet in level three and proceeding to the fourth octet at level six.

Thus, searching down the tree, you can find a domain that matches every possible netid for a Class A, B, or C network. Within the `in-addr.arpa` domains, Pointer (PTR) resource records match the last octet of a host's IP address to its hostname.

After subjecting you to that explanation, I'll point out that you might never need to set up a reverse-naming zone. Very, very few processes perform reverse lookups. I encountered the need for reverse lookup capability once on the Internet when I tried to download some "not for export" encryption software. The host system did a reverse lookup to ensure that I was working from a host that was in a domain registered in the United States. You might run into an occasional process that demands reverse lookups, but they are few in number. (One notable exception is the NSLOOKUP utility described later in the chapter. NSLOOKUP queries DNS to determine the domain names of the DNS servers that correspond to the IP addresses specified in the client's DNS servers configuration parameters.)

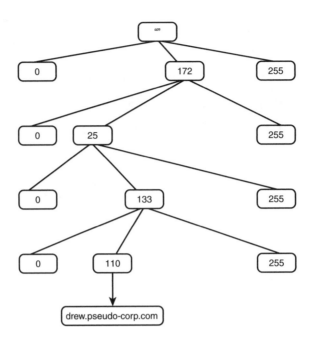

FIGURE 3.8

Structure of the in-addr.arpa *reverse lookup hierarchy.*

NOTE

The domain structure in Figure 3.8 implies that reverse lookups are supported only for class-based IP addresses that divide netids from hostids on eight-bit boundaries. A classless reverse lookup scheme is documented for Windows NT 4.0 DNS.

If your ISP has assigned your organization a classless IP address range, you will probably need to obtain the cooperation of the ISP to maintain your reverse lookup zones on their DNS servers. In some cases the ISP will insist on managing all the reverse lookup zones for the IP addresses they support, but some ISPs are willing to delegate responsibility to the organization using the address range.

The classless reverse lookup scheme for Windows NT 4 is documented in Microsoft Knowledge Base article Q174419, available at http:support.Microsoft.com. I have been unable to find documentation for a similar scheme for Windows 2000, but I have been able to get the Windows NT 4 scheme working on Windows 2000. See the section "Configuring Reverse Lookup Zones to Support Classless IP Addresses" later in the chapter for more information.

Managing DNS in a Small Domain

Now that the basics are covered, we are ready to configure a set of DNS servers. Figure 3.9 shows a simple network with two name servers, a mail server, and a Web server. The network connects to the Internet through a router. Until we discuss Active Directory-integrated DNS zones, Active Directory is not enabled in the examples being displayed, so no Service Location (SRV) resource records will appear in the screen shots.

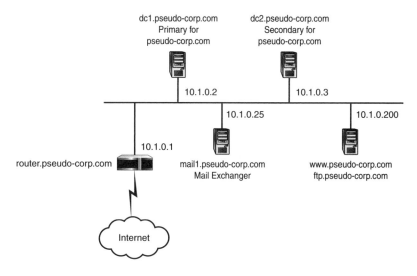

FIGURE 3.9

This simple network illustrates most basic DNS configuration tasks.

The network calls for the following resource records:

- Name Server (NS) RRs for DC1 and DC2, indicating that these hosts are authoritative for the domain
- Host Address (A) RRs for DC1, DC2, mail1, www, ftp, and router
- A Mail Exchanger (MX) RRs for mail1

We are assigning DNS names only to devices that provide services. Because no user's PCs will be configured as servers, it is not mandatory to provide them with DNS names. In any case, the procedure for naming a user's computer is the same as that for naming a server, so you can easily extend the examples to cover non-servers should you desire to do so.

At first, we will configure DNS with standard primary zones on DC1 and standard secondary zones on DC2. We'll see how to configure Active Directory-integrated zones later in the chapter.

Installing the DNS Server Service

Like most Windows 2000 components, the DNS service is installed using the Add/Remove Programs applet in the Control Panel. The procedure is as follows:

1. Open the Add/Remove Programs applet.
2. Click **Add/Remove Windows Components**.
3. Select **Networking Services** in the **Components** list and click the **Details** button.
4. Check the checkbox for **Domain Name System (DNS)**.
5. Click **OK**.
6. Click **Next**. The DNS service components will be installed and configured.
7. Click **Finish**.

NOTE

Windows 2000 DNS servers must be configured with static IP addresses. If you are installing the DNS service on a computer that is dynamically configured through DHCP, you will be prompted to specify a static IP address.

In addition to the DNS service, this procedure adds a DNS snap-in for the MMC. A DNS icon is added to the Start→Program→Administrative Tools menu. Figure 3.10 shows the DNS snap-in as it appears after creation of the zones and resource records necessary for the network in Figure 3.9.

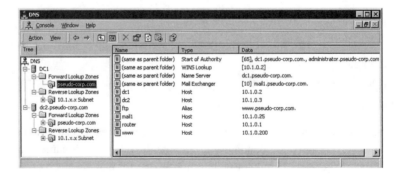

FIGURE 3.10
The DNS management console.

Managing Remote DNS Servers

As Figure 3.10 illustrates, you can manage DNS services on other Windows 2000 Servers by adding the DNS servers to the Microsoft Management Console object tree. To add a server to the object tree:

1. Right-click **DNS** at the top of the object tree.

2. Select **Connect to Computer** from the context menu to open the **Select Target Computer** dialog box, shown in Figure 3.11.

3. Click **This computer** to add the local computer to the object tree

   or

   Click **The following computer** and enter the FQDN of another server that is running the Windows 2000 DNS service.

4. Check **Connect to the specified computer now** to activate the connection immediately.

   Click **OK**.

FIGURE 3.11
Adding a DNS server to the MMC object tree.

Configuring the DNS Server

When the DNS service is installed, the server hosting the DNS server is automatically added to the object tree in the DNS console. Several properties of the DNS server can be configured. To open the server property pages, do the following:

1. Locate the server in the object tree of the DNS console.

2. Right-click the server name in the object tree.

3. Select **Properties** from the context menu to open the DNS Server Properties dialog box.

4. Select the desired property page.

5. After making desired changes, click **OK** to close the dialog box.

The next few sections examine the zone property pages.

Interfaces Properties

By default, the DNS server accepts queries on any of the interfaces installed in the server. You can, if desired, configure the server to accept queries from specific interfaces by selecting **Only the following IP addresses** on the Interfaces properties page, shown in Figure 3.12. The list will contain the IP addresses of all the interfaces that were active on the computer when the DNS service was installed. Use the **Add** and **Remove** buttons to change the IP addresses that appear in the list.

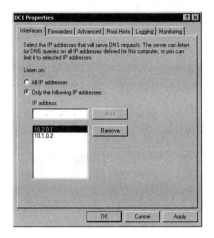

FIGURE 3.12

Interfaces properties determine which interfaces on the DNS server will accept DNS queries.

Forwarders Properties

The DNS server can be configured to forward queries to designated forwarders. This technique is used to enable cache-only servers. As discussed previously, forwarding DNS servers function as focal points for name resolution requests outside an enterprise, resolving all outside queries so that they retain all query results in their cache.

Use of forwarders is enabled on the **Forwarders** properties page, shown in Figure 3.13. If **Enable forwarders** is checked, the server attempts to resolve the query, using the following steps:

1. First, the server attempts to resolve the query using its local cache or data in zones that it is hosting.

2. If the server cannot resolve the request from cache or zone records, it sends the query to the DNS servers that appear in its list of forwarders. After querying a forwarder, the server waits for a timeout interval before trying to resolve the query using the next forwarder in its list.

3. If none of the forwarders responds with a query resolution, the server attempts to resolve the query itself.

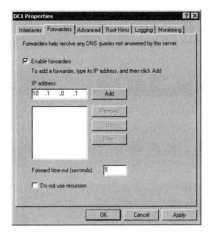

FIGURE 3.13
Configuring forwarders for a zone.

By default, when the forwarders fail, the server will fall back on its normal mode of operation and initiate recursive queries for any queries not answered by the forwarders. In rare instances, you might want to prevent certain name servers from attempting to resolve queries by checking **Do not use recursion**.

Advanced Properties

Figure 3.14 shows the **Advanced** properties tab. You might never need to modify anything on this page and should be aware that most of the settings significantly alter the functionality of the DNS service.

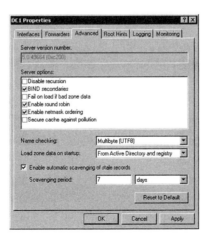

FIGURE 3.14
Configuring advanced properties for a zone.

Six check boxes appear under the heading **Server Options**:

- **Disable recursion.** If you check this option, the server will no longer conduct recursive searches on behalf of DNS clients. If the DNS server cannot resolve a query from its local cache or zones, it can provide a referral to another name server that might be able to resolve the client's query. Typically, recursion is disabled on private networks wherein all DNS RRs exist as internal resources. Recursion is also disabled when a particular DNS server cannot conduct a recursive query. Because DNS clients seldom have the capability to conduct a recursive DNS query on their own, inappropriately disabling recursion can render clients incapable of resolving DNS queries.

- **BIND secondaries.** Determines whether to use a fast transfer format when performing zone transfers to BIND servers. Fast transfer format uses compression and can include multiple RRs per message. Fast transfer format is used on all Windows DNS servers and is available on BIND versions 4.9.4 and later.

- **Fail on load if bad zone data.** If checked, the DNS service requires strict adherence to file format conventions when loading a zone database file. Any errors will prevent the zone from loading. Normally, the Windows DNS service rejects records containing errors and logs the error, but continues to load the database.

- **Enable round robin.** Round robin addressing is enabled by default. See the section "Supporting Round Robin Addressing" for an explanation of how the feature works.

- **Enable netmask ordering.** If a name resolves to more than one IP address, the DNS service can use subnet mask information to prioritize the options. See the Windows 2000 Help for a more thorough explanation.

- **Secure cache against pollution.** When enabled, this option prevents the DNS service from caching responses to queries that are unrelated to the original query. This is usually desirable behavior, and the option is enabled by default.

The value of the **Name checking** field determines the rules restricting the characters that can appear in DNS names. Three options are available:

- **Multibyte (UTF8).** Permits 8-bit ASCII characters and Unicode. Multibyte characters are transformed using the Unicode Transformation Format (UTF-8) support of Windows 2000 Server. This is the default value.

- **Non RFC (ANSI).** Permits names that do not strictly conform to RFC 1123. Permits most displayable ASCII characters.

- **Strict RFC (ANSI).** Permits only names that strictly conform to RFC 1123. Permits ASCII characters a–z, 0–9, and - (hyphen) only. This setting ensures compatibility with all DNS servers and clients and should be selected if names will be resolved through the Internet DNS namespace.

By default, the Windows 2000 DNS server stores zone data in Active Directory (if Active Directory is enabled) and in the Registry. Particularly when importing data from other name servers, you might want to configure the DNS service so that the zone is initialized from another source. Three options are available:

- **From Active Directory and registry.** Standard domains will be loaded from the Registry. Active Directory-integrated zones are loaded from Active Directory.

- **From registry.** Zone data are stored in and loaded from the Registry.

- **From file.** Zone data are loaded from a text database file. See the section "Importing and Exporting BIND Databases" for more about this option.

Automatic scavenging enables the DNS service to discard stale zone records. If you check **Enable automatic scavenging of stale records**, you can specify an interval at which scavenging will take place.

> **NOTE**
>
> You can initiate scavenging manually by right-clicking a DNS server in the DNS Management Console and selecting **Scavenge stale resource records** in the context menu.

Root Hints Properties

As we discussed earlier, when a name server cannot resolve a DNS query using information in its cache or local zone files, it will usually start searching the DNS namespace starting with the root domain. To do this, the server must know the identity of at least one of the servers that is authoritative for the root domain. That information takes the form of root hints, which are defined on the Root Hints properties tab, shown in Figure 3.15.

The root hints are initialized with hints for the Internet root domain servers when the DNS service is installed. The identities of these servers seldom change, and it is unlikely that you will need to modify any of the default entries.

If you are running a private DNS namespace, however, you will need to remove records pertaining to the Internet root name servers. You'll insert hints that identify the servers which are authoritative for your private root domain. Use the **Add** and **Remove** buttons to modify the hints, as required for your network.

3

THE DOMAIN
NAME SYSTEM

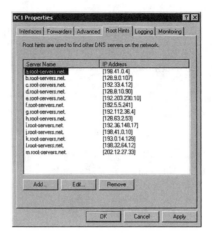

FIGURE 3.15
By default, the root hints identify the Internet root domain servers.

> **NOTE**
>
> Private networks often do not require root name servers because the DNS servers are typically aware of all the DNS domains used in the organization. When all queries are made to known domains, there is no need to send a query to the root domain. If it were not connected to the Internet, the sample network would not require a root domain because all queries are made in the pseudo-corp.com domain, and every name server has a copy of the zone containing that domain.
>
> Chapter 4 describes the procedures required to configure private root name servers.

> **NOTE**
>
> On most DNS servers, RRs pertaining to root name servers are stored in a zone named CACHE. We will discuss the manner in which BIND handles root name servers later in the chapter.

Logging Properties

Figure 3.16 shows the **Logging** properties tab for the DNS server. You can configure the service to maintain logs about the following events:

- **Query.** Queries received from clients
- **Notify.** Notifications received from other servers
- **Update.** Dynamic updates received from other computers
- **Questions.** The contents of the question sections of DNS queries received
- **Answers.** The contents of the answer section of each response the server generates
- **Send.** The number of queries sent by the DNS service to other DNS servers
- **Receive.** The number of queries received
- **UDP.** The number of DNS requests received over a UDP port
- **TCP.** The number of DNS requests received over a TCP port
- **Full packets.** The number of full packets written and sent by the service
- **Write through.** The number of packets written through by the service and back to the zone

FIGURE 3.16
DNS server logging options are configured on the Logging properties page.

Logging is a resource-intensive process that should ordinarily be carried out only when testing and debugging operation of the DNS service. If logging is activated on a live server, performance can suffer, and log files might grow to consume significant amounts of disk space. Unlike with Windows 2000's own log files, there is no provision for configuring DNS logging to discard old records or set a maximum size on log files.

Monitoring Properties

The **Monitoring** properties tab, shown in Figure 3.17, is actually an interface to some tools used to test the DNS service. You can configure two types of tests:

- **A simple query against this DNS server.** This test determines whether the server can resolve queries to local zone databases.
- **A recursive query to other DNS servers.** The DNS server will attempt to query other name servers using a recursive search.

The results of tests are reported in the **Test results** list box.

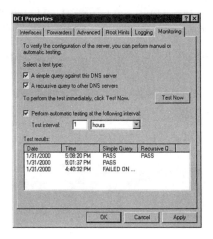

FIGURE 3.17
Tests on the Monitoring tab can be used to report proper operation of the DNS server.

You might want to schedule these tests so that they are performed automatically at specified intervals. If you check **Perform automatic testing at the following interval**, you can specify an interval in seconds, minutes, or hours.

If the most recent tests failed, an Information icon (a yellow warning triangle with an exclamation mark) appears beside the server's name in the DNS console.

NOTE

At the time I am writing this, I have been unable to get these tests to succeed with servers that are not integrated into Active Directory. However, servers that are hosting only standard zones and that are not configured as Active Directory domain controllers do resolve actual queries properly. So, don't panic if you run the tests, and they fail. You can also use the NSLOOKUP utility to test the servers. NSLOOKUP is covered near the end of this chapter.

Creating the Primary Forward Lookup Zone

The first step in configuring the server is to create the forward lookup zone. The following procedure must be performed on the computer that will host the primary zone database:

1. In the DNS console, expand the object tree to locate the DNS server that will host the new zone. Right-click the server name.

> **NOTE**
>
> You can also start creation of a forward lookup zone by right-clicking on the **Forward Lookup Zones** object. The **Forward or Reverse Lookup Zone** dialog box is omitted when you start the wizard in this manner.

2. Choose **New Zone** in the context menu to open the **New Zone Wizard**.

3. Click **Next** to open the **Zone Type** dialog box, shown in Figure 3.18. Because Active Directory is not installed on this server, the **Active Directory-integrated** option would not be active. The option is activated in the figure for clarity.

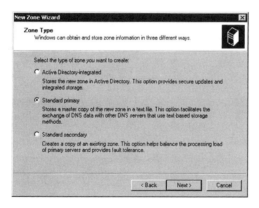

FIGURE 3.18

Specifying the type of zone to be created.

4. Select **Standard Primary**.

5. Click **Next** to open the **Forward or Reverse Lookup Zone** dialog box, shown in Figure 3.19.

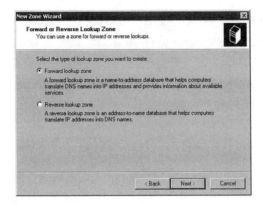

FIGURE 3.19

Specifying whether a forward or reverse lookup zone will be created.

   6. Select **Forward lookup zone**.

   7. Click **Next** to open the **Zone Name** dialog box, shown in Figure 3.20.

   8. To name the zone, enter the FQDN of the topmost domain that will occupy the zone being created.

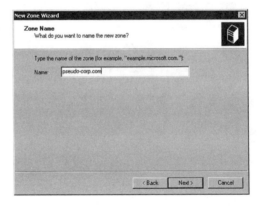

FIGURE 3.20

Zones are named with the FQDN of the topmost domain that will occupy the zone.

   9. Click **Next** to open the **Zone File** dialog box, shown in Figure 3.21.

  10. Data for a standard primary zone are stored in a file with the name you specify. To create a new zone database file, select **Create a new file with this file name**. I suggest that you use the default filename displayed, which consists of the zone's name with a dns file-name extension.

If you want to initialize the zone using data in an existing database file, select **Use this existing file** and enter the filename in the text box. (This option can be used to import data from a BIND database file.)

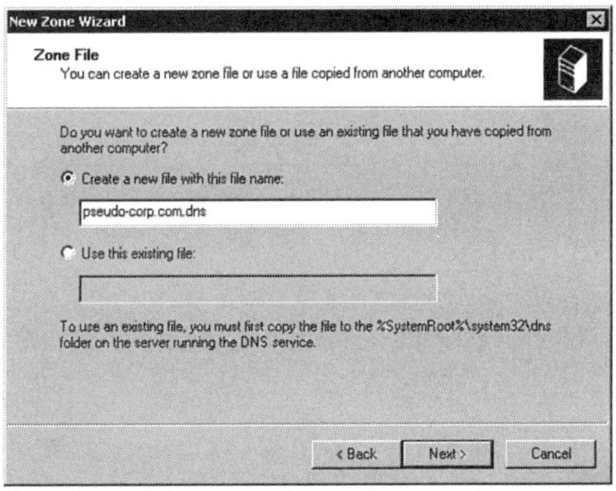

FIGURE 3.21
Specifying the name of the zone database file.

11. Click **Next** to view the closing dialog box (see Figure 3.22), which summarizes the characteristics of the zone you are about to create. Review the zone settings. You can use the Back button to return to any step in the wizard and make changes.

FIGURE 3.22
At the end of the wizard, this box describes the zone settings.

12. Click **Finish** to create the zone.

The database for a new zone is automatically populated with a minimum set of resource records, consisting of

- **Start of Authority.** This RR identifies the administrative contact for the zone and defines several operational parameters.
- **Name Server.** This RR specifies that the server selected in Step 1 is a name server for the zone.
- **Host (Address).** If the selected DNS server has more than one interface, a host address RR will be created for each interface.

The zone is operational as soon as it is created. It can resolve names, and new RRs can be added to the zone database. The next few sections discuss the various types of RRs with which you can expect to work.

Creating the Primary Reverse Lookup Zone

As mentioned earlier, reverse lookup zones are not required fare. If you choose to create them, the DNS console makes your life easier by creating a reverse lookup RR to match each forward lookup Address RR that you create. So it is a good idea to create your reverse lookup zones before you start populating your zones with host records. Reverse lookup primary zones are created as follows:

1. In the DNS Management Console, expand the object tree to locate the DNS server that will be hosting the new zone. Right-click the server name.
2. Choose **New Zone** in the context menu to open the New Zone Wizard.
3. Click **Next** to open the **Zone Type** dialog box.
4. Select **Standard Primary**.
5. Click **Next** to open the Forward or Reverse Lookup Zone dialog box.
6. Select **Reverse lookup zone**.
7. Click **Next** to open the **Reverse Lookup Zone** dialog box, shown in Figure 3.23.

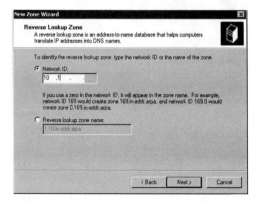

FIGURE 3.23

Specifying the identity of a reverse lookup zone.

8. You can name reverse lookup zones yourself, but the easiest approach is to enter the netid for the zone and let the DNS console name the zone for you.

To specify the zone using the netid, select **Network ID** and enter the netid *only* in the field provided. Any 0 octets that are entered will be included in the zone name. For example, if you enter 10.0, the DNS console will create a zone named `0.10. in-addr.arpa`.

To specify the zone name, select **Reverse lookup zone name** and enter the name.

9. Click **Next** to open the **Zone File** dialog box, shown in Figure 3.24.

10. Data for a standard primary zone are stored in a file with the name that you specify. To create a new zone database file, select **Create a new file with this file name**. I suggest that you use the default filename suggested, which consists of the zone's name with a `.dns` filename extension.

If you want to initialize the zone using data in an existing database file, select **Use this existing file** and enter the filename. This technique enables you to initialize the zone from data in a BIND database file.

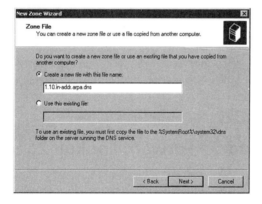

FIGURE 3.24

Specifying the name of a reverse lookup zone database file.

11. Click **Next** to view the closing dialog box. Review the zone's settings. You can use the **Back** button to return to any step in the wizard and make changes.

12. Click **Finish** to create the zone.

Figure 3.25 shows the reverse lookup zone after it has been populated with a few RRs. Notice that a subdomain named 0 has been created in which to place hosts whose IP addresses begin with 10.1.0. The details about establishing subdomains within a parent zone will be covered later in the chapter.

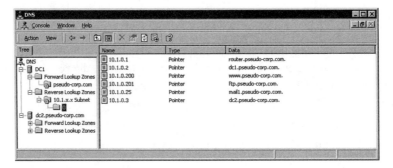

FIGURE 3.25
This reverse lookup zone has been populated with some Pointer resource records.

NOTE

The technique shown in this section assumes that the reverse lookup zone is based on a class-based IP address range wherein the length of the netid field is 8, 16, or 24 bits.

When classless IP addressing is employed, subnetting and supernetting often result in netids with lengths that are not multiples of 8 bits. The Windows 2000 DNS service supports reverse lookup for classless IP address ranges, but the technique requires an understanding of how to support subzones. We'll have to postpone that discussion until later in the chapter. See the section "Configuring Reverse Lookup Zones to Support Classless IP Addresses."

Creating a Secondary Forward Lookup Zone

It is good practice to have at least one secondary zone for each primary zone. Secondary zones require little maintenance beyond the initial effort required to set them up, but they significantly enhance the robustness and performance of a DNS service. The sample network calls for secondary zones running on server DC2.

Before creating the secondary zone, you must add the server to the **Name Servers** list for the primary zone. The procedure for adding name servers to a zone is described in the section "Name Servers Properties" later in this chapter. Unless this is done, the secondary zone cannot start after it is created.

Create a secondary forward lookup zone using the following procedure:

1. Expand the object tree to locate the DNS server that will be hosting the new zone. Right-click the server name.

2. Choose **New Zone** in the context menu to open the **New Zone Wizard**.

3. Click **Next** to open the **Zone Type** dialog box.

4. Select **Standard secondary**.

5. Click **Next** to open the **Forward or Reverse Lookup Zone** dialog box.

6. Select **Forward lookup zone**.

7. Click **Next** to open the **Zone Name** dialog box.

8. Enter the name of the zone.

9. Click **Next** to open the **Master DNS Servers** dialog box, shown in Figure 3.26.

10. Specify the IP address of at least one other DNS server that is authoritative for this zone to serve as a master DNS server for zone transfers. Enter the IP addresses of the DNS masters and click the **Add** button to move the addresses to the list.

    The secondary zone will use the DNS masters in the order they appear in the list. To change the position of an IP address, select it and use the **Up** and **Down** buttons to reposition it.

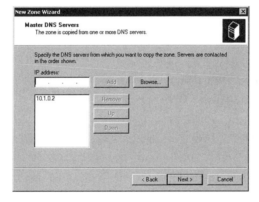

3

THE DOMAIN
NAME SYSTEM

FIGURE 3.26
You must designate one or more DNS servers as masters for a secondary zone.

11. Click **Next** to view the closing dialog box. Review the settings for the zone that is about to be created. You can use the **Back** button to return to any step in the wizard and make changes.

12. Click **Finish** to create the zone.

You must add the server to the **Name Servers** list for the primary zone. The procedure for adding name servers to a zone is described in the section "Name Servers Properties" later in this chapter.

If everything has been configured properly, the secondary zone will be populated with RRs copied from the DNS master. The secondary server requests a zone transfer as soon as it is initialized.

Creating a Secondary Reverse Lookup Zone

Before creating the secondary zone, you must add the server to the **Name Servers** list for the primary zone. The procedure for adding name servers to a zone is described in the section "Name Servers Properties" later in this chapter.

A secondary reverse lookup zone is created much as a secondary forward lookup zone is created. The procedure is as follows:

1. Expand the object tree to locate the DNS server that will be hosting the new zone. Right-click the server name.

2. Choose **New Zone** in the context menu to open the **New Zone Wizard**.

3. Click **Next** to open the **Zone Type** dialog box.

4. Select **Standard Secondary**.

5. Click **Next** to open the **Forward or Reverse Lookup Zone** dialog box.

6. Select **Reverse lookup zone**.

7. Click **Next** to open the **Reverse Lookup Zone** dialog box (refer to Figure 3.23).

8. Select **Network ID** and enter the netid in the field that is provided

   or

   Select **Reverse lookup zone name** and enter the name of the zone.

9. Click **Next** to open the **Master DNS Servers** dialog box.

10. Specify the IP address of at least one other DNS server that is authoritative for this zone to serve as a master DNS server for zone transfers. Enter the IP addresses of the DNS masters and click the **Add** button to move the addresses to the list.

    The secondary zone will use the DNS masters in the order they appear in the list. To change the location of an IP address, select it and use the **Up** and **Down** buttons to reposition it in the list.

11. Click **Next** to view the closing dialog box. Review the settings for the zone that is about to be created. You can use the **Back** button to return to any step in the wizard and make changes.

12. Click **Finish** to create the zone.

If everything has been configured properly, the secondary zone will be populated with RRs copied from the DNS master. The secondary server requests a zone transfer as soon as it is initialized.

Modifying Zone Properties

A number of zone settings are defined as properties, including two types of information that are defined as resource records on most other DNS server implementations: the Start of Authority and the zone name servers. To open the zone property pages, do the following:

1. Right-click the zone in the object tree.
2. Select **Properties** from the context menu to open the zone **Properties** dialog box.
3. Select the desired property page.
4. After making desired changes, click **OK** to close the dialog box.

The next few sections examine the zone property pages.

General Properties

The **General** properties tab appears in Figure 3.27 with options displayed for a standard primary zone. This page reports the status of the zone and enables you to configure several of the zone operational parameters.

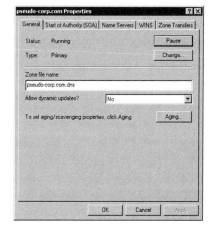

FIGURE 3.27
General properties for a standard primary zone.

General Properties Common to Primary and Secondary Zones

The **Status** field reports whether the zone is Running or Paused. You can pause a zone without stopping the entire DNS service by clicking the **Pause** button. The DNS server will not respond to queries while the zone is paused. Click the **Start** button to resume normal zone operation.

The **Type** field reports the current type of the zone, which can be Primary, Secondary, or Active Directory. You can change the zone type by clicking **Change**. You can convert a zone to the Active Directory-integrated type only if Active Directory is installed on the DNS server.

The **Zone file name** field reports the name of the file in which a primary or secondary server stores its copy of the zone database. You can change this filename, but I recommend that you use the default filename whenever possible.

General Properties of Primary Zones

Some of the properties on the **General** tab apply only to primary zones.

Allow dynamic updates determines whether a primary zone will accept dynamic updates from other services.

The **Aging** button opens the **Zone Aging/Scavenging Properties** dialog box, shown in Figure 3.28. Aging determines whether the DNS service will track the age of RRs created automatically by Dynamic DNS. To keep the DNS database from becoming cluttered, aging can be used to purge old RRs.

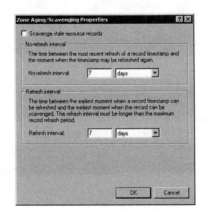

FIGURE 3.28

Aging properties for a primary zone.

If you check **Scavenge stale resource records**, the DNS server maintains a time stamp for RRs defined through DNS and scavenges records that meet the aging criteria you define. In most cases, host records are created and refreshed by DHCP. Therefore, aging characteristics should coordinate with the DHCP lease renewal time. Typically, DHCP leases are configured to renew every few days. The default lease renewal for the Windows 2000 DHCP service is 8 days.

> **NOTE**
>
> Automatic scavenging will not take place on the server unless the option **Enable automatic scavenging of stale records** is enabled on the **Advanced** properties page for the server (refer to Figure 3.14). See the section "Advanced Properties" earlier in this chapter for more about this option.

> **NOTE**
>
> DHCP is discussed in Chapter 5, "Dynamic Host Configuration Protocol."

You can specify two aging parameters:

- **No-refresh interval.** This value specifies the number of days that must elapse following the refresh of an RR and the time when the RR can be refreshed again. Microsoft is rather vague on the purpose of this parameter except to state that increasing the value can result in increased retention of stale RRs. I suggest that you set this parameter to a fairly short value, such as one day, because stale RRs will not be purged until the refresh interval expires.

- **Refresh interval.** This value specifies the number of days that must elapse following the most recent refresh of an RR before the RR can be scavenged. This value should be greater than the maximum refresh interval, which is typically the DHCP lease renewal interval. For example, if your DHCP lease interval is 8 days, set this value to 9 days.

Secondary zones obtain all changes in RRs directly or indirectly from a primary zone. All aging is applied at the primary zone and affects records on secondary zones through zone transfers.

> **NOTE**
>
> Default aging parameters can be set as a property of the DNS server. These default properties apply to all newly created zones unless they are modified for a specific zone. To set default aging properties at the server level, right-click the server name in the object tree and choose **Set Aging/Scavenging for all zones** from the context menu.

General Properties of Secondary Zones

For a standard secondary zone, the **General** zone property tab appears as in Figure 3.29. The **IP Address** list is used to specify the IP address of one or more master DNS servers. You can add or remove IP addresses and change their order. The secondary zone will attempt to initiate zone transfers with master zones in the order that server IP addresses appear in the list.

FIGURE 3.29
The General properties tab for a secondary zone.

Start of Authority Properties

Although the Start of Authority is technically a resource record, it is managed as a zone property. Figure 3.30 shows the **Start of Authority** properties tab on the zone property pages.

> **NOTE**
>
> Secondary zones do not have Start of Authority settings. They use settings received from the primary zone.

The **Serial number** field triggers zone transfers. When a secondary zone server contacts its primary zone server, it checks the zone serial number. A zone transfer is initiated only if the value of the serial number has increased since the last successful zone transfer. After making manual modifications to the zone, click the **Increment** button to add 1 to the current serial number. The serial number is incremented automatically when the zone is modified through Dynamic DNS (DDNS).

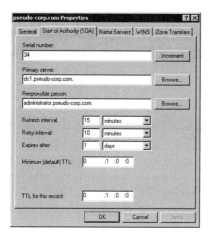

FIGURE 3.30
The Start of Authority properties for a zone.

NOTE

Remember, no zone transfer takes place unless the serial number is incremented! DDNS increments the serial number dynamically, but you must increment it when you make manual changes to the DNS database.

The **Primary server** field specifies the DNS name of the primary master for the zone. This value is defined when the zone is created and seldom requires modification.

By convention, the **Responsible person** field contains the email address of the primary contact person for the zone. There is a catch because the @ character has a special meaning in DNS database files and cannot appear in the email address. A period is entered in place of the @ character, so drew@pseudo-corp.com would be entered as drew.pseudo-corp.com.

The following three parameters determine how any secondary zones should handle data obtained from this primary zone:

- **Refresh interval.** This time specifies the intervals at which the secondary zone server will contact the primary zone server to determine whether its database is current.

- **Retry interval.** If the host of a secondary zone fails to contact a master zone server when it is time to refresh the zone, this parameter specifies the intervals between repeated attempts to contact the zone master server.

- **Expires after.** This value specifies the lifetime of a secondary zone. If the secondary zone host is unable to contact the master zone server before the end of the expiration interval, the secondary zone is to be considered stale, and data should be discarded. Essentially, this value says that after a certain period of time it is better to provide no data at all than to provide data that might be obsolete.

> **NOTE**
>
> The default refresh interval for the Windows 2000 DNS server is a very aggressive 15 minutes, reflecting, I suspect, Microsoft's expectation that Active Directory and DHCP will be making frequent changes to the zone. It is particularly critical to expedite replication of service data to secondaries; otherwise, some clients will be unable to access the services.
>
> The addition of service data changes the nature of DNS significantly. The servers on a network are a fairly stable commodity, and don't come and go. But services can be added, started, stopped, or removed fairly frequently. For example, a print server might be stopped for maintenance and restarted after a few minutes; both changes would need to be available to users with reasonable dispatch.
>
> The primary/secondary approach to providing DNS server redundancy has limitations when frequent changes are made to zones because a zone transfer involves transfer of the complete zone database. With large zones, this can result in significant levels of network traffic.
>
> When zones are integrated with Active Directory, zone replication involves transfer of changes only, with a significant savings in the network traffic generated. For that reason, if for no other, I suggest that you consider using Active Directory–integrated zones whenever possible.

Two parameters affect the TTL value that is returned with the results of each query. The TTL specifies the period of time that the results of a query should be retained in a local cache. You can increase the TTL to reduce the frequency of DNS queries while also increasing the risk that clients will use stale data that have been held in cache. There are two TTL parameters:

- **Minimum (default) TTL.** This parameter specifies the minimum TTL for any RRs that are added to the zone.
- **TTL for this record.** This parameter specifies a TTL for the SOA RR only.

Name Servers Properties

The **Name Server** properties tab (see Figure 3.31) is used to specify the name servers that service a zone. Name servers are listed in Name Server (NS) RRs in the zone database, but you cannot directly edit the RRs. All changes to name servers are made on this properties page.

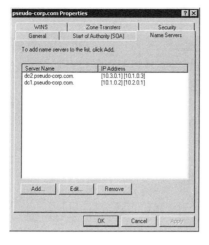

FIGURE 3.31

Name servers assigned to service a zone.

To add a name server to the zone:

1. Create a Host Address resource record for the name server in the appropriate zone. See the section "Adding Host Address Resource Records" for the procedure.

2. Open the properties pages for the name server hosting the primary copy of the zone and select the **Name Servers** page.

3. Click **Add** to open the **Name Server (NS)** dialog box, shown in Figure 3.32.

4. Enter the FQDN for the name server in the **Server name** field. There are a couple of shortcuts you can use in this field:

   - If a Host Address RR already exists, you should be able to browse DNS to find it. Click the **Browse** button to open a browser and browse a zone that contains the Host Address RR. When you select the RR, the **Server name** field will be completed, and the IP address will be inserted into the **IP address** list.

   - If a Host Address RR already exists and you choose to enter the FQDN of the name server, click the **Resolve** button to look up the name server's IP address and stuff it into the **IP address** list.

5. If the IP address has not been specified by browsing or by resolving a name, enter the IP address for the name server in the **IP address** field and click **Add** to copy the IP address to the list.

6. Repeat Step 5 if the name server has additional IP addresses that were not found by browsing or resolving.

7. Click **OK** to add the record to the zone database.

3

**THE DOMAIN
NAME SYSTEM**

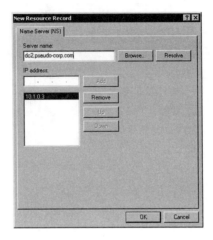

FIGURE 3.32

Creating a new Name Server resource record.

> **NOTE**
>
> Adding a name server to the **Name Servers** properties page does not make it a functioning name server. You must also create a secondary zone on the name server as described in the sections "Creating a Secondary Forward Lookup Zone" and "Creating a Secondary Reverse Lookup Zone."

WINS Properties

Windows 2000 supports WINS for legacy Windows clients. You can configure DNS zones so that the name server will consult WINS if it is unable to resolve a name query using RRs in a zone database. A restriction is that NetBIOS names constitute a flat namespace, and there is no way to allocate NetBIOS names to specific DNS domains. Therefore, you should enable only one zone for WINS lookup so that WINS name resolution reports all NetBIOS names in the same DNS domain.

Forward lookup zones support standard, forward WINS lookup, which is configured in the property page shown in Figure 3.33. Check **Use WINS forward lookup** to enable this feature. You must add the IP address of one or more WINS servers to the list provided.

Reverse lookup zones support reverse WINS lookup, also called WINS-R, which is configured in the property page shown in Figure 3.34. Check **Use WINS-R lookup** to enable this feature. You must add the IP address of one or more WINS servers to the list provided. Because NetBIOS names do not incorporate a domain name, DNS must supply a domain name. All names resolved using WINS-R are reported in the domain you specify in the field **Domain to append to returned name**.

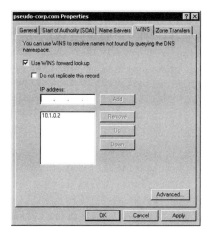

FIGURE 3.33

Configuring forward WINS lookup.

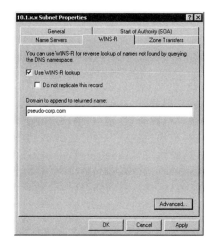

FIGURE 3.34

Configuring reverse WINS lookup.

When you enable WINS lookup, a WINS Lookup RR is added to the zone. This resource record is visible in Figure 3.10.

3

THE DOMAIN
NAME SYSTEM

Zone Transfer Properties

As you have learned, both primary and secondary zones can function as master zones for zone transfers. Use the **Zone Transfers** properties tab, shown in Figure 3.35, to authorize zone transfers. Options on this page can be configured on servers hosting both primary and secondary copies of the zone.

The zone will function as a master zone only if **Allow zone transfers** is checked. This box is checked by default on primary zones and is not checked by default on secondary zones.

If zone transfers are permitted, you can authorize them to all DNS servers or to specified name servers by selecting one of the following options:

- **To any server.** Any server can request a zone transfer.
- **Only to servers listed on the Name Servers tab.** The server permits zone transfers only to name servers that are officially recognized as authoritative for the zone.
- **Only to the following servers.** Use this option if you want to specifically designate secondary zone servers by their IP addresses. Add the IP addresses of authorized servers to the list.

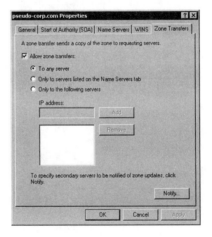

FIGURE 3.35

The zone transfer properties specify which secondary servers can initiate zone transfers for the zone.

Ordinarily, secondary servers wait for the expiration of their refresh timers before checking their masters to determine if a zone transfer is warranted. You can enable the DNS master to notify secondary servers of changes to zone data by clicking the **Notify** button in the Zone Transfers property tab. This opens the **Notify** property page, shown in Figure 3.36.

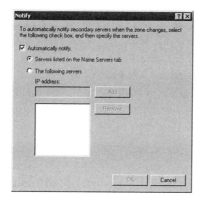

FIGURE 3.36
The Notify properties enable a server to notify secondary servers that zone records have been modified.

Managing Resource Records

At this point, we have a DNS service that works but cannot provide much in the way of useful information. That information must be added in the form of resource records that describe the hosts on the network. We're still doing things the hard way, defining everything by hand. But, even if most of the RRs in your zones will be added by Dynamic DNS, you will often need to manually add, remove, and modify RRs. Some things—such as mail exchangers, round robin addressing, and aliases—just have to be set up manually.

Name Server and Start of Authority RRs are manipulated using the Properties pages for the zone with which they are associated and require no further discussion. There are dozens of types of RRs that are simply beyond the scope of this book. For our purposes, we need to consider three types of RRs for manual entry:

- Address (A) RRs, which identify hosts
- Mail Exchanger (MX) RRs, which identify mail servers
- CNAME RRs, which provide aliases for hosts that already have hostnames

Adding Host Address Resource Records

Address RRs that match a hostname to an IP address will probably be the most populous RRs in your DNS namespace. Every Active Directory domain controller will be identified in DNS with an Address RR. Additionally, if you are configuring your TCP/IP clients using DHCP, you will probably use DDNS to create an Address RR for each DHCP client.

> **NOTE**
>
> If you're used to another implementation of DNS, you might be a bit confused because Microsoft refers to Address RRs as Host RRs. But, when you create a Host record in the Windows 2000 DNS console, an Address resource record is added to the zone database.
>
> To support Microsoft's convention along with everybody else's, I will call them Host Address resource records.

From time to time, however, you will find it necessary to add static Host Address resource records. Many devices cannot or should not be assigned dynamic IP addresses, such as routers and DNS servers. To assign names to these devices, you must create a static Host Address record.

Another reason for creating static Host Address RRs is that RRs created with DDNS are subject to aging and might be scavenged. RRs that you define manually are static and are not subject to scavenging.

The sample network has two servers that might be accessed by outside users: www.pseudo-corp.com and ftp.pseudo-corp.com. Additionally, it will be useful to assign a name to the internal router interface to make it easier to manage the router. Host Address records must be manually created for these devices.

To create a Host Address resource record:

1. Open the DNS console and browse the object tree to select the zone that will contain the Host Address RR.
2. Right-click the zone, or right-click in the Resource Record pane.
3. Select **New Host** in the context menu to open the **New Host** dialog box, shown in Figure 3.37.
4. Because the resource record is created in the zone that was selected in Step 2, it is unnecessary to specify the host's FQDN. Enter the host's name in the **Name** field.

> **NOTE**
>
> An FQDN can be optionally specified in the **Name** field. See the section "Supporting Subdomains" later in the chapter to see one reason why you might do so.

FIGURE 3.37
Creating a new Host Address resource record.

5. Enter the host's IP address in the **IP address** field.

6. Check **Create associated pointer (PTR) record** if you have created a reverse lookup zone and want the DNS Management Console to create an appropriate PTR record. For automatic creation of PTR RRs to work, the primary for the reverse lookup zone must reside on the computer on which the Host Address RR is being created.

7. Click **Add Host** to create the RR.

Adding Mail Exchanger Resource Records

The sample network incorporates a single SMTP mail server. Mail servers that need to deliver mail to any of the domains on our network will query DNS for Mail Exchanger RRs that identify mail servers for the domains. Therefore, a Mail Exchanger RR must be created for
`mail1.pseudo-corp.com`.

To create a Mail Exchanger RR, do the following:

1. Create a Host Address RR that identifies the mail exchanger. The Host Address RR can be in any domain, but the Mail Exchanger RR refers to the computer by name, so the Address RR has to exist or the Mail Exchanger RR won't work properly.

2. Open the DNS console and browse the object tree to select the zone that will contain the Mail Exchanger RR.

3. Right-click the zone, or right-click in the Resource Record pane.

4. Select **New Mail Exchanger** in the context menu to open the New Resource Record dialog box, shown in Figure 3.38.

5. In the **Host or domain** field, enter the name of a host or domain that is a recipient of mail delivered by this mail exchanger. In most cases, this field is left blank, in which case the delivery domain is the same as the domain in which the RR is created.

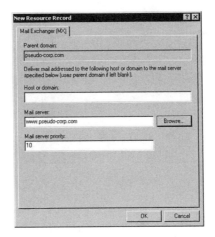

FIGURE 3.38
Creating a new Mail Exchanger resource record.

> **NOTE**
>
> Periods are not allowed in the **Host or domain** field. If you need to create a Mail Exchanger RR for a child domain, add the child domain as described later in the chapter and create the Mail Exchanger RR in the child domain.

6. In the **Mail server** field, specify the FQDN of the mail exchanger. This is a rare instance when you must enter a FQDN, but it makes sense because the mail exchanger could be a machine that handles mail for several domains.

If the Host Address RR for the mail exchanger was created previously, you can click the **Browse** button and browse the domain database and select the host by its resource record.

> **NOTE**
>
> I wish Microsoft would standardize on terminology. It's bad enough that they use the term Host to refer to an RR that everyone else calls an Address RR. But in the same procedure they use the terms mail server and mail exchanger to refer to the same thing. Well, they are the same thing, so don't let the changes in terms throw you.

7. In the **Mail server priority** field, enter a number in the range of 0 through 65535. (Mail exchanger priorities are discussed following this step-by-step procedure.)

8. Click **OK** to create the resource record.

To enable mail delivery to continue when a mail exchanger is shut down, it is common to configure two or more mail exchangers to service a domain. The **Mail server priority** value determines the order in which various mail exchangers will be used.

> **NOTE**
>
> The mail server priority parameter is referred to as a mail server preference in many DNS references. The function is the same regardless of the name being used.

Suppose that a domain is serviced by the following three mail exchangers:

- `mail1.pseudo-corp.com` with a priority of 1
- `mail2.pseudo-corp.com` with a priority of 25
- `mail3.pseudo-corp.com` with a priority of 10

An outside mail program will attempt to send mail addressed to this domain to mail exchangers mail1, mail3, mail2 in that order.

Alternatively, suppose that these three mail exchanger records are defined for the domain:

- `mail1.pseudo-corp.com` with a priority of 10
- `mail2.pseudo-corp.com` with a priority of 5
- `mail3.pseudo-corp.com` with a priority of 10

First, the outside mail program tries to deliver mail to mail2. If mail2 is unavailable, it arbitrarily selects mail1 or mail3. If that server is unavailable, the outside program attempts to contact the remaining priority 10 mail exchanger.

Priority values are purely relative. Priorities of 1 and 10 have exactly the same effect as priorities of 1 and 2. It is common practice to leave gaps in the priorities that are selected to make it easy to insert a new mail exchanger in the middle of the priority sequence.

Supporting Aliases

In the previous section, notice that each of the Web servers has a dual identity. You can add as many Host Address RRs as you want for a given IP address.

3

THE DOMAIN
NAME SYSTEM

In some cases, however, you might want to provide additional names by configuring aliases for existing names. Suppose, for example, that you have set up Microsoft's Internet Information Server on a computer. IIS can provide a wide variety of services, including World Wide Web and FTP. You want to offer the domain names `www.pseudo-corp.com` and `ftp.pseudo-corp.com`. In fact, that is the situation on the sample network.

Yes, you could define each name with a Host Address resource record. But then, what happens if the IIS server is moved to a different subnet and receives a new IP address? You would need to remember to modify every Host Address RR that points to the server.

But aliases point to a hostname, not to an IP address. So one approach would be to create the following RRs:

- A Host Address RR that relates the name `iis.pseudo-corp.com` to the IP address 10.1.0.200
- An alias that associates the name `www.pseudo-corp.com` with `iis.pseudo-corp.com`
- An alias that associates the name `ftp.pseudo-corp.com` with `iis.pseudo-corp.com`

Now, if the IP address for `iis.pseudo-corp.com` is changed, the aliases will still point to the correct host.

In DNS terminology, an alias is called a *canonical name* and is defined in a CNAME resource record. The procedure for creating an alias is as follows:

1. Create a Host Address RR for the device.
2. Browse the object tree in the DNS console to locate the domain in which the alias will be created.
3. Right-click the name of the domain and select **Alias** from the context menu to open the **New Resource Record** dialog box, shown in Figure 3.39.
4. Enter the alias name in the **Alias name** field. Omit a domain name to create the alias in the domain selected in Step 2. Or include the name of a subdomain to create an alias in a child domain.
5. Enter the FQDN of the target host in the **Fully qualified name for target host** field. You can click the **Browse** button to select the target host by browsing the DNS database.
6. Click **OK** to create the resource record.

Aliases make it easier to change host IP addresses. That's the primary reason for using them. But aliases cannot be used to configure round robin addressing. If you require round robin addressing, you will need to create Host Address resource records.

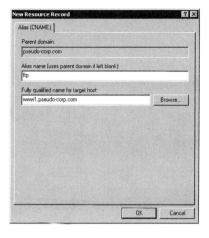

FIGURE 3.39
Creating an alias resource record.

DNS Management: What's Happened So Far

It has taken a lot of steps to get us this far. At this point, the DNS service supports the simple network shown in Figure 3.9. Although it looks like a lot of work is required to establish the basic configuration, the work goes very quickly, particularly after you have a bit of experience. To summarize, the basic sequence of events is as follows:

1. Create the desired primary forward lookup zones.

2. Create the desired primary reverse lookup zones.

3. Review the Start of Authority records in the primary zones. Verify the root name servers and operational parameters. Add the mail address of the primary zone contact.

4. Add PTR resource records to the reverse lookup zones that enable reverse lookups to the zone name servers declared in Steps 1 and 2.

5. Create Host Address resource records for any name servers that will host secondary zones.

6. Create the desired secondary zones anytime after the primary zones are established.

7. Create any other required resource records.

Testing the Name Server

Windows 2000 includes the NSLOOKUP utility, which can be used to query DNS servers and verify their correct operation. But a simple test is simply to ping a host by its domain name. `ping` will attempt to resolve the hostname to an IP address through DNS before attempting to communicate with the target host.

Chapter 2, "TCP/IP Protocol Concepts," introduced ping, which generates ICMP Echo Request messages and attempts to solicit Echo Reply messages from a target host. Figure 3.40 illustrates the result of pinging a host by name. If the DNS lookup succeeds, the resulting IP address is reported in the resulting dialog.

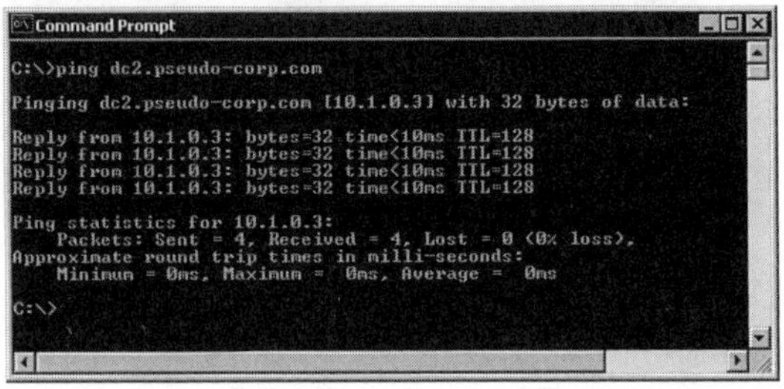

FIGURE 3.40
Pinging a host by name to test DNS operation.

Scaling DNS for Large Networks

Until now we have looked at the most rudimentary of DNS features, features that are essential on all networks. Now we will examine some more advanced features that enable DNS to support larger and busier networks. We will look at two techniques for scaling DNS:

- Methods of supporting subdomains
- Using round robin addressing to distribute access to multiple servers

Figure 3.41 shows a more elaborate network than that in Figure 3.9. In this case, Pseudo Corporation has two sites. The hosts at those sites will be placed in subzones that will be managed locally. For the purposes of this exercise, server dc2 has been relocated to Paris and now has the IP address 192.168.25.2. The following domains are required:

- **pseudo-corp.com.** This zone will contain RRs for all publicly accessed hosts, such as the Web, mail, and FTP servers. The primary for this zone will be in Chicago.
- **chicago.pseudo-corp.com.** This zone will contain RRs for all hosts based in Chicago. The primary for this zone will be hosted by a server in Chicago. A secondary zone will be hosted by a name server in Paris.
- **paris.pseudo-corp.com.** This zone will contain RRs for all hosts based in Paris. The primary for this zone will be hosted by a server in Chicago. A secondary zone will be hosted by a name server in Chicago.
- **1.10.in-addr.arpa.** This is the reverse-naming zone for hosts in Chicago. The primary for this zone will be hosted by a server in Chicago. A secondary zone will be hosted by a name server in Paris.

- **25.168.192.in-addr.arpa.** This is the reverse-naming zone for hosts in Paris. The primary for this zone will be hosted by a server in Paris. A secondary zone will be hosted by a name server in Chicago.

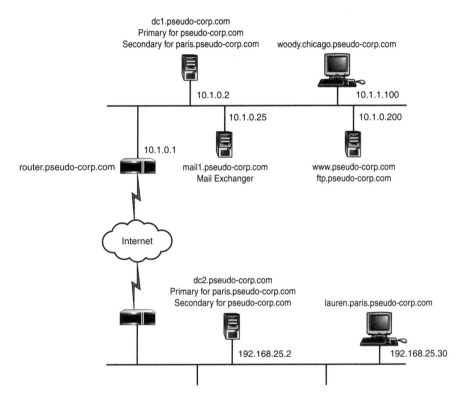

FIGURE 3.41

This DNS namespace has two subdomains and two sites.

All mail will be addressed to the pseudo-corp.com domain, for example, drew@pseudo-corp.com. Multiple mail servers will be located in Chicago.

The corporation has installed three World Wide Web servers to keep up with demand. All Web servers contain the same information, and we want to balance usage across the three servers. The required technique is called *round robin addressing*.

Alias names will be assigned to select hosts. Aliases enable the same host to have more than one DNS name.

The first order of business is to establish support for the subdomains. Then we can populate the namespace with records.

Supporting Subdomains

There are two ways to support hosts in a DNS subdomain:

- Include the child domain in the same zone as the parent domain. This approach separates the domains but requires them to be hosted by the same name server. This is the technique that will be used to establish the chicago.pseudo-corp.com subdomain.

- Create the child domain in a separate zone. This approach separates the domains and enables them to be hosted by separate DNS servers. This technique will be used to support paris.pseudo-corp.com.

Creating a Child Domain in the Parent Domain's Zone

This technique is more commonly employed when the same server will host the primary copies of both the parent and child zones. It is very simple to create the child domain:

1. Open the DNS console and browse the object tree to select the zone that will contain the child domain.

2. Right-click the parent zone.

3. Select **New Domain** in the context menu to open the **New Domain**.

4. Enter the new domain name.

5. Click **OK**.

Figure 3.42 shows the chicago subdomain, hosted in the pseudo-corp.com zone. Notice that the subdomain does not have Start of Authority or Name Server resource records. Those records are assigned at the zone level.

It is also unnecessary to delegate authority for this child domain, as is required when the child domain will be hosted by another name server, as described in the next section.

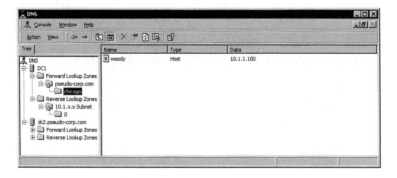

FIGURE 3.42
The chicago *child domain is hosted in the* pseudo-corp.com *zone.*

> **NOTE**
>
> A zone can contain the records for one or more domains. This is the reason DNS terminology distinguishes between domains and zones. The zone is named after the topmost domain in the hierarchy.

Creating a Child Domain in a Separate Zone

If the same DNS server will not host the primary databases for the child domain, it is necessary to add resource records to the parent domain that delegate control to the zone containing the child domain. The procedure for doing so gets a bit involved because appropriate hints must be placed in the parent domain. First, the zone is created to host the child domain. Then the parent domain is configured with the delegation resource records.

Creating the Zone for the Child Domain

The procedure for creating the zone is the same one that we followed earlier in the section "Creating the Primary Forward Lookup Zone." On a name server in Paris, we use the New Domain Wizard to create a zone named `paris.pseudo-corp.com`. Then we add the resource records for the `paris` subdomain. The results are shown in Figure 3.43.

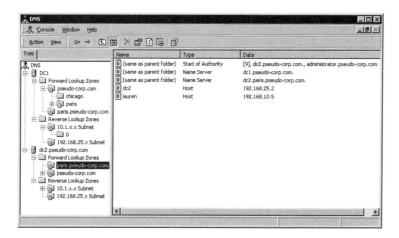

FIGURE 3.43

The `paris.pseudo-corp.com` *primary zone on server dc2.*

Also create at least one secondary zone. A secondary zone can be created on any name server. For our purposes, it will be created on the name server dc1 in Chicago.

Delegating Authority to the Child Zone

Next, the zone delegation records must be added to the `pseudo-corp.com` zone. Here is the procedure:

1. Expand the object tree to locate the parent domain and right-click the parent domain name.

2. Choose **New Delegation** in the context menu to open the New Delegation Wizard.

3. Click **Next** to open the Delegated Domain Name dialog box, shown in Figure 3.44.

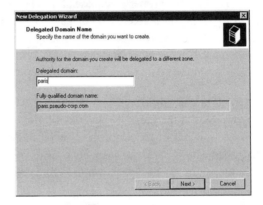

FIGURE 3.44

Delegating authority to a domain.

4. Enter the name of the subdomain in the **Delegated domain** field. The resulting FQDN will be completed for you in the **Fully qualified domain name** field.

5. Click **Next** to open the **Name Servers** dialog box, shown in Figure 3.45.

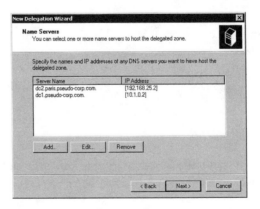

FIGURE 3.45

Specifying name servers that are authoritative for a delegated domain.

6. Use the **Add**, **Edit**, and **Remove** buttons to designate the names and IP addresses of name servers that are authoritative for the delegated zone.

7. Click **Next** and review the delegation settings.

8. Click **Finish** to complete the wizard and add the delegation hints to the domain.

Figure 3.46 shows the `pseudo-corp.com` zone after hints have been added for the `paris` subdomain. The hints consist of two types of entries:

- A subdomain folder, which in the present example is named `paris`

- Within the subdomain folder, Name Server RRs that identify name servers authoritative for the subdomain

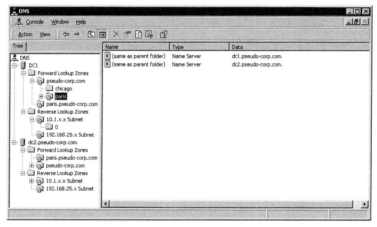

FIGURE 3.46
Domain records showing a delegation of authority.

Notice that delegated name servers are identified by their FQDNs. Consequently, a matching Host Address RR must exist for each name server.

Supporting Round Robin Addressing

As mentioned earlier, the expanded Pseudo Corp network has three Web servers that will share the load of servicing user requests. All three Web servers have identical copies of the Web site, and it's up to DNS to enable users to access them.

The required mechanism is amazingly simple: Create a Host Address resource record for each Web server. Use the same domain name in each Host Address resource record, but point each RR at the IP address of a different computer. Figure 3.47 shows the resource records that are required.

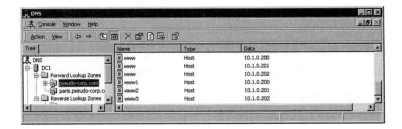

FIGURE 3.47
Resource records providing round robin name support.

Notice that each Web server has an individual name (www1, www2, and www3). These are necessary so that the administrators of the Web servers can access the hosts individually to manage
the computers and to upload copies of the Web files.

But there are also three Host Address RRs for the hostname www, each with a different IP
address. When clients ask DNS to resolve www.pseudo-corp.com, the name servers for
pseudo-corp.com will respond by cycling through the RRs that match the hostname. Thus
some clients will be sent to host 10.1.0.200, some to 10.1.0.201, and some to 10.1.0.202.

> **NOTE**
>
> Round robin addressing is enabled by default. It can be disabled on the Advanced
> Properties page for the zone. See the section "Advanced Properties" earlier in this
> chapter for an explanation.

Configuring Reverse Lookup Zones to Support Classless IP Addresses

Classless address schemes (CIDR; see Chapter 2) are increasingly the rule rather than the
exception when IP address ranges are assigned to organizations. Reverse lookups have always
presented a special problem with classless addressing because reverse lookup domains in the
Internet namespace assume a class-based address scheme with netids having lengths of 8, 16,
or 32 bits.

My small organization has been assigned a /27 address space carved out of a Class C address
range. Until recently, I could only support reverse lookups for my IP addresses by relying on
my ISP to support the reverse lookup zone. This is a problem because most (if not all) ISPs
don't allow Windows to make Dynamic DNS updates to zones on their DNS servers.

But, suppose that the ISP is willing to delegate authority to my name servers for reverse lookups on my IP addresses. Is there a way to configure reverse lookup zones based on classless IP addresses? Yes, there is, and it's a pretty straightforward extension of the subdomain concepts just discussed.

Suppose that an organization has been assigned the IP address range 192.168.5.64/26, which permits the organization to use IP addresses 192.168.5.64 through 192.168.5.127 with a subnet mask of 255.255.255.192. How does the organization configure the reverse lookup zone on its own DNS servers? Here is the procedure:

1. Create a reverse lookup zone for the classful IP address range that contains the CIDR address range. In this case, you would create a reverse lookup zone for the netid 192.168.5, using procedures described earlier in the chapter.

2. Right-click the class-based reverse lookup zone in the DNS Management console and choose **New Domain** from the context menu.

3. In the **New Domain** dialog box, specify the classless address range using the notation *<subnet>*/*<network mask length>* wherein

   - *<subnet>* is the starting IP address in the address range, and

   - *<network mask length>* is the number of bits in the netid portion of the subnet mask.

   For example, you would enter 64/26 to indicate a subnet starting on IP address 192.168.5.64 with a 26-bit subnet mask. (The first three octets of the address range are established by the reverse lookup zone itself.)

4. Click **OK**.

Figure 3.48 shows the DNS Management Console after the subdomain has been established.

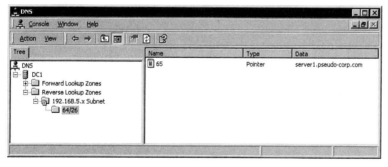

FIGURE 3.48
Reverse lookup has been configured for the address range 192.168.5/26.

NOTE

The procedure for automatically creating PTR RRs while creating Host Address RRs does not work when the IP address falls in a classless range defined in this way. You will need to create the PTR RRs manually.

Importing and Exporting BIND Databases

The data for standard primary zones are stored in database files that are compatible with BIND, making it convenient for you to move zones between BIND and Windows 2000 DNS servers. If you need to work with BIND, you will need to understand the formats of these files.

A BIND database file is required for each zone. The formats are different for forward and reverse lookup zones, so we'll need to consider them separately.

Additionally, BIND stores information about root name servers in a zone named CACHE. The format of the CACHE database file is similar to the format of a forward lookup database, but we will look at the CACHE file separately because of its particular significance.

Importing Data from BIND

If you have copies of the database files for BIND, it is easy to import the data into a zone that is hosted on a Windows 2000 DNS server. Refer back to the discussion about creating primary forward and reverse lookup zones and in particular to Figure 3.21.

In that dialog box, you have the option of supplying the name of a zone database file. Simply copy the BIND database files to the directory %systemroot%\system32\dns on the Windows 2000 Server and supply the name of the file when running the **New Zone Wizard**. When the zone is started, it will be initialized with data from the database file you supplied.

When importing the file, remember that BIND database files are created manually using a text editor. Administrators will have different styles for formatting these files, and you should review the files before attempting to import them to Windows 2000. However, the Windows DNS service should support all the features of BIND, and properly formatted resource records should import to Windows 2000 without problems.

To force an existing primary zone to import data from a text database file, do the following:

1. Place the file in the directory %SystemRoot%\system32\dns.

2. Open the properties for the zone and on the **General** properties tab, edit the **Zone file name** field so that it matches the name of the database file that is to be imported (refer to Figure 3.27).

3. Open the properties pages for the server. On the Advanced tab, select **From file** in the field **Load zone data on startup** (refer to Figure 3.14).

4. Restart the DNS service, or right-click the zone name in the object tree and select **Reload** from the context menu.

5. Reset the value of the **Load zone data on startup** field if you want to store zone data in the Registry or in Active Directory.

The above procedure works only with primary zones. Secondary zones by definition obtain data from primary zones.

Exporting Data to BIND

As mentioned earlier, the data for standard primary and secondary zones are stored in BIND-compatible files. You will have to do more work when exporting to BIND than when importing to Windows 2000. Keep the following things in mind when exporting to BIND:

- Remove any resource records from the database files that BIND does not understand. In particular, remove any WINS resource records.

- Do not place copies of secondary zone database files on the DNS servers. Let BIND build its own database files by transferring the zone from a primary.

- You will need to configure suitable boot configuration files for each server. Boot files are not created by Windows 2000 and are beyond the scope of this chapter.

- Don't forget to set up the root CACHE database file.

NOTE

You can obtain an up-to-date copy of the root domain database file by using FTP to retrieve the file /domain/named.root from FTP.RS.INTERNIC.NET.

To force the Windows 2000 DNS service to update the text database files from its active database, do the following:

1. Right-click a zone name in the DNS Management Console object tree.

2. Select **Update Server Data File** from the context menu.

BIND Database File Formats

BIND database files are text files that are read when the name service is started. The name service on a BIND DNS server is called the Name Daemon. On UNIX systems, a daemon is a background process similar to a service on Windows 2000. The Name Daemon service is invoked using the command named.

The following sections review the formats of the database files for forward lookup, reverse lookup, and root cache zones.

Forward Lookup Database Files

The following listing is a simple database file for a forward lookup zone.

```
;   Database file pseudo-corp.com.dns for pseudo-corp.com zone.
;       Zone version:  25
;
@                       IN  SOA dc1.pseudo-corp.com.  administrator.pseudo-
➥corp.com. (
                        25              ; serial number
                        900             ; refresh
                        600             ; retry
                        86400           ; expire
                        3600        )  ; minimum TTL
;
;   Zone NS records
;
@                       NS   dc1.pseudo-corp.com.
@                       NS   dc2.pseudo-corp.com.
;
;   Delegated sub-zone:  paris.pseudo-corp.com.
;
paris                   NS   dc2.pseudo-corp.com.
;   End delegation
;
;   Zone records
;
@                       MX   10    mail1.pseudo-corp.com.
dc1                     A    10.1.0.2
dc2                     A    10.1.0.3
mail1                   A    10.1.0.25
router                  A    10.1.0.1
www                     A    10.1.0.200
                        A    10.1.0.201
                        A    10.1.0.203
www1                    A    10.1.0.200
www2                    A    10.1.0.201
www3                    A    10.1.0.203
```

If you understand two critical things about the database file, it is easier to relate the listing back to our work with the Windows 2000 DNS server:

- Any text that follows a ; on a line is ignored. This convention enables administrators to format the file and insert comments.

- The @ sign means "this zone," that is, the zone defined by this database file. It has the same meaning as the "(same as parent folder)" notation in resource records on the Windows 2000 DNS server.

Address resource records require little explanation. It is clear, for example, that

```
www                          A    10.1.0.200
```

is a Host Address resource record that maps a hostname to an IP address. By convention, only the hostname is included in an address RR. The domain itself is implied. Fields in the database records are separated by whitespace (spaces or tabs). Typically, administrators supply enough spaces so that columns line up nicely.

To interpret resource records that contain an @ symbol, remember that @ means "this zone." For example,

```
@                     MX    10    mail1.pseudo-corp.com.
```

means that mail1.pseudo-corp.com is a mail exchanger for pseudo-corp.com, because this zone database defines pseudo-corp.com.

The Start of Authority (SOA) RR makes use of both the conventions mentioned previously. First, because it begins with an @, the RR is known to apply to the zone that is associated with the current file.

Second, remember that all text between a ; character and the end of a line is ignored. In the SOA record, helpful comments were added to explain the purposes of the various parameters. Without the comments, the RR would look like this:

```
@                     IN  SOA dc1.pseudo-corp.com.  administrator.pseudo-
➥corp.com. (25 900 600 86400 3600)
```

That isn't very clear unless you are experienced enough with BIND to remember the explanations of the settings.

Zone delegation requires at least two RRs: a Name Server (NS) and an Address (A) record. The following RRs are sufficient to delegate authority for paris.pseudo-corp.com:

```
paris                 NS   dc2.pseudo-corp.com.
```

and

```
dc2                   A    10.1.0.3
```

If the name server were not a host in the pseudo-corp.com zone, we would need to supply its FQDN with something like this:

```
name1.paris.pseudo-corp.com.    A    10.1.0.3
```

Note that this FQDN ends with a period to make it crystal clear that it ends with the root domain. Without the trailing period, it would be placed in the current domain, and the name would be interpreted as name1.paris.pseudo-corp.com.pseudo-corp.com. I warned you early in the chapter that there would be at least one instance where the root domain needs to be explicitly indicated with a trailing period, and this is it.

You shouldn't have much trouble relating the RRs in the text database file to the ones we have discussed. BIND database files aren't all that difficult to work with, when you know a few tricks.

Reverse Lookup Database Files

Here is an example of a BIND database file for a reverse lookup zone:

```
;
;   Database file 1.10.in-addr.arpa.dns for 1.10.in-addr.arpa zone.
;      Zone version:   9
;

@                          IN  SOA dc1.pseudo-corp.com.  administrator.pseudo-
➥corp.com. (
                              9             ; serial number
                              900           ; refresh
                              600           ; retry
                              86400         ; expire
                              3600       )  ; minimum TTL


;
;   Zone NS records
;

@                          NS     dc1.pseudo-corp.com.
@                          NS     dc2.pseudo-corp.com.
dc2.pseudo-corp.com.       A      10.1.0.3


;
;   Zone records
;

1.0                        PTR    router.pseudo-corp.com.
2.0                        PTR    dc1.pseudo-corp.com.
25.0                       PTR    mail1.pseudo-corp.com.
3.0                        PTR    dc2.pseudo-corp.com.
```

The file isn't all that different from a forward looking database except that the bulk of the RRs are PTR records. To interpret the PTR records in the example, remember that the IP addresses for these hosts begin with 10.1. Therefore the RR

```
2.0                     PTR     dc1.pseudo-corp.com.
```

is a pointer for host 10.1.0.2. (Remember that, for reverse lookup zones, the octets in the IP address appear in reverse order.)

There are a couple other things to note here. Notice that a hostname in a PTR RR is a FQDN with an explicit trailing period. Also notice that the database file includes a Host Address RR that enables the DNS server to locate host dc2, which is configured with a secondary copy of the zone.

The Cache Database File

The Cache zone was initially intended to designate frequently used RRs that should be loaded into the DNS server's cache when it was started. In time, however, the purpose of the Cache zone was limited to containing RRs pertaining to the root domain servers.

For the Internet root domain, the cache database contains entries like the following for each of the 13 root name servers:

```
; formerly NS.INTERNIC.NET
;
.                       3600000  IN   NS    A.ROOT-SERVERS.NET.
A.ROOT-SERVERS.NET.     3600000       A     198.41.0.4
```

Integrating DNS Zones with Active Directory

If you have set up Active Directory, integrating zones with Active Directory is a no-brainer. You can select Active Directory-integrated as the type when you create a zone, or you can change the zone type as follows:

1. Open the DNS console and browse the object tree to locate the zone to be modified.
2. Right-click the zone name and select **Properties** from the context menu.
3. Select the **General** properties tab and click the **Change** button.
4. Click the **Active Directory-integrated** radio button in the **Change Zone Type** dialog box.
5. Click **OK**.

Repeat these steps for all the name servers that host primary or secondary copies of the zone. The zone is now integrated with Active Directory.

The most significant operational difference you will observe is that the distinction between primary and secondary zones disappears. All Active Directory-integrated zones function identically, obtaining their data from Active Directory.

Active Directory itself has a significant impact on the zone database because it creates Service Location resource records (abbreviated SRV) and a very elaborate domain structure. Figure 3.49 shows a DNS zone that supports Active Directory. I drilled down through the domains to show you an example of a Service Location resource record.

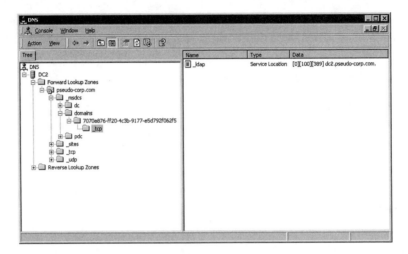

FIGURE 3.49

This domain contains an Active Directory Service Location resource record.

The Service Location domain and resource record structure isn't designed for direct human meddling. Everything is maintained automatically by Active Directory, so look but don't touch. Set up the DNS servers needed by your organization, configure zone support, and sit back. Active Directory will take care of most of the day-to-day maintenance. For example, Windows 2000 Servers operating within the domain will automatically register and deregister their services.

Optionally, you can configure DHCP to dynamically update Host Address resource records as host IP addresses are assigned and revoked. That's a topic for Chapter 5.

You might, of course, need to manually configure some resource records. You will need to intervene if you want to enable round robin addressing, for example, or if you want to have static Host Address RRs for some of your hosts.

Using NSLOOKUP

Included with Windows 2000 is an implementation of the nslookup utility that originated with BIND. nslookup is a fairly elaborate tool that can conduct a wide variety of DNS queries. We'll cover the basics in this section. The Windows 2000 Help utility provides more information.

nslookup is used in a Command Prompt window and works in noninteractive and interactive modes. Let's look at the noninteractive approach first.

Making Noninteractive Queries

In noninteractive mode, the query parameters are included on the command line. Here is a query that seeks to resolve a domain name to an IP address:

```
C:\>nslookup www
Server:  dc1.pseudo-corp.com
Address:  10.1.0.2

Name:    www.pseudo-corp.com
Address:  10.1.0.200
```

> **NOTE**
>
> In the previous query, nslookup used a reverse lookup query to determine the name of the DNS server being used by the client on which the command was run.

This query resolves an IP address to its associated domain name:

```
C:\>nslookup 10.1.0.25
Server:  dc1.pseudo-corp.com
Address:  10.1.0.2

Name:    mail1.pseudo-corp.com
Address:  10.1.0.25
```

Finally, here is a query that fails because nslookup cannot locate a name server that is authoritative for the target reverse lookup zone:

```
C:\>nslookup 10.2.3.4
Server:  dc1.pseudo-corp.com
Address:  10.1.0.2

*** dc1.pseudo-corp.com can't find 10.2.3.4: No
```

Before pursuing a query, nslookup must locate a name server. By default, nslookup uses the DNS servers that are defined in the host's TCP/IP properties, trying DNS servers in the order they appear in the DNS properties tab. What happens if nslookup cannot find an active DNS server? Before starting the following dialog, I stopped the DNS server service:

```
C:\>nslookup www
*** Can't find server name for address 10.1.0.2: No response from server
```

3

THE DOMAIN
NAME SYSTEM

```
*** Can't find server name for address 10.1.0.3: No response from server
*** Can't find server name for address 10.1.0.2: No response from server
*** Can't find server name for address 10.1.0.3: No response from server
*** Default servers are not available
Server:  UnKnown
Address:  10.1.0.2
```

```
*** UnKnown can't find www: No response from server
```

nslookup made two attempts to contact each of the name servers that were in the client's TCP/IP configuration and then reported failure.

Making Interactive Queries

nslookup can also be used interactively. To start an interactive session, invoke the nslookup command as in the following dialog:

```
C:\>nslookup
Default Server:  dc1.pseudo-corp.com
Address:  10.1.0.2
```

```
>
```

The > is the nslookup command prompt. Here you can shape a wide variety of queries. To query a host by name, simply enter the hostname at the prompt. Here's a good example of round robin addressing:

```
> www.microsoft.com
Server:  dc1.pseudo-corp.com
Address:  10.1.0.2
```

```
Name:    microsoft.com
Addresses:  207.46.131.30, 207.46.130.14, 207.46.130.149, 207.46.130.150
            207.46.130.45, 207.46.131.137, 207.46.131.28
Aliases:  www.microsoft.com
```

Notice that the DNS server has responded with all IP addresses that are associated with the target name. The order in which the IP addresses will vary to distribute usage across all the servers.

By default, nslookup queries for Address resource records. You can query for other types of resource records by changing the querytype, abbreviate as q. Here's how you can view the SOA record for a domain:

```
> set q=soa
> pseudo-corp.com
Server:  dc1.pseudo-corp.com
```

```
Address:  10.1.0.2

pseudo-corp.com
        primary name server = dc1.pseudo-corp.com
        responsible mail addr = administrator.pseudo-corp.com
        serial  = 71
        refresh = 900 (15 mins)
        retry   = 600 (10 mins)
        expire  = 86400 (1 day)
        default TTL = 3600 (1 hour)
dc1.pseudo-corp.com     internet address = 10.1.0.2
dc1.pseudo-corp.com     internet address = 10.2.0.1
```

Here is another example that identifies any MX resource records that might be defined for a given hostname:

```
> set q=mx
> mail1
Server:  dc1.pseudo-corp.com
Address:  10.1.0.2

pseudo-corp.com
        primary name server = dc1.pseudo-corp.com
        responsible mail addr = administrator.pseudo-corp.com
        serial  = 71
        refresh = 900 (15 mins)
        retry   = 600 (10 mins)
        expire  = 86400 (1 day)
        default TTL = 3600 (1 hour)
```

I'll leave it to you to experiment further with NSLOOKUP. Use the help option to see a list of available commands. For more detail, use the Windows 2000 Help utility.

Now, You're the DNS Master

DNS is one of those things that takes a lot of time to learn but isn't all that difficult to understand after you get past the basics. The big problem with DNS is that there is so much opportunity for error. It is easy to forget to modify a Host Address RR when a host changes its IP address. It is easy to forget to increment the zone serial number, in which case you might wind up scratching your head, wondering why the zone won't replicate to the secondaries. Take the time to experiment and test your results.

It is difficult to separate DNS and Active Directory. In fact, I had considerable trouble figuring out which to talk about first. Because DNS and Windows domains are merged under Active Directory, when you manage DNS, you're getting involved with Active Directory, and vice versa. Now you know enough about DNS to be able to plan the domain structure for your organization. The next task is to see specifically how DNS domains relate to Active Directory.

Active Directory Concepts

IN THIS CHAPTER

Active Directory (AD) is the technological hub of Windows 2000 Server, providing a distributed, global store for information about servers and services, clients, users, groups, and applications. Although AD doesn't replace the Windows domains that Windows 2000 inherits from Windows NT, AD adds a lot of polish to the domain architecture, making it far easier to manage multidomain enterprises.

The most obvious contribution of Active Directory is that it provides a hierarchical, global directory (one that is available everywhere in the enterprise) that describes every network resource in the enterprise. All the enterprise's domains can be organized under the directory, a capability that greatly simplifies management of multiple domains. Domains added to Active Directory are organized into logical relationships with one another, which reduce much of the domain management drudgery we are used to with Windows NT.

Active Directory isn't a network service, but it is intimately involved in many network services. In particular, because AD stores host identification and service location data in DNS, you need to understand how AD and DNS interrelate. Other relationships between AD and network services will be discussed from time to time in the remainder of the book. For example, Windows 2000 support for secure IP (IPSec) is dependent on Active Directory.

> **NOTE**
>
> Of course, I'm opening a huge can of worms when I try to discuss Active Directory in a single chapter. My goal in this chapter is to provide limited coverage of AD as it relates to the central theme of this book, so please accept my apologies in advance if I have ignored particular aspects of this complex, new directory service.

The Active Directory Architecture

It is easiest to explain the architecture of AD a bit at a time, starting with an explanation of the sorts of things that AD is a directory of and proceeding to the ways those things are related.

Objects, Attributes, Classes, and Schemas

A directory must be a directory of something. A telephone directory, for example, is a directory of users' names along with their street addresses and telephone numbers. The data stored in AD consist of *objects* that have characteristics called *attributes*. Objects are derived from *classes*, which are object templates that are defined by *schemas*. We'll look at objects, attributes, classes, and schemas in the following sections.

Objects

Active Directory is a directory of *objects*, such as user accounts, groups, Windows servers, services, domains, security policies, or any of dozens of other things. Among the types of objects are many things that you will recognize if you've worked with Windows NT, such as domains, user accounts, and groups. But there are new types of objects as well, objects with no parallels in Windows NT domains, such as organizational units.

There are two general types of objects in Active Directory:

- **Container objects** store other objects, including leaf objects and other container objects. (In a file system, directories are container objects that can store files and other directories.)
- **Leaf objects** do not store other objects. A *leaf object* describes a physical or logical network entity such as a server, a user account, or a domain. AD incorporates dozens of types of leaf objects. (In a file system, files are leaf objects.)

Thus, container objects can be nested in other container objects. Just as we build multilayered file systems by nesting directories, we can build AD directories of any required depth by nesting appropriate container objects. An Active Directory hierarchy is constructed primarily of domain container objects.

Attributes

Objects have characteristics that are defined by their attributes. An *attribute* consists of a label and a value that describes a specific attribute of the object. A user object has a couple dozen attributes. Here are some examples:

- First name
- Last name
- Telephone number
- Profile path
- Login script
- Remote access permissions

The idea of attributes isn't all that earthshaking, although we're used to thinking of them as *properties*. We manage user accounts under Windows NT, and every user account is configured by parameters that are managed just like object attributes in AD. But, the way the attributes come to be part of the user object is different under Active Directory. In Windows NT, parameters are hard-wired to objects. In Windows 2000, attributes are extensible characteristics of the objects they describe.

4

ACTIVE
DIRECTORY
CONCEPTS

NOTE

The terms *attributes* and *properties* represent yet another instance of Microsoft's tendency not to settle on a single term when it can use two terms to describe the same thing. Allow me to quote some definitions from Windows 2000 Server Help:

"Attributes describe objects."

A property is "a characteristic or parameter of a class of objects or devices."

Because these things are typically defined in dialog boxes named **Properties**, I've used the term *properties* most often in this book. But be aware that the object properties you define reflect object attributes in the AD database.

Actually, of course, the term *attribute* has a particular meaning in object-oriented data processing technologies, so there's some reason behind the duplicity of terms. If you want to learn more about the formal definition of an object attribute, look in Windows 2000 Help for the topic "Active Directory attributes, definitions."

Classes

A given object is an *instance* (a particular, defined example) of an object *class*. An object class serves as a template for creating new objects. Every object that is created from a class will have the same characteristics. For example, when you create a new user account, you are creating a new instance of the User class.

Schemas

Unlike the parameters associated with a Windows NT object, the properties of a class can be modified to accommodate the needs of applications or organizations. The overall definition of the object classes in an Active Directory database, the ways objects can relate, and the properties associated with objects form the database *schema*.

An AD schema can be modified and extended, for example, to add new object types or new attributes for existing objects. The procedures for modifying a schema are beyond the scope of this book, but it is important to recognize that, because schemas are mutable, it is possible for two AD databases to have different schemas.

Security Principles

Some AD objects are *security principles*, objects that can be assigned permissions to perform specific operations. There are only three categories of AD objects that are security principles:

- Users
- Groups
- Computers

To grant permissions to security principles, objects are configured with *access control lists* (ACLs; also called *discretionary access control lists* or DACLs, in case you're an acronym junkie).

ACLs are lists of *access control entries* (ACEs), wherein each ACE enables or denies a security principle, the right to perform a particular operation on the object that owns the ACL.

Domains

Domains continue to provide the primary means for organizing resources on Windows 2000 networks, but Microsoft has eased many of the limitations, quirks, and rough spots that we chaff against when managing Windows NT. Under Windows 2000, domains have become much more capable and easy to manage.

The chief problem with Windows NT domains is that domains tend to proliferate. With domains, like potato chips, it seems that you can seldom stop with just one. Even small organizations sometimes find it necessary to configure multiple domains. Having multiple domains significantly amplifies the cost and difficulty of supporting a Windows NT network because each domain must have its own servers to function as repositories for the domain database. Under Windows 2000 Active Directory, domains are significantly enhanced in scalability and functionality, so that multidomain networks will be required with less frequency.

Windows 2000 domain functionality improves in other ways as well, eliminating the irksome distinction Windows NT imposed between primary and backup domain controllers, and improving the efficiency of replicating domain databases.

The following sections examine some of the specific ways Windows 2000 enhances Windows domain functionality and flexibility.

NOTE

Sometimes I have to bend over backward to make it clear whether I am discussing Active Directory domains or DNS domains. The task gets especially confusing because there will always be a DNS domain that corresponds to any given AD domain. I'd love it if Microsoft had chosen another term to describe the Active Directory containers, but they didn't, and the potential for confusion is always present.

To distinguish AD domains from DNS domains, I will adhere to these conventions:

- AD domain names will be displayed entirely in uppercase, for example, PSEUDO-CORP.COM.

- DNS domain names will be displayed entirely in lowercase, for example, pseudo-corp.com.

On occasions when a name refers both to an AD domain and a DNS domain, I'll try to make that fact clear in the supporting text.

It is unnecessary to follow these conventions in practice. Also keep in mind that names in AD and in DNS are case-insensitive.

Multidomain Networks

There are three primary reasons for configuring multidomain Windows NT networks:

- Domain scaling
- Controlling domain replication traffic
- Apportioning administrative responsibilities

Let's look at these three concerns and see how Windows 2000 Server has addressed them.

Domain Scaling

Windows NT security is handled by the Security Access Manager (SAM). The SAM database is stored in the Registry under the HKEY_LOCAL_MACHINE\SAM subtree, in the files SAM and SAM.LOG under the directory %SystemRoot%\System32\Config. SAM support is retained in Windows 2000 to ensure compatibility with processes requiring SAM access and to support security for computers that are not configured to use Active Directory to manage security.

Dependency on the SAM database limits the capacities of Windows NT domains. Microsoft recommends that the size of the SAM database not exceed approximately 40MB, but that is an upper limit that is practical only on high-performance servers (at least 500MHz Pentium with 356MB RAM). At this upper limit, a Windows NT domain can be expected to accommodate about 40,000 security principles.

Active Directory, however, blows those limits away. Under AD, a domain can support at least 1.5 million objects, enough capacity that even a very large organization might be able to run its entire network with a single domain. Supporting one and a half million objects isn't a hard-coded limit, by the way, and high-end server hardware can very well enable domains to support more objects than that number. Very large organizations can therefore be able to configure their entire Windows 2000 Server networks with a single domain.

Controlling Domain Replication Traffic

A computer that has a copy of the security database for a domain is a *domain controller*. Users cannot authenticate (log in, have their identities verified, and be granted access permissions) to a domain unless their client computers can communicate with a domain controller. Consequently, we always want to have at least two domain controllers servicing a given domain for the sake of fault tolerance and to distribute domain security processing. If the network spans multiple locations, it is also desirable to have at least one domain controller at each location so that users can be authenticated using a local computer instead of being forced to log in through a slow WAN link.

The problem with having multiple domain controllers is that there must be a mechanism that enables domain controllers to share security information. Replication of security information between domain controllers is something that happens automatically. However, on Windows NT, the process is better suited to LANs than to networks that incorporate WAN links. Windows NT uses the same technique to replicate security data, whether the domain controllers communicate through a high-bandwidth LAN or through a low-bandwidth WAN. In many cases, domain security replication can monopolize a significant portion of the available WAN bandwidth.

There are two undesirable aspects of Windows NT domain replication:

- When a property of an object is modified, the entire object record must be replicated.
- Domain replication is triggered immediately when an object is modified, regardless of the current demands for WAN bandwidth.

Active Directory improves the domain replication process in three ways:

- When a property of an AD object is modified, only the individual property must be replicated.
- Sites can be configured, enabling administrators to determine when domains will replicate through WAN links.
- Data replicated through WAN links are compressed.

Apportioning Administrative Responsibilities

Under Windows NT, a domain administrator is an administrator for the entire domain. It is not possible to limit administrative authority to certain groups of users or resources. (The Windows NT built-in group Account Operators can be used to define users who can manage user and group accounts, but this is a more limited approach than is available under Active Directory.) When you want to have an administrator who has authority over a limited group of objects, you'll need to configure a new domain in which the user is given administrative permissions.

Windows 2000 introduces the concept of the *organizational unit* (OU), which is an administrative subdivision of a domain. Administrative permissions can be assigned and revoked for individual OUs. Suppose that the Accounting department wants to administer its own user accounts and access its own resources. You can configure an Accounting OU without the need to establish and grant authority within the Accounting OU to specific administrators and without the requirement to establish an additional domain.

Because each OU has its own ACL, it is possible to configure in great detail who can administer resources in the OU and the tasks they can perform. Suppose that there is an OU named Accounting in a domain named PSEUDO. It is possible to prevent members of the PSEUDO Domain Admins group from modifying objects in the Accounting OU by modifying the ACEs for Accounting.

The process of enabling a group to manage an OU, called *delegating control*, makes it possible to provide departments with complete autonomy to manage objects in their OUs.

4

ACTIVE
DIRECTORY
CONCEPTS

NOTE

OUs won't provide autonomy if an organization requires total authority over all its computing resources. Suppose that a company's Research And Development unit wants to reduce the likelihood that security leaks can occur. They might need to physically control all their resources including having separate domain controllers. In these circumstances, it is necessary to establish a separate domain.

Domain Controllers

A domain controller stores a copy of the security database for a domain and authenticates user logins, enabling users to gain access to resources in the domain. Access to resources is controlled differently under Active Directory than under Windows NT:

- Under Windows NT, access to resources is granted by assigning an *access control list,* or ACL, to the user after the user's login has been authenticated. The ACL lists all the resources for which the user has access permissions along with the permissions that are assigned. Because a user's ACL is created when the user logs in, changes made to security properties do not affect users until the next time they log in.

- Under Active Directory, ACLs are properties of objects. When an authenticated user attempts to access an object, AD consults the object's ACL to determine whether an ACE provides the user with the required permissions. Consequently, changes made to object ACLs take effect the next time the user accesses the object.

Without access to a domain controller, users cannot be authenticated, and the domain is effectively off-limits. Given the critical nature of the domain controller, it is desirable to have at least two domain controllers active for each domain.

Because users must frequently access domain controllers, it is desirable to have at least one domain controller at each site so that user login traffic does not need to cross the WAN. That requirement might make experienced Windows NT administrators doubt the practicality of establishing large domains on multiple sites. The situation shown in Figure 4.1 is familiar to many NT administrators. Here, domain data must be replicated through the WAN link between the domain controllers in Seattle and Chicago.

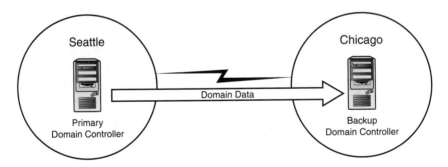

FIGURE 4.1
Windows NT domain controllers complicate replication of the domain security database.

Let's see how the nature of domain controllers changes under Active Directory.

Windows NT Domain Controllers

Under Windows NT, every domain has exactly one *primary domain controller* (PDC) that stores the master copy of the domain security database. The security database can be replicated to *backup domain controllers* (BDCs), which have the capacity to authenticate user logins and grant users access to resources. BDCs support scaling by providing multiple servers that can authenticate users, but they have some undesirable characteristics.

The PDC stores the master copy of the domain database and is the only domain controller into which security changes can be entered. Changes made to the database on the PDC are replicated to BDCs, but database replicas on BDCs are read-only and cannot be directly modified by administrators or users. So although a BDC can process a user's login request, if a user wants to change his password, the change must be sent to the PDC and then replicated to the BDCs. Examine Figure 4.2 and consider the traffic that is required when user Bob in Chicago wants to change his password. Bob's password change request must be sent through the WAN to the PDC in Seattle because the change cannot be recorded on the BDC in Chicago. Then Bob's user account record must be replicated back to Chicago, again through the WAN. Multiply that by password changes for hundreds of users in Chicago, and you can easily see how undesirable levels of WAN traffic might be generated.

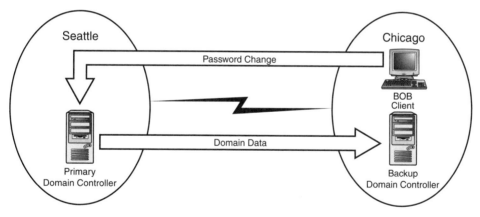

4

FIGURE 4.2

A password change for user Bob in Chicago must be registered on the PDC in Seattle and then replicated to Bob's local BDC in Chicago.

You have already observed how sites enable Windows 2000 domain replication to be scheduled so it does not tie up WAN bandwidth at critical times. But Windows 2000 Active Directory also has two features that significantly reduce traffic when domain replication takes place: multimaster replication and property-based replication.

Multimaster Replication

Under Active Directory, there is no longer a distinction between primary and backup domain controllers. All domain controllers in a domain function as peers, that is, all domain controllers store read-write copies of the domain database. Changes to the domain database can be written to any domain controller (DC) and will be replicated to all other DCs in the domain, a feature that is called *multimaster replication*.

If the servers in Figure 4.1 are configured using Windows 2000 and Active Directory, Bob can make his password change on a DC in Chicago. The change will then be replicated to DCs at other locations. WAN traffic is reduced because the data traverse the WAN only once.

> **NOTE**
>
> One DC in a Windows 2000 Server domain functions as a Windows NT–compatible PDC that can replicate the domain database to Windows NT BDCs.

Multimaster Operations

The majority of changes to domains are multimaster operations that can be performed on any of the DCs in the domain. A potential difficulty of multimaster operations is that conflicting changes might be introduced on different DCs more or less at the same time. In such cases, the conflict must be resolved when domain replication takes place. In most cases, AD resolves these conflicts by accepting the most recent change based on time stamps associated with the changes.

Single-Master Operations

A few changes, by their very nature, should be made only on a single, designated DC. The DC that is designated to perform a particular single-master operation is called the *role master* for that operation. The following are single-master operations:

- **Schema modification.** The schema of a domain defines all the Active Directory data structures for a domain. To prevent conflicting schemas from being introduced on DCs, all schema modifications for a forest are made from a single DC.

- **Domain naming.** A single DC in a forest (a *forest* is a collection of trees) is designated as the domain naming master, with responsibility for ensuring that all domain names are unique in the forest and for maintaining cross-references with other directories.

- **Primary domain controller emulation.** A single DC in a domain can be configured to emulate a Windows NT PDC, compatible with BDCs running Windows NT 3.51 and 4. PDC emulation is included for backward compatibility and as a tool for migrating NT servers to Windows 2000.

- **Relative ID Pool Allocations.** To ensure uniqueness, one domain controller in a domain assigns pools of relative identifiers to other DCs. Relative identifiers (RIDs), along with domain identifiers (no, not DIDs, as far as I can determine) are combined to form the security identifiers (SIDs) that actually identify objects in the security database. SIDs must be unique, so a single DC has the RID master role.

- **Infrastructure changes.** When objects are moved or deleted, a single *infrastructure master* DC updates the security identifiers and the distinguished names in cross-domain references to the object. (An AD *distinguished name* is an object's name including the names of containers that connect the object with the root domain of the AD tree.)

Property-Based Replication

When an object property is modified in a Windows NT domain, the entire object record must be replicated.

When an object property is modified in a Windows 2000 domain, only the property record must be replicated. Entire objects are replicated only when a new DC is added to the domain, and the DC is given a complete copy of the domain database.

Domain Trusts

Even though you might not need to implement multidomain networks under Windows 2000, reasons remain why you might. Part of an organization might require total autonomy for its part of the network, for example. Personnel might not want administrators to have any sort of access to computers storing personnel records that include salary information, for example, or the research department might want to strictly control access to computers storing information about forthcoming, but-for-now-secret, products.

Under Windows NT, managing multidomain networks is painful for a variety of reasons. Let's review the way Windows NT supports multiple domains before examining improvements introduced by Windows 2000.

NOTE

4

In general, your goal should be to get by with the fewest possible domains. The vast majority of organizations can function with a single domain. Each added domain imposes a cost in terms of hardware for domain controllers and administrative complexity.

ACTIVE DIRECTORY CONCEPTS

Windows NT Multidomain Scenarios

Suppose that an organization has offices in Seattle and Chicago. WAN bandwidth between the sites is limited, so it has been decided to implement a separate domain at each site to reduce WAN traffic. We'll call these domains SEATTLE and CHICAGO.

With this approach, there will be a PDC and at least one BDC for the SEATTLE domain, physically located in offices in Seattle. Similarly, there will be a PDC and at least one BDC for the CHICAGO domain, situated in the Chicago facilities. The resulting configuration is shown in Figure 4.3. Users in both sites can now change their passwords on a local server, and WAN traffic is reduced.

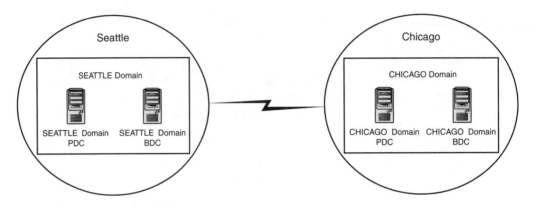

FIGURE 4.3

A local PDC might reduce WAN traffic but increases the number of servers and complicates administration.

The solution in Figure 4.3 works best if users primarily access services on local servers. But what if users in Seattle need to use resources in Chicago? Users who need such access could be given separate user accounts in both domains, but that requires users to log on separately to each domain. The most common solution is to establish a *trust relationship* that configures the CHICAGO domain to trust users that have been authenticated in the SEATTLE domain. The benefit of trust relationships is that users can be given access to resources in several domains based on a single user account in one of the domains.

Windows NT trust relationships have two undesirable characteristics: They operate in one direction only, and they are not transitive.

One-Way Trusts

The disadvantage of one-way trusts is that complete trust between two domains requires two trust relationships. In Figure 4.4, for example, CHICAGO must trust SEATTLE to permit users authenticated in SEATTLE to access resources in the CHICAGO domain. Separately, SEATTLE must trust CHICAGO to enable users authenticated in CHICAGO to access resources in the SEATTLE domain.

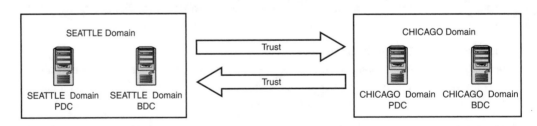

FIGURE 4.4

Two one-way trust relationships are required to establish complete trust between two domains.

Nontransitive Trusts

Trusts are *transitive* when they are passed from one domain to another through intermediate domains. Transitive trusts would probably be on the top ten list of improvements requested by Windows NT administrators, but you have to upgrade to Windows 2000 to get them.

Because Windows NT trust relationships are not transitive, trusts get increasingly complicated when more than two domains must share completely trusting relationships. Consider the domains in Figure 4.5. SEATTLE has a two-way trust with CHICAGO, and CHICAGO has a two-way trust with ATLANTA. It would be great if these trusts automatically configured trust relationships between SEATTLE and ATLANTA, but, under Windows NT, they don't. Nontransitive trusts do not permit trusts to flow through domains to other trusted domains. To establish complete trust between the three domains, six explicit trust relationships are required, as shown in Figure 4.6.

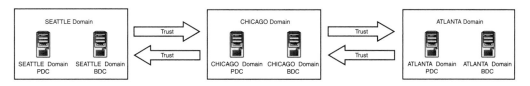

FIGURE 4.5
Under Windows NT, trusts are not transitive, and SEATTLE *does not trust* ATLANTA, *or vice versa.*

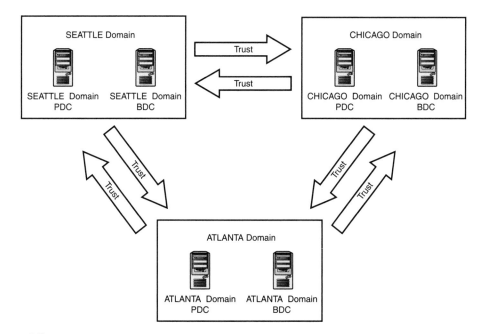

FIGURE 4.6
Windows NT requires six separate trusts to establish complete trust among these three domains.

Figure 4.7 illustrates an extreme case. Here the network consists of five domains. In all twenty, trust relationships are required to establish an environment wherein every domain trusts every other domain. To establish a completely trusting environment requires $n \times (n-1)$ trust relationships, wherein n is the number of domains. Clearly, as the number of domains increases, the number of trust relationships becomes quite large. It can be a real headache to establish and verify the correct operation of all the required trust relationships.

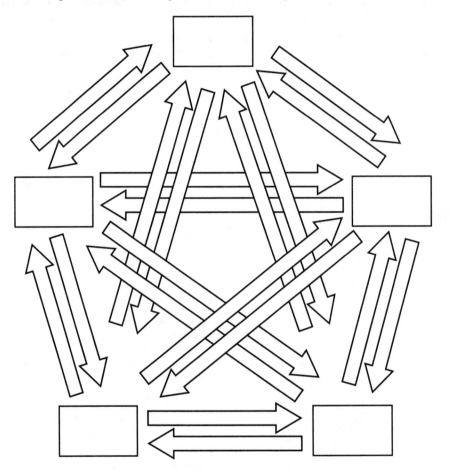

FIGURE 4.7

As domains increase in number, the required number of trust relationships increases rapidly.

Windows 2000 Multidomain Scenarios

Multidomain networks are much easier to manage under Windows 2000 Active Directory, thanks to two new features: two-way trusts and transitive trusts. Let's see how these features work and then examine how they combine to enable us to configure domain hierarchies.

Two-Way Trusts

Although Windows 2000 supports one-way trusts, the predominate type of trust is two-way. A two-way trust relationship is equivalent to two one-way trusts, so this innovation alone reduces by half the number of trust relationships required to support a network such as the one shown in Figure 4.5.

Transitive Trusts

Transitive trusts enable trust relationships to flow through intermediate domains. When transitive trusts are combined with two-way trusts, only two trust relationships are necessary to establish complete trust among the three domains shown in Figure 4.8. Clearly, domains SEATTLE and CHICAGO trust one another, as do domains CHICAGO and ATLANTA. But thanks to transitive trusts, domains SEATTLE and ATLANTA are also in a trusting relationship.

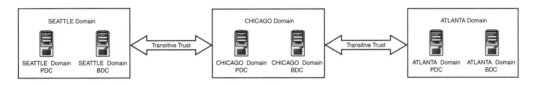

FIGURE 4.8
Windows 2000 transitive trusts enable domains SEATTLE *and* ATLANTA *to trust each other without establishing trusts directly between the two domains.*

Domain Hierarchies

Two-way trusts and transitive trusts enable us to do something under Active Directory that we cannot even dream of doing with Windows NT—establish true hierarchies of mutually trusting domains. As you well know from working with file systems and DNS, hierarchies are almost always the tools of choice when it is necessary to consolidate large numbers of objects in an organized, manageable, easily-searchable data structure. Domain hierarchies, combined with object hierarchies, enable Active Directory to easily and systematically catalog all the objects even on extremely large networks.

Figure 4.9 illustrates an Active Directory domain hierarchy, referred to as an Active Directory *domain tree.* As with all hierarchies, one container is designated as the root container. In Figure 4.9, PSEUDO is the root domain of the tree. With Active Directory, the root domain is always the first domain created in the tree. All other domains are added to expand the hierarchy below the root domain.

Notice that the complete names of child domains are constructed by appending the domain's name to the name of its parent domain. For example, the complete name of the CHICAGO domain is CHICAGO.PSEUDO. We've seen that naming convention in other hierarchies, such as DNS. In fact, Active Directory domain naming conventions are identical to domain naming conventions for DNS. There's a good reason for that, because AD uses DNS as its namespace to store hostname and service location information. For any AD domain hierarchy, there will always be a parallel domain hierarchy in a DNS namespace that has parallel domain names.

4

ACTIVE
DIRECTORY
CONCEPTS

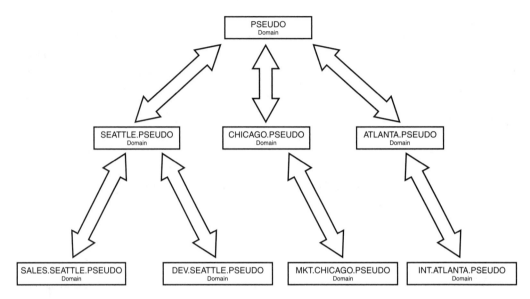

FIGURE 4.9
Under Active Directory, the domains in this tree share a completely trusting relationship.

NOTE

In Chapter 3, "The Domain Name System," it was explained that the Windows 2000 DNS service can be configured to support multibyte (UTF8) character sets, as well as ASCII characters that are not supported by DNS. If you take advantage of these capabilities, you can create AD domain names that do not conform to RFC-compliant DNS name limitations, in which case you must use the Windows 2000 DNS service to support the AD namespace.

Because the whole thrust of using DNS is to bring Windows naming in line with Internet standards, I'm not sure that it is a good idea to violate DNS name restrictions when you name your AD domains. If you use non-standard names, you are closing off the option of incorporating non-Windows DNS servers into your Active Directory namespace.

The domain tree in Figure 4.9 wouldn't be at all practical under Windows NT because individual trust relationships would be required between each pair of domains. Under Windows 2000 Active Directory, however, a small number of trusts are sufficient to bind together a large number of domains. Whereas NT requires $n\times(n\text{-}1)$ trusts to establish a completely trusting network consisting of n domains, Active Directory makes it possible to do the same thing with $n\text{-}1$ trust relationships.

Thanks to two-way, transitive trusts, domain SALES.SEATTLE.PSEUDO trusts domain INT.ATLANTA.PSEUDO, even though no trust relationship is established directly between the two domains.

One of the really nice things about Active Directory is that you don't need to take special pains to establish the trust relationships that configure the domain tree. When you create a new domain under Active Directory, you have the option of configuring the new domain to be the child of an existing domain. AD configures its database and establishes the trust relationship required so the new domain can function in its specified tree location.

> **NOTE**
>
> Besides the costs associated with the root domain itself, there are no added costs for creating an AD tree. The tree is supported by the DCs for the root domain; no additional hardware is required.

Domain Names and Active Directory Trees

In Chapter 3, I explained that Active Directory uses DNS to store name records for servers as clients, as well as service location records for services. Because DNS is used to store information critical to Active Directory, it was a natural decision on Microsoft's part to adopt DNS domain naming conventions for use when naming domains in AD trees. In fact, as stated in the last section, every domain that is defined in AD will have a corresponding domain in the DNS database that AD maintains.

In nearly all its examples, Microsoft assumes that AD tree domain names will integrate with an organization's domain namespace on the Internet. Figure 4.10 illustrates how a hierarchy of names in an AD tree could fit into the Internet namespace.

Every AD tree has a single root domain. In most examples, you will see, it is assumed that the root domain of the AD tree will share the same name as the organization's Internet domain name. For example, if the organization has registered the Internet domain name pseudo-corp.com, it could also name the root domain of its AD tree PSEUDO-CORP.COM.

Note that there is no AD domain that corresponds to the com first level domain or to the Internet root domain. If you integrate the AD tree with the Internet namespace, the AD domain tree always starts at a second- or lower-level domain of the Internet namespace. Thus, the root domain of the AD tree is not necessarily the root domain of the DNS tree that handles the DNS database for the AD tree.

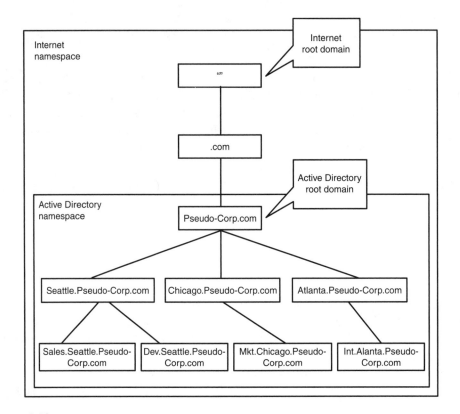

FIGURE 4.10

The root domain in an organization's Active Directory tree can be associated with the organization's Internet domain.

NOTE

Keep in mind that the DNS domain and the AD domain are not the same entities. One is a container object in the DNS namespace, whereas the other is a container object in the AD tree. For every domain in an AD tree, there will be a corresponding domain in the DNS namespace, but the two domains are distinct both in implementation and in concept.

It's a lot like your relationship to the phone book. You have a name, and your phone book entry has the same name, but you and the phone book entry are not the same entities. So that I can blind you with my keen insight into the obvious, I will point out that you are a person, not an entry in a telephone database. Unless you suffer from an identity crisis, that's a significant distinction.

When a new domain is added to the AD tree, the new domain always builds on the hierarchy that begins at the root domain of the AD tree. Suppose we add a child domain named ALPHA just below the PSEUDO-CORP.COM root domain. The FQDN of the new domain would be ALPHA.PSEUDO-CORP.COM. As you know from Chapter 3, DNS domain hierarchies can be extended nearly indefinitely, giving us great flexibility when building AD trees.

As you'll see later in the chapter, it's incredibly easy to add a domain to an AD tree and create the required DNS domains. Both domains are created in a single operation, along with the required resource records.

Groups

Groups are critical administrative tools that enable administrators to manage users in large numbers, instead of one at a time. Groups are closely intertwined with domains, so this is a good place to discuss them. Windows 2000 inherits all the group types that are available under Windows NT, while adding a new type of group that greatly enhances administrative flexibility.

The following types of groups are common to Windows NT and Windows 2000:

- **Machine local groups.** Every Windows NT or Windows 2000 computer that is not a domain controller supports its own groups that can be used to assign permissions for resources on that computer only. Machine local groups are found on Windows NT Workstation and Windows 2000 Professional computers as well as on Windows NT and 2000 servers that are configured as standalone servers. Machine local groups can contain local user accounts, domain user accounts, and global groups.

- **Domain local groups.** Windows domains support domain local groups. They are called *local* because they are used to assign permissions in the domain where the group is created. The primary use for domain local groups is to collect global groups from the local and other domains so that they can be assigned permissions in the local domain.

- **Global groups.** Windows domains support global groups, which are used primarily to export groups of users to other domains so that they can be assigned permissions in those domains. A global group can contain users from its own domain but not from other domains. A global group created in one domain can be given permissions in its own domain or in another domain that trusts the domain that owns the global group.

4

ACTIVE
DIRECTORY
CONCEPTS

> **NOTE**
>
> We didn't see the term *domain local groups* in Windows NT literature where they were referred to simply as *local groups*.
>
> But there is another sort of group that has a local character, groups that are created on Windows clients and standalone servers that are used only on the local machine. Under Windows 2000, these are now referred to as *local groups*. (I've used the term *machine local groups* to distinguish them from *domain local groups*.)

The differences between domain local groups and global groups are subtle, and it is useful to review the following rules about their usage:

- Global groups can contain users from the global group's own domain. If the domain is configured in native mode (described in the next section), global groups can also contain other global groups in the global group's own domain.
- Global groups cannot contain users or global groups from other domains.
- Domain local groups can contain users and global groups from the local domain and from other domains that are trusted by the local group's own domain.
- Domain local groups and global groups can be assigned permissions in the group's own domain.
- Domain local groups cannot be assigned permissions in other domains.

With Windows NT 4, it is the preferred procedure to use both local and global groups to enable users to access resources in trusting domains. Suppose that we want users authenticated in domain ALPHA to be able to access resources in domain BETA. Here is the typical procedure to provide the required access permissions:

- Domain BETA must trust domain ALPHA.
- A global group is created in domain ALPHA, and the desired users in ALPHA are added to the global group. If all users in ALPHA are to have access to resources in BETA, the built-in global group Domain Users can be used, instead of a custom group.
- An administrator of BETA adds the global group from domain ALPHA to a domain local group in domain BETA.
- An administrator of BETA assigns the required permissions to the domain local group in domain BETA.

Domain local and global groups do provide the capabilities required to give users access to resources in trusting domains, but the need to have two types of groups and to use them in precisely the correct way has been rather irksome to many administrators.

That's why universal groups are so welcome. Windows 2000 universal groups can be used anywhere in the domain tree or forest. (A forest consists of one or more domain trees that share a transitive, two-way trust relationship between their root domains.) Universal groups have the following characteristics:

- Universal groups can contain universal groups, global groups, and user accounts from any domain in the domain forest.
- Universal groups can be members of domain local groups and other universal groups.
- Universal groups cannot be members of global groups.

Because universal groups can contain other universal groups, they greatly reduce the confusion involved in managing groups. We can, if we want, build an entire, multidomain group structure using nothing but universal groups.

The catch with universal groups is that they are available only in domains configured to operate in native mode. As the next section explains, this restriction means that Windows NT domain controllers cannot be deployed in domains that offer support for universal groups.

Native and Mixed Mode

By default, new domains operate in *mixed mode*, enabling them to support Windows 2000 Servers and clients as well as downlevel servers and clients (Windows NT 3.51 and 4.0, Windows 95/98, and Windows 3.x). A mixed-mode domain is one in which both Windows 2000 and Windows NT domain controllers are in use. One Windows 2000 DC in a mixed-mode domain functions as a Windows NT–compatible PDC, enabling Windows NT servers to participate in the domain as BDCs. Mixed-mode domain support is offered as a migration tool to enable organizations to move gracefully from Windows NT to Windows 2000.

If all the domain controllers in a domain are upgraded to Windows 2000 Server, the domain can be switched into *native mode*. (The reverse operation is not available. A native mode domain cannot revert to mixed mode.) Native mode domains can still offer SAM-based authentication, enabling them to support downlevel clients, but offer features that are unavailable in mixed-mode domains.

One distinction between domain modes affects client's browsing capabilities:

- Clients in a mixed mode domain can browse only their local domains and domains that are explicitly trusted by their local domains.
- Clients in a native mode domain can browse any domain in their local forest. (Forests are explained in the next section.)

Native mode enhances functionality of groups. In a native mode domain, a global group can contain other global groups that are created in its own domain.

Native mode domains support the new universal group type, described in the previous section. Universal groups require native mode because membership for universal groups is not stored on all domain controllers. Universal group membership information is stored in the global catalog, which is described later in the chapter. Windows NT servers cannot access the Global Catalog.

4

NOTE

Users and groups in mixed-mode domains can be administered using the Windows NT 4.0 User Manager for Domains utility or the Windows 2000 Active Directory Users and Computers MMC snap-in.

Users and groups in native-mode domains can be administered only by the Windows 2000 Active Directory Users and Computers MMC snap-in.

Domain Forests

An Active Directory domain tree consists of a group of domains organized hierarchically under a single root domain, which is always the first domain created in the tree. In the majority of cases, all the domains in an organization will be placed in the same tree, but there might be times when it is necessary to share resources between two or more trees. To improve the efficiency of resource sharing, it is possible to configure multiple trees into a *forest*, such as the one shown in Figure 4.11.

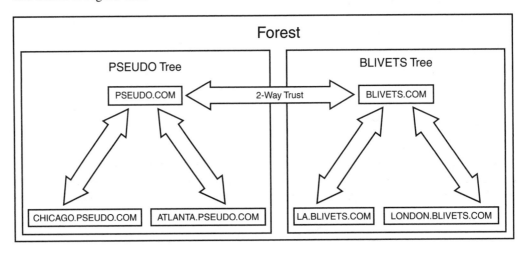

FIGURE 4.11

Two or more AD trees can be associated as members of a forest.

Trees belonging to a forest share a common global catalog and must therefore share the same AD schema. When two trees are associated in a forest, AD establishes a two-way, transitive trust relationship between the root domains of the member trees.

> **NOTE**
>
> Keep in mind that, when you create a forest, it must contain at least one domain. Thus the minimum cost for creating a forest is the cost of the domain controllers required to support the root domain DCs for the new tree.

A forest is not significantly more difficult to manage than a tree. Transitive two-way trusts can be established between any domains in the forest, although the trusts established when domains are created will usually suffice to enable access within a forest. Consequently, it is easy to establish permissions for resource access. And because the forest has a single global catalog, users can easily search for resources in the entire forest.

Multiforest networks are another matter altogether. There are several difficulties involved with managing and using multiple forests:

- AD does not enforce schema consistency between forests, so it is necessary for administrators to manage schema elements directly.

- Two-way transitive trusts are not supported between forests. Administrators must establish explicit one-way, non-transitive trust relationships between domains in different forests if users in one forest are to be given access to domains in another forest. Essentially, trusts between forests behave like trusts under Windows NT.

- By default, users are aware only of resources in the global catalog of their local forest. They can discover objects in other forests only by explicitly querying domains in the forests. To do this effectively, users must be trained to understand the directory structure and to use search tools effectively.

In light of the difficulties, you should avoid creating multiforest networks whenever possible, but they might be necessary when integrating forests from existing organizations.

Global Catalogs

A *global catalog* contains a copy of every object in every domain in a forest but contains only select attributes from each object. The global catalog is used as means of accelerating searches that span the entire forest.

A global catalog server is a server that stores the following information:

- A full, writable copy of the directory for the server's own domain.

- Partial read-only copies of the directories for all other domains in the forest. These copies contain all the objects in the domains but only select object properties.

I mention global catalogs because you should make sure that at least one Global Catalog server is defined for each site. Users log on using Global Catalog servers. If one is not available at the local site, the user logs on with a global catalog server at a remote site. (Cached information is used if no global catalog server is available.) Global catalog support is not enabled automatically but is crucial to some AD functions.

Organizational Units

Organizational units (OUs) enable us to subdivide administrative responsibility inside a domain. OUs are container objects for users, groups, and resource objects such as printers, applications, file shares, and computers. There are three reasons to configure OUs:

- **Delegation of control.** The chief reason for setting up OUs is to create administrative subdivisions of domains. Organizations can establish autonomous groups of resources and delegate control of those resources to users who might not necessarily be the administrators of the domain containing the OU.

4

ACTIVE DIRECTORY CONCEPTS

- **Account Policy.** Account policy is a mechanism for configuring settings for user accounts, such as password policies. Under Windows NT 4, there was a single account policy for the entire domain. Under Windows 2000, each domain and OU can have an individual account policy.

- **Group Policy.** Group Policy is a mechanism for configuring a wide variety of restrictions on users and computers within a domain or an OU, such as the capability to access particular applications or to perform certain operations on their computers. Assigning a separate Group Policy to an OU enables administrators to establish distinct policies for individual groups of users.

You will encounter OUs quite frequently in the AD tree. For example, consider the object tree shown in the AD Users and Computers snap-in that appears in Figure 4.12. Under the PSEUDO domain object, there is an OU named **Domain Controllers**, which is the default container in which Domain Controller objects are created.

It is important to realize that membership in the Domain Controller's OU does not convey to a computer the capability of functioning as a DC. The computer is put into the Domain Controllers OU to group it with other DCs that are managed by the same group of administrators. The only effect of OU membership is to establish administrative control. A computer is a Domain Controller because it is defined by a Domain Controller object created in Active Directory when the computer is promoted.

FIGURE 4.12

OUs under domains organize the objects in the domain.

NOTE

Container objects and leaf objects can be nested into container objects. By now, you recognize that the capability to nest containers conveys the capability to construct hierarchies of unlimited depth.

Each domain and OU has its own ACL so that it can be managed by its own administrators. By default, a domain is managed by the group *domain*/Users Administrators.

Windows 2000 introduces the concept of *inheritance* to Windows security. OUs inherit security properties from their parent containers. For example, as a result of inheritance, the Domain Controllers OU is administered by the same administrators who have authority for the parent domain container. Child containers also have the same Group Policy as their parents. This is a giant advance in Windows administration, enabling us to manage security for entire parts of trees.

But, there are times when we want to block inheritance. In those cases, we can delegate control of an OU to a different group of administrators. We'll see how delegation of control works later in the chapter.

> **NOTE**
>
> Active Directory OUs are primarily administrative tools. Users are largely oblivious to Active Directory OUs, and usually see resources as being grouped at the domain level.

> **NOTE**
>
> If you are an experienced administrator of the Novell Directory Service (NDS), you will need to forget a lot about what you have learned about OUs.
>
> Under NDS, OUs function as natural groups for the objects they contain. Administrators can assign security rights to an OU, for example, and the rights will be inherited by objects in the OU unless inheritance is explicitly blocked by an inherited rights filter. To assign permissions to users in AD OUs, you must add the users to a group and assign permissions to the group.
>
> Another distinction is that OUs do not form full-fledged containers in Active Directory as they do in NDS. All NDS OUs are security groups that offer similar administrative capabilities.
>
> It is very important to understand that, under Windows 2000, OUs do not have the same functionalities as domains. For one thing, each domain is physically associated with a specific group of machines that are designated as domain controllers. OUs are logically associated with domains.
>
> OUs have names and have a place in the AD directory hierarchy, but the DNS namespace will not contain a domain that corresponds to an OU. All the computer and service names within an AD domain will appear in the same DNS domain.

4

ACTIVE
DIRECTORY
CONCEPTS

In fact, even though OUs give the appearance of subdividing the domain namespace, the namespace within a domain is flat. Suppose that the domain pseudo-corp.com has two OUs named Widgets and Blivets. There can be only one user account with the name Drew in the domain. You are not permitted to create an account named Drew in the Widgets OU and another account named Drew in the Blivets OU.

This is another characteristic distinguishing AD from NDS. Each OU under NDS establishes an autonomous namespace in the directory tree hierarchy. Under AD, namespace autonomy is limited by domain boundaries.

Models for Managing Active Directory and DNS Domains

Under Active Directory, DNS has a variety of purposes:

- It enables internal clients using Active Directory to locate Windows servers and services.
- It enables internal clients to resolve DNS domain names inside the organization.
- It enables internal clients to resolve DNS domain names external to the organization.
- It enables external clients to resolve DNS domain names for publicly available servers inside the organization, such as the organization's public Web servers.

In most discussions about Active Directory and DNS, it is assumed that these functions will be performed by a single DNS tree that supports both external DNS name resolution and internal Active Directory name and service location. It turns out, however, that a single DNS tree isn't Microsoft's top recommendation, so we need to spend some time looking at a variety of models you can use when configuring DNS with Active Directory.

Active Directory Using a Domain in the Internet Namespace

Most of the examples you will see of Active Directory configurations assume that the root domain of the AD tree will correspond to a private domain in the Internet DNS namespace. That's the scenario we examined in Figure 4.10, and it has the virtue of simplicity. It practically automates maintenance of DNS, for example, because it is easy to use Dynamic DNS to keep DNS resource records up to date. Additionally, it greatly simplifies network documentation because a computer's identity is the same in AD and in the public DNS namespace. Viewing the DNS and AD domain hierarchies alongside one another, as in Figure 4.13, makes it easy to see how they are related.

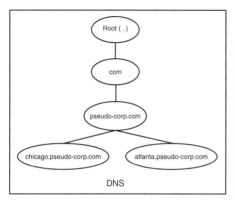
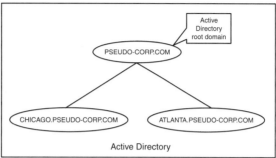

FIGURE 4.13
Here, a single DNS namespace supports external and internal DNS resolution.

But the approach of supporting AD using a tree in the Internet namespace does have some drawbacks. I can think of three:

- You might not want your public DNS domain hierarchy to reflect your private AD domain hierarchy.
- You might not want your entire private namespace to be available to outside users.
- If your organization's private network is behind a network address translating firewall, the internal IP addresses aren't of any value to outsiders and probably shouldn't be published.

Let's look at these concerns.

Should DNS Domains Match AD Domains?

When AD is based on a domain in the Internet namespace, if you create a new AD domain, you will also create a new subdomain in your organization's public DNS namespace. Resource records that are dynamically added to DNS for hosts in the subdomain typically will be created in the DNS subdomain as well.

The crucial question you need to address when you design your Active Directory trees is, "Should I use the same namespace for my Active Directory domains that I use to support public DNS queries for resources in my organizations?"

Because AD domains are not always created for the same reasons as DNS domains, the answer to the question often is "No." AD domains are primarily created as administrative subdivisions of the tree. We can add a domain when one is demanded by the organization's structure, although structural needs can often be satisfied by adding OUs. But when a group requires authority for resources down to the domain controllers, a new domain must be added.

4

ACTIVE
DIRECTORY
CONCEPTS

DNS domains, on the other hand, are added to organize resources accessed by end users. DNS domains often do not reflect departments or organizations. Suppose that the following situation exists:

- The company's World Wide Web server is managed by the Marketing department, which manages its own AD domain. The AD name of the server is `WWW.MARKETING.SEATTLE.PSEUDO-CORP.COM`.

- The company's FTP server is managed by the IS department in Atlanta and has the AD name `FTP.IS.ATLANTA.PSEUDO-CORP.COM`.

It is probable that we wouldn't want to use the AD names to publicly identify the servers. Instead, we would probably create the aliases (CNAME RRs) `www` and `ftp` in the DNS `pseudo-corp.com` domain that point to the RRs created by AD. Aliases must be manually administered. It isn't a big deal to manage aliases, but the necessity is something to remember.

Because Host Address RRs are simply mappings between a domain name and an IP address, a given host IP address can be given names in an unlimited number of domains. This makes it feasible to support external DNS queries and Active Directory DNS usage using the same DNS namespace. Although it is feasible, it might not be desirable to place RRs created by AD in the organization's public DNS namespace. Let's see why.

Protecting the Private Namespace

The big problem with public access to the AD namespace is that it provides anyone who can use a DNS query tool with the ability to discover every server and service on your private network. Typically, security-conscious organizations don't want this information to be available. Often they don't even want the public to know which IP addresses are in use on the private network. Any knowledge about specific server or service addresses provides intruders with information that can simplify their attempts to break into the network.

DNS does not provide security mechanisms that restrict access to information in a namespace, and we can't publish just part of the organization's DNS namespace for public access. Access to a DNS namespace is an all-or-nothing proposition, and, if we don't want outsiders to be able to discover the contents of the `ATLANTA` domain, we have to make sure the domain isn't published in the organization's public DNS namespace. The only way to accomplish that is to have separate namespaces for public and private DNS information.

DNS and Network Address Translating Firewalls

Chapter 2, "TCP/IP Protocol Concepts," introduced network address translating firewalls (NATs), which are used by many organizations to provide a layer of anonymity for hosts on their internal networks. The internal network is configured using non-routable IP addresses, which can be employed locally but are not routed through the Internet. A NAT firewall maps internal IP addresses to IP addresses that can be routed through the Internet, enabling hosts on the private network to communicate with services on the Internet.

If a NAT is used to communicate with the Internet, the DNS database that supports AD will not be of any use to outside users, who need to communicate with servers on the private network. In such cases, it makes little sense to publish the organization's internal DNS tree to outside users.

NATs can enable outside users to access services on internal hosts if administrators configure static mappings between outside and inside IP addresses. Suppose that the organization's DNS database resolves `www.pseudo-corp.com` to w.x.y.23, a valid IP address on the Internet. The NAT can be configured to map w.x.y.23 to the internal IP address 192.168.5.4 (a non-routable IP address). This would enable users to send packets to hosts on the internal network, even though the host's own IP address is non-routable. In these cases, it is the public IP address that we want to make available on the Internet, not the server's internal IP address.

If your organization's network is hiding behind a NAT, you probably want the DNS database outsiders see to be specifically tailored to provide the sort of information they should have. You might want your public DNS namespace to contain only the mappings for specific servers that are used by public users. Doing this would reduce the risk inherent in publishing the full DNS tree of your organization and reduce the likelihood that users will attempt to access resources on servers that have DNS names but that aren't meant for public use.

Active Directory Using a Private DNS Namespace

Suppose that your organization doesn't communicate with the Internet. How do you configure your AD domain tree when you won't be integrating it with the Internet's namespace?

The root domain of the AD tree doesn't necessarily have to correspond with a third- or lower-level domain in the Internet namespace. You can, if you want, construct a private DNS namespace with a private DNS root domain and any domain structure that you choose.

If Pseudo Corp. doesn't communicate with the Internet, we might settle on the AD tree, shown in Figure 4.14. The DNS tree has a *private root* that is recognized only by local name servers. In fact, the root name of the AD domain tree cannot even be used on the Internet. It cannot be integrated into the Internet namespace, but, if there is no Internet connectivity, Internet integration isn't an issue. Insofar as such organizations are concerned, AD functionality is entirely supported by a tree like the one in Figure 4.14.

The arrangement in Figure 4.14 works great if all the subdomains are configured in the same zone as the root domain. In that case, the name server knows about all the domains in the tree and can handle queries for information in other domains in the tree. So the simplest approach when you have a DNS tree with a private root is to support subdomains using the procedure discussed in Chapter 3 in the section "Creating a Child Domain in the Parent Domain's Zone."

4

ACTIVE
DIRECTORY
CONCEPTS

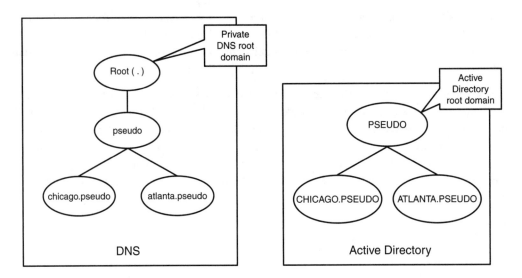

FIGURE 4.14

This domain tree is based on a private root domain.

But, suppose your organization is large and wants to deploy separate DNS servers for some of its subdomains. On a private DNS tree, there's a problem. Consider the situation shown in Figure 4.15. In this simplified example, there are two name servers:

- DNS server name1.pseudo supports a zone that includes the domains pseudo and chicago.pseudo.

- name1.pseudo delegates authority for the atlanta.pseudo subdomain to the DNS server name1.atlanta.pseudo.

Let's consider how client queries work with these two name servers.

Client drew.pseudo is configured to use name1.pseudo for DNS queries. The DNS name1.pseudo can resolve queries to the pseudo and the atlanta.pseudo domains because name1.pseudo understands that authority for atlanta.pseudo has been delegated.

Client lauren.atlanta.pseudo is configured to use name1.atlanta.pseudo for DNS queries. This DNS server can resolve queries in atlanta.pseudo, but might have trouble with queries to the pseudo domain. Although DNS servers can delegate authority for lower-level domains, they cannot delegate authority for higher-level domains. There is no direct mechanism that enables name1.atlanta.pseudo to know that the server name1.pseudo is authoritative for the pseudo domain.

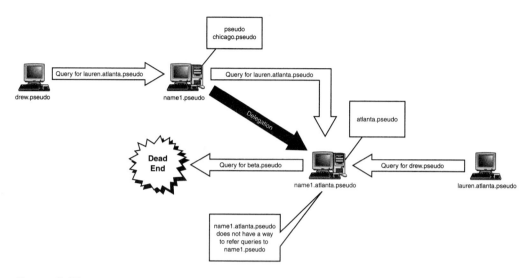

FIGURE 4.15

Unless properly configured, clients using name1.atlanta.pseudo *cannot resolve names in other zones in the organization.*

There are two ways around this difficulty. One is the direct approach. Modify the root hints for name1.atlanta.pseudo, removing the default hints for the Internet root domain servers. Replace them with hints pointing to name1.pseudo and other name servers that are authoritative for the top-level domains in the private network. This approach works fine, but it does render the modified name servers unable to process queries to the public Internet, hence, it's an approach that works only if the network is private and will remain so. The procedure for modifying root hints is discussed in Chapter 3 in the section "Root Hints Properties."

Another approach is to configure name1.atlanta.pseudo to use name1.pseudo as a forwarder. When that is done, any name requests that name1.atlanta.pseudo cannot resolve locally will be forwarded to name1.pseudo, including queries into all other domains in both the private and Internet namespace. Consequently, the use of forwarders enables users to resolve names both locally and on the Internet. The disadvantage of this approach is that DNS forwarders can get very busy because they become focal points for large numbers of queries. In such cases, name1.pseudo should be dedicated to function only as a DNS name server, and it should be equipped with hardware that is up to the task. There should, of course, be at least two name servers for the pseudo zone. Forwarders properties for lower-level name servers should include all the name servers for the pseudo zone in their lists of forwarders. The procedure for configuring forwarders is discussed in Chapter 3 in the section "Forwarders Properties."

NOTE

Incidentally, if you configure a DNS tree with a private root, it is important to remember that the root domain of the AD tree does not correspond to the root domain of the DNS tree. Recall that the root domain of the DNS tree does not have a name and is referred simply as " " or by including a trailing period in the FQDN.

Typically, when the network is configured with a private domain root, the root domain of an AD tree will correspond to a first-level domain in the DNS namespace. So although a rose is a rose, a root is not necessarily a root.

Active Directory and External DNS Using Separate Domains in the Internet Namespace

One approach Microsoft recommends is to use separate Internet DNS domains: one for outside DNS queries and a second for Active Directory. With this approach, Pseudo Corp. would need to register two separate domains on the Internet, perhaps the following, as shown in Figure 4.16:

- `pseudo-corp.com` would support DNS queries for names of servers that are available to the public.
- `pseudo-int.com` would support the private internal Active Directory namespace.

The advantage of this approach is simplicity. The same root hints work for all name servers. Consider the DNS server configuration shown in Figure 4.17. Suppose, for example, that `drew.pseudo-int.com` initiates a query for the company's public Web server `www.pseudo-corp.com` using the name server `name1.pseudo-int.com`. The query must be resolved on `name1.pseudo-corp.com`. Because the DNS server on `name1.pseudo-int.com` is configured with root hints for the Internet name servers, it initiates attempts to resolve `server1.pseudo-corp.com` starting with the Internet root domain. (In practice, `name1.pseudo-int.com` will likely have a record for `www.pseudo-corp.com` in its name cache and will not need to initiate a full query starting with the root name servers.)

That might seem like a roundabout way to resolve a name that is part of the local organization's namespace, but it's the standard mode of attack when a DNS is asked to resolve a query that it cannot resolve from its own cache or zone databases.

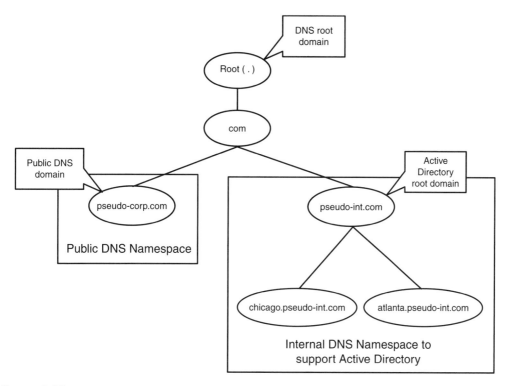

FIGURE 4.16

The internal and external namespaces are separate, but both are in the Internet namespace.

4

ACTIVE
DIRECTORY
CONCEPTS

NOTE

Figure 4.17 shows the more difficult approach of hosting `pseudo-corp.com` and `pseudo-int.com` on separate name servers. But they could easily be hosted on the same name servers, in which case, a query for either domain could be resolved without forcing the name servers to search starting with the Internet root domain.

An advantage of the separate domains approach is that the domain intended to support name resolution for outside users (`pseudo-corp.com`, in this example) contains only RRs that are explicitly placed there by an administrator, such as `www.pseudo-corp.com`. The namespace doesn't contain the organization's Active Directory Service Location RRs, which should preferably have a low profile.

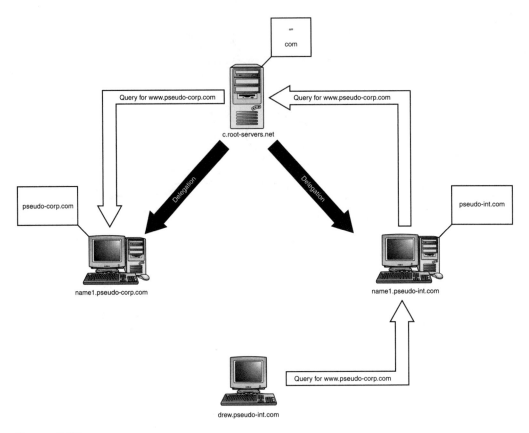

FIGURE 4.17

drew.pseudo-int.com *queries the* pseudo-corp.com *domain via Internet root name servers.*

As with any approach that involves two or more DNS namespaces, one of the namespaces must be administered manually. Dynamic DNS cannot be used to update RRs in both namespaces. But the primary purpose of the external DNS namespace is to support access to servers, and servers are almost always configured with static IP addresses, either in their static configuration parameters or through a reservation in DHCP. Consequently, the external DNS namespace will be much less dynamic than the internal namespace that supports Active Directory, which changes every time a service is stopped or started. The public namespace might, in fact, contain very few entries that describe Web servers, mail exchangers, FTP servers, and servers that are explicitly intended to be accessed by users outside the organization.

If security is the goal, however, this isn't the strongest possible approach because any domain in the Internet namespace is available for public scrutiny. In the example, although we might not give pseudo-int.com much publicity, it would take little effort for an intruder to discover its existence and trace it to your organization using a WHOIS search. (In fact, as soon as you register a new domain, you'll start getting email from vendors who want sell you support services. The Internet namespace—particularly in the .com, .net, and .org domains—is very, very public.)

There are a couple of ways to guard your private namespace. You could register the internal domain under a top-level domain that is receiving a bit less attention than `.com`, `.org`, and `.net`, all of which are cataloged in WHOIS. As mentioned in Chapter 3, some of the country-based, top-level domains are accepting commercial domain registrations and are not cataloged in WHOIS. This approach provides some obscurity, but little genuine protection.

The approach I prefer involves supporting the internal namespace with a separate DNS tree based on a private DNS root. It's more complicated and can require more resources, but it has the virtue of entirely removing your private DNS information from the Internet namespace.

Active Directory Using a Private DNS Namespace, External DNS Using the Internet Namespace

A private root domain might be just the ticket for the Active Directory functions on your network, but what if you need to connect to the Internet after all? If your namespace is private, outside users cannot resolve names in your private DNS namespace because none of the Internet name servers delegate control to your namespace. Bummer, right? Not if you support a second DNS namespace based on a public Internet domain.

My preferred approach for combining AD support with public access is as follows:

- Configure a DNS tree within the public Internet namespace that enables users to access the TCP/IP resources that you choose to make publicly available.
- Configure a DNS tree with a private root that supports Active Directory with a private namespace.

Figure 4.18 shows how these two namespaces might complement each other. Remember as you look at the figure that DNS places no restrictions on the number of names that can map to a given IP address. We could have a dozen resource records in a dozen different trees, all mapping to the same host if that was what we needed.

If you have a NAT firewall, the public DNS namespace can resolve names to the public IP addresses that the NAT router maps to private internal IP addresses. In Figure 4.18, a NAT firewall maps the external IP address 192.168.45.10 to the IP address 10.1.0.25, which identifies the Web server inside the firewall. Mapping of external to internal IP addresses is a valuable and necessary security capability of a NAT firewall. Because IP addresses must be mapped at the NAT in any case, the external addresses have to be identified in the organization's public DNS namespace.

The DNS tree with the public root must be maintained manually, but, as the previous section explained, the public namespace of an organization is not necessarily very large or dynamic, consisting only of RRs that are explicitly intended to be publicly available. These are typically Web, FTP, DNS, and mail servers.

4

ACTIVE
DIRECTORY
CONCEPTS

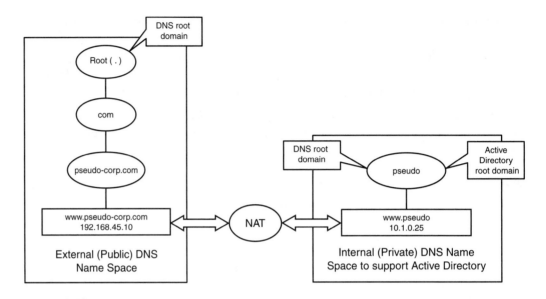

FIGURE 4.18

RRs in the public namespace map to IP addresses of servers that also have identities in the private namespace managed by AD.

Although it does require some additional administrative labor, I am drawn to the dual-root approach. Several advantages speak to me:

- Private information about servers, clients, and services remains entirely private, concealing information about the network from potential intruders. Private name servers can be protected inside the organization's firewall. Private DNS servers can be placed behind the organization's firewall and are therefore resistant to queries from outside computers.
- The AD domain tree can be designed to fit the administrative needs of the organization without raising concerns for its impact on the design of the public DNS namespace.
- The public DNS namespace contains only information that the public needs to have and can be designed to facilitate access to public resources.

Because the two DNS trees used in this approach have different root domains, this approach has a complication that doesn't appear when both AD and external DNS namespaces are part of the Internet namespace. The complication arises because a given DNS server can be configured with only one set of root hints. If the DNS servers in the organization are configured with root hints for the private root, clients cannot resolve queries in the Internet namespace. If the DNS servers in the organization are configured with root hints for the Internet root domain servers, clients will have difficulties with internal queries when the internal namespace is divided into two or more zones that are supported by separate DNS servers. (This situation was explored earlier in the section "Active Directory Using a Private DNS Namespace.")

The problem is how to direct queries to the appropriate namespace. There are essentially two solutions: using forwarding DNS servers or using a Winsock proxy server. Either approach requires two sets of name servers, one for the private internal namespace and one for the public namespace on the Internet. Otherwise, they are significantly different.

Supporting Separate DNS Namespaces Without a Proxy Server

Typically, your internal network will be situated behind a firewall, either a software NAT, such as the one included with Windows 2000 Server, or a separate, hardware-based firewall, which can have NAT capabilities. The name servers supporting the private DNS namespace used by AD should be located inside the firewall to protect them from attack and to prevent unauthorized access to the data they contain. Outside organizations can be given access to resources inside the firewall, including the name servers through a secure, extranet connection.

The most streamlined way to support a private DNS namespace is to keep all the domains in the same zone. When that is done, any name server that is authoritative for the zone can resolve any query in any domain in the zone. Except in small organizations, the DNS servers should be dedicated to DNS services only and there should be at least two DNS servers for the zone.

Figure 4.19 illustrates this simple, effective approach. The root domain of the private AD tree is named PSEUDO. The organization's public Internet namespace is based on the domain pseudo-corp.com.

The name server name1.pseudo is configured as follows:

- It is connected inside the corporate firewall.
- It hosts the zone pseudo, which includes the domains pseudo, atlanta.pseudo, and chicago.pseudo.
- There is no delegation of authority to this server from the Internet first-level domains. (In fact, with the name pseudo, no delegation is possible.)
- Root hints on the server identify the root name servers for the Internet.

The name server name1.pseudo-corp.com is configured as follows:

- It is connected outside the firewall, or the firewall makes the name server available for public access.
- It hosts the zone pseudo-corp.com.
- The Internet com domain delegates authority for pseudo-corp.com to this name server.
- Root hints on the server identify the root name servers for the Internet.

4

ACTIVE
DIRECTORY
CONCEPTS

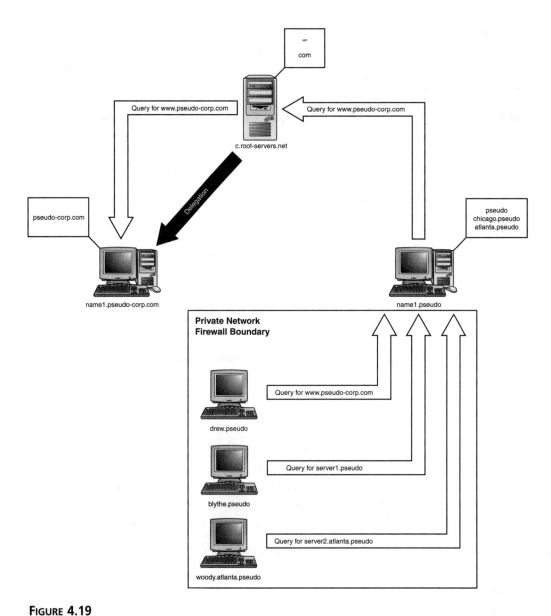

FIGURE 4.19

This network employs a private namespace for internal use and a public Internet namespace for external use.

Client `drew.atlanta.pseudo` can make three types of queries:

- **Queries in the client's own domain.** These queries can be resolved by `name1.pseudo` because it is authoritative for `atlanta.pseudo`.

- **Queries in other domains in Pseudo Corp.'s private namespace.** These queries can also be resolved by `name1.pseudo` because it is authoritative for `pseudo` and for all subdomains of `pseudo`.

- **Queries in domains on the Internet.** Because `name1.pseudo` is configured with root hints for the Internet name servers, `name1.pseudo` can conduct a name resolution query on the Internet.

What happens if the internal DNS namespace is divided into multiple zones on multiple DNS servers? It's a bit more complicated, but it's easy to configure with forwarding name servers. Figure 4.20 illustrates the situation when `atlanta.pseudo` is hosted in a separate zone on the name server `name1.atlanta.pseudo`. This name server is the default name server for `drew.atlanta.pseudo`. Let's see how the same three queries work under these circumstances:

- **Queries in the client's own domain.** These queries can be resolved by `name1.atlanta.pseudo` because it is authoritative for `atlanta.pseudo`.

- **Queries in other domains in Pseudo Corp.'s private namespace.** `name1.atlanta.pseudo` is configured to forward queries that it cannot resolve to `name1.pseudo`. This server can resolve queries in the domains `pseudo` and `chicago.pseudo`.

- **Queries in domains on the Internet.** `name1.atlanta.pseudo` is configured to forward queries that it cannot resolve to `name1.pseudo`. Because `name1.pseudo` is configured with root hints for the Internet name servers, `name1.pseudo` can conduct a name resolution query on the Internet.

In this scenario, `name1.pseudo` could be a very busy name server. Monitor it (and other name servers for the zone `pseudo`) to ensure that they are not bottlenecks in the name query process.

One approach that might have advantages is shown in Figure 4.21. Here an additional forwarding name server is introduced specifically to handle outside name queries. This cache-only name server enables internal name servers to focus on internal queries. It also constructs a single cache of all outside queries, which is available to all internal name servers, thus reducing the number of queries that must actually be conducted using Internet name servers. Cache-only name servers are discussed in Chapter 3.

4

ACTIVE
DIRECTORY
CONCEPTS

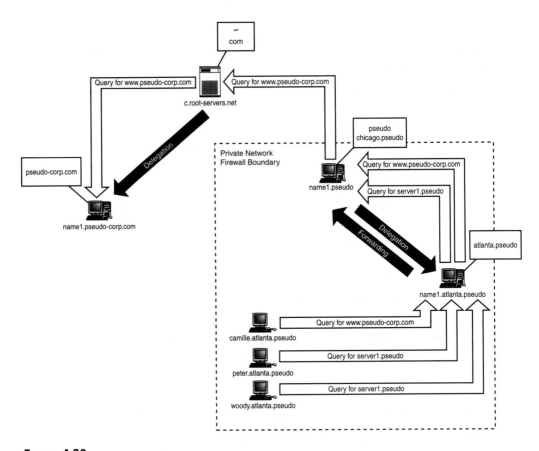

FIGURE 4.20
The authority for the atlanta.pseudo *domain is delegated to* name1.atlanta.pseudo.

Supporting Separate DNS Namespaces with a Windows Sockets Proxy Server

A Windows Sockets (Winsock) proxy server (WSP) is included with the Internet Security and Acceleration server (IAS), a Windows NT/2000 Server add-on that acts as a firewall between the internal network and the public Internet. The WSP component of IAS enables an extensive number of Winsock applications to access the Internet through a firewall.

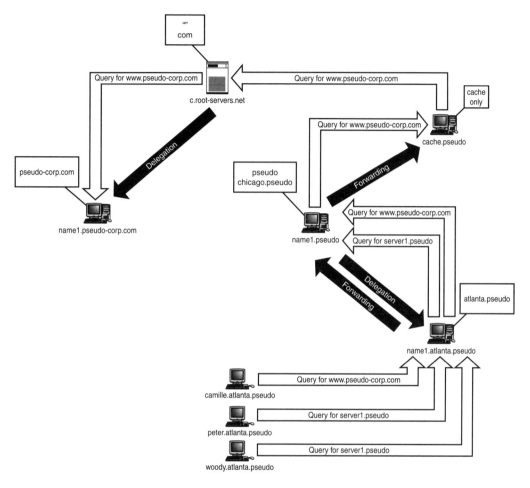

FIGURE 4.21

A cache-only name server can reduce processing loads on internal DNS servers.

4

ACTIVE
DIRECTORY
CONCEPTS

> **NOTE**
>
> The Microsoft Internet Security and Acceleration Server is discussed in the Bonus Chapter for this book, available at `http://www.mcp.com/sams/detail_sams.cfm?item=0672317419`.
>
> The features required in this section are also available in the Microsoft Proxy Server 2.0, which was developed for Windows NT 4.0. Although Proxy Server will run on Windows 2000 Server, it cannot integrate with Active Directory.

To avoid this problem we need to direct external DNS queries to external DNS servers and internal DNS queries to DNS servers that are inside the firewall. IAS provides this capability by enabling administrators to configure Local Domain Tables (LDTs) that list domains that clients are to resolve using internal DNS servers. When a client needs to resolve a name from a domain that does not appear in the LDT, the client directs the query to its IAS server. LDTs can be downloaded automatically to most Web browsers including Microsoft Internet Explorer versions 3.01 and later.

For IAS clients, DNS queries are handled as shown in Figure 4.22.

Suppose that the client `drew.pseudo` needs to resolve the name `server1.pseudo`. This name is internal, a fact that the client can determine by consulting its LDT. Because the client determines that the name is internal, it directs the DNS query to the DNS server that is specified in its TCP/IP client configuration parameters.

Now suppose that the client `drew.pseudo` needs to resolve the name `www.pseudo-corp.com`. This domain does not appear in the LDT. Therefore, the query is sent to the proxy server, which conducts the query on behalf of the client and returns the results to the client.

Which Approach: Forwarders or Winsock Proxy Server?

My sense is that proxy servers are being overtaken in popularity by NAT firewalls in most organizations. NAT firewalls do not require any special configuration on the client and are virtually transparent. And NATs are built in to many routers, so deployment might not require additional hardware.

To use IAS, clients must be configured with a special version of Winsock. Clients must also be configured with lists of local and remote resources so that they can direct packets to Proxy Server when necessary. Consequently, a Winsock proxy server requires extra administrative effort. It might also require additional hardware. Many organizations will maintain routers (usually with firewalls) in addition to any proxy servers they might deploy.

A proxy server does not have the transparency of a NAT, but it does have the capability of maintaining a cache of recently received Web objects. Caching of Web objects can have significant benefits, reducing WAN traffic when several users retrieve the same objects from the Web.

So I guess this is one of the times when my recommendation has to be, "It depends." Learn more about NATs in Chapter 7, "Routing with Routing and Remote Access Service," and about IAS in the Bonus Chapter, available on the Web at `http://www.mcp.com/sams/detail_sams.cfm?item=0672317419`. Then make a decision regarding which you will use, based on the needs of your organization.

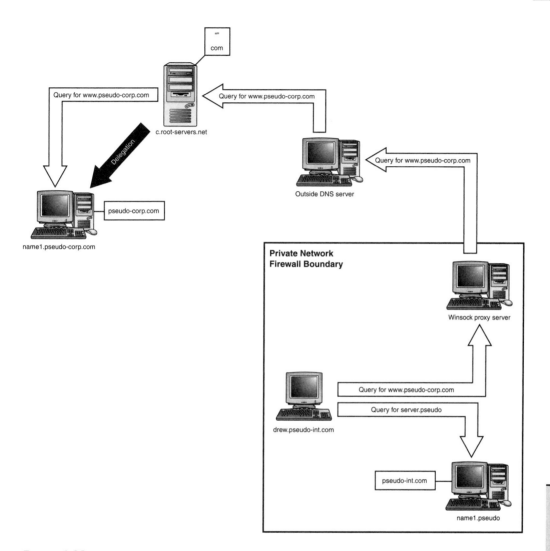

FIGURE 4.22

Clients configured to use a Winsock proxy server can determine for themselves whether to direct packets to local servers or to the proxy server to be forwarded to the Internet.

Configuring Domain Controllers

One of the most welcome improvements of Windows 2000 is that domain controllers can now be reconfigured on-the-fly. You can remove a DC from one domain and add it to another without having to reinstall the operating system. If you're an experienced NT administrator, this capability alone should make your mouth water.

Domain controllers are configured using the **Active Directory Installation Wizard**. Before you configure a DC, you should have answers to the following questions:

- Is this the first DC in a new domain?
- If a new AD domain is being created, will it be created in an existing tree?
- If a new AD domain tree is being created, will the tree be part of an existing forest?
- If a new AD domain tree is being created, does the domain correspond to a DNS domain in a tree with a public or a private root?
- On which device will the DC's own data files be stored? AD maintains a database and a log. Because these files are modified simultaneously, best performance is obtained if they are placed on separate SCSI or Fibre Channel hard disks. (IDE hard disks can perform simultaneous writes only if they are connected to different controllers, but simultaneous write performance probably still will not match that of a SCSI disk subsystem.)

Creating the First DC in a New Domain

A domain is created when you create the first DC in a new domain. In the process of creating the DC, Active Directory is installed on the computer. If you are creating the first DC in a tree, the root domain in the tree must be created first. Subsequent domains in the tree must be appended to the hierarchy. The tree cannot be configured with gaps between domains that are to be filled in later.

In this and the following two sections, I am going to use domain names that are distinctly incompatible with the Internet DNS scheme. The parent domain created in this section will be named PSEUDO. The child domain created in the next section will be named ATLANTA.PSEUDO. Names like these work fine on a private network, but it is, of course, impossible to insert these domains into the Internet namespace. They will be forever private in character.

> **NOTE**
>
> Personally, I like domain names like PSEUDO for use on a private network. They establish a clear distinction between names on the private network and names on the Internet. And they are shorter and therefore easier to remember and type. They can also be the same as NetBIOS names for the domains, simplifying things from the users' perspectives.

Microsoft likes Internet-ready domain names, even if the names won't be available in the Internet DNS namespace. Following their lead, I would use a name such as PSEUDO-INT.COM for my AD root domain, wherein the INT indicates that the namespace is for internal use. I'll show you examples of this naming convention later in the chapter. You can then decide which approach you want to take when naming your internal domains.

CAUTION

Plan your AD tree carefully. You cannot reconfigure the root domain without deleting all domains in the tree and rebuilding the tree.

I concur with Microsoft that whenever possible you should attempt to support your entire organization with a single AD domain. A single domain greatly simplifies tree design and maintenance.

Before you install Active Directory, the following conditions must be met:

- At least one storage volume on the server must support NTFS 5.0.
- The server's TCP/IP client settings must be configured. In particular, the TCP/IP interface settings must be configured with the IP address of at least one DNS server that supports the features required by AD. If desired, the DNS server can be installed on the local machine during the AD configuration process.

CAUTION

I am writing this chapter using Windows 2000 Server prior to the issue of any service packs. With this configuration, Active Directory DCs might have difficulty performing secure updates to remote DNS servers running on Windows 2000 Servers. If the zone used by the domain is hosted on a DNS Server that is running on a remote DC, and you have trouble with dynamic updates, perform the following procedure at the DNS server:

1. In the DNS console, right-click the zone and select **Properties**.
2. In the **General** tab, change the value of the field **Allow dynamic updates?** to **Yes**.

Microsoft's recommended practice is that you have a DNS server in each domain for use by computers in that domain.

Domain controllers are configured using the following procedure:

1. Execute the command DCPROMO at the **Start→Run** menu prompt. This command opens the Active Directory Installation Wizard. Click **Next** to continue.

2. In the **Domain Controller Type** dialog box, select from the following choices to describe the domain controller:

   - **Domain controller for a new domain**
   - **Additional domain controller for an existing domain**

   If the DC is being added to an existing domain, quite a lot of information is deleted from the computer, including local accounts and any locally stored cryptographic keys. The keys can be exported, but you should decrypt any encrypted files or data before continuing with the operation, or the data will not be accessible after the upgrade.

   Click **Next** to continue.

3. In the **Create Tree or Child Domain** dialog box, select one of these choices to describe the domain being created:

   - **Create a new domain tree.** With this choice, the new domain will become the root domain of a new tree.
   - **Create a new child domain in an existing domain tree.** The new domain will be a child domain of a previously created domain.

   Click **Next** to continue.

4. In the **Create or Join Forest** dialog box, select one of these choices:

   - **Create a new forest of domain trees**
   - **Place a new domain tree in an existing forest**

   If you add a new domain tree to an existing forest, the new domain tree will be configured with the schema that is in effect in the forest. A two-way transitive trust will be established between the root domains of the two trees.

   Click **Next** to continue.

5. In the **New Domain Name** dialog box, enter the Fully Qualified DNS Name for the new domain. The dialog box expects the name to contain periods on the assumption that you are specifying a subdomain in the Internet namespace, such as pseudo-corp.com.

   If you enter a domain name without periods, the wizard displays a warning: "The domain name does not appear to be a full DNS name." It is perfectly all right to continue with a name such as PSEUDO, but you will need to click **Yes** in this warning to keep the name.

   Click **Next** to continue.

6. In the **NetBIOS Domain Name** dialog box, the wizard will generate a NetBIOS-compatible name that is derived from the domain name entered in Step 5. This name identifies the domain to non-AD clients. Edit it, if necessary. Some of the automatically generated names are pretty offputting.

Click **Next** to continue.

7. The next dialog box is **Database and Log Locations**, shown in Figure 4.23. Here you specify the locations for the AD database and the AD logs. The default location is %SystemRoot%\NTDS.

As mentioned earlier, to enhance performance, these files should be placed on separate SCSI or Fibre Channel hard disks.

In both fields, you can click the **Browse** button to locate the target directory graphically.

Click **Next** to continue.

8. The next dialog box is **Shared System Volume**. The volume specified here stores the server's copy of the domain database that is shared with other DCs. This must be an NTFS 5.0 volume.

Click **Next** to continue.

9. The wizard attempts to locate a DNS server for the domain you are creating using the DNS servers that are specified in the server's TCP/IP interface configuration. AD requires a DNS server that supports Dynamic DNS updates and Service Location resource records.

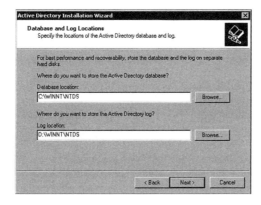

4

ACTIVE
DIRECTORY
CONCEPTS

FIGURE 4.23

Ideally, AD database and log files should be placed on separate physical disks.

If a suitable DNS server is not located, the wizard displays a warning. There are two likely causes of a warning:

- DNS servers that are found do not have the required capabilities.
- No DNS servers are active at the addresses specified in the server's TCP/IP interface properties.

If you know that suitable DNS servers are already configured, check the server's TCP/IP interface properties to ensure that the DNS IP addresses are correct.

If you see this warning and want to configure a new DNS server to support the domain, click **OK** to continue.

10. If a suitable DNS server cannot be located, the wizard brings up the **Configure DNS** dialog box with two choices:

- **Yes, install and configure DNS on this computer.** This is the preferred choice because there will be little doubt that the first DNS server supporting the domain will be properly configured.
- **No, I will install and configure DNS myself.** You can configure the DNS server manually, but it is much easier if you use the **Yes** option the first time you create a new domain so that you see an example of a properly configured DNS server.

Click **Next** to continue.

> **NOTE**
>
> DCPROMO can create a DNS zone to support the new domain only if the DNS server is running on the machine where DCPROMO is running. If the DNS zone will be hosted on another machine, you must create the zone manually.

11. The next dialog box is **Permissions** and offers two choices:

- **Permissions compatible with pre-Windows 2000 Servers.** Choose this option if you have applications that are not running on Windows 2000 Servers or that are running in Windows 3.x or 4.0 domains, particularly if the domain includes Remote Access Servers running on Windows 4.0 servers, or SQL Servers running on Windows 3.x or 4.0. With this choice, the built-in group Everyone is given the permissions required to log in anonymously. This is the default option.
- **Permissions compatible with only Windows 2000 Servers.** Choose this option if all applications are running on Windows 2000 Servers that are in Windows 2000 domains.

Click **Next** to continue.

12. The next dialog box is titled **Directory Services Restore Mode Administrator's Password.** Enter and confirm a password that restricts access to Directory Services Restore Mode when restarting the server. In this mode certain server functions are unavailable. If the server is not physically secure, you should specify a password.

   Click **Next** to continue.

13. A **Summary** box describes the configuration you have defined. Review the configuration and use the **Back** button to return to any dialog boxes that require modification.

   Click **Next** to continue.

14. The wizard configures AD. If you configured it to do so, it will install DNS. You will need to supply a Windows 2000 Server installation CD-ROM to provide the required files.

15. Restart the system to activate Active Directory.

When you install Active Directory, you get a lot of new MMC snap-ins as a bonus. Look under **Start→Programs→Administrative Tools** for shortcuts to the following:

- **Active Directory Domains and Trusts.** Lists domains and enables administrators to directly manage the domain mode, domain trusts, and change the domain manager.

- **Active Directory Sites and Services.** Defines sites and specifies how AD data will be replicated between sites.

- **Active Directory Users and Computers.** Describes and manages computers, domain controllers, users, groups, and connections to pre-Windows objects such as print shares. (Replaces Windows NT User Manager for Domains and Server Manager. Many new functions are specific to Windows 2000.)

- **Domain Controller Security Policy.** A policy console that manages the Security Policy for a single DC.

- **Domain Security Policy.** A policy console that manages the Security Policy for an entire domain.

4

ACTIVE
DIRECTORY
CONCEPTS

NOTE

After creating a new domain, tree, or forest, you should configure administrators. Using the Active Directory Users and Computers snap-in, configure users in the following groups:

- *root domain*\Users\Enterprise Admins. By default, users in this predefined group are made members of the Administrators built-in group of the domain. This group is predefined only in the first root domain of a tree. Unless you use a different group structure, add users to this group who have administrative permissions for all domains in the forest.

- *domain*\Builtin\Administrators. Add local users and global groups that are to have administrative permissions for the domain container.

AD Child Domains and Resource Records in DNS

When AD is installed, quite a few special domains and RRs are added to the DNS domain associated with the AD domain. Figure 4.24 shows a DNS domain supporting a private AD root domain named PSEUDO, a name I chose to emphasize the fact that this is a private DNS namespace that cannot appear on the Internet. I've expanded one subtree of the domain records to show the structure of the tree that supports a set of AD Service Location RRs.

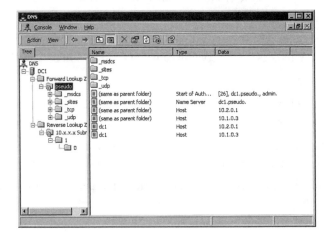

FIGURE 4.24

AD maintains several subdomains in every DNS domain that supports an AD domain.

You will see four special subdomains in every DNS domain that supports AD: _msds, _sites, _tcp, and _udp. These subdomains are used to organize Service Location resource records. The structure of these subdomains and the details about Service Location RRs are beyond the scope of this book, and it is seldom necessary to manually manipulate any of these objects. Everything should be taken care of by AD.

It is important that the domains and RRs be there, however. If they are not, it is an indication that AD is improperly configured or is unable to perform dynamic DNS updates to the zone. After the DNS zone is created initially, it takes a few minutes for AD to populate the zone with subdomains and RRs. If the objects fail to appear in the DNS console, try the following operations before you conclude that AD is not working properly with DNS:

- Press F5 to refresh the display. If that doesn't work, wait a few minutes and press F5 again.

- Close the DNS console. Then use the Services snap-in under **Start→Programs→ Administrative Tools** to stop the DNS Server. Stop the NetLogon service, restart the NetLogon service, and restart the DNS Server. Restart the DNS console to see if the records appear.

- If the DNS server is not running on the computer that is being configured as the DC, in the DNS console open the zone **Properties** dialog box and change the value of **Allow dynamic updates?** to **Yes**. (As mentioned in an earlier note, for some reason the **Only secure updates** option might not allow AD to update a zone on a remote Windows 2000 DNS Server.)

Adding a DC to a Domain

After a domain has been created, it is a simple matter to add another domain controller to the domain. Active Directory will be installed on the new DC, and the computer must meet the preconditions mentioned in the preceding section.

The procedure for adding a DC to a domain is merely a simplified version of the numbered steps in the previous section, and I won't provide a complete run through. In Step 2, choose **Additional domain controller for an existing domain**. Remember that this option results in the removal of all local accounts, cryptographic keys, and all encrypted information. Take steps to decrypt essential files and to export keys if they must be preserved.

> **NOTE**
>
> When you add a computer to a domain, be sure that the computer's DNS server parameters include the IP address of a DNS server that can perform updates to the zone. If the zone is Active Directory-integrated, this can be any DNS server that is authoritative for the zone. Otherwise it must be the primary DNS server for the zone.
>
> Because multiple DNS servers are preferable, you should install the DNS server service on two or more servers, preferably at least one in each domain and at each site. Active Directory–integrated zones are supported only on DNS servers that are configured as Active Directory domain controllers.

Creating a Child Domain

The procedure for creating a child domain is nearly identical to the procedure for creating the root domain of a tree. A child domain cannot be created unless the parent domain is already in existence.

The process of creating an Active Directory child domain differs from the process of creating the root domain primarily in that DNS servers are already active and support at least the zone that includes the organization's root domain. Consequently, when adding a child domain, you must plan ahead regarding the mechanism for integrating DNS for the child domain with DNS for the parent domain. There are two ways to proceed:

- Placing the child domain in the same zone as the parent domain, in which case the same DNS name servers support the child and the parent. In this situation, the DNS servers supporting the new domain will already be in operation.

4

ACTIVE DIRECTORY CONCEPTS

- Placing the child domain in a zone that is separate from the zone containing the parent domain, in which case separate DNS servers must be configured to support the child zone. Authority must be delegated to the new DNS servers. In this case, the domain can be configured using existing DNS servers, or it can be configured with a new DNS server, perhaps running on the new DC.

Minimally, the TCP/IP interface parameters for the new DC must specify the IP address of at least one DNS server that supports features required by Active Directory and that can resolve names in the root domain of the AD tree. The child domain cannot be created unless a suitable DNS server is available. It is a good idea to use NSLOOKUP to verify communication with the target DNS server before you start to configure the domain.

Installing the DNS server on the local DC won't support installation of a child DC when the child domain is in the same zone as the DNS parent because DCPROMO cannot integrate the new DC with the DNS zones that support the parent domain. Start by using the DNS server that supports the root domain. After the child domain is created, you can install a DNS server on the new DC and configure zones and authority delegation as necessary.

NOTE

Most of the problems I have encountered with setting up and maintaining domains relate to DNS communication. It is essential that DCs be able to communicate with the DNS servers supporting writable copies of their domains. Given the critical nature of DNS, it is essential to have two DNS servers supporting each zone that contains a domain used by AD. Be extremely careful not to delete DNS domains that support AD. They can be deleted when it is necessary to move or reconfigure the zones, but AD cannot function properly unless the domains are re-established in DNS.

I have experimented with moving child domains between zones, for example, from a parent zone to a child zone on a new DNS server. As long as authority is properly delegated, AD copes well with such changes.

Although I haven't found anything in Microsoft literature stating that this as a requirement, I've encountered problems when a DC's default DNS server does not support the zone containing the domain in which the DC is defined. The simplest and most trouble-free approach is to host all your internal domains in the same zone.

Create the child domain as follows

1. Execute the command DCPROMO at the **Start→Run** menu prompt. Click **Next** to continue.

2. In the **Domain Controller Type** dialog box, select **Domain controller for a new domain**.

3. In the **Create Tree or Child Domain** dialog box, select **Create a new child domain in an existing domain tree**.

4. In the **Network Credential** dialog box, specify the user name, password, and domain of a user account that has the authority to add the domain to the AD tree.

5. In the **Child Domain Installation** dialog box (see Figure 4.25), complete the following fields:

   - **Parent domain.** Type or browse for the full DNS name of the parent domain. In this example, I am adding a child domain to a tree with a private DNS root. Hence the name does not include an Internet first-level domain.

   - **Child domain.** Enter the name of the child domain.

   The FQDN of the domain that is being created will be constructed in the **Complete DNS name of new domain** field.

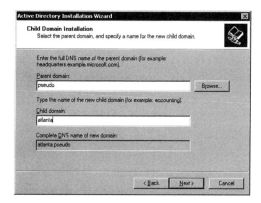

FIGURE 4.25

To create a child domain, specify the FQDN of the parent domain and the name of the child domain.

6. In the **NetBIOS Domain Name** dialog box, edit the NetBIOS name that is generated by the wizard if you desire to do so.

7. Complete the **Database and Log Locations** dialog box, as described in Step 7 in the previous section.

8. Complete the **Shared System Volume** dialog box, as described in Step 8 in the previous section.

9. The wizard attempts to locate a DNS server for the child domain you are creating. If a DNS server cannot be found that supports the features required by Active Directory, a warning is displayed. You can either proceed to Step 10 and install a DNS server on the

4

ACTIVE
DIRECTORY
CONCEPTS

local computer, or you can correct the problem with the DNS server. Here are some things to check:

- The local computer's DNS server IP addresses. On multihomed servers, configure all interfaces with the same DNS server IP addresses.
- The child domain on the DNS server. If the child domain is to be created in a new zone, be sure that it has been created. Verify the Name Server properties for the zone. Child domains that are in the same zones with their parent domains should not include Name Server (NS) RRs.

10. If a suitable DNS server cannot be located and you cannot fix the problem, you can install the DNS server service on the local computer. If you will be configuring a local DNS Server, the wizard brings up the **Configure DNS** dialog box. Choose **Yes, install and configure DNS on this computer**.

11. In the **Permissions** dialog box, select one of the following:

- **Permissions compatible with pre-Windows 2000 Servers**
- **Permissions compatible with only Windows 2000 Servers**

12. In the **Directory Services Restore Mode Administrator's Password** dialog box, enter and confirm a password that restricts access to Directory Services Restore Mode when restarting the server.

13. A **Summary** box describes the configuration you have defined. Review the configuration and use the **Back** button to review to any dialog boxes that require modification.

14. The wizard proceeds to configure AD and to install DNS if you enabled that option.

15. Restart the system to activate Active Directory.

Figure 4.26 depicts a DNS server with a zone named pseudo. DC1.PSEUDO is a domain controller for the domain PSEUDO and is also running the DNS service that hosts the pseudo zone. In the figure, I have created a subdomain named atlanta, which has an AD domain controller named DC2.ATLANTA.PSEUDO.

It takes several minutes for AD to populate the DNS zone with all its RRs. You can, of course, refresh the display by clicking F5. But don't assume that there are problems with the DNS configuration for the new domain until you have given the domain time to create all its records. When I created this domain, it was several minutes before a Host Address RR for dc2.atlanta.pseudo appeared in the atlanta.pseudo domain.

Configuring a Private DNS Root Name Server

There might be times when you want to configure a DNS server as a private root name server, which ensures that it will not use Internet root hints to direct DNS queries to the Internet.

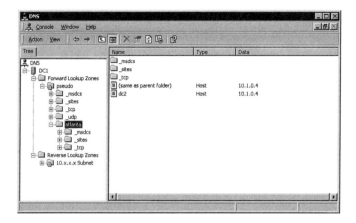

FIGURE 4.26

The `atlanta.pseudo` *DNS subdomain contains the RRs required to support the* `ATLANTA.PSEUDO` *child domain in Active Directory.*

Establishing a Private DNS Root Name Server

To configure a private DNS root name server, do the following:

1. Create a root zone. In the **Root Name** dialog box, enter a single period for the domain name. (Recall from Chapter 3 that a period can be used when it is necessary to explicitly name the root domain of a DNS namespace.)

2. Close the DNS console.

3. Using the **Services** snap-in under **Start→Programs→Administrative Tools**, stop the DNS Server service and restart it.

4. Open the DNS console and verify that the server is a root name server by examining the **Root Hints** tab of the DNS server **Properties** dialog box. The Internet root hints are deleted and the dialog box displays the message "Root hints are not required because the server is a root server."

5. Begin to create zones by right-clicking **Forward Lookup Zones**. Do not begin to create zones by right-clicking the . zone.

Figure 4.27 shows the DNS console for a DNS server that is configured as a private root name server. In addition to the root zone ("."), there is one zone supporting a domain named `pseudo-int.com`. If you expand the . zone, you will notice several things:

- A subdomain named `com` is created when the root (.) zone is created. A `com` subdomain is created even if it is not in use on the private network.

- A subdomain is created under the root (.) zone for each zone and child domain that is hosted by the server. As shown in Figure 4.27, this copy of the subdomain does not contain a complete set of domain records. For example, it will not contain copies of the

Service Location RRs created by Active Directory. This copy of the domain is used only for the purpose of authority delegation. It is not used to resolve queries.

- The actual, working domain is found in the separate zone that was created for the domain. The zone pseudo-int.com contains the AD RRs for the corresponding domain. All queries are resolved against this zone.

At the risk of belaboring a point (all right, already, I admit it, I'm a nag.), I want to emphasize that the DNS server shown in Figure 4.27 cannot resolve names on the Internet because it no longer has copies of the Internet root name hints. As shown, the DNS server can resolve names only if they are found in the pseudo-int.com domain or in lower-level domains under pseudo-int.com.

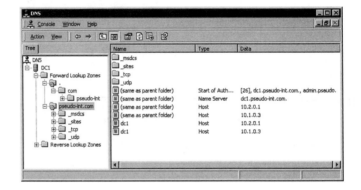

FIGURE 4.27
This DNS server is configured as a private root name server.

Restoring Root Name Hints

To restore root name hints to a DNS server and enable it to resume resolving names on the Internet, do the following:

1. Delete the . zone.
2. Close the DNS console.
3. Using the **Services** snap-in, stop the DNS Server service and restart it.
4. Open the DNS console and verify that Internet root hints have been restored to the **Root Hints** tab of the DNS server **Properties** dialog box.

Creating a New Tree in an Existing Forest

If you are creating a root domain for a new tree, you have the option of adding the tree to an existing forest by selecting **Create a new child domain in an existing domain tree** in the **Create Tree or Child Domain** dialog box.

There are three ways DNS can be configured for multi-tree forests:

- Each AD tree can be supported by a separate DNS domain that is in the public Internet namespace. This option enables clients to access RRs in the private and public namespaces because queries to all DNS domains can be resolved using Internet root hints. This procedure simplifies DNS support if the root domain DCs are at different sites, but it does open up the private DNS data to public scrutiny.

- If the DNS namespaces supporting AD trees are to be private and clients are not configured to use Winsock proxy servers, the DNS domains corresponding to the AD root domains of all trees must be hosted on the same DNS servers. Because the local DNS namespaces aren't registered on the Internet, a DNS server cannot use Internet root hints to direct queries to a private DNS domain that is hosted on a different DNS server.

  With this approach, the DNS servers can resolve names in any of the private domains (because they support zones for all the private domains) as well as in the public Internet (by using Internet root hints). If DNS servers are located at separate sites, you will want to place copies of all zones on all DNS servers, probably accomplishing zone transfers through a VPN or a private WAN link that connects the sites.

- Proxy servers can be deployed to enable clients to direct DNS queries to internal or external DNS servers as appropriate. Because internal name servers can be configured with a private DNS root domain, it is possible with this approach to support the DNS trees corresponding to AD trees on separate DNS servers if necessary.

When you add the first DC in the root domain of an additional tree in a forest, the following preconditions must be met:

- The default DNS server IP address of the server being configured must identify a DNS server that hosts the primary zone containing the first root directory created in the forest. If the zone is Active Directory-integrated, you can use any DNS server that is authoritative for the zone.

- You should manually create a zone for the root directory of the new tree on the same server that hosts the root domain for the first tree in the forest. Configure the **Allow dynamic updates?** property for the zone (on the **General** tab under **Properties**) with the value **Yes**.

- All reverse lookup zones that support hosts in the new tree should be configured with the **Allow dynamic updates?** property for the zone set to a value of **Yes**.

During or after the process of creating the root domain for the new tree, you can install the DNS service on the new server and create copies of the zones.

When the new tree is added to the forest, a two-way, transitive trust is created between the root domains of the trees. Figure 4.28 is a composite of two windows, showing the Active Directory Domains and Trusts snap-ins after a second tree has been added to a forest. I have opened the **Domain Properties** dialog box for PSEUDO-INT.COM and selected the **Trusts** tab so that you can see the trusts that are established between the root domains of the trees.

4

ACTIVE
DIRECTORY
CONCEPTS

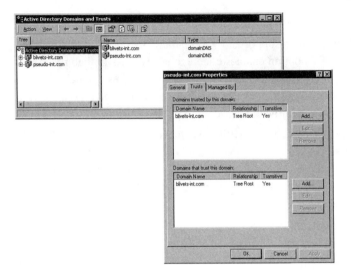

FIGURE 4.28

A forest has been configured with two trees. Note that a two-way transitive trust has been established between the root domains.

Figure 4.29 illustrates a DNS server after external and internal DNS zones have been established. In this example, I have named the AD root domains PSEUDO-INT.COM and BLIVETS-INT.COM (wherein INT stands for "internal"). Although they are not public domains in this example, the domain names could be registered on the Internet if that is desirable. Although previous examples of private DNS trees used domain names that cannot be registered on the Internet (such as PSEUDO), it can be desirable to use names that are valid on the Internet and to register the domain names. If you do not have the Internet domain records configured to delegate authority to a DNS server that is authoritative for the domains, the domain remains effectively private because outside name queries cannot be directed to valid DNS servers.

Why would you want to take this approach of registering Internet domains without configuring the Internet name servers to delegate authority to your name servers? You might want to do it this way to preserve the option of activating these domains on the Internet in the future. After a root domain name has been configured for an Active Directory tree, there is no way to change the domain name without re-creating the entire tree. By using Internet-ready domain names, activating Internet access to the domain is a simple matter of updating the domain registration with the addresses of valid DNS servers. This tactic is only worthwhile if you are willing to go to the trouble of registering domains on the Internet that you do not currently intend to expose to public access. In doing so, you can guarantee that the domains will be available in the future. In the long run, the benefits can outweigh the administrative effort and small cost of registering the domains.

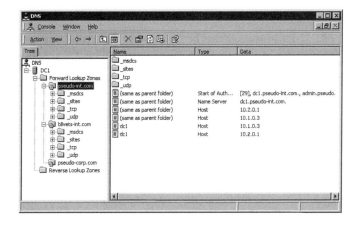

FIGURE 4.29
*This DNS server supports two private zones (*pseudo-int.com *and* blivets-int.com*) for internal AD trees and one public zone in the Internet namespace (*pseudo-corp.com*).*

Demoting a Domain Controller

To change the role of a DC, it must be demoted to the status of standalone server, a process that removes Active Directory from the computer. After the DC has been demoted, it can be promoted into a DC role in a new or different domain.

Communication with DNS servers supporting the DC's domain (either the primary zone server or a server with an AD-integrated zone) is essential when demoting a DC. If you are deleting a domain, delete all the DCs in a domain before you delete domain records from DNS. In most cases, demoting the last DC in the domain results in removal of DNS domains associated with the domain.

4

> **NOTE**
>
> If a server cannot communicate with a DNS server that supports the domain associated with the server's AD domain, DCPROMO cannot promote or demote the server. If you need to demote a server for which the required DNS zone is unavailable, you must reinstall Windows 2000 Server.
>
> Microsoft recommends that each DC be configured to use a DNS server in its own domain. If you have trouble demoting a DC, install the DNS Server service on the DC, configure it with the appropriate zone(s), wait for RRs to replicate to the DNS Server, and try once more to demote the DC.

To demote a DC, do the following:

1. Execute the command DCPROMO at the **Start→Run** menu prompt. Click **Next** to continue.

2. If you are demoting the last DC in a domain, be aware that this deletes the domain itself. All domain records will be lost, and clients currently configured in the domain will be unable to access the network.

   If this is the last DC, check **This server is the last domain controller in the domain**. Click **Next**.

3. In the **Network Credentials** dialog box, specify the account name, password, and domain for a user that has administrative permissions for the forest. Typically this user is a member of the Enterprise Administrators built-in group, which, by default, conveys administrative permissions for all domain containers in the tree.

4. In the **Administrator Password** dialog box, enter and confirm the password for the Administrator user account that will be in effect when the server is configured in a stand-alone role.

5. In the **Summary** dialog box, verify the tasks that DCPROMO will accomplish and click **Next** to begin the procedure of demoting the DC.

6. Restart the computer.

The server will start back up as a standalone server.

Managing Organizational Units

Organizational units are useful tools for improving the granularity of control over Windows NT security. They are easy to create and manage.

Creating OUs

OUs are created using the **Active Directory Users and Computers** snap-in. To create a new OU

1. Right-click the domain object.

2. In the context menu, choose **New→Organizational Unit**.

3. In the **New Object–Organizational Unit** dialog box, supply a name for the OU.

4. The OU is created when you click **OK**.

You can create Computer, Contact, Group, Organizational Unit, Printer, User, and Shared Folder objects in a domain or in any OU in the domain. In Figure 4.30, an OU named Personnel has been created. In the OU, I have created a sampling of objects that might by useful in that department.

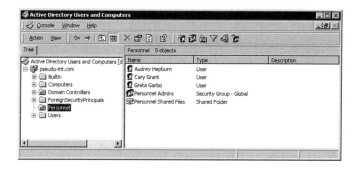

FIGURE 4.30
The Personnel OU contains objects used and managed by the Personnel department.

Delegating Control in OUs

By default, an OU inherits security settings from its parent container. You can grant administrative permissions for various operations to users and groups.

> **NOTE**
>
> To manage security in **Active Directory Users and Computers**, open the utility and select **View→Advanced Features**. When this menu item is checked, new containers are listed under the domain (Lost and Found and System). In addition **Security** and **Group Policy** tabs are added to the Property pages for domain and OU objects.

To delegate control for a domain or OU

1. Create any groups that you want to have control over some or all the security functions for the container.
2. Right-click the container object and choose **Delegate Control** in the context menu.
3. Click **Next** to open the **Users or Groups** dialog box, shown in Figure 4.31.
4. Click **Add** and select the users or groups in the **Select Users, Computers, or Groups** dialog box.
5. Click **Next** to open the **Tasks to Delegate** dialog box, shown in Figure 4.32.

4

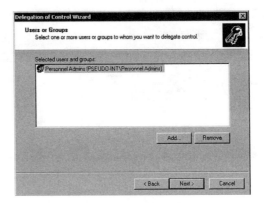

FIGURE 4.31

Select the users or groups that are to be given control over operations in the container.

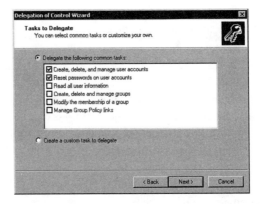

FIGURE 4.32

Specify the functions to be performed by the selected users or groups.

6. If the desired tasks are included in the **Tasks to Delegate** dialog box, check the tasks that are to be delegated and click **Next**. Skip to Step 10.

   To have greater control over tasks being delegated, select **Create a custom task to delegate** and click **Next** to open the **Active Directory Object Type** dialog box, shown in Figure 4.33.

7. To delegate control for all objects in the container and for the container itself, select **This folder, existing objects in this folder, and creation of new objects in the folder**.

   To delegate control for specific objects, select **Only the following objects in the folder** and check the desired objects.

   Click **Next** to open the **Permissions** dialog box, shown in Figure 4.34.

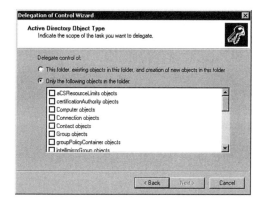

FIGURE 4.33

For advanced delegation, specify whether delegation is for all objects in the container or for specific objects.

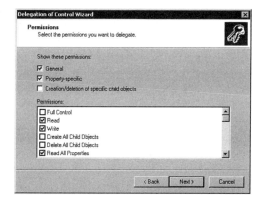

FIGURE 4.34

Specify the permissions to be granted for the objects that have been selected.

8. In the **Permissions** dialog box:

- Check **General** to display permissions of a general nature such as **Read**, **Write**, and **Full Control**.

- Check **Property Specific** to display permissions for specific properties, such as **Read adminDescription**.

- Check **Creation/deletion of specific objects** to display permissions to create and delete specific types of objects such as **Create Computer objects**.

9. In the **Permissions** list of the **Permissions** dialog box, check the specific permissions to be delegated. Then click **Next**.

> **NOTE**
>
> **Full Control** of a class of objects conveys all available permissions for the class.

10. The next dialog box summarizes the actions you have specified. Click **Finish** to carry out the actions or click **Back** to return to an earlier dialog box and modify it.

> **NOTE**
>
> Delegation of control is simply a convenient means of constructing Access Control Lists for OUs and domains.
>
> There are two categories of security capabilities:
>
> - **Permissions** are rules associated with objects that determine which users can access the object and what operations they can perform on the object. Permissions are recorded as ACEs in ACLs.
> - **User rights** describe tasks a user can perform on a computer system or domain, such as backing up files, creating or deleting user objects, or shutting down a computer. Rights can be assigned to user accounts or to groups.

Managing Object Security

The **Delegation of Control Wizard** is a convenient tool for assigning permissions, but it does not support all the security choices that can be made in a container, nor does it provide a way to examine the permissions that are currently defined in the object's ACL.

To perform detailed security management, open the object's properties dialog box and select the **Security** tab, an example of which is shown in Figure 4.35. After selecting a user or group in the **Name** list, you can view and modify the permissions assigned to the user or group. The permissions listed in this dialog box are general in nature and in many cases correspond to the **General** permissions displayed in the **Delegation of Control Wizard** (refer to Figure 4.34).

Controlling Inheritance from the Parent Container

Inheritance of permissions can greatly simplify security administration. Under normal circumstances, when a user or group has a permission in the parent container, the user or group inherits the permission in the child container.

If you want to configure a child container to be administered autonomously, you might want to block inheritance of permissions from the parent. To do that, remove the check for **Allow inheritable permissions from parent to propagate to this object**.

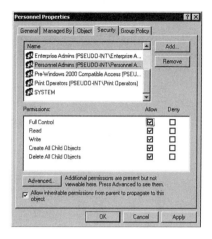

FIGURE 4.35
The Security tab lists general categories of permissions that are in force for the selected object.

A similar check box is found in the **Access Control Settings** dialog box considered in the next section, enabling you to determine whether detailed ACEs will be inherited.

Advanced Object Security

The initial **Security** tab supports permissions of a very general nature. You can directly manage the ACL for an object by clicking the **Advanced** button to open the **Access Control Settings** dialog box, shown in Figure 4.36. Each item in the **Permission Entries** list is an ACE in the ACL.

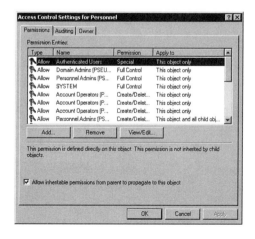

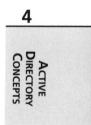

FIGURE 4.36
Individual ACEs can be modified in the Access Control Settings dialog box.

To view and edit an existing ACE, double-click the entry to open the **Permission Entry** dialog box, shown in Figure 4.37.

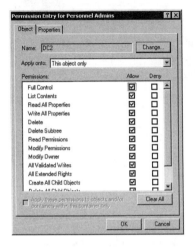

FIGURE 4.37

Detailed editing of ACEs can be performed in the Permission Entry dialog box.

Click **Change** to modify the user or group associated with the ACE.

The **Apply to** field determines the scope of application for the ACE. Options for this field include

- This object and all child objects
- Child objects only
- Computer objects
- Connection objects
- Contact objects
- Group objects

The **Permissions** list provides permissions control at a very detailed level. If you browse the lists for a variety of ACEs, you will identify permissions that correspond to options selected in the Delegate Control Wizard.

Given the complexity of the **Security** dialog boxes, it's pretty obvious why Microsoft provided the **Delegate Control** Wizard. Not many of us will want to learn the details about ACEs or want to take the time to manage them at this level. But there is one "blunt instrument" use for these dialog box. Ordinarily, administrators and users with permissions in the parent container have permissions in the child container as well. If you want to create an OU that is highly independent from the parent, you can delete unwanted users and groups from the ACL, including Administrators, Domain Admins, and so forth.

To complete the *coup d'etat*, administrators of the OU need to take ownership of the OU, which is done on the **Owner** tab on the **Advanced Control Settings** dialog box. Ownership of an object conveys total control and should be allocated carefully. For example, ownership of a domain should be entrusted only to a small group of highly trusted administrators.

There is an escape hatch in case an OU becomes unmanageable because of messed up permissions: Owners of the parent container can take ownership of the OU. Doing so leaves an audit trail because ownership can be taken, but it can't be given away. An administrator who takes ownership to commit mischief is stuck with the evidence.

Group Policy

Group Policy is a collection of policy options that can be applied to sites, domains, or organizational units. Group Policy is a complex topic, and I'm not going to try to achieve full coverage. But some network security functions are defined in Group Policy, so we need to address the topic at a basic level.

Group Policy has nothing to do with groups. Group Policy is a group of policies (Clever, huh?) that can be applied to sites, domains, and OUs. Group Policy can provide very exacting control over the operations that can be performed by a user or on a computer.

Windows NT offers capabilities that superficially resemble Windows 2000 Group Policy. For example, Windows NT supports the establishment of a user account policy that defines, among other things, password requirements. But these policy settings apply to the entire domain. There is no option to allocate different policy settings to different groups of users in the domain.

Windows NT also offers Security Policy, which can be used to configure a variety of user environment settings. But these settings are stored in the Registry on the user's local machine and consequently can be overridden by the user.

Windows 2000 Server Group Policy is different. Group Policies can be established for individual containers, and settings defined in Group Policies override settings made locally on the client. Consequently, Windows 2000 Server administrators have a very high level of control over the working environments of Windows 2000 clients.

4

ACTIVE
DIRECTORY
CONCEPTS

NOTE

To manage Group Policy in **Active Directory Users and Computers**, open the utility and select **View→Advanced Features**.

Group Policy Inheritance

Group Policies are defined in Group Policy Objects that are, in turn, linked to sites, domains, and OUs. It commonly happens that Group Policies will be active at several levels in the AD hierarchy. When that happens, policy settings are applied in the following order:

1. Local computer settings
2. Site
3. Domain
4. OU
5. Nested OUs

If the same property is configured at more than one level, the client is configured with the last value encountered. Consider this situation

- In the Group Policy for the domain, the **Minimum password length** policy's property value is 6.
- In the Group Policy for the user's OU, the **Minimum password length** policy's property value is 8.

The policy defined in the OU overrides the policy defined in the domain, and users whose User objects are in the OU must supply passwords that are at least eight characters in length.

A policy in Group Policy takes effect only when an administrator explicitly assigns a value to it. By default, all policies in a new OU have a value of Not defined. Consider the following situation:

- In the Group Policy for the domain, the **Minimum password length** policy's property value is 6.
- In the Group Policy for the user's OU, the **Minimum password length** policy's property value is Not defined.

In this situation, the effective value of the **Minimum password length** is 6.

A given policy has one of three status settings:

- **Not defined**. The policy has no effect at this level.
- **Enabled**. The policy at this level replaces any policy inherited from the previous level.
- **Disabled**. The policy at this level blocks inheritance of the policy, but this leaves the policy without an effective value.

There is no neat way to determine the policies in effect for a particular user, taking into account all Group Policies defined at all levels. Consequently, it is desirable to implement as few Group Policies as possible. Don't assume that just because you can have a Group Policy at the site, domain, and OU levels that it is desirable to actually implement all three Group Policies. If you do implement two or more layers of Group Policies, it is essential to plan, document, plan, document, and plan again. Otherwise you won't know what policies you've actually got in place.

Overriding Group Policy Inheritance

Implicit in the previous section is the capability of administrators to override policies that are inherited from parent containers. In fact, there is an explicit **Block Policy inheritance** capability that enables the administrator of an OU to prevent policies from being inherited from the parent container. **Block Policy inheritance** makes it easy for the administrator of an OU to ensure that the OU's Group Policy defines all policies for a domain.

That gives administrators of OUs a lot of power over policies, and, when administrators have authority, they have the nagging habit of using it whether they should or not. It's a lot easier to block inheritance entirely than it is to review policies on an individual basis and ensure that desirable policies are making their ways to users' configurations.

Suppose that the corporate policy requires passwords to have a minimum length of eight characters, and that this is enforced with a Group Policy at the site container level. Users in the Marketing OU don't like messing with eight-character passwords, so they bribe their administrator with football tickets that were bought to entertain customers, and he defines a Group Policy for Marketing that has a minimum password length of 2. Because the domain administrators are blocked from accessing policies in Marketing, they cannot even verify that policies in the OU meet with corporate standards.

When it is important to prevent blocking or modification of a policy, the Group Policy can be configured with a **No override** option. Under this option, any policies defined in the Group Policy cannot be modified by policies that appear later in the Group Policy priority order. If you enable **No override** for a site or domain Group Policy, administrators in OUs cannot change the policies that are mandated for the organization.

No override takes precedence over **Block Policy inheritance**, so the domain administrators always get the last word. (Eventually, Marketing might try to bribe the domain administrators with football tickets, but we administrators simply have too much integrity to accept. We do, don't we?)

Managing Group Policy

A Group Policy is defined in a Group Policy Object (GPO) that is, in turn, linked with a site, domain, or OU. You can create GPOs separately using a Group Policy snap-in, but my favorite way to manage Group Policies is to access them in the properties for sites, domains, and OUs.

> **NOTE**
>
> To manage Group Policy in **Active Directory Users and Computers**, open the utility and select **View→Advanced Features**.

4

ACTIVE
DIRECTORY
CONCEPTS

To manage Group Policy for an object

1. For a site, open **Active Directory Sites and Services**, and right-click a Site object.

    For a domain or OU, open **Active Directory Users and Computers** and right-click a Domain or OU object.

2. Select **Properties** in the context menu to open the object **Properties** pages.

3. Select the **Group Policy** tab, shown in Figure 4.38. This tab lists any Group Policy Objects that are presently linked to the container being managed.

Manage Group Policy for the container as described in the following sections.

Creating a Group Policy Object

A domain has a default GPO named **Default Domain Policy**, which defines default policies in a number of areas such as password policies. You must create GPOs for sites and OUs and can create new GPOs for domains as well.

To create a new Group Policy:

1. Click **New** in the **Group Policy** tab. A new entry will appear under **Group Policy Object Links** with the title New Group Policy Object.

2. Edit the title of the new GPO as desired.

The new GPO is automatically linked to the container in which it is created.

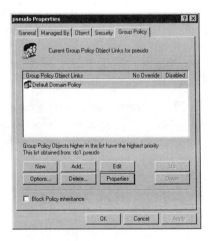

FIGURE 4.38

The Group Policy tab in a domain's property sheets.

Editing the Group Policy

No policies are activated in a new GPO, so you must edit the GPO after it's created to establish or modify policies. Select a GPO and click **Edit** to open the Group Policy window, shown in Figure 4.39.

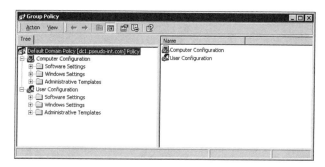

FIGURE 4.39

Policies are divided into two major categories: Computer Configuration and User Configuration.

A tremendous number of policies are defined in a GPO, and I'm not going to try to list them. Some of the capabilities of a Group Policy, such as installing packages, are not in keeping with the theme of this book. But, let me show you a couple examples of policies so that you can get an idea of the organization of a GPO.

Figure 4.40 shows objects under **Computer Configuration→Windows Settings→Security Settings→IP Security Policies on Active Directory**. These policies relate to the use of IPSec for network communication, and we will encounter them again in Chapter 11, "Securing IP Communication."

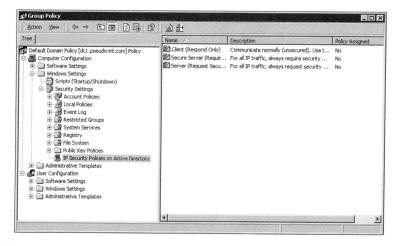

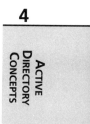

4

**ACTIVE
DIRECTORY
CONCEPTS**

FIGURE 4.40

Policies displayed here relate to configuration of IPSec.

Figure 4.41 shows objects under **User Configuration→Administrative Templates→ Network→Network and Dial-Up Connections**. These policies restrict user access to a variety of capabilities related to network communication. If you don't want users configuring their TCP/IP connection properties, for example, you can disable `Enable access to properties of components of a LAN connection`. Clearly, policies such as this one, which prevent users from mucking with their network interface configurations, are a very, very good thing.

To modify a policy, right-click it and select **Properties** from the context menu to open a **Properties** dialog box, such as the one shown in Figure 4.42.

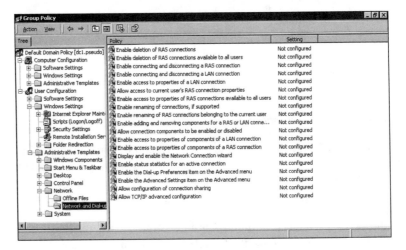

FIGURE 4.41

These policies determine the network connection features that users can configure.

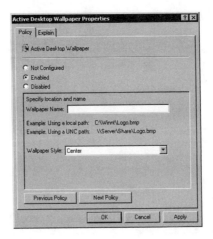

FIGURE 4.42

Properties for a sample policy.

All policies have one of three status settings:

- **Not Configured**
- **Enabled**
- **Disabled**

I selected the **Active Directory Wallpaper** policy in Figure 4.42 because this policy has additional properties that must be defined when the policy is enabled. In this example, if an AD wallpaper is enabled, you must specify the name and style of the wallpaper to be used.

Simply close the **Group Policy** window to save changes to the Group Policy.

Editing Group Policy Object Properties

There are several GPO properties that can be managed. To open the property sheets shown in Figure 4.43, select the GPO on the **Group Policy** tab (refer to Figure 4.38) and click **Properties**.

The **General** tab has two options that disable parts of the Group Policy:

- **Disable Computer Configuration settings**
- **Disable User Configuration settings**

When a user logs on, all the Group Policies that affect the user must be processed in sequence. If several Group Policies must be processed, users might experience significant delays during the logon process. You can speed GPO processing by disabling parts of the GPO that aren't being used.

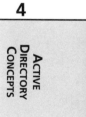

FIGURE 4.43

General properties for a GPO.

The **Links** tab lists sites, domains, and OUs that are linked to the GPO. If desired, you can create a single GPO that is linked to multiple containers.

The **Security** tab displays the ACL for the GPO. You can modify ACEs as necessary.

Options on the **Properties** tabs affect the GPO itself and therefore apply to all instances when the GPO is linked to a site, domain, or OU.

Editing Group Policy Object Options

If you select a GPO on the Group Policy tab and click **Options**, the dialog box shown in Figure 4.44 is displayed. This box has two check boxes:

- **No Override: prevents other Group Policy Objects from overriding policy set in this one**
- **Disabled: the Group Policy Object is not applied to the container**

These options affect only the specific linkage that is being configured.

FIGURE 4.44
Options for a GPO.

Blocking Group Policy Inheritance

At the bottom of the **Group Policy** tab is a check box labeled **Block Policy inheritance** (see Figure 4.38). Check this box if you do not want policies to be inherited from Group Policy Objects linked to parent containers.

Managing Sites

Windows 2000 uses the concept of *sites* to improve communication through wide area networks. Recall from earlier discussion that a site consists of network segments that communicate reliably and at LAN speeds.

AD directory replication is managed by the Knowledge Consistency Checker (KCC), which runs on every DC. The KCC creates a replication topology for the forest and enables replication to take place automatically between DCs at the same site.

When the network is divided into multiple sites that must communicate through low-bandwidth networks, site links must be established. A *site link* is a low-bandwidth or unreliable connection between sites. The KCC uses site link configurations to determine how best to replicate directory data between sites. By configuring sites and site links, administrators have considerable control over the directory replication process.

Directory replication is accomplished using one of three methods:

- High-speed Remote Procedure Call (RPC) over IP within a site.
- Synchronous, low-speed RPC over IP between sites that communicates through a continuously available link. In this context, *synchronous communication* means that the source and destination DCs engage in a request-and-acknowledgment dialog while synchronization takes place.
- Asynchronous, low-speed SMTP between sites that do not communicate through a real-time transport.

Inter-site replication is optimized for efficiency. Windows 2000 Server compresses all data being replicated between sites.

A site is defined by the IP subnets that it contains. After two sites are defined, we can define site links that specify the methods Windows 2000 Server uses to communicate between sites. Essentially sites are established as follows:

1. Sites are defined.
2. Subnets are defined and associated with subnets.
3. Servers are associated with sites.
4. Site links are defined to connect sites to sites.

Actually, these tasks can be performed in any order, but the preceding sequence is a good way to get started. Sites are managed using the **Active Directory Sites and Services** snap-in.

Let's consider the site configuration for the network, shown in Figure 4.45. This example consists of two private networks that communicate through a WAN link. To optimize communication between DCs, we want to define sites for Seattle and Atlanta.

Defining Sites

A site identifies the servers and subnets that constitute a reliable, high-performance network. When AD is installed, an initial site is created named `Default-First-Site-Name`. All servers are associated with this site, but new sites can be defined, and the site associations of servers can be changed. All subnets must be defined manually. Figure 4.46 shows the initial objects in Active Directory Sites and Services.

We can start by renaming the default site to Seattle. Just double-click the name to open it for editing and type the desired site name.

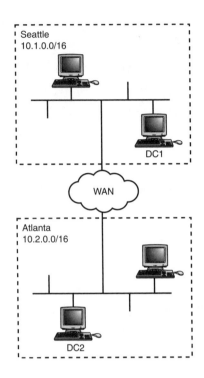

FIGURE 4.45

This network requires two sites.

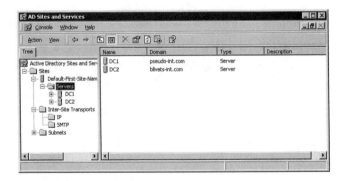

FIGURE 4.46

AD Sites and Services before sites are configured.

To create the Atlanta site, do the following:

1. Right-click the **Sites** container and choose **New Site** from the context menu to open the **New Object—Site** dialog box, shown in Figure 4.47.

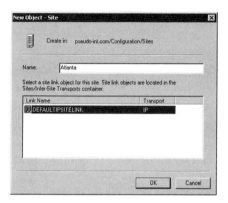

FIGURE 4.47
Defining a new site.

2. In the **Name** field, enter a name to describe the site.
3. In the **Link Name** list, select a site link object to be used for this site.
4. Click **OK**.

To modify site properties, right-click the site object and choose **Properties** from the context menu to display the site **Properties** dialog box. There are five tabs:

- **Site.** The **Description** field accepts free-form text that describes the site. This is a good place to document the site purpose, creation date, or other information regarding the site's purpose.
- **Location. Location** specifies text that is displayed to users when they start a search for printers. This feature is active only when the `Pre-populate printer search location tool` policy is enabled in **Group Policy**.
- **Object.** This tab displays the fully qualified name of the object, documents the dates and times when the object was created or modified, and displays update sequence numbers that are used to track changes for the object.
- **Security.** This tab enables you to edit the ACL for the object.
- **Group Policy.** This tab enables you to link a Group Policy Object to the site and to edit the Group Policy.

> **NOTE**
>
> A *site* is an island of high-performance network connections that communicate with other sites through unreliable or low-bandwidth means. Therefore, steps should be taken to ensure that a site can operate with some level of autonomy. Here are some suggestions for site design:
>
> - Have at least one DC at each site.
> - Have at least one additional DC at the site if the WAN connection is deemed insufficient for normal operation of the site in the event of a DC failure.
> - Enable at least one global catalog server at each site. If a global catalog server is not available at the local site, users will log on using a global catalog server at a remote site.
> - Have at least one DNS server at each site, configured with zones required at the site.
> - Have a second DNS server at each site if feasible.
>
> The ideal minimum configuration for a site is to have two DCs, each running the DNS Server service, and each configured as a Global Catalog server.

Figure 4.48 shows **AD Sites and Services** after two sites have been configured.

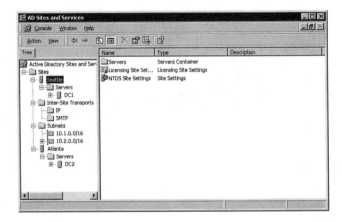

FIGURE 4.48

Two sites have been configured on this network.

Defining Subnets

A Subnet object must define every subnet range in use in the organization. To define a new subnet, do the following:

1. Right-click the **Subnets** container and choose **New Subnet** from the context menu to open the **New Object—Subnet** dialog box, shown in Figure 4.49.

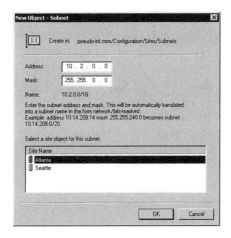

FIGURE 4.49
Defining a new subnet.

2. In the **Address** field, enter an IP address used on the subnet. All that is required is the netid portion of the IP address range.

3. In the **Mask** field, enter the network mask used on the subnet.

4. In the **Site Name** list, select the site where the subnet is located.

5. Click **OK**.

To modify subnet properties, right-click the subnet object and choose **Properties** from the context menu to display the site **Properties** dialog box. There are four tabs:

- **Subnet.** The **Description** field accepts free-form text that describes the site. This is a good place to document the site purpose, creation date, or other information regarding the site's purpose.

  The **Site** field can be used to change the site associated with the subnet. The network and mask for the subnet cannot be modified after they are established. To change address information you must delete the Subnet object and create a new one.

4

**ACTIVE
DIRECTORY
CONCEPTS**

- **Location.** Refer to the description of this tab in the previous section "Defining Sites."
- **Object.** Refer to the description of this tab in the previous section "Defining Sites."
- **Security.** This tab enables you to edit the ACL for the object.

Managing Servers

Servers, as referred to in the **AD Sites and Servers** snap-in, are domain controllers. I don't know why the container isn't named Domain Controllers. After all, the whole purpose of configuring sites is to optimize replication of AD data between DCs at different locations. Servers are automatically added to the sites' object hierarchies when DCPROMO creates an AD domain controller. You will need to associate servers with the appropriate sites and to define the properties of the server, particularly the transport technologies supported by the server.

Associating Servers with Sites

By default, all DCs are added to the Default-First-Site-Name site. To move a server to a different site

1. Expand the Site object for the site currently associated with the server.
2. Expand the **Servers** container.
3. Right-click a server and choose **Move** from the context menu to open the **Move Server** dialog box, shown in Figure 4.50.
4. Choose the site where the server is physically located.
5. Click **OK**.

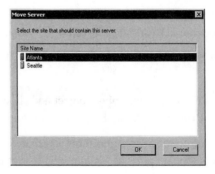

FIGURE 4.50

Moving a server to a different subnet.

Managing Server Properties

To modify subnet properties

1. Expand the **Site** object for the site currently associated with the server.

2. Expand the **Servers** container.

3. Right-click a server and choose **Properties** from the context menu to open the **Properties** pages, shown in Figure 4.51.

4. Modify the desired properties.

5. Click **OK**.

The **Server** properties tab is shown in Figure 4.51.

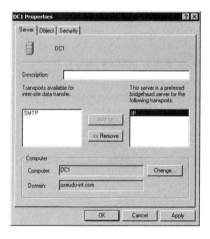

FIGURE 4.51

The Server property pages for a domain controller.

Servers will replicate directory data between sites without configuration, but there are two ways to configure inter-site communication that provide advantages under certain circumstances.

The first method of configuring inter-site communication is to designate a *preferred bridgehead server*, which functions as the preferred point of contact for a site. The KCC will select bridgehead servers automatically, but it might be preferable in some circumstances to designate a preferred bridgehead server. A good choice for a bridgehead server is a computer that has access to high-bandwidth communication or is dedicated to the task of replicating data between sites. Multiple preferred bridgehead servers can be configured for a site, but only one will be active at a given time and for a given protocol.

4

ACTIVE
DIRECTORY
CONCEPTS

> **NOTE**
>
> A preferred bridgehead server *must* be configured if a site is protected behind a firewall.

A second way of managing inter-site communication is through the protocols enabled for that purpose. As discussed earlier, communication between sites can be performed synchronously using RPC over IP or asynchronously using SMTP. Synchronization via SMTP can even be accomplished using dial-up links when necessary.

If you want the selected server to be a preferred bridgehead server, copy either or both protocols to the list **This server is a preferred bridgehead server**.

Managing Site Links

Site links establish the details of communication between sites. Site links are defined individually for RPC over IP and for SMTP transports. Site links are defined under the **Inter-Site Transports** container in the AD Sites and Services snap-in.

IP Site Links

Because most inter-site communication will use RPC over IP, a default IP site link (cleverly named DEFAULTIPSITELINK) is defined. You can modify the default site link or create a new one as required.

To create a new IP site link, right-click the **IP** object under the **Inter-Site Transports** container and choose **New Site Link** from the context menu.

To modify an existing site link, select the IP object. Then double-click the existing site link object in the Details pane of the snap-in.

An **IP Site Link Properties** dialog box is shown in Figure 4.52.

To configure the site link

- Copy the desired sites to the **Sites in this Site link** list.
- If desired, adjust the value of the **Cost** parameter. If multiple site links are available between sites, the KCC will choose the site link with the lowest cost.
- Adjust the value of the **Replicate every** parameter, if you want to replicate between sites at an interval other than every three hours.
- To schedule when replication can be performed, click the **Change Schedule** button to open the **Schedule** dialog box shown in Figure 4.53. Directory replication will be performed through this link only during time periods marked in blue. To change the status of a time period, drag a selection frame through the time period and click **Replication Not Available** or **Replication Available**.

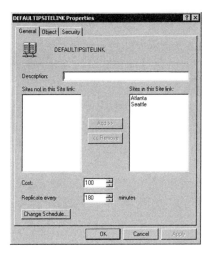

FIGURE 4.52

Properties for an IP site link.

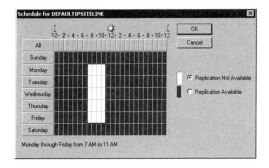

FIGURE 4.53

A site link can be used for directory replication during time periods marked in blue on the screen (black in the figure).

SMTP Site Links

SMTP site links are useful when there is no available communication channel to support RPC over IP. For example, SMTP site links enable directory replication to take place through network backbones and WAN links that are not based on TCP/IP.

No SMTP site links are established by default. To create a new SMTP site link, right-click the **SMTP** object under the **Inter-Site Transports** container and choose **New Site Link** from the context menu.

The **SMTP Site Link** dialog box is shown in Figure 4.54. The only configuration issue is to copy sites into the **Sites in this site link** list.

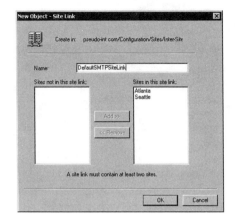

FIGURE 4.54
Properties for an SMTP site link.

Site Link Suggestions

It is possible to configure multiple site links that enable replication to take place without negatively impacting bandwidth. Suppose that the WAN link between two sites has limited bandwidth. You could schedule replication to take place only after business hours.

You might, for example, configure an SMTP dial-up site link with a higher **Cost** parameter than the cost of an IP site link. Then, replication will take place via SMTP if the IP connection is down.

When bandwidth is limited, SMTP can be more efficient because the SMTP transport enables multiple transmissions to be outstanding without acknowledgment. With the IP transport, every transmission must be acknowledged before the next transmission is sent.

Active Directory Afterthoughts

Active Directory is an incredibly key technology for Windows 2000 and an incredibly complex one. It would be easy to write a book as large as this one on nothing but AD. Consequently, there is a lot of subtlety that I have been forced to gloss over. My focus in this chapter has been to provide an overview of AD with a focus on network-related issues. The information contained in this chapter should be enough to get you through any AD-related issues in the rest of the book.

In the next chapter, we move back to TCP/IP itself. Before you deploy a large-scale TCP/IP internetwork, you need to know how to make TCP/IP management a bit easier on yourself. That's the purpose of the Dynamic Host Configuration Protocol (DHCP), which is the focus of the next chapter.

Dynamic Host Configuration Protocol

IN THIS CHAPTER

The Dynamic Host Configuration Protocol (DHCP; RFC 2131 and 2132) is to TCP/IP administration what aspirin is to headaches. DHCP's most obvious benefit is that it automates IP address assignment while simultaneously eliminating most of the errors that can result when addresses are configured manually. But IP address assignment is just the start of DHCP's capabilities. Along with its IP address, a DHCP client can be given most of the configuration parameters it requires to communicate with the network, such as its subnet mask, router addresses, addresses of DNS name servers, and so forth. Think of DHCP as a TCP/IP client construction set that you can use to build almost any type of client network configuration.

If you are familiar with the Windows NT DHCP service, you will have no trouble making the transition to Windows 2000, but you will find some significant enhancements in the new DHCP implementation. We'll consider the following new features in this chapter:

- **Dynamic DNS updates.** The Windows 2000 DHCP service can dynamically update Address and Pointer DNS resource records as hosts receive and surrender IP addresses. Windows NT 4 had a similar capability, but it was based on giving DNS the capability of obtaining host information from WINS.

- **User- and vendor-specified options.** The standard set of client configuration options can be augmented by options defined to meet special user and vendor requirements. This new feature eliminates an old DHCP limitation that required all clients on the same subnet to be configured with the same options.

- **Detection of unauthorized DHCP servers.** Windows 2000 DHCP servers are defined in Active Directory and a new DHCP server cannot be added unless it is authorized by an administrator. This reduces the possibility that "rogue" DHCP servers will be configured.

- **Support for superscopes.** This enables DHCP to assign IP addresses from multiple address ranges to clients on the same physical network.

- **Support for clustering.** Because DHCP servers cannot share their databases, in the past it has been impossible to configure a backup DHCP server to take over if a primary DHCP server fails. The Windows 2000 DHCP service supports server clustering, enabling you to configure a fallback DHCP server that springs into action if a primary DHCP server malfunctions. (Server clustering is a feature of Windows 2000 Advanced Server.)

As you might expect, we can't just jump directly into DHCP service management. We have to cover a bit of theory first. If you're new to DHCP management, you should take the time to read the next section. If you're an experienced DHCP administrator, you probably only need to read the section about superscopes.

DHCP Concepts

The DHCP service can assign client IP addresses in two ways. Clients can lease an IP address for a specified duration, in which case they must renew the lease when it approaches expiration. Or clients can be assigned a permanent IP address that is associated with a unique client identifier, such as its network hardware address. Because leasing is the method most commonly employed to manage IP addresses, we'll start this section by taking a look at the procedures clients use to obtain, renew, and release their DHCP leases.

After that, we'll take a look at some network design issues. DHCP has special implementation requirements when a network is segmented by routers, and routers must be specially configured to enable DHCP clients to communicate with remote DHCP servers. We'll also look at superscopes and how they enhance our ability to assign IP addresses.

> **NOTE**
>
> The Windows 2000 DHCP service can also be used to configure clients with the BOOTP protocol, an older configuration protocol that is now used primarily to configure terminals. Because all Windows computers function as DHCP clients, we won't be looking at the BOOTP support features in this chapter.

DHCP Leases

By far the most common means of assigning an address to a DHCP client is in the form of a limited-duration lease. There are several advantages to address leasing:

- If IP addresses are scarce, the IP address of an inactive client will be returned to the assignment pool, making it available for use by another host.
- Clients are forced to periodically contact the DHCP server to renew their leases. At these times, clients receive any changes that have been made to their configuration parameters. This feature enables administrators to manage the configurations of clients centrally and in groups rather than individually.
- After the addressing for a network is properly configured, IP address errors are practically eliminated. While initializing, a client will automatically obtain an IP address, subnet mask, and other settings appropriate to the client's subnet. DHCP makes it easy to change the location of a client because it will automatically obtain new network settings when it is activated in the new setting.

DHCP leases can be made permanent, but the more common practice is to provide leases for a limited duration, in which case a DHCP client must negotiate a lease life cycle as the lease is obtained, expired, and renewed. To manage DHCP servers and clients effectively, you should understand the lease life cycle.

There are several lease life cycle processes that you need to understand:

- Obtaining a new DHCP lease
- Configuring an IP address automatically
- Renewing an existing lease
- Restarting a DHCP client
- Expiring a lease
- Releasing an existing lease

These processes are examined in the following sections.

Obtaining a New DHCP Lease

Until a DHCP client obtains an IP address from a DHCP server, it has very limited communication abilities. Its first order of business, therefore, is to negotiate with a DHCP server to obtain an IP address. Let's look at the steps involved in leasing an IP address, depicted in Figure 5.1:

1. Until a client successfully leases an IP address, it is in an *unbound state* and has limited communication capabilities. Specifically, it can send and receive broadcast messages, but it cannot send a unicast message because it cannot supply a source IP address.

2. A client that that is not bound to an IP address enters an *init state* when it attempts to obtain an IP address from a DHCP server. The unbound DHCP client broadcasts a DHCPDiscover message with a source IP address of 0.0.0.0. The DHCP client then enters a *selecting state* and awaits lease offers from DHCP servers.

3. All DHCP servers on the subnet receive the DHCPDiscover message. They determine whether they are authorized to provide an IP address on the client's subnet.

4. All DHCP servers that are authorized to provide IP addresses on the DHCP client's subnet broadcast a DHCPOffer message that contains an unleased IP address and associated configuration parameters.

5. The DHCP client evaluates the DHCPOffer messages that it receives. One of two things happens:
   - The DHCP client determines that one of the offered leases is suitable, sends a DHCPRequest message that specifies the selected IP address, and requests a lease after which the client is in a *requesting state*. The DHCP lease process continues at Step 6.

- The DHCP client determines that none of the offered leases is acceptable and transmits DHCPDecline messages that notify the DHCP servers that the leases are not accepted. The client remains in an unbound state and must begin the DHCP lease process again at Step 1.

6. The DHCP server that offered the lease responds to the DHCPRequest message with a DHCPAcknowledge (DHCPAck) message that includes any DHCP configuration options that should be included with the IP address.

7. The client receives the DHCPAck message, binds to the IP address lease and enters a *bound state*. The client now has an IP address and can communicate normally on the network.

Typically, DHCP leases expire after a time interval that is determined when the lease is assigned. The default lease duration for the Windows 2000 DHCP service is eight days. If a DHCP client cannot renew its lease before the lease expires or obtain a new lease, the client loses its ability to communicate on the network using IP unicast messages. (It can still send and receive broadcast packets, enabling it to continue attempts to obtain a DHCP lease.)

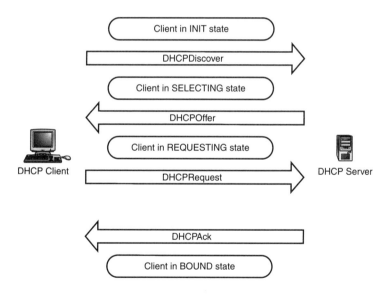

FIGURE 5.1

Steps required to obtain a DHCP lease.

IP Address Automatic Configuration

Traditionally, when a DHCP client fails in its attempt to obtain an IP address lease, it remains in an unbound state. A feature that Microsoft introduced with Windows 98 and extended to Windows 2000 is that DHCP clients that are unable to lease an IP address from a DHCP server will select one from a pre-specified IP address range. Microsoft calls this feature *Automatic Private IP Addressing* (APIPA, just in case you need to add another ugly acronym to your vocabulary).

The default auto-configuration address range is subnet 169.254.0.0/16, a Class B address range reserved by Microsoft. A client that selects an IP address through auto-configuration pings the network to determine whether the address is in use, in which case it selects another address and again tests for availability. A client that obtains an IP address through auto-configuration continues to check every five minutes for the availability of a DHCP server.

As a consequence of IP address auto-configuration, Windows 98 and 2000 clients will never report a failure to obtain an IP address lease. However, the automatically selected IP address is of dubious value unless it is supported by the client's network segment, and automatic configuration is no guarantee that a client will be able to communicate successfully. IP address auto-configuration appears to be most useful on small networks that do not communicate with the Internet (or that communicate with the Internet through an address-translating firewall), in which case, clients can be configured without the necessity of running a DHCP server. Also, because routers require careful planning of IP addressing, the random nature of APIPA makes it difficult to deploy usefully on a routed network.

The range of IP addresses that is available for use with auto-configuration can be redefined by editing Registry values under the following key:

```
HKEY_LOCAL_MACHINE\
  SYSTEM\
  CurrentControlSet\
  TCP/IP\
  Parameters\
  Interfaces\
  {interface number}
```

The interface number refers to Windows 2000 internal identification of the systems network interfaces. By browsing through the available keys, you can identify which location pertains to a given interface.

Under the preceding key, automatic IP address assignment is configured by a variety of values:

- **IPAutoconfigurationEnabled (REG_DWORD).** A value of 1 enables IP auto-configuration, which is the default setting. A value of 0 disables IP auto-configuration.

- **IPAutoconfigurationAddress (REG_DWORD).** The default subnet for IP auto-configuration is 169.254.0.0. This value can be modified if IP addresses are to be selected from another IP address range. This parameter is effective only if IP auto-configuration is enabled.
- **IPAutoconfigurationMask (REG_DWORD).** The default subnet mask is 255.255.0.0. This parameter is effective only if IP auto-configuration is enabled.

These values are also found in the Parameters subkey. The values in the Parameters subkey define settings for all interfaces that are not explicitly configured under a specific Interfaces subkey.

You could modify these values to enable IP auto-configuration to provide IP addresses that are appropriate for the client's subnet, one of the few techniques that provides a fail-safe backup in the event of the failure of a DHCP server. Because clients run tests to determine whether an IP address is in use, clients will not bind to an IP address that conflicts with addresses configured through DHCP.

Renewing a DHCP Lease

A client must renew its lease in two situations:

- When it is restarted
- When the predefined lease renewal interval is reached

The *lease renewal interval*, also known as the T1 interval, is typically about 50% of the total lease duration. When the T1 interval is reached, the client begins to take steps to ensure that its IP address lease will be renewed before it expires.

The client must renew its lease before reaching the *lease rebinding interval*, also known as the T2 interval. The T2 interval is typically 87% of the total lease duration. If the client cannot renew its lease before encountering the T2 interval, it must obtain a new lease from another DHCP server.

The following is the lease renewal procedure, which is depicted in Figure 5.2:

1. When the T1 interval is reached, the client enters a *renewing state* and broadcasts a DHCPRequest message to the DHCP server that issued its current lease.
2. Depending on the availability of the DHCP server, one of two things can happen:

   - If the DHCP server is available, it returns a DHCPAck message that includes any updated configuration options that the client should use. The client updates its lease configuration and remains in a bound state. The lease has been successfully renewed.

5

- If the DHCP server is unavailable, the client periodically retransmits the DHCPRequest message. If the T2 interval is encountered, the client enters a *rebinding state* and must begin the process of requesting a new DHCP lease, as described in the previous section.

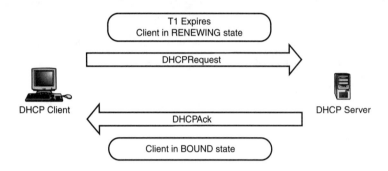

FIGURE 5.2
Steps required to renew a DHCP lease.

Restarting a DHCP Client

A DHCP client that is restarting represents a special case because the client might have been inactive long enough for its least to expire. Additionally, its old IP address might have been reassigned, the client might have moved to a different subnet, or the network configuration settings might have changed.

If a client's lease can be renewed by the DHCP server, the client receives a new set of configuration parameters with the lease renewal.

If a client attempts to renew a lease for an IP address that has been assigned to another client, or if the client attempts to renew a lease for an IP address that is no longer valid, the DHCP server responds with a DHCPNak (DHCP negative acknowledgment) message. The DHCP client remains in an unbound state and must initiate the process of obtaining an IP address. This situation might arise if the client is moved to a different subnet. It is unable to renew its previous lease, which is invalid for the new subnet, and must lease a new IP address.

Expiring a DHCP Lease

If a client is unable to renew its lease before the lease expires, the client must stop using the lease, in which case it enters an unbound state. Windows 98 and 2000 clients can use IP address auto-configuration to obtain an IP address if a DHCP server is unavailable.

Releasing a DHCP Lease

In some cases, it may be useful to have the DHCP client voluntarily release its current lease. On Windows NT and Windows 2000 DHCP clients, a lease is released with the following command:

```
IPCONFIG /RELEASE
```

On Windows 95/98 clients, release the client's current lease for the selected interface by clicking the **Release** button in the WINIPCFG utility. Click **Release All** to release DHCP leases for all of the client's interfaces.

When the lease is released, the client sends a DHCPRelease message to the DHCP server that granted its current lease. The client then enters an unbound state, and the DHCP server frees up the client's former IP address for reassignment.

DHCP Relay Agents

The point has been made that DHCP relies heavily on broadcast messages, but in Chapter 2, "TCP/IP Protocol Concepts," we determined that TCP/IP routers do not forward broadcasts. If that is the case, how does a DHCP client communicate with a DHCP server that resides on a remote subnet?

DHCP was designed to take advantage of forwarders designed for the older BOOTP client configuration protocol. When enabled on routers, forwarders (called *DHCP relay agents* in Windows 2000 and *BOOTP forwarders* in Windows NT) function as intermediaries between DHCP clients and servers. Figure 5.3 illustrates how BOOTP forwarders operate.

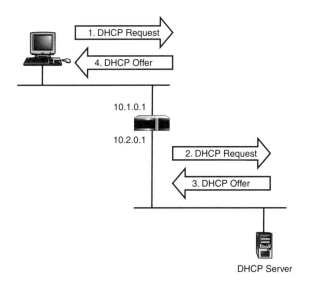

5

DYNAMIC HOST CONFIGURATION PROTOCOL

FIGURE 5.3

DHCP relay agents enable DHCP clients to communicate with remote DHCP servers.

When the DHCP relay agent receives a DHCPRequest message from the DHCP client, it learns the netid of the client's network from the configuration information for the router's interface on the network that received the message. The relay agent then sends a request to the DHCP server for an IP address on the client's network, forwarding all responses from the DHCP server to the client.

> **NOTE**
>
> DHCP must not be used to configure routers or DHCP servers, and Figure 5.3 illustrates one reason why. If the router or DHCP server does not have fixed IP addresses, it cannot determine the netids of the subnets to which it is attached.
>
> Configuration of the DHCP relay agent is discussed in Chapter 7, "Routing with Routing and Remote Access Service."

Scopes and Superscopes

The IP address pool that is available for dynamic assignment on a subnet is called a DHCP *scope*. An individual scope must be defined for each subnet that will be serviced by a DHCP server.

The network in Figure 5.4 presents an interesting problem for DHCP. The client's subnet supports too many hosts for a single Class C address, so it is assigned two Class C address ranges, 192.168.1.0/24 and 192.168.16.0/24. The problem encountered on this network arises because neither the BOOTP forwarders nor the DHCP server has complete knowledge both of the network configuration and of the DHCP addresses that have been assigned.

Working as a proxy for clients on the remote network, the DHCP forwarder will request IP address leases based on the netid of the first IP address that is bound to the interface. On the network in Figure 5.4, assume that the primary IP address for the network interface is 192.168.1.1. BOOTP forwarding will request IP addresses on network 192.168.1.0.

What happens when all of the IP addresses on network 192.168.1.0 have been assigned? The DHCP server must respond to additional DHCPRequests by denying the requests for leases. The DHCP server does not know that there is another network address range that could be used for clients on the subnet. Additionally, the DHCP forwarder does not have access to the database of active leases and so does not know that network 192.168.1.0 is fully leased. Therefore, the forwarder does not know that it should start requesting IP addresses on subnet 192.168.16.0.

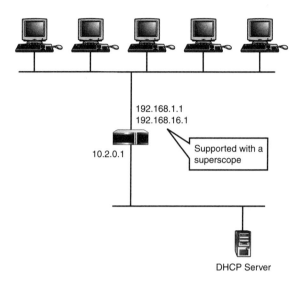

192.168.1.1
192.168.16.1

Supported with a
superscope

10.2.0.1

DHCP Server

FIGURE 5.4

Superscopes enable DHCP to assign IP addresses from multiple address ranges to remote subnets.

That's where superscopes come in. By bundling network address ranges 192.168.1.0 and 192.168.16.0 into a superscope, the DHCP service is informed that it can respond to lease requests for network 192.168.1.0 by providing IP address leases from network 192.168.16.0. When 192.168.1.0 is fully leased, the DHCP server begins to lease addresses on 192.168.16.0, all without skipping a beat.

Managing the DHCP Service

As with nearly all Windows 2000 services, the DHCP service is installed using the **Add/Remove Programs** applet in the **Control Panel**. To install the service, follow the procedures in Chapter 1, "Installation: Planning and Execution," in the section titled "Installing Windows 2000 Components."

When the DHCP service is installed, a DHCP snap-in is configured for the MMC. An icon for the DHCP console snap-in is added to the **Administrative Tools** program group of the **Start** menu. Figure 5.5 shows the DHCP console after a variety of DHCP objects have been created.

To supervise the DHCP server, you need to manage the following types of DHCP objects:

- Servers
- Scopes
- Reservations

5

**DYNAMIC HOST
CONFIGURATION
PROTOCOL**

- Options
- Superscopes

We'll discuss these activities during the remainder of this chapter.

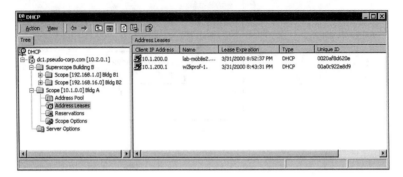

FIGURE 5.5
Editing scope properties with the General tab.

Managing DHCP Servers

To manage a DHCP server, it must be added to the DHCP administrator object tree. A Windows 2000 DHCP server cannot be activated until it has been authorized to Active Directory. So the first thing we need to look at are the procedures for managing DHCP servers in the DHCP console.

Adding DHCP Servers to the DHCP Console

You can manage the DHCP service on the local server or on remote servers by adding the servers to the DHCP snap-in. If the server you need to manage does not appear in the Active Directory object tree, add it to the tree as follows:

1. Right-click the **DHCP** object at the top of the tree and select **Add Server** from the context menu. The **Add Server** dialog box will be displayed (see Figure 5.6).

2. If the DHCP server has not been authorized to Active Directory, select **This server** and specify the server name. Click the **Browse** button to search for the server.

   If the DHCP server has been authorized, select **This authorized DHCP server** and select the server from the list that is provided.

3. Click **OK**.

The DHCP server will now appear in the object tree. Double-click the DHCP server object to see the objects that are automatically created for every DHCP server.

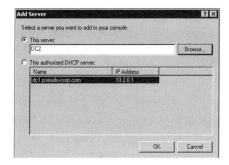

FIGURE 5.6
Adding a DHCP server to the DHCP console.

Authorizing DHCP Servers

A Windows 2000 DHCP server cannot actively service scopes until it has been authorized to Active Directory, a procedure that prevents the deployment of rogue DHCP servers. Unauthorized DHCP servers are problematic because clients communicate with DHCP using broadcast messages and a rogue DHCP server is as likely to receive a client's attention as an official one. (Unfortunately, DHCP server authorization functions only for DHCP servers that authenticate to Active Directory, and it can't detect or prevent the configuration of DHCP servers on Windows NT Servers, UNIX, Linux, NetWare, or other operating systems.)

Unauthorized DHCP servers are identified in the DHCP console by a red, downward-pointing arrow.

To authorize a DHCP server, do the following:

1. Add the DHCP server to the object tree of the DHCP console.
2. Right-click the server and choose **Authorize** from the context menu.

Authorized DHCP servers are identified in the DHCP console by a green, upward-pointing arrow. You will need to press the F5 key to refresh the display so that it reflects a change in the status of a DHCP server.

Configuring DHCP Server Properties

To view the properties pages for a DHCP server, right-click the DHCP server's object icon in the object tree and select **Properties** from the context menu.

Logging and Statistics

The **General** properties tab is shown in Figure 5.7. Two settings on this tab configure statistics collection and auditing.

5

- **Automatically update statistics every.** Statistics updating is disabled by default and it should be unnecessary to enable it on a permanent basis. Enable statistics updates when testing a new DHCP server and when troubleshooting performance and operational problems. You can specify the interval at which the statistics are updated. To view statistics, right-click the DHCP server and select **Display Statistics** from the context menu. A sample statistics display is shown in Figure 5.8.

- **Enable DHCP audit logging.** Audit logging is enabled by default. When audit logging is enabled, each DHCP event is recorded in a comma-delimited log file, which can be imported into a variety of applications for analysis. The format of the audit log and the details of the data fields are described in the Windows 2000 DHCP help under the heading "audit logging, analyzing log files."

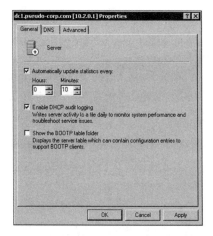

FIGURE 5.7

The General properties tab for a DHCP server.

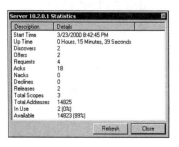

FIGURE 5.8

Statistics for a DHCP server.

The following listing contains an edited example of a DHCP audit log file. At the beginning of the file are definitions of the various Event IDs that can be recorded. The database includes records generated when a client released and then reobtained a DHCP address lease.

```
                Microsoft DHCP Service Activity Log

Event ID  Meaning
00        The log was started.
01        The log was stopped.
02        The log was temporarily paused due to low disk space.
10        A new IP address was leased to a client.
11        A lease was renewed by a client.
12        A lease was released by a client.
13        An IP address was found to be in use on the network.
14        A lease request could not be satisfied because the scope's
          address pool was exhausted.
15        A lease was denied.
16        A lease was deleted.
17        A lease was expired.
20        A BOOTP address was leased to a client.
21        A dynamic BOOTP address was leased to a client.
22        A BOOTP request could not be satisfied because the scope's
          address pool for BOOTP was exhausted.
23        A BOOTP IP address was deleted after checking to see it was
          not in use.
50+       Codes above 50 are used for Rogue Server Detection information.

ID Date,Time,Description,IP Address,Host Name,MAC Address
63,03/08/00,00:16:40,Restarting rogue detection,,,
51,03/08/00,00:17:40,Authorization succeeded,,pseudo-corp.com,
12,03/08/00,11:06:44,Release,10.1.200.1,W2KPROF-1.,00A0C922E8D9
10,03/08/00,11:06:52,Assign,10.1.200.1,W2KPROF-1.,00A0C922E8D9
```

Locations of the audit log file and the DHCP database are defined on the **Advanced** properties tab, shown in Figure 5.9.

Address Conflict Detection

Another field on the **Advanced** tab is **Conflict detection attempts**. If this feature is enabled, then prior to leasing an IP address, the DHCP server will ping the IP address the number of times specified in this field. The IP address will be offered to clients only if there is no response to the pings. If the DHCP server receives a response to the ping attempt it assigns a BAD_ADDRESS label to the IP address in its database. The BAD_ADDRESS label remains in effect for the duration of the lease time configured for the scope containing the address, but you can manually delete the lease if the source of the conflict is corrected.

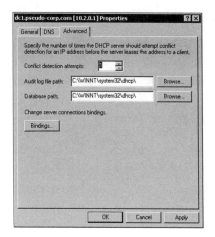

FIGURE 5.9

Advanced DHCP server properties include locations of data and audit files.

Conflict detection slows the process of assigning an IP address because the DHCP server must wait for its pings to time out before deciding that the IP address is not in use. Requiring more than one collision detection attempt will slow the leasing further.

Conflict detection also generates extra network traffic that may be undesirable. Besides, Windows clients make their own collision detection attempts, pinging before they use their assigned IP addresses.

Still, a single conflict detection attempt on the part of the DHCP server is probably a good use of resources. Without conflict detection, the DHCP server will continue trying to assign the IP addresses in response to further DHCP requests.

Dynamic DNS Updates

As mentioned earlier, the Windows 2000 DHCP server has the capability of dynamically updating DNS Host Address (A) and Pointer (PTR) resource records as DHCP leases are granted and released. The functionality of the dynamic DNS update capability is configured on the DNS properties tab, shown in Figure 5.10.

- **Automatically update DHCP client information in DNS.** Dynamic DNS updates are enabled by default. The updates can be performed in one of two ways:
    - **Update DNS only if DHCP client requests.** By default, Windows 2000 clients are configured to request updates transparently in the background. Configuration of the client options related to dynamic DNS update are discussed later in this chapter in the "Configuring Windows 2000 DHCP Clients" section.

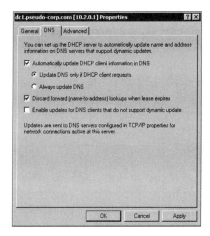

FIGURE 5.10

DNS update properties for a DHCP server.

- **Always update DNS.** If this option is enabled, dynamic DNS updates take place without an explicit client request. Use this option if DHCP is supporting clients that cannot generate the required request, which is the case with Windows clients prior to Windows 2000.

- When **Update DNS only if DHCP client requests** is enabled, the DNS update process for a Windows 2000 client is as follows:

    - The Windows 2000 client communicates directly with DNS to request a dynamic DNS update of its associated Host Address (A) resource record. The client requests creation of its Host RR in the domain that is specified in the host's configuration parameters.

    - The DHCP server requests a dynamic DNS update of the Pointer (PTR) resource record associated with the client.

    Windows clients prior to Windows 2000 and other types of DHCP clients are incapable of communicating with DNS to request dynamic updates of RRs. For these clients, the DHCP server must perform Dynamic DNS updates on behalf of the client.

- **Discard forward (name-to-address) lookups when lease expires.** If this option is checked, Host Address (A) resource records are deleted from the DNS forward-lookup zone database when the client associated with the RR loses its lease for the IP address. This option is enabled by default, and I can't think of a good reason to disable it.

5

DYNAMIC HOST CONFIGURATION PROTOCOL

- **Enable updates for DNS clients that do not support dynamic updates.** If the DHCP server must support clients that cannot request dynamic DNS updates, enable this option so that the DHCP server will request updates of both the Host Address (A) and Pointer (PTR) resource records associated with clients configured through DHCP. Host Address RRs are created in the domain specified by the DNS Domain Name option (option 15) of the scope used to assign an IP address to the client.

> **NOTE**
>
> When the DHCP server updates Host Address (A) resource records on behalf of a client, all clients in a given scope are placed in the same domain. This behavior is often undesirable. If your organization makes use of DNS subdomains, there is a distinct advantage in using Windows 2000 clients because each client's domain can be individually configured.

Creating and Managing Scopes

You must create a scope for each range of IP addresses that is assigned by DHCP. From a scope, you can carve out ranges of addresses that are available for dynamic assignment, designated for fixed client address reservations, or excluded from assignment by DHCP.

Defining Scopes

New scopes are defined using (Do I need to say it?) a wizard. The procedure is as follows:

1. Right-click a DHCP server in the DHCP console object tree and select **New Scope** from the context menu to open the New Scope Wizard.

2. Select **Next** to move on to the **Scope Name** dialog box, which has two fields in which you can enter any desired descriptions for the scope you are creating:

    - **Name.** The name you enter will label the scope object in the DHCP object tree. This is a required field.

    - **Description.** Enter any descriptive information you feel is appropriate. This is an optional field.

3. Select **Next** to open the **IP Address Range** dialog box, shown in Figure 5.11.

4. Specify the address range of the scope in the **Start IP Address** and **End IP Address** fields. The wizard will not accept start or end IP addresses that have all-0s or all-1s hostids.

5. The subnet mask for the scope can be defined in either of two ways:

    - Enter the length of the netid portion (the number of netid bits) of the subnet mask in the **Length** field.

    - Enter a dotted-decimal subnet mask in the **Subnet mask** field.

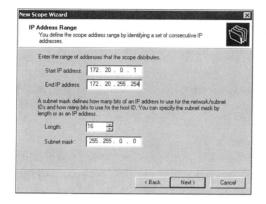

FIGURE 5.11

Defining the IP address range for a new scope.

6. Click **Next** to continue to the **Add Exclusions** dialog box, shown in Figure 5.12.

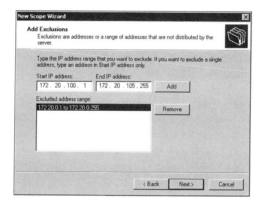

FIGURE 5.12

Specific IP addresses in a scope's address range can be excluded from dynamic assignment.

7. *Exclusions* are ranges of IP addresses in a scope's IP address range that the DHCP server will not assign to dynamic DHCP clients. Use exclusions to reserve IP addresses for devices that must have fixed IP addresses such as routers and DNS servers. Exclusions are optional.

If you need to define an exclusion range, specify the range of addresses in the **Start IP address** and **End IP address** fields and click **Add** to copy the address range to the **Excluded address range** list.

8. Click **Next** to continue to the Lease Duration dialog box where you specify the lifetime of leases defined in this scope in hours, minutes, and seconds. The default lease duration is eight hours.

NOTE

Use long lease durations (a week or two) if the scope contains enough IP addresses to support all your clients on a continuous basis. But don't be tempted to define very long lease durations, because clients do not check in with the DHCP server for updated option parameters unless they are restarted (which in my experience will be required infrequently with Windows 2000) or the lease reaches the T1 interval.

Use short lease durations (sometimes as short as a few hours) if you have more clients than IP addresses. Suppose you have a large mobile workforce that occasionally visits the office and jacks their notebooks into the network. With short leases, IP addresses are promptly recycled so that addresses remain available as clients come and go.

---

9. Click **Next** to open the **Configure DHCP Options** dialog box where you choose between these two radio buttons:

   - **Yes, I want to configure these options now.** Take this choice if you want to configure options for default routers, DNS servers, and WINS servers at this time.

   - **No, I will configure these options later.** Take this choice if you want to define the options at a later time. Then skip to Step 14.

10. Click **Next** to continue.

11. The **Router (Default Gateway)** dialog box is used to create a list of one or more default routers for the subnet. Use the Add and Remove buttons to determine the IP addresses that appear in the list. The order in which router addresses appear is significant, with routers at the top of the list having highest priority. Select an entry in the list and use the Up and Down buttons to adjust its position. (This dialog box defines DHCP option 3, "Router.")

12. The next dialog box is **Domain Name and DNS Servers**, shown in Figure 5.13. Complete this dialog box as follows:

   - **Parent domain.** Specify a parent domain for clients on this subnet. This domain is used by clients that do not have a domain name defined in their static configuration parameters. This is also the domain that the DHCP server will specify when it performs Dynamic DNS updates on behalf of DHCP clients that cannot perform DNS updates themselves. (This field defines DHCP option 15, "DNS Domain Name.")

   - **IP address.** Define a list of one or more DNS servers that will support clients on this subnet. The order in which servers are identified in the list is significant, and priority is given to the DNS server at the top of the list. (This list defines DHCP option 8, "DNS Servers.")

   - **Server name.** If desired, you can enter the FQDN of a DNS server in this field and click the Resolve button to resolve the name to an IP address.

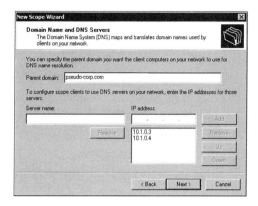

FIGURE 5.13

Specifying the domain name and DNS servers for scope options.

13. The next dialog box is **WINS Servers**, which contains **IP address** and **Server name** fields similar to those shown in Figure 5.13. If clients on this subnet are to use WINS to perform NetBIOS name resolution, define a list of the IP addresses of WINS servers to be used. WINS servers at the top of the list have priority.

This dialog box defines DHCP option 44, "WINS/NBNS Server." When WINS servers are defined, the wizard also defines DHCP option 46, "WINS/NBT Node Type" with a node type of 0×8, which configures clients to use the H-node algorithm for resolving NetBIOS names.

NOTE

WINS and NetBIOS node types are discussed in Chapter 6, "NetBIOS Name Support: LMHOSTS and WINS."

---

14. **Activate Scope** is the final dialog box in the New Scope Wizard. A scope will not service client requests unless it is activated. In the majority of cases, you will want to choose **Yes, I want to activate this scope now.** Click **Next** after making your selection to create the scope.

Figure 5.14 shows the details of a scope with the Scope Options object selected. Options defined for the scope are listed in the right-hand panel.

FIGURE 5.14
A DHCP scope, shown with enabled options.

Scope Management Tasks

Right-click a scope in the DHCP object tree to display the scope context menu. Several scope management tasks can be initiated from this menu.

Displaying Scope Statistics

Select **Display Statistics** to open the Scope Statistics window shown in Figure 5.15. These statistics are updated at intervals. Click **Refresh** to force statistics to be updated.

Clearly, the statistics for a scope are limited in usefulness. Use the statistics for the server in conjunction with the audit log if you need to troubleshoot scope operation.

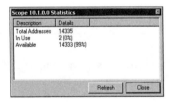

FIGURE 5.15
Statistics for a scope.

Activating and Deactivating a Scope

There may be times when you need to disable a scope so that clients cannot obtain new leases or renew existing ones. Choose the **Deactivate** option in the scope context menu to temporarily stop a scope without stopping the DHCP service. A deactivated scope is tagged with a red, downward-pointing arrow.

Choose **Activate** to activate a deactivated scope. An active scope is tagged with a green, upward-pointing arrow.

Reconciling a Scope

It may happen that the database for a DHCP server can become inconsistent with leases that are in use by clients. The DHCP server maintains a duplicate of DHCP scope information in the Registry. When a scope is reconciled, the scope database is made consistent with scope data in the Registry.

By default, scope data are backed up to the Registry at 60-minute intervals (although the DHCP help files specify a 15-minute interval). You can modify the backup interval by changing the value of BackupInterval (which specifies the backup interval in a range of 1 to 71583 minutes) in the following Registry key:

```
HKEY_LOCAL_MACHINE\
   SYSTEM\
   CurrentControlSet\
   Services\
   DHCPServer\
   Parameters
```

To rebuild a damaged scope database using data in the Registry, do the following:

1. Stop the DHCP Service using the Services console in the Administrative Tools folder of the Start menu, or by entering the command NET STOP DHCPSERVER at a command prompt.

2. Delete the file %SystemRoot%\System32\dhcp\dhcp.mdb.

3. Start the DHCP Service using the Services console or by entering the command NET START DHCPSERVER at a command prompt. When the service is started, it will create a new dhcp.mdb database file.

4. To rebuild the database of active leases, right-click a scope in the object tree of the DHCP console. Then choose **Reconcile** from the context menu. Manually reconcile any conflicts that are identified.

Editing Scope Properties

To edit scope properties, right-click the scope object in the DHCP object tree and select **Properties** from the context menu. The **General** tab, shown in Figure 5.16, enables you to redefine the scope name, IP address range, and lease duration.

CAUTION

Be cautious about choosing the **Unlimited** lease duration. If any scope parameters change, you will be forced to visit each client with an unlimited lease duration to manually force the client to renew its lease.

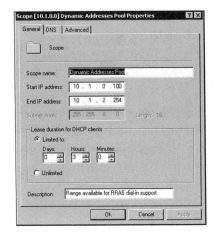

FIGURE 5.16
Editing scope properties with the General tab.

Parameters on the **DNS** tab duplicate options seen in properties for a DHCP server, enabling you to configure individual DNS support settings for each scope if desired. See the discussion related to Figure 5.10 for information about these properties.

Managing Reservations

There may be times when you want to ensure that a particular host always has the same IP address, but you don't want to lose the advantage of configuring the host using DHCP options. In such cases, you can assign the client's IP address through a *reservation*, which establishes a fixed relationship between a particular IP address and the client's network hardware address.

Before establishing a reservation, you need to learn the client's MAC address. Depending on the type of client, some methods are as follows:

- On Windows NT or 2000, enter the command IPCONFIG /ALL at a command prompt.
- On Windows 95/98, use the WINIPCFG utility.

Once the MAC address is known, setting up a reservation is a piece of cake:

1. Under the scope object supporting the IP address to be assigned to the reservation, right-click the **Reservations** object.

2. Choose **New Reservation** from the context menu to open the **New Reservation** dialog box, shown in Figure 5.17.

3. Enter a name in the **Reservation Name** field. One possibility is to enter the DNS domain name of the host.

4. Enter the IP address to be assigned to the client in the **IP address** field.

5. Enter the client's hardware address in the **MAC address** field.

6. Enter any desired descriptive information in the **Description** field. You might want to enter the name of the administrator who established the reservation and the date.

7. Select **Both**, **DHCP only**, or **BOOTP only**, depending on the type of client being supported.

FIGURE 5.17
Defining a DHCP reservation.

Managing DHCP Options

DHCP options enable DHCP to be used as a central clearinghouse for TCP/IP client configuration parameters. New features in the Windows 2000 DHCP service significantly enhance the flexibility of options assignment, enabling options to be assigned on the basis of client or vendor classes. After looking at some useful DHCP options, we'll discuss the means of using options to configure clients.

Common DHCP Options

RFC 2132 defines the standard set of DHCP options, but additional options can be defined as required. Expect to encounter options that aren't mentioned in the RFCs. There is a plethora of options, and many of them do not apply to Windows clients. Let's limit discussion to options that you are likely to use. By convention, option numbers are expressed in decimal form, but I'll include the hex representation because that's what you'll see if you look at the packets in Network Monitor.

- **Option 1 (0x01): Subnet Mask.** This option accepts a single, 32-bit subnet mask. Naturally, the subnet mask should be appropriate for the IP addresses being assigned.

- **Option 3 (0x03): Router.** This option accepts an array consisting of the IP addresses of one or more default routers. When multiple IP addresses are specified, clients use the routers in the order in which they appear in the list.

5

DYNAMIC HOST CONFIGURATION PROTOCOL

- **Option 6 (0x06): DNS Server.** This option accepts an array consisting of the IP addresses of one or more DNS servers. When multiple IP addresses are specified, clients use the DNS servers in the order in which they appear in the list.

- **Option 12 (0x0C): Host Name.** This option specifies a hostname for the client with a length up to 63 characters. Windows clients are not configured using this parameter, but may use the option to inform the DHCP server of their hostnames. Windows clients obtain their hostnames from the Computer Name in their network properties.

- **Option 15 (0x0F): DNS Domain Name.** This option specifies the default domain name that the client should use when attempting to resolve hostnames with DNS.

- **Option 43 (0x2B): Vendor Specific Information.** Vendors can use this option to supply options that are specific to their systems. Microsoft uses the vendor-specific information to support options grouped in vendor classes.

- **Option 44 (0x2C): WINS Server.** This option accepts an array consisting of the IP addresses for one or more WINS servers. Clients use the WINS servers in the order in which they appear in the list.

- **Option 46 (0x2E): NetBIOS Node Type.** This option specifies the method used by the client when resolving NetBIOS names. (NetBIOS name resolution is discussed in Chapter 6.) Values are entered as hexadecimal representations of a 4-bit bitmap. Available values are

  - **0x1. b-node.** Client uses broadcasts to resolve NetBIOS names.

  - **0x2. p-node.** Client uses point-to-point (unicast) communication with a WINS server.

  - **0x4. m-node.** Client uses broadcasts and then uses unicast communication if broadcasts fail to resolve the name.

  - **0x8. h-node.** Client uses unicasts and then uses broadcasts if unable to resolve the name with a WINS server. This is the preferred NetBIOS node type for networks where WINS is deployed.

- **Option 47 (0x2F): NetBIOS Scope ID.** This option specifies the name of a NetBIOS scope that is to be used by the client.

- **Option 51 (0x33): Lease Time.** This option specifies the lifetime of a lease that is being granted to a client.

- **Option 53 (0x35): DHCP Message Type.** This option specifies the type of the DHCP message.

- **Option 58 (0x3A): Renewal (T1) Time Value.** This option specifies the time in seconds from the time a lease is granted to the time the client must initiate attempts to renew the lease. By default, this value is 50% of the lease time specified in option 51. Some clients ignore this option and use a time that is coded in their local TCP/IP stack parameters.

- **Option 59 (0x3B): Rebinding (T2) Time Value.** This option specifies the time in seconds from the time a lease is granted to the time the client must initiate attempts to bind to a new lease if it is unable to renew its current lease. By default, this value is 87% of the lease time specified in option 51. Some clients ignore this option and use a time that is coded in their local TCP/IP stack parameters.
- **Option 60 (0x3C): Vendor Class Identifiers.** DHCP clients can use this option to inform the DHCP server of specific vendor-based client characteristics.

Option Assignment Levels

Option assignment levels enable administrators to determine the range of clients that will be affected by a given option assignment. You can configure options at the server level, in which case they affect every client that obtains an IP address lease from the server. At the other end of the scale, you can configure options for reservations, in which case a single client is affected by the options being specified.

The levels of option assignment are as follows:

- **Predefined options** do not actually result in option assignments, but they do determine which options are available and can establish default values for options.
- **Server options** are assigned to every client that obtains an IP address from a DHCP server unless they are overridden by options assigned to scopes or reservations.
- **Scope options** are assigned to every client in a scope unless they are overridden by options assigned to reservations.
- **Client options** apply to an individual client that is configured through an IP address reservation. Client options override all options that are assigned at server or scope levels.

In addition to the option assignment levels, Windows 2000 DHCP service introduces the new tools of client and vendor classes, added to the DHCP standard, as revised in RFC 2131/2132:

- **Client class** options are assigned to all clients that identify themselves as members of the client class and can be specified at the server, scope, and client levels.
- **Vendor class** options are assigned to all clients that identify themselves as members of the vendor class, for example, clients running a particular operating system. Vendor class options can be specified at the server, scope, and client levels.

We'll start by discussing predefined options and then move on to increasingly specific levels of option assignment.

Predefined Options

You can edit the predefined options to add or remove options from the list of available options or to establish default values that apply to all new option assignments that are configured on a given DHCP server.

5

DYNAMIC HOST
CONFIGURATION
PROTOCOL

The Predefined Options and Values dialog box is shown in Figure 5.18. To open the dialog box, right-click a DHCP server in the DHCP object tree and choose **Set Predefined Options** in the context menu.

FIGURE 5.18
Default values can be established for predefined options.

Predefined options fall into four classes. To view options in a class, select the class in the **Option class** field. The option classes are discussed in the "Vendor Class Options" section later in this chapter.

To view a particular option:

1. Select the option class in the **Option class** field.
2. Select the option in the **Option name** field.

You cannot delete options in the DHCP Standard Options class and, in general, I don't recommend that you delete any options at all.

You can add options if a new vendor package requires options that aren't part of the basic option classes. For example, if you need the Windows 2000 DHCP server to support clients of NetWare 5 servers, you may need to add options that support Novell Directory Services (NDS; RFC 2610) and the Service Location Protocol (SLP; RFC 2241). Some options you might require are:

- **Option 78 (0x4E): Directory Agent.** This option specifies a list of SLP directory agents that can be used by the client.
- **Option 79 (0x4F): Service Scope.** This option specifies a list of SLP scopes with which an SLP client is to communicate.
- **Option 85 (0x55): NDS Server.** This option provides a list of IP addresses of NDS servers.

- **Option 86 (0x56): NDS Tree Name.** This option specifies the client's NDS tree name.
- **Option 87 (0x57): NDS Context.** This option specifies the client's initial NDS context.

When an option is selected, a **Value** field displays any default values that have been assigned to the option. For options with single values, edit the value field directly. For options that accept multiple values, such as 003 Router shown in Figure 5.18, click the Edit Array button to open a dialog box where you can add, remove, and edit array entries.

Server Options

Server options (also called *default global options* in Microsoft documentation) are applied to every DHCP client of the server unless they are overridden by options at a different level. That makes server options a good place to specify options that will be the same for most or all clients, such as the WINS node type or the addresses of DNS servers.

Server options are stored in the Server Options container object under the DHCP server object. Figure 5.19 shows a Server Options container in which options have been defined.

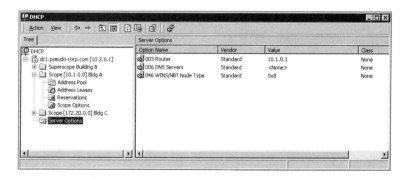

FIGURE 5.19

Several options have been defined under the Server Options heading.

To edit options, right-click the **Server Options** object and choose **Configure Options** from the context menu. The **Server Options** dialog box is shown in Figure 5.20.

To enable an option, check the options check box.

When you select an option, a data entry form is provided in which you can modify the value assigned by the option.

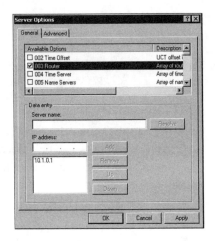

FIGURE 5.20
Standard DHCP options are configured on the General options tab.

Vendor and user class options are configured on the **Advanced** tab shown in Figure 5.21. After selecting the vendor class and user class, select and configure options in the same manner as on the General tab.

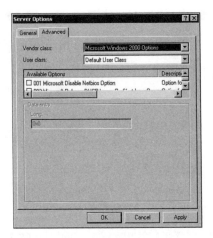

FIGURE 5.21
Vendor and user class options are configured on the Advanced tab.

Scope Options

Scope options override server options and apply to all clients receiving leases from the scope. Options for a scope are stored in the Scope Options container under a scope.

To configure scope options, right-click the **Scope Options** object under the desired scope and choose **Configure Options** from the context menu. Scope options are configured in the same manner as server options, using **General** and **Advanced** tabs in the **Scope Options** window.

Reservation Options

Reservation options override options from all other sources and apply only to the specific client that is specified in the reservation properties.

To configure reservation options, open the **Reservations** container and right-click the reservation object. Then choose **Configure Options** from the context menu. Reservation options are configured in the same manner as server options, using **General** and **Advanced** tabs in a Scope Options window.

Vendor Class Options

Vendor options can be applied at the server, scope, and reservation levels. Four vendor option classes are defined by default:

- **DHCP Standard Options** contains RFC-based DHCP options.
- **Microsoft Options** contains options defined by Microsoft that do not pertain to a particular client type.
- **Microsoft Windows 2000 Options** includes the same options as the Microsoft Options class. The separate class enables you to configure Windows 2000 clients independently of other Microsoft clients.
- **Microsoft Windows 98 Options** is available as a class, however no options are installed.

Vendor class options (called *vendor specific information* in RFC 2132) are returned to clients in DHCP option 43 (0x2B).

Clients request vendor options by sending a vendor class ID using option 60. Windows 2000 clients are identified by the string "MSFT 5.0" in the option 60 data fields. The vendor class of a client is not user configurable.

The use of vendor class options is determined by vendors themselves, and you will only need to create or modify vendor classes if a new vendor class is required for non-Microsoft devices on your network.

User Class Options

User class options enable administrators to define client groups that receive special DHCP option assignments. While you may never have a need to define new vendor option classes, user option classes solve a longstanding DHCP limitation, enabling you to assign different options to clients on the same subnet. You might want to create classes based on types of clients, or you could create classes for different departments.

Three user classes are standard on the Windows 2000 DHCP service:

- **Default User Class.** This class is applied to all clients that do not specify a user class when placing DHCP requests.
- **Default BOOTP Class.** This class is applied to BOOTP clients only.
- **Default Routing and Remote Access Class.** This class is applied to clients being configured to access the network remotely.

To utilize custom user classes, you must create a new class, configure options for the class, and configure clients to use the class.

Defining User Classes

It is a simple matter to add a user class to the DHCP service:

1. Right-click a DHCP server object in the DHCP object tree and choose **Define User Classes** in the context menu to open the **DHCP User Classes** list box, shown in Figure 5.22. (The figure includes the new Software Engineering user class that I am adding as an example.)

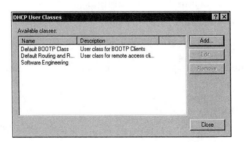

FIGURE 5.22

DHCP user classes can be viewed and managed in this dialog box.

2. To create a new user class, click **Add** to open the **New Class** dialog box shown in Figure 5.23.

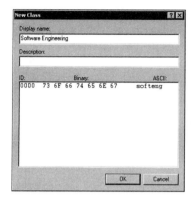

FIGURE 5.23
Defining a new user class.

3. In the **Display name** field, enter the name that will identify the user class in DHCP dialog boxes.

4. In the **Description** field, enter any descriptive information you feel is desirable. This is a good place to document the user class and could contain an explanation of its purpose and the date it was created.

5. Under the **ID** heading, enter the identifier that clients will send when requesting options from this user class. Typically, this will be an ASCII text string. The value can be entered either in hex or in ASCII. You will need to type this value when changing a client's user class affiliation, so enter an ID string that is convenient to type. (The identifier is not case dependent.)

   To enter the class ID in hexadecimal, click under the **Binary** heading and enter the ID in the form of a sequence of two-digit hexadecimal numbers. The corresponding ASCII characters will be placed in the **ASCII** column.

   To enter the class ID in ASCII, click under the **ASCII** heading and enter the character string that identifies the class. The corresponding hex values will be placed in the **Binary** column.

6. Click **OK** to close the **New Class** dialog box. The class you created will be listed in the **DHCP User Classes** list.

Defining User Class Options

After a user class has been created, you can assign options to it at the server, scope, or reservation level. Class options are assigned from the **Advanced** tab in the **Options** dialog box. Simply select the custom user class in the **User class** field and specify options per usual procedures.

In Figure 5.24, options are being assigned to the Software Engineering user class created in Figure 5.23.

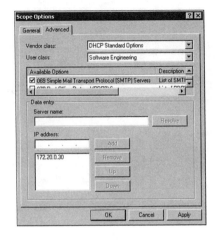

FIGURE 5.24

Options are assigned to custom user classes on the Advanced tab of the Options dialog box.

Options assigned to a user class at a given level (server, scope, or reservation) override options assigned on the General tab at the same level for users in the user class. You can define options that apply to all clients on the **General** tab and then override the options on a class-by-class basis.

Changing the Client's User Class

By default, clients do not include a user class identifier in their communications with the DHCP server. The Windows 2000 DHCP service associates clients that don't specify a user class with the Default DHCP Class.

The class affiliation for a Windows 2000 client is changed using the IPCONFIG command with the following syntax:

IPCONFIG /SETCLASSID *ADAPTERNAME CLASSNAME*

ADAPTERNAME corresponds to the name by which the adapter is identified in the Control Panel **Network and Dial-Up Connections** applet. The default name for a LAN adapter is Local Area Connection.

CLASSNAME is the class ID string that you defined when creating the class.

NOTE

If either the *ADAPTERNAME* or the *CLASSNAME* strings include spaces, you must enclose them in quotation marks when entering them at the command line.

On a single-homed DHCP client, you can enter * in place of the adapter name.

NOTE

If the /SETCLASSID option is specified without a class name, any existing class association is removed.

An example of the command is as follows:

```
IPCONFIG "Local Area Connection" SOFTENG
```

You can verify the user class of a Windows 2000 client by entering the command IPCONFIG /ALL. The class is identified under the heading DHCP Class ID. You can also use the command IPCONFIG /SHOWCLASSID to display class IDs. To use the /SHOWCLASSID option, an adapter must be specified by name as in the following example:

```
IPCONFIG /SHOWCLASSID "Local Area Connection"
```

The class established by the /SETCLASSID option is persistent and remains in effect when the computer is restarted. The class ID is stored in the following Registry value:

```
HKEY_LOCAL_MACHINE/
  SYSTEM/
  CurrentControlSet/
  Services/
  Tcpip/
  Parameters/
  Interfaces/
  {interface number}
  DhcpClassId
```

Managing Superscopes

You won't often need superscopes but, when you need them, there is no substitute. Creating a superscope is a simple matter of adding predefined scopes to the superscope definition. The procedure is as follows:

1. Create the scopes to be added to the superscope.
2. Right-click the DHCP server object that is to be associated with the superscope and choose **New Superscope** from the menu to open the **New Superscope Wizard**.
3. Enter a name for the superscope in the **Name** field and click **Next**.
4. In the **Select Scopes** dialog box (see Figure 5.25), select the scopes to be added to the superscope. (Ctrl+click to select multiple items.) Then click **Next**.
5. Click **Finish** to create the superscope.

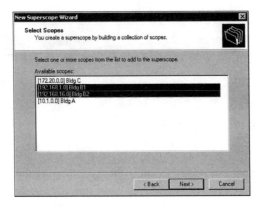

FIGURE 5.25

A superscope combines two or more scopes.

Configuring Windows 2000 DHCP Clients

To enable DHCP configuration on a Windows client, select the option **Obtain an IP address automatically** in the client's network configuration properties. Figure 5.26 shows the properties dialog box for a Windows 2000 client.

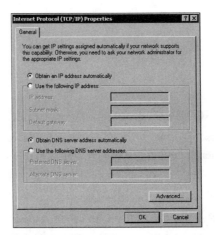

FIGURE 5.26

DHCP client configuration is enabled in the client network properties.

Static client properties take precedence over settings received from DHCP. Therefore, you should not configure a default gateway, DNS servers, DNS zone, or WINS servers on clients that are to be configured through DHCP.

If **Obtain DNS server address automatically** is selected, the client expects to learn the IP addresses of DNS servers from DHCP. (On non-Windows 2000 clients, simply do not define DNS server IP addresses to enable configuration through DHCP.)

The following client properties should be blank if the parameter is to be configured through DHCP:

- **Default gateways (IP Settings tab).** Configure through DHCP option 3 (Router).
- **Interface metric (IP Settings tab).** Configure through DHCP using option 3 (Microsoft Default Router Metric Base) in the Microsoft Options and Microsoft Windows 2000 Options vendor classes.
- **DNS server addresses (DNS tab).** Configure through DHCP option 6 (DNS Servers).
- **DNS suffix for this connection (DNS tab).** Configure through DHCP option 15 (DNS Domain Name).
- **WINS addresses, in order of use (WINS tab).** Configure through DHCP option 44 (WINS/NBNS Servers).
- **Enable NetBIOS over TCP/IP or Disable NetBIOS over TCP/IP (WINS tab).** If you enable **Use NetBIOS setting from the DHCP server**, NetBIOS support is configured through DHCP option 1 (Microsoft Disable Netbios Option) in the Microsoft Options and Microsoft Windows 2000 Options vendor classes.

The IPCONFIG Utility

This is the best place in the book to look at the IPCONFIG utility because most of the IPCONFIG command options relate to DHCP.

IPCONFIG is used to report the client's TCP/IP configuration settings and to change some of those settings that cannot be modified from the GUI. The syntax of IPCONFIG is as follows:

```
ipconfig [ /?
         | /all
         | /release [adaptername]
         | /renew [adaptername]
         | /flushdns
         | /registerdns
         | /setclassid adaptername [classname]
         | /showclassid adaptername ]
```

5

DYNAMIC HOST
CONFIGURATION
PROTOCOL

In this syntax diagram, replace *adaptername* with the name of a network adapter, as identified in the Network and Dial-Up Connections applet in the Control Panel. Replace *classname* with the string that identifies a DHCP user class.

NOTE

The * wildcard character can be entered in place of the *adapter* parameter. On a multihomed host, the * wildcard matches all network interfaces.

Entered without parameters, IPCONFIG generates a simple report like the following:

```
C:\>ipconfig

Windows 2000 IP Configuration

Ethernet adapter Local Area Connection:

        Connection-specific DNS Suffix  . : pseudo-corp.com
        IP Address. . . . . . . . . . . . : 10.1.200.1
        Subnet Mask . . . . . . . . . . . : 255.255.0.0
        Default Gateway . . . . . . . . . : 10.1.0.1
        DHCP Class ID . . . . . . . . . . : SOFTENG
```

If a client has more than one network interface, IPCONFIG generates a separate report for each interface. To generate a more thorough report, include the /ALL option:

```
C:\>ipconfig /all

Windows 2000 IP Configuration

        Host Name . . . . . . . . . . . . : W2KPROF-1
        Primary DNS Suffix  . . . . . . . :
        Node Type . . . . . . . . . . . . : Broadcast
        IP Routing Enabled. . . . . . . . : No
        WINS Proxy Enabled. . . . . . . . : No
        DNS Suffix Search List. . . . . . : pseudo-corp.com

Ethernet adapter Local Area Connection:

        Connection-specific DNS Suffix  . : pseudo-corp.com
        Description . . . . . . . . . . . : Intel 8255x-based PCI Ethernet Adapter
➥(10/100)
        Physical Address. . . . . . . . . : 00-A0-C9-22-E8-D9
        DHCP Enabled. . . . . . . . . . . : Yes
```

```
Autoconfiguration Enabled . . . . : Yes
IP Address. . . . . . . . . . . . : 10.1.200.1
Subnet Mask . . . . . . . . . . . : 255.255.0.0
Default Gateway . . . . . . . . . : 10.1.0.1
DHCP Class ID . . . . . . . . . . : SOFTENG
DHCP Server . . . . . . . . . . . : 10.1.0.2
DNS Servers . . . . . . . . . . . : 10.1.0.99
Lease Obtained. . . . . . . . . . : Wednesday, March 15, 2000 4:40:39 PM
Lease Expires . . . . . . . . . . : Thursday, March 23, 2000 4:40:39 PM
```

The client reported above is a DHCP client. As you can see, `ipconfig /all` reports the status of the client's DHCP lease as well as many settings that are configured by DHCP options.

The `/RELEASE` and `/RENEW` options are used to force a Windows NT or 2000 client to release or renew its lease. The following commands release the client's DHCP lease and then initiate the process of acquiring a new lease:

`ipconfig /release`

`ipconfig /renew`

On hosts with multiple network interfaces, these commands affect the leases of all interfaces that are configured through DHCP. To manage the lease of a particular interface, you can include the adapter name in the command, for example:

`ipconfig /renew "Local Area Connection"`

DHCP class membership is managed with the `/SETCLASSID` and `/SHOWCLASSID` options, which are discussed earlier in this chapter in the "Changing the Client's User Class" section.

Three `IPCONFIG` options relate to DNS. The `/REGISTERDNS` option refreshes the client's DHCP lease and then updates the client's RRs in DNS.

The `/DISPLAYDNS` option displays the contents of the client's DNS cache.

The `/FLUSHDNS` option purges the contents of the client's DNS cache, which may be necessary if the cache contains results of old queries that are no longer valid. Because a client consults its DNS cache before sending a query to a DNS server, obsolete data in cache can result in invalid results from DNS queries.

Building a Fault-Tolerant DHCP Service

By itself, DHCP does not offer any mechanisms for establishing redundant or back-up servers. You cannot establish two DHCP servers to support the same subnet address range because DHCP servers have no way to share their databases. If two DHCP servers have scopes covering overlapping IP address ranges, it is likely that they will attempt to assign the same IP address to different clients.

A single DHCP server per subnet represents a single point of failure, something we would like to avoid as often as possible. If only one DHCP server supports a subnet, failure of that server means that clients on the subnet will be unable to obtain new leases or renew existing ones. This lack of fault tolerance is probably one reason some administrators resist implementing a DHCP client configuration solution.

There are ways to improve the robustness of DHCP. One way is to split the address range on a subnet among two or more DHCP servers. Another is to rely on address conflict detection to enable multiple DHCP servers to support overlapping address ranges. But probably the best, if your budget permits it, is to rely on Windows 2000 clustering to build a fault-tolerant DHCP server cluster. We'll look at each of these options in the following sections.

Splitting a Subnet Address Range Among Multiple DHCP Servers

The traditional method of improving DHCP fault tolerance is to assign two or more DHCP servers to provide address leases on a subnet, dividing the subnet address range among them. If one of the DHCP servers fails and another DHCP server has addresses available, DHCP clients will continue to be able to obtain and renew leases.

You will often encounter the 80/20 rule: When two DHCP servers support a subnet, assign 80% of the addresses to the DHCP server you want to be primarily responsible for the subnet (which is usually physically attached to the subnet) and 20% of the addresses to the backup DHCP server (which is often remote). This approach works particularly well if you have multiple subnets, as with the network shown in Figure 5.27. The DHCP server on each subnet is assigned to offer 80% of the IP addresses on the local subnet and 20% of the IP addresses on the remote subnet. If you have two or more DHCP servers overlapping in this way, you improve the likelihood that a DHCP server will be available to service DHCP clients.

Splitting a subnet works best when you have a surplus of IP addresses. It doesn't work well if 80% or more of the available IP addresses are leased out at a given time. Also, because both servers will offer leases in response to client requests, it is entirely possible that all of the IP addresses on the secondary DHCP server will be leased when the primary DHCP server fails. (In practice, the client is more likely to select an IP address that is offered by a DHCP server that resides on its local subnet.)

DHCP Fault Tolerance Using Address Conflict Detection

Recall that DHCP servers can be configured to ping an IP address before it is assigned. (See the "Address Conflict Detection" section earlier in the chapter.)

If address conflict detection is enabled, it is possible to have two or more DHCP servers that provide leases in the same address range. Each DHCP server will test addresses for conflicts before leasing them, noting conflicting addresses in their databases so that they won't continue attempting to lease them.

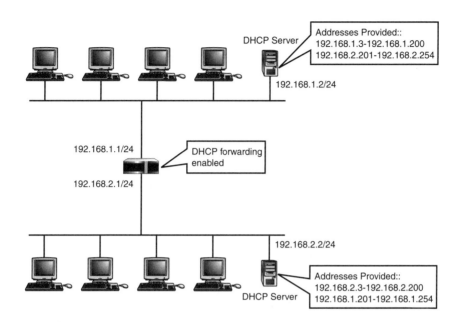

FIGURE 5.27
The 80/20 rule on a network with two subnets.

The primary drawback to this approach is the extra network traffic that address conflict detection generates. Also, because conflicts may be encountered somewhat frequently, clients may experience somewhat slower responses to requests for new DHCP leases. Nevertheless, this is a low-budget approach that improves DHCP server availability.

DHCP Fault Tolerance Using Server Clusters

The strongest approach to DHCP fault tolerance is server clustering, a feature that is supported on Windows 2000 Advanced Server. Clustering is a fault-tolerant technology that enables a service running on one server to continue running on a backup server if the first server fails. The process of switching to an alternative server in the event of a server failure is called a *failover*.

Windows 2000 clustering has both hardware and software components. A cluster consists of two servers that share a common storage bus so that they can both have access to the same disk drives. A Cluster service mediates access to the shared disk drives, coordinates communication between the member servers, and enables applications to fail over to the alternate cluster server if a server fails. Finally, the service must support clustering, which is the case of the Windows 2000 DHCP service.

We'll discuss things in the following order:

- Configuring the cluster hardware
- Configuring the first member of the cluster
- Configuring the second member of the cluster
- Configuring DHCP cluster support

> **NOTE**
>
> The Cluster service has a lot of nuances that are beyond the scope of this book. In this chapter, I'm taking a cookbook approach, focusing on the steps required to configure a working DHCP server cluster. If your organization relies on clustering, you will want to read further on the subject, starting with all the information that is included in the Windows 2000 Advanced Server help facility under the heading Windows Clustering.

Configuring Cluster Hardware

Figure 5.28 illustrates the physical components of a server cluster. There are two unusual features in a cluster: the shared disk channel and the secondary network that connects the server.

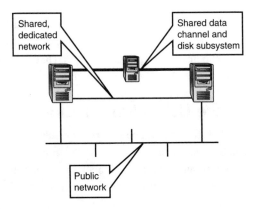

FIGURE 5.28
Components of a server cluster.

The shared disk channel enables both servers to have access to the same disk drives. The shared disk channel can be configured using either SCSI or fibre channel hardware. A server cluster represents a significant investment, and you may want to run more than the DHCP service on the cluster. Fibre channel running in full-duplex mode supports data transfers at rates up to 200Mbps with as many as 125 devices on a controller. At present, the best SCSI hardware offers data transfer rates of 160Mbps and remains limited to 8 devices per controller. Fibre channel controllers cost in the neighborhood of $1400, two-to-four times the cost of high-end SCSI controllers, but the drives themselves are not significantly more expensive.

> **NOTE**
>
> Because the shared disk drives represent a single-point of failure, you should consider using a RAID drive array. The RAID drive must be hardware-based, and cannot be implemented using the software-based RAID support offered by Windows 2000.

The shared disk channel is unusual because it is configured with two controllers. In the case of SCSI, the controllers must be configured with SCSI addresses 6 and 7.

Figure 5.29 illustrates Microsoft's recommendation for cabling a SCSI disk channel for a server cluster. Ordinarily, the devices at the ends of the SCSI cable bus are configured to terminate the bus. The problem this presents with regard to a server cluster is that disconnecting either end device removes termination from the bus. If you have to replace a SCSI device and the controller provides SCSI bus termination, the entire server cluster will be down while repairs are being performed.

FIGURE 5.29
Microsoft recommends wiring the shared SCSI channel with Y-cables at the end-nodes.

That's why Microsoft recommends making the end connections using SCSI Y-cables with terminators connected to the end connectors. If you disconnect a Y-cable from a device, the bus remains terminated and operational. The Y-cables can be external or internal. Inline terminators are available for both types of cables, but you will probably find it easier to locate internal ribbon-type Y-cables and terminators.

> **CAUTION**
>
> Use PCI controllers to implement the shared disk channel. ISA controllers are unsuitable due to their greater throughput latency.

> **NOTE**
>
> Adding a second hard disk controller to a system can screw up the drive boot sequence. If you add a controller and the system is no longer able to find the Windows boot files, you will need to reconfigure the system so that it boots from the original controller. On some motherboards, the boot sequence depends on the interrupts that are assigned to the SCSI adapters; try reversing the interrupt values. On most modern motherboards, however, the boot sequence is a BIOS setting. On my Phoenix BIOS systems, the option is on the Boot page under the Hard Drive selection.

> **NOTE**
>
> A good source of disk drives, controllers, and cables is www.megahaus.com.

Microsoft recommends that you implement a separate, dedicated network connection to support cluster communication between the servers. A second network connection isn't essential. Cluster communication can travel through the public network. But a dedicated network connection minimizes latency and provides a redundant path that enables the cluster to continue operating if a network adapter fails. (The idea of clustering is to create as much redundancy as possible to eliminate single points of failure.)

The dedicated network connection can be implemented using a hub, but the extra hardware does introduce one more thing that could fail. On an Ethernet, you can connect directly between two network adapters directly using a cable that crosses over wire pairs so that the transmit circuits on one adapter connect to the receive circuits on the other. Most Ethernet cables are wired straight-through.

> **NOTE**
>
> Category 5 crossover cables, as well as nearly everything else to do with computer cabling, are available from www.blackbox.com. Black Box is also a good source of SCSI hardware and offers great technical support for its products.

The servers in the cluster need not be equipped with identical hardware. It is probably a good idea to use identical SCSI controllers on the shared SCSI bus so that small differences in implementation don't become an issue. Otherwise, the systems can consist of any hardware that will support Windows 2000.

All of the hardware you select, most particularly the components of the shared disk channel, should be chosen from the Windows 2000 hardware compatibility list. Research hardware compatibility for Windows 2000 at `http://www.microsoft.com/windows2000/upgrade/ compat/default.asp`.

Configuring the First Member of the Server Cluster

Before configuring the Cluster service on the first server in the cluster, do the following:

1. Install Windows 2000 Advanced Server on both servers.

2. Configure both servers with computer accounts in the same Windows domain.

3. Configure the shared storage bus. Turn on one server at a time and ensure that it can communicate with the shared hard disk.

4. Create partitions on the drives on the shared storage bus. Determine drive letters for the partitions that do not conflict with drive letters that are in use on either of the cluster servers. If necessary, reconfigure the drive letters on the servers.

5. Configure the dedicated network connection and ensure that the servers can communicate through it.

6. When the shared storage bus and network connections have been tested, shut down one of the servers.

Now that the hardware is configured and tested, you can install the Cluster service on the first server. The procedure is as follows:

1. Create a user account for use by the Cluster service. This account will be given administrative permissions when it is configured for use by the Cluster service. In my examples, the user account is named ClusterUser. Select the **User cannot change password** and **Password never expires** options. Because this account will have administrator permissions, give it a secure password.

2. Open the **Add/Remove Programs** applet in the Control Panel and select **Add/Remove Windows Components**.

3. In the **Windows Components** dialog box, check **Cluster Service** and click **Next**. After files are copied, the Cluster Service Configuration Wizard will be started.

4. Click **Next** to open the **Hardware Configuration** dialog box, which reminds you to review the Hardware Compatibility List for information about hardware that Microsoft supports with regard to the Cluster service. Click **I Understand**, and then click **Next**.

5. Select the radio button labeled **The first node in the cluster** and click **Next**.

6. In the **Cluster Name** dialog box, enter a name for the cluster. In my examples, the cluster is named CLUSTER1 (although I was tempted to name it PEANUT_CLUSTER, clearly a tip-off that I shouldn't listen to my own sense of humor). Click **Next**.

5

DYNAMIC HOST CONFIGURATION PROTOCOL

7. Enter the following information in the **Select an Account** dialog box:

   - **User name.** Enter the username for the user account you created in Step 1.

   - **Password.** Enter the password for the user account.

   - **Domain.** Select the domain that contains the user account.

   Click **Next**.

8. If the user account specified in Step 7 is not a member of the Administrators group on the computer, it must be given the required permissions. Click **Yes** to make the user account a member of the Administrators group.

9. The **Add or Remove Managed Disks** dialog box, shown in Figure 5.30, is used to determine which disks will be managed by the Cluster service. All disks listed in the **Managed disks** list will be controlled by the Cluster service. Use the **Add** and **Remove** buttons to select desired disks. Then click **Next**.

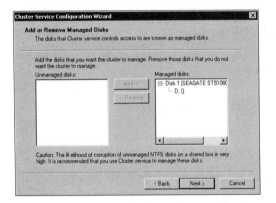

FIGURE 5.30

The Add or Remove Managed Disks dialog box determines which disks will be managed by the Cluster service.

10. One of the managed disks specified in Step 9 must be selected as the location where the Cluster service stores its checkpoint and log files. In the **Cluster File Storage** dialog box, select one of the disks in the **Disks** field. Then click **Next**. (The disk you select is referred to as the *quorum resource*. By default, files will be stored in the directory \MSCS\ on the quorum resource.)

11. The next dialog box is informational, describing the options for using private and public networks to support cluster communication. After reading the message, click **Next**.

12. Next you will see a **Network Connections** dialog box for each interface on the computer. As Figures 5.31 and 5.32 illustrate, each interface can be configured with the following options:

- **Enable this network for cluster use.** In general, all networks should be made available to the cluster so that alternative paths exist in the event of a network failure.
- **Client access only (public network).** This option disables the network interface for cluster communication.
- **Internal cluster communications only (private network).** This option should be enabled only on the interface that connects with the cluster's private network.
- **All communications (mixed network).** This is the recommended setting for the interface with the public network, enabling users to access cluster resources and making an alternative communication channel available to the cluster.

After specifying the network connection type, click **Next**. Repeat Step 12 for each interface.

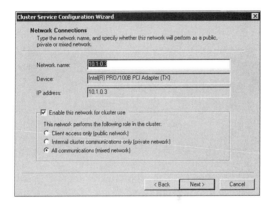

FIGURE 5.31
Network connection settings recommended for the network interface that connects with the public network.

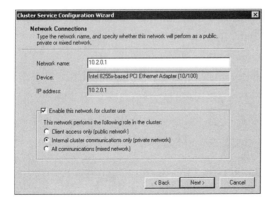

FIGURE 5.32
Network connection settings recommended for the network interface that connects with the cluster's private network.

13. The next dialog box is **Internal Cluster Communication**, shown in Figure 5.33. Use it to specify the priorities in which the Cluster service will use the interfaces that are available for cluster communication as determined in Step 12. The interface to the cluster's private network should appear at the top of the list, followed by interfaces to public networks. Use the **Up** and **Down** buttons to adjust the order in which network interfaces are listed.

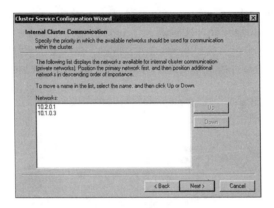

FIGURE 5.33

The cluster's private network should have the highest priority for cluster communication.

14. Next, you must specify an IP address for the cluster itself, a task that is performed in the **Cluster IP Address** dialog box, shown in Figure 5.34.

In the **Network** field, select the network that clients will use to access cluster resources. Only networks that are enabled for client access will be listed, as determined by settings applied in Step 12.

Then specify an IP address and subnet mask that will identify the cluster on the network. Naturally, the IP address should not conflict with IP addresses in use on the network.

Click **Next** to continue.

15. This completes configuration of the Cluster service. Click **Finish** to complete the wizard. After completing system configuration, the wizard attempts to start the Cluster service.

NOTE

If you cancel the **Cluster Service Configuration Wizard** before completing all the steps, the cluster software is installed but not started. You can return to the wizard by opening **Add/Remove Windows Components** in the Add/Remove Programs applet. A **Configure Cluster service** option remains available until the **Cluster Service Configuration Wizard** is completed. Click **Configure** to restart the wizard.

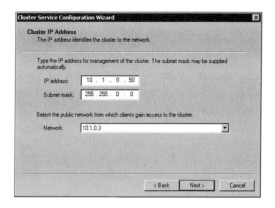

FIGURE 5.34
The cluster is identified by its own IP address.

Using the Cluster Administrator

After the Cluster service is successfully installed, a Cluster Administrator snap-in is added to the MMC. You can access the Cluster Administrator console through an option that is added to **Administrative Tools** in the **Start Menu**. Figure 5.35 illustrates the Cluster Administrator after both members of the cluster have been configured.

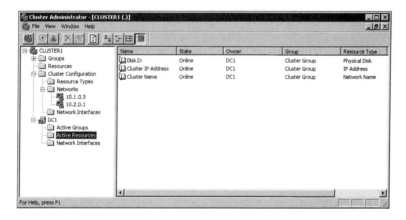

FIGURE 5.35
Cluster Administrator after the first cluster has been configured.

I selected the **Active Resources** object under the server to introduce you to concept of *cluster resources*, which consist of physical and logical objects that are required by the Cluster service or by applications that rely on clustering. As you can see, the cluster disks, IP address, and name are considered cluster resources.

Resources are organized into *groups* that define the units of resource failover. A resource group is always owned by one server at a given time, and a resource is always owned by one group. Consequently, all the group's resources will reside on a single server at any given time.

Resource groups, such as the default Cluster Group, establish virtual servers that clients use to access resources in the cluster. A *virtual server* is typically a group consisting of all the resources required to support a clustered application.

> **NOTE**
>
> One thing worth noting is that because a given resource can belong to only one group, a cluster with a single cluster disk will have only one cluster group.

Unless you get involved with more elaborate uses of the Cluster service than I am covering in this book, you will probably not need to make many modifications to cluster resources and groups. Later, I'll show you how to add the DHCP service as a resource and how to force a cluster server failover.

Configuring the Second Member of the Server Cluster

After you have installed the Cluster service on the first server and have confirmed that it is running successfully using the Cluster Administrator, you can add the second server to the cluster. Here's the procedure:

1. Start installing the Cluster Service using **Add/Remove Windows Components** in the Add/Remove Programs applet. When the Cluster Service Configuration Wizard starts, proceed to the **Create or Join a Cluster** dialog box.

2. In the **Create or Join a Cluster** dialog box, select **The second or next node in the cluster**. Then click **Next**.

3. The next dialog box is **Cluster Name**, shown in Figure 5.36, which you complete as follows:

   - **Type the name of the cluster you want to join.** Enter the name of the cluster that you defined in Step 6 when the first cluster server was established.

   - **Connect to cluster as.** If you are not logged in with the permissions required to administer the Cluster service, check this box. Then complete the **User name**, **Password**, and **Domain** fields to specify a user account that has the required permissions.

   Click **Next** to continue.

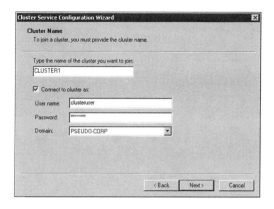

FIGURE 5.36

To join a cluster, specify the cluster name and optionally identify an account with administrator permissions.

4. The next dialog box is titled **Select an Account.** Enter the password of the user account that is being used by the Cluster service, as specified in Step 7 in the procedure used to configure the first member of the cluster.

5. That's it. Finish the wizard, and the second server will be added to the cluster.

The cluster is now operational. Both servers will appear in the Cluster Administrator object tree. You can now configure applications to take advantage of clustering.

Configuring DHCP Cluster Support

Before DHCP can take advantage of clustering, you must add DHCP as a Cluster service resource. After installing the DHCP service, the procedure is very straightforward:

1. In the Cluster Administrator, right-click the **Resource** object under the cluster name and select **Configure Application** from the context menu to start the **Cluster Application Wizard**.

2. Advance to the **Select or Create a Virtual Server** dialog box, shown in Figure 5.37. You created a virtual server named Cluster Group when you set up the Cluster service, and there's no need to create a new one. Select **Use an existing virtual server** and click **Next**.

3. The next dialog box is named **Create Application Cluster Resource** and offers two choices:

   - **Yes, create a cluster resource for my application now**
   - **No, I'll create a cluster resource for my application later**

   Choose **Yes** to create the cluster resource.

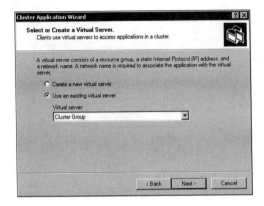

FIGURE 5.37

An application can be configured using an existing virtual server or a new one.

4. The next dialog box is **Application Resource Type**, shown in Figure 5.38. In the **Resource type** field, select **DHCP Service** from the drop-down list. (I opened the list so that you could get an idea of the types of Windows 2000 services that come ready for clustering.)

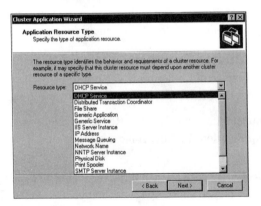

FIGURE 5.38

A resource in this list can be selected for addition to the cluster group.

5. The next dialog box is titled **Application Resource Name and Description** and is shown in Figure 5.39. Here you can enter a name that identifies the cluster resource and a description. The name should clearly identify the cluster resource. The description is a good place to document the resource, perhaps by including the name of the administrator who created it and the date it was created.

FIGURE 5.39

The name and description identify the service for administrators.

6. Click the **Advanced Properties** button to open the **Advanced Resource Properties** dialog box, shown in Figure 5.40. The **Name** and **Description** fields duplicate fields on the last wizard dialog box. The **Possible owners** field identifies servers in the cluster and should require no modification.

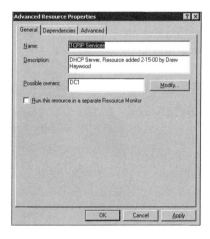

FIGURE 5.40

Cluster Resource Properties: The General tab.

7. You must specify the dependencies for the resource being installed. Dependencies are other resources to which the new resource requires access. Figure 5.41 shows the Dependencies tab after dependencies have been added for the DHCP service.

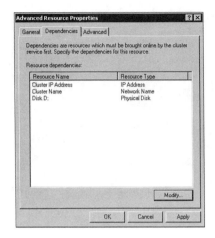

FIGURE 5.41
Dependencies are other resources that a resource requires.

To add dependencies, click the **Modify** button to open the Modify Dependencies dialog box, shown in Figure 5.42. The DHCP service requires the Cluster IP Address, Cluster Name, and Physical Disk resources. Move these items from the **Available resources** list to the **Dependencies** list. Click **OK** to close the **Modify Dependencies** dialog box. Click **OK** to return to the **Application Resource Name and Description** dialog box. Then click **Next** to move to the next step in the wizard.

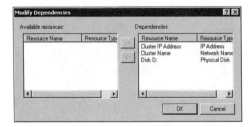

FIGURE 5.42
These dependencies are required for the DHCP service.

8. The next dialog box is titled **DHCP Service Parameters**. As shown in Figure 5.43, three file paths must be specified for the DHCP service. These paths must rely on a cluster disk resource and must be specified with a final \ character. Three directory paths must be specified:

- **Database path.** The directory that will store the DHCP database.
- **Audit file path.** The directory in which DHCP audit files are stored. By default, this is the same as the database directory.
- **Backup path.** The directory in which the backup DHCP database is stored.

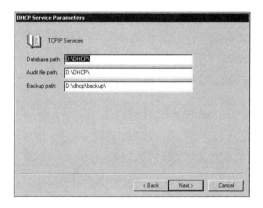

FIGURE 5.43

Directory paths used by the DHCP service must be specified.

9. Finish the wizard.

10. Open the Cluster Administrator in the MMC. Under the Groups object, locate the group that contains the **TCPIP Services** resource that was just installed. At first, the group object is marked with a red X icon and the state of the **TCPIP Services** resource is Offline, as shown in Figure 5.44.

   To bring the service online, right-click the group name object and select **Bring Online** from the context menu. After a few seconds, the red X should be cleared and the state of the **TCPIP Services** resource should change to Online.

The DHCP service should now be fully operational on the cluster. Open the DHCP Console and the cluster will be listed as a DHCP server, as shown in Figure 5.45. From this point on, you administer the DHCP service normally, using procedures described earlier in the chapter.

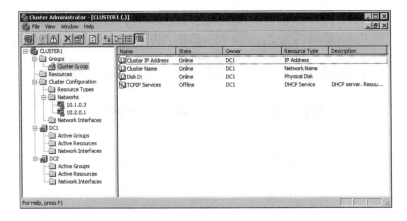

FIGURE 5.44
When first installed, the TCPIP Services resource is offline.

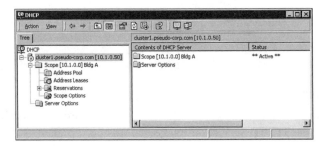

FIGURE 5.45
This DHCP server is running on a Windows 2000 server cluster.

Testing Cluster Failover

You may want to test the cluster failover process before you rely on it to support your critical services. First, verify which server node owns the cluster group resources by examining the Owner column for the resources in the group. In Figure 5.40, resources are owned by server DC1.

To test a failure of a cluster node, you can shut down the server that currently owns the cluster group, or simply stop the Cluster service using the Services console under Administrative Tools. Use the Cluster Administrator console to watch the process. You will see the resources go offline on the current server and then restart on the other cluster server.

DHCP on the Wire

Before we leave DHCP, I want to look at a couple of DHCP packets so that you gain some familiarity with the message format.

Figure 5.46 illustrates a DHCPDiscover packet. Take note of the following features:

- The DHCP message type is defined by the third byte of the three-byte field provided for option 53 (0x35). Table 5.1 defines the codes associated with each message type.
- The various IP address fields are set to 0.0.0.0. The client does not as yet have an IP address, and it doesn't know the IP address of a DHCP server, so the client's only option is to communicate via broadcasts.
- In the past, the client has owned a lease to IP address 10.1.200.1. It is requesting a lease for the same IP address.
- The client did not need to communicate through a BOOTP forwarder, as indicated by a value of 0.0.0.0 in the Relay IP Address field.
- Options have varying lengths. In many cases, the length is defined by the option definition (see RFC 2132). In some cases, options contain a parameter that specifies the length of the option in bytes.
- Option numbers are not included in the decodes. If you select an option in the decode pane, the associated data is highlighted in the hex pane. The option number is the first hex byte in the highlighted area. In the Client Class Information option, the option number is 0x3C (60 decimal). Recall from earlier discussion that option 60 is used to transmit the client class identifier to the DHCP server.
- The Client Class Information field has been selected so that you can see how it is represented in hex and ASCII.

TABLE 5.1   DHCP Message Types and Corresponding Option 53 Codes

Value	Message Type
1	DHCPDiscover
2	DHCPOffer
3	DHCPRequest
4	DHCPDecline
5	DHCPAck
6	DHCPNak
7	DHCPRelease
8	DHCPInform

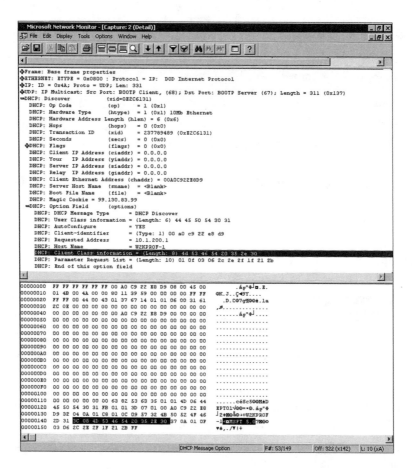

FIGURE 5.46

Details of a DHCPDiscover packet.

Figure 5.47 shows the contents of a DHCPOffer packet. Notice that the format is essentially the same as the format of the DHCP Discover packet. All DHCP packets share a common structure. Their functions are determined by the value of the Op Code field wherein

- 0x1 identifies a boot request (originated by the DHCP client).
- 0x2 identifies a boot reply (originated by the DHCP server).

The DHCPOffer packet offers an IP address to the client in the field Your IP Address (yiaddr). With the offer, the packet includes a variety of options that define the terms under which the lease is being offered, including the T1 and T2 times, as well as the IP address of the DHCP server in the Server IP Address (siaddr) field.

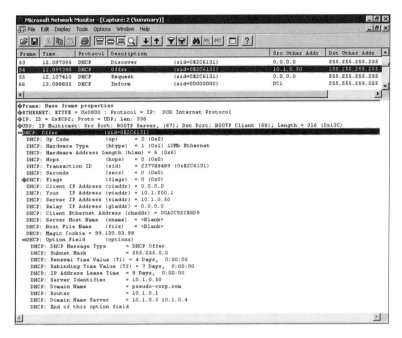

FIGURE 5.47
Details of a DHCPOffer packet.

NOTE

The packet captures used in this chapter are available online. Download the file
`dh_win2k-networks_5-1.cap` from `http://www.mcp.com/sams/detail_sams.`
`cfm?item=0672317419`.

What a Relief!

DHCP is an effective cure for lots of TCP/IP administrator headaches. Astoundingly, you may encounter networks of significant size where client's TCP/IP configurations have been defined statically. With a small amount of effort, however, you can set up a DHCP infrastructure that can flexibly configure all of your hosts that don't require static IP addresses, a small investment that pays significant dividends over time.

In the next chapter, we return to the topic of host naming and service location. Windows 2000 supports legacy Windows clients that depend on NetBIOS names. Because you probably won't be moving all your clients and servers to Windows 2000 overnight, you will need to support NetBIOS naming while developing a plan for migrating to an environment that eliminates WINS and relies entirely on Active Directory.

NetBIOS Name Support: LMHOSTS and WINS

IN THIS CHAPTER

Imagine for a moment what it would be like to use a network without a naming service. To access a service, you would need to know the network address of a server that offered the service you required. There would be no way to search, no way to browse, and no way to easily remember a computer's identity when the right server was identified. Imagine the World Wide Web without links. Pretty dreary, even for those of us with a lot of network experience.

Very early in the game, LAN designers realized that ordinary users couldn't use LANs unless the environment was friendlier. To make networks friendly to users, it became common practice to maintain naming services that enabled users to identify computers by names rather than numbers. The name served as an alias for the computer so that the user didn't need to remember an IP address such as 10.1.55.88 or an Ethernet address such as 00 6A 4B 30 2E 7F.

Networks also had to support a mechanism that enabled users to easily locate the services they required. If they needed to print, for example, they needed to be able to search for a print server. We've already encountered this sort of thing, which falls under the general heading of service location.

Traditionally, Microsoft networks have identified computers with names based on NetBIOS. NetBIOS makes it easy to develop applications that interact with the network by providing an application programming interface (API). An API enables the applications to access the network without worrying about the folderol of network communication. NetBIOS naming is simple and efficient, and works so smoothly that it is practically invisible. Additionally, by dedicating an extra byte of the NetBIOS name to identify types of services, NetBIOS names support service location as well as host naming.

But when Microsoft began to move their network products toward TCP/IP, they were faced with a problem, because TCP/IP networks do not use NetBIOS names. The result has been a long evolution of technologies that have gradually simplified the process of supporting a naming service on a Microsoft TCP/IP network. The latest is Active Directory, which uses DNS for both host naming and for service location.

Until all the nodes on your networks are running Windows 2000, however, you're stuck with two systems for naming computers. That complicates our lives as Microsoft network administrators, and you need to understand the complications to deal with the problems that inevitably arise. In this chapter, we will be taking a close look at NetBIOS naming and how Windows 2000 Server supports it.

NetBIOS Names

Every computer on a Microsoft network is associated with a NetBIOS name (with the exception that NetBIOS can be disabled on Windows 2000 computers). These NetBIOS names appear in browse lists. For example, if you open **My Network Places** (**Network Neighborhood** on down-level operating systems), computers are identified by their NetBIOS names.

NetBIOS names also can be used in native NetBIOS applications, such as the NET command. For example, you might map a network share with the command **net use m: \\drew\docs** to map network drive m: to the docs share on the computer with the NetBIOS name drew.

Expressions such as \\drew\docs are UNC (Universal Naming Convention) names. A UNC name consists of a NetBIOS name followed by a share name. Backslashes must appear as shown in the example.

Apart from systems that are enabled for Active Directory, NetBIOS names comprise the backbone of Microsoft network communication. Unfortunately, NetBIOS doesn't mate naturally with TCP/IP, and the naming architecture gets pretty involved. To understand the techniques Microsoft has devised to support NetBIOS over TCP/IP, we need to look at NetBIOS naming in some depth.

The Structure of NetBIOS Names

You might think you know all about NetBIOS names. After all, isn't a NetBIOS name simply the computer name you specify when you install the operating system? Not quite. The name you enter during setup is only part of the NetBIOS naming picture.

At any given time, a Microsoft computer will be known by as many as 16 NetBIOS names. Why so many? Well, a NetBIOS name identifies more than the physical computer. It also identifies a specific service running on that computer. Let's look at two examples for a computer named WOODY. Like every networked Microsoft computer, WOODY is running a Workstation service, the service that enables the computer to interact with network resources. WOODY also is sharing resources and is therefore running a Server service. Suppose that WOODY is communicating with a computer named BLYTHE. If BLYTHE wants to send a message to WOODY's Server service, BLYTHE must address the message so that the message doesn't go to the Workstation service instead.

To differentiate between services, each service is given a different NetBIOS name, which is generated by adding a byte (usually expressed as a hex number in the range 0x00 through 0xFF) to the end of the computer's basic machine name. This byte is typically referred to as "the 16th byte character" of the NetBIOS name. The Workstation service on the computer named WOODY has the NetBIOS name WOODY[00h], wherein [00h] is the 16th byte, the hexadecimal digit 00.

A computer registers the NetBIOS names it is using with the network. You can view the NetBIOS names that have been registered by a computer by entering the command **nbtstat -n** at a command prompt. Here is an example of the output:

```
Node IpAddress: [209.51.67.15] Scope Id: []
          NetBIOS Local Name Table
   Name              Type         Status
---------------------------------------------
WOODY          <00>  UNIQUE      Registered
PSEUDO         <00>  GROUP       Registered
WOODY          <03>  UNIQUE      Registered
WOODY          <20>  UNIQUE      Registered
```

The output of nbtstat reports the 16th byte in angle braces (such as <03>). As you can see, the computer WOODY is known by three NetBIOS names. WOODY<00> identifies the computer's Workstation service, WOODY<03> is associated with the Messenger service, and WOODY<20> identifies the Server service. These names are identified as UNIQUE because they are uniquely identified with a specific computer.

In the output of nbtstat, you can observe the way NetBIOS names are padded with spaces if the computer name portion contains fewer than 15 characters. Thus all NetBIOS names have exactly 16 characters when the computer name and service byte are taken into account.

Notice that another NetBIOS name appears in the list. PSEUDO<00> is the name of the domain the computer is logged on to. A domain is a GROUP NetBIOS name because it can be associated with more than one computer.

NetBIOS computer names can consist of up to 15 characters, and must conform to the following rules:

- The following characters are allowed: A–Z, a–z, 0–9, and the dash (-).
- The first and last characters must be alphanumeric (A–Z, a–z, or 0–9).

The 16th byte is assigned by the operating system. NetBIOS names are categorized in three groups:

- Computer names
- Domain/workgroup names
- Other and special names

NetBIOS names can be categorized in another way as well:

- *Unique names* associated with a specific machine
- *Group names* associated with groups of machines

Let's look at some examples of the NetBIOS names you are likely to encounter.

NetBIOS Computer Names

Computer names are associated with processes and services running on the computer that has registered the names. Here are some examples of NetBIOS computer names:

- *<computername>*[00]. This unique name registers the computer's Workstation service. This is the basic client NetBIOS name, registered by every NetBIOS client computer.

- *<computername>*[03]. This unique name registers the computer's Messenger service, enabling the client to receive and send messages.

- *<computername>*[06]. This unique name registers the RAS server service if that service is running.

- *<computername>*[1F]. This name is registered for the Network Dynamic Data Exchange (NetDDE) service and appears when NetDDE is started. By default, NetDDE is not started.

- *<computername>*[20]. This name is registered for the Server service, which is active on all computers that are configured to share resources, and provides a sharepoint for share access.

- *<computername>*[21]. This name is registered if an RAS server service is running on the computer.

- *<computername>*[BE]. This name is registered if the Network Monitor is running on the computer. (See Chapter 10, "Managing and Monitoring Connections," for information about the Network Monitor.)

- *<computername>*[BF]. This name is registered if the Network Monitoring Agent is running on the computer.

NetBIOS Domain Names

NetBIOS names are also used to register domains. Here are some Domain NetBIOS names you are likely to encounter:

- *<domainname>*[00h]. The Workstation service registers this name, enabling it to receive browser broadcasts.

- *<domainname>*[1Bh]. This unique name is registered by the computer that is the domain master browser, which is always the PDC if the PDC is available. The domain master browser is explained later in this chapter in the section "Naming Versus Browsing."

- *<domainname>*[1Ch]. This group name registers the IP addresses of up to 25 computers that are domain controllers for the domain. One IP address will be the PDC, and an IP address will be included for each BDC in the domain. The [1Ch] domain name enables BDCs to locate the PDC and enables pass-through logon validation to take place.

- **<*domainname*>[1Dh].** This group name registers a master browser. On NWLink or NetBEUI networks, there will be a single master browser for the domain. On TCP/IP networks, there will be a master browser for each subnet.

- **<*domainname*>[1Eh].** This group name is registered by all browser servers and potential browser servers in a domain or workgroup. The master browser uses this name to address requests to fill up its browse lists. This name is also used in election request packets used to force an election.

Special NetBIOS Names

A few NetBIOS names don't fit neatly into categories. The ones you are most likely to encounter are

- **<*username*>[03h].** The currently logged-on user is registered with this name, enabling the user to receive messages. If a user logs on to more than one computer, only the first computer will register the name.

- **_MSBROWSE_[01h].** The master browser registers this name, which is used to broadcast and receive domain announcements on the local subnet. This name enables master browsers of different domains to learn the names of different domains and the names of other domains' master browsers.

The NetBIOS Namespace

The NetBIOS namespace (the totality of NetBIOS names being used on a network) is flat, meaning that all the names are registered in a single name pool. This has some perplexing consequences.

For example, two computers cannot share a NetBIOS computer name, even if the computers log on to different domains. Also a computer cannot share its name with a domain (or workgroup). Let's emphasize that point:

- If a computer named BLYTHE logs on to the PSEUDO domain, there cannot be another computer named BLYTHE that simultaneously logs on to the WIDGETS domain. All computers in all domains are recorded in the same NetBIOS namespace.

- If your network has a domain (or workgroup) named PSEUDO, you cannot create a computer with the machine name PSEUDO.

- A network cannot have a domain and a workgroup that have the same name.

The flat nature of the NetBIOS namespace has a number of liabilities. Perhaps the greatest inconvenience arises when the Microsoft DNS server is configured to obtain NetBIOS names from WINS. Because the WINS namespace is flat and all names are mushed together, all names obtained from WINS must be registered in a single DNS domain.

NetBIOS Name Resolution Modes

On NetBEUI and NWLink networks, NetBIOS names must be resolved to machine physical addresses, such as the Ethernet MAC address, before communication can take place. On TCP/IP networks, NetBIOS names must be resolved to IP addresses. (IP addresses will be resolved to MAC addresses at a later time by using the ARP protocol.)

Resolution of NetBIOS names on TCP/IP environments is the responsibility of the NetBIOS-over-TCP/IP (abbreviated NetBT or NBT) service. NBT name resolution can be accomplished in three ways:

- By broadcasting name resolution requests to computers that maintain name databases. These name databases are called *browse databases* because they support the activity of browsing on the network, and the computers that store copies of the browse database are called *browsers*.
- By querying an LMHOSTS file, a text database file that contains name-to-IP address name mappings.
- By querying a NetBIOS Name Server (NBNS) such as WINS, which maintains a dynamic database of registered NetBIOS names.

Clients can be configured to use any or all of these methods. The resolution method a client uses depends on its *node type*. Three node types[m]b-node, p-node, and m-node—are defined in RFCs 1001 and 1002. The newer h-node type is currently an Internet-draft. Microsoft supports an extension to b-node called *enhanced b-node*, which will also be discussed.

> **NOTE**
>
> Microsoft likes to emphasize the fact that the NBNS is defined in RFCs 1001 and 1002, but, in fact, the NBNS as implemented in WINS is essentially proprietary. Microsoft has extended the RFCs in several areas, such as enhanced b-node and in replication of data between WINS servers. Consequently WINS would be incompatible with other NBNS servers. This isn't a serious problem, however, because WINS is the only NBNS implementation.

B-Node

NetBIOS name resolution using broadcast messages (b-node) is the oldest method employed on Microsoft networks. Figure 6.1 illustrates b-node name resolution. When HOSTA needs to communicate with HOSTB, the sequence of events is as follows:

1. HOSTA consults a local cache, maintained in its memory, of recently resolved names. If the required name is found there, name resolution stops. A local cache is maintained to reduce the amount of network traffic that will be caused by name resolution requests.

2. HOSTA sends a broadcast message that interrogates the network for the presence of HOSTB. The broadcast is received by all hosts on the local network.

3. If HOSTB receives the broadcast, it sends a response to HOSTA that includes its IP address. If HOSTA does not receive a response within a preset period of time, it "times out," and the attempt fails.

4. If a browser receives the broadcast and can supply the required information, the browser replies to HOSTA with the IP address of HOSTB. Browser name resolution works somewhat differently under different network protocols. The section "Naming Versus Browsing" later in this chapter describes the operation of browsers.

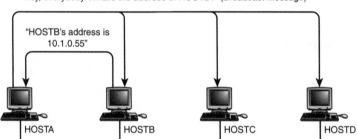

FIGURE 6.1

B-node name resolution.

B-node name resolution works well in small, local networks, but poses two disadvantages that become critical as networks grow:

- As the number of hosts on the network increases, the amount of broadcast traffic can consume significant network bandwidth.

- IP routers do not ordinarily forward broadcasts, and the b-node technique cannot propagate names through an internetwork. As Figure 6.2 illustrates, b-node broadcasts cannot resolve the NetBIOS names of computers that reside on remote subnets.

Broadcast messages are necessary when the IP address of the destination host is not known. But high levels of broadcast messages are undesirable because every host that sees the message must expend some processing power decoding the message to see whether it is the intended destination for the message. So every broadcast message generates some activity on every computer, and the overall processing cost of many broadcasts can be significant. Therefore, b-node is not the most desirable name resolution method, and is best used only on small networks.

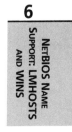

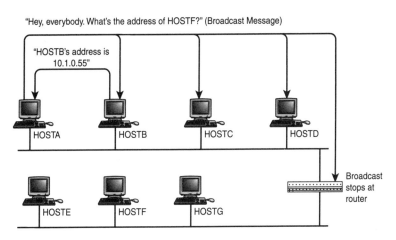

FIGURE 6.2

B-node name resolution is blocked by routers.

> **NOTE**
>
> The utility `nbtstat` is useful for diagnosing broadcast mode name resolution, and is discussed later in this chapter. The command `nbtstat -r` is particularly useful, reporting the number of b-node broadcasts that are occurring on the network. This information is useful if you suspect that b-node broadcasts are degrading network performance.

Enhanced B-Node

In its own implementations, Microsoft provides an extension to b-node name resolution. If an enhanced b-node host cannot resolve a NetBIOS name through b-node broadcasts, it will consult a local LMHOSTS file if one has been configured. LMHOSTS files are text database files that map NetBIOS names to IP addresses. The format of the LMHOSTS file is described later in this chapter.

B-node is the default name resolution mode for Microsoft hosts not configured to use WINS for name resolution. In pure b-node environments, hosts can be configured to use LMHOSTS files to resolve names on remote networks. Enhanced b-node is enabled by checking the **Enable LMHOSTS Lookup** check box on the WINS tab of the **Advanced TCP/IP Properties** dialog box. (If WINS server addresses are specified on the WINS tab, the computer will be configured for h-node name resolution, even if the **Enable LMHOSTS Lookup** check box is checked.)

P-Node

Hosts configured for p-node (point-to-point) use WINS for name resolution. All p-node communication is via point-to-point messages, and no broadcast traffic is generated. P-node computers register themselves with a WINS server, which functions as a NetBIOS name server. The WINS server maintains a database of NetBIOS names, ensures that duplicate names do not exist, and makes the database available to WINS clients. Figure 6.3 illustrates how WINS clients resolve names.

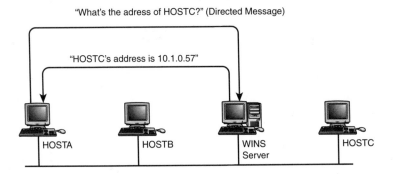

FIGURE 6.3
P-node name resolution.

Notice in Figure 6.4 that routers are not barriers to WINS operation. Each WINS client is configured with the address of a WINS server, which can reside on the local network or on a remote network. WINS clients and servers communicate via directed messages that can be routed. No broadcast messages are required for p-node name resolution.

P-node name resolution has two liabilities:

- All computers must be configured using the address of a WINS server, even when communicating hosts reside on the same network.
- If a WINS server is unavailable, name resolution fails for p-node clients.

Because both b-node and p-node address resolution present disadvantages, two address modes have been developed that form hybrids of b-node and p-node. These hybrid modes are called m-node and h-node.

> **NOTE**
>
> Microsoft network clients can be configured to use p-node or m-node only if they obtain their configuration settings from DHCP. See the section "Configuring DHCP Clients as WINS Clients" later in this chapter for details.

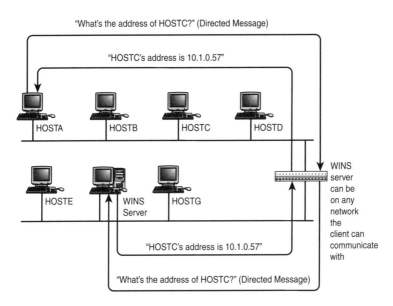

"What's the address of HOSTC?" (Directed Message)

"HOSTC's address is 10.1.0.57"

HOSTA   HOSTB   HOSTC   HOSTD

HOSTE   WINS   HOSTG
         Server

WINS
server
can be
on any
network
the
client can
communicate
with

"HOSTC's address is 10.1.0.57"

"What's the address of HOSTC?" (Directed Message)

FIGURE 6.4
P-node name resolution is unaffected by routers.

M-Node

M-node (mixed) computers first attempt to use b-node (broadcast) name resolution, which succeeds if the desired host resides on the local network. If b-node resolution fails and LHHOSTS lookup (enhanced b-node) is configured, an attempt is made to resolve the name through a local LMHOSTS file. If b-node fails, m-node hosts then attempt to use p-node to resolve the name.

M-node enables name resolution to continue on the local network when WINS services are down. B-node resolution is attempted first on the assumption that in most environments, hosts communicate most often with hosts on their local networks. When this assumption holds, performance of b-node resolution is superior to p-node. Recall, however, that b-node can result in high levels of broadcast traffic.

Microsoft warns that m-node can cause problems when network logons are attempted in a routed environment.

H-Node

Like m-node, h-node is a hybrid of broadcast (b-node) and directed (p-node) name resolution modes. Nodes configured with h-node, however, first attempt to resolve addresses using WINS. Only after an attempt to resolve the name using a name server fails does an h-node computer attempt to use b-node, with LMHOSTS lookup if that option is configured. H-node computers, therefore, can continue to resolve local addresses when WINS is unavailable. When operating in b-node mode, h-node computers continue to poll the WINS server and revert to h-node when WINS services are restored.

H-node is the default mode for Microsoft TCP/IP clients configured using the addresses of WINS servers. As a fallback, Windows TCP/IP clients can be configured to use LMHOSTS files for name resolution.

> **NOTE**
>
> Although networks can be configured using mixtures of b-node and p-node comput-ers, Microsoft recommends this only as an interim measure. P-node hosts ignore b-node broadcast messages, and b-node hosts ignore p-node directed messages. Two hosts, therefore, conceivably could be established using the same NetBIOS name.

Name Resolution with LMHOSTS Files

Although a complete name resolution system can be based on LMHOSTS files, static naming files (called "static" because they are not automatically updated as the network evolves) can be a nightmare to administer, particularly when they must be distributed to several hosts on the network. Nevertheless, LMHOSTS files might be necessary if WINS will not be run on a net-work or if it is desirable to have a backup plan in case the WINS service fails.

Although LAN Manager LMHOSTS files supported little more than mappings of NetBIOS names to IP addresses, starting with Windows NT there are several new options that make LMHOSTS considerably more versatile.

Format of LMHOSTS Files

A sample LMHOSTS file named `LMHOSTS.SAM` is installed in the directory `C:\Winnt\ system32\drivers\etc`. You can consult this file for formatting examples, but should create your LMHOSTS file from scratch. The LMHOSTS file is processed line-by-line, and the sample file contains numerous comments and extraneous lines that slow name resolution. When you create your own LMHOSTS file, it must be named `LMHOSTS` (no filename exten-sion), and it must be stored in `C:\%SystemRoot%\system32\drivers\etc`.

> **NOTE**
>
> Most Windows-based editors automatically append an extension to the filename when they save a file. If you save a file named `LMHOSTS` in Notepad, for example, the `.txt` extension is automatically added to the saved file.
>
> In Notepad, you can override this behavior by enclosing the filename in quotation marks when you save it.

In any case, if LMHOSTS name resolution doesn't appear to work, use Windows NT Explorer to examine the filenames. To see filename extensions, you need to open the Options dialog box (choose **Options** in the **View** menu) and check **Hide file extensions for known file types**.

The format of an LMHOSTS entry is

```
ip address      name
```

The IP address must begin in column one of the line. Here is an example of a basic LMHOSTS file:

```
10.1.0.100      LAUREN
10.2.0.101      BLYTHE
10.1.0.155      WOODY
```

Windows NT LMHOSTS files can be enhanced by a variety of keywords, discussed in the next section.

NOTE

The entries in the LMHOSTS file are examined sequentially. To speed the name resolution process, place the most-used names toward the beginning of the LMHOSTS file.

LMHOSTS Keywords

Here is an example of an LMHOSTS file augmented using keywords:

```
10.1.0.100   LAUREN
10.1.0.101...BLYTHE
10.1.0.155   WOODY
10.1.0.3     DC1    #PRE  #DOM:PSEUDO     #Primary DC
10.1.0.4     DC2    #PRE  #DOM:PSEUDO     #Backup DC
10.1.0.1     ROUTER1 #MH
10.2.0.1     ROUTER1 #MH

#BEGIN_ALTERNATE
#INCLUDE \\DC1\PUBLIC\LMHOSTS          #Primary source for file
#INCLUDE \\DC2\PUBLIC\LMHOSTS          #Backup source for file
#END_ALTERNATE
```

The #PRE keyword specifies that the entry should be preloaded into the name cache. Ordinarily, LMHOSTS is consulted for name resolution only after WINS and b-node broadcasts have failed. Preloading the entry ensures that the mapping will be available at the start of the name resolution process. #PRE is often used to ensure that domain names loaded with the #DOM keyword will be cached.

The #DOM keyword identifies domain controllers, information that is often used to determine how browsers and logon services behave on a routed TCP/IP network. #DOM entries can be pre-loaded into cache by including the #PRE keyword.

The #INCLUDE keyword makes loading mappings from a remote file possible. One use for #INCLUDE is to support a master LMHOSTS file stored on logon servers and accessed by TCP/IP clients during startup. Entries in the remote LMHOSTS file are examined only when TCP/IP is started. Entries in the remote LMHOSTS file, therefore, must be tagged with the #PRE keyword to force them to be loaded into cache. There's a trick to using #INCLUDE that is explained in the next section.

If several copies of the included LMHOSTS file are available on different servers, you can force the computer to search several locations until a file is successfully loaded. This is accomplished by bracketing #INCLUDE keywords between the keywords #BEGIN_ALTERNATE and #END_ALTERNATE, as was done in the sample file just presented. Any successful #INCLUDE causes the group to succeed.

> **NOTE**
>
> In the sample listing, note that the hosts DC1 and DC2 are explicitly defined so that the names can be used in the parameters of the #INCLUDE keywords.

The #MH keyword designates entries for a multihomed host. One #MH entry can be included for each interface on the host.

It is useful to have copies of the master LMHOSTS file on several computers so that computers can obtain a backup copy if the primary server is down.

Organizing Entries in LMHOSTS

When the LMHOSTS file is consulted, Windows reads entries sequentially starting from the beginning of the file. Windows stops when it encounters the first entry that matches the NetBIOS name it is searching for. Because of this behavior, the arrangement of entries in the LMHOSTS file has an effect on the speed of LMHOSTS name resolution. Here are some recommendations:

- Place the entries that will be needed most often at the beginning of the LMHOSTS file.
- Place entries tagged with the #PRE keyword after standard entries. #PRE entries are loaded into cache when LMHOSTS is processed during logon (or when you enter the command **nbtstat -R**), and there is no need to process them again.

- Place #INCLUDE entries at the end of the LMHOSTS file, following #PRE statements that they depend upon. #INCLUDE statements are processed only during logon or when you enter the command **nbtstat -R**.

In large LMHOSTS files, it is possible to have two entries for the same NetBIOS name. In such cases, only the first entry will be processed. You need to be aware of this behavior when editing the file. If you add an entry for a host when an entry already exists in the LMHOSTS file, only the first entry in the file will be effective.

Enabling #INCLUDE Statements to Succeed During Logon

When a user fires up a network computer, the LMHOSTS file is processed before the user logs on to the network. The #INCLUDE statement must process a file in a shared directory but cannot connect with the share because the user has not been authenticated and therefore does not have security access.

To enable the user to access a share before logon authentication has been accomplished, you must configure the Windows computer offering the share to support *null sessions*. These enable users to connect to specified shares with null credentials. Windows versions later than 3.1 do not support null sessions by default; null sessions must be explicitly enabled. This can be done on a per-share basis, and properly configured null sessions do not jeopardize security.

To enable null sessions support, add a Registry value named NullSessionShares of type REG_MULTI_SZ to the following Registry key:

```
HKEY_LOCAL_MACHINE
   \System
   \CurrentControlSet
   \Services
   \LanmanServer
   \Parameters
```

Registry values of type REG_MULTI_SZ accept multiple data entries. To enable null session support for a share, open the NullSessionShares value entry and add the name of the share, for example, PUBLIC, as in the sample LMHOSTS file. You must restart the server to activate any changes made to the Registry.

Alternatively, you can force the client to load the LMHOSTS file after the user has logged on, by executing the command **nbtstat -R** (the -R parameter must be uppercase). The #INCLUDE statement can now succeed because the user has been authenticated to the network. If desired, the **nbtstat -R** statement can be executed in a logon script.

Enabling Clients to Use LMHOSTS Files

Generally speaking, LMHOSTS files are unnecessary on networks that have a properly functioning WINS name service. If an internetwork does not use WINS, LMHOSTS lookups should be enabled, and LMHOSTS files should be configured to enable computers to find critical hosts.

Any Windows TCP/IP client can be enabled to use LMHOSTS files by checking the **Enable LMHOSTS Lookup** check box. On Windows 2000, the check box is found in the **WINS** address tab of the **Advanced TCP/IP Settings** dialog box. (See Chapter 1, "Installation Planning and Execution," for more about this setting.)

Guidelines for Establishing LMHOSTS Name Resolution

B-node computers are not configured to use WINS name resolution and must use LMHOSTS to resolve names on remote networks. If the majority of name queries are on the local network, it is generally not necessary to preload mappings in the LMHOSTS file. Frequently accessed hosts on remote networks can be preloaded using the #PRE keyword.

#DOM keywords should be used to enable non-WINS clients to locate domain controllers on remote networks. The LMHOSTS file for every computer in the domain should include #DOM entries for all domain controllers that do not reside on the local network. This ensures that domain activities, such as logon authentication, continue to function.

To browse a domain other than the logon domain, LMHOSTS must include a #DOM entry that defines the name and IP address of the primary domain controller of the domain to be browsed. Include backup domain controllers in case the primary fails, or a backup domain controller is promoted to primary.

LMHOSTS files on backup domain controllers should include mappings to the primary domain controller name and IP address, as well as mappings to all other backup domain controllers.

All domain controllers in trusted domains should be included in the local LMHOSTS file.

When Should You Use LMHOSTS to Resolve NetBIOS Names?

LMHOSTS can be a useful means of resolving names of stable computers, such as servers. By preloading caches with addresses for Windows servers, you can speed the name resolution process by reducing NetBIOS and WINS queries. LMHOSTS can provide a backup to WINS, and entries preloaded from LMHOSTS and held in cache continue to be available if WINS servers fails.

Still, if the network is large or changes frequently, it is very difficult to keep LMHOSTS files current and distributed to users. Given the facts that there are few circumstances in which LMHOSTS is required and WINS is a more flexible, more easily managed solution for NetBIOS naming, you are likely to find that the effort required to support LMHOSTS files is difficult to justify.

NetBIOS Naming with WINS

WINS, the Windows Internet Name Service, is Microsoft's implementation of the NetBIOS Name Service (NBNS) defined in RFCs 1001 and 1002. As we have already seen, WINS provides a mechanism for working around the limitations imposed by the use of broadcast communication to resolve NetBIOS names.

Architecture of WINS

WINS uses one or more WINS servers to maintain a database that provides name-to-address mappings in response to queries from WINS clients. The WINS database can be distributed across multiple WINS servers to provide fault-tolerance and better service on local networks. A replication mechanism enables WINS servers to share their data on a periodic basis.

WINS is a particularly good fit when IP addresses are assigned by DHCP. Although the DHCP lease renewal process results in a certain stability of IP address assignments, IP addresses can change if hosts are moved to different networks, or if a host is inactive for a time sufficient to cause its address to be reassigned. WINS automatically updates its database to respond to such changes.

Because WINS clients communicate with WINS servers via point-to-point messages (no broadcasts), no problems are encountered when operating in a routed environment. Figure 6.5 shows an internet with three networks. WINS servers are configured on two of the networks. The WINS servers can both resolve name queries, and are configured to periodically replicate their databases. WINS clients on all three networks can communicate with a WINS server to resolve names to addresses.

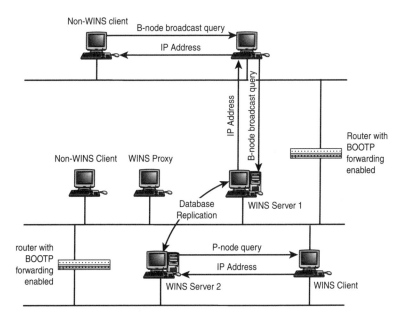

FIGURE 6.5

Architecture of a WINS name service.

WINS proxies enable non-WINS clients to resolve names on the internetwork. When a WINS proxy receives a b-node broadcast attempting to resolve a name on a remote network, the WINS proxy directs a p-node (point-to-point) name query to a WINS server and returns the response to the non-WINS client.

> **NOTE**
>
> WINS will not detect NetBIOS names that are already in use on the network by non-WINS clients, giving rise to a potential source of conflict. The same name could be used by a WINS and a non-WINS client. WINS proxy agents enable non-WINS client names to be registered with WINS and prevent such conflicts.

WINS makes it possible to maintain unique NetBIOS names throughout the internetwork. When a WINS client computer attempts to register a NetBIOS name with WINS, it is permitted to do so only if the name is not currently reserved in the WINS database. Without WINS, unique names are enforced only through the broadcast b-node mechanism on local networks, and it becomes possible to have the same NetBIOS name in use on two or more subnets.

When a WINS client is shut down in an orderly manner, it releases its name reservation in the WINS database, and the name is marked as *released*. After a certain time, a released name is marked as *extinct*. Extinct names are maintained for a period of time sufficient to propagate the information to all WINS servers, after which the extinct name is removed from the WINS database. The process of marking a name as *extinct* is referred to as *tombstoning*.

If a computer has released its name through an orderly shutdown, WINS knows that the name is available, and the client can immediately reobtain the name when it reenters the network. If the client has changed network addresses (by moving to a different network segment, for example), a released name can also be reassigned.

If a computer is not shut down in an orderly fashion, its name reservation remains active in the WINS database. When the computer attempts to reregister the name, the WINS server challenges the registration attempt. If the computer has changed IP addresses, the challenge fails, and the client is permitted to reregister the name with its new address. If no other computer is actively using the name, the client is also permitted to reregister the name.

All names in the WINS database bear a time stamp that indicates when the reservation will expire. If a client fails to reregister the name when the reservation expires, the name is released. WINS supports definition of static name assignments that do not expire.

The WINS Name Life Cycle

WINS accomplishes NetBIOS to IP address resolution through a four-step process:

- NetBIOS name registration
- NetBIOS name renewal
- NetBIOS name release
- NetBIOS name query and resolution

Each of these processes is examined in the following sections.

NetBIOS Name Registration

When a WINS client initializes, NetBIOS-over-TCP/IP (NBT, also known as NetBT) sends a *name registration query* (called a NAMEREGISTRATIONREQUEST) message directly to the primary WINS server for that client. The name registration query includes the source (WINS client) IP address, the destination (WINS server) IP address, and the NetBIOS name to be registered.

If the WINS server is available and the NetBIOS name is not already registered in the database, the server replies to the client with a *positive name registration response* message (also called a NAMEREGISTRATIONRESPONSE). This response includes the IP address of the WINS client and WINS server (in order to route the message to the WINS client); the NetBIOS name that has been registered; and the renewal interval, which is a Time-to-Live (TTL) duration for the NetBIOS name registration. After the renewal interval expires, the NetBIOS name is removed from the database unless the WINS client renews the registration and is given a new renewal interval.

If the WINS server is available and the database already contains a duplicate of the NetBIOS name that was requested to be registered by the WINS client, the WINS server sends a challenge to the currently registered owner of the NetBIOS name. The challenge is sent as a *name query request* (NAMEQUERYREQUEST) three times at intervals of 500 milliseconds. The purpose of the challenge is to see whether the original owner of the NetBIOS name is still using that NetBIOS name. For example, if a computer tries to register its computer name in a WINS server that already has that computer name registered, the WINS server sends a message to the original owner of the computer name to see whether that computer name is still in use on the network.

A multihomed computer in TCP/IP terminology has more than one network interface installed and bound to TCP/IP. If the registered owner of a NetBIOS name is a multihomed computer, the WINS server sends up to three challenges to each network interface on the multihomed computer, to ensure that the challenge message reaches the multihomed host.

If the current owner of a registered NetBIOS name responds to the name query challenge from the WINS server, the WINS server sends a *negative name query response* (NAMEQUERYRESPONSE) to the WINS client that is attempting to register the duplicate NetBIOS name. The offending WINS client is not allowed to register that name, and an error message is displayed or recorded at the offending WINS client.

If the WINS server does not respond to the first name registration request, the WINS client sends two more requests. It then sends up to three requests to the secondary WINS server, if one has been configured for the WINS client. If neither WINS server responds, the WINS client initiates a b-node broadcast to register its NetBIOS names on the local network. If a router on the network is configured to forward b-node broadcasts, then the registrations can be relayed to remote networks as well.

NOTE

LAN Manager 2.2 MS-DOS clients and Microsoft Network Client 3.0 WINS clients do not register NetBIOS names with a WINS server, although they can use the WINS server database for NetBIOS name resolution.

NetBIOS Name Renewal

To continue using a registered NetBIOS name, a WINS client must periodically renew its WINS name registrations in the WINS server database. If the client does not renew its registrations before the renewal interval (TTL) of the name registration expires, that NetBIOS-name-to-IP-address mapping is marked as *released* (no longer registered) in the WINS server database. The renewal interval is set on the WINS server in the **Intervals** tab of the **Properties** box in the WINS console. By default, the renewal interval established on Windows 2000 Server is six days.

TIP

The renewal interval represents a compromise between network traffic generated by WINS and timely updating of the WINS database. The default renewal interval is probably a good compromise value. You should always ensure that the renewal interval is the same for primary and backup WINS servers, so that the backup WINS server is not used until necessary.

When it has consumed one-half of its WINS refresh interval, the WINS client sends a *name refresh request* directly to its primary WINS server. The name refresh request contains the source (WINS client) and destination (WINS server) IP addresses and the NetBIOS name to be refreshed. If the WINS client gets no response, it tries again every ten minutes for a total of one hour. If the client is unable to refresh its name with its primary WINS server, it starts sending name refresh requests to the secondary WINS server (if one is configured), using the same procedure. Then the WINS client goes back to trying to register with the primary WINS server. If the WINS client is unable to refresh its name with its secondary WINS server, it again attempts to renew with its primary WINS server. If the client is still unable to refresh its name, it releases its name.

When a WINS server receives a name refresh request, it sends a *name refresh response* directly to the WINS client. The name refresh response contains the WINS client IP address, as the destination; the WINS server IP address, as the source; the NetBIOS name registered; and the new renewal interval, which by default is 144 hours on Windows 2000 Server.

NetBIOS Name Release

When a WINS client initiates a normal shutdown of the host, meaning that the operating system is shut down before rebooting, the WINS client sends one *name release request* directly to the WINS server for each of its registered NetBIOS names. The NetBIOS name release request contains the WINS client and WINS server IP addresses , as well as the NetBIOS name to be released in the WINS database.

When the WINS server receives a name release request, it consults the local WINS database to ensure that the name exists and is registered to the WINS client that sent the name release request. If the name requested to be released is found in the database and is mapped to the IP address of the client sending the name release request, the WINS server marks that database entry as *released*. The server then sends a *positive name release response* to the WINS client that sent the name release request. The positive name release response is directed to the WINS client IP address. It contains the released NetBIOS name and a renewal interval or TTL of zero.

If the NetBIOS name requested to be released was not registered in the WINS database, or was registered with a different IP address, the WINS server replies with a *negative name release response* to the WINS client that sent the name release request.

The WINS client treats a negative name release response the same as a positive name release response. After the WINS client receives either type of name release response from the WINS server, it no longer responds to name request registration challenges sent from the WINS server when another host wants to register the same NetBIOS name.

If the WINS client does not receive a name release response from the primary WINS server, it sends up to three b-node broadcasts of the name release request to the local network, and any remote networks attached by routers forwarding b-node broadcast. All b-node–enabled clients, including WINS clients, receiving the name release request then make sure that the NetBIOS name is removed from their local NetBIOS name cache.

NetBIOS Name Query and Resolution

When a host running NetBIOS-over-TCP/IP attempts to execute a command containing a NetBIOS name, that NetBIOS name must be resolved to an IP address. For example, if the command **net use p: \\SERVER01\PUBLIC** is executed, NBT must make a connection to the computer SERVER01 in order to map the drive p: to the PUBLIC share on SERVER01. To make this connection, NBT must know the IP address of the computer SERVER01. In other words, NBT must *resolve* the NetBIOS name to an IP address.

The process of NetBIOS name resolution involves checking the NetBIOS name mapping tables in various places until an entry is found that maps the NetBIOS name to an IP address. The NetBIOS-name-to-IP-address mappings can be found in some or all of the following places, depending on which of the following components are implemented on the internetwork:

- The local NetBIOS name cache, found in memory on the local or source host.
- A WINS server database.
- An LMHOSTS file.
- A HOSTS file.
- A Domain Name Service (DNS) database, which will also contain hostname-to-IP-address mappings and can be used if the client is configured to use DNS for NetBIOS name resolution.
- The host that owns the particular NetBIOS name can respond to a b-node broadcast name query if that host is on the same subnet as the source host or on a subnet connected by a b-node broadcast forwarding router.

Depending on the configuration of the NBT implementation, any number of the preceding methods of resolving NetBIOS names can be used in an order determined by the NetBIOS node type.

> **NOTE**
>
> If a host is configured to use WINS for NetBIOS name resolution, then, by default, the host uses the h-node (hybrid) NetBIOS name resolution order.

To verify which NetBIOS name resolution node type is being used by a host, enter
ipconfig /all from a command prompt. For example

```
C:\>ipconfig /all

Windows 2000 IP Configuration

        Host Name . . . . . . . . . . . . : W2KPROF-1
        Primary DNS Suffix  . . . . . . . : pseudo
        Node Type . . . . . . . . . . . . : Hybrid
        IP Routing Enabled. . . . . . . . : No
        WINS Proxy Enabled. . . . . . . . : No
        DNS Suffix Search List. . . . . . : pseudo

Ethernet adapter Local Area Connection:

        Connection-specific DNS Suffix  . : pseudo
        Description . . . . . . . . . . . : Intel 8255x-based PCI Ethernet
➥ Adapter (10/100)
        Physical Address. . . . . . . . . : 00-A0-C9-22-E8-D9
        DHCP Enabled. . . . . . . . . . . : No
        IP Address. . . . . . . . . . . . : 10.1.0.75
        Subnet Mask . . . . . . . . . . . : 255.255.0.0
        Default Gateway . . . . . . . . . : 10.1.0.1
        DHCP Class ID . . . . . . . . . . : DEPT01
        DNS Servers . . . . . . . . . . . : 10.1.0.3
                                            10.1.0.4
        Primary WINS Server . . . . . . . : 10.1.0.3
        Secondary WINS Server . . . . . . : 10.1.0.4
```

In the preceding sample output, the NetBIOS node type is configured to use Hybrid, or h-node
NetBIOS name resolution.

After the NetBIOS name has been resolved to an IP address, NBT adds the NetBIOS name
and IP address mappings to the local NetBIOS name cache and does not need to query by
using any of the other methods. The NetBIOS names are periodically cleared from the
NetBIOS name cache.

The NetBIOS name cache contains several names registered by the local host—including the
computer name, username, and domain name—plus any other names that have been recently
resolved and added to the NetBIOS name cache. To view the current contents of the NetBIOS
name cache, enter the command **nbtstat -c** from a command prompt. Sample output is
shown here:

```
C:\>nbtstat -c
```

```
Local Area Connection:
Node IpAddress: [10.1.0.75] Scope Id: []

              NetBIOS Remote Cache Name Table

        Name            Type      Host Address    Life [sec]
        ----------------------------------------------------
        DC1         <20>  UNIQUE      10.1.0.3        470
        DC2         <20>  UNIQUE      10.1.0.4        465
        PSEUDO      <1B>  UNIQUE      10.1.0.3        465
        DC1.PSEUDO  <20>  UNIQUE      10.1.0.3         22
```

When the NetBIOS node type is h-node, a NetBIOS name query is performed in the following order (see Figure 6.6):

1. The local name cache is consulted for a NetBIOS-name-to-IP-address mapping.

2. If no mapping is found, a *name query request* is sent directly to the configured primary WINS server. The name query request contains the NetBIOS name to be resolved as well as the source (WINS client) and destination (WINS server) IP addresses.

   If the primary WINS server does not respond to the name query request, the WINS client resends the request two more times to the primary WINS server. If the primary WINS server still does not respond, the WINS client then sends up to three name query requests to the secondary WINS server, if one is configured on the WINS client.

   If either WINS server resolves the name, a *name query response* is sent to the WINS client along with the requested NetBIOS-name-to-IP-address mapping. The name is added to the local cache, and name resolution is complete.

   If a WINS server receives the name query request but the name does not exist in the WINS database, the WINS server sends a *requested name does not exist response* to the WINS client that initiated the request.

NOTE

Windows 2000 client properties accept IP addresses for as many as twelve WINS servers. Windows 9.x, NT, and Windows for Workgroups clients accept two IP addresses for primary and secondary WINS servers.

---

3. If no WINS server can satisfy the name query request, or a WINS server returns the response that the requested name does not exist, the WINS client then sends three b-node broadcasts of the name request query to the local network, and to any networks attached by b-node broadcast–forwarding routers. If the required name is reported, the name and IP address are recorded in the local name cache and name resolution is complete.

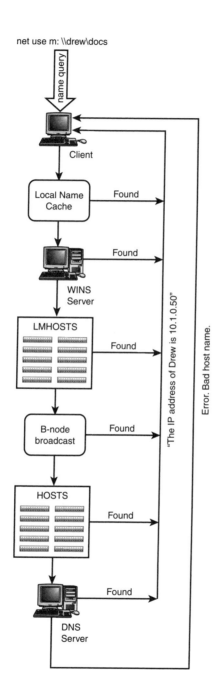

FIGURE 6.6

Resolving a NetBIOS name on an h-node client.

4. If b-node broadcasts do not succeed, the WINS client checks its local LMHOSTS file, if one is configured, and LMHOSTS lookup is enabled. If the required name is found, the name and IP address are recorded in the local name cache, and name resolution is complete.

5. Next, the computer consults its HOSTS file if one is configured.

6. In a final effort to resolve the name, the client queries a DNS server.

7. If no methods can resolve the name, an error is reported.

After the WINS client has received a mapping for the NetBIOS name, it adds the mapping to its local NetBIOS name cache. It can then use IP to route datagrams to the destination NetBIOS host.

If the requested NetBIOS name cannot be resolved to an address, NetBIOS cannot use TCP/IP to communicate with that host. If TCP/IP is the only protocol capable of reaching that host—for example, if the NWLink protocol is not being used—the requested NetBIOS command fails, and the host might report an error message such as "The network path was not found."

When Name Resolution Fails

Suppose that your WINS and DNS services are running, and your HOSTS and LMHOSTS files are in place. And yet you encounter a name that won't resolve or resolves incorrectly. Why? Here are some common culprits:

- **A name server is offline, and the name isn't in the appropriate static file.** Static files are useful backups to dynamic name servers. But are they worth the effort required to keep them current? It's up to you to decide. Most organizations are happy to chuck LMHOSTS files as soon as WINS goes active.

- **A name is misspelled.** HOSTS and LMHOSTS entries, as well as many DNS name entries, are made by people banging on keyboards. Typing errors are common causes of name resolution failures.

- **Duplicate entries.** If the host is described in two places, the entry that is retrieved is determined by the search order, which is different for NetBIOS and TCP/IP names.

- **The IP address has changed.** Static files are a nuisance to keep current, and obsolete entries are common.

To debug naming problems, you need to possess a thorough understanding of Microsoft's naming technologies. Then it's a matter of detective work and elbow grease. You need to get your hands dirty and dig into the service databases and the static files.

Implementing a WINS Service

That's enough theory. Now we can move on to the procedures for implementing WINS. We'll start by looking at some planning issues and move on to procedures for installing, configuring, and managing the WINS server.

Planning for WINS Installation

The chief question when planning for WINS is, how many WINS servers does the network require? According to Microsoft guidelines, a dedicated WINS server can support up to 10,000 computers.

However, WINS resolution increases network traffic, and you should consider distributing WINS servers throughout the network. Consider placing a WINS server on each network segment, or at least at every site, for example, to reduce the WINS traffic that must be routed, particularly through slow WAN links.

At a minimum, you should have two WINS servers, configured to mutually replicate their databases. This provides a measure of fault tolerance in case a WINS server fails. Be sure that your clients are configured with the IP addresses of each of the WINS servers on the network. The easiest way to do that is to configure the clients using DHCP.

When a WINS client is turned off, it releases its WINS registration. When the client restarts, it registers its name with the WINS server, receiving a new version ID. This reregistration results in entries in the WINS database that must be replicated with other WINS servers. Recall from earlier in the chapter that a given NetBIOS computer can be associated with multiple NetBIOS names, which are associated with the services running on the client. Each NetBIOS name that is registered with WINS increases the WINS replication traffic.

Roving WINS clients generate traffic in a different way. When a client moves to a different network and is restarted, it attempts to register its name with WINS. A registration already exists for that client on the old network. WINS must challenge the existing name registration before the name can be released for use by the client on the new network. This challenge is another source of increased traffic generated by WINS.

All of this is to say that you must be sensitive to WINS traffic demands when planning and monitoring your network. On small networks, WINS traffic will probably be trivial. As networks grow to many hosts, however, WINS traffic can become significant. Proper placement of WINS servers can reduce routed WINS traffic. Additionally, scheduling WINS replication for periods of low network demand can reduce WINS bandwidth requirements.

WINS servers that are separated by WAN links should be replicated infrequently whenever possible. Consider a WAN consisting of sites in New York and San Francisco. Typically, clients will be configured so that their primary services are provided by local servers, and WINS servers would be located at each site. Each site should have at least two WINS servers, which should be synchronized frequently, perhaps at 15-minute intervals. With proper planning, it should be sufficient to synchronize the WINS servers between New York and San Francisco at longer intervals, such as six to 12 hours. Remember, however, that with long replication intervals, the time required to converge the entire network on a change is extended as well. It might be necessary to force replication to take place when significant alterations take place.

Installing the WINS Server Service

Like nearly all Windows 2000 services, the WINS service is installed using the Add/Remove Programs applet in the Control Panel. Follow the procedures in Chapter 1, in the section "Adding and Removing Windows Components" to install the service.

Configuring a Statically Addressed WINS Client

Clients configured using static IP addresses are enabled as WINS clients by supplying one or more WINS server addresses for the client's TCP/IP configuration. Figure 6.7 shows the **WINS** tab for the advanced TCP/IP properties of a Windows 2000 computer.

To enable WINS client functionality, you must specify the IP address of at least one WINS server in the **WINS addresses, in order of use** box.

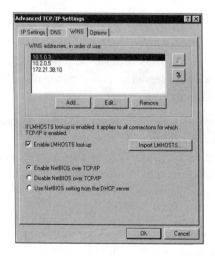

FIGURE 6.7
Configuring a TCP/IP host as a WINS client.

NetBIOS naming can be disabled on Windows 2000 computers. Radio buttons to enable and disable use of NetBIOS are found on the **WINS** tab of **Advanced TCP/IP Settings**.

> **NOTE**
>
> Microsoft highly recommends that WINS servers be configured with themselves as primary and secondary WINS servers.
>
> Microsoft highly recommends that WINS clients be configured with the IP addresses of all WINS servers operating on the network. Windows 2000 clients can be configured with the IP addresses of up to 12 WINS servers.

Renewing a Client Registration

You can force a client to renew its WINS reservation without restarting by entering the command `nbtstat -rr`. The `-rr` option is new with Windows 2000.

Configuring WINS Proxies

Windows 2000, NT, Windows 95, and Windows for Workgroups (WfW) computers can be configured as WINS proxies, enabling them to receive broadcast b-node name requests from non-WINS clients and to resolve them using directed h-node queries to WINS servers. WINS proxies enable b-node computers to obtain name resolutions from WINS.

For WfW computers, the WINS proxy feature is enabled in the **Advanced Microsoft TCP/IP Configuration** dialog box by checking the box labeled **Enable WINS Proxy Agent**.

For Windows 2000 and NT computers, you must edit the Registry. Create the value entry `EnableProxy`, and assign it a value of 1 (type `REG_DWORD`). Place this value entry under the following Registry key:

```
HKEY_LOCAL_MACHINE
  \SYSTEM
  \CurrentControlSet
  \Services
  \Netbt
  \Parameters
```

You might find it necessary to create the `Netbt` key.

Configuring DHCP Clients as WINS Clients

To enable DHCP clients to make use of WINS, the clients must be assigned the following two DHCP options:

- **044 WINS/NBNS Servers.** This option specifies the WINS servers that the computers will attempt to use. Because hosts in different scopes will probably access different scopes, this option should probably be assigned at the scope level.

- **046 WINS/NBT Node Type.** This option specifies the address resolution mode that the WINS client will employ. In the vast majority of cases, all hosts should be configured in h-node mode, and it might be appropriate to assign this as a global option that applies to all scopes on a DHCP server.

The procedures for defining DHCP options are described in Chapter 5, "Dynamic Host Configuration Protocol," under the heading "Managing DHCP Options."

> **NOTE**
>
> To force Windows 2000, NT, and Windows 3.1x DHCP clients to renew their current leases, enter the command `ipconfig /renew` at a command prompt on the client computer.
>
> To force Windows 95 to renew its DHCP lease, enter the command `winipcfg` at a command prompt and choose the **Renew** button in the dialog box.

Naming Versus Browsing

Users of Windows products in network environments become so familiar with browsing network resources that mistaking the Windows Browser for a name service becomes rather easy. Browsers, however, maintain databases only of hostnames. Addresses must still be derived from a name resolution process.

Browsing works somewhat differently on TCP/IP networks than on networks running NetBIOS and NWLink, although the difference becomes apparent only when routing is involved. Windows browsing is based on browse lists, which catalog all available domains and servers. When a user opens a **Connect Network Drive** dialog box (in Windows for Workgroups), a **Network Neighborhood** dialog box (Windows 95 and NT), or a **My Network Places** dialog box in Windows 2000, the information that appears has been retrieved from a browse list. (Windows 2000 clients can, of course, also retrieve computer information from Active Directory.)

Browse lists are maintained by browsers. By default, all Windows 2000 and NT Server computers are browsers. Windows 2000 Professional and NT Workstation computers are potential browsers, and can become browsers if required. Windows 95/98 and WfW computers also are potential browsers.

Each domain has one master browser that serves as the primary point for collecting the browse database for the domain. Servers (any computer that offers shared resources) that enter the network transmit server announcements to the master browser to announce their presence. The master browser uses these server announcements to maintain its browse list.

Backup browsers receive copies of the browse list from the master browser at periodic intervals. Backup browsers introduce redundancy to the browsing mechanism and distribute browsing queries across several computers. An election process among the various browsers determines the master browser. In domains, the election is biased in favor of making the primary domain controller (PDC) the master browser, which always is the master browser if it is operational.

All Windows 2000 Server and Windows NT Server computers function as master or backup browsers. Windows NT Workstation computers can function as browsers. In the presence of sufficient Windows 2000/NT Server computers, no Windows 2000 Professional or Windows NT Workstation computers will be configured as browsers. When no Windows 2000/NT Server computers are available, at least two Windows 2000 Professional or Windows NT Workstation computers will be activated as browsers. An additional browser will be activated for every 32 Windows 2000 Professional and Windows NT Workstation computers in the domain.

Servers must announce their presence to the master browser at periodic intervals, starting at 1-minute intervals and increasing to 12 minutes. If a server fails to announce itself for three announcement periods, it is removed from the browse list. Therefore, up to 36 minutes might be required before a failed server is removed from the browse list.

Domains are also maintained in the browse list. Every 15 minutes, a master browser broadcasts a message announcing its presence to master browsers in other domains. If a master browser is not heard from for three 15-minute periods, other master browsers remove the domain from their browse lists. Thus, 45 minutes might be required to remove information about another domain from a browse list.

Internetworks based on NetBIOS and NWLink protocols can route broadcast name queries across routers. Maintaining a single master browser for each domain, therefore, is sufficient.

Internetworks based on TCP/IP do not forward broadcast name queries between networks. Therefore, Microsoft TCP/IP networks maintain a master browser for each network or subnetwork. If a domain spans more than one network or subnetwork, a *domain master browser* running on the PDC has the special responsibility of collecting browse lists from the master browser on each network and subnetwork. (Even on an Active Directory network, one domain controller is designated as a PDC to support interaction with downlevel domain controllers.) The domain master browser periodically rebroadcasts the complete domain browse list to the master browsers, which in turn update backup browsers on their networks.

> **NOTE**
>
> To enable browsing on a TCP/IP internetwork, at least one Windows 2000/NT Server computer must be present on each network (or subnetwork, if subnetting is used). If WINS is not enabled for the network, each browser must be configured with an LMHOSTS file that contains entries for domain controllers on the internetwork.

The browsing service is a convenience but is not required to enable clients to access servers on the internetwork. Client processes still can use shared resources by connecting directly with the UNC (Universal Naming Convention) name of the resource. If host BLYTHE shares its CD-ROM drive with the share name cd-rom, you can specify the resource as \\blythe\cd-rom in the **Folder** box of a **Map Network Drive** dialog box (see Figure 6.8). In Windows 2000, this dialog box is produced when you choose the **Map Network Drive** command in the **Tools** menu of Windows Explorer.

FIGURE 6.8
Entering a UNC path to connect to a resource.

Alternatively, you can connect the resource using a net use command at a command prompt, for example

```
net use f: \\blythe\cd-rom
```

It is not necessary to browse BLYTHE to connect using the UNC name. It is, however, necessary to obtain the IP address for BLYTHE. On a TCP/IP internetwork, that makes WINS a near necessity. Browsing, on the other hand, is very convenient but is not essential.

> **NOTE**
>
> Multihomed hosts often present an ambiguous face to the network community. Different hosts can use different IP addresses to access services running on the host, with unpredictable results. One case in which this unpredictability seems to appear is browsing when the PDC for a domain is multihomed. Clients are not hard-wired with the addresses of browsers, and a multihomed master browser appears to confuse things, causing various clients to see different browse lists. More consistent results seem to be obtained when the PDC has a single IP address. In any case, the PDC cannot serve as a master browser for more than one network or subnetwork.

Managing WINS Servers

WINS functions are managed using the WINS console snap-in. The WINS console is used to monitor WINS servers, establish static address mappings, and manage database replication. A few WINS database management tasks, such as compacting the database, are initiated from the command line.

Adding WINS Servers to WINS Server Manager

Figure 6.9 shows the main window for the WINS console. In this case, the WINS console has been configured to manage two WINS servers. A single WINS console can be used to monitor all WINS servers on the internet. In Figure 6.9, I selected the **Server Status** icon, which configures the Details pane to display a status summary for each WINS server that is being managed.

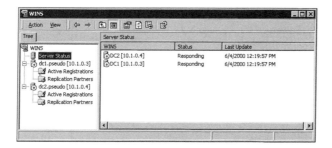

FIGURE 6.9
The WINS Server Manager main window.

If the WINS console is run on a computer running the WINS Server service, the computer is automatically listed in the **WINS** object tree. To add a WINS server to the list of managed servers:

1. Right-click the **WINS** icon in the object tree and choose **Add Server** from the context menu.

2. Enter the IP address of the new WINS server in the **Add Server** entry box and choose **OK**. The server is added to those in the object tree of the WINS console.

To remove a WINS server from the list, right-click the server and choose the Delete WINS Server command in the Server menu.

Monitoring WINS

You can monitor the status of a WINS server as follows:

- If the WINS console is able to communicate with the WINS server and the WINS server service is active, the WINS server's icon will be tagged with a green, upward-pointing arrow.

- If the WINS console is unable to communicate with the WINS server or the WINS server service is inactive on the computer being referenced, the WINS server's icon will be tagged with a red, downward-pointing arrow.

Select the **Server Status** icon to display summary information about the status of each WINS server being monitored by the WINS console. A sample server status display is shown in Figure 6.10.

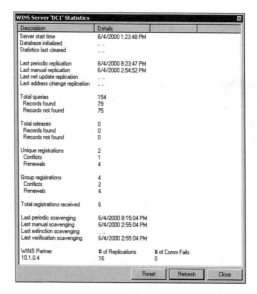

FIGURE 6.10

The WINS server status summary.

Detailed statistics for a specific WINS server can be displayed by right-clicking the WINS server's icon and selecting **Display Server Statistics** from the context menu. Figure 6.10 shows a sample **Server Statistics** window. Some of the statistics that appear are

- **Server start time.** The date and time when the WINS Server was started. This is the time the computer was started. Stopping and starting the WINS Server service does not reset this value.

- **Database initialized.** Static mappings can be imported from LMHOSTS files. This value indicates when static mappings were last imported.

- **Statistics last cleared.** The date and time when the server's statistics were cleared with the **Reset** button in the **Server Statistics** window.

- **Last periodic replication.** The last time the WINS database was updated by a scheduled replication.

- **Last manual replication.** The last time a WINS database replication was forced by an administrator.

- **Last net update replication.** The last time the WINS database was updated in response to a push request from another WINS server.

- **Total queries.** The number of name queries this WINS server has received from WINS clients. Statistics indicate the number of queries that succeeded (records were found) and failed (records were not found).

- **Total releases.** The number of messages indicating an orderly shutdown of a NetBIOS application. Statistics indicate the number of names the WINS server released successfully and the number that it failed to release.

- **Unique registrations.** The number of NetBIOS names that have been registered for individual computers.

- **Group registrations.** The number of names that have been registered for NetBIOS groups.

- **Total registrations received.** The number of registration messages received from clients.

- **Scavenging statistics.** Scavenging is the process of removing WINS registrations that have been released or have been transferred from other WINS servers that have removed the registrations from their own databases. Scavenging occurs automatically at scheduled intervals, but can also be initiated by an administrator. Scavenging intervals are determined by properties found on the **Intervals** tab of the WINS server **Properties** dialog box (see Figure 6.13). There are four statistics related to scavenging:

  - **Last periodic scavenging.** The last scheduled scavenging event that took place (defined by the **Renew interval** property.)

  - **Last manual scavenging.** The last scavenging that was initiated by an administrator.

- **Last extinction scavenging.** The last scavenging of tombstoned records, released records that have aged past the time specified by the **Extinction timeout** property.
- **Last verification scavenging.** The last scavenging based on the **Verify interval** property.

- **WINS Partner.** This item lists any WINS partners that have been established for this server and reports the numbers of successful and failed replications.

To refresh the statistics, click the **Refresh** button.

To clear the statistics, click the **Reset** button.

Setting WINS Console Properties

Right-click the **WINS** icon in the object tree and select **Properties** from the context menu to open the **WINS Properties** dialog box, shown in Figure 6.11. Options in this dialog box are as follows:

- **Display servers in the console by.** Select **Name** or **IP address** to determine the order in which WINS servers will be listed in the WINS console object tree.
- **Show DNS names for WINS servers.** Select this check box if you want WINS servers to be identified in the WINS console by their FQDNs. When this box is not checked, WINS servers are identified by their NetBIOS names.
- **Validate cache of WINS servers at startup.** The WINS console maintains a cache of all WINS servers that were added to its configuration the last time the console was saved. By default, this cache is not validated to verify whether remote WINS servers are online. If cache validation is enabled, additional time is required to start up the WINS console.

Configuring WINS Server Properties

A number of properties can be adjusted for each WINS server. These properties are configured by right-clicking a WINS server in the WINS console and choosing the **Properties** in the context menu.

WINS Server General Properties

Figure 6.12 shows the **General** tab of a WINS server **Properties** dialog box.

By default, statistics for a WINS server are refreshed every 10 minutes. To disable automatic updating of statistics, uncheck the **Automatically update statistics every** box. To adjust the statistics update interval, edit the **Hours**, **Minutes**, and **Seconds** fields. Updating statistics imposes a small processing load on the WINS server. You might want to increase the update interval on a busy WINS server.

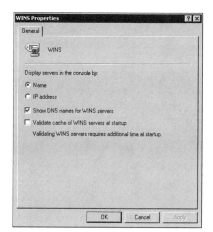

FIGURE 6.11
WINS console properties.

When clients have registered with WINS, the WINS database becomes a valuable asset, enabling clients to enter the network without imposing on NetBIOS names that are already in use. To reduce the likelihood of data loss, you can configure backup procedures for the database.

Specify a directory path in the **Default backup path** field. Automatic backup of the WINS database is enabled when a default backup path is specified. By default, backups are performed at three-hour intervals.

To force backup of the WINS database when the WINS service is stopped, check the **Back up database during server shutdown** box. Although this option is not enabled by default, it should be selected in most circumstances.

WINS Server Intervals Properties

Figure 6.13 shows the **Intervals** tab of a WINS server **Properties** dialog box. This tab is used to configure the following WINS events:

- **Renewal interval.** This option determines how frequently a client must reregister its name. By default, clients initiate attempts to reregister their names when 50% of the renewal interval is reached. A name not reregistered within the renewal interval is marked as released. Forcing clients to reregister frequently increases network traffic. The default value for this field is 6 days.

- **Extinction interval.** This option determines how long a released name will be retained in the database before it is marked extinct and is eligible to be purged. The default value for this field is 4 days.

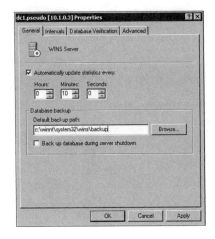

FIGURE 6.12
General properties for a WINS server.

- **Extinction timeout.** Specifies the interval between the time a record is marked extinct and the time when the record is actually purged from the database. The default value for this field is 6 days.

- **Verification interval.** Specifies how frequently the WINS server must verify the correctness of names that are owned by other WINS servers. The default value is 24 days.

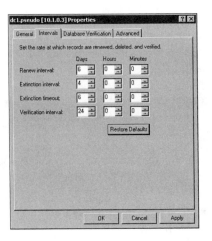

FIGURE 6.13
Intervals properties for a WINS server.

> **NOTE**
>
> Setting renewal and extinction intervals is a balancing act between the needs of your users, keeping the WINS database up-to-date, and generation of network traffic. If you force renewal and extinction to occur at frequent intervals, network traffic increases, and users can lose their name reservations if they are away from the office for a few days. On the other hand, if these intervals are too long, the database becomes cluttered with obsolete entries.

WINS Server Database Verification Properties

Figure 6.14 shows the **Database Verification** tab of a WINS server **Properties** dialog box. Database verification enables the WINS server to consult other WINS servers to determine whether its own database is consistent with other WINS databases. The following fields are used to enable and configure database verification:

- **Verify database consistency every *nn* hours.** If this box is checked, database consistency is checked at the specified interval.

- **Begin verifying at**. This setting determines the time of day at which database verification will be initiated. This enables you to schedule database verification for times when the WINS server and the network are less busy.

- **Maximum number of records verified each period.** If you are worried about the impact of database consistency checking on the network, you can limit the number of records that will be checked in a given replication period.

- **Verify against.** Records in the local database can be verified against the owner of the record (the WINS server that originally accepted the client's registration) or against randomly selected replication partners.

Database verification provides a useful check against errors in network communication or WINS operation. I recommend that you enable this feature only if problems are being encountered.

WINS Server Advanced Properties

Figure 6.15 shows the **Advanced** tab of a WINS server **Properties** dialog box. These properties determine a variety of WINS server operational characteristics:

- **Log detailed events to Windows event log.** Check this box to log details about WINS operations. Because detailed logging can be a drain on system resources, it should be enabled only when testing or troubleshooting WINS server operation.

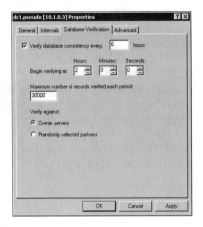

FIGURE 6.14
Database verification properties for a WINS server.

- **Enable burst handling.** Burst handling supports high volumes of client requests to WINS. With burst handling, the WINS server can respond positively to client requests before it has processed and entered updates in the database (starting with a 5-minute TTL for the first 100 requests, and adding 5 minutes to the TTL for each 100 additional requests). When **Enable burst handling** is checked, the radio buttons below specify the size of the queue that the WINS server will permit before burst handling is used to handle traffic. The size of the burst queue can be configured to **Low** (300 requests in the burst queue), **Medium** (500 requests), **High** (1000 requests), or **Custom** (the number of requests is specified by the administrator). By default, burst handling is enabled with a Medium burst queue size. Burst handling improves response time to clients in high-demand situations at the risk that clients might be allowed to function with an invalid registration.

- **Database path.** Specifies the path of the directory in which WINS stores its database.

- **Starting version ID (hexadecimal).** Specifies the beginning version ID (in hexadecimal) for the WINS server database. This value must be adjusted only if the WINS database is corrupted and must be restarted. In that case, set the value higher than the version number for this WINS server as it appears on all the server's replication partners, to force replication of records for this server. The maximum value of this parameter is $2^{31} - 1$. The highest version number for a server can be determined on the **Active Registrations** list.

- **Use computer names that are compatible with LAN Manager.** Check this option to force WINS to enforce NetBIOS naming rules compatible with LAN Manager (15 characters plus a 16th character to indicate a computer role). Some NetBIOS implementations use all 16 characters for computer names, but all Windows clients are compatible with LAN Manager name conventions. Do not disable this option unless non-Windows computers are identified using NetBIOS.

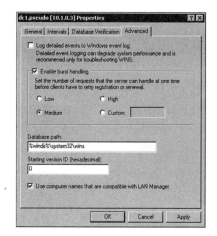

FIGURE 6.15
Advanced properties for a WINS server.

Configuring Static Mappings

Sometimes dynamic name-address mappings are undesirable. At such times, creating static mappings in the WINS database proves useful. A static mapping is a permanent mapping of a computer name to an IP address. Static mappings cannot be challenged and are removed only when they are explicitly deleted.

> **NOTE**
>
> Reserved IP addresses assigned to DHCP clients override any static mappings assigned by WINS.
>
> Microsoft highly recommends that you do not configure static mappings for WINS clients.

To add static mappings in a WINS console, use the following procedure:

1. Right-click the **Active Registrations** icon for the desired WINS server and choose **New Static Mapping** from the context menu to open the **New Static Mapping** dialog box, shown in Figure 6.16.

FIGURE 6.16
Adding static mappings.

2. Type the computer name in the **Computer name** box.

3. If NetBIOS scope names are deployed on the network, enter the name of the scope in the **NetBIOS scope (optional)** field.

> **NOTE**
>
> When a computer is assigned a NetBIOS scope, it will communicate only with computers that have the same scope. Scopes are seldom used and provide additional opportunities to make configuration errors. By default, all NetBIOS clients are configured with an empty scope name.
>
> Windows 2000 implements a "NetBIOS-less" transport for Server Message Block (SMB) traffic that directly hosts SMB traffic on the TCP protocol. Because this transport does not use NetBIOS, scope IDs (which are implemented at the NetBIOS level) do not apply to the transport. NetBIOS Scope IDs still limit traffic that travels over the NetBIOS-over-TCP/IP (NBT) transport.
>
> At the time of this writing, Microsoft is reporting that communication might be inconsistent between Windows 2000 computers using scopes. Until a fix is posted, you should avoid deploying scopes.

4. Choose one of the options in the **Type** box. (Group, internet group, and multihomed names are discussed further in the next section, "Special Names.") The following choices are available:

- **Unique.** The name will be unique in the WINS database and will have a single IP address.

- **Group.** Groups are targets of broadcast messages and are not associated with IP addresses. If the WINS server receives a query for the group, it returns FFFFFFFF, the IP broadcast address. The client then broadcasts on the local network.

- **Internet Group.** A group associated with the IP addresses of up to 24 Windows NT Servers, plus the address of the primary domain controller, for a total of 25.

- **Multihomed.** A name that can be associated with up to 25 addresses, corresponding to the IP addresses of a multihomed computer.

- **Domain Name.** A name associated with a domain. This type of WINS mapping is new to Windows 2000.

5. Enter IP addresses as required **IP Address** box. A single IP address is required for a unique or group static mapping. Multiple IP addresses are accepted for an internet group, domain name, or multihomed static mapping.

6. Click **OK**.

NOTE

You will seldom need to add group, internet group, domain, or multihomed static mappings, but there are several situations that might call for unique static mappings. Here are two examples:

- Your network includes non-Microsoft hosts, such as UNIX hosts, that do not announce NetBIOS names. You can advertise the names of these hosts in the NetBIOS namespace by adding a static mapping.

- You are configuring an IIS WWW server that will support multiple virtual sites. You can assign a NetBIOS name to each site by adding a static mapping to WINS, enabling NetBIOS clients to access these sites without relying on DNS for name resolution.

Static mappings for unique and special group names can be imported from files that conform to the format of LMHOSTS files, described earlier in this chapter. To import static mappings, follow this procedure:

1. Right-click the **Active Registrations** icon for the desired WINS server and select **Import LMHOSTS File** in the context menu.

2. Browse for the desired LMHOSTS file. Click **Open** when the file is selected to import static mappings from the file.

Special Names

WINS recognizes a variety of special names, identified by the value of the 16th byte of LAN Manager-compatible names. Special names are encountered when setting up static mappings and when examining entries in the WINS database. The special names recognized by WINS are discussed in the following sections.

Normal Group Names

Normal group names are tagged with the value 0x1E in the 16th byte. Browsers broadcast to this name and respond to it when electing a master browser. In response to queries to this name, WINS always returns the broadcast address FFFFFFFF.

Multihomed Names

A multihomed name is a single computer name that stores multiple IP addresses, which are associated with multiple network adapters on a multihomed computer. Each multihomed name can be associated with up to 25 IP addresses. This information is established when TCP/IP configuration is used to specify IP addresses for the computer.

When the WINS Server service is running on a multihomed computer, the WINS service is always associated with the first network adapter in the computer configuration. All WINS messages on the computer, therefore, originate from the same adapter.

CAUTION

Multihomed computers with connections to two or more networks should not be configured as WINS servers. If a client attempts a connection with a multihomed WINS server, the server might supply an IP address on the wrong network, causing the connection attempt to fail.

Internet Group Names

An internet group name is used to register Windows NT Server computers in internet groups, principally Windows NT Server domains. If the internet group is not configured statically, member computers are registered dynamically as they enter and leave the group. Internet group names are identified by the value 0x1C in the 16th byte of the NetBIOS name. An internet group can contain up to 25 members, preference being given to the nearest Windows NT Server computers. On a large internetwork, the internet group registers the 24 nearest Windows

2000/NT Server computers, plus the primary domain controller. Windows NT Server v3.1 computers are not registered to such a group dynamically, and must be added manually in WINS Manager. Manually adding computers to the group makes the group static—it no longer accepts dynamic updates.

Replicating the WINS Database

It is desirable to have two or more WINS servers on any network. A second server can be used to maintain a replica of the WINS database that can be used if the primary server fails. On large internetworks, multiple WINS servers result in less routed traffic and spread the name resolution workload across several computers.

Pairs of WINS servers can be configured as replication partners. WINS servers can perform two types of replication actions: *pushing* and *pulling*. And a member of a replication pair functions as either a *push partner* or a *pull partner*.

All database replication takes place by transferring data from a push partner to a pull partner. But a push partner cannot unilaterally push data. Data transfers can be initiated in two ways.

A pull partner can initiate replication by requesting replication from a push partner. All records in a WINS database are stamped with a version number. When a pull partner sends a pull request, it specifies the highest version number that is associated with data received from the push partner. The push partner then sends any new data in its database that has a higher version number than was specified in the pull request.

A push partner can initiate replication by notifying a pull partner that the push partner has data to send. The pull partner indicates its readiness to receive the data by sending a pull replication request that enables the push partner to push the data.

NOTE

Windows 2000 Server introduces the concept of a push/pull relationship between two WINS servers. When two WINS servers share a push/pull relationship, either WINS server can function as a pull or a push partner.

In summary:

- Replication cannot take place until a pull partner indicates it is ready to receive data. A pull request indicates a readiness to receive data as well as the data the pull partner is prepared to receive. Therefore, the pull partners really control the replication process.

- All data are transferred from a push partner to a pull partner. Data are pushed only in response to pull requests.

Pulls generally are scheduled events that occur at regular intervals. *Pushes* generally are triggered when the number of changes to be replicated exceeds a specified threshold. An administrator, however, can manually trigger both pushes and pulls.

Planning the Replication Topology

Microsoft highly recommends a hub-and-spoke replication topology for WINS. Figure 6.17 illustrates a simple replication topology involving five WINS servers. Notice that there are no loops in the topology, for example, WINS1-to-WINS2-to-WINS3-to-WINS1. Loops can cause inconsistencies in the various copies of the WINS database.

> **NOTE**
>
> Microsoft strongly recommends a hub-and-spoke WINS replication topology. Loops in the replication topology are specifically not recommended and can result in inconsistencies among the copies of the WINS database.

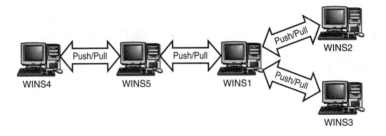

FIGURE 6.17
A simple WINS replication topology.

When multiple sites are involved, Microsoft recommends designating a single WINS server at each site to replicate to other sites. Figure 6.18 illustrates a network that incorporates three sites with several WINS servers at each site. In all cases, WINS servers are configured as push/pull replication partners.

Adding Replication Partners

To add a new replication partner for a WINS server:

1. In the WINS console, right-click the **Replication Partners** object under the desired WINS server and choose **New Replication Partner** from the context menu to open the **New Replication Partner** dialog box.

2. Enter the IP address of the replication partner in the **WINS server** field and click **OK**.

You must repeat this procedure on the replication partner even if the partners are in a push/pull relationship. Both partners must understand that they share a replication partner relationship.

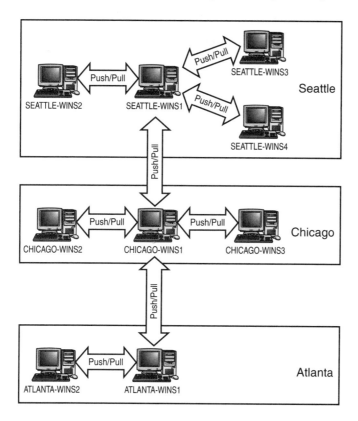

FIGURE 6.18
A multi-site WINS replication topology that maintains a hub-and-spoke architecture.

To view the replication partners for a WINS server, select the **Replication Partner** container under the desired server in the WINS console object tree. Replication partners are listed in the Details pane.

Configuring Replication Partners

After a replication partner has been established, the properties of the partnership can be configured. To configure a replication partnership, do the following:

1. Select the **Replication Partners** icon under the desired WINS server.

2. In the Details pane, right-click the partnership to be configured and select **Properties** from the context menu to open the **Properties** dialog box.

3. The **General** tab displays only information that is available in the Details pane, none of which can be edited. Select the **Advanced** tab to display the **Properties** page, as shown in Figure 6.19.

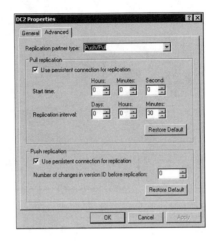

FIGURE 6.19

Configuring a replication partnership.

4. Select the desired replication relationship in the **Replication partner type** field. The fields that are available for modification depend upon the replication partner type that is selected.

   If the **Replication partner type** value is **Push**, fields within the **Push replication** box can be modified.

   If the **Replication partner type** value is **Pull**, fields within the **Pull replication** box can be modified.

   If the **Replication partner type** value is **Push/Pull**, all fields can be modified.

5. Pull replication is initiated when a pull partner sends a request to a push partner requesting that replication be started. Pull replication is initiated at prespecified time intervals. Configure pull replication with these **Pull replication** options:

   - **Use persistent connection for replication.** Check this box to enable WINS to establish a persistent connection between WINS partners. Persistent connections are new to Windows 2000. They improve replication efficiency and reduce CPU overload required to establish connections. Persistent connections are recommended when both WINS partners are running on Windows 2000 Server computers.

- **Start time.** Specify the time of day when pull replication can begin. By default, the value is 0 hours, 0 minutes, 0 seconds, and pull replication does not take place. *You must increase this time from 0:0:0 to enable pull replication to take place.*

- **Replication interval.** Specify the intervals at which the pull partner will request replication. By default the pull interval is 30 minutes.

6. Push replication is initiated when changes to the database of a push partner exceed a pre-defined threshold. A change is indicated by incrementing the version ID on the push partner. The push partner sends a replication trigger to its pull partner. Replication can commence when the pull partner sends a replication request to the push partner. Configure push replication with these **Push replication** options:

- **Use persistent connection for replication.** As with pull partners, persistent connections are recommended when both WINS partners are running on Windows 2000 Server computers.

- **Number of changes in version ID before replication.** Enter a value specifying the number of changes that must take place before the push partner attempts to initiate replication.

7. Click **OK** when the partnership is configured.

Replication Partners Properties

Right-click a **Replication Partners** icon and choose **Properties** from the context menu to open the **Replication Partners Properties** pages, shown in Figure 6.20. Some values on these properties pages establish default values that can be overridden for specific replication partners.

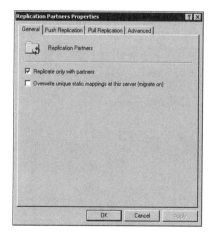

FIGURE 6.20

General replication partner properties.

Replication Partner General Properties

The **General** tab has two check boxes:

- **Replicate only with partners.** If this box is checked (the default), replication can take place only between explicitly configured replication partners. If the box is cleared, replication can be initiated between any two WINS servers.

- **Overwrite unique static mappings at the server (migrate on).** If this box is not checked (the default), static WINS database entries cannot be overwritten. If this box is checked, static WINS database entries can be overwritten during replication or record migration.

Replication Partner Push Replication Properties

The **Push Replication** tab (see Figure 6.21) has the following options:

- **Start push replication at service startup.** If this box is checked, a push replication trigger is sent when the WINS server starts up. By default, this option is not checked.

- **Start push replication when address changes.** If this box is checked, a push replication trigger is sent when the IP address of a WINS record is modified. By default, this option is not checked.

- **Number of changes in version ID before replication.** The version ID is incremented every time a WINS record is modified. This option specifies the number of changes that must take place before the WINS server sends a push trigger. By default, the value is 0, and no WINS push triggers are initiated by changes in version ID.

- **Use persistent connections for push replication partners.** If this box is checked (the default), persistent connections are used whenever communicating with a push partner.

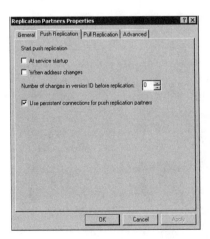

FIGURE 6.21

Push partner replication partner properties.

Replication Partner Pull Replication Properties

The **Pull Replication** tab (see Figure 6.22) has the following options:

- **Start time.** Establishes the default time of day when pull replication can be initiated with all partners. If the time is 0:0:0, no automatic pull replications take place.

- **Replication interval.** Establishes the default intervals at which pull replication events are initiated with all partners.

- **Number of retries.** Establishes the default retries that will be made when trying to initiate a pull replication event.

- **Start pull replication at service startup.** If this box is checked, a pull replication trigger is sent when the WINS server starts up. By default, this option is checked.

- **Use persistent connections for pull replication partners.** If this box is checked (the default), persistent connections are used whenever communicating with a pull partner.

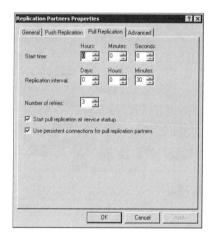

FIGURE 6.22
Pull partner replication partner properties.

Replication Partner Advanced Properties

The **Advanced** tab (see Figure 6.23) has the following options:

- **Block records for these owners.** Particularly when WINS partner automatic discovery is used, you might want to prevent partnerships from being established with specific WINS servers. Enter server to be blocked to this list.

- **Enable automatic partner configuration.** A new feature of Windows 2000 WINS is the capability for WINS servers to automatically discover their replication partners. When automatic partner configuration is enabled, WINS servers periodically send a multicast message to address 224.0.1.24, which is reserved for WINS. WINS servers with autodiscovery enabled listen for these announcements, learn about other WINS servers on the network, and automatically add these servers as push/pull partners. WINS server autodiscovery should be used only when you are sure there will be no unauthorized WINS servers on the network. Check this box (the default) to enable automatic partner detection. Remove the check to prevent automatic discovery. You might want to disable automatic discovery if you want to enforce a specific replication topology.

- **Multicast interval.** Specify the interval at which WINS servers multicast announcements to other WINS servers. The default interval is 40 minutes.

- **Multicast Time to Live (TTL).** Specifies the number of seconds that the WINS multicast messages are to be propagated on the network. Increase this value if the network is physically large, and multicast announcements are being discarded by routers.

FIGURE 6.23

Advanced replication partner properties.

NOTE

WINS partner automatic discovery must be enabled on all WINS servers that will participate in the process.

A multicast router infrastructure must be established to enable WINS multicasts to propagate through an internetwork. This feature is not enabled by default on Windows 2000 routers. See Chapter 7, "Routing with Routing and Remote Access Service," for information about multicast routing.

Manually Triggering Replication

After adding a WINS server, updating static mappings, or bringing a WINS server back online after shutting it down for a period of time, forcing the server to replicate its data with its replication partners might be advisable. WINS Manager enables administrators to manually trigger both push and pull replications.

There are three ways to initiate replication manually:

- Right-click the **Replication Partners** icon under the desired WINS server and select **Replicate Now** from the context menu. The request is queued, but it might be a few minutes before replication begins.

- Right-click a WINS server and select **Start Push Replication** to send a push notification to the server's pull partners.

- Right-click a WINS server and select **Start Pull Replication** to send a pull request to the server's push partners.

Maintaining the WINS Database

After it is configured, WINS generally requires little maintenance. Some tasks should be performed periodically, however, to improve the efficiency of WINS and to reduce the size of WINS database files. Additionally, when clients experience name resolution problems, you might need to view the contents of the WINS database to diagnose problems.

Figure 6.24 shows an Active Registrations Details pane listing a small WINS database. The listing can be sorted according to any of the column headers. For example, to sort the display according to IP address, click the header of the IP Address. Alternate clicks sort the list in ascending or descending order, as indicated by a pointer that appears in the column header.

As discussed in the section "Special Names," NetBIOS names fall into several categories, identified by byte 16 of a LAN Manager-compliant NetBIOS name. Each name in the **Mappings** box of the **Show Database** dialog box is tagged with the value assigned to byte 16 of its name, along with a description of the service type.

Finding WINS Database Records by NetBIOS Name

There are two ways to search for WINS database records, either by NetBIOS name or by record owner.

Finding them by name is the best way to locate the WINS database records for a particular computer. To search by NetBIOS name, do the following:

1. Right-click the **Active Registrations** icon for a WINS server and select **Find by Name** in the context menu to open the **Find by Name** dialog box, shown in Figure 6.25.

2. In the **Find names beginning with** field, enter the initial characters of the names to be displayed. Enter up to 15 characters.

3. Check **Match case** to require an exact match for characters and case.

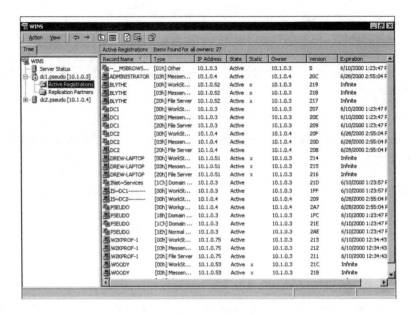

FIGURE 6.24
The database of a WINS server.

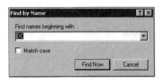

FIGURE 6.25
Searching for WINS records by NetBIOS name.

Finding WINS Database Records by Owner

Every WINS database record has an owner, which is the WINS server where the registration was originally recorded. Finding records by owner is a good way to conduct broad or targeted searches.

To find by owner, do the following:

1. Right-click the **Active Registrations** icon for a WINS server and select **Find by Owner** in the context menu to open the **Find by Owner** dialog box, shown in Figure 6.26.

2. Select **All owners** to display all records in the database, regardless of ownership.

   or

   Select **This owner** and specify a WINS server to display only records owned by a particular server.

3. Select the **Record Types** tab if you want to find only certain types of records. As Figure 6.27 illustrates, you can select which types of NetBIOS records will be included in the search. (You can add your own record types to the list or edit existing record types.)

4. Click **Find Now** to initiate the search.

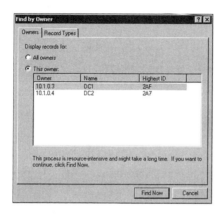

FIGURE 6.26

Searching for WINS records by owner.

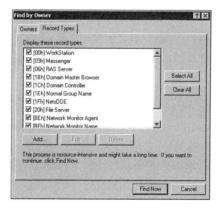

FIGURE 6.27

When searching by owner, you can specify which types of WINS records are to be displayed.

Backing Up the Database

WINS performs a complete backup of its database every 24 hours. The procedure for defining the directory in which backup files are stored is discussed in the section, "WINS Server General Properties," earlier in this chapter. On occasion, you might want to execute an unscheduled backup. The procedure, which must be performed on the computer running the WINS Server service, is as follows:

1. Right-click the icon of the WINS server to be backed up.

2. Choose **Back Up Database** from the context menu.

3. Specify the path for the backup directory.

Restoring the WINS Database

If users cannot connect to a server running the WINS Server service, the WINS database probably has become corrupted. In that case, you might need to restore the database from a backup copy. This can be done using menu commands or manually. The procedure must be performed on the computer running the WINS service.

To restore the WINS database using menu commands, perform the following procedure on the computer that is running the WINS server to be restored:

1. Stop the WINS Service using one of these methods:

    • Stop the Windows Internet Server Service using the Services console in Administrative Tools.

    • Open a command prompt and enter the command **net stop wins**.

2. Start the WINS Console. Ignore the warning message Cannot find WINS Server.

3. Right-click the icon of the WINS server to be backed up.

4. Choose **Restore Database** from the context menu. (This option is available only when the WINS service is stopped.)

5. Specify the path for the backup directory.

6. After the database is restored, the WINS service is restarted.

Scavenging the Database

The key WINS database files are stored by default in the directory \%SystemRoot%\system32\wins (typically C:\winnt\system32\wins). If your system files are stored in a different directory, substitute the appropriate directory path. The files are as follows:

    • **WINS.MDB.** The WINS database file

    • **WINSTMP.MDB.** Used by WINS to store temporary working data

    • **J50.LOG.** Records transactions performed on the database

CAUTION

Never remove or modify the WINS files.

Over time, the WINS database becomes cluttered with released and old entries from other WINS servers. Scavenging the WINS database clears these old records. WINS database scavenging first occurs after the server is started when 50% of the renewal interval has expired. The renewal interval is defined on the **Intervals** tab of the WINS servers **Properties** dialog box. Scavenging recurs at intervals of 50% of the renewal interval or can be initiated manually.

To scavenge the database, right-click the WINS server in the WINS console object tree and choose **Scavenge Database** in the context menu.

Compacting the Database

When records are deleted from the WINS database, gaps are left in the database file structure that must be removed by compacting the database. Compacting takes place automatically during periods when the WINS server is experiencing low demand, but Microsoft recommends manually compacting the database offline from time to time.

The WINS database is stored in the file named WINS.MDB, which is stored by default in the directory \%*SystemRoot*%\System32\Wins. To compact the WINS database, do the following:

1. Open a command prompt.
2. Enter the command **net stop wins** to stop the WINS Server service on the computer. Users cannot resolve names on this server while the WINS Server service is stopped.
3. Change to the WINS directory. If the directory is in the default location, enter the command **cd \winnt\system32\wins**.
4. Enter the command **jetpack wins.mdb temp.mdb** to compact the database. wins.mdb is the file to be compacted, whereas temp.mdb is a name for a temporary file that jetpack uses during the compacting process.
5. After receiving the message jetpack completed successfully, restart WINS using the command net start wins.

CAUTION

jetpack should be used to compact the WINS.MDB file only. Do not compact the SYSTEM.MDB file.

Checking WINS Database Consistency

It is recommended that you periodically check the WINS database for consistency, a process that maintains database consistency among WINS servers running on large networks. When you initiate a consistency check on a WINS server, all records are pulled from the record owners, including WINS servers that are indirect replication partners. The pulled records are compared to local records. If the records are identical, the local time stamp is updated. If the version ID of the local record is lower than the version ID of the pulled record, the local database is updated.

Consistency checking can be performed automatically at periodic intervals. Configuration of automatic consistency checking is discussed in the section "WINS Server Database Verification Properties" earlier in this chapter.

To manually initiate consistency checking for a WINS server, right-click the desired WINS server and select **Verify Database Consistency** in the context menu. Verify the results by consulting the System Log in the Event Viewer.

Managing Manual Tombstoning

Tombstoning is the process of marking a WINS record so that it will be removed by the next scavenging process. With earlier versions of the WINS service, records were not deleted simultaneously on multiple servers. Consequently, for a certain period of time, replication could take place between servers that had inconsistent records, making it possible for records to be restored to a WINS server from which they were just deleted.

Manual tombstoning eliminates this problem because the length of the tombstoned state is longer than the propagation delay encountered when replication takes place. When the time limit is reached, tombstoned records are removed through the scavenging process.

When a tombstoned record is replicated, the tombstoned status is replicated with it. Therefore, all WINS servers are informed of the status of the record, enabling all WINS servers to scavenge the records.

To manually tombstone a WINS record, select a record in a WINS database (see Figure 6.24) and press the Delete key to open the **Delete Record** dialog box, shown in Figure 6.28. This dialog box has two radio buttons:

- **Delete the record only from this server.** If you choose this option, the record is not marked for deletion on other servers that receive the record by replication.
- **Replicate deletion of the record to other servers (tombstone).** If you select this option, the record is tombstoned, and its tombstoned status is replicated to all the WINS server's partners.

FIGURE 6.28
Deleting a WINS record.

Managing Remote WINS Servers Through Firewalls

You can manage remote WINS servers by adding the WINS server to WINS Manager using the **Add WINS Server** command in the **Server** menu. When managing a WINS server through the Internet, you might encounter difficulty because firewalls or routers might block ports that are required.

WINS Administrator uses "dynamic endpoints" in remote procedure call (RPC) communication. When opening a remote WINS session, an initial session is set up on port 135. Then a second session is set up on a randomly selected port with a higher number than 1024. Because the second port is not consistent, it is difficult to configure a firewall to pass traffic for the required port.

To enable remote administration of WINS to take place through a firewall, you must supply WINS with a list of all ports that are supported by the firewall. This is done by configuring the Registry.

The required parameters are stored in the following Registry key:

```
HKEY_LOCAL_MACHINE
  \Software
  \Microsoft
  \Rpc
  \Internet
```

The following Registry value entries contain RPC configuration parameters:

Ports

Data Type:	REG_MULTI_SZ
Range:	Valid port ranges (0–65535 inclusive)

Specifies a set of IP port ranges describing either all ports that are available from the Internet or all ports that are not available. Each string represents a single port or a range of ports (for example, `"1030-1055" "1068"`). If any ports are outside the range 0–65535, or if any errors are encountered, the RPC runtime ignores the entire value entry.

`PortsInternetAvailable`

> Data Type: REG_SZ
>
> Range: Y or N (not case-sensitive)

If Y, the ports specified in the Ports value entry are Internet-available ports. If N, the ports specified in the `Ports` value entry are not Internet-available ports.

`UseInternetPorts`

> Data Type: REG_SZ
>
> Range: Y or N (not case-sensitive)

Specifies the default policy. If Y, the processes using the default will be assigned ports from the ports defined in the `Ports` and `PortsInternetAvailable` value entries. If N, processes using the default will be assigned ports from the set of intranet-only ports.

What's in a Name?

From the users' perspectives, quite a lot. If naming support goes down, network services are inaccessible for all practical purposes. Consequently, if you are supporting non-Windows 2000 computers on your network, you need to ensure that NetBIOS naming is supported.

This chapter explored two methods of providing friendly names for computers on Microsoft TCP/IP networks. Although LMHOSTS can do the job, static LMHOSTS files have the disadvantage of being difficult to manage on large networks. After it is set up, however, WINS, has the virtue of being dynamic. Names are registered automatically, and the database is updated without hands-on intervention. Yes, WINS demands some knowledge on the administrator's part, and a bit of effort to keep things working smoothly, but WINS remains easier to manage than LMHOSTS on a large network.

It's time now to start looking at ways to grow the network. We've alluded to routers in practically every chapter, and it's time to see how routing is configured on Windows 2000 Servers. Chapter 7, "Routing with Routing and Remote-Access Service," takes a close look at routing with the Windows 2000 Routing and Remote Access Service.

Routing with Routing and Remote Access Service

IN THIS CHAPTER

Chapter 2, "TCP/IP Protocol Concepts," pays considerable attention to routing, and by now, you should have a good grasp of basic routing concepts, including how IP delivers datagrams through an internetwork. You have yet to learn how Windows 2000 Server computers can be configured as routers and how to configure a large, routed network. This chapter examines configuration of Windows 2000 routers in simple and complex internetworks.

The Routing and Remote Access Service (RRAS) is responsible for packet routing and for switched network connectivity in both dial-out and dial-in modes. Windows 2000 RRAS is a very complex component, enhancing its Windows NT predecessor in several ways.

RRAS is actually the hub of a variety of capabilities, including dial-up connectivity and virtual-private networks (VPNs), which enable you to establish secure communication channels through public networks such as the Internet. We'll take up those topics in the two chapters that follow this one.

> **NOTE**
>
> I mentioned this bit of terminology in Chapter 2, but let me emphasize that the term *gateway* was originally used to describe a device that functioned as a TCP/IP router. The term *router* is now more widely applied (with *gateway* reserved as a term for devices that forward traffic for protocols above the Internet protocol layer), but gateway crops up quite often, for example, in the **Default gateway** field of a network connection **TCP/IP Properties** dialog box. I will attempt to be consistent and to use the terms router and default router unless I am referring to a data entry field that explicitly uses the term gateway.

Rules of Routing

Before you examine the procedures for configuring routers, take a moment to review the basic rules of routing:

- When two hosts have the same netids (as determined by their IP addresses and subnet masks) and are connected to the same cable segment, the hosts can communicate by sending packets directly between themselves.
- When two hosts have different netids, they must communicate through a router, even if the hosts are connected to the same cable segment.
- When two hosts have the same netids and are connected to different network segments, the hosts cannot communicate.

Let's look at routing in some detail, starting with the simple case of routing packets between hosts that are separated by a single router.

Routing with Two Networks

Figure 7.1 illustrates a basic internet with two networks: 10.1.0.0/16 and 10.2.0.0/16. The common element that connects the two networks is Windows 2000 Server host A, which is equipped with a network adapter on each of the two networks. Recall from Chapter 2 that a host that connects to two or more networks is called a *multihomed* host. To turn a multihomed Windows 2000/NT Server computer into an IP router, the IP Routing feature must be turned on.

> **NOTE**
>
> All examples in this chapter assume a network mask of 255.255.0.0.

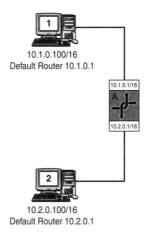

FIGURE 7.1
Routing between adjacent networks.

After routing is activated on a multihomed Windows 2000 or NT computer, the computer forwards IP datagrams from one of its connected networks to another connected network. (Because TCP/IP routing takes place at the Internet protocol layer, we are dealing with IP protocol data units. Hence, we use the term *datagram* rather than *packet* in this discussion.) Here is an example of what happens:

1. Host 1 needs to send a datagram to host 2, which is not on the local network. Host 1 does not know how to reach 2, and therefore sends the packet to its default gateway, 10.1.0.1.

2. Router A receives the packet on interface 10.1.0.1. The packet is identified by the physical address of A, but the destination IP address is 10.2.0.2. Router A knows that it is not the ultimate destination and proceeds to forward the datagram.

3. Router A consults its routing table and determines that it has a route to network 10.2.0.0. (This route is automatically added to the computer's routing table because the computer has a route on that network.)

4. Router A resends the datagram from its interface 10.2.0.1. The packet is addressed with the physical address and the IP address of host 2.

5. Host 2 receives the packet and recovers the datagram.

Two things must be done to enable this simple routing system to work:

• A router (A in the example) must be installed between the networks, configured with network adapters on each network, and have its routing function enabled.

• Other hosts must be configured with a default gateway.

Those tasks are performed in the following sections.

Enabling Routing Support on a Windows 2000 Router

A *router* is a multihomed host that has its routing function turned on. Three steps are involved in setting up a Windows 2000 Router:

1. Install a second network adapter and configure it for the desired protocols.

2. Activate routing.

3. Test the routing configuration.

Installation and configuration of network adapters is covered in Chapter 1, "Installation Planning and Execution." After the adapter hardware and drivers are installed, configure protocol support as required. For TCP/IP, you must configure each interface with a suitable IP address and subnet mask. For IPX, you must configure each adapter with the network number for the attached network. After that is done, you can enable routing and test the system.

CAUTION

A multihomed TCP/IP host should be configured with only one default router, which should be defined on the interface connected to the network to which the default router is attached.

Although it is possible to define a default router on each interface, leave the **Default Gateway** field on other interfaces blank. Inconsistent communication can result when default gateways are defined on interfaces that do not communicate with the network on which the router resides, even if all interfaces are configured with the same default gateway IP address.

It's difficult to troubleshoot Windows systems that have default routers defined on more than one interface because only one default router appears in the routing table (discussed later). If you run the command `ipconfig /all` in a command prompt window, it's easy to spot all the default router addresses.

Enabling Routing

Unlike most other Windows 2000 services, the Routing and Remote Access Service is installed on every Windows 2000 Server. There is no need to visit the Add/Remove Programs applet to add the service to the server's configuration.

Unlike in Windows NT, however, routing is not enabled by default on multihomed servers. NT supported simple routing based on static routing tables that was available without setting up RRAS (which did not ship with the product and became available with Windows NT 4.0 Service Pack 4). However, Windows 2000 Server manages all routing using RRAS, and RRAS must be configured before any routing can take place. The procedure for enabling IP routing on a multihomed server is as follows:

1. Install any protocols that will be supported by the router. Protocols are installed using the **Properties** dialog box for interfaces defined in **Network and Dial-up Connections**. See Chapter 1 for more information. Make sure that the protocols are enabled on all interfaces that will be providing routing support. (Remember that NetBEUI is not routable, so it isn't covered by this discussion.)

2. Open **Routing and Remote Access** in the **Administrative Tools** program group. (An RRAS console is shown in Figure 7.2. In the figure, routing has been enabled, and several of the objects have been expanded to illustrate the object hierarchy.)

3. Right-click the local server in the object tree of the MMC console and select **Configure and Enable Routing and Remote Access** to start the **RRAS Server Wizard**.

4. Skip the wizard's introductory screen to open the **Common Configurations** dialog box, shown in Figure 7.3. You can configure any feature of RRAS at any time, but the options in this dialog box enable you to easily select the most appropriate standard configuration. If you select **Manually configured server**, no initial configuration is established.

5. The next dialog box is **Routed Protocols**, shown in Figure 7.4. Initially, the list includes protocols that are already configured on the machine.

   If you select **No, I need to add protocols**, you will see a warning message informing you that protocols must be added using **Network and Dial-up Connections** before they can be configured in RRAS. You must stop the wizard, configure the desired protocols, and begin again at Step 3.

7

ROUTING WITH
RRAS

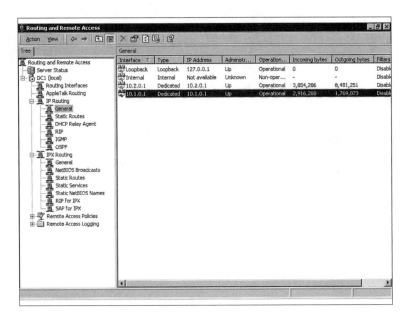

FIGURE 7.2

The RRAS console.

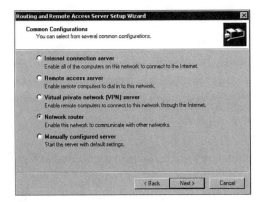

FIGURE 7.3

Selecting a starting RRAS configuration.

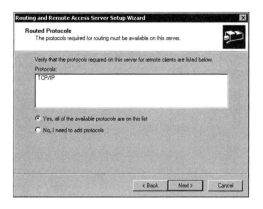

FIGURE 7.4
Protocols to be installed in RRAS.

7

6. The next dialog box is **Demand-Dial Connections**. Select **Yes** if you want to configure RRAS to establish demand-dial connections to remote networks. Select **No** if you do not want to configure demand-dial connectivity at this time. Demand-dial connections are discussed in Chapter 8.

7. Complete the wizard to configure RRAS.

NOTE

If you want to reconfigure RRAS using the wizard, first disable RRAS using the **Disable Routing and Remote Access** option in the context menu for the server. Then use **Configure and Enable Routing and Remote Access** again to configure RRAS as desired.

Testing the IP Routing Configuration

After routing is enabled, IP routing can be tested using the ping utility. When pinging through routers, the -r parameter can be handy. This parameter configures ping to report the route through which the test packets are directed. Figure 7.5 shows an example in which host 1 in Figure 7.1 pings host 2 (10.2.0.100) with the -r option. Notice that ping -r reports a route via router interfaces 10.2.0.1 (the forwarding interface when the request is outbound to 10.2.0.100) and 10.1.0.1 (the forwarding interface when the reply is returned to 10.1.0.100).

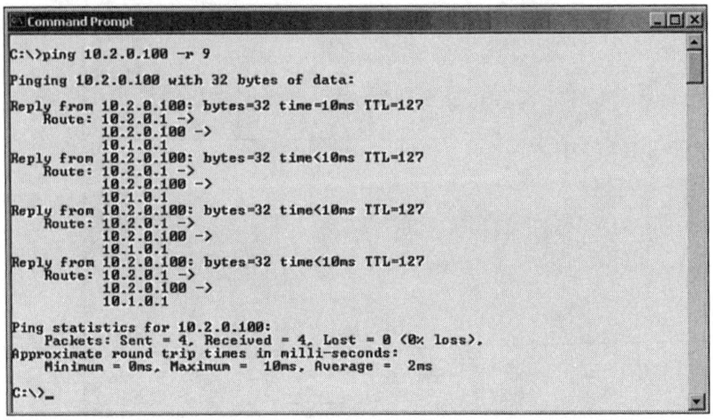

FIGURE 7.5

Pinging through a router using the -r parameter.

> **NOTE**
>
> As shown in Figure 7.5, the ping -r option requires an integer parameter in the range of 1 through 9, which specifies the maximum number of hops that will be allowed when attempting to reach the destination.

Configuring IP Unicast Routing

IP unicast routing is responsible for routing unicast datagrams through internetworks. Broadcast datagrams are not routed, and multicast datagrams are routed using a multicast router function.

Unicast routing is dependent on default routers and on static and dynamic routes that are recorded in a routing table. Let's see how far we can push routing using only default routers. Then we'll see how network routing can be enhanced using static routes and dynamic routes that are supplied with routing protocols.

Configuring Default Gateways on Internets with Three Networks

Figure 7.6 illustrates an internet that consists of three networks connected by two gateways. On this network, all required routing can be performed using default gateways. Arrows on the figure illustrate the paths that are followed when datagrams are routed from host 1 to host 2 and from host 1 to host 3.

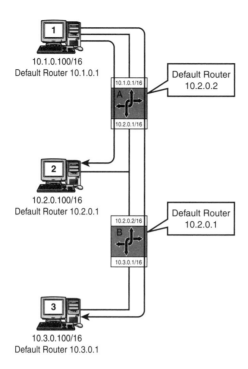

FIGURE 7.6
Routing can be performed on this network using only default routers.

Consider the behavior of router A when it receives a datagram to be delivered from host 1 to host 2. Router A has direct knowledge of network 10.2.0.0, on which host 2 resides, and uses that knowledge to address the datagram to host 2 and route it to network 10.2.0.0.

Now consider what happens when host 1 needs to send a datagram to host 3. Router A examines the destination IP address and determines that 10.3.0.100 does not reside on either of the subnets to which A is connected. Therefore, A uses its default router and routes the datagram to 10.2.0.2 on router B. Router B can deliver the datagram to network 10.3.0.0.

A mirror of this process occurs when 3 sends a datagram to 1. Host 3 sends the datagram to its default router, 10.3.0.1 on B. B sends the datagram to its default router, 10.2.0.1 on A, and A can deliver the datagram because it is connected to the destination network.

Finally, the case of routing datagrams from host 2 must be examined. When 2 sends a datagram to 1, 2 sends the datagram to its default router A, and A can deliver the datagram.

The route from 2 to 3 is a bit more indirect (see Figure 7.7). Host 2 sends to its default router A. A is not aware of the network 10.3.0.0 and sends the datagram to its default router B, from which the datagram can be delivered. Therefore, even though network 10.2.0.0 is separated from network 10.3.0.0 by only one router, routing from 2 to 3 requires an extra hop.

7

ROUTING WITH
RRAS

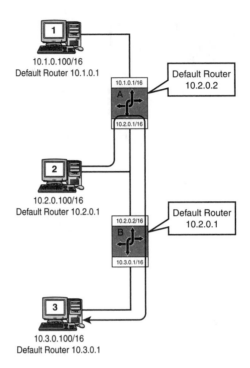

FIGURE 7.7

Routing from host 2 to host 3 on a three-network internet.

NOTE

The route taken from 2 to 3 in Figure 7.7 is clearly not the most efficient route possible, but it is the best you can do if host 2 routes by its default route only. Later in this chapter, you will learn how to add static routes to a host's routing table. Clearly, efficiency could be improved if you added a static route to host 2's routing table, instructing it to route datagrams destined for network 10.3.0.0 through 10.2.0.2. The question is, should you use static routes in this case?

The question is one of administrative versus routing efficiency. In all likelihood, 10.2.0.100 is but one of several dozen hosts on network 10.2.0.0. You could easily add a static route to each host on the network during initial configuration, enabling the hosts to route directly to 10.3.0.0. But suppose the route changes? You would be required to visit each host to reconfigure its routing table. On networks that change with any regularity, the administrative burden would soon become overwhelming. In such cases, the default gateway is a simple mechanism that reduces administrative complexity. Only the routers must be reconfigured when a change is made in the network topology.

Configuring Default Gateways on Internets with More Than Three Networks

Can default gateways be used to route datagrams to internetworks that include more than three networks? To see, it is necessary to examine an internetwork such as the one illustrated in Figure 7.8.

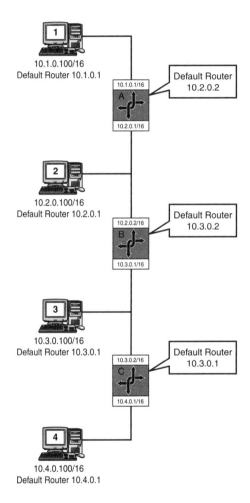

7

ROUTING WITH
RRAS

FIGURE 7.8

Routing on an internetwork with four networks.

As Figure 7.8 illustrates, routing datagrams to network 10.4.0.0 can be performed using default routers. If you trace the routes, you will find that the following situations all are covered:

- 1 can route to 2, 3, and 4.
- 2 can route to 1, 3, and 4.
- 3 can route to 2 and 4.

The sting in the tail of this diagram is apparent when 3 attempts to route a datagram to 1. Here is the sequence, which is illustrated in Figure 7.9:

1. Host 3 sends the datagram to its default router, 10.3.0.1.
2. Router B has no direct knowledge of network 10.1.0.0. Router B therefore routes the datagram to B's default router, 10.3.0.2.
3. Router C has no direct knowledge of network 10.1.0.0. Router C therefore routes the datagram to C's default router, 10.3.0.1. The datagram has now arrived back at router B.
4. B routes the datagram to its default router, C.
5. C routes the datagram to its default router, B.

The datagram cannot be delivered to network 10.1.0.0 because it never reaches a router that is aware of the destination network. A loop has developed between B and C that could continue indefinitely. To resolve this problem, we need to intervene manually by defining a static route.

> **NOTE**
>
> Loops are the reason for including the Time To Live parameter in the IP header. Time To Live is decremented by some amount each time it passes through a router. For any datagram not delivered, Time To Live eventually reaches 0, and the datagram is removed from the network.

Building Static Routing Tables

The default router mechanism is extremely limited. Although hosts can be configured with default routers, backup default routers are used only when the primary default router is unavailable. In other words, any given host is limited to a single default route at any given time, which is why the network shown in Figure 7.9 occasionally fails to deliver datagrams properly.

To solve problems such as the one shown in Figure 7.9, you need to improve the knowledge that hosts and routers possess of possible routes to remote networks. You can do so by adding static routing entries to the computer's routing tables.

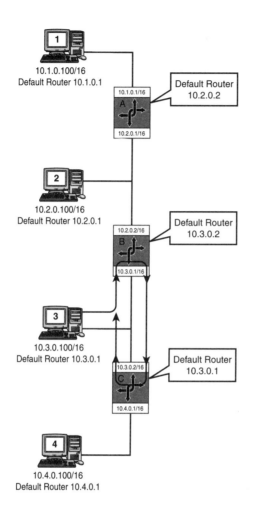

FIGURE 7.9

A routing loop.

The problem in Figure 7.9 is that router B is unaware of the existence of network 10.1.0.0. To eliminate the problem, B's routing table is updated with a path to network 10.1.0.0.

Figure 7.10 shows the same network, but this time router B has been configured with a static routing table entry that supplements the default gateway specifications. The routing table describes the next hop on the route to network 10.1.0.0 on the internet.

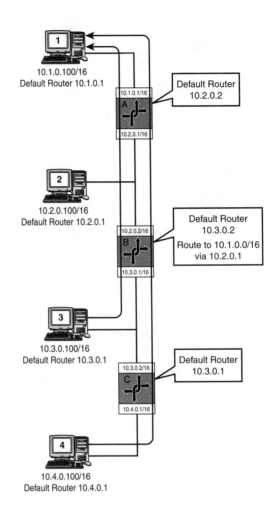

FIGURE 7.10

To implement routing on this network, a static route must be defined in router B.

Returning to the problem of routing a datagram from host 3 to host 1, now the sequence of events is as follows:

1. Host 3 sends the datagram to its default router, 10.3.0.1.

2. Router B has an entry in its routing table for network 10.1.0.0. Any datagram directed to 10.1.0.0 will be routed to 10.2.0.1 on router A.

3. Router A is attached to the destination network and can deliver the packet.

Figure 7.10 illustrates the routes from hosts 3 and 4 to host 1, showing how the routing table entry in router B also enables host 4 to reach any network.

Viewing and Interpreting Routing Tables

Figure 7.11 shows a router table for router B in Figure 7.10. The table includes information about default routers and routing to adjacent networks. To view the IP routing table for a router, do the following:

1. In the RRAS console, expand entries under the router being managed. Then expand the **IP Routing** header.

2. Right-click **Static Routes** and choose **Show IP Routing Table** from the context menu.

DC2 - IP Routing Table						
Destination	Network mask	Gateway	Interface	Metric	Protocol	
0.0.0.0	0.0.0.0	10.3.0.2	10.3.0.1	1	Network ma...	
10.2.0.0	255.255.0.0	10.2.0.2	10.2.0.2	1	Local	
10.2.0.2	255.255.255.255	127.0.0.1	Loopback	1	Local	
10.3.0.0	255.255.0.0	10.3.0.1	10.3.0.1	1	Local	
10.3.0.1	255.255.255.255	127.0.0.1	Loopback	1	Local	
10.255.255.255	255.255.255.255	10.3.0.1	10.3.0.1	1	Local	
10.255.255.255	255.255.255.255	10.2.0.2	10.2.0.2	1	Local	
127.0.0.0	255.0.0.0	127.0.0.1	Loopback	1	Local	
127.0.0.1	255.255.255.255	127.0.0.1	Loopback	1	Local	
224.0.0.0	240.0.0.0	10.3.0.1	10.3.0.1	1	Local	
224.0.0.0	240.0.0.0	10.2.0.2	10.2.0.2	1	Local	
255.255.255.255	255.255.255.255	10.3.0.1	10.3.0.1	1	Local	
255.255.255.255	255.255.255.255	10.2.0.2	10.2.0.2	1	Local	

FIGURE 7.11

A routing table with adjacent routing entries only.

7

ROUTING WITH RRAS

> **NOTE**
>
> The routing table in Figure 7.11 is shown as reported by the Routing and Remote Access console. Routing tables can also be viewed by entering the command route print in a command prompt window. Under Windows NT, the route command is used to view and manage the routing table. The route command is supported by Windows 2000, but all routing table maintenance functions can be performed within the RRAS console, and that is the utility we will be using in this chapter. route print does not report all routes that are established in RRAS and should not be relied on as a tool for troubleshooting routing problems on Windows 2000 Servers.
>
> Windows 2000 Professional does not include RRAS or the RRAS console. Therefore, routing tables must be managed using the route command, which is described later in the chapter.

The routing table display is arranged in six columns:

- **Destination**. Specifies the IP address of a destination network or host.

- **Network mask.** Determines the number of bits in the corresponding Network Address that must match the destination address. In the case of the network address 10.2.0.0, a netmask of 255.255.0.0 indicates that only the first 16 bits are matched against the destination IP address. In other words, it is only necessary for the netid portion to match the destination address for the route to apply. For the host address 10.2.0.2, however, a netmask of 255.255.255.255 indicates that all bits must match between the destination address and the network address in the routing table entry.

- **Gateway.** Specifies the IP address of the router to which datagrams must be forwarded for delivery to the destination.

- **Interface.** Specifies the interface on the local computer through which datagrams should be transmitted that are directed to the specified router.

- **Metric.** A value that declares the cost of routing datagrams through the specified gateway. A lower cost indicates a higher preference for using the route. By default, all metrics are 1. Different metrics might be defined by routing protocols and, in the case of static routes, by administrators.

- **Protocol.** Specifies the source from which the route was learned. In this case, all routes but 0.0.0.0 are defined statically on the local machine.

> **NOTE**
>
> Although it is not shown in the display, a Time to Live (TTL) parameter is included with each routing table entry. When a route is learned from a routing protocol, the TTL value determines the length of time that the route is to be regarded as valid. Unless they are refreshed, routes are removed from the routing table when their TTLs expire.

All the entries shown in Figure 7.11 were created when the host's network interfaces were configured using **Network and Dial-Up Connections**. It is worth examining the entries in the table:

- **0.0.0.0.** The address 0.0.0.0 in a routing table identifies a default route, in this case router 10.3.0.2 through interface 10.3.0.1.

- **10.2.0.0.** A network address. Datagrams destined for that network are routed through adapter 10.2.0.2.

- **10.2.0.2.** A network adapter on the router. Notice that datagrams sent to that address are routed through the loopback address because they are targeted for the local host.

- **10.3.0.0.** The other attached network. The routing table includes entries for 10.3.0.0 that are similar to the entries discussed for 10.2.0.0.

- **10.3.0.1.** The second network adapter on the router. Notice that datagrams sent to that address are routed through the loopback interface because they are targeted for the local host.

- **10.255.255.255.** A broadcast address for network 10.0.0.0. Notice that a routing table entry is included for interfaces 10.3.0.1 and 10.2.0.2. A broadcast to network 10.0.0.0 will not be sent through both interfaces, however. IP will send the broadcast to the first entry in the routing table that matches the target specification.

- **127.0.0.0.** The loopback network. Any datagrams sent to 127.0.0.0 are routed to 127.0.0.1 and reflected back to the protocol stack.

- **127.0.0.1.** A loopback IP address. Any datagrams sent to this address are routed to the loopback network 127.0.0.0.

- **224.0.0.0.** A multicast address that is used to route any multicast messages directed to the host interface associated with the entry. An entry is included for each network interface.

- **255.255.255.255.** The local broadcast address. (Routers do not forward broadcasts to other networks.) An entry is included for each network interface.

When IP consults the routing table, it proceeds in order from the most explicit to the least explicit entries, searching for routes in the following order:

1. First, IP looks for a host address entry that matches the destination host address. (A host address entry has a network mask of 255.255.255.255.)

2. Second, IP looks for a network address entry that matches the destination netid.

3. Finally, IP looks for a default route.

4. If none of these routes are identified, IP reports an error.

> **NOTE**
>
> Notice that the router attempts routes in a very definite sequence. It is, therefore, not necessary to specify metrics that make the preferences explicit. You might think, for example, that it is necessary to specify a higher metric for the default route to ensure that it will be used only if all else fails. But the default route can have a metric of 1, as with other standard routes, because it will be used only if an explicit route entry has not been made for the destination host or network.

Figure 7.12 illustrates two routing attempts using `ping`, both performed on router B. In the first attempt, it proves possible to ping 10.2.0.2. This is not surprising because that host is attached to a network directly attached to B.

An attempt to ping 10.1.0.1 fails, however. B attempts to reach 10.1.0.1 via its default router, 10.3.0.2, which is not configured with a route to the target network. This attempt does not succeed and times out.

```
Command Prompt                                              _ □ ×

C:\>ping 10.2.0.2

Pinging 10.2.0.2 with 32 bytes of data:

Reply from 10.2.0.2: bytes=32 time<10ms TTL=128
Reply from 10.2.0.2: bytes=32 time<10ms TTL=128
Reply from 10.2.0.2: bytes=32 time<10ms TTL=128
Reply from 10.2.0.2: bytes=32 time<10ms TTL=128

Ping statistics for 10.2.0.2:
    Packets: Sent = 4, Received = 4, Lost = 0 (0% loss),
Approximate round trip times in milli-seconds:
    Minimum = 0ms, Maximum =  0ms, Average =  0ms

C:\>ping 10.1.0.1

Pinging 10.1.0.1 with 32 bytes of data:

Request timed out.
Request timed out.
Request timed out.
Request timed out.

Ping statistics for 10.1.0.1:
    Packets: Sent = 4, Received = 0, Lost = 4 (100% loss),
Approximate round trip times in milli-seconds:
    Minimum = 0ms, Maximum =  0ms, Average =  0ms

C:\>
```

FIGURE 7.12
Pinging routed and nonrouted addresses.

Defining a Static Route

To solve the problem, an entry must be added to the router table for B. This entry must specify that network 10.1.0.0 can be reached via router 10.2.0.1. A static routing entry is created as follows:

1. In the RRAS console, expand entries under the router being managed. Then expand the **IP Routing** header.

2. Right-click **Static Routes** and select **New Static Route** from the context menu to open the **Static Route** dialog box, shown in Figure 7.13.

FIGURE 7.13
Defining a static routing table entry.

3. In the **Interface** field, select the network interface that is to be used to direct datagrams to the destination being defined.

4. In the **Destination** field, enter the network or host address of the route destination.

5. In the **Network mask** field, enter the netmask that determines which bits in the destination address must be matched in order to select this route. Typically, network masks for network addresses are the same as the subnet mask that is in use on the network. Host masks will be 255.255.255.255, so the entire destination address must be matched.

6. In the **Gateway** field, specify the IP address of the router that is trusted to forward datagrams to the destination.

7. In the **Metric** field, specify a metric for the route. The default metric is 1.

8. If demand-dial support is enabled, you can check **Use this route to initiate demand-dial connections**. When the option is enabled, a demand-dial connection is established whenever a datagram is forwarded to the destination specified in the route.

Figure 7.14 illustrates the routing table for router B after a static entry has been added for network 10.1.0.0. Note that the route is described as Static (non demand-dial) in the Protocol column.

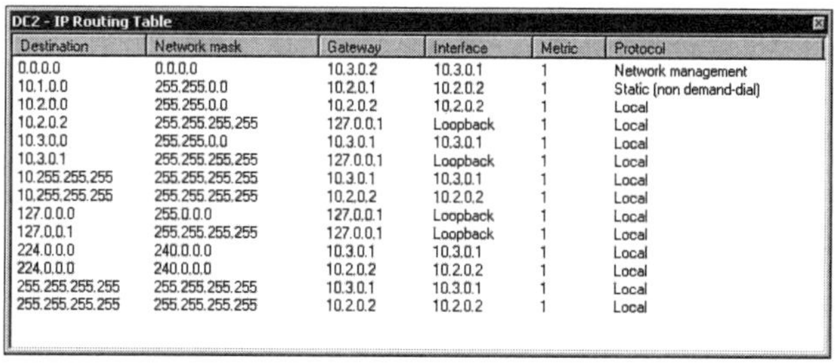

Destination	Network mask	Gateway	Interface	Metric	Protocol
0.0.0.0	0.0.0.0	10.3.0.2	10.3.0.1	1	Network management
10.1.0.0	255.255.0.0	10.2.0.1	10.2.0.2	1	Static (non demand-dial)
10.2.0.0	255.255.0.0	10.2.0.2	10.2.0.2	1	Local
10.2.0.2	255.255.255.255	127.0.0.1	Loopback	1	Local
10.3.0.0	255.255.0.0	10.3.0.1	10.3.0.1	1	Local
10.3.0.1	255.255.255.255	127.0.0.1	Loopback	1	Local
10.255.255.255	255.255.255.255	10.3.0.1	10.3.0.1	1	Local
10.255.255.255	255.255.255.255	10.2.0.2	10.2.0.2	1	Local
127.0.0.0	255.0.0.0	127.0.0.1	Loopback	1	Local
127.0.0.1	255.255.255.255	127.0.0.1	Loopback	1	Local
224.0.0.0	240.0.0.0	10.3.0.1	10.3.0.1	1	Local
224.0.0.0	240.0.0.0	10.2.0.2	10.2.0.2	1	Local
255.255.255.255	255.255.255.255	10.3.0.1	10.3.0.1	1	Local
255.255.255.255	255.255.255.255	10.2.0.2	10.2.0.2	1	Local

FIGURE 7.14
The routing table after a static route has been added.

Static routes are also listed in the details pane of the RRAS console when the **Static Route** icon is selected, as shown in Figure 7.15.

Effective Use of a Default Router

In many cases, non-routing hosts need be configured only with the address of a default router. Consider the network in Figure 7.16.

Notice an important detail in the figure. Routing on the Internet is not performed with a protocol that can exchange routing information with LAN-based routers using RIP or OSPF. (Routing on the Internet is performed using the Border Gateway Protocol, or BGP.) Consequently, every host and router must be configured so packets destined for unknown destinations (presumably on the Internet) are sent to a router on the Internet, most likely a router that is operated by the organization's ISP. Routing of datagrams to the Internet is handled through the default routing mechanism because default routes are used precisely when an explicit route isn't known.

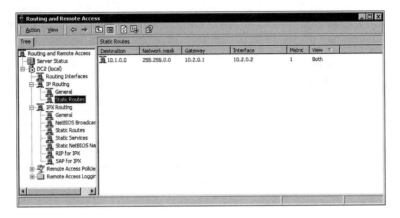

FIGURE 7.15

Static routes are listed in the details pane for the Static Route icon.

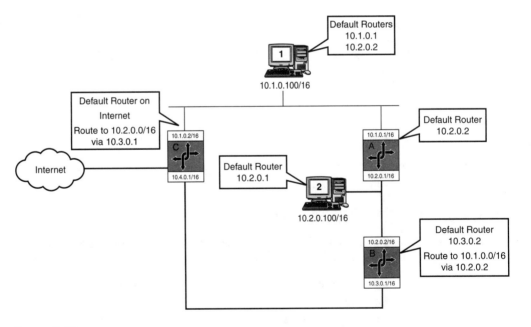

FIGURE 7.16

Host 1 requires only a default route to reach all destinations.

Let's see how the default routing mechanism works in this case:

- Router C is configured with a default router that is at the organization's ISP. Consequently, when C must forward a datagram that does not match an entry in C's routing table, the datagram is directed to the Internet.
- Router A is configured with a default router address of 10.1.0.2 on router C. A can route to the Internet via C.
- Router B is configured with a default router address of 10.2.0.2 on router C. B can route to the Internet via C.
- Hosts on network 10.1.0.0 are configured with default router addresses of 10.1.0.2.
- Hosts on network 10.2.0.0 are configured with a default router address of 10.2.0.2.
- Hosts on network 10.3.0.0 (not shown) can be configured with a default router address of 10.3.0.2.

All the devices can communicate with every destination, including the Internet, but there are at least two ways in which the situation is less than optimal:

- Although each device has two paths available to the Internet, a device can take advantage of only one. For example, if network 10.1.0.0 fails, hosts dependent on router A cannot communicate with the Internet.
- A host's default router might not be the most efficient way to reach a destination.

To correct the first situation, we can take advantage of Windows' capability of accepting multiple default routers in its TCP/IP configuration. To correct the second situation, we might elect to configure static routes.

Routing with Multiple Default Gateways

Any Windows TCP/IP host can be configured with more than one default router. Unfortunately, only the first configured default router will be used for routing. The additional default routers are used only if the primary router becomes unavailable. Consequently, multiple gateways cannot be used to take better advantage of network bandwidth. On the other hand, they do provide a greater degree of network fault tolerance.

NOTE

Besides configuring multiple default routers, ICMP provides another mechanism that enables hosts to learn new routes. The Windows 2000 and NT router services can use the ICMP Router Discovery Protocol to notify hosts that a router knows of a better route to a given destination. The router sends an ICMP *redirect* message to the host that originated the datagram.

> Unfortunately, ICMP redirection is effective only for the first-hop router. ICMP redirect messages from later gateways are ignored. The host is not concerned with remote routers, and, because the redirect message is directed to the host that originated the datagram, it is not processed by the router that could benefit from its information. Therefore, a dynamic routing protocol remains a superior solution to the problem of automatically configuring the network.

Suppose that network 1 fails in Figure 7.16. Router A is configured to use 10.1.0.2 as its default router. But if we add a second default router address of 10.2.0.2 to the router's configuration, datagrams can be routed through router B if there are problems with network 10.1.0.0.

Microsoft TCP/IP detects dead routers by sending packets to the default router until an acknowledgment is received or until it exceeds one-half of the TcpMaxDataRetransmissions parameter. If the default router is unresponsive and the host is configured with multiple default routers, the next default router is used.

Additional default routers are configured using Advanced TCP/IP Configuration. To add a default router:

1. Open the **TCP/IP Properties** dialog box for the network connection to be configured.
2. Click the **Advanced** button to open the **Advanced TCP/IP Settings** dialog box.
3. Add the default router addresses to the **Default gateway** list on the **IP Settings** tab. The preference for using default routers is determined by their positions in the list, with the most preferred routers appearing at the beginning of the list.

Managing Routing Tables with route

On a Windows 2000 Professional workstation (or any Windows NT computer), managing static routes requires the use of the route utility. The syntax for route is as follows:

```
route [-f][-p]
    [command]
    [destination]
    [mask netmask]
    [gateway]
    metric metric
```

route accepts four command options:

- **add** adds a route to a table.
- **delete** removes a route from a table.

- **change** modifies the routing for a table entry.
- **print** displays the router table.

destination is an optional parameter that specifies the network address that is the destination to be specified in the routing table entry. It must be supplied with the add, delete, and change options.

mask is an optional parameter. When mask appears, it specifies that the following IP address is an address mask. The default value for netmask is 255.255.255.255. Other values must be fully specified.

gateway is an optional parameter that specifies the IP address of the gateway that is to be used when routing datagrams to the destination.

metric is an optional parameter. When metric appears, then *metric* is a number that specifies the cost metric for the route being specified. If the metric parameter is omitted, a cost of 1 is assumed. The metric parameter is required only when multiple routes exist to the destination network, in which case the lowest metric identifies the preferred route.

-f is an optional parameter that specifies the routing table is cleared of all entries. It can be included with routes to clear the table before the routes are entered.

-p is an optional parameter that is used with the add option to make an entry persistent. Persistent entries remain in effect after the router restarts. If this parameter is not specified, the table entry does not appear after the router restarts.

NOTE

The -p option is available beginning with Windows NT version 3.51. With earlier versions, the route commands must be reentered when the computer restarts. Persistent routes are stored in the Registry under the key:

```
HKEY_LOCAL_COMPUTER\SYSTEM\CurrentControlSet\Services\
Tcpip\Parameters\PersistentRoutes
```

The metric parameter was new in Windows NT version 4.

The following commands can be used to configure the static routes that enable host 1 in Figure 7.16 to route to networks 10.2.0.0 and 10.3.0.0:

```
route add 110.2.0.0 mask 255.255.0.0 10.1.0.1 metric 1 -p
route add 10.3.0.0 mask 255.255.0.0 10.1.0.2 metric 2 -p
```

These commands add static routing table entries for networks 10.2.0.0 and 10.3.0.0 with a network mask of 255.255.0.0. The router to be used to reach 10.2.0.0 is 10.1.0.1, and the cost for the route is 2. The router to be used to reach 10.3.0.0 is 10.1.0.2, and the cost for the route is 2. (A metric of 2 was used in this example to illustrate use of the metric parameter. Because only one route is defined for each of the destination networks, however, any metric would have the same effect. The default metric would work just as well.)

Figure 7.17 shows the routing table for host 1 after these static routes have been defined. Notice that persistent, statically defined routes are listed separately in the routing table printout.

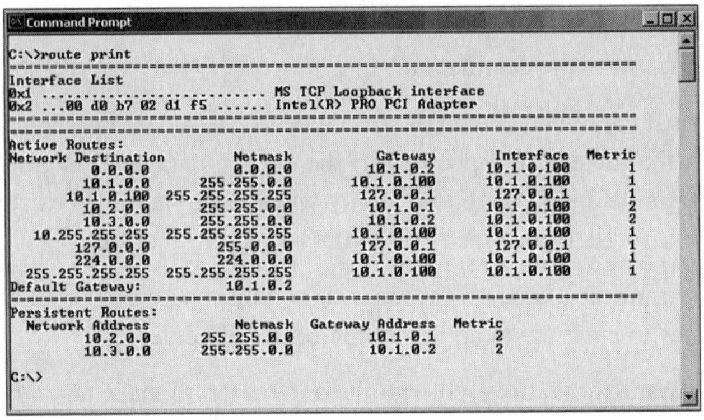

```
Command Prompt                                                          _ |□| x|

C:\>route print
========================================================================
Interface List
0x1 ........................... MS TCP Loopback interface
0x2 ...00 d0 b7 02 d1 f5 ...... Intel(R) PRO PCI Adapter
========================================================================
Active Routes:
Network Destination        Netmask          Gateway       Interface  Metric
          0.0.0.0          0.0.0.0          10.1.0.2      10.1.0.100    1
         10.1.0.0      255.255.0.0         10.1.0.100     10.1.0.100    1
       10.1.0.100  255.255.255.255         127.0.0.1      127.0.0.1     1
         10.2.0.0      255.255.0.0          10.1.0.1      10.1.0.100    2
         10.3.0.0      255.255.0.0          10.1.0.2      10.1.0.100    2
   10.255.255.255  255.255.255.255        10.1.0.100     10.1.0.100    1
        127.0.0.0        255.0.0.0          127.0.0.1      127.0.0.1     1
        224.0.0.0        224.0.0.0         10.1.0.100     10.1.0.100    1
  255.255.255.255  255.255.255.255        10.1.0.100     10.1.0.100    1
Default Gateway:        10.1.0.2
========================================================================
Persistent Routes:
  Network Address          Netmask   Gateway Address   Metric
         10.2.0.0      255.255.0.0         10.1.0.1       2
         10.3.0.0      255.255.0.0         10.1.0.2       2

C:\>
```

FIGURE 7.17
The routing table for host 1 in Figure 7.16.

Assuming that the default router for host 1 is 10.1.0.2, that takes care of all possibilities. It is no longer necessary to run RIP (or another routing protocol) on the routers, so routing traffic is eliminated. And host 1 will now route messages directly to the appropriate router.

Should you go to this much trouble to set up routing? It depends on whether your network changes frequently. If your network relies on static routes, you need to visit each host every time the network is reconfigured. That can mean a lot of one-on-one sessions with your hosts, and can be an inefficient use of your time. The downside is that all hosts must be configured with static routes to enable the scheme to work to its optimal efficiency. (You might consider including appropriate route commands in login scripts to simplify distribution and maintenance.) In most cases, you'll make better use of resources by running RIP or OSPF, however.

Testing Routing with tracert

The tracert (trace route) utility is included with Windows 2000 and NT as a tool for debugging routing, using ICMP messages to report the routes between two hosts on an internetwork. When you query a destination with tracert, it will report the route taken together with a variety of statistics. If the destination cannot be reached, tracert reports which router failed.

The following is an example of `tracert` output, showing the route to `ftp.internic.net`.

```
C:\>tracert ftp.internic.net

Tracing route to ftp.internic.net [198.41.0.6]
over a maximum of 30 hops:

  1    30 ms   <10 ms    10 ms  209.51.67.1
  2   260 ms   140 ms   221 ms  206.251.67.17
  3    20 ms    20 ms    20 ms  gw-f0-0.ptld.transport.com [209.222.130.254]
  4    60 ms   270 ms   220 ms  gw2.transport.com [209.222.140.50]
  5    90 ms    20 ms    20 ms  216.67.147.193
  6    20 ms    20 ms    20 ms  207.170.193.161
  7    30 ms    20 ms    31 ms  sl-gw4-sea-5-0-T3.sprintlink.net [147.228.96.9]
  8    40 ms    30 ms    20 ms  sl-bb10-sea-4-2.sprintlink.net [147.232.6.49]
  9    20 ms    30 ms    30 ms  sl-bb10-tac-7-0.sprintlink.net [147.232.18.41]
 10   110 ms   120 ms   111 ms  sl-bb10-sj-4-0.sprintlink.net [147.232.9.213]
 11   180 ms   190 ms   171 ms  sl-bb12-rly-5-0.sprintlink.net [147.232.9.217]
 12   210 ms   170 ms   171 ms  sl-bb10-rly-8-0.sprintlink.net [147.232.7.209]
 13   170 ms   180 ms   211 ms  sl-gw2-rly-0-0-0.sprintlink.net [147.232.17.42]
 14   190 ms   180 ms   201 ms  sl-netsolut-2-0-0.sprintlink.net
➥[147.232.187.78]
 15   170 ms   180 ms   171 ms  216.168.227.4
 16   190 ms   220 ms   191 ms  rs.internic.net [198.41.0.6]

Trace complete.
```

Notice that `tracert` uses DNS reverse lookups to determine the hostnames of routers that it discovers.

The route is determined by sending ICMP echo request packets with varying Time to Live values to the destination. Each router that forwards the packet must decrement the TTL before forwarding it. The result serves as a hop count to the destination. When the TTL times out, the router is required to return an ICMP time-exceeded packet.

`tracert` determines the route by sending the first echo request packet with a TTL of 1, thus learning the first router in the route. Then `tracert` repeatedly sends the echo request, incrementing the TTL with each datagram sent, until the target host is reached. Consequently, each time `tracert` sends an echo request, the TTL expires at the router that is next in line to the destination. This enables `tracert` to reconstruct the route path from the ICMP time-exceeded datagrams that are returned.

`tracert` will fail to determine the route when it encounters some older routers that simply drop packets whose TTL has expired (so-called "black hole" routers).

NOTE

Because of the way it works, tracert can produce inconsistent results on networks that have multiple paths to a destination. The route tracing process expands the route one hop at a time. If multiple routes exist, the ping packet might go through a different route with each iteration. Consequently, the list of routers that is reported might not be accurate and might differ when tracert is executed on different occasions.

The ping -r option works in much the same way and shares the same limitation as tracert.

Configuring RIP for IP

RRAS supports three dynamic routing protocols for TCP/IP:

- Routing Information Protocol (RIP) version 1 (RFC 1058)
- Routing Information Protocol (RIP) version 2 (RFC 1723)
- Open Shortest Path First (OSPF)

RIP and OSPF are very different routing protocols that need to be considered separately. Because it is the most commonly encountered and the easiest to configure, we'll consider RIP first, starting with some theory about RIP, which comes under the category known as *distance vector protocols*.

Operational Characteristics of RIP

RIP is the protocol most commonly used to maintain routing tables on TCP/IP internets. If you have experience on Novell networks, you probably are familiar with the Novell RIP protocol, which is similar in function to Internet RIP but not interchangeable with it. (Both were derived from the XNS protocol that Xerox originated.)

RIP is a distance vector routing protocol. *Distance vector routing protocols* represent routing information in terms of the cost of reaching destination networks. *Cost* is a fairly simple metric (measure) that represents the efficiency of a route with a number from 1 through 15. In general, each network that a route must traverse is represented by a cost of 1, although higher metrics can be used to discourage the use of certain routes. RIP is used to discover the costs of various routes to destination networks and store that information in a routing table, enabling IP to select the lowest-cost route.

In a router, RIP builds and maintains its routing table using a mechanism that is, at its heart, quite simple. Each router periodically broadcasts its entire RIP routing table, which other routers use to update their route information.

Route Convergence

Figure 7.18 illustrates an internetwork with four routers. Assume that the entire internet has just come up and that all router tables have been newly initialized. The following steps describe how router A initializes its routing table and how its information propagates through the internet.

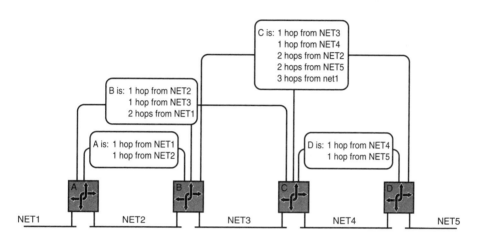

FIGURE 7.18

Route convergence on a simple internetwork.

1. After initialization, A knows only of the directly attached networks. A is 1 hop from NET1 and 1 hop from NET2. (1 is the minimum cost metric.) A broadcasts a RIP response packet containing this information to its attached networks.

2. B receives A's broadcast. B is directly attached to NET2 at a cost of 1, and discards the route learned from A. Because B is attached to a network that is attached to A, B learns that it is 1 hop from A. B determines the cost to reach NET1 by adding its cost to reach A (1) to A's cost to reach NET1 (1). Consequently, B's cost to reach NET1 is 2.

   B broadcasts a RIP response packet using its routing table, including its attached networks. A learns from this table that it has a route to NET3 at a cost of 2. C learns that it has routes to NET1 (cost 3) and to NET2 (cost 2).

Meanwhile, other routers have not been idle. D has broadcast its RIP routing table as well, informing the other routers of routes to NET5. In this way, routers arrive at a complete picture of the network in terms of the costs to each destination and the routers through which a message should next be routed to reach a given destination. The process of bringing all routers up-to-date on the state of the network is called *convergence*.

Each router broadcasts a route response packet to its neighbors at 30-second intervals. The general rule is that a router updates its route tables after it discovers a route that has a lower cost. Routers eventually converge on the lowest-cost routes.

When a new router is started on an established network, the new router can solicit routing information from nearby routers by issuing a RIP request packet, which reduces the time required to converge the new router and informs other routers of new routes the new router makes available.

Potential Convergence Problems with RIP

The RIP algorithm, as described to this point, has some potential for problems. Before examining techniques for alleviating the problems, the problems themselves must be examined.

Figure 7.19 illustrates an internetwork. Each of the networks shown is associated with a cost of 1, with one exception. The cost from C to D is 10, which might be the result of crossing many routers. Or it might result because the link is a low-speed link that should be used only in emergencies, and the network administrator has manually assigned a high cost to it.

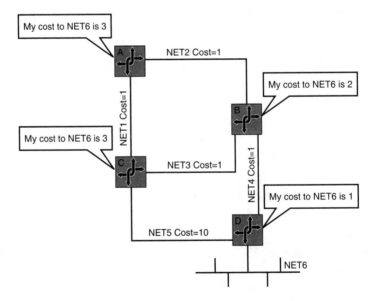

FIGURE 7.19

Example of a fully converged network.

When the network is working properly, the routing information for the routers with respect to NET6 is as follows:

- A can reach NET6 through B at a cost of 3.
- B can reach NET6 through D at a cost of 2.

- C can reach NET6 through B at a cost of 3.
- D can reach NET6 directly at a cost of 1.

If NET4 fails between B and D, current routes are invalidated on A, B, and C. It takes some time, however, for the routers to converge on new routes. B rids itself of the old route fairly quickly by using a time-out mechanism. If B fails to receive a route response packet from D after 90 seconds (three 30-second intervals), B times out the entries in its tables that route through D.

Timing out solves the immediate problem for B. But RIP routers have specific route knowledge only of the networks to which they are directly attached, causing problems in this instance because neither A nor C is aware that NET4 has failed and that B's route is invalid. A and C advertise that they have routes to NET6 with a cost of 3, but do not specify that the routes require the link between B and D. Therefore, C assumes it can use A's route and A assumes it can use C's route.

After B advertises that its route is gone, C looks for the least costly route available and discovers that A offers a route with a cost of 3, making C's cost to reach NET6 4, including C's cost to reach A. Similarly, A selects the route advertised by C, with a cost of 3, making A's cost to reach NET6 4. When A and C broadcast their routing tables, B sees routes to D through A or C with a cost of 4 and makes those entries in its routing table. Figure 7.20 shows the new routing status.

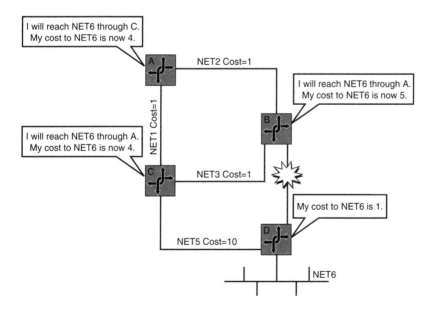

FIGURE 7.20
Reconverging after a network failure.

B's routing information causes A and C to update their costs to reach NET6, revising their costs to 6. This information, when received by B, prompts B to assign a cost of 7 to the routes through A and C. In this way, the cost metrics in the routing tables gradually ratchet up until the direct route from C to D, through NET5, becomes the low-cost route. Because RIP updates occur at 30-second intervals, considerable time might elapse before the network reconverges on the new route.

The Count to Infinity Problem

A more sinister scenario can take place if a network becomes inaccessible. In Figure 7.21, the connection between router B and NET1 has failed. B has been advertising itself as a router to A, with a cost of 1 to reach NET1. Also, because A advertises its entire routing table, A advertises that it can reach NET1 at a cost of 2.

When B loses its route to NET1, it examines incoming RIP advertisements to determine if another route exists. Because A is advertising a route to NET1 at a cost of 2, B assumes that it can route through A to reach NET1 at a cost of 3. Because NET1 is no longer connected, a suitable route never becomes available, and the counting process can proceed indefinitely, giving rise to the term used to describe the problem: the *count to infinity problem*.

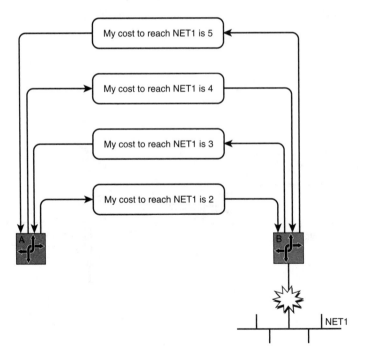

FIGURE 7.21

Counting to infinity.

The technique for breaking this loop is to make "infinity" a suitably low number that is reached fairly rapidly. For RIP, the number chosen to represent infinity is 16. Any network that has a cost of 16 is considered unreachable. Any counting loop stops feeding itself when the metrics reach 16. Only when the metric reaches 16 do A and B realize that NET1 is not reachable.

Convergence is simplified by making a simple change in B's behavior when a route times out. When B's table entry for NET1 times out, B is aware that the route is invalid. Rather than simply discarding the table entries, B assigns a cost of 16 to its routes to NET1. When A does its next route update, A arrives at a cost of 17 to reach NET1 through B. Consequently, all routers quickly become aware that NET1 cannot be reached through B.

With distance-vector algorithms, the value used for "infinity" is a compromise between the capability to support a reasonably complex network and the need to promote speedy convergence. RIP's designers did not feel that diameters larger than 15 were appropriate for networks using the RIP protocol.

7

ROUTING WITH
RRAS

> **NOTE**
>
> The Windows 2000 RIP router considers all routes not learned from RIP to have a fixed hop count of 2, including static routes that are obtained from the router's interface configuration. Consequently, networks based on Windows 2000 RIP routers have a maximum diameter of 14 routers.

Split Horizon and Poison Reverse

Although setting infinity to 16 eventually stops hop counts from incrementing, eliminating the count to infinity problem altogether would be better. One technique for doing so is called *split horizon*. Examining the preceding scenarios reveals one source of error. In Figure 7.20, for example, router A relies on routes advertised by B, whereas B accepts routes advertised by A. The self-referential nature of this relationship generates loops. Split horizon is a technique that helps routers be a bit more careful about the routing information they send.

If A advertises a route to B, it is never beneficial for B to advertise that route back to A. The split horizon technique prevents a router from advertising routes through the interface from which it has learned the routes, thereby keeping two routers from getting into a self-referential loop. Figure 7.22 illustrates the split horizon in action. In the figure, B learns that A is 1 hop from NET1. After adding this information to its routing table, B passes the route along to C. However, B does not advertise the route back to A.

A technique called *poison reverse* (see Figure 7.23) amplifies the safeguard provided by split horizon. If B can reach D through A, A's route cannot go back to B without forming a self-referential loop. Therefore, when A advertises its routes to B, B advertises to A that NET1 is unreachable by advertising a metric of 16 to reach NET1. A, thus, cannot attempt to route to NET1 through B because the distance through B is infinite. Poison reverse informs attached routers that a route is invalid immediately, without the delay required for the route entries to time out. Poison reverse is useful on many complex internetworks and generally is safer than split horizon. A cost is associated with poison reverse, however, in the form of increased network traffic.

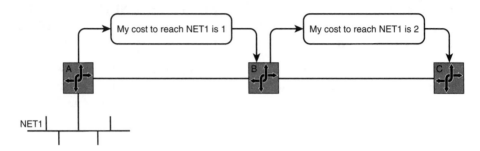

FIGURE 7.22
Split horizon.

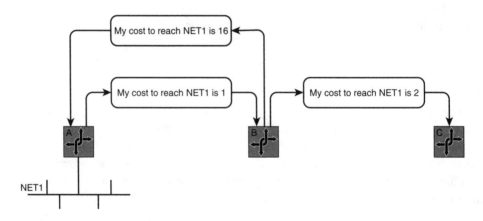

FIGURE 7.23
Poison reverse.

Complex Routing Loops

Split horizon and poison reverse can prevent self-referential loops from being created between any pair of routers. But even with those safeguards, RIP remains vulnerable to loops that are formed by three or more routers. Consider the situation in Figure 7.24.

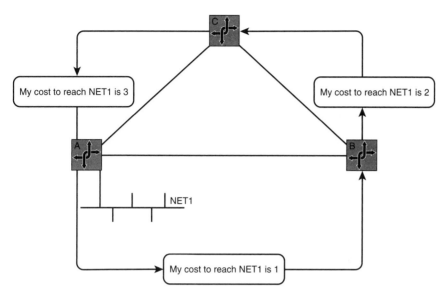

FIGURE 7.24

A multi-router RIP routing loop.

A advertises to B that it can reach NET1 in 1 hop. Split horizon prevents B from advertising the route back to A, but B does advertise to C that it can reach NET1 at a cost of 2. C is unaware that the route originates with A, and C has no inhibitions about advertising to A that it can reach NET1 in 3 hops. Now, if A loses its connection to NET1, a loop has been established involving all three routers, and it will be necessary for the loop to count to 16 before all routers become aware that NET1 is unavailable.

Redundant paths are desirable in internetworks, providing fault tolerance and alternative routes should certain paths become overburdened with traffic. RIP has great difficulty, however, dealing with the loops that can be established when redundant paths are present. RIP's inability to cope with redundant paths is one of the reasons OSPF is preferred over RIP, particularly on larger networks with redundant paths. OSPF develops routing information in a more intelligent manner and cannot establish self-referential routing loops.

RIP-1 and RIP-2

RIP version 1 (RIP-1), as specified in RFC 1058, has some significant limitations, the most critical of which is that it does not comprehend subnets and subnet masks. If all the non-netid bits in an address are 0, then RIP-1 can determine that the address is a network address and that the default subnet mask is in effect. If, however, any of the non-netid bits are 1, RIP cannot determine whether it is the address of a subnet or a host.

As you observed in the discussion of subnetting earlier in this chapter, careful design can conceal the structures of subnets from outside hosts and routers. In these circumstances, RIP-1 can function adequately as a router. If, however, routers must comprehend subnets to facilitate routing, RIP-1 is inadequate.

RIP version 2 (RIP-2) is specified in RFC 1723, a standards track document that updates RFC 1058. RIP-2 adds several enhancements to RIP-1:

- The message format is extended to include subnet masks.
- Authentication enables network managers to configure password authentication of messages exchanged by RIP routers.
- Route tags enable RIP to interface more smoothly with routing protocols outside a RIP autonomous system (a routing region using the RIP protocol). Route tags determine which routes should be advertised to external autonomous areas.

Not all routers support RIP-2. If RIP-2 will be deployed on your network, you must examine the specifications for each router to determine compliance with RFC 1723.

Limitations of RIP

RIP functions reliably and provides reasonably rapid route convergence. RIP does, however, have some undesirable traits.

The necessity for declaring some hop count to represent infinity places a size limitation on networks. RIP cannot provide routing on networks that have diameters of greater than 15 hops. Without declaring a metric to signify infinity, however, loops can develop that prevent routers from reaching convergence in the event of a network change.

RIP's method of advertising routes results in slow convergence and high traffic. RIP requires routers to advertise their routing tables every 30 seconds. When many routers are present on a network, a significant amount of network bandwidth can be monopolized to send the many RIP response packets required.

For these reasons, the network community is gradually moving toward routing based on link-state algorithms. The protocol developed for the Internet community is Open Shortest Path First (OSPF), which is described later in this chapter.

Adding RIP for IP to RRAS

To add RIP for IP, do the following:

1. Right-click the **General** icon under the **IP Routing** object and choose **New Routing Protocol** in the context menu.

2. In the **New Routing Protocol** dialog box, select **RIP Version 2 for Internet Protocol** and click **OK**.

An icon labeled **RIP** is added in the **IP Routing** container.

Adding Interfaces to RIP

Before RIP is functional, you must specify each interface that RIP is to support. Perform the following procedure for each interface:

1. Right-click the **RIP** icon and choose **New Interface** in the context menu.

2. Select an interface that is listed in the **New Interface for RIP Version 2 for Internet Protocol** dialog box and click **OK**.

> **NOTE**
>
> In most situations, RIP will function well using the default interface properties. Modify interface properties only if you have a specific reason for making a change.

3. The next dialog box, named **RIP Properties**, is used to configure the properties of the RIP interface, as described in the next section.

Configuring RIP Interface Properties

After an interface is added, it will be listed in the details pane of the RRAS console when the **RIP** icon is selected, as shown in Figure 7.25. You can modify the properties of an interface by right-clicking the interface and choosing **Properties** from the context menu.

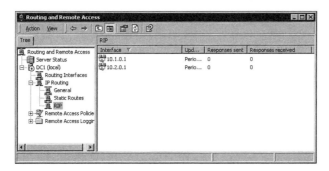

FIGURE 7.25
Interfaces defined for a RIP router.

RIP Interface Properties: The General Tab

The **General** properties tab for a RIP interface (see Figure 7.26) defines the following properties:

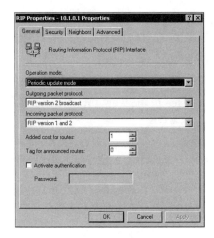

FIGURE 7.26
RIP Interface Properties: The General tab.

Operation mode. Select one of the following choices:

- **Periodic update mode.** In this mode the interface will transmit periodic RIP advertisements at intervals specified by the **Periodic announcement interval** field on the **Advanced** tab. This is the default selection for permanently connected interfaces.

- **Auto-static update mode.** When this mode is selected, the interface will transmit a RIP announcement only when one is requested by another router. Routes that are learned over a RIP interface operating in auto-static mode are marked as Static in the routing table. If the router from which the route was learned becomes unavailable, these static routes will not expire and must be deleted manually when they become obsolete. Auto-static mode is the default for demand-dial interfaces, enabling these interfaces to retain routing information without the need to establish a connection at periodic intervals.

Outgoing packet protocol. Select one of the following options:

- **RIP version 1 broadcast.** All RIP announcements are sent in RIP version 1 format, compatible with all RIP routers. Remember that RIP 1 does not include subnet information in announcements and cannot support some subnetted network configurations.

- **RIP version 2 broadcast.** All RIP announcements are sent in RIP version 2 format. All routers on the network must support RIP version 2. IP subnetting is supported as well as other RIP 2 features. This is the default setting.

- **RIP version 2 multicast.** All RIP announcements are sent as RIP version 2 multicasts. All RIP routers must support RIP 2 and must be configured to communicate in multicast mode. All routers must be configured to forward multicast datagrams.

- **Silent RIP.** The router listens for incoming RIP announcements but does not originate RIP announcements. It is useful to enable this option on non-routers so that they can maintain more detailed routing tables based on RIP announcements that traverse the network.

Incoming packet protocol. Select one of these options:

- **Ignore incoming packets.** The RIP router does not process incoming RIP announcements.
- **RIP version 1 and 2.** The RIP router processes incoming RIP 1 and RIP 2 announcements. This is the default setting.
- **RIP version 1 only.** The RIP router ignores incoming RIP 2 announcements.
- **RIP version 2 only.** The RIP router ignores incoming RIP 1 announcements.

Added cost for routes. When a route that is learned from another router is added to the local routing table, RIP adds a value to the route metric to represent the cost of reaching the router that advertised the route. By default, the advertised cost is incremented by one, but the cost increment can be increased by adjusting the value of this field. You might want to increase the added cost to discourage use of a busy route when another route is available.

Tag for announced routes. RIP version 2 permits route advertisements to be identified by an integer tag. Route tags can be used to distinguish routes learned from RIP ("internal routes") from routes learned from another protocol, such as OSPF or EGP ("external routes"). See RFC1723 for more information about uses for this field.

Activate authentication. Check this box if you want to include a plaintext password in RIP announcements. RIP routers configured to use authentication will process only packets that contain the expected password. Note: The password is transmitted as clear text and can be easily decoded in a network analyzer. It is provided as a mechanism for establishing groups of mutually communicating routers and for reducing the likelihood that unauthorized RIP routers will be placed on the network, but should not be considered a security mechanism.

Password. If RIP authentication is enabled, enter the password that is to be included in RIP announcement packets.

RIP Interface Properties: The Security Tab

The **Security** tab is shown in Figure 7.27. To define security options for routes coming in through this interface, select **For incoming routes** in the **Action** field and configure the options as follows:

- **Accept all routes.** Select this option to accept routes to all addresses.
- **Accept all routes in the ranges listed.** Select this option to accept routes for destinations in the ranges specified in the **From...To** list.
- **Ignore all routes in the ranges listed.** Select this option to reject routes for destinations in the ranges specified in the **From...To** list.

7

ROUTING WITH RRAS

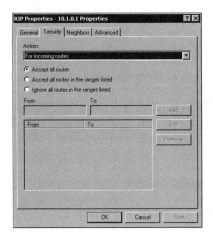

FIGURE 7.27
RIP Interface Properties: The Security tab.

To define security options for route announcements sent from this interface, select **For outgoing routes** in the **Action** field and configure the options as follows:

- **Announce all routes.** Select this option to announce routes learned by this router.
- **Announce all routes in the ranges listed.** Select this option to announce routes for destinations in the ranges specified in the **From...To** list.
- **Do not announce all routes in the ranges listed.** Select this if the router should not announce routes for destinations in the ranges specified in the **From...To** list.

RIP Interface Properties: The Neighbors Tab

The **Neighbors** tab is shown in Figure 7.28. *Neighbors* are routers with which this router has made explicit communication arrangements. The advantage of having neighbors is that communication between neighbors can be explicitly configured, including the capability to communicate with unicast messages. The disadvantage of having neighbors is that the neighbors list is static and must be maintained by an administrator. Select one of the following options regarding neighbors that communicate through this interface:

- **Use broadcast or multicast only.** Neighbors are not defined.
- **Use neighbors in addition to broadcast or multicast.** Neighbors can be explicitly defined in the **IP address** list. The router continues to transmit broadcast or multicast advertisements to disseminate RIP advertisements to non-neighbors.
- **Use neighbors instead of broadcast or multicast.** The router will communicate using unicast messages and only with RIP routers that are listed in the **IP address** list. An advantage of this mode is that routers can exchange routing information directly with routers on remote networks.

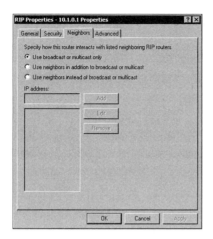

FIGURE 7.28
RIP Interface Properties: The Neighbors tab.

RIP Interface Properties: The Advanced Tab

The **Advanced** tab is shown in Figure 7.29. This tab contains properties for a variety of RIP settings:

Periodic announcement interval (seconds). This timer determines the frequency with which the router will advertise routes through this interface. The default for IP RIP is 30 seconds. This parameter is effective only if **Periodic update mode** is selected on the General tab. All RIP routers should be configured with the same periodic announcement interval.

Time before route expires (seconds). Routes learned from other routers must be refreshed periodically. External routes that are not refreshed within the period specified by the route expiration timer are marked as expired in the routing table. The default value of this field is 180 seconds (three RIP announcement intervals). This parameter is effective only if **Periodic update mode** is selected on the General tab.

Time before route is removed (seconds). This parameter specifies the interval between the expiration of a route and the time the route is removed from the routing table. This parameter is effective only if **Periodic update mode** is selected on the General tab.

Enable split-horizon processing. When this option is checked, split-horizon processing is used to determine which interfaces will be used to advertise routes learned from outside routers. When split horizon is in effect, a route will not be advertised through the interface from which the route was learned.

Enable poison-reverse processing. This option is available when split-horizon processing is enabled. When poison-reverse processing is in effect, a route is advertised through the interface from which the route was learned, but it is advertised with a cost of 16.

Enable triggered updates. When triggered updates are enabled, if the router learns a route or metric change, it advertises the change immediately without waiting for the interval specified by the periodic announcement timer. The minimum interval for triggered updates is specified on the General tab of the RIP for Internet Protocol Configuration dialog box, described earlier in this chapter. Triggered updates are enabled by default. Although triggered updates speed network convergence, they result in higher levels of router traffic.

Send clean-up updates when stopping. When this option is selected, a router that is shutting down announces its entire routing table with all metrics set to 15, thereby informing other routers that all its routes are unreachable. Other routers can immediately update their routing tables without waiting to discover the change in periodic router announcements. This option is enabled by default.

Process host routes in received announcements. By default, RIP updates its routing table with network routes learned from other routers' route advertisements. Host routes, however, are ignored. Enable this option if RIP should process host routes that are learned from other routers.

Include host routes in sent announcements. By default, RIP advertises only the network routes in its routing table. Host routes are not advertised. Check this option if RIP should advertise the host routes in its routing table.

Process default routes in received announcements. By default, default routes in incoming route advertisements are not recorded in the local routing table. Enable this option if incoming default routes should be processed for addition to the local routing table.

Include default routes in sent announcements. By default, the router does not advertise default routes in its own routing table. Enable this option if default routes should be advertised.

Disable subnet summarization. If the **Outgoing packet protocol** on the **General** tab is set to **RIP version 2 broadcast** or **RIP version 2 multicast**, the router can summarize multiple subnets in the form of a single, class-based route announcement. Use of subnet summaries requires careful attention to subnet design and in most cases should be disabled.

Configuring RIP Properties

The RIP router has a variety of properties that can be configured. To open the **RIP Properties** dialog box shown in Figure 7.30, right-click the RIP icon and select **Properties** from the context menu.

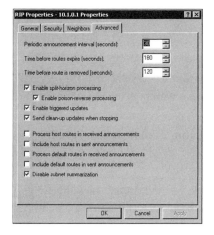

7

ROUTING WITH
RRAS

FIGURE 7.29
RIP Interface Properties: The Advanced tab.

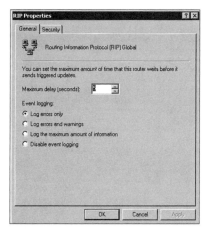

FIGURE 7.30
RIP Properties: The General tab.

RIP Properties: The General Tab

The **General** tab of the **RIP Properties** dialog box configures the following properties:

Maximum delay (seconds). This parameter determines the length of time the RIP router will wait before sending a triggered update in response to a route change. Increasing the interval might reduce network traffic at the cost of delaying the process of converging the network. The default value is 5 seconds.

Event logging. There are four options that determine the types of log records that will be recorded for the RIP router. RIP log messages are recorded in the System Log.

- **Log errors only.** This is the most appropriate choice for day-to-day operation. Most errors describe fatal events that interfere with RIP functionality.

- **Log errors and warnings.** Warnings report noncritical events that take place during router operation.

- **Log the maximum amount of information.** Logging will be verbose. Because this is demanding and can cause the System Log to fill up rapidly, select this mode only when testing or troubleshooting RIP.

- **Disable event logging.** In general, I don't recommend that you disable logging entirely. When RIP irregularities occur, it is useful to be able to check the System Log for recent critical events.

RIP Properties: The Security Tab

The **Security** tab of the **RIP Properties** dialog box (see Figure 7.31) determines which announcements the router will accept from other RIP routers. The following options are available:

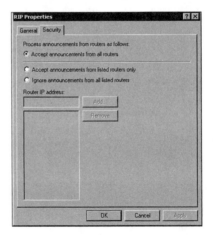

FIGURE 7.31

RIP Properties: The Security tab.

- **Accept announcements from all routers.** Select this option to accept all announcements received.

- **Accept announcements from listed routers only.** Select this option to accept announcements only from routers specified in the **Router IP address** list.

- **Ignore announcements from all listed routers.** Select this option to reject announcements from routers specified in the **Router IP address** list.

RIP Routes in the Routing Table

Figure 7.32 shows a RRAS routing table that includes routes learned from RIP. To obtain this figure, I enabled RIP support on all three routers shown in Figure 7.10 and captured the routing table for router A. Examine Figure 7.10 and then note the metrics shown in the routing table in Figure 7.32. Notice that the metrics for routes to networks 10.3.0.0 and 10.4.0.0 are 3 and 4, respectively, whereas we might expect them to be 2 and 3. (For example, packets from router A cross network 10.2.0.0 and 10.3.0.0 to reach a host on network 10.3.0.0, hence an anticipated metric of 2.)

The increased value of the metric results because of a characteristic of the Windows 2000 RIP service mentioned in an earlier Note. Windows 2000 RIP regards all routes not learned from RIP as having a metric of 2, including routes learned from static interface configuration data.

DC1 – IP Routing Table

Destination	Network mask	Gateway	Interface	Metric	Protocol
0.0.0.0	0.0.0.0	10.2.0.2	10.2.0.1	1	Network ma...
10.1.0.0	255.255.0.0	10.1.0.1	10.1.0.1	1	Local
10.1.0.1	255.255.255.255	127.0.0.1	Loopback	1	Local
10.2.0.0	255.255.0.0	10.2.0.1	10.2.0.1	1	Local
10.2.0.1	255.255.255.255	127.0.0.1	Loopback	1	Local
10.3.0.0	255.255.0.0	10.2.0.2	10.2.0.1	3	RIP
10.4.0.0	255.255.0.0	10.2.0.2	10.2.0.1	4	RIP
10.255.255.255	255.255.255.255	10.2.0.1	10.2.0.1	1	Local
10.255.255.255	255.255.255.255	10.1.0.1	10.1.0.1	1	Local
127.0.0.0	255.0.0.0	127.0.0.1	Loopback	1	Local
127.0.0.1	255.255.255.255	127.0.0.1	Loopback	1	Local
224.0.0.0	240.0.0.0	10.2.0.1	10.2.0.1	1	Local
224.0.0.0	240.0.0.0	10.1.0.1	10.1.0.1	1	Local
255.255.255.255	255.255.255.255	10.2.0.1	10.2.0.1	1	Local
255.255.255.255	255.255.255.255	10.1.0.1	10.1.0.1	1	Local

FIGURE 7.32
Routes learned from RIP appear in this routing table.

Configuring Silent RIP

Silent RIP enables computers to listen in on RIP announcements so that they can modify their routing tables as the network's routing configuration changes. Silent RIP does not increase network traffic, but it can greatly improve routing efficiency on networks that have redundant routing paths.

On Windows 2000 Servers, silent RIP is enabled as a property of the network interfaces. Silent RIP is enabled by opening the **Properties** dialog box for a RIP network interface, selecting the **General** tab, and selecting **Silent RIP** in the **Outgoing packet protocol** field.

To enable silent RIP on a Windows 2000 Professional client, do the following:

1. Open the **Add/Remove Programs** applet in the Control Panel.
2. Select **Add/Remove Windows Components**.
3. Install the **RIP Listener** component, which is listed under **Networking Services**.

There is nothing to configure regarding silent RIP. You can view the routing table on a Windows 2000 Professional client by entering the command **route print** in a command prompt window. Routes learned from RIP will have metrics greater than 1.

Configuring OSPF

OSPF (RFC 1583) is a protocol on the Internet Standards track that is becoming increasingly popular for routing within autonomous systems. An *autonomous system* (AS) is a group of routers that share a common routing protocol. An entire TCP/IP internetwork does not have to use a common routing protocol, and can be configured into several ASes that exchange routing information.

> **NOTE**
>
> The name Open Shortest Path First is often misconstrued. OSPF is an *open* implementation (that is, the implementation is public and non-proprietary) of the *shortest path first* routing algorithm. Consequently, *open* in this context is an adjective, not a verb.

OSPF is a link-state routing protocol, meaning that each router maintains a database that describes the topology of the local autonomous system. This topological database takes the form of a tree, with each router placed at the root of its own tree. Data to construct the database come from link-state advertisements sent by the routers in the AS.

To illustrate this process, consider the network illustrated in Figure 7.33. As shown, link-state algorithms can use more flexible metrics than RIP. The network administrator can assign the cost of any given link, and the total cost for a path does not necessarily have a limit, which enables link-state routing to model ASes that are indefinitely large. The upper limit for the metric used with OSPF is 65,535, which is sufficient to support networks of considerable scope.

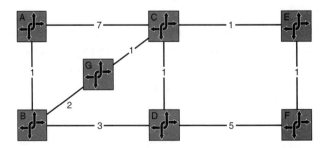

FIGURE 7.33
A network illustrating the OSPF algorithm.

Each node places itself at the root of its tree. The tree constructed for router B is shown in Figure 7.34. The link-state database contains information about the most efficient route available to each destination. The tree contains the route B-G-C (cost 3) but has discarded the route B-A-C (cost 6). (The algorithm for determining the least-cost path is called the *Dijkstra algorithm*.)

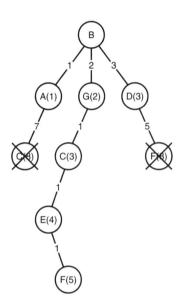

FIGURE 7.34

A router's link-state database tree.

NOTE

When multiple routes of the same cost are available to a destination, OSPF routers can perform load balancing by distributing traffic across the available routes. RIP lacks this capability.

OSPF routers have the following two relationships:

- *Neighboring routers* connect to a common network.
- *Adjacencies* are relationships among selected neighboring routers used to share routing information. Not all neighboring routers become adjacent.

A router that starts up uses the OSPF Hello Protocol to acquire neighbors. On networks that support broadcasts, routers can dynamically discover neighbors; Hello packets are multicast to all routers on the local network. If a network does not support broadcast messaging, some level of manual configuration is required before the router can identify its neighbors.

Routers attempt to form adjacencies with newly acquired neighbors. Adjacent routers synchronize their topological databases. Adjacencies then are used to distribute routing protocol packets. A router advertises its state by transmitting a link state update packet to its adjacencies.

Link-state advertisements flood the routing area. Reliable delivery is used to ensure that each router in the area has identical information. Each router uses this information to calculate its own shortest-path tree.

OSPF operates directly above IP, unlike RIP, which uses UDP as a transport. When the fragmentation of OSPF protocol packets is necessary, the responsibility falls to IP.

OSPF uses several techniques to reduce the amount of messaging required to maintain the routing database:

- Although routers periodically transmit link-state advertisements, this is done at infrequent intervals. This contrasts sharply with RIP, which requires each router to send its entire routing table every 30 seconds.
- Apart from those infrequent updates, a router advertises its state only when it detects a change in the network.
- Link-state update packets can contain routing information for multiple routers.
- Link-state update packets are sent only to adjacencies. Adjacencies are responsible for forwarding the information until it has been flooded throughout the AS. Consequently, each OSPF packet travels a single IP hop.

This overview of OSPF has been necessarily brief. A full description in the RFC requires more than 200 pages. The goal has been to illuminate the areas in which OSPF improves on RIP. In particular, OSPF eliminates incidents of self-referential routing information by enabling each router to build an unambiguous routing database. Also, maintenance of OSPF routing places more modest demands on network bandwidth than RIP, a capability of special importance on WAN links of limited bandwidth. Finally, OSPF does not impose an artificial size limit on the network, as with the 15-hop limit specified for RIP.

> **NOTE**
>
> Although OSPF makes more efficient use of network bandwidth than RIP, it places higher demands on the processing capabilities of the router. Because many inexpensive or older routers do not have the capability of supporting OSPF, RIP remains the dominant IP routing protocol.

Like RIP, OSPF configuration has two procedural components: configuration of the OSPF router's general parameters, and configuration of the interfaces. Before you actually implement an OSPF network, you need to know how to configure OSPF routing areas.

Planning OSPF Routing Areas

Figure 7.35 shows a diagram of a network that uses OSPF routing. The diagram focuses on routers, and, of course, many more TCP/IP hosts would appear on the networks that the routers join. Now, let's review the components of the network, with an emphasis on concepts that you must consider when configuring OSPF routers.

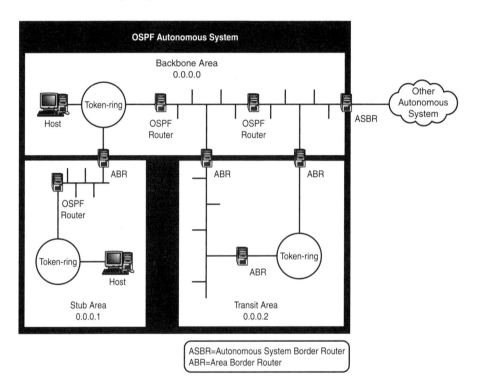

FIGURE 7.35

Diagram of an OSPF network.

An *autonomous system* (AS) is a collection of networks that share a common routing protocol. Figure 7.34 includes one OSPF AS.

Areas define groups of OSPF routers that share a common link-state database. OSPF advertises routes using link-state advertisements (LSAs), which are flooded throughout an area. *Flooding* describes the process of distributing LSAs to all OSPF routers in an area. On small-to-medium size networks, the entire AS can be configured as a single area.

One router in an area is identified as the *designated router* through an election process that can be configured by setting priorities for individual routers. The designated router is responsible for preparing LSAs for the area.

Within an area, OSPF routers communicate with *neighbors*, which are peer OSPF routers. On broadcast networks, OSPF routers can discover their peers using Hello packets. Only routers that exchange Hello packets establish themselves as neighbors. On non-broadcast networks, such as X.25 and packet relay, the addresses of neighbors must be added manually to the routers' configurations.

A *designated router* is established for each network that attaches through two or more routers. The designated router is selected through an election process, and becomes adjacent to all other routers on the network. The designated router originates all link-state advertisements for the network.

As areas grow in size, OSPF performance diminishes in two areas: It takes longer to recompute the new routes that result from link-state changes, and increasing amounts of network traffic are devoted to distributing link-state advertisements. Consequently, the design of OSPF accommodates partitioning the AS into multiple areas. This has two advantages:

- Areas can be configured around organizational or geographical relationships, limiting the sharing of routing information and making the network more secure.
- The number of LSAs in the areas is reduced, and they are limited to the information users require most often.

NOTE

A good rule of thumb is to limit the size of an AS to 200 routers.

Areas must be organized hierarchically, with one area designated as a backbone area. All other areas must connect to the backbone area. Each area is identified by an area ID, a four-byte number, which is usually expressed in dotted-decimal form. These area IDs are not IP addresses and don't need to follow IP address restrictions. The backbone area is always assigned the area ID 0.0.0.0.

Areas must be configured out of contiguous groups of routers and networks. In other words, parts of an area must not be separated by another area. Because most areas typically support a localized subset of hosts, it is seldom a problem to configure areas out of contiguous components. Because only one backbone is permitted, however, it can be difficult to configure a backbone contiguously on a geographically dispersed network.

It is possible to partition the backbone area into multiple physical areas, and to enable the backbone partitions to communicate using a virtual link through another area. The area that supports the virtual link is called a virtual-link transit area. Because virtual-links are complex and trouble prone, I regard them as advanced tools that are beyond the scope of this introductory chapter.

Area border routers (ABRs) connect areas and advertise destinations across area boundaries in the form of *summary link advertisements*.

Two types of areas can connect to the backbone area:

- *Stub areas* connect to the backbone through a single ABR. The ABR of a stub area does not advertise external routes. Instead, because all external traffic must go through the ABR, a single default route is advertised. Configuration of stub areas reduces the memory, processing, and bandwidth requirements of the ABR but obviously makes the area subject to a single point of failure.

- *Transit areas* connect to the backbone with more than one ABR. Processing, memory, and bandwidth requirements are higher for ABRs that support transit areas. Routing within an area, called *intra-area routing*, can take place without knowledge of external routes. Routing between areas, *inter-area routing*, requires ABRs to exchange routing information about their areas.

Autonomous system border routers (ASBRs) are responsible for routing traffic between the OSPF AS and ASes based on other routing protocols such as RIP. External routes are advertised through *external link advertisements*.

7

ROUTING WITH
RRAS

NOTE

OSPF gives different preferences to routes that are obtained from the local AS (internal routes) and from remote ASes (external routes). On a network that includes OSPF and RIP routers, for example, an OSPF router prefers a route that it learns internally from another OSPF router over a route that it learns externally from a RIP router.

If your network includes multiple brands of routers, you need to ensure that all routers employ the same preferences. Consult the TCP/IP Reference manual for more information about OSPF protocol preferences.

Adding OSPF to RRAS

To add OSPF to RRAS, do the following:

1. Right-click the **General** icon under the **IP Routing** object and choose **New Routing Protocol** in the context menu.

2. In the **New Routing Protocol** dialog box, select **Open Shortest Path First (OSPF)** and click **OK**.

An icon labeled **OSPF** is added in the **IP Routing** container.

Adding OSPF Interfaces

Before OSPF is functional, you must specify each interface that OSPF is to support. Perform the following procedure for each interface:

1. Right-click the **OSPF** icon and choose **New Interface** in the context menu.

2. Select an interface that is listed in the **New Interface for Open Shortest Path First (OSPF)** dialog box and click **OK**.

3. The next dialog box, named **OSPF Interface Properties**, is shown in Figure 7.36. Configure the options as described in the next section.

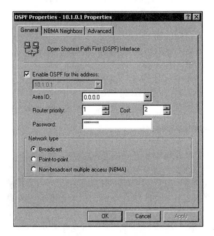

FIGURE 7.36
OSPF Interface Properties: The General tab.

Configuring OSPF Interface Properties

After an interface is added, it will be listed in the details pane of the RRAS console when the **OSPF** icon is selected. You can modify the properties of an interface by right-clicking the interface and choosing **Properties** from the context menu.

OSPF Interface Properties: The General Tab

The OSPF interface properties **General** tab is shown in Figure 7.36. The settings on this tab are as follows:

Enable OSPF for this address. This box is checked by default, enabling OSPF support on the interface. If multiple IP addresses are bound to the interface, select an IP address in the drop-down list. Each IP address must be configured individually.

Area ID. Select the OSPF area associated with the network that connects to this interface. Before areas can be selected in this field, they must be defined in the OSPF router general configuration.

Router priority. The router priority establishes preferences for the election of the designated router for a network. In general, the router that has the highest router priority will be selected as the designated router.

Cost. This parameter defines the cost for sending a packet out through this interface. Lower-cost interfaces will be preferred over higher-cost interfaces. The default cost is 2. The maximum cost is 32,767.

Password. If passwords are enabled for an area (**Enable plaintext password** is checked on the **OSPF Area Configuration** dialog box), all routers that communicate with that area must be configured to use the same area password. (As with RIP, passwords are transmitted in clear text and should not be regarded as a security mechanism.)

Network type. This box offers the following three options that specify the type of interface:

- **Broadcast.** Select this option for a broadcast interface, such as Ethernet, token ring, FDDI, or another LAN protocol.
- **Point-to-point.** Select this option for a point-to-point link such as a T1, T3, or dial-up connection.
- **Non-broadcast multiple access (NBMA).** Select this option for a *non-broadcast multiaccess* (NBMA) network such as X.25, frame relay, or ATM. Use the **NBMA Neighbors** tab to define neighbors for this router.

OSPF Interface Properties: The NBMA Neighbors Tab

On broadcast networks such as Ethernet and token ring, OSPF routers use the Hello protocol to establish adjacencies and neighbor relationships. The Hello protocol relies on broadcast messages that are not supported on non-broadcast networks such as X.25, frame relay, and ATM (without LAN emulation). On non-broadcast networks, neighbors must be explicitly defined. This is done on the **NBMA Neighbors** tab, shown in Figure 7.37. A neighbor definition has two fields, which are active only when **Non-broadcast multiple access (NBMA)** is selected on the **General** tab:

Address. Enter the neighbor's IP address.

Router priority. Specify a priority. The router with the highest priority on a given network will be preferred in elections to determine the designated router for the network.

7

ROUTING WITH
RRAS

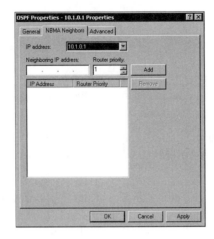

FIGURE 7.37

OSPF Interface Properties: The NBMA Neighbors tab.

OSPF Interface Properties: The Advanced Tab

The OSPF interface properties **Advanced** tab is shown in Figure 7.38. In most cases, you will not need to adjust the parameters on this tab. The following parameters are available:

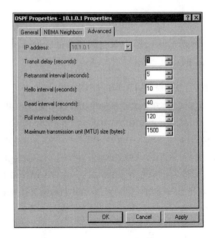

FIGURE 7.38

OSPF Interface Properties: The Advanced tab.

IP Address. If multiple IP addresses are bound to the interface, select an IP address in the drop-down list. Each IP address must be configured individually.

Transit delay (seconds). This parameter is an estimate of the time in seconds required to deliver a link-state advertisement through this interface. The default value is 1 second.

Retransmit interval (seconds). This parameter specifies the number of seconds between retransmission of LSAs and should exceed the round-trip time between this router and its adjacencies. This parameter should be adjusted to reflect the type of network, and must be increased for slow networks and virtual links. If the retransmit interval is too short, LSAs might be needlessly retransmitted.

Hello interval (seconds). This parameter specifies the interval between transmission of Hello packets, and must be the same for all routers on a given network. A shorter interval results in faster propagation of network changes but also results in greater levels of network traffic. A Hello interval of 30 seconds might be used on a low-bandwidth network such as X.25, whereas 10 seconds might be used on a LAN.

Dead interval (seconds). This parameter determines how long this router will wait before declaring a silent router to be dead. A silent router is a router that fails to respond to Hello packets. Typically, this parameter should be several multiples of the Hello interval. If the Hello interval is 10 seconds and the Dead interval is 40 seconds, the router will transmit four unacknowledged Hello packets before declaring a given router to be dead.

Poll interval (seconds). On non-broadcast networks, routers cannot use broadcast Hello packets to determine that a dead router has been reactivated. This parameter is specified on NBMA networks to establish the interval between attempts to contact the dead router. The poll interval should be at least twice the dead interval.

Maximum transmission unit (MTU) size (bytes). This parameter specifies the *maximum transfer unit* (MTU), which is the maximum packet size to be used when sending OSPF packets from this interface. The default value of 1500 is appropriate for 10Mbps Ethernet. The standard MTU for FDDI networks is 4096. Adjust this parameter to reflect the maximum packet size and reliability of the attached network.

Configuring OSPF Properties

The OSPF router has a variety of properties that can be configured. To open the **OSPF Properties** dialog box shown in Figure 7.39, right-click the OSPF icon in the object tree and choose **Properties** from the context menu.

OSPF Properties: The General Tab

When you add OSPF, the dialog box shown in Figure 7.39 enables you to configure general OSPF parameters.

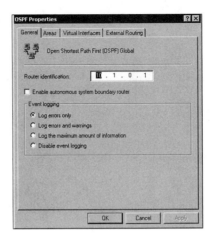

FIGURE 7.39
OSPF Properties: The General tab.

Router identification. In this field, enter a 32-bit number in dotted-decimal notation that uniquely identifies this OSPF router. The default approach for defining the router identification is to select the IP address that is assigned one of the router's interfaces. You are not restricted to using IP addresses, however, and can devise your own standards for identifying routers if you want.

Enable autonomous system boundary router. Check this field if this router functions as an ASBR.

Event logging. The radio buttons in this box determine the types of messages that will be recorded in the Event Viewer. Options are the same as for the RIP protocol, and are explained earlier in this chapter in the section "RIP Properties: The General Tab."

OSPF Properties: The Areas Tab

The **Areas** tab is shown in Figure 7.40. The **Areas** list is configured with a list of all areas that interfaces on this router connect to. The first area in an OSPF autonomous system is designated as the backbone area and is assigned area number 0.0.0.0.

Click the **Add** button to define a new area using the **OSPF Area Configuration** dialog box, shown in Figure 7.41. The **General** tab has the following fields:

- **Enable plaintext password.** If this field is checked, passwords will be used to determine which OSPF routers will communicate with one another. When passwords are used, each interface must be configured with a password.

- **Stub area.** Check this box if this router is an area border router servicing a stub area. The backbone (area 0.0.0.0) cannot be configured as a stub area. Virtual links cannot be configured as stub areas.

- **Stub metric.** If **Stub area** is checked, this field specifies the routing cost that the ABR will advertise to outside areas.

- **Import summary advertisements.** By default, routing within a stub area (*intraarea routing*) makes use of default routes. If this option is checked, the ABR will import routes learned from outside areas (non-intraarea routes) and will advertise non-intraarea routes within the area.

FIGURE 7.40
OSPF Properties: The Areas tab.

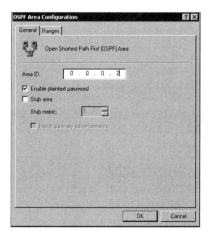

FIGURE 7.41
OSPF Area Configuration: The General tab.

Areas are explicitly configured to service ranges of IP addresses. This is done on the **OSPF Area Configuration Ranges** tab, shown in Figure 7.42. To add an IP address range to an area:

1. Enter an IP subnet address in the **Destination** field.

2. Enter the subnet mask in the **Network mask** field.

3. Choose **Add**.

Enter all the address ranges that are encompassed by the area being defined.

FIGURE 7.42

Defining address ranges for an area.

NOTE

Typically, a given area will be serviced by two or more OSPF routers. There is no mechanism that enables OSPF routers to exchange information about the configuration of an area. It is up to the administrator to manually review the area configurations on each router to ensure consistency.

OSPF Routes in the Routing Table

OSPF routes are listed in the **IP Routing Table** with the protocol identified as OSPF. As illustrated earlier in the chapter, the **IP Routing Table** is displayed by right-clicking the **Static Routes** object under IP Routing and selecting **Show IP Routing Table** from the context menu.

Configuring IP Interfaces

IP interfaces are listed in the details pane when the **General** icon is selected in the **IP Routing** container. Some of these properties relate to IP multicast routing and will be discussed in the section "Configuring IP Multicast Routing."

To view the **Properties** dialog box for an interface, select the **General** icon in the **IP Routing** container, right-click the desired interface, and choose **Properties** from the context menu. Figure 7.43 shows the **Properties** dialog box for an interface with the **General** tab selected.

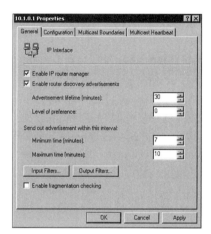

FIGURE 7.43

IP Interface Properties: The General tab.

IP Interface Properties: The General Tab

The **General** tab has the following options:

Enable IP router manager. If this option is checked, TCP/IP is functional on this interface. Remove the check to disable TCP/IP support for the interface. The **Administrative Status** column of the details pane reports the status of each interface as Up or Down.

Enable router discovery advertisements. By default, this box is not checked, and the router does not attempt to discover other routers using multicast ICMP router discovery advertisements. Therefore, if this feature is enabled, a multicast routing environment must be configured. When router discovery advertisements are enabled, the following fields can be configured:

- **Advertisement lifetime (minutes).** Determines the amount of time that a router discovery advertisement is considered to be valid. The default value is 30 minutes.
- **Level of preference.** Establishes the priority clients will use to determine whether this interface should be their default router if the interface is discovered through ICMP route

advertisements. Higher values indicate that the interface has a higher usage preference. On networks with two or more routers, you can use the level of preference to determine which interface clients will select as their default routers.

- **Send out advertisements within this interval, Minimum time (minutes).** Specifies the minimum time in minutes between router advertisements. The default is 7 minutes.

- **Send out advertisements within this interval, Maximum time (minutes).** Specifies the maximum time in minutes between router advertisements. The default is 10 minutes.

Input Filters. This button opens dialog boxes where input filters can be configured for this interface. See the next section for information about configuring input filters.

Output Filters. This button opens dialog boxes where output filters can be configured for this interface. See the next section for information about configuring output filters.

Enable fragmentation checking. If this option is checked, IP will not forward fragmented datagrams. Fragmentation filtering applies to incoming packets only. Fragmentation filtering can prevent the Ping of Death attack, which involves sending one or more ICMP messages with sizes of 64KB, requiring the messages to be fragmented when sent and to be reassembled by the receiving device. The receiving host must allocate resources to buffer and reassemble the large datagrams, which can impair performance significantly. It is, therefore, useful to enable fragmentation checking on any interface that connects with an outside public network.

> **NOTE**
>
> Although IP supports datagram fragmentation and reassembly, well-designed TCP/IP stacks avoid sending fragmented datagrams. IP does not perform error checking, and cannot request retransmission of a fragment. Therefore, if one fragment of a datagram is damaged, TCP must request retransmission of the entire datatagram. It is far more efficient for TCP to provide IP with message segments that are sized so that fragmentation will not be required.
>
> Since a well-behaved TCP/IP stack doesn't send fragmented datagrams, enabling fragmentation checking usually will have no ill effects. But there's always a chance that IP fragments will be generated, and enabling fragmentation checking is not entirely without risks. Only protocol analysis can tell you what's really going on.

Defining Input and Output Filters

RRAS can filter packets being received and transmitted by an IP interface based on the following criteria:

- **IP address and subnet mask.** Filters can be based on the source network or the destination network.

- **TCP.** Filters can be based on the source port and/or destination port.
- **UDP.** Filters can be based on the source port and/or destination port.
- **ICMP.** Filters can be based on the ICMP message type and ICMP code.
- **Other.** Filters can be based on protocol numbers appearing in the IP header.
- **Any.** Filters can allow all datagram types to be received or blocked.

Viewing Filter Lists

Active filters are displayed by clicking **Input Filters** or **Output Filters** in the IP interface **General Properties** tab. Figure 7.44 shows an **Input Filters** list. There are two options that determine how these filters will be interpreted:

- **Receive all packets except those that meet the criteria below**
- **Drop all packets except those that meet the criteria below**

Suppose that you are configuring IP filtering on a Windows 2000 Server running the Internet Information Service and that you want to block all packets except those related to the WWW server. WWW servers rely on the HTTP protocol, which by default is configured to use TCP port 80. To allow only HTTP traffic, you would need to configure input and output filters that permit only that protocol to be routed. Figure 7.44 shows an **Input Filters** list configured to allow datagrams for TCP port 80. The filter in place drops all packets that are not being delivered to destination port 80.

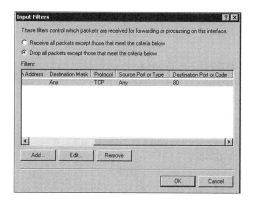

FIGURE 7.44

An Input Filters list that accepts only datagrams for port 80.

The **Output Filters** dialog box is similar to the **Input Filters** box shown in Figure 7.44, but the options are as follows:

- **Transmit all packets except those that meet the criteria below**
- **Drop all packets except those that meet the criteria below**

Figure 7.45 shows an Output Filters dialog box that limits the interface to sending HTTP datagrams (port 80).

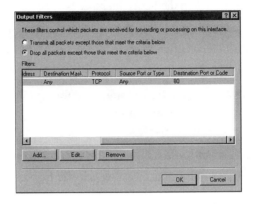

FIGURE 7.45

An Output Filters list that transmits only datagrams for port 80.

CAUTION

Of course, 80 isn't the only port used for Web servers. Sites can be configured with custom ports, and different ports will be used when communicating using the Secure HTTP protocol. So don't forget that you've applied port-based filters to an interface.

Defining a Filter

To add a new filter to a filter list, click the **Add** button in either the **Input Filters** or **Output Filters** list box. The **Add IP Filter** dialog box is shown in Figure 7.46. Configure a filter as follows:

1. To filter based on the source network, check **Source network** and complete the **IP address** and **Subnet mask** fields to specify the network. Filtering on the source network is optional.

2. To filter based on the destination network, check **Destination network** and complete the **IP address** and **Subnet mask** fields to specify the network. Filtering on the destination network is optional.

3. In the **Protocol** field, select the protocol to be configured:

   - **Any.** All protocols are filtered. Choose this protocol to base filtering solely on the source network and/or the destination network.

   - **TCP.** Specify a port number in the **Source port** and/or **Destination port** fields.

   - **UDP.** Specify a port number in the **Source port** and/or **Destination port** fields.

FIGURE 7.46
Defining an IP filter.

> **NOTE**
>
> RRAS does not provide a means of filtering ranges of TCP or UDP port numbers. You must define each port to be filtered separately.

> **NOTE**
>
> See http://www.iana.org for definitive listings of TCP and UDP ports, ICMP types and codes, and registered protocol numbers.

- **ICMP.** Specify an ICMP message type in the **ICMP type** field. If the ICMP message type supports codes, you can optionally specify an ICMP code in the **ICMP code** field. Table 7.1 lists some common ICMP message types and codes.

- **Other.** Enter the protocol number to be filtered in the **Protocol number** field.

TABLE 7.1   Common ICMP Message Types

Type	Code	Name
0	0	Echo Reply
3	0	Network Unreachable
3	1	Host Unreachable
3	2	Protocol Unreachable
3	3	Port Unreachable

TABLE 7.1   Continued

Type	Code	Name
3	4	Fragmentation Needed and Don't Fragment Was Set
3	5	Source Route Failed
3	6	Destination Network Unknown
3	7	Destination Host Unknown
3	8	Source Host Isolated
3	9	Communication with Destination Network Is Administratively Prohibited
3	10	Communication with Destination Host Is Administratively Prohibited
3	11	Destination Network Unreachable for Type of Service
3	12	Destination Host Unreachable for Type of Service
4	0	Source Quench
3	0	Redirect Datagram for the Network or Subnet
3	1	Redirect Datagram for the Host
3	2	Redirect Datagram for the Type of Service and Network
3	3	Redirect Datagram for the Type of Service and Host
6	0	Alternate Host Address
8	0	Echo
9	0	Router Advertisement
10	0	Router Selection
11	0	Time to Live Exceeded in Transmit
11	1	Fragment Reassembly Time Exceeded
12	0	Parameter Problem
12	0	Pointer Indicates an Error
12	1	Missing a Required Option
12	2	Bad Length
15	0	Information Request
16	0	Information Reply
17	0	Address Mask Request
18	0	Address Mask Reply
30	0	Traceroute, datagram successfully forwarded
30	1	Traceroute, no route for packet, packet discarded

IP Interface Properties: The Configuration Tab

This tab provides another means of configuring the interface properties that are ordinarily modified in the Network and Dial-Up Connections applet in the control panel.

Configuring IP Multicast Routing

IP multicast datagrams are routed separately from unicast datagrams using a mechanism that is mediated by the Internet Group Messaging Protocol (IGMP). RRAS includes an IGMP multicast router.

The IP multicast router has two modes: router mode and proxy mode.

In router mode, the IP multicast router performs the following functions:

- Listens in *multicast promiscuous* mode. If multicast promiscuous mode is not supported by the network adapter, the IP Router Management event number 10157 is entered in the System Log.
- Receives IGMP multicast group membership reports from hosts on attached networks. Hosts report when they are joining or leaving a group.
- Sends IGMP queries to attached networks to update membership status.
- Forwards multicast datagrams as required by host group memberships.

Notice that router mode makes no provision for exchanging multicast group information with other multicast routers. Router mode is used on interfaces that service locally attached networks, such as the intranet environment shown in Figure 7.47.

> **NOTE**
>
> Because RRAS multicast routers cannot exchange group information, they can support multicast routing only on small networks that have a single router hop. To implement an enterprise multicast routing infrastructure, you will need to deploy third-party routers, which you will probably need to do in any case to support routing performance requirements.

In proxy mode, a router interface functions as a host, enabling the IP router to connect to a multicast-enabled IP internetwork such as the Internet's multicast backbone (the MBone) or another network that is using multicast routing protocols. Multicast proxy mode is enabled on a network that communicates with a multicast core router that is running multicast routing protocols, such as the network shown in Figure 7.48.

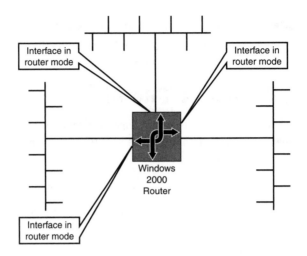

FIGURE 7.47

Multicast routing support on a single router intranet.

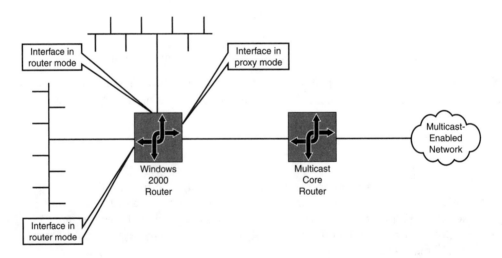

FIGURE 7.48

Multicast proxy mode enables the multicast router to exchange multicast group information with a multicast core router.

Adding IGMP Multicast Support to RRAS

To add IGMP multicast support to RRAS, do the following:

1. Right-click the **General** icon under the **IP Routing** object and choose **New Routing Protocol** in the context menu.

2. In the **New Routing Protocol** dialog box, select **IGMP Version 2 Router and Proxy** and click **OK**.

An icon labeled **IGMP** is added in the **IP Routing** container.

Adding and Configuring IGMP Interfaces

Before IGMP multicasting is functional, you must specify each interface that is to be supported. Perform the following procedure for each interface:

1. Right-click the **IGMP** icon and choose **New Interface** in the context menu.

2. Select an interface that is listed in the **New Interface for IGMP Version 2**, **Router and Proxy** dialog box and click **OK**.

3. The next dialog box, named **IGMP Properties**, is shown in Figure 7.49. Configure options as described in the following two sections.

After an interface is added, it will be listed in the details pane of the RRAS console when the **IGMP** icon is selected. You can modify the properties of an interface by right-clicking the interface and choosing **Properties** from the context menu.

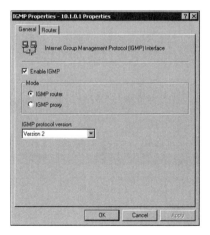

FIGURE 7.49
IGMP Interface Properties: The General tab.

7

ROUTING WITH RRAS

IGMP Interface Configuration: The General Tab

The IGMP interface properties **General** tab is shown in Figure 7.49. The settings on this tab are as follows:

Enable IGMP. Check this box to enable IGMP for this interface.

Mode. Select one of the following modes:

- **IGMP router.** The interface functions as an IGMP multicast listener and forwarder.
- **IGMP proxy.** The interface functions as an IGMP proxy and communicates with external routers running IP multicast protocols.

IGMP protocol version. Select **Version 1** or **Version 2**, where **Version 2** is the default value. IGMP version 2 is backward-compatible with version 1 but simplifies operation by electing a single IGMP router to transmit multicast queries for a given subnet. IGMP version 2 also introduces some new message types that streamline group management.

IGMP Interface Configuration: The Router Tab

Options on the **Router** tab (see Figure 7.50) can be configured only for interfaces configured to operate in IGMP router mode.

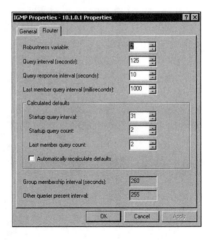

FIGURE 7.50
IGMP Interface Properties: The Router tab.

The following options are available:

Robustness variable. Determines the number of lost IGMP packets that will be tolerated on the interface. This value should be increased on networks that are known to occasionally drop packets.

Query interval (seconds). Specifies the interval that will elapse between IGMP general queries.

Query response interval (seconds). Specifies the time in seconds that the router will wait for responses to IGMP general queries.

Last number query interval (milliseconds). Specifies the time in milliseconds (!) that the IGMP router waits for responses to IGMP group-specific queries.

Calculated defaults.

- **Startup query interval.** Specifies the interval in seconds between successive general query messages sent during startup. The default interval and the automatically calculated value are one-fourth of the query interval.

- **Startup query count.** Specifies the number of general queries that are sent at startup. The default value is 2. When calculated automatically, this value is the same as the robustness variable.

- **Last member query count.** Specifies the number of group-specific query messages that are sent before the router assumes that there are no members on the network attached to the interface. When calculated automatically, this value is the same as the robustness variable.

- **Automatically recalculate defaults.** If this box is checked, values in the **Calculated defaults** section are defined automatically based on values entered in the **Robustness variable** and **Query interval** fields.

Group membership interval (seconds). Displays the group membership interval, which is calculated using the formula, (robustness variable)×(query interval)+(query response interval). This value cannot be edited directly.

Other queries present interval (seconds). Displays the calculated other queries present interval according to the formula, (robustness variable)×(query interval)+(query response interval)/2.

Displaying the Interface Group Table

You can determine the groups that are registered by an interface by displaying the **Interface Group Table**, an example of which appears in Figure 7.51. To display the **Interface Group Table,** right-click an IGMP interface and choose **Show Interface Group Table** from the context menu.

FIGURE 7.51

An IGMP Interface Group Table.

Configuring Interface Multicast Boundaries

You can define limits to the areas in which information will be propagated for multicast groups. You might want to define multicast boundaries to prevent multicast messages from WAN links, for example. Or you can use *multicast scopes* to establish groups of hosts that will exchange multicast information only with each other. These characteristics are configured on the **Multicast Boundaries** tab of the **Properties** dialog box for an IP interface, shown in Figure 7.52. Open this tab by selecting the **General** icon in the **IP Routing** container, right-clicking an interface, choosing **Properties** from the context menu, and selecting the **Multicast Boundaries** tab.

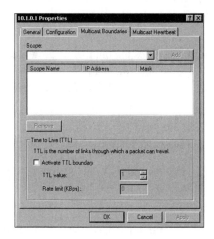

FIGURE 7.52
IP Interface Properties: The Multicast Boundaries tab.

A multicast scope is assigned a name and an IP address range that is shared by all members of the scope. After an interface is configured with a scope name, it will exchange multicast communication only with other interfaces that are members of the same scope.

TTL boundaries provide a mechanism for limiting the propagation of multicast datagrams.

NOTE

A thorough discussion of multicast scopes and TTL boundaries is beyond the scope of this book. See RFC 2365 for more information.

Configuring the DHCP Relay Agent

If DHCP forwarding is required on your network (see Chapter 5 for information about DHCP), you must configure the DHCP relay agent (also known as a *BOOTP forwarder*) on RRAS.

Adding the DHCP Relay Agent to RRAS

To add the DHCP Relay Agent to RRAS, do the following:

1. Right-click the **General** icon under the **IP Routing** object and choose **New Routing Protocol** in the context menu.

2. In the **New Routing Protocol** dialog box, select **DHCP Relay Agent** and click **OK**.

An icon labeled **DHCP Relay Agent** is added in the **IP Routing** container.

Adding and Configuring DHCP Relay Agent Interfaces

Before DHCP forwarding is functional, you must specify each interface that is to be supported. Perform the following procedure for each interface:

1. Right-click the **DHCP Relay Agent** icon and choose **New Interface** in the context menu.

2. Select an interface that is listed in the **New Interface for DHCP Relay Agent** dialog box and click **OK**.

3. The next dialog box, named **DHCP Relay Properties**, is shown in Figure 7.53. Configure the DHCP Relay properties as follows:

   - **Relay DHCP packets.** Check this box if this interface should be used to forward packets to DHCP servers.

   - **Hop count threshold.** This field specifies the maximum hop count allowed for DHCP packets originating at this router. The maximum value is 16 hops.

   - **Boot threshold (seconds).** This parameter specifies the period of time the relay agent will wait before forwarding DHCP requests. This delay provides a time interval in which a local DHCP server can respond before an attempt is made to contact a remote DHCP server. The default value is 4 seconds.

Configuring DHCP Relay Agent Properties

After the DHCP relay agent is added, you must specify the DHCP servers to which the DHCP relay agent will forward DHCP messages. This is done in the **DHCP Relay Agent Properties** dialog box, shown in Figure 7.54.

7

ROUTING WITH RRAS

To edit DHCP relay agent properties, right-click the **DHCP Relay Agent** icon and choose **Properties** from the context menu. Then add the IP addresses of DHCP servers to the **Server address** list.

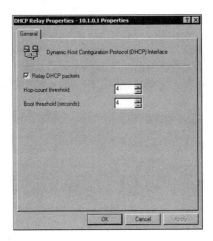

FIGURE 7.53

DHCP relay agent interface properties.

FIGURE 7.54

DHCP relay agent properties.

Configuring IPX Routing

Compared to IP, IPX routing is a snap to configure. There is a particularly significant difference between routing on IP and IPX servers, however. IP routing directs datagrams to a particular interface, which is identified by an IP address. The TCP/IP protocol stack delivers the datagram payload to the correct upper-layer protocol using port numbers associated with specific processes.

When a packet is being sent to a server, IPX routing directs packets to an internal IPX network number that is defined on all IPX servers. The internal IPX network is a virtual network that is "connected" to all the services the server has to offer.

RRAS supports the RIP routing protocol for IPX, which functions quite similarly to RIP on IP. The primary difference you will notice is that RIP for IPX broadcasts route advertisements at 60-second intervals as opposed to the 30-second intervals that are standard with RIP for IP.

7

ROUTING WITH
RRAS

NOTE

RRAS does not support the Novell Link State Protocol (NLSP), Novell's link state protocol for IPX networks. Beginning with version 5, NetWare servers default to NLSP routing with RIP/SAP capability for the IPX routing configuration, which supports both NLSP and legacy RIP/SAP protocols. NLSP is definitely the protocol of choice for NetWare IPX routing. If it is deployed on your NetWare network, you will need to configure NetWare servers to propagate routing information to Windows-based RIP routers.

NetWare uses the Service Advertising Protocol (SAP) to enable network clients to locate services on NetWare servers running on IPX networks. Each server maintains a Service Information Table (SIT; Microsoft calls them SAP tables), which it broadcasts periodically. SAP is a broadcast-based protocol, and because broadcast packets ordinarily don't cross routers, each IPX router maintains its own SIT, enabling it to advertise services to remote networks.

Windows propagates Windows service information on IPX networks using NetBIOS over IPX. NetBIOS over IPX relies on broadcast packets often referred to as *type 20* broadcast packets. The RRAS IPX routers can be configured to accept and optionally to forward type 20 broadcast packets, enabling NetBIOS names to be propagated by IPX routers. Consequently, on IPX networks there is no need for a service comparable to WINS.

Before we look at the procedures for managing RIP for IPX, we need to look at IPX network numbers in greater detail.

Adding and Configuring IPX Interfaces

In most cases, IPX interfaces are added to the IPX routing configuration when RRAS is enabled. IPX interfaces are listed in the details pane when the **General** icon is selected in the **IPX Routing** container.

To add new interfaces to the IPX routing configuration, right-click the **General** icon in the **IPX Routing** container and choose **New Interface** in the context menu. Follow the prompts to add the interface.

Figure 7.55 shows RRAS with the objects under **IPX Routing** expanded.

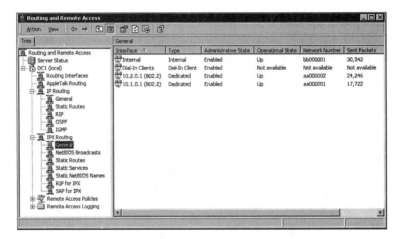

FIGURE 7.55

Interfaces for the IPX router are placed in the General container under the IPX Routing object.

NOTE

My convention for naming interfaces after their IP addresses might be a bit misleading under IPX. Just remember that the interface names in Figure 7.55, such as 10.2.0.1, are names only, and do not imply IP functionality in this context.

It's easy to spot an IPX interface in RRAS because the interface name includes a parenthetical notation that identifies the frame type used on the interface, for example, (802.2) for IEEE 802.3 Ethernet with support for the IEEE 802.2 Logical Link Control, which Novell refers to as the Ethernet_802.2 frame type.

IPX Interface Properties

To modify the properties for an IPX interface, right-click the interface and select **Properties** in the context menu to open the **Properties** dialog box shown in Figure 7.56. Options on the **General** tab are as follows:

- **Enable IPX on this interface**. IPX routing is functional on the interface only when this box is checked.

- **Dial-in control protocol.** The IPX router supports two dial-in control protocols:

  - **IPX CP** is used to support dial-up connections using the Point-to-Point Protocol (PPP) and is supported for dial-up connections to Windows 2000 routers and for dial-up clients.

  - **IPX WAN** is used to support dial-up connections to NetWare remote access services. IPX WAN is not supported for dial-up clients.

- **Input Filters.** Click this button to open a dialog box in which input filters can be configured.

- **Output Filters.** Click this button to open a dialog box in which output filters can be configured.

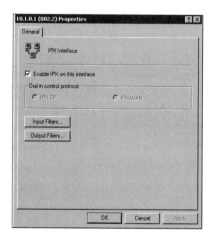

FIGURE 7.56

IPX Interface Properties.

IPX Interface Input and Output Filters

IPX interfaces can be configured to filter incoming and outgoing packets. Filtering is based on three parameters:

- **Network number**. A 4-byte (32-bit) number that provides a globally unique identification of each external and internal IPX network.

- **Node number.** A 6-byte (48-bit) number that is usually derived from the burned-in address of the network adapter.
- **Socket number.** A 2-byte (16 bit) number that uniquely identifies each service on a server.

On IPX networks, all addresses are typically expressed in hexadecimal notation. A given IPX service is uniquely identified by the combination of its network number, node number, and socket number, which is usually expressed in the following format:

(network number):(node number):(socket number)

The server's node number on the internal network is always 000000000001. If you analyze packets on an IPX network, you will see many server packets addressed to or from node 1 on the internal network. Common socket numbers are listed in Table 7.2. For a server with a network number of AA000001, the NCP service is identified by the following address:

AA000001:000000000001:0451

Consequently, every node on an IPX network is uniquely identified by the combination of its network number and its node number. And every service is uniquely identified by including the socket number in the address.

In my examples, external network numbers have the format AA00000n. Internal network numbers have the format BB00000n.

TABLE 7.2   Common IPX Socket Numbers

Socket	Service
0x0451	NetWare Core Protocols (NCP)
0x0452	Service Advertising Protocol (SAP)
0x0453	Routing Information Protocol (RIP)
0x0455	NetBIOS
0x9001	Novell Link State Protocol (NLSP)

NOTE

This is not the place to provide a thorough technical discussion of IPX. For more complete information, consult the Web site http://www.packet-level.com, which is also a good source of information about TCP/IP and protocol analysis. In this chapter, we will be focusing on IPX only insofar as is required to configure the IPX routing component of RRAS.

> **NOTE**
>
> See Chapter 1 for information about configuring network connections for IPX.

IPX packets also include a one-byte "packet type" number in the header. In theory, the packet type is intended to identify the type of IPX communication, but the type field has not been used consistently. In the majority of cases, this field is set to a value of 0x00 for "unknown." Table 7.3 lists some common IPX packet types. Of the packet types listed, only 0x05 (SPX) and 0x14 (NetBIOS over IPX, decimal value 20) can be considered reliable.

TABLE 7.3   Common IPX Packet Types

Packet Type	Protocol
0x00	Unknown or NLSP
0x01	RIP
0x04	Service Advertising Protocol (SAP)
0x05	Sequenced Packet Exchange (SPX)
0x11	NetWare Core Protocol (NCP)
0x14	NetBIOS over IPX ("Type 20 packets")

When you click **Input Filters** or **Output Filters** in the IPX interface **General Properties** dialog box, you open an **IPX Packet Filters Configuration** dialog box similar to the one in Figure 7.57. This box lists filters that are defined for the interface. When filters are defined, the following radio buttons are active:

- **Receive all packets except those that meet the criteria below.** Choose this option to block specific types of packets.
- **Drop all packets except those that meet the criteria below.** Choose this option to block all packets except those you choose to allow.

To define a filter, click the **Add** button to open the **Add IPX Filter** dialog box shown in Figure 7.58. Filters can be defined based on the sources or destinations of packets. The following fields must be defined for a filter:

- **Network number.** Enter the IPX network number up to 4 bytes in length (8 hex digits).
- **Network mask.** Enter a network mask of up to 8 characters that defines a range of IPX network numbers based on the specified network number. Enter a 0 (zero) in the network mask to match any hex digit. Enter an F in the network mask for a digit that requires an

exact match. Network masks are discussed in greater detail in the following section. (Since this field defines a mask, you cannot omit leading zeros.)

- **Node.** Enter a node number 6 bytes (12 hex digits) in length. The source and destination node numbers are optional values.

- **Socket.** Enter an IPX socket number 2 bytes (4 hex digits) in length.

- **Packet type.** Enter a 1-byte (2 hex digits) IPX packet type number that identifies the type of IPX packet. As discussed earlier, packet types are not used consistently. If you want to filter based on packet types, use a protocol analyzer to verify the contents of the Packet Type fields of packets you want to filter. Socket numbers are a more reliable means of identifying specific packet types.

FIGURE 7.57

Active IPX packet filters.

FIGURE 7.58

Defining an IPX packet filter.

NetBIOS Broadcast Statistics

If you select the **NetBIOS Broadcasts** object under the **IPX Routing** container, the details pane lists the status of each interface with regard to broadcast support and traffic. The IPX SAP and RIP protocols are fairly broadcast intensive, so don't be too surprised at the numbers of broadcast packets reported.

Defining IPX Static Routes

In most cases, IPX routes are maintained by RIP, however, there might be circumstances in which you want to add static routes to the router configuration. Static routes are listed in the details pane when the **Static Routes** icon is selected in the **IPX Routing** container.

> **NOTE**
>
> Static routes should be necessary only if RIP has been disabled on all or part of the network. For example, if RIP packets are filtered out of traffic crossing a WAN link, you would need to configure static IPX routes on the routers that communicate with the WAN link. In such cases, however, I would prefer to use the NLSP routing protocol, which preserves a dynamic routing environment and makes better use of WAN bandwidth.
>
> Because clients use RIP to learn how to communicate with the internal networks on NetWare servers, RIP must be enabled even on networks having a single cable segment.

To define a static route, right-click **Static Routes** and choose **New Route** from the context menu to open the **Static Route** dialog box, shown in Figure 7.59. Complete the following fields to define a static route:

- **Network number (hex).** Enter the destination IPX network number up to 4 bytes (8 hex digits) in length.
- **Next hop MAC address (hex).** Enter the node address of the next router to which the packet should be sent.
- **Tick count.** Enter the approximate time required for packets to reach the destination network in ticks (1/18-second intervals). The tick count is used to establish route preferences. If multiple routes are available for a network, the router prefers the route with the lowest tick count.

- **Hop count.** Enter the number of routers that must be crossed to reach the destination network. IPX networks with a hop count of 16 or greater are not reachable. The hop count is used as a tie-breaker when two or more routes have the same tick count. If two or more routes for a network have the same tick count, the router prefers the route with the lowest hop count.
- **Interface.** Specify the interface over which the packet is to be transmitted.

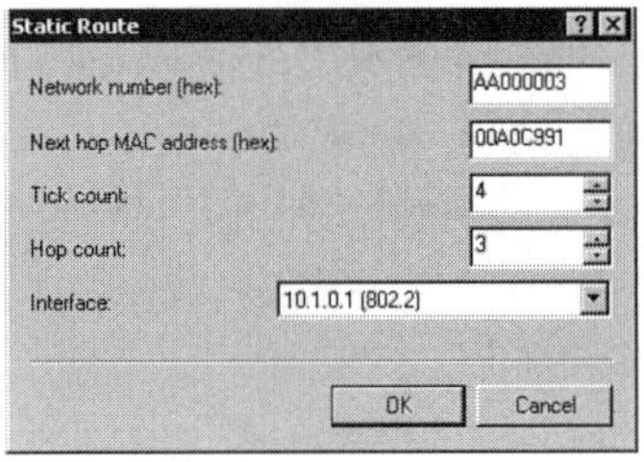

FIGURE 7.59
Defining an IPX static route.

NOTE

View the IPX routing table by right-clicking the **Static Services** icon and choosing **Show IPX Routing Table** from the context menu.

Defining IPX Static Services

In most cases, service information is propagated by the SAP protocol. Because service information propagates by broadcast messages, each IPX router maintains a Service Information Table so that it can provide service information to remote networks. Static service table entries are visible in the details pane when you select the **Static Services** icon under the **IPX Routing** container.

NOTE

Static service routes should be necessary only if SAP has been disabled on all or part of the network. For example, if SAP packets are filtered out of traffic crossing a WAN link, you would need to configure static services on the routers that communicate with the WAN link.

To define a static service, right-click **Static Services** and choose **New Service** from the context menu to open the **Static Services** dialog box, shown in Figure 7.60. Complete the following fields to define a static route:

- **Service type (hex).** Enter a 2-byte service type (4 hex digits).
- **Service name.** Enter the SAP service name, up to 48 characters in length.
- **Network address (hex).** Enter the destination IPX network number up to 4 bytes (8 hex digits) in length.
- **Node address (hex).** Enter the node address of the next router to which the packet should be sent.
- **Socket address (hex).** Enter the 2-byte IPX socket number (4 hex digits).
- **Hop count.** Enter the number of routers that must be crossed to reach the destination service. IPX networks with a hop count of 16 or greater are not reachable.
- **Interface.** Specify the interface over which the packet is to be transmitted.

FIGURE 7.60
Defining an IPX static service.

> **NOTE**
>
> View the IPX routing table by right-clicking the **Static Services** icon and choosing **Show IPX Routing Table** from the context menu. Services will be listed only if NetWare servers are active on the network. Windows computers advertise services using NetBIOS over IPX.

Defining Static NetBIOS Names

In most cases, NetBIOS names are maintained by NetBIOS over IPX. In some cases, it might be desirable to define static NetBIOS names. Static NetBIOS name entries are visible in the details pane when you select the **Static NetBIOS Names** icon under the **IPX Routing** container.

To define a static NetBIOS name, right-click **Static NetBIOS Names** and choose **New NetBIOS Name** from the context menu to open the **Static NetBIOS Name** dialog box shown in Figure 7.61. Complete the following fields to define a static route:

- **Name.** Enter the text portion of the NetBIOS name, up to 15 characters.
- **Type (hex).** Enter the type of NetBIOS name as a 2-digit hexadecimal number. This is the 16th byte of the NetBIOS name. See Chapter 6 for more information about NetBIOS name types.
- **Interface.** Specify the interface over which the NetBIOS name query for this name is broadcast.

FIGURE 7.61

Defining a static NetBIOS name.

Modifying RIP for IPX Properties

The only properties of RIP for IPX are logging properties. Right-click **RIP for IPX** and select **Properties** from the context menu to modify RIP for IPX logging properties.

Modifying RIP for IPX Interface Properties

Interfaces for RIP for IPX are displayed in the details pane when **RIP for IPX** is selected. To modify properties for an interface, right-click the interface and choose **Properties** from the context menu to open the dialog box shown in Figure 7.62. The following properties can be defined:

- **Enable RIP on this interface.** Check this box to enable RIP for IPX support on this interface.
- **Advertise routes.** Check this box if RIP should advertise routes through this interface.
- **Accept route advertisements.** Check this box if this interface should accept RIP advertisements.

- **Update mode.** Update mode settings determine how routing information will be updated. The following settings are available.

  - **Standard.** Routing table entries are updated in response to RIP advertisements. This is the default setting for a LAN interface.

  - **No update.** Routing table entries are not updated.

  - **Autostatic.** Routing table entries are updated but recorded as static entries. This is the default setting for demand-dial interfaces.

- **Update interval (sec).** This field specifies the interval in seconds between periodic RIP advertisements. The default interval for RIP for IPX is 60 seconds. This field is active only if the **Update mode** setting is **Standard**.

- **Aging interval multiplier.** This field specifies the number of update intervals that learned routes are considered valid before they are purged. The default value is 3, meaning that, by default, routing table entries learned from RIP are considered valid for 180 seconds.

- **Input Filters.** Click this button to open a dialog box where you can define filters to determine which incoming routes RIP will accept.

- **Output Filters.** Click this button to open a dialog box where you can define filters to determine which routes RIP will advertise.

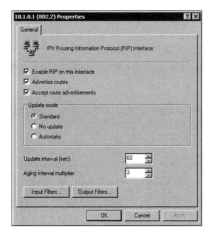

FIGURE 7.62
RIP for IPX interface properties.

Modifying SAP for IPX Properties

The only properties of SAP for IPX are logging properties. Right-click **SAP for IPX** and select **Properties** from the context menu to modify SAP for IPX logging properties.

Modifying SAP for IPX Interface Properties

Interfaces for SAP for IPX are displayed in the details pane when **SAP for IPX** is selected. To modify properties for an interface, right-click the interface and choose **Properties** from the context menu to open the dialog box shown in Figure 7.63. The following properties can be defined:

- **Enable SAP on this interface.** Check this box to enable SAP for IPX support on this interface.

- **Advertise services.** Check this box if SAP should advertise services through this interface.

- **Accept service advertisements.** Check this box if this interface should accept SAP advertisements.

- **Reply to get nearest server requests.** Check this box if this interface should respond to "SAP get nearest server" (GNS) requests. Clients send GNS requests to network 00000000, indicating that the packets should not be forwarded. Routers must typically respond to GNS requests if servers are located on remote networks.

- **Update mode.** Update mode settings determine how routing information will be updated. The following settings are available:

    - **Standard.** Service table entries are updated in response to SAP advertisements. This is the default setting for a LAN interface.

    - **No update.** Service table entries are not updated.

    - **Autostatic.** Service table entries are updated but recorded as static entries. This is the default setting for demand-dial interfaces.

- **Update interval (seconds).** This field specifies the interval in seconds between periodic SAP advertisements. The default interval for SAP is 60 seconds. This field is active only if the **Update mode** setting is **Standard**.

- **Aging interval multiplier.** This field specifies the number of update intervals that learned services are considered valid before they are purged. The default value is 3, meaning that, by default, routing table entries learned from SAP are considered valid for 180 seconds.

- **Input Filters.** Click this button to open a dialog box where you can define filters to determine which incoming service advertisements SAP will accept.

- **Output Filters.** Click this button to open a dialog box where you can define filters to determine which services SAP will advertise.

FIGURE 7.63

SAP for IPX interface properties.

Network Address Translation Firewalls

RRAS includes Network Address Translation (NAT) capability that can provide firewall protection for small organizations. As Chapter 2 explains, a NAT acts as an interface between an internal, private network and the Internet. To enable internal clients to communicate with the Internet, the NAT must map two types of resources in a process that is illustrated in Figure 7.64:

- IP addresses on the private network must be mapped to IP addresses in the Internet address space.

- Ports being used by clients must be mapped to ports that are available on the NAT host.

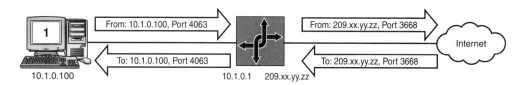

FIGURE 7.64

A NAT firewall translates IP addresses and ports between internal and external networks.

The NAT keeps track of these mappings and edits packet headers as required when they are routed between the Internet and the private network. This imposes some processing load on the computer supporting the NAT service, and the performance of the NAT is dependent on the performance of the computer hardware.

Some protocols embed IP addresses in headers for protocols above the Internet layer. To support these protocols, the Windows 2000 RRAS NAT supports editors the following protocols: FTP, ICMP, PPTP, and NetBIOS over TCP/IP.

Configuring Interfaces for NAT

Interfaces must be properly configured on the server providing NAT capability, specifically:

- The interface that connects to the Internet must be configured with a default router address for a router that communicates with the Internet.
- The interface that connects to the private network must not be configured with a default router address.

Adding Network Address Translation to RRAS

To add Network Address Translation to RRAS, do the following:

1. Right-click the **General** icon under the **IP Routing** object and choose **New Routing Protocol** in the context menu.
2. In the **New Routing Protocol** dialog box, **select Network Address Translation (NAT)** and click **OK**.

An icon labeled **Network Address Translation (NAT)** is added in the **IP Routing** container.

Adding NAT Interfaces

Before NAT is functional, you must specify one interface on the internal (private) network and one interface that communicates with the external (public) network. Perform the following procedure for each interface:

1. Right-click the **Network Address Translation (NAT)** icon and choose **New Interface** in the context menu.
2. Select an interface that is listed in the **New Interface for Network Address Translation (NAT)** dialog box and click **OK**.
3. The next dialog box, named **Network Address Translation Properties**, is used to configure the interfaces (see Figure 7.65).

After an interface is added, it will be listed in the details pane of the RRAS console when the **Network Address Translation (NAT)** icon is selected. You can modify the properties of an interface by right-clicking the interface and choosing **Properties** from the context menu. The interfaces on the public and private networks are configured differently. Procedures for configuring the interfaces are discussed in the next two sections.

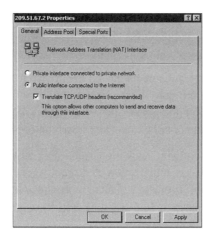

FIGURE 7.65
NAT Interface Properties: The General tab, illustrating configuration for the interface that communicates with the public network.

Configuring NAT Interface Properties for the Private Interface

Initially, both interfaces are configured as private interfaces. There is little to configure on the NAT's private interface, but let's review the procedure in case you need to change the status of an interface.

To configure the private interface for the NAT:

1. Test the interface and make sure that it can communicate on the private network. Do not configure a default router on the private interface. If routing is necessary, configure static routes or enable a dynamic routing protocol.

2. Open the **Properties** page for the interface.

3. Select **Private interface connected to private network**.

Configuring NAT Interface Properties for the Public Interface

The interface on the public network can be configured in a number of ways. Figure 7.65 shows the **General** tab for the interface that communicates with the public network.

To configure the public interface for the NAT:

1. Configure the interface with a default router on the Internet. Test the interface and make sure that it can communicate with the Internet normally.

2. Open the **Properties** page for the interface.

3. Select **Public interface connected to the Internet**.

4. Check **Translate TCP/UDP headers (recommended)**. (It's unclear to me what circumstances would warrant disabling this option. If header translation is disabled, hosts on the private network will be unable to communicate through the NAT to the Internet.)

At this point, the NAT is functional, and clients on the private network should be able to communicate with the Internet. If difficulty is encountered, make sure that the NAT computer can communicate properly with both the public and private networks. Most NAT difficulties arise because the NAT computer cannot communicate properly in one direction or the other.

With the basic NAT in operation, you need to consider more advanced configuration issues. Do you want to enable the NAT to communicate with more than one public IP address? Then you must configure an address pool. If outside clients need to be able to communicate with servers on your private network, you need to map public IP addresses and ports to the private IP addresses and ports configured on servers.

Defining an Address Pool

The NAT can function with a single public IP address, but in some cases you will want to configure a pool of IP addresses. This pool can be used for dynamic address translation. It also serves as a source of IP addresses that can be statically mapped to servers inside the firewall. To define an address pool:

1. Select the **Network Address Translation (NAT)** icon, right-click the NAT's public interface in the details pane, and choose **Properties** from the context menu.

2. In the interface **Properties** dialog box, select the **Address Pool** tab shown in Figure 7.66. To enable the NAT to communicate using addresses in a pool, click **Add** to open the **Add Address Pool** dialog box where you specify the following for each address range:

   - **Start address.** The first IP address in the range of addresses that is available to the NAT. (The example is prepared with private IP addresses, which, of course, can't be used in practice to communicate on the Internet.)

   - **Mask.** The subnet mask that applies to the addresses being used.

   - **End address.** The last IP address in the range of addresses. (The **End Address** field is filled in as you enter the subnet mask. Edit it manually if you don't want to assign all the available addresses to the NAT.)

NOTE

You can also make multiple IP addresses available to the NAT by adding them statically to the **Advanced TCP/IP Properties** of the public interface. Access TCP/IP properties from the RRAS console by right-clicking an interface in the **General** container and selecting **Properties** from the context menu.

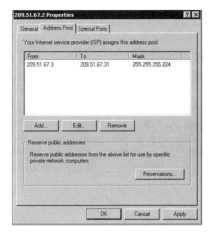

FIGURE 7.66
NAT Interface Properties: The Address Pool tab.

Mapping Public IP Addresses to Private IP Addresses

In some cases, users on the Internet might need to be able to initiate connections with servers on your private network. Ordinarily, the NAT prevents attempts to communicate with hosts on the private network, but it is possible to map an IP address in an address pool, enabling outside users to access the server using its public address.

Suppose that you want to enable a user on the public network to access a Web server on the private network. Two major steps are required:

- A mapping must be established between the public IP address 209.51.67.5 and the Web server address 10.1.0.35.

- DNS must be configured with a Host Address RR that maps the Web server's name to its public IP address.

After an address pool is established, define an IP address mapping as follows:

1. In the interface **Properties** dialog box for the public interface, select the **Address Pool**.

2. Click the **Reservations** button to open the **Reserve Addresses** dialog box shown in Figure 7.67.

3. To add a reservation, click **Add** to open the **Add Reservation** to open the **Add Reservation** dialog box shown in Figure 7.68. Complete the dialog box as follows:

   - **Reserve this public IP address.** Enter an IP address that is defined in an address pool for the public NAT interface.

- **For this computer on the private network.** Enter an IP address that is assigned to a host on the private network. Naturally, this IP address should be stable, defined either through static interface properties or through a DHCP reservation.

- **Allow incoming sessions to this address.** If this box is checked, clients on the public network can initiate connections with the host on the private network.

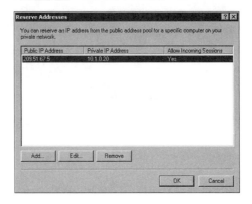

FIGURE 7.67

IP address reservations for a NAT public interface.

All that remains is to add the Host Address RR to your public DNS servers, and then users can access the service from outside the firewall.

CAUTION

It's worth remembering that servers accessed in this way effectively receive no firewall protection from the NAT. Therefore, if you need to permit this sort of access, you should implement a commercial firewall between the NAT and the Internet.

FIGURE 7.68

An IP address reservation associates a public IP address with the IP address of a host on the private network.

Mapping Public Ports to Private Ports

On rare occasions, servers inside your firewall might be configured with non-standard ports. If users are to access these servers, they must either be aware of the port numbers to be used (so that they can, for example, include the port in a URL accessing a Web server) or you must configure the NAT to map ports between the inside and outside environments.

Port mappings are established on the **Special Ports** tab of the **Properties** pages for the NAT external interface. This tab, shown in Figure 7.69, lists port mappings for TCP or UDP, depending on the selection made in the **Protocol** box.

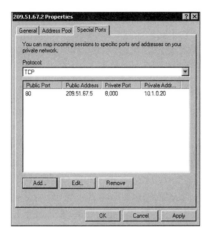

FIGURE 7.69

Port mappings are listed on the Special Ports tab.

To add a port mapping, click **Add** to open the **Add Special Port** dialog box shown in Figure 7.70, which is completed as follows:

- **On this interface.** Select this option to specify a mapping for the IP address statically defined for this interface.

- **On this address pool entry.** Select this option to specify an IP address, which must have been previously added to an address pool.

- **Incoming port.** Specify the port that outside users will use to access the private service.

- **Private address.** Specify the IP address of the server on the private network that provides the service being accessed.

- **Outgoing port.** Specify the port associated with the service as it is accessed on the private network.

FIGURE 7.70
Port mappings are created in the Add Special Port dialog box.

Building a High-Performance Routing Infrastructure

With RRAS, Microsoft has made it possible to implement sophisticated routing at moderate cost by taking advantage of Windows NT running on a microcomputer. If you are running a large, busy network, however, a software-based router such as RRAS will probably not provide the routing throughput that you require, and you might experience slow traffic throughput or dropped packets. Better performance is available with dedicated, hardware-based routers such as those offered by Cisco Systems and other vendors. If you are networking on a budget, however, RRAS is a very capable tool for connecting your network.

We've only begun to look at the capabilities RRAS has to offer. In fact, it's going to take three chapters to cover everything. In Chapter 8, we take a look at the options RRAS provides for communicating through dial-up connections. Then, in Chapter 11, we take up the topic of VPNs.

Supporting Dial-Up Connections with Routing and Remote Access Service

IN THIS CHAPTER

Many organizations that have multiple sites face a dilemma. They need to enable computers to communicate with remote locations—to transmit email, for example—but they don't have enough traffic to justify the expense of full-time leased lines. In many such cases, a demand-dial router can be an ideal solution. RRAS supports demand-dial routing for IP and IPX.

Windows 2000 RRAS's dial-up capability includes many more options than were available with Windows NT. The following connection types are supported out of the box:

- Analog modems work via Public Switched Telephone Network, or PSTN, also referred to as Plain Old Telephone Service, or POTS. The fastest standard service available in North America is V.90, offering customers the capability of sending data at 33.6Kbps and receiving data at 53Kbps. The maximum receive rate is limited by FCC rules. To use V.90, the dial-in server must be using a V.90 digital switch and be connected to the PSTN using a digital link, such as a T-carrier leased circuit or ISDN.

- Integrated Services Digital Network (ISDN) is a digital replacement for PSTN, supporting voice, data, fax, and other services. Data rates for ISDN vary. The most common rate is Basic Rate ISDN (BRI) offering two 64Kbps channels. Primary Basic Rate ISDN (PRI) supports twenty-three 64Kbps channels.

- X.25 is an international standard packet switching network. X.25 clients support the use of X.25 smart cards, which connect directly with the X.25 network. X.25 smart cards communicate using X.25 protocols, as well as via a modem communicating with the X.25 network through a packet assembler/disassembler. X.25 servers require use of an X.25 smart card. X.25 is an old technology that limits data rates to 64Kbps.

- Asynchronous Transfer Mode (ATM) over Asymmetric Digital Subscriber Line (ADSL) is a new technology that offers subscribers the capability of receiving data at megabit speeds. Typically, clients send data at 64Kbps and receive at 1.544Mbps.

Clearly, both ends of the connection must be configured to use the same connection type.

Some of these technologies have costs based on data transferred, connect time, distance, or a combination of those factors. Careful efforts must be made to analyze the costs in the context of anticipated traffic and connection duration. In many cases, communication through a virtual private network (VPN) involving local connections to the Internet and a secure communication channel through the public network will be the most cost-effective way of connecting distant sites. We'll see how RRAS supports VPNs in Chapter 11.

Windows 2000 also supports a variety of techniques for using dial-up connections. We'll consider those capabilities in the following order:

- Configuring a NAT dial-out connection to the Internet
- Configuring RRAS to support dial-in connections to a Windows network
- Configuring RRAS to support dial-up routing connections between two private networks

New with Windows 2000 Server is the capability to establish *remote access policies* that enable you to establish separate policies for groups and users. Unlike Windows NT 4, which applied the same policy to all users, you can now create many separate policies that satisfy different user and security requirements. Dial-in connections are not accepted unless they are supported by an appropriate remote access property.

We'll look at remote access policies in considerable detail, but first let's get the hardware working and configure RRAS to support dial-out connections.

> **NOTE**
>
> Microsoft documentation uses two terms to describe the dial-up component of RRAS. One is Remote Access Server, a name that harks back to the time when dial-up services were separate from routing services. That changed when the Windows NT 4 Option Pack was released. The Option Pack included the Routing and Remote Access Service, which enhanced the routing capabilities of NT and bundled routing with a more sophisticated Remote Access Server. This server replaced the RAS implementation that was included with NT Server.
>
> When referring to remote access services generically, Microsoft uses the term *Network Access Server*, or NAS, an acronym that pops up in some unexpected places. Remote Access Server (RAS) is Microsoft's implementation of a NAS. Consequently, I'll use RAS when I want to specify the dial-in remote access server that is built into RRAS. I'll use NAS when I need to make a generic comment about dial-in access servers.

Installing and Configuring Dial-Up Hardware

If your organization requires multiple dial-up connections, you will want to investigate multi-port communication adapters. Some adapters provide multiple serial ports to be connected to external modems. Some build multiple modems into a single card. Most recent multi-port devices permit the ports to share IRQs and memory ports, enabling you to configure a considerable number of working dial-up connections on a single Intel architecture server. These days, the approach of building multiple modems into a single card appears to have advantages from the standpoints of cost and reliability. These cards eliminate the serial cables and power connections required for external modems. (Cable problems are among the most common causes of hardware difficulties.)

Thanks to the inclusion of USB support in Windows 2000, there is a new option for creating modem pools that doesn't require the installation and configuration of hardware cards. Several companies make multi-modem devices that connect through USB, enabling you to configure many modems through a single USB bus connection.

> **TIP**
>
> One source of excellent USB communications hardware is Inside Out Networking at www.ionetworks.com. Their Rapidport/4 product incorporates four V.90 modems and has received the Designed for Windows 2000 certification.

Most communication devices used with Windows offer Plug-and-Play (PnP) configuration. In most cases, PnP devices and drivers are installed automatically when they are detected by Windows 2000, using drivers supplied with Windows 2000 or disks provided by the vendor. In such cases, modems become available as soon as PnP configuration is complete.

With non-PnP hardware, and with hardware that does not configure properly using PnP, you will need to intervene manually. Start by consulting the vendor of your equipment to see whether they have published procedures for installing their device on Windows 2000. The fact that it didn't install properly with PnP is a good indication that special procedures are required. In many cases, the required procedure might not be obvious. (For example, my Boca Research Tidalwave modem required device drivers selected from the Rockwell vendor category in the device configuration dialog boxes. Although the modem is PnP capable, PnP did not find the proper drivers for Windows 2000. Instead, it attempted to configure the modem using Windows NT 4 drivers that would not function on Windows 2000. Boca's Web site gave me the information I needed to get the modem working when I upgraded to Windows 2000.)

Installing a Modem

To install a modem manually:

1. If it is an external modem, connect it to a COM port and make sure that the modem is on. To determine which COM ports are enabled, use the **Computer Management** console in **Administrative Tools**. Open **System Tools→Device Manager→Ports** to view available ports and ascertain their status. If the port you are using is hardwired to the motherboard, you might need to enable it by configuring the system's BIOS.

2. Open the **Add/Remove Hardware Wizard**. In most cases Plug-and-Play devices will have been detected already, so they will not be detected when the wizard searches for new ones.

3. The next window is titled **Choose a Hardware Device**.
   - If the device you are configuring is listed in the **Devices** list, you can reconfigure it by selecting the device and clicking **Next**.
   - If the device you are configuring is not listed, select **Add a new device** and click **Next**. That is the path we will follow in the remaining steps.

4. If you are adding hardware, the **Find New Hardware Wizard** gives you the option of having Windows automatically search for non-PnP devices. To bypass the search, select **No, I want to select the hardware from a list**. Again, if you have reached this point, you will probably need to select the hardware manually.

5. In the **Hardware Type** dialog box, select **Modems** in the category list. When you click **Next**, the **Install New Modem Wizard** is started.

6. To try to detect your modem, click **Next**. To skip modem detection, check **Don't detect my modem**. **I will select from a list**, and click **Next**. In this procedure, we are assuming that automatic procedures aren't working.

7. In the **Install New Modem** dialog box, select the modem's vendor in the **Manufacturer** list. Then select the modem model in the **Model** list.

   If your drivers are not included with Windows 2000, click **Have Disk**. Specify the path to the drivers provided by the vendor, supplying a disk if necessary.

8. In the **Install New Modem** dialog box, select the port to which the device is connected.

Configuring Communications Ports

You should review the properties of all COM ports to ensure that they are configured as desired. To view the property pages for a port, open the **Computer Management** console in the **Administrative Tools** menu. Select **Device Manager**→**Ports** and then double-click the port to be examined.

The **General** property tab (see Figure 8.1) reports the port type, manufacturer, location (if specified), and status. Click **Troubleshooter** to open Help pages relevant to port configuration and problem solving. Selections in the **Device usage** field enable or disable the port. (You might want to disable unused COM ports to free up IRQs or memory addresses.)

FIGURE 8.1

Communications Port Properties: The General tab.

The **Port Settings** tab is shown in Figure 8.2. Configurable options on this page are

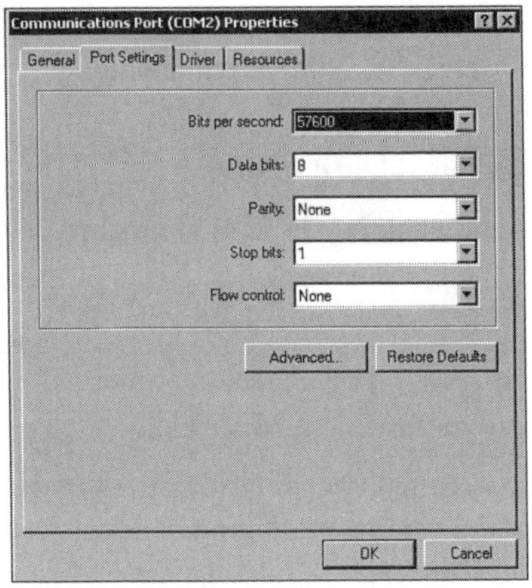

FIGURE 8.2

Communications Port Properties: The Port Settings tab.

- **Bits per second.** For some unaccountable reason, the default bps setting is 9600. Practically all COM ports included in equipment being made today support higher speeds. To achieve the best performance available with your modem, the value in this field should be greater than the modem's top speed and flow control should be enabled. With a V.90 modem, it should be set to a speed of 57600 or higher. Flow control will prevent the port from sending data faster than the modem can accept it. (See the description of the Flow Control option.)

NOTE

Most if not all computers, internal modems, and serial port cards currently being manufactured are equipped with a 16550 UART (Universal Asynchronous Receiver Transmitter) that supports speeds to 115200Kbps.

Equipment that uses the older 8250 or 16450 UARTs typically will not support data rates higher than 9600bps, which probably explains the default value for the **Bits per second** field.

- **Data bits.** Determines the number of bits that will be included in each character transmitted; can be set in a range from 4 to 8. The default value of 8 is appropriate under nearly all circumstances.

- **Parity.** Determines how the parity bit will be interpreted. When used, the parity bit is set to an even (0) or odd (1) value that is used at the receiving end to determine whether the data have been modified during transmission. In recent years it has become common practice not to use the parity bit, hence None is the default value. With this setting, error checking is disabled. See the help message for this field to learn about the other available values.

- **Stop bits.** Serial communication pauses briefly between each character to ensure that the receiving device has reset itself for the next character. The duration of the pause is measured in the number of bits that would be transmitted in the interval. Older equipment required as many as 2 stop bits, but 1 stop bit is the rule on modern equipment.

NOTE

In almost all situations, serial communication is now performed using 8 data bits, no parity, and 1 stop bit, a configuration that is conventionally abbreviated as 8-N-1.

- **Flow control.** To ensure that the modem is operating at peak capacity, the COM port should send data to the modem at the modem's maximum speed, or even a bit faster. Modems are equipped with buffers that enable them to store characters that are queued up for transmission. But if the buffer is full, any characters sent to the modem will be discarded, so it is necessary to have a flow control mechanism that enables the modem to communicate the status of its input buffer to the serial port. Flow control has three possible values:

  - **None.** Flow control is disabled, and there is no protection against buffer overflow. Use this setting only when the port speed is less than the speed the modem uses for communication. This is the default setting, but there are few situations in which this is the most appropriate setting.

  - **Hardware.** Hardware flow control relies on the *clear to send* (CTS, an input to the serial interface) and *ready to send* (RTS, an output used by the modem) lines in the serial interface to enable the modem to inform the port when it can and cannot accept more data. Most if not all modern communications equipment supports hardware-based flow control, and I recommend that you select this option.

  - **Xon/Xoff.** This is a software-based flow control method that relies on the transmission of the ASCII control characters *transmit on* (Xon, ASCII value 0x11) and *transmit off* (Xoff, ASCII value 0x13). The modem sends an Xon character when it is ready to receive and sends an Xoff character when it is unable to accept more data. Software flow control does waste some bandwidth because of the extra characters that must be transmitted and is not as efficient as hardware flow control.

8

SUPPORTING DIAL-
UP CONNECTIONS
WITH RRAS

- **Advanced.** This button opens the **Advanced Settings** dialog box shown in Figure 8.3. Configure its options as follows:

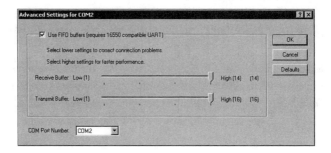

FIGURE 8.3

Communications Port Properties: Advanced Settings accessed through the Port Settings tab.

- **Use FIFO buffers.** If the COM port has a 16550-compatible UART, buffers significantly enhance performance. Disable this option if the COM port hardware does not have a 16550 UART.
- **Receive Buffer** and **Transmit Buffer.** These sliders can be used to reduce the sizes of the COM port's buffers. Larger buffers improve performance. Reduce buffer sizes if connection problems are encountered.
- **COM Port Number.** Windows 2000 supports COM ports 1–256, enabling the server to support multi-port serial devices.

The **Driver** tab of the COM Port property pages has three buttons:

- **Driver Details.** Reports the driver files being used by the COM port.
- **Uninstall.** Removes drivers for the COM port.
- **Update Driver.** Initiates the **Update Device Driver Wizard**, which enables you to install new or different drivers for the device.

The **Resources** tab of the COM Port property pages is shown in Figure 8.4. Fields in this tab are

- **Resource settings.** Reports the IRQ, memory, and other resources designated for use by the port.
- **Settings based on.** Specifies the Windows configuration from which the settings are derived.

FIGURE 8.4
Communications Port Properties: The Resources tab.

- **Use automatic settings.** Enabled by default so that the port is configured automatically by Windows. Uncheck this option to enable manual configuration.

- **Change Setting.** Click to open a dialog box where you can manually select settings. Manual configuration is not possible with all hardware or configurations.

- **Conflicting device list.** Reports any conflicts that exist between this device and other devices. This is a good place to start when troubleshooting an inoperative device.

Modem Properties

The property pages for a modem can be used to review a modem's configuration, test its operation, specify operational parameters, and change the modem drivers.

To view the property pages for a modem, open the **Computer Management** console in the **Administrative Tools** menu. Select **Device Management→Modems** and then double-click the modem to be examined.

The **General** property tab (see Figure 8.5) reports the modem type, manufacturer, location (if specified), and status. Click **Troubleshooter** to open Help pages relevant to modem configuration and problem solving. Selections in the **Device usage** field enable or disable the modem.

The **Modem** tab has three settings:

- **Speaker volume.** Used to adjust the volume of the modem's built-in speaker.

- **Maximum Port Speed.** Selections enable you to specify the maximum speed in bps supported by the interface.

- **Wait for dial tone before dialing.** In most cases, this option should be enabled.

FIGURE 8.5

Modem Properties: The General tab.

The **Diagnostics** tab is shown in Figure 8.6. If you click the **Query Modem** button, Windows sends a variety of control strings to the modem and reports the results in the **Command/Response** list. If any responses are received, it can be safely assumed that the computer is able to communicate with the modem.

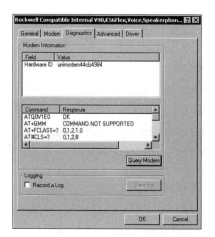

FIGURE 8.6

Modem Properties: The Diagnostics tab.

Creating a Dial-Up Connection to the Internet

Before you get fancy and try to integrate the dial-up router into a connection, it's useful to configure a manual dial-up connection. It introduces you to a lot of the configuration issues, is a good way to test your hardware, and ensures that you have the credentials and settings required to communicate with your ISP's dial-in servers. After you have the experience of configuring a dial-up connection to your ISP, you will have little trouble configuring the client to dial into a remote access server on your network.

We'll start by creating a dial-up connection to the Internet. Later we'll see how to modify dial-up connections to communicate with RAS. To create a dial-up connection to the Internet:

1. Open the **Network and Dial-Up Connections** applet and double-click the **Make New Connection** icon to open the **Network Connection Wizard**.

2. Click **Next** to skip the introductory window and open the **Network Connection Type** dialog box.

3. Select the **Dial-up the Internet** radio button and click **Next** to open the **Internet Connection Wizard**.

4. You can sign up for a new Internet account, or let the wizard search for communication parameters for an existing account. In this example, we are going to follow the manual setup method. To configure manually, select **I want to set up my Internet connection manually**.

5. The next dialog box is titled **Setting up your Internet connection**. The following choices are available:

   - **I connect through a phone line and a modem.** Choose this option to configure an intermittent, dial-up connection.

   - **I connect through a local area network (LAN).** Choose this option to configure a persistent connection through a directly connected network.

6. The next dialog box is shown in Figure 8.7. Enter the following information:

   - **Area code.** Specify the area code of your Internet provider's dial-in access number.

   - **Telephone number.** Specify the dial-in access number of your Internet provider.

8

SUPPORTING DIAL-UP CONNECTIONS WITH RRAS

- **Use area code and dialing rules.** In most cases, your local area code is specified in your telephony dialing properties. If dialing rules are enabled, Windows will not include an area code when it is dialing a local telephone number.
- **Country/region name and code.** This value enables Windows to dial using the rules required for the ISP's location.

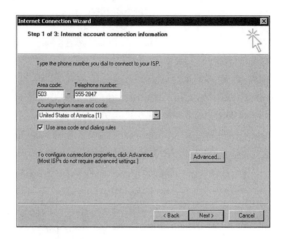

FIGURE 8.7

Configuring the Internet dial-in account access number.

7. Click the **Advanced** button to open the **Advanced Connection Properties** dialog box shown in Figure 8.8. The **Connection** tab has the following fields:
    - **PPP (Point to Point Protocol).** PPP is the most commonly used protocol for TCP/IP dial-up service and the default choice. PPP is more efficient than SLIP, offers better performance, and enables clients to be assigned dynamic IP addresses by the dial-up site. PPP can be used for all supported protocols.
    - **Disable LCP Extensions.** LCP extensions are supported for most PPP communication but are not supported by older PPP implementations. Try disabling LCP extensions if problems occur when using PPP.
    - **SLIP (Serial-Line Internet Protocol).** SLIP suffers from many deficiencies and is now seldom used for TCP/IP connections. When SLIP is selected, only TCP/IP protocols can be used. Windows 2000 remote access servers do not support SLIP.
    - **C-SLIP (Compressed Serial-Line Internet Protocol).** C-SLIP is an implementation of SLIP that supports some data compression. Like SLIP, it is seldom used on modern dial-up services.

FIGURE 8.8
Configuring the Internet dial-in account connection properties.

Under the **Logon procedure** heading are three options that enable special logon procedures after the connection is established:

- **None.** No logon script is executed. This is the default and will work on most PPP servers.
- **Log on manually.** If this option is selected, a terminal window will be opened when the connection is established to present the dial-in host's logon dialog.
- **Use logon script.** If this option is selected, enter the path name for the script file.

8. The **Addresses** tab is shown in Figure 8.9. Settings on this tab determine how the dial-in client will be assigned its IP address and DNS address.

Options under the **IP address** heading are

- **Internet service provider automatically provides one.** This is the correct selection in almost all instances.
- **Always use the following.** If the dial-up provider has assigned a fixed IP address, select this option and enter the IP address here. To conserve scarce IP addresses, ISPs assign fixed IP addresses to users. Although dynamic address assignment is prevalent on private dial-in services, some implementations may assign fixed IP addresses to some or all clients.

8

SUPPORTING DIAL-
UP CONNECTIONS
WITH RRAS

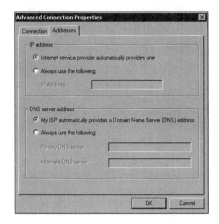

FIGURE 8.9

Configuring the Internet dial-in account address properties.

Options under the **DNS server address** heading are

- **My ISP automatically provides a Domain Name Server (DNS) address.** Some do; many don't. Check with your ISP.

- **Always use the following.** If you are required to enter static DNS server addresses, select this option and specify the addresses of one or two DNS servers.

9. After exiting the **Advanced Connection Properties** dialog box, click **Next** to move on to the next dialog box in the **Internet Connection Wizard**. Supply the following account information, as provided by the dial-in service provider:

- **User name**
- **Password**

10. The next dialog box in the **Internet Connection Wizard** prompts you for a connection name. This will be the name of the icon in the **Network and Dial-in Connections** applet and will identify the connection when it is used in RRAS.

11. The next prompt is **Do you want to set up an Internet Mail account now?** Choose **Yes** or **No**. We are not setting up a mail account in this example.

12. The next dialog box completes the wizard and gives you the option of connecting to the Internet immediately. Click **Finish** to create the connection.

Reviewing and Modifying Dial-Up Connection Properties

Dial-out connections have different properties than the LAN connections we examined in Chapter 1. To review the properties for a dial-out connection, right-click the dial-out connection icon in **Network and Dial-out Connections** and choose **Properties** from the context menu.

Dial-Up Connection Properties: The General Tab

The **Internet Dial-Up Properties General** tab is shown in Figure 8.10. This tab has the following properties:

- **Connect using.** This field identifies the device used to establish the connection. You cannot change the device here, but you can click the **Configure** button to open the **Modem Configuration** dialog box shown in Figure 8.11. Options in this dialog box are as follows:

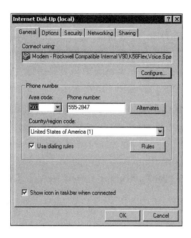

FIGURE 8.10

Internet Dial-Up Properties: The General tab.

8

SUPPORTING DIAL-
UP CONNECTIONS
WITH RRAS

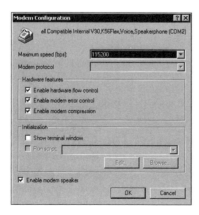

FIGURE 8.11

The Modem Configuration dialog box specifies the modem settings that will be used for this connection.

- **Maximum speed (bps).** You can specify a speed in excess of the maximum modem capacity. When the connection is established, the modems will negotiate a mutually agreeable speed that is compatible with line conditions.

- **Modem protocol.** Options in this field depend on the modem. Consult the modem documentation if options appearing in this field must be modified.

- **Enable hardware flow control.** By default, this option is checked, and hardware flow control is used.

- **Enable modem error control.** Specifies whether cyclic redundancy checks (CRCs) are used by modems to perform error control. Modem error control is supported by the MNP4 and the V.42 protocols, which enable modems to retransmit corrupted data. These protocols are supported by most modems, and modems will negotiate error control protocols when the connection is established. Check documentation for your modem to determine support for this feature.

- **Enable modem compression.** Most modems can compress data in the modem-to-modem data stream. Hardware compression is less effective than software compression, however, and should be disabled in most cases. It is unproductive and unnecessary to enable both hardware (modem) and software (protocol) compression. Software compression is not supported by the SLIP protocol.

- **Show terminal window.** If this option is checked, a terminal window will be opened after the connection is established. The terminal window might be required in some instances to complete the logon dialog.

- **Run script.** Specifies whether a logon script is executed after a connection is established. Specify the path to the logon script if this option is enabled.

- **Enable modem speaker.** Check if the modem's speaker should be enabled while the connection is being established.

- The **Phone Number** fields display the phone number that is used for this connection. These fields can be edited as required.

- **Show icon on taskbar when connected.** It is very useful to add the icon to the taskbar, enabling you to monitor and control the connection without needing to open **Network and Dial-Up Connections**.

Dial-Up Connection Properties: The Options Tab

The **Internet Dial-Up Properties Options** tab is shown in Figure 8.12. This tab has the following properties:

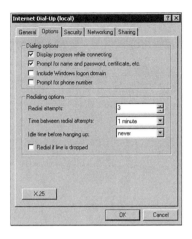

FIGURE 8.12
Internet Dial-Up Properties: The Options tab.

- **Display progress while connecting.** When this feature is enabled, a message box reports events that take place while a connection is being established. You might want to disable this feature if a user's workstation is doubling as a shared dial-on-demand connection to the Internet.

- **Prompt for name and password, certificate, etc.** In most cases, a dialog box should be displayed in which the user can enter a password and credentials. If dial-up is automated, the logon dialog box can be suppressed.

- **Include Windows logon domain.** If the dial-up connection is directed to a dial-up server on a Windows network, a domain is required to establish a connection. For an Internet connection, a Windows domain should not be specified.

- **Prompt for phone number.** This option is probably included to enable mobile users to enter a local dial-up number. It should seldom, if ever, be required for a dial-up router.

- **Redial attempts.** Windows will make the specified number of attempts to connect before reporting failure.

- **Time between redial attempts.** This parameter specifies the time Windows waits after failing to connect before making another attempt.

- **Idle time before hanging up.** By default, the connection is left up until it is manually disconnected. If desired a time can be specified. If the connection is idle for the specified time it will be closed.

- **Redial if line is dropped.** If the connection is broken because of this error, enabling this option causes Windows to attempt to redial the connection.

Dial-Up Connection Properties: The Security Tab

The **Internet Dial-Up Properties Security** tab is shown in Figure 8.13. Windows supports a wide variety of security options, so this tab and its subordinate dialog boxes gets pretty involved. This tab contains typical security settings but can be configured to enable access to advanced options. First, we'll look at settings on the **Security** tab itself. Then we'll examine the advanced options.

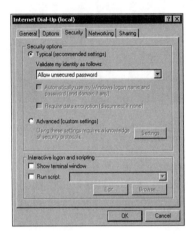

FIGURE 8.13
Internet Dial-Up Properties: The Security tab.

Settings on the Security Tab

Typical (recommended settings). This is the default setting. When selected, the following fields are available:

- **Validate my identity as follows.** Four validation options are available:
    - **Allow unsecured password.** This is the typical setting when establishing an Internet dial-up connection through an ISP. This option is available for unsecured dial-up connections only.
    - **Require secured password.** This option requires a user to enter a password, which is transmitted in secure form to the server. Secure passwords are supported for standard dial-up connections and for VPN connections.
    - **Use smart card.** This option requires a user to be authenticated by presenting a smart security card. Smart cards are supported for standard dial-up connections and for VPN connections.
    - **Require secured password.** This option requires a user to enter a password, which is transmitted in secure form to the server. Secure passwords are supported for standard dial-up connections and for VPN connections.

Advanced (custom settings). If this option is selected, the **Settings** button is illuminated, enabling you to access the **Advanced Security Settings** dialog box, discussed in the next section.

Show terminal window. If this option is checked, a terminal window will be opened after the connection is established so that the logon can be completed from a terminal interface.

Run script. If this option is checked, the specified script file will be executed after a connection is established.

Settings in the Advanced Settings Dialog Box

The **Advanced Settings** dialog box, shown in Figure 8.14, is accessed by selecting **Advanced (custom settings)** on the **Security** tab and clicking the **Settings** button.

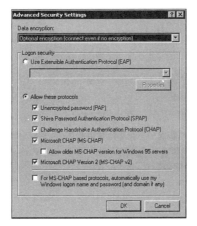

8

SUPPORTING DIAL-
UP CONNECTIONS
WITH RRAS

FIGURE 8.14
Advanced dial-up security settings.

The **Data encryption** field accepts the following options:

- **Optional encryption (connect even if no encryption).** Encrypted and unencrypted authentication methods are supported. This is the default setting.

- **No encryption (server will disconnect if it requires encryption).** Encrypted authentication is not supported.

- **Require encryption (disconnect if server is required).** Requires use of an encrypted protocol. PAP, SPAP, and CHAP are not supported.

If **Use Extensible Authentication Protocol (EAP)** is selected, click the **Properties** button to configure EAP settings. EAP is discussed in the "RRAS Authentication Protocols" sidebar and later in this section. (See the discussion related to Figure 8.15).

If **Allow these protocols** is selected, you can enable any or all of the following authentication protocols, which are described in the sidebar "RRAS Authentication Protocols":

- **Unencrypted password (PAP)**
- **Shiva Password Authentication Protocol (SPAP)**
- **Challenge Handshake Authentication Protocol (CHAP)**
- **Microsoft CHAP (MS-CHAP)**
- **Microsoft CHAP Version 2 (MS-CHAP v2)**
- **For MS-CHAP based networks, automatically use my Windows logon name and password (and domain if any).** This option attempts to log the user on to the remote access server with the username and password that were entered to log on to Windows.

RRAS Authentication Protocols

Authentication protocols enable RAS to verify clients' identities with varying levels of security. Unless dial-up clients and servers share at least one authentication method, clients are unable to authenticate to the dial-in server. RAS supports a variety of authentication methods, ranked here from most to least secure:

- **Extensible Authentication Protocol (EAP).** EAP is an extension of PPP that varies the sequence of messages that are presented in a user authentication dialog. Rather than using a fixed sequence of messages, as is done by MS-CHAP and SPAP, the devices negotiate the use of a specific EAP authentication scheme while the connection is being established. The details of EAP are beyond the scope of this book, but one clear feature is that EAP supports digital certificates as an authentication method.

- **Microsoft encrypted authentication version 2 (MS-CHAP v2).** This Microsoft protocol uses a challenge-response method with encryption performed on the response. MS-CHAP v2 corrects several shortcomings found in MS-CHAP v1, but is not supported on Windows 95. It is consistent with standard CHAP, but the message format is designed for Windows 2000, NT, and 9x or later.

- **Microsoft encrypted authentication (MS-CHAP).** This is version 1 of MS-CHAP. It must be enabled to support Windows 95 dial-up connections.

- **Encrypted authentication (CHAP).** With CHAP (Challenge Handshake Authentication Protocol), the server responds to a logon request with a random challenge to the client. The challenge is used to process the user's password via the Message Digest 5 (MD5) hash algorithm, and the resulting hash is returned to the server. The server can use this hash to verify that the client knows its password. Thus authentication is performed without actually transmitting the password through the connection. Because the challenge is different each time, an eavesdropper cannot forge the authentication and play it back to the server at a later time. CHAP can be used to authenticate to most PPP servers.

- **Shiva Password Authentication Protocol (SPAP).** SPAP is an implementation of PAP on Shiva remote client software, and enables the client to dial in to and be authenticated by the SHIVA server. If this option is enabled, you cannot enable **Require encryption (disconnect if server declines)** in the **Data encryption** field.

- **Unencrypted password (PAP).** Passwords can be sent in the clear and be authenticated by the Password Authentication Protocol. PAP is used by most ISPs to authenticate Internet dial-up clients.

Additionally, RAS can request authentication of clients from a Remote Authentication Dial-In User Service (RADIUS; RFCs 2138 and 2139). Microsoft includes an implementation of RADIUS with Windows 2000 Server, called the Internet Authentication Server (IAS), which is discussed later in this chapter. RADIUS-based authentication is invisible to the user and does not need to be enabled on the dial-in client.

If EAP is enabled, you can click the **Properties** button to open the **Smart Card or other Certificate Properties** dialog box shown in Figure 8.15. Certificates can be used to enable the server to authenticate the client and the client to authenticate the server. A client using a smart card can still authenticate the server by examining the server's certificate. Options in this dialog box are as follows:

FIGURE 8.15

Configuring smart card or digital certificate authentication.

- **Use my smart card.** The user's smart card can be used as authentication.
- **Use a certificate on this computer.** The client sends its digital certificate as authentication.

- **Validate server certificate.** Typically, digital certificates expire after a prespecified time. They can also be revoked. If this option is checked, the client will consult the certificate authority that issued the certificate to ensure it is still valid.
- **Connect only if server name ends with.** When this option is enabled, you can specify a domain name in the accompanying field. The client will connect with a server only if the server's domain name matches the domain name specified.
- **Trusted root certificate authority.** Digital certificates are issued and verified by certificate authorities that are related hierarchically. The root certificate authority can be used to locate a lower-level certificate authority that can validate the server's certificate.
- **Use a different user name for the connection.** Ordinarily your Windows username is used. Check this box if you want to use a different name.

Dial-Up Connection Properties: The Networking Tab

The networking properties of a dial-up interface are configurable in the same manner as a LAN interface. If you select the **Networking** tab in the **Dial-Up Properties** dialog box, you will access the dialog box shown in Figure 8.16. From here you can enable, disable, install, and configure protocols that are supported on this interface. For example, if the dial-up site doesn't provide the client with the IP address of a DNS server, you can enter the DNS server addresses statically here.

Here are some things to remember:

- Components such as **Client for Microsoft Networks** have no use on interfaces connected to the Internet and should be disabled.
- **Client for Microsoft Networks** should be enabled if you are dialing in to a Microsoft network.
- Not all protocols are supported with all connection types. For example, IPX/SPX is not supported by a SLIP connection.

Dial-Up Connection Properties: The Sharing Tab

The **Sharing** tab can be used to support Internet Connection Sharing, an easy way to enable clients on the local network to access the Internet through a dial-up connection.

I'm not going to discuss Internet Connection Sharing because Windows 2000 Server provides much more versatile techniques for sharing a dial-up connection. Internet Connection Sharing is useful if you have only Windows 98 or Windows 2000 Professional, but if you have Windows 2000 Server available, RRAS is the preferred method of sharing connections.

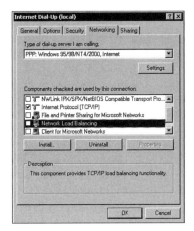

FIGURE 8.16
Internet Dial-Up Properties: The Networking tab.

> **NOTE**
>
> A significant limitation of Internet Connection Sharing is that the dial-up device must have the IP address 192.168.0.1. Clients sharing the connection must be configured to obtain their IP addresses through DHCP so that the dial-up computer can assign IP addresses. Consequently, Internet Connection Sharing drives the entire addressing scheme of the network. That approach is suitable for a home network or a small office, but doesn't scale to larger organizations.

Testing the Dial-Up Connection

The dial-up connection is now ready to test. If you double-click the connection's icon in **Network and Dial-Up Connections**, the **Connect Internet Dial-Up** dialog box is presented, as shown in Figure 8.17.

While a connection is active, you can observe its status by right-clicking the connection's icon in **Networking and Dial-Up Connections**, or in the taskbar if you enabled that option, and selecting **Status** from the context menu. Figure 8.18 shows the **General** and **Details** tabs of the **Status** dialog box.

FIGURE 8.17

The Connect Internet Dial-Up dialog box.

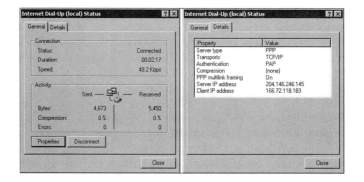

FIGURE 8.18

Statistics for a dial-up connection.

Close a dial-up connection by clicking the **Disconnect** button in the **Status** dialog box, or by right-clicking the connection icon and choosing **Disconnect** in the context menu.

CAUTION

Although a given dial-up connection can be used by RRAS and by a user, it cannot be used by both at the same time. For example, if you have connected manually, RRAS cannot use the connection. You will have to disconnect and then reconnect through RRAS.

Configuring RRAS Server Properties

Before you proceed to configure RRAS for dial-in or dial-out connectivity, you should review the RRAS server properties. To view the property pages, right-click the RRAS server icon in the RRAS console object tree and choose **Properties** from the context menu. The RRAS server **Properties** dialog box is shown in Figure 8.19.

> **NOTE**
>
> The default RRAS server properties are suitable in most instances. You should review them, however, to ensure the defaults are appropriate for your organization.

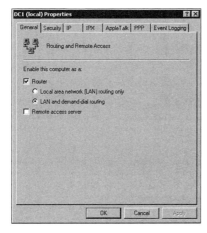

FIGURE 8.19

RRAS Server Properties: The General tab.

RRAS Server Properties: The General Tab

The **General** tab, shown in Figure 8.19, contains the following properties:

- **Router.** Enable this property if RRAS will function as a network router. If **Router** is enabled, select one of the following router modes:
    - **Local area network (LAN) routing only.** Select this option if all routing will be performed on the local area network.
    - **LAN and demand-dial routing.** Select this option if the router will also be configured to establish on-demand router connections with remote networks.

- **Remote access server.** Enable this property if RRAS will be configured as a dial-in access point that enables users to access the network remotely.

RRAS Server Properties: The Security Tab

The **Security** tab, shown in Figure 8.20, contains settings for authentication and accounting. Let's consider the two categories separately.

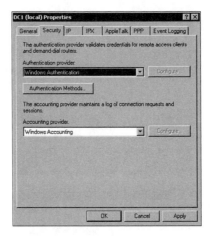

FIGURE 8.20

RRAS Server Properties: The Security tab.

RRAS Authentication Providers

The **Authentication provider** drop-down list on the **Security** tab offers two options that determine how dial-in users will be authenticated:

- **Windows Authentication.** If this option is selected, Windows is responsible for authentication.
- **RADIUS Authentication.** With this option, RRAS requests authentication of users from a RADIUS server, such as the Windows 2000 Server IAS, discussed later in this chapter.

NOTE

You must restart the **Routing and Remote Access** service to activate changes made to the RRAS authentication provider or accounting provider. This can be done using the **Services** console in the **Administrative Tools** folder of the **Start** menu.

The **Authentication Methods** button opens the **Authentication Methods** dialog box shown in Figure 8.21. One or more of the available authentication methods can be enabled. These choices are

- **Extensible authentication protocol (EAP)**
- **Microsoft encrypted authentication version 2 (MS-CHAP v2)**
- **Microsoft encrypted authentication (MS-CHAP)**
- **Encrypted authentication (CHAP)**
- **Shiva Password Authentication Protocol (SPAP)**
- **Unencrypted password (PAP)**
- **Allow remote systems to connect without authentication**

The last option enables clients to authenticate without a username or password. Obviously, unauthenticated access must be permitted only when the actions the user can perform are strictly limited.

FIGURE 8.21
Authentication methods available for the RAS server.

If **Extensible authentication protocol (EAP)** is selected in the **Authentication Methods** dialog box, click the **EAP Methods** button to view a dialog box that lists authentication methods supported by EAP. The RRAS implementation of EAP supports the following two methods:

- **MD5 Challenge.** EAP Message Digest 5 Challenge Handshake Authentication Protocol (EA-MD5 CHAP) uses the CHAP protocol, sending the challenges and responses as EAP messages. This protocol is used to authenticate users by username and password.
- **Smart Card or Other Certificate.** This method supports hardware- or software-based digital signatures.

RADIUS Authentication Methods

If `RADIUS Authentication` is selected in the Authentication provider field of the Security tab (refer to Figure 8.20), RRAS must be configured with information identifying at least one RADIUS authentication server. Click the **Configure** button to open the **RADIUS Authentication** dialog box that lists RADIUS servers in this server's configuration. Click **Add** to open the **Add RADIUS Server** dialog box shown in Figure 8.22. Complete the dialog box as follows:

- **Server name.** Enter the FQDN of the RADIUS server or its IP address in dotted-decimal form.

- **Secret.** RADIUS servers maintain security by encrypting communication between them. The encryption key is a *shared secret*, a text string that is known only to the RADIUS servers. Because RADIUS servers and clients must transmit passwords through the network, it is extremely important that the shared secret be difficult to guess. I suggest a mixture of upper- and lowercase characters, along with some numeric and punctuation characters.

- **Time-out (seconds).** This parameter specifies the length of time RAS will wait for a response from a RADIUS server before trying to contact another RADIUS server.

- **Initial score.** The *score* is a measure of the responsiveness of a RADIUS server and is adjusted by RAS as it interacts with the RADIUS server. RAS uses the scores to determine the order in which it will query the available RADIUS servers. The initial value can be adjusted, enabling you to establish starting priorities in using multiple RADIUS servers.

- **Port.** This is the UDP port value for the RADIUS authentication server. Per RFC 2138, the default value is 1812, which is also the default value for the Windows 2000 Server IAS implementation of RADIUS. Older RADIUS servers use a default port value of 1645.

- **Always use digital signatures.** *Digital signatures*, also known as *digital certificates*, serve to enhance the security of RADIUS communication. Digital certificates are supported by a public key infrastructure (PKI), which will be discussed in detail in Chapter 11. If digital signatures are enabled, a public or private Certificate Authority must be available that can issue digital certificates for your organization.

RRAS Accounting Providers

Accounting maintains a log of connection activity. Three accounting options are available in the **Accounting providers** drop-down list (refer to Figure 8.20):

- None. An accounting log is not maintained.
- Windows Accounting.

- RADIUS Authentication. With this option, RRAS requests authentication of users from a Remote Authentication Dial-In User Service (RADIUS; RFCs 2138 and 2139). Microsoft includes an implementation of RADIUS with Windows 2000 Server, called the Internet Authentication Server (IAS), which is discussed later in this chapter.

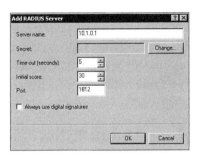

FIGURE 8.22
Adding a RADIUS authentication server to the RRAS configuration.

If RADIUS Accounting is selected as the accounting method, RRAS must be configured with information identifying at least one RADIUS authentication server. Click the **Configure** button to open the **RADIUS Accounting** dialog box, which lists RADIUS servers in this server's configuration. Click **Add** to open the **Add RADIUS Server** dialog box shown in Figure 8.23. Complete the dialog box as follows:

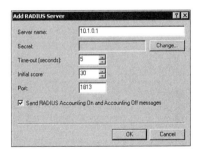

FIGURE 8.23
Adding a RADIUS account server to the RRAS configuration.

- **Server name.** Enter the FQDN of the RADIUS server or its IP address in dotted-decimal form.
- **Secret.** RADIUS accounting security is maintained by defining a secured secret on the RADIUS client and the RADIUS server. This does not have to be the same shared secret that is used for communication of RADIUS authentication messages.

- **Time-out (seconds).** This parameter specifies the length of time RAS will wait for a response from a RADIUS server before trying to contact another RADIUS server.

- **Initial score.** RADIUS accounting clients use the score to rank the responsiveness of the available RADIUS servers. You can enter an initial value to establish initial priorities.

- **Port.** This is the UDP port value for the RADIUS accounting server. Per RFC 2139, the default value is 1813, which is also the default value for the Windows 2000 Server IAS implementation of RADIUS. Older RADIUS servers use a default port value of 1646.

- **Send RADIUS Accounting On and Accounting Off messages.** These messages are sent to the RADIUS accounting server when the RAS service is stopped or started. Disable these messages if they are not supported by your RADIUS server.

RRAS Server Properties: The IP Tab

The RRAS server properties **IP** tab is shown in Figure 8.24. There are two options that determine the functions RRAS will support for IP:

- **Enable IP routing.** If this option is checked (the default setting), RRAS will route IP traffic.

- **Allow IP-based remote access and demand-dial connections.** If this option is checked (the default setting), RRAS will accept dial-in connections from clients configured with TCP/IP protocol stacks.

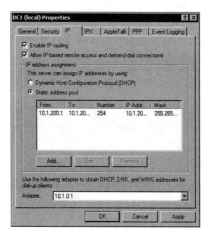

FIGURE 8.24

RRAS Server Properties: The IP tab.

In most cases, when the remote access server grants a connection to a TCP/IP client, RAS dynamically assigns the client an IP address that is valid on the local network. The IP addresses that are assigned can be selected in either of the following ways:

- **Dynamic Host Configuration Protocol (DHCP).** RRAS will request an IP address from DHCP.
- **Static address pool.** RRAS will assign IP addresses from a pool that is defined by the administrator. If this option is selected, click **Add** to open a dialog box where you can specify the starting IP address, the ending IP address, and the number of IP addresses available for use in the address pool. Multiple ranges of IP addresses can be added to the pool if necessary. This address pool is shared by all dial-in clients and routers.

> **NOTE**
>
> If the configured address source does not provide an IP address, an address is assigned to the client using Automatic Private IP Addressing. See the section "IP Address Automatic Configuration" in Chapter 5 for more information about this feature.

RRAS Server Properties: The IPX Tab

The RRAS server properties **IPX** tab is shown in Figure 8.25. There are two options that determine the functions RRAS will support for IP:

- **Allow IPX-based remote access and demand-dial connections.** Enable this option to configure the Remote Access Service to support IPX for dial-in and dial-out connections.
- **Enable network access for remote clients and demand-dial connections.** If this option is enabled, clients dialing in to RAS are permitted to access the private network to which the RRAS server is connected.

IPX clients do not need to be assigned host numbers. A unique node number is generated by RAS for each dial-in connection.

Besides the host number, IPX clients need to be assigned a network number. The manner in which IPX network numbers are assigned is determined by options under **IPX network number assignment** as follows:

- **Automatically.** RRAS will discover a network number that is not in use on the private network and use it to configure IPX nodes connecting through the dial-in interface.

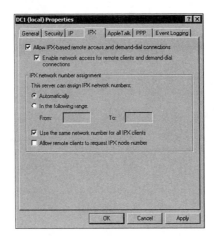

FIGURE 8.25
RRAS Server Properties: The IPX tab.

- **In the following range.** When this option is selected, you can specify a range of hexadecimal network addresses that can be assigned. Of course, addresses in this range should not conflict with internal or external network addresses already in use on the network. So that you know the network numbers for dial-in clients, I recommend that you select this option even if you are going to use a single network number.

- **Use the same network number for all IPX clients.** In most cases, I recommend leaving this option in its default-enabled state. There is seldom a need for more than one network number on the dial-in interface.

- **Allow remote clients to request IPX node number.** As mentioned previously, RAS normally assigns IPX node numbers automatically. If this option is enabled, the dial-in client can request a specific IPX node number. This option is disabled by default, and there is seldom a need to enable it.

RRAS Server Properties: The AppleTalk Tab

The sole option on the RRAS server properties **AppleTalk** tab is the check box **Enable AppleTalk remote access**.

RRAS Server Properties: The PPP Tab

The **PPP** tab has four options that affect the Point-to-Point protocol (PPP) features that the RRAS server will support. PPP communication settings can be determined on a case-by-case basis by options in remote access profiles. The following check boxes are available on this tab:

- **Multilink connections.** *Multilink connections* enable clients to open more than one communications channel when additional bandwidth is required. This is especially useful with ISDN connections that typically provide multiple digital channels in increments of 64Kbps each.

- **Dynamic bandwidth control using BAP or BACP.** Allocation and deallocation of multilink channels can be managed dynamically by the **Bandwidth Allocation Protocol** (BAP) and the **Bandwidth Allocation Control Protocol** (BACP).

- **Link Control Protocol (LCP) extensions.** LCP extensions (RFC 1570) enhance PPP with Identification and Time-Remaining packets that are useful when configuring and testing the data-link communication. Most PPP implementations support LCP extensions.

- **Software compression.** PPP can compress data sent through the dial-up connection. This is highly advantageous and should be enabled unless it is not supported by a device.

RRAS Server Properties: The Event Logging Tab

The Event Logging tab offers four logging modes:

- **Log errors only.** Select this option if only critical failures should be logged.

- **Log errors and warnings.** Select this option to log critical failures and non-critical problems. This is the default and is usually the preferred setting for a production RRAS server.

- **Log the maximum amount of information.** Verbose logging is useful when testing and troubleshooting but can result in very large log files. Enable this option only during initial setup of RRAS, when testing a new feature, or when tracking down sources of errors.

- **Disable event logging.** In most cases, event logging should not be disabled.

Determine whether PPP events will be logged by enabling or disabling the **Enable Point-to-Point (PPP) logging** check box.

Configuring a RRAS Demand-Dial Interface

Demand-dial interfaces provide RRAS with the capability to dial out and connect with remote networks. RRAS treats a dial-up interface much like any router interface. When configured, the interface can be included in the interfaces for any routing protocol. With proper configuration, RRAS will initiate dialing on the demand-dial interface automatically when traffic needs to be routed through the dial-up link.

We will look at two varieties of demand-dial interfaces. First, we will look at an interface that can be used by NAT to establish a dial-in connection to the Internet. Later in the chapter, we'll look at demand-dial interfaces that enable routers to establish demand-dial router connections.

Creating a New Demand-Dial Interface

Create a new demand-dial interface from within the RRAS console by right-clicking the **Routing Interface** icon and choosing **New Demand-Dial Interface** in the context menu. The **Demand Dial Interface Wizard** is easy to complete. It proceeds as follows:

1. The **Interface Name** dialog box prompts for a name to identify the interface. The default name is Remote Router. A good practice is to name the interface after the network or location that it is dialing.

2. The **Connection Type** dialog box offers two radio buttons:

    - Connect using a modem, ISDN adapter, or other physical device. That is the route we are taking in this chapter.

    - Connect using virtual private networking (VPN). We'll be exploring VPNs in Chapter 11.

3. In the **Phone Number** dialog box, enter the phone number to be dialed. Click the **Alternates** button if there are back-up phone numbers for the destination.

4. In the **Protocols and Security** dialog box, enable any or all of the following features:

    - **Route IP packets on this interface.** Enable this option if IP traffic will be routed.

    - **Route IPX packets on this interface.** Enable this option if IPX traffic will be routed.

    - **Add a user account so a remote router can dial in.** All dial-in connections are authenticated using a Windows user account. Check this option to create the user account within the wizard. Don't check this option if you are creating an interface that will be used to dial out to another network such as the Internet.

    - **Send a plain-text password if that is the only way to connect.** Most remote access servers support encrypted passwords. Plain-text passwords are seen most often when dialing into the Internet through an ISP.

    - **Use scripting to complete the connection with the remote router.** If a script must be executed to complete the connection, select this option.

5. If you checked **Use scripting to complete the connection with the remote router** in Step 4, the next dialog box is **Router Scripting**. Check **Run Script** to enable scripting and enter the pathname for the file that contains the script.

6. If you checked **Add a user account so a remote router can dial in** in Step 4, the next dialog box is **Dial-In Credentials**. The name of the user account is the same as the interface name specified in Step 1. You must enter and confirm a password to be used with this account.

7. The next dialog box is titled **Dial-Out Credentials**. Here you specify the following information that is used to authenticate this router when it dials in to the remote router:

- **User name.** On a RRAS demand-dial interface, this is the interface name that is specified in Step 1 when the demand-dial interface is created on the remote router.

- **Domain.** If dialing in to a Windows network, the Windows domain must be specified.

- **Password** and **Confirm Password.** Enter the password associated with the user account.

When the **Demand Dial Interface Wizard** is finished, a new dial-up connection is added to the **Routing Interfaces** container in the RRAS console.

Configuring RRAS Dial-Out Credentials

To configure or modify the credentials for a RRAS dial-up interface, right-click the interface in the **Routing Interfaces** details pane and choose **Set Credentials** from the context menu to open the **Interface Credentials** dialog box. There you can specify the username, domain, and password used to authenticate the dial-up connection to the remote dial-in access server.

The **Domain** field applies only if you are dialing in to a Windows domain-based network. For connections to the Internet through an ISP, the field should be blank.

Configuring RRAS Dial-Up Properties

To configure properties for a RRAS dial-out port, right-click the interface in the **Routing Interfaces** container and choose **Properties** to open the properties dialog box.

The **General** tab has two fields:

- **Connect using.** Specifies the device to be used for this connection. Click **Configure** to modify the device's hardware-based properties.

- **Phone number.** Specifies the telephone number that is to be called. Click **Alternates** to enter back-up phone numbers.

The **Options** tab is shown in Figure 8.26. Options on this tab are as follows:

- **Demand dial—Idle time before hanging up.** Because dial-up connection charges are often based on connect time, you might want to force disabled connections to hang up after a specified period of inactivity. This is particularly feasible with ISDN connections, which can re-establish the connection in just a few seconds.

- **Persistent connection.** If this option is used, a connection will not be terminated after it is established.

- **Redial attempts.** Specifies the number of dial attempts RRAS will make before it determines that the connection is unavailable.

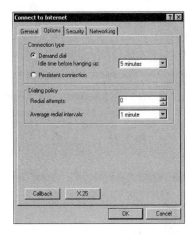

FIGURE 8.26
Dial-Up Connections: The Options tab.

- **Average redial intervals.** Specifies the time interval allowed to elapse between dial-out attempts.
- **Callback.** Many dial-up servers have the capability of calling back to establish a connection with a user. Callback can be enabled so that long-distance connection charges are centralized, or it can be done as a security precaution. If you click this button, the **Router Callback** dialog box is opened, as shown in Figure 8.27. If you select **Always call me back at the number(s) below**, you can specify a phone number for each device that is listed.
- **X.25.** Click this button to configure X.25 logon settings. See Windows 2000 Help for more information about these settings.

The **Security** tab is the same as is shown in Figure 8.13 and has the same options.

The **Networking** tab is similar to the **Network** properties tab for a network connection.

Testing the Dial-Up Interface

After the dial-up interface is configured, it can be tested from the RRAS console. Right-click the interface in the **Routing Interfaces** container and choose **Connect** from the context menu. RRAS immediately attempts to establish the connection and reports its progress in a message box.

If the connection is established, the **Connection Status** column in the details pane reports the status of the interface as Connected.

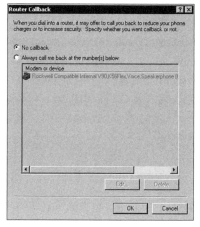

FIGURE 8.27
Dial-Up Connections: Configuring callback.

If the interface connects, you can observe its operational details by right-clicking the interface icon in the **Ports** container and choosing **Status** from the context menu.

If the interface fails to connect, you can determine the reason by right-clicking the interface and choosing **Unreachability Reason** from the context menu.

Some reasons for connection failures are

- **Hardware failure.** Run the modem communication tests listed earlier in the section "Modem Properties." The **Query Modem** command on the **Diagnostics** tab of the modem is an excellent way to see whether the modem hardware is configured properly.

- **Port configuration.** Check the port communication properties. Modem communication almost always is based on 8-N-1 serial communication properties.

- **Protocol configuration.** TCP/IP in particular has many options that affect dial-up communication. One thing to suspect when using PPP is the setting for LCP extensions. Review the PPP Settings with your dial-up provider and make sure that the settings are appropriate. (In the interface properties pages, see **Networking→Settings** to review the options for PPP.)

- **Telephony parameters.** Yes, I know I'm stating the obvious, but it's amazing how often dial-up connections fail just because the telephony parameters are incorrect. Is the phone number correct? Is your dialer dialing long distance when it should, or locally when that is appropriate? If the dialer needs to request an outside line, is it including the access code? There are lots of things that can go wrong. That's why it's useful to test your setup with a manual dial-out connection before you try to enable dial-up on the router.

8

SUPPORTING DIAL-
UP CONNECTIONS
WITH RRAS

- **Security and authentication.** Verify that the authentication methods required by the dial-up host are enabled at the client. Most ISPs allow unencrypted passwords, but most private dial-up sites use some form of encrypted authentication.

- **Credentials.** Make sure that the username and password are correct. Re-enter the password if you are uncertain. Don't configure a domain unless you are dialing in to a Windows, domain-based network.

Setting IP Demand-Dial Filters

If desired, you can configure RRAS so that it will only open a demand-dial connection for particular IP network destinations. To establish filters for a dial-up interface, right-click the interface in the **Routing Interfaces** container and choose **Set IP Demand-dial filters.** As with the routing filters discussed in Chapter 7, "Routing with Routing and Remote Access Service," there are two options that determine how filters will be interpreted:

- **Only for the following traffic.** The dial-up connection will be opened only for traffic directed to the destinations you specify.

- **For all traffic except.** The dial-up connection will not be opened for traffic directed to the destinations you specify.

Setting Dial-Out Hours

If desired, you can limit the hours during which RRAS will permit dial-out operations to take place on an interface. To modify dial-out hours for a dial-up interface, right-click the interface in the **Routing Interfaces** container and choose **Dial-out Hours** in the context menu. In the **Dial-out Hours** dialog box, specify the hours during which dial-out is permitted (blue time blocks) or denied (white time blocks). (Figure 8.35 shows a similar dialog box.)

Configuring Remote-Access Logging

Remote-access logging behavior is configured by modifying properties of the log file. To modify log file properties, do the following:

1. Select the **Remote Access Logging** container in the RRAS console object tree.

2. Double-click **Local File** object in the details pane to open the **Local File Properties** dialog box.

3. On the **Settings** tab, enable the desired logging behaviors from the following list:

   - **Log accounting requests.** Enable this option to log events such as starting or stopping the accounting service.

   - **Log authentication requests.** This option is always enabled. RRAS will log access accept and access deny events.

- **Log periodic status.** Enable this option to log interim accounting requests. This option is not recommended because it can result in rapid growth of log files.
4. On the **Local File** tab under **Log file format**, make one of the following choices:
   - **Database compatible file format.** Select this option to generate log files in ODBC-compatible format.
   - **IAS Format.** Select this option to generate log files that can be imported into IAS.

   Under **New log time period**, select a period that specifies when a new log should be generated (Daily, Weekly, Monthly, Unlimited file size, or When log file reaches).

   For **Log file directory**, specify the path for the directory where log files are to be stored.

Enabling NAT Dial-Out Networking

In most cases, a modem dial-up connection to an ISP can only be shared if a NAT is used because the ISP will route back to only the single IP address that is dynamically assigned to the connection. A NAT, of course, enables a single computer to act as a proxy for multiple clients. NAT technology is included in the Internet Connection Sharing capability that Windows 2000 carries over from Windows 98 Special Edition, but a dial-out connection from the NAT component of RRAS is much more versatile and will be the focus of this section.

If you have followed the procedures so far, you now have a dial-out networking connection that has been tested. This connection can be employed by the NAT router to establish a demand-dial routing connection to the remote network.

Before you attempt to enable NAT to use a demand-dial interface, be sure that you understand the essentials of NAT configuration as described in Chapter 7.

Creating a Demand-Dial Interface to the Internet

Typically, a demand-dial interface that connects to the Internet through an ISP has properties similar to the following:

- On the **Security** properties tab under **Security options**, the **Typical (recommended settings)** radio button is selected with a setting of Allow unsecured password.
- On the **Networking Tab**, for the **Type of dial-in server I am calling**, PPP is selected. In the vast majority of cases, all the PPP options accessed by the **Settings** button can be enabled.
- On the **Networking Tab**, the **Internet Protocol (TCP/IP)** component must be enabled. In most cases, that is the only required component. For most ISPs, configure TCP/IP as follows:

8

SUPPORTING DIAL-
UP CONNECTIONS
WITH RRAS

- **Obtain an IP address automatically.** Few ISPs permit clients to specify their IP addresses.
- **Use the following DNS server addresses.** This is selected by default. You must specify the IP address of at least one DNS server supported by the ISP. (The option **Obtain DNS server address automatically** works with DHCP but not with most PPP dial-in servers.)

Before you try to use the demand-dial interface with NAT, test the interface manually as described in the section "Testing the Dial-Up Interface" earlier in the chapter.

Enabling a Demand-Dial NAT Interface

After you have created and tested a demand-dial interface to the Internet, it can be used as an interface for NAT, enabling the NAT to initiate dial-out connections to remote networks.

To add a demand-dial interface to NAT:

1. Configure the dial-out interface as previously described.
2. In RRAS, right-click **Network Address Translation (NAT)** in the **IP Routing** container and choose **New Interface** from the context menu.
3. Open the properties pages for the demand-dial interface object in the **Network Address Translation (NAT)** container. On the **General** page, select **Public interface connected to the Internet** and **Translate TCP/UDP headers**.

As explained in Chapter 7, the NAT should be configured as the default router for clients that will use it to access the Internet.

Creating a Default Route to the Demand-Dial Interface

Typically you will want RRAS to dial the connection automatically when it receives a datagram to be routed to the Internet. Enabling automatic connection is a simple matter of configuring RRAS with a default route that has the demand-dial connection as its outbound interface.

To configure the default route:

1. Right-click the **Static Route** icon in the RRAS console.
2. Select **New Static Route** from the context menu to open the **Static Route** dialog box.
3. Configure the static route as follows (see Figure 8.28):
    - **Interface.** Select the dial-up interface.
    - **Destination.** Enter **0.0.0.0**.
    - **Network mask.** Enter **0.0.0.0**.
    - **Gateway.** Leave blank.

- **Metric.** Enter any value.
- **Use this route to initiate demand-dial connections.** Check this option.

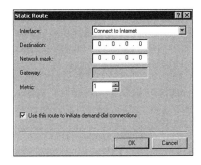

FIGURE 8.28
Configuring a default route to enable automatic dial-up connectivity.

Test the Demand-Dial Interface

Start simply by executing a command on the NAT computer that requires Internet access, such as opening a Web browser and accessing an Internet URL. NAT should initiate dialing.

You can monitor the status of demand-dial connections by selecting the **Routing Interfaces** container in the RRAS console. In the **Connection State** column of the details pane, a demand-dial interface can be in one of the following states:

- **Connected.** The interface has been authenticated by its dial-in server and can access the remote network.
- **Disconnected.** The interface is idle.
- **Unreachable.** The last connection attempt failed after being repeated the specified number of times. This interface will not be used for demand-dial connections until the administrator corrects the reason for failure.

You can view details about the interface by double-clicking the port in the **Ports** container. Figure 8.29 shows a **Port Status** box. In addition to statistics, the **Port Status** box has these buttons:

- **Refresh.** Statistics in this box do not refresh dynamically. You must click the **Refresh** button to refresh the data. (F5 doesn't work.)
- **Reset.** This button clears all the statistics.
- **Disconnect.** This button disconnects the port if it is in a connected state.

FIGURE 8.29
This box shows the status and traffic for a connected demand-dial port.

After assuring yourself that the connection will be established when it is requested, close the connection by clicking the **Disconnect** button in the **Port Status** box.

Next, try to access the Internet from a client that is configured to use the NAT. The NAT router should auto-dial and enable the client to connect.

> **NOTE**
>
> The difficulty with modem connections is that many client processes will time out before the connection is established. Users must be made aware that they might need to retry their connection attempt if timeouts are encountered.
>
> In some cases, the modem connection will time out and then immediately reconnect. This happens because some local traffic is being routed by the NAT server's default route when it should be routed by local router table entries. You may need to configure static routes or a dynamic routing protocol to properly route local traffic. Also, because they can generate spurious traffic, you should disable unneeded network protocols on the demand-dial interface. Typically, Internet Protocol (TCP/IP) is the only required protocol.

RRAS Dial-In

We haven't yet looked at the dial-in capabilities of RRAS. In addition to providing routing services with the potential for establishing outgoing demand-dial connections, RRAS can function as a very serviceable dial-in server for your network. This capability offers these benefits:

- Mobile clients can dial in to the network while in the field.

- Routers can automatically establish dialed connections between distant networks, enabling networks to exchange data without the need for a full-time connection.

Let's look at client dial-in first. We have already examined the procedures used to configure client dial-out functionality. The next thing to add is the configuration of the RRAS dial-in service.

Obviously, to support dial-in, RRAS must be configured with at least a modem. The best way to test the modem hardware is to dial out through it. If that works, you shouldn't encounter any hardware problems when configuring the modem to accept dial-in connections.

Configuring the Remote Access Server

As mentioned earlier, the RRAS dial-in service is the Remote Access Server (RAS). In most cases, modems supporting dial-in client access should be dedicated to that purpose. If they are also used for dial-out connections, users might have trouble finding an available modem. So the first thing to do is to configure the port properties as follows:

1. In the RRAS console, right-click the **Ports** icon on the server you want to manage and select **Properties** from the context menu to open the **Ports Properties** dialog box. Select a port you want to use for dial-in access and click **Configure** to open the **Configure Device** dialog box, shown in Figure 8.30.

2. Check **Remote access connections (inbound only)**.

8

Supporting Dial-
Up Connections
with RRAS

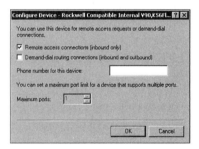

FIGURE 8.30
Dial-up connections: Configuring the port.

3. Uncheck **Demand-dial routing connections (inbound and outbound).**

- You are configuring the **Called Station ID** property in a remote access policy, in which case the phone number entered here must match the number entered in the remote access policy.

- The phone service or hardware do not support identification of the called number.

4. On devices that support multiple ports, the field **Maximum ports** will be active. Enter the number of ports being used on the device.

Dial-In User Authorization Models

Every dial-in user must be authenticated with a user account. To do this, users must know the username and password of a valid Windows 2000 user account, and the user account must be authorized to dial in to the network.

There are two places where access properties must be configured to enable dial-in users to access the network: the **Dial-In** tab of a user's account properties and the remote access policy that is in force for the user. Let's look at each set of properties before we see how to configure a working remote access system.

NOTE

By default, policies are defined on a server-by-server basis. If the organization has multiple RRAS servers, it is possible to manage authentication and remote access policies for all RRAS servers in a central location by implementing a Remote Authentication Dial-In User Service (RADIUS; RFCs 2138 and 2139).

Windows 2000 Server includes an implementation of RADIUS called the Internet Authentication Server (IAS), which is discussed later in the chapter. For now, we will look at the procedures used to manage dial-in clients taking a domain-by-domain and server-by-server approach.

User Account Dial-In Properties

The properties for each user account include properties that allow or deny dial-in permissions for the user. To configure the dial-in properties for a user account, open the properties pages for the User object in the **Active Directory Users and Computers** console and select the **Dial-in** tab shown in Figure 8.31. Configure the properties on this tab as follows:

- Under **Remote Access Permission (Dial-in or VPN),** select one of the following radio buttons:
  - **Allow access.** This option permits the user to dial in to the server.
  - **Deny access.** This option prevents the dial-in server from granting dial-in access to the user.
  - **Control access through Remote Access Policy.** This option is available only on RRAS servers operating in native mode domains.

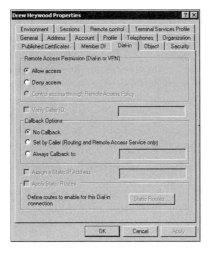

FIGURE 8.31

User properties: The Dial-in tab.

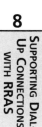

- Under **Callback Options,** select one of these radio buttons:
    - **No Callback.** The user is permitted to connect directly without being required to accept a return call from RRAS.
    - **Set by Caller (Routing and Remote Access Service only).** The user is permitted to request callback when attempting to establish a connection and can specify the number that is to be called. This option is most often enabled so that long distance telephone connections are charged to a single location.
    - **Always Callback to.** This option requires callback to a specific phone number to establish the connection. This approach is typically used to enhance security because the user is required to be at a particular location in order to dial in to the network.
- **Assign a Static IP Address**, if enabled, permits the administrator to specify a particular IP address for the user, overriding any IP address that might be assigned by a remote access policy.
- **Apply Static Routes**, if enabled, permits the administrator to define one or more static routes that will be applied to the client's routing table, overriding any static routes that might be assigned by a remote access policy. Click the **Static Routes** button to open a dialog box where static routes can be defined.

We will examine the use of the options on the **Dial-In** tab when we examine the procedures for implementing the three dial-in authentication models.

Remote Access Policies

Remote access policies are managed using the **Routing and Remote Access** console. Select the **Remote Access Policies** container under a particular server to see policies that are in effect on that server. Figure 8.32 shows the RRAS console with the default remote access policy in the **Remote Access Policies** Details pane.

NOTE

The **Remote Access Policies** container appears in the RRAS console only if Windows Authentication is selected in the **Authentication provider** field of the **Security** tab in the RRAS server **Properties** dialog box. See the section "RRAS Server Properties: The Security Tab" earlier in the chapter for more information about this setting.

If RADIUS is configured as the authentication provider, remote access policies will be created and managed on the IAS server, as described later in the chapter in the section, "Managing the Internet Authentication Service."

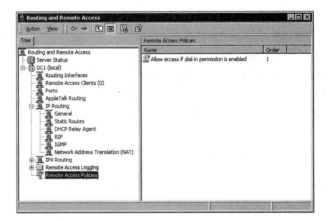

FIGURE 8.32

One or more remote access policies must be defined to enable remote users to connect to the network.

When RRAS is first installed, a single policy is included, named **Allow access if dial-in permission is enabled**. This policy applies to all clients.

The order in which policies appear in the list is significant. When a client attempts to connect to the network, RAS attempts to match the client to a policy, starting with the first (top) policy and proceeding to the last. Access permissions are determined by the first policy that matches the client.

Double-click a policy in the **Remote Access Policies** Details pane to display the **Properties** dialog box for the policy, shown in Figure 8.33. This dialog box has one tab named **Settings**, which has the following fields:

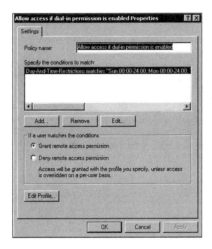

FIGURE 8.33
Remote Access Policy Properties.

- **Policy name.** The name of a policy is simply a friendly label that describes the policy to administrators. It does not determine which clients are affected by the policy. That function is performed by conditions, which are defined in the next field.

- **Specify the conditions to match.** A policy applies to clients that meet conditions defined in this field. Conditions are simply too varied and important to discuss briefly within a list. We'll look at conditions in considerable detail in the next section.

- **Grant remote access permission.** If this radio button is selected, users who meet the conditions defined for the policy are permitted remote access to the network.

- **Deny remote access permission.** If this radio button is selected, users who meet the conditions defined for the policy are prevented from accessing the network remotely.

From the **Settings** tab, you can define policy conditions and the policy profile. We'll take up those tasks in the following sections.

Defining Remote Access Policy Conditions

Policy conditions specify one or more tests that are applied to a client attempting to connect to the network. The policy applies to a client if the client matches all the conditions in the policy.

Existing conditions are listed in the **Specify the conditions to match** list in the **Settings** tab (refer to Figure 8.33). The conditions are identified with very descriptive titles that make it easy to determine a condition's characteristics.

To add a condition to the policy, do the following:

1. Click the **Add** button to open the **Select Attribute** dialog box shown in Figure 8.34. We'll discuss the available conditions after covering the basic procedure for adding them to the policy.

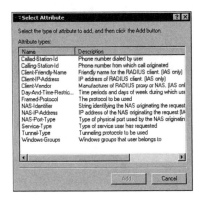

FIGURE 8.34

Thirteen conditions can be added to a remote access policy.

2. Click the **Add** button to open a dialog box where you can enter parameters for the condition.

3. Click **OK** to add the condition to the policy.

Thirteen types of conditions can be added to a policy. Let's discuss each of them. These conditions fall into two categories: general-purpose conditions and conditions that are applicable when RAS is using an IAS server to authenticate users.

General-Purpose Conditions

General-purpose conditions include

- **Called-Station-Id** accepts a text string that identifies the telephone number of the RAS port. The telephone service, dial-up hardware, and Windows drivers must support identification of the called ID, otherwise the connection attempt will be denied. You might use this condition on a multi-port, dial-in server to apply a remote access policy to users who dial in to a specific telephone number of a multi-port RAS server.

- **Calling-Station-Id** accepts a text string that identifies the telephone number of the caller. The telephone service, dial-up hardware, and Windows drivers must support identification of the calling ID, otherwise the connection attempt will be denied. This policy can be used to ensure that a dial-up client calls from a particular location.

- **Day-And-Time-Restrictions** defines blocks of times that determine when the policy is in effect. When you add this option, day and time blocks are defined in the **Time of day constraints** dialog box shown in Figure 8.35. Access is permitted during the times corresponding to the blue time blocks. Access is denied during the times corresponding to the white time blocks. By default, permissions are denied for all time blocks. To permit access, drag a selection box around the desired time blocks and click **Permitted**. To deny access, drag a selection box around the desired time blocks and click **Denied**.

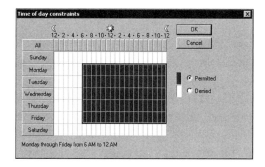

FIGURE 8.35

Time and day constraints for a remote access policy.

- **Windows-Groups** accepts a list of Windows domain global groups to which the policy applies. If this condition is added, the **Groups** dialog box is displayed as shown in Figure 8.36. Click the **Add** button to select domain global groups from a Windows browse list. Domain local groups do not appear in the list. Universal groups can be used in native-mode domains.

Conditions Used with IAS

The following conditions apply only when RAS is using an IAS server to authenticate users:

- **Client-Friendly-Name** accepts a text string that identifies the RADIUS client computer that is requesting a connection. In this context, "client" refers to a RAS server that is configured as an IAS client.

- **Client-IP-Address** specifies the IP address of the RAS server, and is used when requesting authentication from the IAS server. In the context of the Remote Access Policy, "client" refers to a RAS server that is configured as an IAS client.

FIGURE 8.36
The Windows-Groups condition includes one or more Windows groups.

- **Client-Vendor** accepts a text string that identifies the vendor of the RAS server that is requesting authentication from an IAS server. The Windows 2000 Remote Access Server is identified as "Microsoft RAS."

- **Framed-Protocol** specifies one or more frame protocols that are supported for the policy. If this condition is added, the **Framed-Protocol** dialog box is displayed, as shown in Figure 8.37. The **Selected types** list identifies protocols that are included in the condition. Use the **Add** and **Remove** buttons to move protocols between the **Available types** and **Selected types** lists.

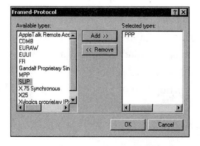

FIGURE 8.37
The Framed-Protocol condition includes framed protocols that appear in the Selected types list.

- **NAS-Identifier** accepts a text string that identifies the remote access server. This field is used to provide the identity of the remote access server to an IAS server.

- **NAS-IP-Address** accepts the IP address that identifies the remote access server to an IAS server.

- **NAS-Port-Type** identifies the media used to communicate with the client. If this condition is added, the **NAS-Port-Type** dialog box is displayed as shown in Figure 8.38. The **Selected types** list identifies port types included in the condition. Use the **Add** and **Remove** buttons to move protocols between the **Available types** and **Selected types** lists. The NAS port types are described in RFC 2138.

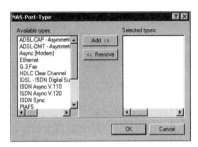

FIGURE 8.38

The NAS-Port-Type condition includes port types that appear in the Selected types list.

- **Service-Type** identifies types of services that can be selected by the client. If this condition is added, the **Service-Type** dialog box is displayed as shown in Figure 8.39. The **Selected types** list identifies service types that are included in the condition. Use the **Add** and **Remove** buttons to move service types between the **Available types** and **Selected types** lists. The service types are described in RFC 2138.

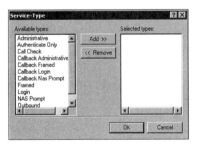

FIGURE 8.39

The Service-Type condition includes service types that appear in the Selected types list.

- **Tunnel-Type** identifies types of protocol tunnels that can be used by the client. If this condition is added, the **Tunnel-Type** dialog box is displayed as shown in Figure 8.40. The **Selected types** list identifies tunnel types included in the condition. Use the **Add** and **Remove** buttons to move tunnel types between the **Available types** and **Selected types** lists. The tunnel types are described in RFC 2138.

8

SUPPORTING DIAL-
UP CONNECTIONS
WITH RRAS

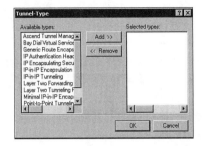

FIGURE 8.40
The Tunnel-Type condition includes tunnel types that appear in the Selected types list.

TIP

The values in the **Client-Friendly-Name**, **Client-IP-Address**, and **Calling-Station-Id** can be entered using UNIX-style pattern-matching syntax. See the topic "pattern-matching syntax" in Windows 2000 Server Help for more information.

Examples of Conditions

Let's look at some policy condition scenarios.

Suppose that you want to set one pattern of connection inactivity during business hours and another pattern for after business hours. This requires two policies, configured as follows:

- One policy has a **Day-and-Time-Restrictions condition** that permits access during business hours. This policy would be configured with properties appropriate for users dialing in during the business day.

- The second policy has a **Day-and-Time-Restrictions condition** that permits access during non-business hours. This policy would be configured with properties appropriate for users dialing in during the non-business day.

If you want to restrict dial-in access to users who are members of a group named DialInUsers, create a policy that includes a **Windows-Groups** condition. Add the DialInUsers group to the groups listed in the **Windows-Groups** condition.

If you want to require a user to dial in from her home, create a policy that includes a **Calling-Station-Id** condition. Enter the user's home phone number in the **Calling-Station-Id** condition.

Editing the Remote Access Policy Profile

Click the **Edit Profile** button in the remote access profile **Properties** dialog box (refer to Figure 8.33) to open the **Edit Dial-in Profile** dialog box shown in Figure 8.41. There's quite a lot to a remote access policy profile, so let's discuss things one tab at a time.

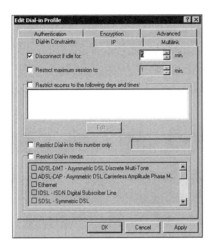

FIGURE 8.41
Remote access policy profile: The Dial-in Constraints tab.

Remote Access Policy Profile: The Dial-in Constraints Tab

The following properties are defined on the **Dial-in Constraints** tab shown in Figure 8.41:

- **Disconnect if idle for.** If enabled, RAS will close any connection that does not transport data for the number of minutes specified.

- **Restrict maximum session to.** If enabled, RAS will close any connection after the number of minutes specified.

- **Restrict access to the following days and times.** Click **Edit** to open a **Dial-in Hours** dialog box (refer to Figure 8.35) where you can edit the times and days when dial-in access is permitted under this profile.

- **Restrict Dial-in to this number only.** If the RAS server supports multiple dial-in ports, select this option and enter the dial-in phone number if clients should dial in to a particular port under this profile.

- **Restrict Dial-in media.** If the RAS server can be accessed through more than one type of network medium, select this option and select the media types that clients should dial in to under this profile.

Remote Access Policy Profile: The IP Tab

Figure 8.42 shows the **IP** tab. Under the **IP Address Assignment Policy** heading, one of the following radio buttons must be selected:

- **Server must supply an IP address.** The client must use the IP address assigned to it by the server.
- **Client may request an IP address.** The client can request a specific IP address, which can be assigned to the client if it is available. Otherwise, the client must use the IP address assigned to it by the server.
- **Server settings define policy.** The IP address assignment method is defined by settings on the **IP** tab of the RRAS server's property pages, shown in Figure 8.24.

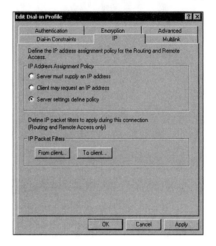

FIGURE 8.42

Remote access policy profile: The IP tab.

If you select **Server settings define policy**, RRAS will use the IP address assignment method defined for the server. This is often the preferred approach, particularly when addresses are assigned from a pool maintained by RRAS. To configure an address assignment method for the server, open the properties pages for the RRAS server object and select the **IP** tab shown in Figure 8.24.

Remote Access Policy Profile: The Multilink Tab

Some dial-up media enable clients to open multiple communication links with the server. This is a particularly useful technique with ISDN connections, which can be opened and closed with little delay. Many types of ISDN service provide multiple communication channels. The **Multilink** tab, shown in Figure 8.43, has two groups of properties:

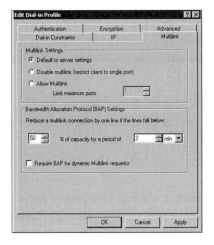

FIGURE 8.43

Remote access policy profile: The Multilink tab.

Multilink Settings determine whether and how multilink communication will be supported. Multilink operation is available only if it is enabled on the **Multilink** tab of the RRAS server **Properties** dialog box. The following options are available:

- **Default to server settings.** If this option is selected, multilink operation is configured by the **Multilink connections** property on the **PPP** tab of the RRAS server's property pages. If the **Multilink connections** property is enabled for the RRAS server, multilink connections are supported unless they are disabled by the remote access profile applied to the connection.

- **Disable multilink (restrict client to single port).** If this option is selected, multilink connections are disabled for clients affected by this profile.

- **Allow Multilink.** If this option is selected, multilink connections are enabled for clients affected by this profile. The number of connections clients can establish is determined by the value of the **Limit maximum ports** field.

Bandwidth Allocation Protocol (BAP) Settings determine how BAP will determine when multiple links are closed.

- A multilink connection will be reduced by one line when the usage falls below the specified percentage for the specified time period.

- If the **Multilink connections** property is enabled on the **PPP** tab of the RRAS server's property pages, the **Dynamic bandwidth control using BAP or BACP** property can be enabled on the same tab. If the **Dynamic bandwidth control using BAP or BACP**

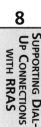

8

SUPPORTING DIAL-
UP CONNECTIONS
WITH RRAS

property is enabled for the RRAS server, bandwidth control is supported unless it is disabled by the remote access profile applied to the connection.

- **Require BAP for dynamic Multilink requests** determines whether the client must support BAP in order to negotiate a multilink connection.

Remote Access Policy Profile: The Authentication Tab

RRAS supports a variety of remote access authentication protocols. Support for one or more of these protocols can be enabled on the **Authentication** tab of the remote access profile, shown in Figure 8.44. The various protocols were discussed earlier in the chapter in the section "Settings on the Security Tab."

Allow remote PPP clients to connect without negotiating any authentication method, when enabled, effectively overrides all efforts to authenticate the user.

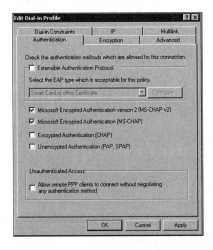

FIGURE 8.44

Remote access policy profile: The Authentication tab.

Remote Access Policy Profile: The Encryption Tab

RRAS supports secure, encrypted communication between the client and the remote access server. When encryption is enabled, only clients that encrypt data they send are permitted access to the RAS. Encryption can be enabled on the **Encryption** tab, which has four options:

- **No Encryption.** Encryption is not supported for clients affected by this policy.
- **Basic.** If this option is selected, clients can use IPSec with encryption based on 56-bit Data Encryption Standard (DES) or 40-bit Microsoft Point-to-Point Encryption (MPPE). Basic encryption is compatible with older software products that do not support 56-bit encryption.

- **Strong.** If this option is selected, clients can use encryption based on 56-bit Data Encryption Standard (DES) or 56-bit Microsoft Point-to-Point Encryption (MPPE).

- **Strongest.** If this option is selected, clients can use encryption based on 128-bit Data Encryption Standard (DES) or 128-bit Microsoft Point-to-Point Encryption (MPPE).

Settings on this tab affect RRAS only. Other services that support encryption must be configured separately.

> **NOTE**
>
> Encryption methods are discussed in Chapter 9.
>
> 128-bit encryption requires installation of the High Encryption Pack, available for download from www.microsoft.com/downloads/. Thanks to January 2000 relaxation of United States' restrictions regarding the export of strong encryption from North America, the High Encryption Pack is available for export to all countries except to U.S.-embargoed destinations. Some countries have local regulations regarding the use of strong encryption technologies.

Remote Access Policy Profile: The Advanced Tab

When RAS requests client authentication from a RADIUS server, it can request the RADIUS server to return values for attributes that it requires. These attributes are specified on the **Advanced** tab, shown in Figure 8.45. Click **Add** to open the **Add Attributes** dialog box shown in Figure 8.46. Here you can select from the list of attributes that is included with Windows 2000 Server, or you can add attributes required for a particular application or piece of hardware. Some of the attributes are defined in the RFCs that describe the RADIUS protocol, whereas others provide vendor-specific information.

RAS Client Authentication Models

Before authorizing dial-in users, you need to decide which of the following authentication models you will employ:

- Access control by user account property settings
- Access by policy on a Windows 2000 mixed-mode domain
- Access by policy on a Windows 2000 native-mode domain

The default policy **Allow access if dial-in password is enabled** (refer to Figure 8.33) has a single condition that includes all available time blocks. In the default policy, the **Deny remote access permission** radio button is selected. Depending on the authentication method that is being used, this policy might need to be deleted.

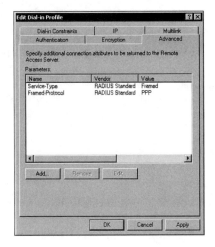

FIGURE 8.45

Remote access policy profile: The Advanced tab.

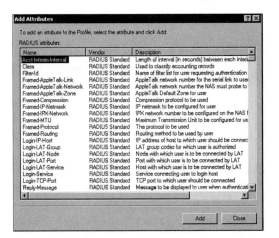

FIGURE 8.46

Remote access policy profile: Predefined attributes.

The following sections examine the RAS client authentication models and the procedures used to set them up. Figure 8.47 presents a flowchart that traces the logic followed by the access control methods.

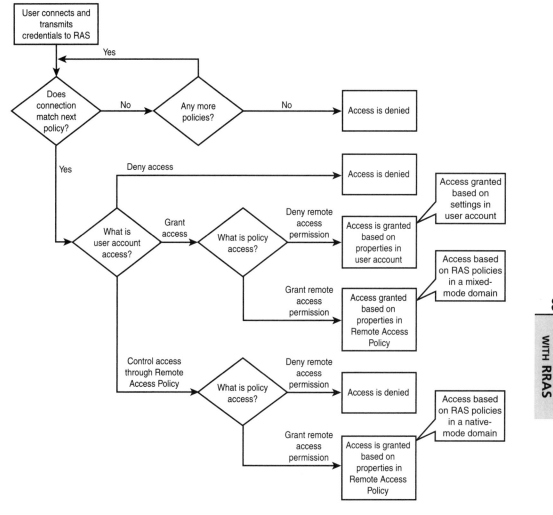

FIGURE 8.47

This flowchart illustrates the authentication models that can be employed with RAS.

Access Control by User Account Property Settings

Under this model, properties in the user's account properties determine whether the user will
be granted dial-in access. The logic used to authenticate a user is as follows:

1. RRAS evaluates the default policy **Allow access if dial-in password is enabled**. The
   policy conditions match the user because they permit the user to dial in to the network at
   any time. However, because **Deny remote access permission** is selected, the policy is
   not used to determine the user's access permissions.

2. The properties under **Remote Access Permission (Dial-in or VPN)** in the user's account (refer to Figure 8.31) are evaluated as follows:

- If **Allow access** is selected, the client is connected subject to settings in the user account dial-in properties.
- If **Deny access** is selected, the client is not connected.

With this model, a client cannot connect unless a remote access profile is present with conditions that match the user's connection attempt. However, the remote access policy is not used to configure the connection.

To summarize, this model is in use when the following conditions apply:

- **Allow access** is selected on the user account Dial-in properties.
- **Deny remote access permission** is selected in the first remote access policy with conditions matching the connection attempt.

This approach is essentially the same as the authentication model used in Windows NT 4. Each user must be individually configured to allow or deny dial-in access, and the same settings are applied regardless of the conditions under which the connection is attempted. This model of user access control can be manageable on small-to-moderately-sized networks, but definitely resists scaling to larger networks.

Access by Policy on a Windows 2000 Mixed-Mode Domain

If your network still incorporates non–Windows 2000 servers and clients and therefore must be configured to operate in mixed-mode, you can still use remote access policies to control dial-in access.

Perform the following steps to implement this access model:

1. In the user account properties for dial-in users, select **Allow access** on the **Dial-in** tab.
2. In the RRAS console, delete the default policy named **Allow access if dial-in permission is enabled**.
3. Create a new remote access policy. Give it a name that suggests the conditions established in the policy.

   For example, suppose that you have established a group named DialInUsers and created a policy that allows access to members of that group. A descriptive name for the policy might be **Allow access if member of DialInUsers group**.
4. In the new policy, select the **Grant remote access permission** property on the **Settings** tab (refer to Figure 8.33).
5. Define the conditions for the policy. The policy must have at least one condition that matches users attempting to connect to RRAS.

For the example mentioned in step 3, you would need to add the condition **Windows-Groups** and add the group DialInUsers to the condition.

The logic used to authenticate a user under this model is as follows:

1. RAS evaluates the policies that have been created. The first policy having conditions that match the connection is used to determine the user's dial-in permissions and connection characteristics.

2. If a remote access policy is found that applies to the client, RAS checks the **Remote Access Permission (Dial-in or VPN)** setting for the user account (refer to Figure 8.31) and determines whether the client should be given access as follows:

   - If **Allow access** is selected, the client is connected subject to settings in the remote access policy.

   - If **Deny access** is selected, the client is not connected.

3. RAS examines the setting **If a user matches the conditions** on the remote access policy **Settings** properties page (refer to Figure 8.33), and proceeds as follows:

   - If **Grant remote access permission** is selected, RAS connects the client based on properties in the remote access policy.

   - If **Deny remote access permission** is selected, RAS connects the client based on properties in the user account.

It is worth emphasizing the critical distinction between policy-based access on a mixed-mode domain and user account–based access. The distinction lies in the setting for **If a user matches the conditions** on the remote access policy **Settings** properties page. The model being used can be determined as follows:

- If **Deny remote access permission** is selected in the remote access property and **Allow access** is selected in the user account **Dial-in** properties, the model being used is Access by Policy on a Windows 2000 Mixed-Mode Domain.

- If **Grant remote access settings** is selected in the remote access property and **Allow access** is selected in the user account **Dial-in** properties, the model being used is Access Control by User Account Property Settings.

Access by Policy on a Windows 2000 Native-Mode Domain

If all computers in a domain run Windows 2000, the domain can be configured to operate in mixed-mode. One advantage of native-mode domains is that control of remote access clients is somewhat simpler.

> **NOTE**
>
> This model also applies to standalone servers that are not members of domains.

> **CAUTION**
>
> If you use this model and do not use groups to determine which users are granted access, make sure that the remote access permission of the Guest user account is set to **Deny access**.

Chapter 4, "Active Directory Concepts," explained the procedure used to convert domains to native-mode. When the conversion has been completed, the property **Control access through Remote Access Policy** is added to the user account properties on the **Dial-in** tab.

Perform the following steps to implement this access model:

1. In the user account properties for dial-in users, select **Control access through Remote Access Policy** on the **Dial-in** tab.

> **CAUTION**
>
> If you base user access on remote access policies and configure user accounts with the **Control access through Remote Access Policy** setting, you must either modify the default remote access policy or delete it and create another. The default remote access policy is configured with the setting **Deny remote access permission**. All clients will match the condition in the default remote access policy and be denied remote access permissions.

2. In the RRAS console, delete the default policy named **Allow access if dial-in permission is enabled** (refer to Figure 8.32).

3. Create a new remote access policy. Give it a name that suggests the conditions established in the policy.

4. In the new policy, select the **Grant remote access permission** property on the **Settings** tab.

5. Define the conditions for the policy. The policy must have at least one condition that matches users attempting to connect to RRAS.

The logic used to authenticate a user under this model is as follows:

1. RAS evaluates the policies that have been created. The first policy having conditions that match the connection is used to determine the user's dial-in permissions and connection characteristics.

2. If a remote access policy is found that applies to the client, RAS examines the **Remote Access Permission (Dial-in or VPN)** setting in the user account **Dial-in** properties and determines whether the client should be given access as follows:

   - If **Control access through Remote Access Policy** is selected, continue to Step 3a.

   - If **Allow access** is selected, continue to Step 3b.

   - If **Deny access** is selected, the client is not connected.

3a. RAS checks the setting **If a user matches the conditions** on the remote access policy **Settings** properties page, and proceeds as follows:

   - If **Grant remote access permission** is selected, RAS continues to step 4.

   - If **Deny remote access permission** is selected, the client is not connected.

3b. RAS examines the setting **If a user matches the conditions** on the remote access policy **Settings** properties page, and proceeds as follows:

   - If **Grant remote access permission** is selected, RAS proceeds to step 4.

   - If **Deny remote access permission** is selected, RAS connects the client based on properties in the user account.

4. RAS searches the list of remote access policies and proceeds as follows:

   - If a policy is found with conditions matching the user, the user is connected with settings defined in the policy.

   - If no policy is found with conditions matching the user, the user connection is denied.

Considerations for Remote Access Client and Server Configuration

There are a number of ways that remote access connection attempts can fail. Many are the same ones mentioned earlier in the section "Testing the Dial-Up Interface." There are two chief sources of difficulty that can arise because you now have the opportunity to misconfigure the dial-in server as well as the dial-out client.

The first source of difficulty is that RAS supports a huge variety of connection hardware and communication protocols. Verify the following configuration settings:

8

SUPPORTING DIAL-UP CONNECTIONS WITH RRAS

- Does the RAS server support the protocol stack being used by the client?
- Are the client and the server configured to use the same framing protocol (PPP or SLIP)? If PPP, do client and server agree on the PPP settings to be used?
- Does the RAS server assign IP addresses in a manner the client will accept? In most cases, the RAS server should assign IP addresses, and clients should accept dynamic configuration.
- Are the modems at both ends of the connection configured with the same settings (usually 8-N-1)? Speed is negotiated during connection setup.

In addition to hardware and protocol concerns, you also need to ensure that security methods are correct. Here are some things to look for:

- Do the RAS server and client support at least one common authentication protocol? Preferred protocols for dialing into a Windows network are EAP and MS-CHAP.
- Is **Allow access** selected on the **Dial-in** tab of the user account's properties?
- Are the client's credentials correctly specified and entered?
- If multiple remote access profiles are defined, is the client using the desired profile to establish a connection? If not, either the desired profile is configured with conditions that do not match the connection, or a profile higher on the list has conditions that match the client.

I suggest that you start testing a new dial-in server as simply as possible, using the Access Control by User Account model. There are only three important security concerns with this model:

- Use the default remote access policy that is installed with RRAS.
- Authenticate to RAS using a valid Windows username and password.
- Select **Allow access** on the **Settings** tab of the user account properties.

After you can reliably dial in and connect with this simple setup, you can proceed to implement policies if that is desirable on your network.

If you can't create a working remote access client and server configuration, try establishing a generic configuration, as discussed in the next section.

Using Wizards to Configure the Dial-Up Client and Server

Simple, no frills dial-up client and server configurations can be implemented using the appropriate wizards. If you are setting up your first RAS dial-in server, the wizards practically guarantee that you will produce a dial-up client and server that can connect.

Configuring the Dial-Up Client with a Wizard

Configure the client using the **Network Connection Wizard** as follows:

1. In **Network and Dial-Up Connections**, double-click **Make New Connection** to open the **Network Connection Wizard**.

2. In the **Network Connection Type**, choose **Dial-up a private network**.

3. In the **Phone Number to Dial** dialog box, enter the phone number of the RAS server. If you check **Use dialing rules**, you must specify the area code and country for the dialing destination.

4. In the **Connection Availability** dialog box, choose **For all users** to make the connection available to all users who log on to this computer. Choose **Only for myself** to make the connection available only for your user account.

5. In the **Internet Connection Sharing** dialog box, I suggest that you disable Internet Connection Sharing.

6. In the **Completing the Network Connection** dialog box, enter a name that identifies the connection.

This procedure creates a dial-up connection that has the following properties (see the section "Reviewing and Modifying Dial-Up Connection Properties" earlier in this chapter for more information about these properties):

- On the **Security** tab (refer to Figure 8.13), `Allow unsecured password` is selected. This is fine for testing, but I suggest that you change the setting to `Require secured password` so that RAS will use a secure authentication protocol. Alternatively, select `Advanced (custom settings)` so that you can manually enable or disable the available authentication protocols.

- On the **Networking** tab (refer to Figure 8.16), PPP is selected as the dial-up server type.

- On the **Networking** tab, all available protocol stacks are enabled for the dial-up interface. **Client for Microsoft Networks** is enabled so that the client can access services on the Windows network as permitted by RAS. **File and Printer sharing for Microsoft Networks** is disabled, as it should be for most dial-up interfaces, because clients typically should not share their files and printers through a slow, on-demand network connection.

Configuring the Dial-Up Server with a Wizard

You can use RRAS as a remote access server using the **Routing and Remote Access Server Setup Wizard**. We first met this wizard in Chapter 7 in the section "Enabling Routing Support on a Windows 2000 Router." There the wizard was used to establish a basic RRAS router configuration that could be customized manually. The **Routing and Remote Access Server Setup Wizard** can also be used to configure RRAS as a remote access server, but there's a catch. You

8

SUPPORTING DIAL-UP CONNECTIONS WITH RRAS

can use the wizard to establish one of five initial RRAS configurations, but the wizard cannot add capabilities to an operational RRAS server. To re-run the wizard, you must first disable RRAS, which returns RRAS to its unconfigured state.

Still, if you're having trouble getting a first RAS server to work, and you have a non-production server you can experiment on, the wizard isn't a bad way to establish a standard RAS configuration that will almost certainly work. You can then see how a working RAS server is configured and customize it or add routing features from there.

To reconfigure RRAS using the wizard, do the following:

1. If RRAS is currently enabled, right-click the RRAS server icon and choose the command **Disable Routing and Remote Access** in the context menu. All configured RRAS services will be disabled.

2. Right-click the RRAS server icon and choose **Configure and Enable Routing and Remote Access** in the RRAS server's context menu to start the **Routing and Remote Access Server Setup Wizard**.

3. In the **Common Configurations** dialog box, choose **Remote access server**.

4. In the **Remote Client Protocols** dialog box, verify that all the required client protocol stacks appear in the **Protocols** list. If a protocol stack is missing, exit the wizard, install the protocol stack on one of the server's network interfaces, and return to Step 2.

5. If AppleTalk is supported, the next dialog box is **Macintosh Guest Authentication**. If you check **Allow unauthenticated access for all remote clients**, Macintosh and other clients can connect to the network through the Guest user account without entering a username and password. I recommend that you leave this option in its default, disabled state.

6. If TCP/IP is supported, the next dialog box is **Network Selection**. If the RRAS server has more than one LAN interface, you must choose one of the IP address ranges as the range to which dial-in client IP addresses will be assigned.

7. If TCP/IP is supported, the next dialog box is **IP Address Assignment**. This dialog box has two radio buttons:

   - **Automatically**. Select this option if client IP addresses will be provided by DHCP.

   - **From a specific range of addresses.** Select this option if you want to allocate a range of IP addresses that RRAS can assign to clients.

8. If you selected **From a specific range of addresses** in step 7, the next dialog box is titled **Address Range Assignment**. You must define at least one range of IP addresses that is reserved specifically for dynamic assignment to clients by RRAS.

9. The next dialog box is **Managing Multiple Remote Access Servers**, which determines how dial-up clients will be authenticated. There are two choices:

  - **No, I don't want to set up this server to use RADIUS now.** If this radio button is selected, client authentication will be done by RAS.

  - **Yes, I want to use a RADIUS server.** If this option is selected, a RADIUS server must be available.

  - In this example, it is assumed that RADIUS is not used to authenticate clients.

10. Click **Finish** for the wizard to set up RRAS as a remote access server. The RRAS service will be started when configuration is complete.

The RAS server that is configured by the wizard has the following characteristics (see the section "Configuring RRAS Server Properties" earlier in the chapter for more information about these properties):

- On the RRAS server **General** property tab, **Router** is disabled and **Remote access server** is enabled.

- On the RRAS server **Security** property tab, Windows Authentication is selected in the **Authentication provider** field. MS-CHAP version 2 and MS-CHAP version 1 are enabled in the **Authentication Methods** dialog box. All other authentication methods are disabled.

  Windows Accounting is selected in the **Accounting provider** field.

- On the RRAS server **IP** property tab, options are configured as follows:

  - **Enable IP routing** is enabled so that outside clients can access the private network via the RAS server.

  - **Allow IP-based remote clients access and demand-dial connections** is enabled so that remote access clients can connect to the RAS server using TCP/IP protocols.

- On the RRAS server **IPX** property tab, options are configured as follows (if the RAS server supports IPX):

  - **Allow IPX-based remote clients access and demand-dial connections** is enabled so that remote access clients can connect to the RAS server using IPX protocols.

  - **Enable network access for remote access and demand-dial clients** is enabled so that outside clients can access the private network via the RAS server.

  - The IPX network address assignment method is **Automatically**.

  - **Use the same network number for all IPX clients** is enabled.

  - Allow remote clients to request IPX node number is disabled.

8

SUPPORTING DIAL-
UP CONNECTIONS
WITH RRAS

- On the RRAS server **AppleTalk** property tab, **Enable AppleTalk Remote Access** is enabled (if the RAS server supports AppleTalk).

- On the RRAS server **PPP** property tab, all available PPP features are enabled.

This is a highly generic configuration for a Windows remote access server that should accommodate nearly all Windows dial-up clients.

Configuring Dial-Up Router Connections

Two RRAS routers on unconnected networks can be configured to dial one another if it is necessary to establish a routed connection between the networks. We've already seen most of the pieces that are required to route through dial-up connections. To configure the routers for dial-up connections, you need to do the following:

- Configure at least one port to support demand-dial routing.

- Configure each router to support demand-dial routing.

- Configure each router with a dial-out connection. Dial-out router connections are similar to dial-out NAT connections, which we examined in the section "Enabling NAT Dial-Out Networking," but we'll cover them again and highlight the differences.

The chief differences we must consider when establishing dial-up router connections are

- The name of the user account used to dial in to the router must be identical to the name of the demand-dial routing interface that accepts the connection.

- Authentication should always be performed using a secure authentication protocol. NAS dial-up connections to the Internet typically are authenticated using PAP, which does not encrypt passwords.

- The routing table must be configured to initiate a demand-dial connection when required. Routers that communicate between dial-up links present special routing table concerns.

NOTE

RAS can accept remote router connections and remote access clients through the same interface, but it is necessary to treat these connection types differently. Specifically:

- Remote router connections support routing between two separate networks.

- Client remote access connections enable a single client to communicate with the RRAS server and, if routing is enabled, with the private network to which the RRAS server is connected.

Connection types are distinguished in the following manner:

- If the user account used to authenticate the dial-in router has the same name as the demand-dial interface that accepts the connection, RAS treats it as a dial-in router connection.
- If the user account used to authenticate the dial-in router has a different name than the demand-dial interface that accepts the connection, RAS treats it as a client remote access connection.

Figure 8.48 illustrates a typical demand-dial routing situation consisting of two networks that do not share a full-time connection:

- In Seattle, Network 10.1.0.0/16 includes RRAS server DC1.
- In Atlanta, Network 172.16.0.0/16 includes RRAS server DC3.

We want to enable either RRAS server to initiate or accept a demand-dial connection. Let's see what is required.

8

SUPPORTING DIAL-
UP CONNECTIONS
WITH RRAS

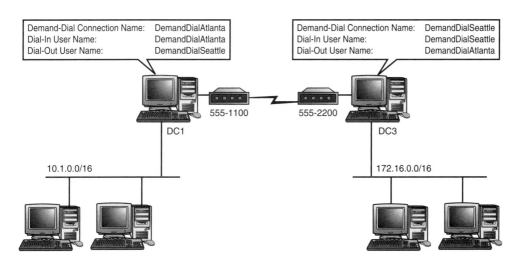

Demand-Dial Connection Name:	DemandDialAtlanta
Dial-In User Name:	DemandDialAtlanta
Dial-Out User Name:	DemandDialSeattle

Demand-Dial Connection Name:	DemandDialSeattle
Dial-In User Name:	DemandDialSeattle
Dial-Out User Name:	DemandDialAtlanta

555-1100   555-2200

DC1   DC3

10.1.0.0/16   172.16.0.0/16

FIGURE 8.48

Example of a network supporting two-way, demand-dial routing.

RRAS on both routers is configured with the following characteristics:

- It supports both LAN and demand-dial routing.
- IP routing is enabled.

- It supports demand-dial routing on the port being used.
- It has a remote access policy that permits remote routers to connect.

RRAS on DC1 is configured as follows:

- It has a LAN connection on network 10.1.0.0/16.
- The phone number for incoming connections is 555-1100.
- It has a demand-dial connection that is configured as follows:
  - The demand-dial connection name is DemandDialAtlanta. (This connection is used to dial out to the RRAS server in Atlanta.)
  - The username used to authenticate a dial-in connection from Atlanta is DemandDialAtlanta. (This username is the same as the connection name for the demand-dial interface.)
  - The username used to authenticate when dialing out to network 176.16.0.0/16 is DemandDialSeattle. (This username is the same as the connection name for the demand-dial interface on DC3 in Atlanta.)

RRAS on DC3 is configured as follows:

- It has a LAN connection on network 172.16.0.0/16.
- The phone number for incoming connections is 555-2200.
- It has a demand-dial connection that is configured as follows:
  - The demand-dial connection name is DemandDialSeattle.
  - The username used to authenticate a dial-in connection from Seattle is DemandDialSeattle.
  - The username used to authenticate when dialing out to network 10.1.0.0/16 is DemandDialAtlanta. (This username is the same as the connection name for the demand-dial interface on DC1 in Seattle.)

We'll use a wizard to set up the demand-dial connections and user accounts, but first we need to make sure the RRAS server is configured to support demand-dial routing.

Configuring RRAS Server Properties for Demand-Dial Routing

Several RRAS server properties need to be configured to support demand-dial routing. See the section "Configuring RRAS Server Properties" earlier in this chapter for screen shots of the RRAS server property pages and descriptions of the properties.

On the **General** tab, make the following settings:

- Check **Router**.
- Select **LAN and demand-dial routing**.
- Uncheck **Remote access server** if the RRAS server will not support remote access client connections. (On sufficiently powerful hardware, RRAS is capable of supporting a large number of both routing and client connections.)

On the **Security** tab, click **Authentication Methods** and verify that at least one secure authentication protocol is enabled. EAP and MS-CHAP v2 are the most secure. If your network supports a public key infrastructure (see Chapter 10), EAP can use digital certificates as authentication credentials. I do not recommend that you enable authentication protocols that are less secure than MS-CHAP. And don't try to get fancy with EAP until you have things working reliably with MS-CHAP.

If TCP/IP will be supported, make these settings on the **IP** tab:

- Check **Enable IP routing**.
- Check **Allow IP remote access and demand-dial connections**.

If IPX will be supported, make these settings on the **IPX** tab:

- Check **Enable IPX-based remote access and demand-dial connections**.
- Check **Enable network access for remote clients and demand-dial connections**.

Configuring RRAS Ports for Demand-Dial Routing

To configure a port to support demand-dial routing, make the following settings in the port properties:

- Disable **Remote access connections (inbound only)**. Although a port can support demand-dial routing and remote access, it is preferable to disable remote access connections on ports used for demand-dial routing.
- Enable **Demand-dial routing connections (inbound and outbound)**. This option must be enabled.

See the section "Configuring Communications Ports" earlier in the chapter for more information about port configuration.

Creating the Demand-Dial Routing Interface

After the RRAS server properties are configured and a port has been configured to support demand-dial routing, you need to create a demand-dial interface on each router. This is most easily done using the **Demand Dial Interface Wizard**. If desired, the required user accounts and dial-up credentials can be created within the wizard.

8

SUPPORTING DIAL-UP CONNECTIONS WITH RRAS

To create the demand-dial interface, perform the following procedure on each router:

1. Right-click the **Routing Interfaces** object in the RRAS console object tree and choose **New Demand-dial Interface** in the context menu.

2. In the **Interface Name** dialog box, enter a descriptive name. For example, an interface used to establish a demand-dial connection with Atlanta might be called DDAtlanta or DemandDialAtlanta.

3. In the **Connection Type** dialog box, select **Connect using a modem, ISDN adapter, or other physical device**. (We'll explore the use of VPNs in Chapter 11.)

4. In the **Select a device** dialog box, select one of the available adapters or modems.

5. In the **Phone Number** dialog box, enter the phone number of the remote router that is used by this interface. Click **Alternates** if you need to enter additional phone numbers for the destination.

6. In the **Protocols and Security** dialog box, select the following options:

   - **Route IP packets on this interface.** Select if TCP/IP is supported for the demand-dial routing connection.

   - **Route IPX packets on this interface.** Select if IPX is supported for the demand-dial routing connection.

   - **Add a user account so a remote router can dial in.** Select if the router accepts incoming demand-dial connections from the remote router that is used by this interface.

7. In the **Dial In Credentials** dialog box, enter the interface name specified in Step 2 in the **User name** field. Remember that, with demand-dial routing connections, the username used to dial in to the interface must be identical to the name of the interface. Enter the password in the **Password** and **Confirm Password** fields.

8. Complete the **Dial Out Credentials** dialog box with the credentials of the user account used to authenticate to the remote router. The username must be identical to the name of the demand-dial interface used to access the remote router.

The newly created user account has the following property settings:

- Logon is permitted at all times on the **Account** tab.
- **Password never expires** is enabled on the **Account** tab.
- Under **Account expires** on the **Account** tab, **Never** is selected.
- Under Remote Access Permission on the Dial-in tab, Allow access is enabled.

After the previously described procedures have been completed on both routers, you can test the router-to-router connection.

Testing the Demand-Dial Connection

In the example, it's assumed that either router can initiate a demand-dial connection. When that is the case, the connection should be tested from both ends. To initiate a connection manually, right-click the demand-dial interface in the **Routing Interfaces** container of the RRAS console object tree and choose **Connect** in the context menu.

If you configured the connection using the **Demand-Dial Interface Wizard**, it is very likely to connect the first time. The wizard establishes most configuration settings so that demand-dial routing will be properly configured. If problems are encountered, they will most likely have to do with security. Here are some things to look for:

- If custom remote access policy objects have been defined, make sure that there is a policy with conditions that match the dial-in connection and that the policy conveys dial-in access rights to the user account being used to authenticate the connection. If no suitable policy is found, the connection will be refused.
- Make sure that the name of the user account specified in the dial-out credentials is identical to the name of the demand-dial interface that receives the connection attempt.
- Verify that the domain and password supplied in the dial-in credentials are correct.
- If the user account existed before you ran the **Demand-Dial Interface Wizard**, it can be configured with properties that are inappropriate for a demand-dial connection.

Test the connection from both directions, ensuring that the routers can communicate, before you worry about routing packets to the private networks behind the routers.

Configuring Routes for Demand-Dial Connections

It is not desirable to support dynamic routing protocols such as RIP and OSPF on low-speed, demand-dial router connections because these protocols generate network traffic that steals valuable bandwidth. Therefore, you should never configure demand-dial interfaces to have their routing tables dynamically updated by RIP for IP, RIP for IPX, or OSPF.

Two alternatives to dynamic routing protocols are useful on demand-dial routing connections:

- Static routes can be manually entered by an administrator.
- Auto-static routes can be exchanged by routers and then stored as static routes in the routing tables. Auto-static updates enable demand-dial routers to exchange routes learned from RIP without sending RIP route advertisements through the dial-up connection.

Static and auto-static routes never expire and are not advertised. Therefore, provided there are no changes in the network topology, no network traffic is generated for routing table maintenance.

8

SUPPORTING DIAL-
UP CONNECTIONS
WITH RRAS

Static Routes

As we saw when discussing NATs, static routes can be used to initiate demand-dial connections. When configuring the NAT, we used a default route to initiate dialing, but that might not always be possible with a demand-dial routing connection.

Typically, users of LANs will spend most of their time accessing local resources. Consequently, the default routes might be needed to simplify client routing on the local network. That means that explicit static routes might be needed to support routing to networks on the remote end of the demand-dial routing connection. The procedure for configuring static routes on demand-dial connections was described earlier in the chapter in the section "Creating a Default Route to the Demand-Dial Interface."

Explicit static routes can still be used to automatically initiate a demand-dial connection startup. Consider, for example, router DC1 in Figure 8.48. To initiate a connection to network 172.16.0.0, the route specified in Figure 8.49 is required.

FIGURE 8.49
A static route that triggers setup of a demand-dial connection on RRAS server DC1 in Figure 8.48.

Similarly, the static route in Figure 8.50 must be defined on RRAS server DC3 to initiate a connection to network 10.1.0.0.

Auto-Static Routes

Manually defined static routes are fine if there are relatively few networks but become difficult to manage when there are many networks at either or both ends of the connection. Auto-static routes enable the demand-dial interface to learn routes from RIP routers on the LAN and transmit those routes to the remote router.

To configure support for auto-static routes, do the following:

1. Add RIP Version 2 for Internet Protocol to the RRAS configuration. (See "Adding RIP for IP to RRAS" in Chapter 7.)

2. Add all LAN interfaces and the demand-dial interface to RIP. (See "Adding Interfaces to RIP" in Chapter 7.)

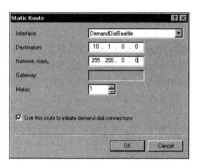

FIGURE 8.50
A static route that triggers setup of a demand-dial connection on RRAS server DC3 in Figure 8.48.

Examine the RIP interface properties, particularly the **General** tab. (See "Configuring RIP Interface Properties" in Chapter 7.) Note that the default value of the **Operational mode** field is configured as follows:

- On LAN interfaces, the mode is `Periodic update mode`. In this mode, the interface will transmit periodic RIP advertisements at intervals specified by the **Periodic announcement interval** field on the **Advanced** tab. This is the default selection for permanently connected interfaces.

- On WAN interfaces such as demand-dial routing interfaces, the mode is `Auto-static update mode`. When this mode is selected, the interface will transmit a RIP announcement only when another router requests one. Routes that are learned over RIP in auto-static mode are marked as `Static` in the routing table. If the router from which the route was learned becomes unavailable, these static routes will not expire and must be deleted manually when they become obsolete. Auto-static mode is the default for demand-dial interfaces, enabling these interfaces to retain routing information without the need to establish a connection at periodic intervals.

Manually Initiating Auto-Static Updates

Unless the topologies of the networks change frequently, it is typically sufficient to have an administrator initiate auto-static route updates manually. Here is the procedure:

1. Establish a connection between the routers.

2. In the RRAS console, right-click the **General** container object under **IP Routing**.

3. Right-click a demand-dial interface in the Details pane and choose **Update routes** in the context menu.

When you view the host's routing table (see "Viewing and Interpreting Routing Tables" in Chapter 7), routes learned through auto-static updates are identified by the label Auto-static in the **Protocol** column.

> **Caution**
>
> When the **Update routes** command is executed, RRAS purges all auto-static routes before it initiates the auto-static update. If the update does not succeed in communicating with the remote router, necessary routes might be lost.

Automating Auto-Static Updates

If the network topology is subject to changes, you might want to schedule auto-static updates to occur automatically at periodic intervals. This is done by creating a script file that can be executed by the Windows 2000 Task Scheduler utility.

A script file that initiates auto-static updates for the demand-dial interface DemandDialSeattle is as follows:

```
netsh interface set interface name DemandDialSeattle connect=connected
netsh routing ip rip update DemandDialSeattle
netsh interface set interface name DemandDialSeattle connect=disconnected
```

Create this script file in a text editor and save it with a .scp filename extension. (If you create the file with Notepad, enclose the filename in quotation marks when you save it. Without the quotes, Notepad adds the extension .txt to any filename you specify.)

The interface in the script file is installed on router DC3 in Atlanta, so we might name the script file AtlantaRoutes.scp. The script file can be executed with the following command:

```
netsh –f AtlantaRoutes.scp
```

This command can executed as a scheduled task. Open **Start→Programs→Accessories→ System Tools→Scheduled Tasks** to access the Windows 2000 task scheduler.

Remote Access Properties and Demand-Dial Connections

With demand-dial routing as with remote access clients, RAS must find a remote access policy with conditions matching the remote access client before it permits the client to establish a connection. I recommend that you create a remote access policy that applies only to dial-in routers. An easy way to define the conditions for dial-in routers is to use the Windows-Groups condition as follows:

1. Create a domain global or universal group for use in the policy. I named my group `RemoteRouters`.

2. Add all the user accounts used to authenticate dial-in routers to the group created in Step 1.

3. Create a new remote access policy. In the conditions list, add a `Windows-Groups` condition and include the group created in Step 1 to the condition. The description I used for the remote access policy is `Allow access if member of RemoteRouters group`.

After the group is created and is added to the conditions of the remote access policy, allowing or denying remote access to a remote router is a simple matter of adding the router's user account to, or removing the user account from, the group.

Testing Automatic Demand-Dial Connections

Now that static routes are configured, you should run tests to see whether demand-dial connections are established when they are required. You can try pinging a destination on a remote network, for example. The `ping` command will probably time out before a modem-based connection can be established, but the modems should initiate dialing when there are packets to be routed to the remote network.

You've already tested the demand-dial connections, so any security issues should be taken care of by now. At this point your only concern should be configuring the static routes required to instigate dialing when a connection is required.

Persistent Connections

Demand-dial connections configured using the **Demand-Dial Connection Wizard** will disconnect if the connection is idle for five minutes. This is usually desirable on dial-up connections that accrue charges based on the connect time.

There might be times, however, when you want an established connection to remain in effect, even when it is idle. For example, the dial-up connection might be local so that there are no time-based charges. To establish that sort of behavior, you must configure the connection as a *persistent connection*.

To configure a demand-dial connection as persistent:

1. Right-click the demand-dial interface in the **Routing Interfaces** container of the RRAS console object tree. Then choose **Properties** from the context menu.

2. Select the **Options** tab.

3. Select the **Persistent connection** radio button.

Controlling Demand-Dial Connections

Automatic disconnection of demand-dial connections is desirable in most cases. The fly in the ointment, however, is that unless you take special steps, a demand-dial connection will almost never be idle for more than a few seconds. Unless steps are taken to prevent it, there is always a slow trickle of communication between Active Directory domain controllers and perhaps between other services as well.

The solution to controlling traffic between demand-dial connections is to configure sites and to schedule the replication of data between sites. Sites were introduced in Chapter 4. The section "Managing Sites" showed how to create and manage sites and the objects associated with them. Here, we'll concentrate on the specifics that apply to demand-dial connections.

The sample network of Figure 8.48 requires two sites:

- Seattle is the site for the following objects:
  - Domain controller DC1
  - Subnet 10.1.0.0
- Atlanta is the site for the following objects:
  - Domain controller DC3
  - Subnet 172.16.0.0

We also need to configure a site link that specifies how replication will take place between the sites. A variety of questions must be answered before site links are configured.

NOTE

Before you change site settings, establish a connection between the sites that will be affected.

Do Domains Span Multiple Sites?

Will any domains span two or more sites? That is, will there be domain controllers for the same domain that are separated by the demand-dial connection? The domain topology has implications for the selection of the inter-site transport:

- If a domain spans multiple sites, an IP site link must be defined.
- If there are no domains that span multiple sites, either an IP or an SMTP site link can be set up. SMTP cannot replicate domain directories, but can be used to replicate the Active Directory (AD) schema, Global Catalog, and configuration.

If a domain spans a WAN link, there should be at least one, and preferably two, domain controllers (DCs) for the domain at each site.

Generally speaking, I don't recommend that you configure domains to span slow demand-dial connections. These low-speed connections are not suitable for supporting users. For example, they won't enable several users at one site to do work on a server located at another site. Typically, this sort of connection is useful for administration and for small amounts of data transfer. An administrator could manage a server at a remote site, for example, or Web pages could be copied between Web servers at various sites so that users could access them locally.

An exception to the previous recommendation might exist if you want all your users to be authenticated by the top-level domain of your tree. Because AD domains employ multi-master replication between DCs, users can log on to a local DC, changing their password or other user information as required. Then scheduled replication based on site definitions could be used to replicate user account changes to DCs at other sites.

When all the servers and clients for a domain are at the same site, there is a lot of data that doesn't need to be replicated between sites. The domain database doesn't require replication, for example. The schema is replicated only when it changes, and the Global Catalog is replicated very efficiently.

When Must Replication Take Place?

How much replication latency can users tolerate? Can AD replication take place only at night, or must it take place during business hours as well? How much time can be allowed to elapse between database replication events? You can control when replication takes place in two ways:

- Adjust the **Replicate every** value on the **General** tab of the Site Link property pages to determine the replication interval.
- Click the **Change Schedule** button on the **General** tab to open a schedule dialog box where you can specify the times and days when replication is permitted.

The replication schedule can be a very useful tool. Suppose that your network includes domains that span two or more sites. Users will authenticate to a local DC, and you want to prevent replication from taking place until after 9 a.m., by which time most users will have logged on, changing their passwords if necessary. Similarly, most dynamic DNS updates will have been performed, so that they can be replicated together. Simply use the replication schedule to block replication from occurring between 8:00 and 9:00 a.m.

Distributing the Global Catalog

At least one Global Catalog server should be enabled at each site so that users can authenticate and browse using a local Global Catalog. If there is no local Global Catalog server, the demand-dial link will be started so that the user can access one on the remote network.

To configure a DC as a Global Catalog server, do the following:

1. In **AD Sites and Services**, expand the object tree for the site.
2. Right-click **NTDS Settings** under the server to be configured and select **Properties** in the context menu.
3. Check **Global Catalog** on the **General** tab of the **NTDS Settings Properties** dialog box.

Configuring DNS for Multiple Sites

There should be at least one DNS server at each site, configured with the zones required to resolve local names.

DNS servers must replicate zone data. To minimize the impact of DNS replication on the WAN link, use Active Directory–integrated domains so that AD takes care of replicating zone data.

Using Demand-Dial Filters

For demand-dial connections supporting IP, demand-dial filters can be configured to determine which types of packets are permitted to initiate a demand-dial connection.

Demand-dial filters do not apply to traffic routed through the connection after it is established. To filter traffic through the interface, use the **Input Filters** and **Output Filters** buttons.

To configure demand-dial filters, do the following:

1. In the RRAS console, select **Routing Interfaces**.
2. In the Details pane, right-click the demand-dial interface and choose **Set IP Demand-dial Filters** to open the **Set Demand-dial Filters** dialog box.
3. Add filters to the list. The procedure for adding filters is discussed in Chapter 7 in the section "Defining Input and Output Filters."
4. Under **Initiate connection**, select one of the following radio buttons:
    *   **Only for the following traffic.** Demand-dial connections will be established only for traffic matching one of the filters.
    *   **For all traffic except.** Demand-dial connections will not be established for traffic matching one of the filters.

Demand-dial filters do not apply to traffic routed through the connection after it is established. To filter traffic through the interface, right-click the demand-dial interface in the **General** tab, select **Properties** in the context menu, and use the **Input Filters** and **Output Filters** buttons on the **General** tab.

RRAS Support for IPX

The procedures for configuring IPX demand-dial connections are not very different from those we have covered for IP. Here are some general guidelines:

- IPX must be installed on the RRAS server and dial-in client, or, in the case of demand-dial routing, on both RRAS servers by enabling IPX on at least one interface on each computer.

- LAN and demand-dial connections must be added to the **General** container under **IPX Routing**.

- IPX routing must be enabled in the RRAS server properties, as described earlier in the chapter in the section "RRAS Server Properties: The IPX Tab."

- Open the properties of the IPX demand-dial interface in the **General** tab and make the following settings:

  - Check **Enable IPX on the interface**.

  - Under **Dial-in control protocol**, select **IPX CP** when the demand-dial connection will communicate with Windows clients or routers.

  - Under **Dial-in control protocol**, select **IPX WAN** when the demand-dial connection will communicate with NetWare dial-in clients or routers.

NOTE

NetWare servers periodically send out *watchdog packets* to verify that idle clients are still alive on the network. If there is no reply to the watchdog packet, NetWare closes the client's connection to the server.

If a NetWare client were separated from its NetWare server by a demand-dial router connection, a watchdog packet would be sent to the client, resulting in traffic that would prevent the demand-dial connection from ever being disconnected.

Consequently, RRAS on the server's network "spoofs" watchdog packets, responding on behalf of the remote client. If the connection is closed because of inactivity, RRAS continues to respond to watchdog packets sent to the remote client, enabling the client to retain its connection to the NetWare server. As a result of spoofing, watchdog packets do not cross the WAN link and therefore do not prevent the connection from timing out and do not force the connection to be re-established.

8

SUPPORTING DIAL-UP CONNECTIONS WITH RRAS

Managing the Internet Authentication Service

The Internet Authentication Service (IAS) included with Windows 2000 Server is an implementation of the RADIUS authentication and accounting standards. If your organization has two or more RRAS servers supporting dial-in connections, IAS can greatly simplify management by centralizing authentication and accounting in a single, easily managed place.

Additionally, IAS provides some authentication services that are unavailable with RRAS authentication, such as Dialed Number Identification Service (DNIS), which verifies the number that the remote access client was calling, and Automatic Number Identification Service (ANI), which determines the phone number from which the connection request originated.

IAS is managed very similarly to the authentication and accounting components of RRAS, so there is little additional information you need to deploy IAS.

Installing IAS

Install IAS using the **Add/Remove Programs** applet in the Control Panel. Choose **Add/Remove Windows Components→Networking Services→Internet Authentication Service**.

An icon to open the **Internet Authentication Service** console is added to the **Administrative Tools** folder in the **Start** menu. Figure 8.51 shows the IAS console.

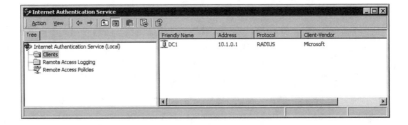

FIGURE 8.51
The Internet Authentication Service console.

Configuring IAS Server Properties

Unless you require the advanced capability offered by IAS realms, which we won't discuss in this chapter, you might never need to modify the IAS server properties. Let's familiarize ourselves with some of the properties, however.

To open the IAS server properties pages, right-click **Internet Authentication Service** in the IAS console object tree and choose **Properties** from the context menu. The **Internet Authentication Service Properties** dialog box, shown in Figure 8.52, has three tabs. We will discuss the **Service** and **RADIUS** tabs.

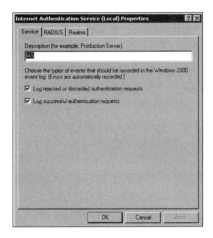

FIGURE 8.52
IAS Server Properties: The Service tab.

IAS Server Properties: The Service Tab
The **Service** tab has the following fields:

- **Description.** This is an optional friendly name for the IAS server. The default value is IAS.

- **Log rejected or discarded authentication requests.** Typically this option should be enabled so that you can determine whether attempts are being made to circumvent security, perhaps by guessing passwords for user accounts.

- **Log successful authentication requests.** This option is useful when confirming IAS operation, but will result in large log files. Although enabled by default, it should usually be enabled unless stringent security requirements require logging of all connections.

IAS Server Properties: The RADIUS Tab
The **RADIUS** tab specifies the UDP ports that are used by the authentication and accounting components of IAS. IAS clients and servers must be configured to use the same port numbers. You should not need to modify the ports on either the IAS server or the IAS client.

RADIUS ports were discussed earlier in the chapter in the section "RADIUS Authentication Methods."

Adding IAS Clients

An IAS client is any network access system that relies on IAS for RADIUS authentication of dial-in clients. To configure a RAS server as an IAS client, do the following:

1. Right-click the **Clients** object in the IAS console object tree and choose **New Client** from the context menu to open the **Add Client Wizard**.

2. The **Name and Protocol** dialog box has the following fields:

    - **Friendly name.** Enter a descriptive name for the RAS server. This need not be the same as the Active Directory or NetBIOS name of the server.

    - **Protocol.** The only value available for this field is RADIUS.

3. The **Client Information** dialog box is shown in Figure 8.53. Complete the dialog box as follows:

    - **Client address (IP or DNS).** IAS must know the IP address of the IAS client. You can enter the IP address directly, or you can enter the FQDN of the client and click **Verify** to resolve the domain name to an IP address.

    - **Client-Vendor.** There are many different network access systems that can use RADIUS for authentication and accounting. A number of vendors can be selected in this field, enabling RADIUS to be tailored to particular vendor requirements. The default value is RADIUS Standard. You can select Microsoft to optimize IAS for use with RRAS clients.

    - **Client must always send the signature attribute in the request.** If this option is enabled, IAS clients must include the shared secret in every communication with IAS.

    - **Shared secret** and **Confirm shared secret.** The shared secret is a text string known only to the IAS client and the IAS server, enabling them to communicate securely. The same shared secret must be entered in RAS, as described in the section "RADIUS Authentication Methods" earlier in this chapter.

When the wizard is completed, the network access server is added to the **Clients** container.

Registering the IAS Server in Active Directory

IAS must be registered with Active Directory so that it can obtain the user account information required to authenticate dial-in users. Registration adds the server running IAS to the Active Directory **RAS and IAS Servers** group.

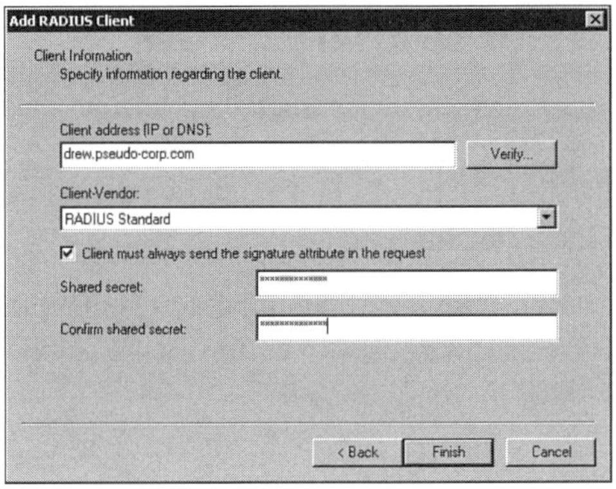

FIGURE 8.53
RADIUS client information.

The IAS server can be registered with Active Directory in two ways:

- Use **Active Directory Users and Computers** to add the server to the **Members** property of the **RAS and IAS Servers RAS and IAS Servers** group.
- In the IAS console, right-click **Internet Authentication Service** and choose **Register Service in Active Directory**.

Managing IAS Remote Access Policies

In the same manner as RRAS, IAS uses remote access policies to configure connections. When you add a RRAS server as an IAS client, any remote access policies on the RRAS server are copied over to the IAS server.

The chief difference between IAS and RAS remote access policies is that more conditions are available with IAS. The section "Conditions Used with IAS" earlier in the chapter lists these conditions and describes their uses.

Configuring RRAS for IAS Authentication and Accounting

The RRAS server must be configured to use a RADIUS server for authentication and accounting. See the section "RRAS Server Properties: The Security Tab" earlier in the chapter for the procedures that are required.

IAS Logging

IAS logging procedures are defined by the properties of the **Local File** object in the **Remote Access Logging** procedure. The contents of the properties pages were discussed earlier in the section "Configuring Remote-Access Logging."

Onward to VPNs and Encryption

This is only the second of three chapters centered on the Windows 2000 Server Routing and Remote Access Service. We haven't exhausted the capabilities of RRAS, because we haven't started to talk about Virtual Private Networks (VPNs) that enable us to securely route data through a public network such as the Internet.

VPNs bring us to the subject of encryption, so we'll take on both topics in the next chapter. We'll discuss the ways encryption can be used to ensure secure communication and then we'll use encryption in an applied way by configuring VPNs.

Data Communication Security Concepts

IN THIS CHAPTER

The ARPAnet, which became the Internet, was developed as an alternative to fixed-leased lines. Because the Internet uses packet-switching technology, a computer that is connected to the Internet can communicate with any other computer that is also connected to the Internet. The only requirement is that both computers must have some method of communicating with a local Internet access point such as an ISP. One local connection buys an organization communication with virtually every place in the world.

If there's a fly in the Internet ointment, it's that the Internet wasn't originally intended to provide secure communication. Most protocols used on the Internet have been extremely open to casual scrutiny. I can read your SMTP email if I simply have the means to intercept your packets because every SMTP mail message is sent in clear text. You can look at my FTP file transfers to see whether I'm retrieving anything interesting from my corporate FTP server.

But the Internet is just too good a way to move data around to let security worries keep it down. Businesses want to do business on the Internet. Customers want to be able to make credit card purchases without having to fax in their credit card numbers. Users want to send email without being concerned about privacy. The need for data communication security is pervasive and is likely to become more so as our desire for privacy grows.

Consequently, significant efforts have been made in the data communication industry to develop methods that enable us to communicate freely without being concerned about data being compromised. Along the way, whole new tools have sprung up, such as digital signatures that are being recognized as legal proof of identity in increasing numbers of local and national governments. It is now possible to send data, know that they have not been viewed or modified, and verify from whom the data were sent.

The tools that provide this security and flexibility take the form of advanced cryptography technologies along with network protocols that take advantage of them. In many cases, the result is so smooth and seamless that users are unaware of the level of protection they are experiencing. When you access a secure Web site, it is likely that your only tip-off is that `http://` changes to `https://` in the URL.

Cryptography consists of two mirror processes:

- *Encryption* is the process of processing input data, often called *plaintext*, to generate an unreadable form of the data, often called *ciphertext*.
- *Decryption* is the process of processing ciphertext to recover the initial plaintext.

This is the first of three chapters that discusses several key data communication security technologies that are supported by Windows 2000 Server.

- This chapter discusses the goals of communication security and the technologies that we will rely on when we build a secure network infrastructure.
- Chapter 10, "Planning and Implementing a Public Key Infrastructure," explains how to establish a public key infrastructure that can issue and validate public key certificates. These

certificates are used by many security processes for identification and for exchanging encrypted data.

- Chapter 11, "Securing IP Communication," explores two methods of securing data in IP communication: the Secure Sockets Layer (SSL) and Internet Protocol Security (IPSec).

- Chapter 11 also covers virtual private networking, a method of transporting data through a public data network while maintaining security and communications transparency.

Before we get involved in implementation details, some general discussion is in order. Let's start by examining the three general classes of techniques that are employed in data security, along with the primary algorithms for implementing the techniques. In the course of the chapter, we'll see how these techniques are used alone and in combination to meet a variety of security goals.

The Tools of Digital Data Security

In most cases, if we're concerned about security at all, it's because we don't want unauthorized people to have access to data. The solution to that problem is as old as civilization: Use some technique to encrypt the data so that, hopefully, only the sender and receiver of the data can decrypt them. Until the advent of digital encryption techniques, most encryption techniques were not terribly effective. Good encryption could be done before computers became widespread, but the vast majority of codes eventually were cracked. (Interesting exceptions were the German Enigma machine of World War II, which was only cracked when a coding machine was stolen, and in the same war the use by the United States Marines of Navajo-speaking communicators in the Pacific theater. The latter technique remained effective throughout the conflict.)

The modern tools of choice involve digital cryptographic techniques. One reason digital encryption is so secure is that there is no such thing as being "close" to the solution. Remember those substitution ciphers we all played with in grade school? You know, A=1, B=2, and so forth? The solution to substitution ciphers lies in knowing the most common letters and words and then applying some judicious guesswork. If we see a lot of 5s in the code, then 5 is likely to correspond to E or T, the most common letters in English. After we solve several letters, we can probably guess some of the words, which gives us some more letters. Thus we can gradually work closer to the solution.

With digital encryption, however, if you're trying to crack the cipher with a key that is just one digit different from the real one, your results will be as garbled as if the key were 100% incorrect. The only way to crack a digitally encrypted message is to use a brute-force attack that tries all the available keys. If the algorithm is carefully designed and the key is long enough, guessing (using very fast computers, of course) won't get you anywhere in your lifetime or a thousand generations to come. For example, it takes on average 2^{55} (36,028,797,018,963,968 decimal!) attempts to crack DES, which is no longer regarded as a particularly strong encryption algorithm.

That doesn't mean that an encryption technique can rest on its laurels. Cryptanalysts are constantly working to refine techniques for breaking encryption. From 1977 until recently, the U.S. standard for encrypting non-secret data was the Data Encryption Standard (DES), which relies on 56-bit keys. In 1977, cracking DES was considered theoretically possible, but only given a concerted and expensive effort at a government level. Today, however, DES can be cracked in a matter of hours using hardware costing less than a million dollars. Cracking DES still isn't easy, but it's getting easier. That's why work is being done to develop a next-generation encryption technique that has been dubbed the Advanced Encryption Standard.

Windows 2000 supports three primary digital encryption algorithms:

- *DES* (Data Encryption Standard) is a symmetrical encryption algorithm, released in 1977 by the U.S. National Bureau of Standards.

- *3DES* is a more secure form of DES, developed in response to the growing vulnerability of the original DES algorithm.

- *RSA* (Rivest-Shamir-Adelman) is an asymmetrical encryption algorithm that relies on pairs of keys. RSA is the foundation of most public key infrastructures.

There are many things that we seek to achieve with data security, but everything is accomplished with three types of encryption tools: message digests, secret key (symmetric key) cryptography, and public key (asymmetric key) cryptography. When you configure IPsec and VPNs, you need to make choices between the available methods so that you can meet your security goals while keeping processing and communication costs under control.

NOTE

As you read this chapter, keep these general rules in mind:

- For a given algorithm, longer keys result in greater security.
- Because longer keys require more processing, a more secure implementation of a given algorithm requires more processing than a less secure implementation of the same algorithm.
- Security is a moving target. Techniques that once were considered secure are now vulnerable to low-cost attacks. New penetration techniques might exploit loopholes and weaknesses in algorithms that were not apparent when the algorithm was published.
- As a corollary to the previous point, nothing is ever completely secure. Given enough processing power, it is theoretically possible to crack the most secure forms of encryption.
- There will always be a need for vigilance. Users who don't protect their account passwords can be the chinks in your security armor. And remember that insiders perform most espionage. Be as concerned about the people you let in as you are about the people you are trying to keep out.
- Digital cryptography never eliminates the need for physical security. The most secure cryptographic techniques can be circumvented if a computer or disk that contains cryptographic keys is stolen or simply used surreptitiously.

NOTE

Until January 2000, U.S. export laws prohibited export of strong encryption products outside of North America. As a result, several security algorithms had to be hobbled in exported versions of software products such as Windows NT and 2000. For example, the export versions of Windows supported 40-bit encryption, whereas domestic versions supported 56-bit encryption.

In all but a few cases regarding specifically embargoed countries, export restrictions on strong encryption were rescinded in January 2000. To configure Windows 2000 to support strong encryption (128-bit or greater), you must install the High Encryption Pack, available for download from `www.microsoft.com/downloads/recommended/encryption/download.asp`.

Message Digests

When we receive data we often require assurance that the data were not modified in transit. Suppose that you arrange for a funds transfer between bank accounts. Unless precautions are taken, an intruder could intercept the message, change the destination of the transfer to his bank account, and send the message on to the bank. Even if the contents of a message are encrypted, it might still be possible for an intruder to modify the contents in such a way as to invalidate the data.

Message digests are the primary tools for ensuring *message integrity*, the process of ensuring that data have not been modified, either through error or malice. Message digests are digital signatures that uniquely describe a bundle of data. Although message digests are not cryptographic in nature—they cannot be used to encrypt and decrypt data—they are vital tools in data security and are often used in parallel with data encryption.

Message digests are generated in a process usually called *hashing*. A *hashing algorithm* is a computational process that takes variable-length input data and generates a fixed-length *hash code*, also called a *hash signature*, that is a cryptographic checksum of the data. Message digests go by a variety of names. Three have been mentioned already, and you need to know a fourth. A message digest is also sometimes called a *Message Integrity Code* (MIC).

When used for data security, a good hashing algorithm has several characteristics:

- The same hash code will seldom, if ever, be produced for different input data.
- Although it is easy to process the input data to generate the hash code, it is computationally inefficient (read "very, very difficult") or even impossible to generate the input data by working backward from the hash code.
- The same input data should produce a different hash code each time they are hashed.

Given these characteristics, the chain of events illustrated in Figure 9.1 can be used to determine whether data have changed between the time they are created and the time they are used. Suppose that Andy wants to send a message to Betty so that Betty can be sure the message wasn't modified. The process would look like this:

1. Andy processes the data with a hash algorithm to produce a message digest that is included in the packet with the data.

2. Betty applies the same hash algorithm to the data that are received, generating her own hash signature for the data.

3. Betty compares her hash signature to the one she received from Andy. If the two hash signatures are identical, it is reasonable to conclude that the data were not modified.

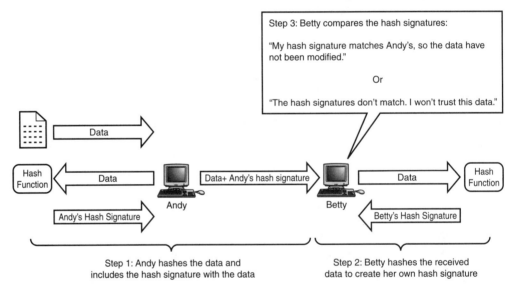

FIGURE 9.1

Testing message integrity with message digests.

NOTE

It's common when writing cryptography scenarios to use wording that suggests the users are manually performing each step. Although users do need to personally request some security functions, for example, when they want their email program to secure a message, the secure networking protocols discussed in Chapter 11 function invisibly from the standpoint of the end user.

Because hashing algorithms work in one direction only, hashing cannot be used to encrypt data for later decryption. Nevertheless, message digests are vital components of many data security processes. Hash signatures go by several different names. Because they function as encrypted summaries of the input data, hash signatures are often referred to as *message digests*. And, because the hashing algorithm is nonreversible, the resulting signatures are sometimes called *one-way transforms*.

If you have looked at data communication protocols, you have seen the way checksums are used to verify the integrity of packets and messages. For example, as was explained in Chapter 2, "TCP/IP Protocol Concepts," every Ethernet packet includes a Frame Check Sequence (FCS), which is a checksum that is calculated when the packet is sent and again when it is received. If the receiver generates a value that is identical to the FCS in the received packet, the receiver can presume that the packet was probably not modified.

Requirements for a Secure Hashing Algorithm

The checksum calculation for an Ethernet packet cannot provide security for two reasons:

- The FCS value is too short to ensure that two packets cannot bear the same checksum value.
- The same FCS value is generated every time the checksum calculation is made for the same data.

Because the checksum algorithm is well known, it would be relatively easy for an intruder to modify a packet either in such a way as to produce the same checksum value or by replacing the FCS field altogether.

That's why secure hash algorithms use three inputs to the hash algorithm:

- The data to be signed.
- A secret key known only to the sender and receiver. The secret key ensures that an intruder cannot modify the data and generate a new message digest.
- A randomly-generated *initialization vector*, a "seed" value that is different for each calculation, ensuring that a different hash code will result even if the same data are processed multiple times.

The initialization vector is there for randomization, not for security, and it can be sent in the clear. The secret key is commonly negotiated between the correspondents before a message or series of messages is exchanged. Because the initialization vector ensures there will be no patterns in the resulting message digests, the same secret key can be used for a reasonable period of time without jeopardizing security. (Which is great, because the most troublesome aspect of sharing secret keys is the task of exchanging them while keeping the keys secret.)

9

DATA
COMMUNICATION
SECURITY CONCEPTS

An additional requirement is that secure message digests must be long enough to make them resistant to attack. The 16-bit FCS of an Ethernet packet is far too short to provide security even if it were generated by a secure algorithm. With only 64,536 possible values, an intruder could crack the code with a trivial computer-based attack. Secure message digests algorithms use keys that are 128 bits in length or greater.

Message Digests Standards Supported by Windows 2000

RFC2104 describes the Hashed Message Authentication Code (HMAC), the standard message authentication algorithm for Internet communications. HMAC can make use of several message digest algorithms. Windows 2000 supports two message digest standards:

- *HMAC-MD5*, also referred to as *Message Digest 5* (RFC1321), corrects several shortcomings in the older MD4 standard. MD5 makes four passes through the data, using a different numeric constant with each pass. Using the equivalent of 64, 32-bit constants, MD5 generates a 128-bit message digest. Because MD5 uses shorter keys, it is faster but less secure than SHA.

- *HMAC-SHA* uses the *Secure Hash Algorithm* developed by the U.S. National Institute of Standards and Technology. Although modeled on MD5, SHA uses an equivalent of 72, 32-bit constants to generate a 160-bit message digest. Because longer keys provide better security, SHA is regarded as being stronger than MD5, but has greater processing requirements.

The default message digest used for Windows 2000 is HMAC-SHA, usually identified simply as SHA or SHA1.

Secret Key Cryptography

Secret key cryptography performs encryption and decryption with the same key, which must be guarded as a shared secret known only to the communication partners. Because the same key is used to encrypt and decrypt, secret key cryptography is also called *symmetrical key cryptography*.

Symmetrical encryption is the oldest encryption technique. Over the centuries, shared secrets have taken many forms, from rolling strips of paper around sticks of the same size to using formulas to pick words out of a book that was known only to the parties involved, but the type of shared secret we are interested in here is the digital key.

A *digital key* is simply a pattern of bits that is input to the encryption algorithm along with the data to be encrypted. With a symmetric key algorithm, the resulting encrypted data can be decrypted only when the decryption algorithm is supplied with the key used to encrypt the data.

There are two general types of secret key cryptography algorithms:

- *Block* cipher algorithms transform fixed-size blocks of plaintext into ciphertext blocks of the same size. Today the typical block size is 64 bits, but the trend is toward 128-bit blocks. When the plaintext is longer than the block size, there must be a mechanism for chaining blocks together. The most commonly used block encryption is DES. RC2 is a block cipher, developed by RSA Security as a drop-in replacement for DES. RC2 has been subject to less stringent export controls than DES and has been used by developers of products that are distributed internationally, such as export versions of Windows.

- *Stream cipher* algorithms generate a *keystream*, a sequence of bits that is used as a key. The keystream is combined with the plaintext (usually by an XOR operation) to produce the ciphertext. DES can function as a stream cipher in certain modes but generally offers poorer performance than the RC4 cipher developed by RSA Security, which is probably the most commonly used stream cipher.

Symmetrical encryption is efficient and very secure, and is used in nearly all instances when large amounts of data must be encrypted. Symmetric keys are also used as *session keys* in a wide variety of data protocols, for example:

- Secure Socket Layer (SSL) and Transport Layer Security (TLS), which is being developed as an Internet standard to replace SSL

- Internet Protocol Security (IPSec)

- Secure/Multipurpose Internet Mail Extensions (S/MIME)

- Microsoft's Encrypting File System (EFS)

The most commonly used symmetrical encryption algorithm is DES or its more secure variant, 3DES, which we should look at in a bit more detail.

DES

DES makes use of a 56-bit key. (Although the key appears to have 64 bits, 8 bits provide parity.) The key is used to map a 64-bit input block into a 64-bit output block.

9

DATA
COMMUNICATION
SECURITY CONCEPTS

NOTE

Windows products packaged for export use a 40-bit cipher that is considerably less secure than standard DES. Export restrictions have been eliminated (except for to a few embargoed countries), so the High Encryption Pack makes DES available worldwide.

There are several things we don't want an encryption algorithm to do. One is to leave patterns in the ciphertext that reflect patterns in the plaintext, perhaps by producing the same ciphertext for material that is repeated in the plaintext. Another is to use the same key to encrypt for too long. The more material that is encrypted by the same key, the more likely a code breaker will be to find something that can be used to crack the code.

Initialization Vectors

Like secure message digests, DES makes use of a randomly determined *initialization vector* that is separately generated for each encryption event. The initialization vector is provided to the encryption algorithm along with the shared key and the data to be encrypted. Thus, every time a message is encrypted, different ciphertext will result.

Cipher Block Chaining

To prevent patterns and excess use of keys, DES employs *Cipher Block Chaining* (CBC), which works as follows:

1. The first block of plaintext is encrypted using the key and the initialization vector.
2. Before being encrypted, the plaintext for each subsequent block is XORed with the ciphertext for the previous block, a process that obscures any patterns that might be found in the plaintext.

Robustness of DES

As mentioned earlier in the chapter, there have been a variety of successful public efforts (and who knows how many secret ones) to crack DES encryption. The vulnerability of DES is not due to its algorithm, which has withstood intense analysis since it was published in 1977, but rather to the relatively short key length. All efforts to crack DES rely on the brute-force approach of trying all available keys. Although it takes an average 2^{55} attempts to crack a DES cipher, that number is small enough to make DES vulnerable to cracking on the affordable, clustered microcomputers and workstations that have become readily available in recent years. Consequently, the United States federal government certifies DES for use only on legacy systems.

Nevertheless, DES encryption is efficient and fast, and DES remains a useful method for encrypting data that have a relatively short useful lifetime.

3DES

The DES standard makes no provision for lengthening the encryption key past 56 bits. To enable DES encryption to function with the equivalent of longer keys, it has been necessary to adopt a strategy that uses multiple keys instead of longer keys.

3DES, or triple-DES, relies on the basic DES algorithm. To increase the effective key length, however, 3DES makes three passes through each block with three independent keys. One sequence processes data as follows:

1. The block is encrypted with key 1.
2. The block is decrypted with key 2.
3. The block is encrypted with key 3.

That process is reversed when decrypting the block. Other encryption-decryption sequences are possible, but this appears to be the sequence that Microsoft is using in its products.

3DES is regarded as highly secure given the current state of computers and decryption techniques. No successful 3DES decryptions have been demonstrated publicly, although proposals have been floated that remain impractical on computers presently available. Consequently, it is likely that 3DES will remain uncracked in the near future. 3DES is the default encryption algorithm used in the Windows 2000 implementation of IPSec.

Vulnerabilities of Symmetric Keys

For a given key length, symmetrical ciphers are more secure than asymmetrical ciphers. Because of the shorter keys that are required, symmetrical cryptography algorithms are much more efficient than asymmetrical ciphers and are therefore almost always used when it is necessary to encrypt large amounts of data.

But there has always been a troublesome aspect to symmetric keys. For the system to work, it is necessary for both correspondents to possess the shared secret key. If the key is obtained by a third party, the ciphertext is compromised. Some of the great victories in code breaking have simply involved the interception or theft of a shared secret key.

Yes, we could hire a beefy security guard with a briefcase handcuffed to his wrist to deliver secret keys around the organization, but the goals of data processing include both speed and flexibility. For encryption to work on a widespread basis, there has to be a mechanism for exchanging secret keys through the network without risk that the keys will be compromised.

There are two common mechanisms that accomplish just that: Diffie-Hellman Key Agreement, and public key encryption. There will be an entire section on public key encryption in just a bit, but let's take a moment to examine the Diffie-Hellman algorithm.

Diffie-Hellman Key Agreement

Whitfield Diffie and Martin Hellman of Stanford University were the first researchers to publicly propose the use of public key cryptography in a 1975 paper. (A method for public key cryptography was actually described long ago by two analysts working for British intelligence, but their proposals were not, of course, made public until much later and were, in fact, largely ignored within the intelligence community.) Among other things, Diffie and Hellman proposed a method for securely exchanging cryptographic keys. The exchange algorithm is not itself cryptographic in nature, but is based on mathematical transformations that enable two parties to arrive at the value of a secret key without actually exchanging the key through the network.

The potential of Diffie and Hellman's work was not fully appreciated until it became necessary to implement security protocols that could be publicly available without infringing on the rights of RSA Security, Inc., which until recently held patents to the RSA public key encryption algorithms and charged for their use. (RSA surrendered their patents into the public domain in September 2000.) We will encounter the use of Diffie-Hellman Key Agreement to negotiate shared secret keys in IPSec in Chapter 11.

NOTE

The mathematical formulas employed by the Diffie-Hellman Key Agreement algorithm are not particularly complex, but it isn't appropriate or necessary to discuss them here. If you want to know more, RSA Security, Inc. maintains a Public Key Cryptography Standard regarding Diffie-Hellman Key Agreement. The RSA standards are described in a sidebar in the following section.

Public Key Cryptography

Public key cryptography relies on pairs of keys: a private key that is kept secret and a public key that can be freely distributed. Because different keys are required to encrypt and decrypt data, public key cryptography is also described as *asymmetrical cryptography*.

Both the public and the private key can be used to encrypt messages, but a key that was used to encrypt a message cannot be used to decrypt it. The message must be decrypted by the other key in the key pair. Specifically

- The public key can decrypt ciphertext that was encrypted by the private key.
- The private key can decrypt ciphertext that was encrypted by the public key.

The private and public keys are stored and used in very different ways.

The private key is held as a secret that is known only to the owner of the key pair and is stored in a place or manner that reduces the likelihood it will be compromised. It might be stored in a smart card, on a removable computer disk, or in an encrypted data store on the computer.

The public key is stored in a digital *public key certificate* (usually referred to simply as a *certificate*), a digitally-signed electronic document. Among other things, the public key identifies the owner of the public key, the organization that issued the digital certificate, the time period for which the certificate is valid, and the purposes for which the certificate can be used. Public keys can be distributed freely and can always be verified by the authority that issued them.

Public-private key pairs can be useful in many ways, such as providing identification, creating digital signatures, and exchanging small amounts of confidential information. When deployed in a well-designed public key infrastructure (PKI), public-private key pairs can be the cornerstones of an organization's data security.

The most widely deployed public key algorithms are known by the initials of their developers, Rivest, Shamir, and Adelman (RSA). The RSA algorithms are based on factoring with large prime numbers and have proven to be extremely robust.

A particularly useful advantage of the RSA algorithms is that the lengths of keys can be extended as it becomes necessary to strengthen encryption. Thus RSA public key encryption has adapted to improvements in code cracking technology with greater agility than DES.

RSA Cryptography Standards

The Web site for RSA Security, Inc. is an excellent source of information about digital cryptographic methods. The RSA Laboratory Web site is accessed at
`http://www.rsasecurity.com/rsalabs/`.

Their FAQ pages provide excellent, brief descriptions of a wide variety of encryption technologies. To access the RSA Laboratories FAQ pages, follow the link `Crypto FAQ` at the previously mentioned Web site.

RSA Security is also the coordinator of the Public Key Cryptography Standards (PKCS). The following PKCS standards are currently defined:

- PKCS #1: RSA Cryptography Standard
- PKCS #2: Incorporated into PKCS #1 version 2
- PKCS #3: Diffie-Hellman Key Agreement Standard
- PKCS #4: Incorporated into PKCS #1 version 2
- PKCS #5: Password-Based Cryptography Standard
- PKCS #6: Extended-Certificate Syntax Standard
- PKCS #7: Cryptographic Message Syntax Standard
- PKCS #8: Private-Key Information Syntax Standard
- PKCS #9: Selected Attribute Types

- PKCS #10: Certification Request Syntax Standard
- PKCS #11: Cryptographic Token Interface Standard
- PKCS #12: Personal Information Exchange Syntax Standard
- PKCS #13: Elliptic Curve Cryptography Standard
- PKCS #15: Cryptographic Token Information Format Standard

You will often encounter references to these standards. For example, a client transmits a PKCS #10 certificate request when requesting a public key certificate. When issued, the certificate is returned in a PKCS #12 file.

To obtain the PKCS standards, follow the link PKCS at the RSA Laboratories Web site.

Techniques for Using Public Key Cryptography

Broadly speaking, there are two sorts of processes in which public key encryption is used: verifying identity and securely exchanging data. Notice that both of these techniques work only if it is valid to assume that the private key remains a closely guarded secret of the key holder.

Secure Data Exchange

Figure 9.2 illustrates how Andy can send Betty data in secure, encrypted form:

1. Andy encrypts the data using Betty's public key.
2. Only Betty can decrypt the data because only she has access to her private key.

Notice that unlike secret key encryption, public key encryption does not face the problem of securely sharing a secret key. As a result, public key encryption can provide a mechanism for secure exchange of secret encryption keys. After the secret key is exchanged using public key methods, secret key encryption can be used to efficiently encrypt the bulk of the data that must be exchanged.

NOTE

Figure 9.2 uses common shorthand for indicating encryption, by specifying the key and enclosing the encrypted data in parentheses. For example,

Betty's public key (Data)

indicates that the data is encrypted using Betty's public key.

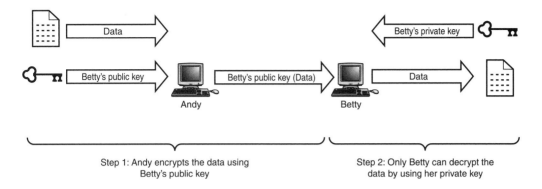

Step 1: Andy encrypts the data using
Betty's public key

Step 2: Only Betty can decrypt the
data by using her private key

FIGURE 9.2

Ensuring confidentiality with asymmetric keys.

On occasion, data might be encrypted more than one time to satisfy special requirements. Suppose Andy wants to send a digitally signed document to Betty while ensuring that only Betty can read the document. First, Andy digitally signs the document using his private key. Then he encrypts the document using Betty's public key.

To recover the original document, Betty first decrypts the ciphertext with her private key. Then she uses Andy's public key to verify that Andy is the originator of the document.

For a given level of security, public key cryptography requires longer keys than do private key cryptography methods. Consequently, public key cryptography requires more processing and is not suitable to the encryption of large amounts of data. When it is necessary to encrypt large messages, a symmetric key algorithm such as DES is employed, and public key methods can be used to securely exchange the symmetric key.

Digital Signatures

As we seek to do more and more business electronically, the need is increasing for ways to "sign" electronic documents. Suppose that we receive a contract in electronic form. We don't want the other party to the contract claiming that it is a forgery. We need a digital signature method that cannot be repudiated by its originator (a security goal often referred to as *non-repudiation*). But we also need a digital signature mechanism that doesn't require excessive amounts of computation or storage space.

Digital signatures (also popularly called *electronic signatures* or even *e-signatures*) require two technologies that we have already discussed: hash algorithms and public key cryptography. The following process creates a signed data document whose ownership can be verified by the recipient:

1. The document is processed by a hash function to generate a hash signature. As we know, a given hash signature can be produced for only a particular document.

2. The hash signature is encrypted using the private key owned by the creator of the document. (It is seldom possible to create a digital signature by encrypting the entire document because the signature would be as large as the original document. Also, public key encryption is not well suited to encrypting large amounts of data.)

3. The receiver of the document uses the document owner's public key to decrypt the message hash signature. If the public key successfully decrypts the hash signature, the recipient can be certain that only the sender's private key could have encrypted the document. This success verifies that the owner of the key pair is the only person who could have encrypted the digital signature.

4. The receiver then checks the decrypted hash signature to determine if it is valid for the document received. If the hash signature is verified, the document has not been modified, and the hash code must be the one that was prepared for the original document.

Another method of supporting digital signatures is the Digital Signature Security Standard (DSS) developed by the United States National Security Agency. DSS defines the Digital Signature Algorithm (DSA), which is the digital signature standard of the United States government. Although DSA- and RSA-based digital signatures offer similar levels of security, DSA is a more complex, processing-intensive algorithm, in part because it requires SHA-1 message digests to provide the needed security.

Digital signatures have gained enough credibility that they are recognized as legally binding in many legal jurisdictions including, as I am writing, 40 of the United States and the United States federal government.

RSA Key Length and Encryption Strength

RSA keys can be as short as 384 bits and, in strong implementations, as long as 16,384 bits. RSA Security runs frequent assessments of the security offered by various key lengths.

In 1997, ciphertext encrypted with 512-bit RSA keys was broken in about seven months using a computer system costing about $1 million. It is prudent to presume that decryption can be performed more quickly with each passing year. Consequently, RSA recommends the use of 512-bit keys only when encrypting data that has a short useful life. At present, their recommendation is to use keys with a minimum length of 1024 bits to encrypt any critical data.

Of course, longer keys require greater processing effort, so it's probably premature to use 16,384-bit keys in all your public key cryptography. At this time, keys in the range of 1024–4096 bits probably offer the best compromise between security and processing overhead.

One problem with digital encryption is that you can't enhance the security of older encrypted material simply by using longer keys. Only keys in the key pair that was originally used for encryption can decrypt a given ciphertext. If the security level of existing material must be increased, the ciphertext must be decrypted and then encrypted using stronger keys. No doubt, this will present significant logistical problems for organizations that want to maintain secure, long-term archives of their documents in electronic form. (Another problem with long-term storage is the impermanence of all available methods for storing digital data. No digital medium today can reliably store documents for 2,000 years, something that has been accomplished with a few handwritten documents on parchment.)

Public Key Infrastructures

To provide all its possible benefits, public key cryptography must be implemented so that well-defined procedures support the following processes:

- Generating a public-private key pair
- Requesting a public key certificate for a user, computer, or process
- Verifying the identity of the user, computer, or process that is requesting a certificate
- Issuing a public key certificate by a suitable authority
- Verifying a public key certificate at the time of use to ensure that the certificate is properly authorized and has neither expired nor been revoked

These are not informal processes. Security never is. There must be clear protocols and authorities for each process, or effectiveness and security are brought into question.

That is the purpose of a public key infrastructure, which consists of Certificate Authorities (CAs) to issue and verify certificates and public key–enabled clients that can exploit the capabilities that the PKI offers.

The public key infrastructure for the Internet is based on standards developed by the PKIX (Public-Key Infrastructure [X.509]) working group of the Internet Engineering Task Force (IETF). The PKI standards are derived from the X.509 standards issued by the International Telecommunications Union (ITU).

The IETF PKI is documented in about two dozen RFCs and Internet-Drafts and is clearly too vast to be addressed in a single chapter. You can find more information at the RSA Laboratories Web site mentioned earlier in the chapter, or on the PKIX pages on the IETF Web site at http://www.ietf.org/html.charters/pkix-charter.html.

We'll be coming back to public key infrastructures in Chapter 10.

Authentication

All the security in the world won't accomplish much if we let anyone walk through the front door. Consequently, the first step in any security plan is to verify the identity of the user or system that is attempting to access secure data.

Authentication ensures that the person or computer seeking to send or receive data is who or what it purports to be. We're used to dealing with authentication issues with user accounts, where a user is authenticated by a username and password. But the need for authentication goes much further than the user logon process. Here are a couple of examples:

- A user wants to gain access to a computer that contains very sensitive data. How can we be especially sure that the user is authorized to see the data?

- You are shopping on a Web site and are asked to enter your credit card. How do you know that the Web site is genuine and hasn't been compromised?

- A computer wants to establish a dial-in network connection. How do we ensure that the computer is authorized to connect?

Windows 2000 supports a variety of authentication methods:

- *Kerberos v.5* is the protocol used to authenticate users on Windows 2000 computers. For example, when a user logs on and enters a username and password, Kerberos is used to verify the user security data and to grant tickets that enable the user to access secured objects.

- *Windows NT LAN Manager (NTLM)* is the authentication mechanism supported by Windows NT 4. Windows 2000 supports NTLM to authenticate downlevel Windows clients and servers. But NTLM is no longer the protocol of choice for authenticating Windows users and computers, so we won't be considering it further in this book.

- *Public key certificates* provide a very secure means of identification. The Extensible Authentication Protocol (EAP) discussed in Chapter 8, "Supporting Dial-Up Connections with Routing and Remote Access Service," can be configured to authenticate users based on public key certificates.

- *Smart cards* add a physical authentication device to the logical password. A smart card is a credit card–sized electronic device that can be issued public key certificates. A user attempting to be authenticated with a smart card must present the card to a card reader and know the password or PIN associated with the card. Both the smart card and the password must be compromised before an intruder can gain access to the system.

The advantage of using a public key certificate for authentication is that the process of authenticating a connection can be made entirely automatic. That's usually what happens when you connect to a secure Web site. The Secure Sockets Layer protocol that enables secure HTTP communication to take place requires the Web server to have a public key certificate. The browser receives the site's public key certificate and validates it with the authority that issued it, usually without any involvement by the user. The methods used to issue and validate public key certificates are discussed at length in Chapter 10.

We've already discussed the manner in which public key certificates can be used to verify their owners' identities. But we haven't touched on the improvements in user authentication that arise through the adoption of Kerberos as the Windows 2000 authentication protocol. Because our confidence in many Windows 2000 services depends on our confidence in the method used to authenticate users, let's take a look at Kerberos to illuminate its approach to authentication and its advantages.

Kerberos

Kerberos version 5 (RFC 1510) is a network authentication protocol developed at the Massachusetts Institute of Technology (see `http://web.mit.edu/kerberos/www/`). Named after the three-headed dog that guarded the underworld of Greek mythology, Kerberos is designed to provide high-security authentication on untrustworthy networks. Kerberos is an improvement over NTLM authentication in several ways:

- Strong encryption ensures that authentication data cannot be compromised.
- Two-way authentication authenticates the client to the server and the server to the client. With Kerberos, the client is assured that it is connecting with the desired server, not a decoy.
- Time codes embedded in requests protect against replay attacks. Because request packets are time-stamped, an intruder cannot collect packets and retransmit them at a later time in order to gain access to a system.
- Kerberos uses tickets to authorize access to resources.

With Kerberos, a client does not authenticate directly to a particular server. Kerberos functions as a trusted intermediary that enables servers and clients to be mutually authenticated. The trusted intermediary is called the Key Distribution Center (KDC). Under Active Directory, a KDC is established on every domain controller.

NOTE

Kerberos can subdivide large networks into *realms*, which function much like Windows domains. Within Windows, realms always correspond to domains. Consequently, I'll use the term *domain* to describe Kerberos authentication boundaries.

CAUTION

Shortly before I was writing this chapter, a controversy was circulating regarding the Microsoft implementation of Kerberos. It appears that Microsoft has used some of the fields in a manner not described in the MIT Kerberos specification. I have no idea how this issue will play out, but you should be aware that some adjustments might be required if non-Windows Kerberos clients are authenticating with the Windows Kerberos implementation. Similarly, non-Windows Kerberos servers do not fully support Windows authentication requirements.

If you search http://www.microsoft.com for the keyword Kerberos, the results include dozens of articles describing Kerberos-compatibility issues. Start with these articles if you are implementing Kerberos with a mixture of Windows and non-Windows clients. A FAQ regarding Microsoft's Kerberos implementation can be found in Knowledge Base article Q266080. This article provides references to Internet-Drafts that describe Microsoft's modifications.

Key Distribution Center Services

The KDC provides two services: the authentication service and the ticket-granting service.

The *authentication service* verifies the identities of the server and client and issues *session tickets* that authorize the client to communicate with the server. Authentication relies on two types of keys:

- *Long-term keys* uniquely identify security principles. A long-term key is created for each security principle and is known only to the security principle and the KDC. The user's account password is processed with a hash function to generate the long-term key. Long-term keys for Active Directory users are derived from the users' passwords.

- *Session keys* enable servers and clients to authenticate each other so that clients can access services. Session keys are encrypted using the long-term keys of the associated security principles. Session keys enable users to request session tickets from the KDC.

The *ticket-granting service* issues *tickets* that authorize access to services in the KDC's own domain or to KDCs in other domains. Three types of tickets are employed:

- *Session tickets* contain a server's session key, encrypted with the server's long-term key. When a client is authenticated, the KDC sends a session ticket to the client, which in turn presents the session key to the server.

- *Ticket-granting tickets* (TGTs) are session tickets for the ticket-granting service of the KDC, issued by the KDC to authenticated clients. The TGT is encrypted with the KDC's secret key and cannot, therefore, be decrypted except by the KDC. This ensures that the contents of the TGT remain confidential, and that, once issued, the TGT cannot be modified. A TGT includes a session key along with the user's authorization data. Presenting the TGT to a KDC enables the client to request a session ticket for a particular service.

- *Referral tickets* are TGTs to KDCs in other domains. If a client needs to access services in another domain, the client must request a TGT from a local KDC for a KDC in the target domain.

All Kerberos tickets include a start time and an expiration time that determine the lifetime of the ticket. A session ticket can be used any number of times during its valid time span. Kerberos tickets are configured to expire after a certain period of time so it is less likely that the tickets will be compromised.

Authorizing Client Access to Services

The various keysand tickets are used in three Kerberos exchanges, which operate in the following sequence:

1. The *Authentication Service* (AS) exchange enables clients to log on and to obtain TGTs. The AS exchange, illustrated in Figure 9.3, consists of the following events:

   a. The client sends the KDC an AS request that specifies the username and the service that is required. The request includes *preauthentication data*, usually a time stamp that is encrypted with the user's long-term key.

   b. The KDC retrieves the user's long-term key from its local store and recovers the time stamp by decrypting the preauthentication data. The time stamp is used to decide whether the request is valid or might be a replay of an earlier request. If the time stamp of the preauthorization data is suspect or the KDC's copy of the user's long-term key does not decrypt the preauthorization data, the logon attempt is rejected.

   c. After the KDC determines that the client is genuine, it creates a logon session key that is encrypted with the user's long-term key. A second copy of the logon session key is embedded in a TGT. The logon session key and the TGT are returned to the client.

   d. The client uses its long-term key to decrypt the logon session key and stores the session key and the TGT in a local credentials cache. These credentials can be reused out of cache until they expire.

   The client now possesses a logon session key that is stored in its cache. From now on, all exchanges are authenticated using session keys instead of the client's long-term key. The client also has a TGT.

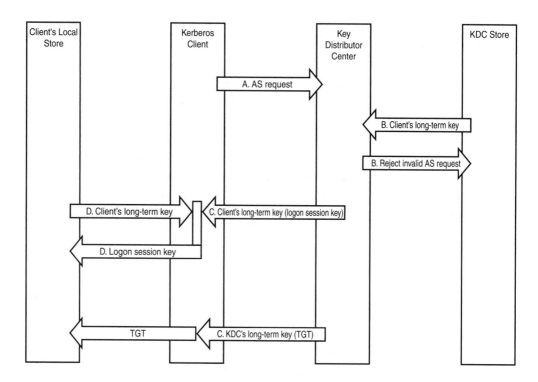

FIGURE 9.3

The Kerberos Authentication Service exchange.

2. The *Ticket-Granting Service* (TGS) exchange enables clients with TGTs to obtain session tickets in the following manner, as depicted in Figure 9.4.

   a. The client sends the KDC a Ticket-Granting Service Request that includes the user's name, an authenticator encrypted by the client's logon session key, the TGT issued during the AS exchange, and the identity of the service for which access is requested.

   b. The KDC decrypts the TGT using the KDC's secret key and extracts the client's logon session key. The logon session key enables the KDC to decrypt the logon session authenticator included in the TGT.

   c. The logon session authenticator enables the KDC to extract the client's authorization data.

   d. If authorization is successful, the KDC creates a session key.

   e. One copy of the session key is encrypted with the client's logon session key.

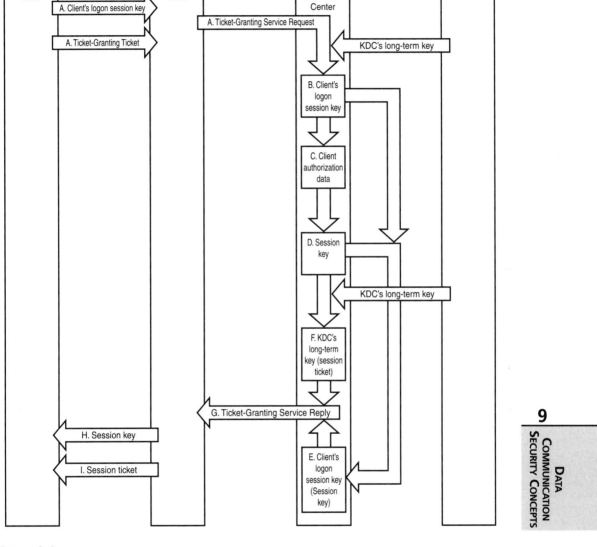

FIGURE 9.4
The Kerberos Ticket-Granting Service exchange.

f. A second copy of the session key and the client's authentication data are embedded in a session ticket, which is encrypted using the long-term key of the server on which the service resides.

g. A Ticket-Granting Service Reply is sent to the client. It contains the session key encrypted in the client's logon session key (Step 2e) and the session ticket (Step 2f).

h. The client decrypts the session key and stores the key in its credentials cache.

i. The client extracts the session ticket and stores it in its credentials cache.

The client now has a session ticket that can be used to request access to the desired service on the desired server.

3. The *Client/Server* (CS) exchange, shown in Figure 9.5, enables clients with session tickets to access services using this procedure:

a. The client sends the server an Application Request that contains an authenticator encrypted with the session key for the service, the session ticket obtained during the TGS exchange, and a mutual authentication flag indicating whether the client requires authentication of the server. (Windows 2000 clients always request mutual authentication.)

b. The server decrypts the session ticket using its long-term key, extracting the user's authentication data and the session key.

c. The server decrypts the authenticator using the session key and examines the time stamp.

d. If the time stamp is valid, the server examines the mutual authentication flag. If mutual authentication is requested, the server uses the session key to encrypt the time from the client's authenticator. The result is a server authenticator that is returned to the client in an Application Reply. The client authenticates the server by decrypting the server authenticator to recover the time stamp. If the time stamp is identical to the time stamp the client sent to the server, the server is authenticated.

e. After the client and (optionally) the server are authenticated, the session proceeds. The session key can be used to encrypt data during the session, or another key or encryption protocol can be used.

Configuring Kerberos Policy Settings

Several parameters related to Kerberos can be edited in Group Policy (see Chapter 4, "Active Directory Concepts"). These settings are found in Group Policy settings for domains and OUs.

To access Group Policy, do the following:

1. Open **Active Directory Users and Computers**.

2. Right-click a domain or OU container and choose **Properties** from the context menu.

3. Select the **Group Policy** tab.

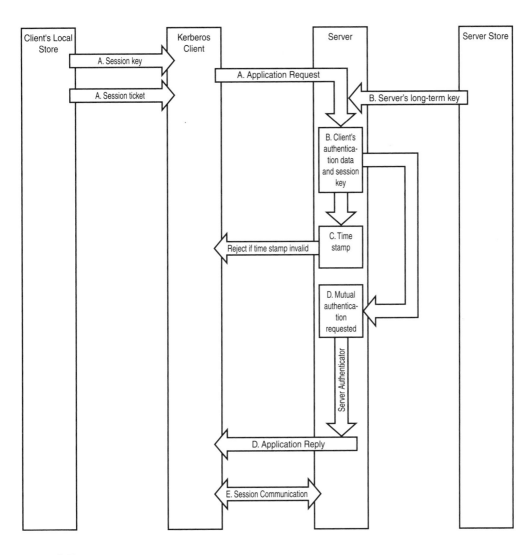

FIGURE 9.5

The Kerberos Client/Server exchange.

4. Edit an existing policy or create an existing one as discussed in Chapter 4 in the section "Managing Group Policy."

5. To expose the policies related to Kerberos, follow this path: **Computer Configuration→Windows Settings→Security Settings→Account Policies→Kerberos Policy**. The **Kerberos Policy** container is shown in Figure 9.6.

9

DATA COMMUNICATION SECURITY CONCEPTS

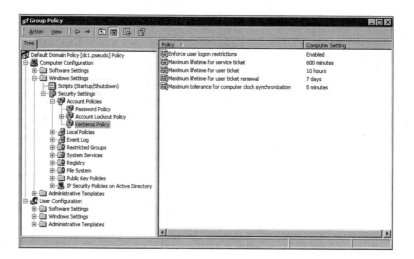

FIGURE 9.6

Group Policy settings related to Kerberos.

Five Group Policy parameters affect Kerberos (and yes, once again Microsoft uses two terms to refer to the same thing, their own and the term used in the Kerberos standard):

- **Enforce user logon restrictions.** When this option is enabled (the default setting), the KDC validates every request for a session ticket by verifying with the target server that the requester has the right to log on locally or to access the computer from the network, as appropriate. The KDC also checks that the user account is still valid. The policy can be disabled because these verifications can slow access to services.

- **Maximum lifetime for service ticket.** This policy setting specifies the maximum life-time for a session ticket. The default value is 600 minutes (10 hours). This setting must be more than 10 minutes and less than the setting for **Maximum lifetime for user ticket**.

- **Maximum lifetime for user ticket.** This policy setting specifies the maximum lifetime for which a TGT is valid. After the lifetime expires, the TGT must be renewed to remain valid. The default value is 10 hours.

- **Maximum lifetime for user ticket renewal.** This policy specifies the maximum life for both TGTs and session tickets, despite the fact that only user tickets are specified in the policy title. When the specified lifetime expires, the tickets cannot be renewed. The default value for this policy is 7 days.

- **Maximum tolerance for computer clock synchronization.** Recall that the KDC evaluates the time stamp that is included in the user preauthentication data (Step 1b in the previous section) and rejects requests for authentication that are judged to be too old. This policy allows some wiggle room between the clocks of the Kerberos client and the KDC, enabling clients to be authenticated even if their clocks do not agree exactly. The default tolerance is 5 minutes.

Windows Time Synchronization

Several Windows 2000 processes depend on having reasonable time agreement between Windows computers in an organization. Kerberos time stamp evaluation is one such process. If the Kerberos server and client disagree on the time by more than a few minutes, the server will reject authentication requests that were generated just seconds ago by the client.

Another example is the manner in which Active Directory arbitrates between changes that are made to the same object property on two different domain controllers. When it comes time to synchronize AD, the time stamps of the modified properties are used as tiebreakers, with the most recent change taking precedence.

Time synchronization is automatically provided by the W32Time service, an implementation of the Simple Network Time Protocol (SNTP; RFC 1769). The time service might need to be configured for proper operation on large LANs and particularly on internetworks that incorporate WAN links.

Within an AD tree, an election process identifies the PDC of the root domain as the master time server for the tree. Time propagates down the tree hierarchically.

Ideally, the PDC for the root domain should synchronize its time with a reliable external SNTP time server. The U.S. Naval Observatory operates two suitable time servers, which are identified as follows:

- ntp2.usno.navy.mil at 192.5.41.209

- tock.usno.navy.mil at 192.5.41.41

To configure a Windows 2000 computer to reference these SNTP computers, enter the following command at a command prompt:

```
net time /setsntp:"ntp2.usno.navy.mil tock.usno.navy.mil"
```

IP addresses can be entered instead of domain names. The quotation marks can be omitted if only one time server is specified. The time server identification is stored in the Registry and is therefore persistent.

> The default time synchronization setting produces queries for a time server three times at 45-minute intervals until a time server is contacted, after which the time is checked at eight-hour intervals.
>
> For detailed information about W32Time, including Registry settings, search `http://support.Microsoft.com` for Knowledge Base articles Q224799, Q2231894, and Q216734. Alternatively, search for W32Time.

Configuring Password Policy Settings

All the strength of Kerberos turns to mush if users aren't vigilant about their passwords. Password policies are also enforced in Group Policy at the location **Computer Configuration→Windows Settings→Security Settings→Account Policies→Password Policy**. The **Password Policy** container is shown in Figure 9.7.

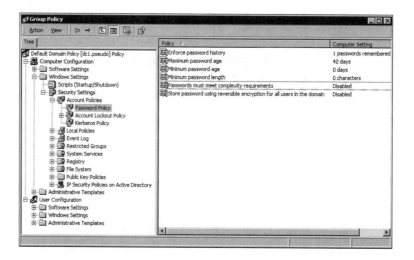

FIGURE 9.7

Group Policy settings that affect password strength.

The default password policy settings shown in Figure 9.7 establish the level of security that a cardboard box would provide for the Hope diamond. Here are the policies with some recommendations for settings:

- **Enforce password history.** Password history prevents users from repeatedly selecting the same password. A password cannot be reused until it has cycled through the history queue. Increase the password history value to establish the level of security that is required. The minimum value should be 5 or greater. 10 or greater results in considerable password variety.

- **Maximum password age.** This policy setting determines the number of days a password can be used before it can be reused. 42 is not a bad starting value, but you should reduce the password lifetime if higher levels of security are required.

- **Minimum password age.** Some users who don't want to change their passwords will simply enter enough passwords to remove the old password from the history list, enabling them to use their favorite password again. A minimum password age makes it difficult to engage in that practice. A minimum password that is one-half of the maximum password age ensures that passwords will not be reused too frequently.

- **Minimum password length.** Short passwords are easy to guess. Under normal circumstances, a minimum password length of 7 or 8 provides reasonable security. Increase the minimum length to strengthen passwords, but don't make passwords so long that users have trouble remembering them (which often means that passwords will be posted on sticky notes attached to the user's monitor).

- **Passwords must meet complexity requirements.** Lots of users will select passwords that are easy to remember and type, such as "aaaaaaaa," "drew," or "qwerty." You can eliminate such weak passwords by enabling this policy. A nearby note defines the requirements that must be met by passwords to meet complexity requirements. Users might find it objectionable to create and enter passwords that meet these requirements, so don't just spring it on users without warning. Make sure that use of the policy has the support of your organization and that users understand the necessity.

- **Store passwords using reversible encryption for all users in the domain.** This policy enables support for the Challenge Handshake Authentication Protocol (CHAP), but applies only to passwords stored on a standalone remote access server. Passwords used in Windows 2000 domains are always encrypted when stored.

NOTE

When **Passwords must meet complexity requirements** is enabled in Group Policy, passwords must meet these requirements:

1. Passwords must be at least six characters long.
2. Passwords must contain characters from at least three of the following four classes:
   - English uppercase letters (A, B, C,...Z)
   - English lowercase letters (a, b, c,...z)
   - Westernized Arabic numerals (0, 1, 2,...9)
   - Nonalphanumeric characters such as punctuation symbols
3. Passwords cannot contain your username or any part of your full name.

9

DATA COMMUNICATION SECURITY CONCEPTS

Now That You Know the Concepts, Let's Get Busy

You now know enough about cryptography to implement a public key infrastructure and to configure secure IP communications. Naturally, cryptography is much more vast than I've even hinted at in this chapter. If you're inclined to dig deeper, the RSA Laboratories Web site is one of the best places to start looking for accessible but authoritative information. Cryptography standards are pretty complex, so if your curiosity leans in that direction, prepare to set aside quite a bit of time to figure them out. Most of us would benefit by having a bottle of NoDoze handy as well.

The next two chapters focus on putting cryptography theory into practice. You'll see how the various hash and encryption algorithms go together to create secure network communications infrastructures.

We'll start in Chapter 10 by implementing a public key infrastructure using the Windows 2000 Certification Services. You never know when you'll need a good certificate, so it's useful to take up PKIs before we start working with secure network protocols in Chapter 11. Two of the technologies discussed in that chapter, Secure Sockets Layer and Internet Protocol security, use certificates for authentication.

Planning and Implementing a Public Key Infrastructure

IN THIS CHAPTER

From the discussion in the previous chapter, it should be clear that public key cryptography can be useful, even vital, in an organization, providing secure, versatile mechanisms for identifying users, computers, and services and making it easy to exchange data with an assurance of confidentiality. When deployed in a well-designed public key infrastructure (PKI), public-private key pairs can be the cornerstones of an organization's data security. Several secure communication methods cannot be implemented until a method for issuing public key certificates is established.

The most widely deployed public key algorithms are known by the names of their developers: Rivest, Shamir, and Adelman (RSA). The RSA algorithms are based on factoring with large prime numbers and have proven to be extremely robust. The Windows Certification Services is an easily managed service for supporting a PKI based on RSA public key cryptography.

As mentioned earlier, public keys are distributed in public key certificates. These certificates are of value only if their veracity can be established. Is the owner of the certificate who or what it purports to be? Is the certificate valid now, or has it expired or been revoked? Who issued the certificate, and can I trust them? To see how PKIs enable users to have confidence in digital certificates, we need to examine Certification Authorities.

NOTE

I've more material about Certification Services than you really need to support secure network protocols. But a PKI is seldom established simply to support network security, and if you're going to start using certificates, I wanted to provide enough information to enable you to get a solid start. It's difficult to modify a PKI once it is in place, so rather than showing you something simple that you'd have to rip out later, I wanted to help you build something substantial that has the potential to last.

Certification Authorities

A *certification authority* (CA) is a service that issues public key certificates and validates them when they are used. Because clients rely on CAs to determine whether a certificate is valid, the question arises of how a client can be assured that a particular CA is itself trustworthy. The trustworthiness of CAs becomes of greater concern in organizations that require multiple CAs in their PKIs. The entire mechanism of trust falls down if CAs don't issue certificates properly and if clients cannot rely on CAs.

We need to look at several issues regarding CAs:

- How CAs issue certificates to clients
- How CAs validate certificates at the time of use
- How multiple CAs can be deployed in an organization
- How clients can determine the trustworthiness of a CA

Issuing Public Key Certificates

The processes of requesting, receiving, and installing a public key certificate is called *enrollment*. On a Windows 2000 CA, certificate enrollment functions as follows:

1. The client generates a public-private key pair and prepares a *certificate request* that includes the locally generated public key, client authentication data, and the characteristics of the desired certificate. The certificate request is sent to a CA. The format of certificate requests generated by Windows clients is defined in PKCS #10. (PKCS standards are described in the sidebar "RSA Cryptography Standards" in Chapter 9.)

    In most cases, certificate requests are transmitted in real time through the network. They can be delivered by other means, for example as email attachments or on portable storage media such as a floppy disk.

2. The Windows 2000 CA processes the incoming request using an *entry module* that determines how the certificate request will be disposed of. The entry module determines whether certificate request processing will be handled automatically or an administrator must manually process the request.

3. Before issuing a certificate, the CA must authenticate the client. This can be done in two ways:

    - Automatic client authentication can be performed if a suitable mechanism is available. Windows 2000 Certification Services can be configured to authenticate certificate requests using Active Directory.

    - Manual authentication can be performed by an administrator, in which case incoming requests are held in a queue until they can be attended to. After the certificate administrator is satisfied of the identity of the requestor, the administrator confirms or denies the request.

4. If the certificate request is approved, the CA prepares an X.509v3 certificate. The certificate includes the client's public key, client identification information, begin and end dates for the period in which the certificate is valid, and CA identification information. The CA applies a digital signature to the certificate, attesting to the validity of the binding between the client public key and the client.

10

PLANNING AND
IMPLEMENTING A PUBLIC
KEY INFRASTRUCTURE

5. The certificate is published to the CA's certificate database and to other destinations specified by an *exit module* that specifies optional actions to be taken after a certificate is published. On Windows 2000 CAs, the exit module may specify that certificates are to be published to Active Directory.

6. The client obtains the certificate from the CA's certificate database and stores the certificate in its local certificate store. A given client may have several certificates in its certificate store that are used for different purposes.

Validating the Certificate

When a certificate is used, it is not accepted at face value. The user of the certificate contacts the CA that issued the certificate to ensure that the certificate is valid and remains in force.

A certificate may be invalidated for several reasons:

- It may have been forged by another CA. The client obtains a copy of the CA's certificate and uses the CA's public key to decrypt the digital signature. If the signature is valid, the origin of the certificate is verified. Assuming that the client trusts the CA, the client trusts certificates issued by the CA.

- It may have been tampered with. This can be determined by processing the message digest that is included with the certificate.

- It may have expired. Certificates include dates the user can read that determine when they are valid.

- It may have been revoked. For various reasons, the certificate may have been cancelled by the CA. The CA maintains a *Certificate Revocation List* (CRL) that publishes the identities of certificates that have been revoked. Clients can obtain these CRLs and store them locally.

CA Hierarchies

Many organizations are too large to be properly serviced by a single CA. When multiple CAs are deployed, typically they are organized in *certification hierarchies* because this greatly simplifies the process whereby clients trust CAs.

Figure 10.1 shows a certification hierarchy that illustrates some of the possible relationships that can be established among CAs. There are three types of CAs in the hierarchy:

- The top CA in the hierarchy is called the *Trusted Root* or simply the root CA. Typically, when certification hierarchies are implemented, the Trusted Root CA is used only to certify lower-level CAs.

- *Intermediate* CAs are *subordinate* (child) CAs that certify other CAs but typically are not used to issue client certificates.

- *Issuing* CAs are subordinate CAs that certify clients and issue certificates.

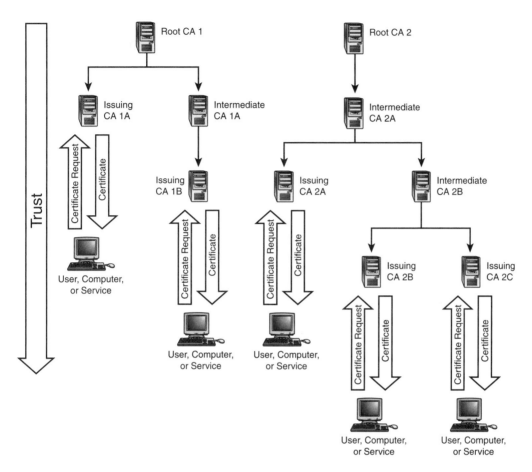

FIGURE 10.1

A simple certification hierarchy.

When a subordinate CA is added to the hierarchy, it must be certified by a parent CA, which the parent CA accomplishes by issuing and signing a subordinate CA certificate. Every subordinate CA must have a certificate that permits it to function in its defined role in the certification hierarchy. The root CA certifies the second level of subordinate CAs, which certify third-level CAs, and so forth.

As a result, one or more certificate links establish a *certification path* that establishes trust between every subordinate CA and the root CA. If a client trusts the root CA, by implication the client trusts subordinate CAs that are certified by the root CA and the certificates they issue.

> **NOTE**
>
> Certification hierarchies are not required to implement a functional PKI. Everything we are doing in subsequent chapters can be implemented with a single root CA.

You may have noticed that this process leaves one CA uncertified by another. The Trusted Root CA is at the top of the hierarchy, with no parent CA to certify it.

Root CAs are the only CAs in the hierarchy that are *self certified*. When the first CA in a hierarchy is defined, it issues a certificate to itself.

There are no special installation procedures for intermediate CAs. They are regarded as intermediate CAs because administrators permit them to be used only to certify lower-level subordinate CAs and are entirely optional. There are several reasons why you might want to include intermediate CAs in your certification hierarchy:

- Access to the all-important root CA can be closely restricted, but administration permissions for the intermediate CAs can be distributed to staff in different departments or at different locations.
- Intermediate CAs offload and distribute processing that would otherwise need to be performed by a single root CA.
- Stand-alone intermediate CAs can be assigned different certificate lifetime parameters, which in turn determine the lifetimes that subordinates of the intermediate CA can assign to certificates they issue. See the section "Managing Certificate Lifetimes" later in this chapter for more information on the roles of intermediate CAs in certificate lifetime control.

> **NOTE**
>
> Certification hierarchies can be expensive propositions. CAs need to be very secure, their data must be protected, and in most cases they should be run on computers dedicated to that function. If your organization makes extensive use of public key certificates, a multi-tier certification hierarchy may be expensive but indispensable.
>
> But for a small organization or one that makes limited use of certificates, you may be able to get by with one or two CAs: an enterprise root CA to support internal Active Directory users and, if needed, a stand-alone root CA to support outside users and users of non-AD systems. If the root CAs will be issuing certificates to users, their Registry settings should limit certificate lifetimes appropriately.

The problem with the single-tier approach is that it may back you into a corner. If you decide at a future time that you need to move toward a multi-tier certification hierarchy, you will have to reissue new certificates to replace all existing ones. In that case, planning becomes essential. You will need to keep the old CAs around until new certificates have been issued to all clients.

Should You Support Your Own Root CA?

You have to begin trusting somewhere, and the Trusted Root is the place. The first two questions you need to answer when your organizations start relying on public key certificates are

- Do we want to manage the certification authorities ourselves?
- If the response is yes to the first question, do we want to manage our own Trusted Root CA?

First let's figure out whether we want to manage any of the CAs in-house. There are a few good reasons to rely on a third party to issue certificates to your organization:

- Certificates issued by a well-known certification authority are more likely to be trusted by users outside your organization. If you are entering your credit card number on an e-commerce site, who would you rather see as the certification authority, SecureNet or Joe's Primo Pet Supplies?
- Commercial certificate issuers are experts at security and secure storage of certificates. It takes some time and experience to become skilled at managing a PKI.
- Active users may access dozens or hundreds of secure resources in the course of using the Internet. To enable clients to verify certificates transparently, their computers are configured with lists of Trusted Root CAs. (Microsoft Internet Explorer includes certificates for several dozen CAs that Microsoft deems trustworthy.) If every company has its own Trusted Root CA, users will find it irritating at best to be forced to add each Trusted Root certificate to their client configurations.

But there are also good reasons to manage your own PKI:

- Commercial CAs provide a service and must charge a fee. These services are best used when the credibility of third-party certification is desirable.
- Commercial CAs must verify the clients to whom certificates are issued. Because CAs cannot rely on an authentication service such as Kerberos to verify clients' identities, client enrollment usually requires manual auditing. Consequently, some processing delay is encountered.

- Flexible internal security may require an internal PKI that is equally flexible. In some cases, certificates are issued automatically to satisfy known requirements. In others they must be requested manually but client enrollment is an automated process that is completed in little time.

There is a hybrid method for configuring a certification hierarchy that gives you control while maintaining public trust. The Trusted Root CA could be a CA operated by a trusted, commercial certification authority. The commercial CA can issue certificates from its CAs that certify one or more subordinate CAs in your organization. When that is done, your private CAs have a certification path that extends to a Trusted Root CA at the commercial certificate provider. Consequently, users who trust the commercial CA will trust certificates issued by your CAs. With this approach, your organization has the flexibility of issuing and revoking certificates as required, and outside users can satisfy themselves that certificates you issue are trustworthy.

However, there are several circumstances in which an organization might establish its own root CA, for example:

- The organization is in the business of certifying clients and issuing certificates. If the organization is well-known and follows rigorous certification procedures, public users will trust certificates issued by CAs in the organization's certificate hierarchy. Some well-known examples of commercial certification authorities are SecureNet, VeriSign, and Thawte.

- An organization may be prominent enough that users are likely to trust their CAs. Microsoft operates private Trusted Root CAs that validate certificates used for a variety of public functions, such as verifying digital signatures for software that Microsoft has tested for Windows compatibility. Still, for some functions, Microsoft continues to use certificates issued by VeriSign.

- An organization may want control of an entire business process. For example, a financial institution that provides online banking may operate its own CAs so that it can control the entire security process. After all, if you're going to trust a bank with your money, you ought to be willing to trust certificates the bank issues.

- An organization may set up CAs for its own internal use. An organization that uses certificates to authenticate dial-in users, users who connect through a virtual private network connection to the Internet, or simply to provide in-house network security may deploy a PKI with a private Trusted Root because public trust isn't an issue.

CAUTION

Remember that anyone can put up a Certification Authority. Don't add a new Trusted Root CA to your client configuration unless you are confident that it is legitimate.

Should You Create Subordinate CAs?

While a single root CA can support an entire organization, there are times when it is desirable to configure subordinate CAs, in which case the root CA may be used only for the purpose of certifying subordinate CAs.

Here are several reasons why you might want to deploy subordinate CAs:

- The root CA can be subjected to more rigid security and access to it can be restricted. Special security hardware might be used to protect the root CA that would complicate the process of issuing certificates by subordinate CAs.

- Different policies can be implemented on different CAs, which in turn can support different parts of the organization.

- The cost of a CA failure is reduced.

- Demand for Certification Services is distributed.

- The CA servicing part of an organization can be disabled without interrupting Certification Services for the entire organization.

- CAs can be placed locally at sites that communicate through WANs.

Cryptographic Service Providers

Cryptographic service providers (CSPs) are packages that convey specific cryptographic capabilities to a Windows 2000 Server CA. Microsoft includes two CSPs with Windows 2000 Server:

- **Microsoft Base Cryptographic Provider v1.0.** This CSP provides basic capabilities and relies on RSA technology. This CSP was designed to be in compliance with U.S. export restrictions before they were relaxed. Consequently, the algorithms it supports are rather weak.

- **Microsoft Base DSS Cryptographic Provider.** This CSP supports data signing and signature verification based on SHA and DSA. It was developed as a CSP that was not subject to U.S. export restrictions. If it is available to you, select the **Microsoft Base Cryptographic Provider** in preference to this option.

Two more options are available if the High Encryption Pack is installed on the local computer. (See the section "Remote Access Policy Profile: The Encryption Tab" in Chapter 8 for more information.) The new CSPs are

- **Microsoft Enhanced Cryptographic Provider.** Compatible with the Base CSP, this enhanced version offers much stronger encryption and, when available, should always be chosen over the Base CSP.

- **Microsoft Strong Cryptographic Provider.** I have been unable to determine the specific ways this CSP differs from the Enhanced Cryptographic Provider.

Table 10.1 summarizes the differences between the Base and Enhanced CSPs.

TABLE 10.1   Features Comparison of the Base and Enhanced CSPs

Algorithm	Base CSP	Enhanced CSP
RSA public key signature algorithm	Key length: 512 bits	Key length: 1,024 bits
RSA public key exchange algorithm	Key length: 512 bits	Key length: 1,024 bits
RC2 block encryption algorithm	Key length: 40 bits	Key length: 128 bits Salt length: Settable
RC4 stream	Key length: 40 bits	Key length: 128 bits Salt length: Settable
DES	Not supported	Key length: 56 bits
Triple DES (2-key)	Not supported	Key length: 112 bits
Triple DES (3-key)	Not supported	Key length: 168 bits

CAUTION
As I am writing this, there is a known bug with the High Encryption Pack Enhanced Cryptography Provider in that the CA's private key is protected by only a 40-bit RC4 algorithm (see Microsoft Knowledge Base article Q260219). This problem is corrected in Windows 2000 Service Pack 1.

Policy Modules

Policy modules determine how CAs will process certificate requests. Two types of CAs can be defined using Certification Services as it ships with Windows 2000:

- *Enterprise CAs* integrate with Active Directory and are intended to support certificate requests from Windows clients in Active Directory domains.
- *Stand-Alone CAs* function independently from Active Directory and primarily support non-Windows users who need certificates.

Third-party vendors can write custom policy modules to support special cryptography products such as secure storage devices or smart cards.

> **NOTE**
>
> Although the Windows 2000 documentation mentions two policy modules, named `Enterprise Policy Module` and `Stand-Alone Policy Module`, as it ships Windows 2000 Server the Certification Service has a single policy module named `Enterprise and Stand-Alone Policy Module` that implements policy for both enterprise and stand-alone CAs.

Exit Modules

Exit modules specify how a certificate is to be distributed after being issued by a CA. The process of storing certificates after they are issued is referred to as *publication.* Certification Services includes the `Enterprise and Stand-Alone Exit Module` that supports publishing of certificates to Active Directory or to the file system, depending on whether the CA is running with an enterprise or a stand-alone configuration.

Certificate Templates

Certificate templates are used by enterprise CAs to define the types of certificates that can be issued to a given type of requester. Certificate templates contribute several capabilities to enterprise CAs:

- Specific credential checks are defined for each certificate template so that the CA will issue certificates based on that template only to objects with the required properties and permissions. Some types of certificates are appropriate for users, while others are appropriate for computers.
- A certificate subject name is automatically generated.
- Predefined lists of certificate extensions are added to certificates that are issued, reducing the information a user must provide to create a certificate request.

Stand-alone CAs do not use certificate templates. When a user requests a certificate from a stand-alone CA, the user must provide all information required to define the certificate.

Default Certificate Templates

By default, the following certificate templates appear in the **Policy Settings** folder of the **Certification Authority** console:

- **Administrator.** Certificates are issued to users for client authentication, Encrypting File System (EFS), certificate trust list (CTL) signing, and code signing.
- **Basic EFS.** Certificates are issued to users for EFS operations.
- **Computer.** Certificates are issued to computers to authenticate clients, servers, and services.
- **Domain Controller.** Certificates are issued to computers to authenticate domain controllers. When an enterprise CA is installed, a certificate of this type is installed on every domain controller in the domain to support public key operations when DCs are supporting Certification Services.
- **EFS Recovery.** Certificates are issued to users for recovery of EFS encrypted data.
- **Subordinate Certificate Authority.** Certificates are issued to computers to authenticate subordinate CAs.
- **User.** Certificates are issued to users for user authentication, EFS, and signing secure mail.
- **Web Server.** Certificates are issued to computers to authenticate Web servers.

Additional Template Types

All of the secure operations described in this chapter can be performed with only the default certificate templates. However, several more templates are included with Windows 2000 Server:

- **Authenticated Session.** Certificates are issued to users to authenticate clients.
- **CEP Encryption (offline request).** Used to enroll Cisco routers for IPSec authentication certificates issued by a Windows 2000 CA.
- **Code Signing.** Certificates are issued to users for generating digital signatures for applications, dlls, controls, and other executables.
- **Enrollment Agent.** Certificatesare issued to users to authenticate administrators requesting certificates for smart card users.
- **Enrollment Agent (computer).** Certificates are issued to computers to authenticate services requesting certificates for other computers.
- **Exchange Enrollment Agent (offline request).** Certificates are issued to users to authenticate Exchange administrators requesting certificates for secure mail users.

- **Exchange Signature Only (offline request).** Certificates are issued to computers and are used by Exchange Server to authenticate clients and sign secure email.

- **Exchange User (offline request).** Certificates are issued to computers and are used by Exchange Server for client authentication and secure email (signing and confidentiality).

- **IPSec.** Certificates are used for IPSec authentication.

- **IPSec (offline request).** Certificates are used for IPSec authentication.

- **Root Certificate Authority.** Certificates are issued to root CAs during installation of Certification Services. This certificate type cannot be issued from a CA.

- **Router (offline request).** Certificates are issued to computers for router authentication.

- **Smart Card Logon.** Certificates are issued to users for authentication and smart card logon.

- **Smart Card User.** Certificates are issued to users for authentication, smart card logon, and logging on with a smart card.

- **Trust List Signing.** Certificates are issued to users for signing certificate trust lists.

- **User Signature Only.** Certificates are issued to users for client authentication and signing secure email. Certificates support the Digital Signature Standard (DSS).

> **NOTE**
>
> As mentioned earlier, stand-alone CAs do not use certificate templates. By default, a stand-alone CA can issue the following certificates for the following purposes:
>
> - Client authentication
> - Email protection
> - Server authentication
> - Code signing
> - Time stamp signing
> - IPSec
>
> Other types of certificates can be requested, as explained later in the chapter in the section "Requesting Certificates with the Web Enrollment Pages."

Installing and Managing a Certification Authority

It is surprisingly easy to set up a working PKI. The first step is to install a Trusted Root CA (which may be your only CA). Amazingly, you may not need to configure the CA at all, particularly a CA that is linked to Active Directory. But we will still look at the configuration and policy issues related to managing CAs and PKI clients.

Protecting CAs

Certification authorities are extremely important assets and should be protected accordingly. The private key for a CA provides the basis for trusting certificates issued by the CA. If that key is lost, certificates issued by the CA can no longer be validated. The need for precautions is particularly important for the root CA. Without the private key for the root CA, the entire certification hierarchy is invalidated.

Ideally, CAs should be physically secured in a controlled-access area, preferably one that is equipped with computer-safe fire protection. If you can't secure all CAs, at least pay special attention to the security of the root CA.

Certification Services stores certificates and keys in encrypted form in Active Directory. To provide for other methods of certificate storage, Certification Services accepts cryptographic hardware modules from other vendors. Some vendors provide secure storage devices particularly intended for storing certificate-related data.

Enterprise Versus Stand-Alone CAs

Before configuring a new CA, you need to determine which type of CA you require. Two standard types of CAs are supported by Windows 2000: enterprise CAs and stand-alone CAs.

Within each type, a new CA can be installed as the root CA of a new certification hierarchy or as a subordinate CA in an existing hierarchy. A certification hierarchy can consist of any mixture of enterprise and stand-alone CAs.

Enterprise and stand-alone CAs are based on the `Enterprise and Stand-Alone Policy Module`. The policy module for an enterprise CA policy cannot be modified. To install a CA with a custom policy module, you must first install a stand-alone CA and then replace the stand-alone policy module with a custom policy-module. (We will be examining only the standard policy modules in this book.)

Enterprise CAs

Enterprise CAs are integrated with Active Directory and can only be installed on Windows 2000 Server computers that are members of Active Directory domains. Because CAs are critical resources and may be very busy, Microsoft does not recommend installing an enterprise CA on a domain controller.

Enterprise CAs have the following features:

- When an enterprise root CA is configured, it is automatically added to the Trusted Root Certification Authorities certificate store for all users and computers in the domain. Consequently an enterprise root CA may be installed only by Domain Administrators or users who have write permissions for Active Directory.

- Only users in domains that are trusted by the CA's domain can request certificates.

- Certificate requesters do not need to supply identification information or request a particular certificate type because that information is already present in Active Directory.

- Enterprise CAs issue certificates based on certificate templates and will only issue certificate types they are authorized to offer.

- Enterprise CAs always issue a certificate or deny the certificate request immediately. No requests are held pending administrator attention.

- Certificates can be issued that enable users to log on to Windows 2000 using smart cards.

- The exit module publishes certificates and the certificate revocation list to Active Directory. To enable AD publication, the CA's server must be a member of the Cert Publishers group in the domain where the certificate is published.

Enterprise CAs are clearly the tools of choice for issuing certificates to Active Directory users, computers, and services.

Stand-Alone CAs

The primary reason for using stand-alone CAs is to issue certificates to users, computers, and services that are not objects in Active Directory. Often, these will be entities outside your organization, perhaps on the Internet or on a company extranet. Stand-alone CAs have these features:

- Stand-alone CAs can issue most of the certificate types that are offered by enterprise CAs with the exception of certificates used to authenticate logons to Active Directory using a smart card.

- Users requesting certificates from stand-alone CAs must supply identification information and the type of certificate that is requested.

- By default, certificate requests sent to stand-alone CAs are held in a pending state until an administrator verifies the requester's identity and approves the request. Stand-alone CAs have no mechanism for automatically verifying the credentials of certificate requesters.

- Certificate templates are not supported.

- An administrator or the requester must manually distribute certificates to the user's certificate store, a process that involves exporting the certificate to a file, delivering the file to the client, and having the client import the certificate to the appropriate user's or computer's certificate store.

If the stand-alone CA is installed by a user who is a member of the Domain Admins group or who has write access to Active Directory, the CA is automatically added to the Active Directory Trusted Root Certification Authorities certificate store, from which it is added to the Trusted Root Certification Authorities certificate store for all users and computers in the domain.

CAUTION

Microsoft documentation states that, if a stand-alone CA is installed by a user who has write access to Active Directory, the CA can publish certificates and certificate revocation lists to Active Directory. I have been informed by Microsoft technical support that this information is in error.

Mixing CA Types in a Certification Hierarchy

It is not necessary for all CAs in a hierarchy to be of the same type. The certification path that validates a CA does not determine the CA's functionality.

If you are establishing a CA hierarchy, in most cases the root CA will be used only to certify intermediate and issuing CAs. If root and intermediate CAs are configured as stand-alone CAs, all certificates issued by the CA require approval by an administrator, enabling administrators to closely monitor the CAs that are added to the certification hierarchy.

Enterprise CAs can be installed in subordinate roles without affecting their ability to automatically approve and issue certificates to Windows clients.

Managing Certificate Lifetimes

Every certificate is assigned a beginning and end date that determine when the certificate is valid. Certificates must be renewed by their owners before they expire. By default, certificates are renewed with their existing key pairs. Periodically, however, keys should be regenerated before the certificates are renewed. Key length is an indicator of the frequency with which new keys should be generated.

The default lifetime for a certificate issued by a stand-alone CA is one year. By default, enterprise CAs issue certificates with two-year lifetimes.

These default lifetimes can be overridden by editing value entries in the Registry. It may be necessary to create the value entries. The value entries are stored in this Registry key:

```
HKEY_LOCAL_MACHINE\
   SYSTEM\
   CurrentControlSet\
   Configuration\
   CA name
```

The value entries affecting certificate lifetimes are

- `ValidityPeriod` is of type REG_SZ and accepts the strings "Days", "Weeks", "Months", or "Years", which determine the unit of time that specified by the `ValidityPeriodUnits` value entry.
- `ValidityPeriodUnits` is of type REG_DWORD and accepts a numeric value that specifies the lifetime of certificates in terms of the number of units that are specified by the `ValidityPeriod` value entry.

All certificates issued by a stand-alone CA are assigned the lifetime specified in these Registry values. Consequently, if it is necessary for stand-alone CAs to issue certificates with different lifetimes, a separate stand-alone CA must be configured for each desired lifetime.

It is common to configure root and intermediate CAs in stand-alone mode so that an administrator must approve all certificates that are created for issuing CAs. If the stand-alone CA's certificate lifetime isn't changed, however, certificates issued by other CAs will have lifetimes of one year or less. (You are only permitted to specify a certificate lifetime when installing a root CA. Certificate lifetimes for all subordinate CAs are determined by Registry settings on the parent CA.) The next section suggests some certificate lifetimes for different types of CAs.

For enterprise CAs, the Registry values determine the greatest lifetime that can be assigned to certificates issued by the CA. If an enterprise CA must issue certificates with a five-year lifetime, the `ValidityPeriodUnits` value must be changed to 5.

As discussed earlier, enterprise CAs support certificate templates that define the characteristics for the types of certificates that can be issued by the CA. Certificate templates specify lifetimes to be assigned to certificates modeled on them. The majority of certificate templates specify a one-year lifetime. The following types of certificates specify two-year lifetimes:

- CEP Encryption (offline request)
- Enrollment Agent
- Enrollment Agent (computer)
- Enrollment Agent (offline request)
- IPSec
- IPSec (offline request)
- Web Server

There are two certificate templates that specify lifetimes of five years:

- Domain Controller
- Subordinate Certificate Authority

10

PLANNING AND
IMPLEMENTING A PUBLIC
KEY INFRASTRUCTURE

Planning CA Configuration Parameters

Two critical parameters must be considered when configuring a CA: the length of the CA's key and the lifetime of its certificate. In general, CAs should be assigned longer keys and longer lifetimes as they are placed higher in the certificate hierarchy.

As important as the certificate lifetime is the certificate renewal interval. A CA cannot issue certificates with lifetimes that extend beyond the expiration date of the CA's own certificate. Therefore, it is important to renew a CA's certificate to ensure that certificates being issued are granted the full desired lifetimes.

To simplify your planning, Table 10.2 offers some suggestions offered by Microsoft for configuring CA and client certificates.

TABLE 10.2   Suggested Settings for Keys and Certificates

Certificate Use	Key Length (bits)	Certificate Lifetime	Certificate Renewal
Root CA	4,096	20 years	10 years. Renew with new key at least every 20 years.
Intermediate CA	3,072	10 years	5 years. Renew with new key at least every 10 years.
Issuing CA (except smart card certificates)	2,048	5 years	Renew every 3 years to ensure issued certificates can be issued with 2 year lifespan. Renew with new key at least every 5 years.
Enterprise issuing CA for smart card certificates	2,048	5 years	Renew every 4 years to ensure issued certificates can be issued with 1 year lifespan. Renew with new key at least every 5 years.
SSL certificates for mail and browsers	1,024	1 year	Renew with new key every 2 years.

TABLE 10.2   Continued

Certificate Use	Key Length (bits)	Certificate Lifetime	Certificate Renewal
Smart card certificates	1,024	1 year	Renew with new key every 2 years.
Administrator certificates	1,024	1 year	Renew with new key every 2 years.
Secure Web server certificates	1,024	2 years	Renew with new key every 2 years.
Outside users given extranet access	1,024 (Microsoft suggests 512, but I'm not comfortable recommending keys under 1,024 bits in length.)	6 months	Renew with new key every year.

As the certification hierarchy increases in depth, the lifetimes that can be assigned to certificates are progressively restricted. Because the lifetime of a certificate cannot be changed, even when renewing with a new key, it is very important to plan the hierarchy for your organization in some detail so that you aren't forced to reconfigure the entire hierarchy from scratch.

There is no direct way to control key lengths of certificates requested by users. As we will see, when requesting certificates users can specify keys as short as 384 bits and as long as 16,384 bits depending on the CSP they elect to use. 384-bit keys can no longer be considered secure, and keys longer than 1,024 bits are impractical for most end-user applications. There is also no efficient way to determine the lengths of certificates that have been issued.

It is essential that the organization establish clear policies governing public key lengths. In some cases, the delay inherent in approving certificates sent to stand-alone servers may be justified by the need to enforce key length standards.

Installing a CA

The computer on which an enterprise CA is installed must be a member of a Windows 2000 domain so that the CA has access to Active Directory. After you install the enterprise CA, you cannot rename the computer or change its domain membership.

Stand-alone CAs can be installed on domain member servers, but because stand-alone CAs do not require Active Directory they can be installed on servers that are not domain members. If a stand-alone root CA is installed on a domain member server by an Administrator or a user with AD write permissions, the CA is automatically added to the Trusted Root Certification Authorities certificate store for all users and computers in the domain.

NOTE

While you're learning, I suggest you start with enterprise CAs. Some operations such as certificate issue are a bit more complicated on stand-alone CAs, particularly when installing a child CA with a stand-alone CA parent.

Installing a Root CA

The procedures for installing enterprise and stand-alone CAs are very similar, so we'll cover them together. Installation of root and subordinate CAs differs in that a root CA generates its own certificate while a subordinate CA must obtain its certificate from its parent CA. First we'll follow the process for installing a root CA. Then we'll see how subordinate CAs are configured.

CAUTION

If you wish to use the Enhanced CSP, install the High Encryption Pack and Windows 2000 Service Pack 1 before you install Certification Services.

CAUTION

If an Internet Information Server is running on the server that is being configured as a CA, the **Windows Components Wizard** will automatically configure IIS with a site for use when requesting certificates. IIS must be stopped during this configuration process, and you should plan installation of a CA for a time when users will not be connected to IIS.

Here is the procedure for installing a root CA:

1. Many certificate request options are available only by requesting the certificate through the Web. If IIS will be running on the Web server, it is best to install IIS before installing Certification Services so that IIS can be customized to provide the Web certificate enrollment site. (The Web enrollment site can be added to an IIS server that is running on a different computer. See the section "Installing the Web Enrollment Pages" later in the chapter.)

2. Use the **Add/Remove Programs** applet in the Control Panel to add the **Certification Services** component. While the software is installed the **Windows Component Wizard** is used to configure the CA. The remaining steps are performed in the wizard.

   While installing Certification Services the **Windows Component Wizard** is started. Operational settings for a CA are established during installation and cannot be modified thereafter.

3. The first dialog box in the **Windows Component Wizard** is **Certificate Authority Type,** shown in Figure 10.2. Here you select the type of CA that is being installed. For this procedure select either **Enterprise root CA** or **Stand-alone root CA**.

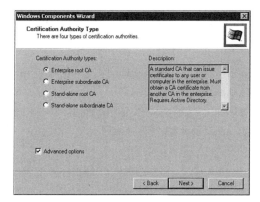

FIGURE 10.2

Selecting the type of CA that will be installed.

4. I recommend that you always check **Advanced options** in the **Certificate Authority Type** dialog box so that the wizard displays the **Public and Private Key Pair** dialog box shown in Figure 10.3. I don't think you should ever blindly rely on the default settings when installing a new CA.

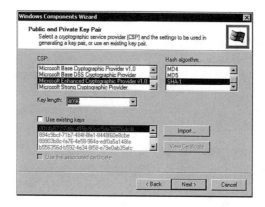

FIGURE 10.3

During the installation, the characteristics of the CA's own key pair can be customized.

5. The **Public and Private Key Pair** dialog box, shown in Figure 10.3, determines the characteristics of the key pair that is defined for the CA itself. Before selecting any options, select an entry in the **CSP** list. The CSPs that are available depend on whether the High Encryption Pack is installed on the local computer. The CSP that is selected determines the options that are available in the **Key length** and **Hash algorithm** fields. I recommend that you install the High Encryption Pack and select either the Microsoft Enhanced CSP or the Microsoft Strong CSP.

6. Select a hash algorithm. SHA-1 is the strongest hashing algorithm and is the preferred choice when supported by the CSP.

7. In the **Key length** field select a value to specify the length of the keys that will be created for the CA. The earlier section "Planning CA Configuration Parameters" offers suggestions on CA key lengths.

8. Check **Use existing keys** if the CA will be configured using an existing key pair. This option is used most often when restoring a failed CA. When **Use existing keys** is selected, several actions can be taken:

   - Select a key pair that is already on the computer by selecting an entry in the **Use existing keys** list.

   - Import a key pair from an archive by clicking **Import**.

   - Examine the certificate for the key pair by clicking **View Certificate**.

   - Check **Use the associated certificate** to use a certificate that was previously created for the key pair. You need to use an existing certificate when restoring a failed CA.

9. The next dialog box is **CA Identifying Information**, shown in Figure 10.4. Information entered here is included in the certificate that is generated for the CA. Most of these fields are self explanatory, but there are two things to keep in mind:

- The **CA name** identifies the CA and its private key. The name entered cannot be assigned to an existing key pair unless the existing private key is deleted before completing CA configuration.

- The lifetime of the CA's certificate is specified in the **Validity duration** field, which may be modified only for root CAs. It is important to plan certificate life-times carefully. The earlier section "Planning CA Configuration Parameters" offers some suggestions.

  When you click **Next** to complete this step, the cryptography keys are generated.

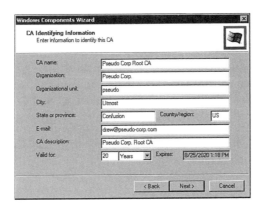

FIGURE 10.4

This information identifies the CA and appears in the CA's certificate.

10. The next dialog box is **Data Storage Location**, shown in Figure 10.5. **Certificate database** and **Certificate database log** define pathnames to directories where database and log files are stored. These files can be placed on any local drive. Once established, the locations cannot be modified without uninstalling the CA, moving the files, and rein-stalling, so I suggest you define locations that will be used for the lifetime of the CA.

Store configuration information in a shared folder applies only to stand-alone CAs. Data stored in this folder enable users to find information about CAs. The Administrators group is given Full Control permissions for this folder. The Everyone group is given Read permissions to the shared folder.

Preserve existing certificate database is active only if a key pair is being reused, as determined by selections in the **Public and Private Key Pair** dialog box. Select this option when restoring a failed CA.

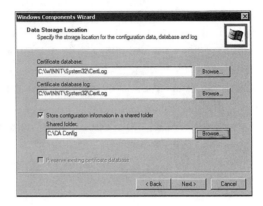

FIGURE 10.5

Defining CA data storage locations.

11. Installation of the CA starts when you click **Next** in the **Data Storage Location** dialog box. If the Internet Information Server is running, it will be stopped so that the Certificate server can be added to the IIS configuration, after which IIS is restarted. Installation of both enterprise and stand-alone root CAs will be completed without further input.

The root CA is now operational. Proceed to the section "Managing Certification Authorities" and review the CA's configuration.

> **NOTE**
>
> None of the fundamental characteristics of a CA can be modified once it is installed. If you want to change the type of the CA or the characteristics of its keys and certificate, you must remove Certification Services and reinstall it with the desired settings.

Installing a Subordinate CA with an Enterprise Parent CA

Because a subordinate CA must obtain a certificate from its parent CA, some additional steps are required following Step 10 in the previous procedure. When the parent is an enterprise CA, the required certificate can be requested and installed by the **Windows Components Wizard**. The procedure in this section applies under the following conditions:

- The parent is an enterprise CA.
- The parent CA is online.
- The child CA is running on a server that is a member of an Active Directory domain that is trusted by the CA's domain. (Enterprise CAs cannot issue certificates to non-Active Directory computers. Trust is required so that the parent CA can authenticate the certificate request.)

To install the subordinate CA, do the following:

1. Perform Steps 1–10 of the procedure described in the section "Installing a Root CA" with the following exceptions:

    • In the **Certificate Authority Type** dialog box (see Figure 10.2) select either **Enterprise subordinate CA** or **Stand-alone subordinate CA**.

    • In the **CA Identifying Information** dialog box, you will be unable to specify a certificate lifetime in the **Valid for** field.

2. After the **Data Storage Location** (Step 10; Figure 10.5) dialog box, the **CA Certificate Request** dialog box is shown (see Figure 10.6). Select **Send the request directly to a CA already on the network**. (This choice should be used only if the parent is an enterprise CA and is online.)

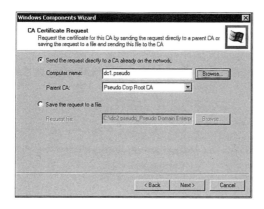

FIGURE 10.6
When the parent is an enterprise CA, the certificate request can be submitted during installation of a child CA.

3. Complete the following fields:

    • **Computer name.** Enter the Active Directory name for the parent CA's computer.

    • **Parent CA.** Enter the CA's name. This is the name specified in the **CA name** field of the **CA Identifying Information** dialog box (see Figure 10.4).

    The easiest way to complete these fields is to click the **Browse** button to open a **Select Certification Authority** list that includes all CAs that are currently installed. When you select an entry, both fields are completed.

4. After you complete the **CA Certificate Request** dialog box and click **Next**, installation begins.

The certificate request is submitted and approved automatically, and the certificate is installed on the new CA without further input. The CA will start after the certificate is installed. Look for a green check mark on the CA's icon in the **Certification Authority** console to verify that the CA started properly. (See "Managing Certification Authorities" for thorough coverage of the **Certification Authority** console.)

Installing a Subordinate CA with a Stand-Alone Parent CA

Installing a child CA under a stand-alone parent CA is a bit more involved than the procedure discussed in the previous section. The certificate for the subordinate CA cannot be received or installed from the **Windows Component Wizard**. During CA installation, the best procedure is to have the wizard prepare a certificate request file. After the CA is installed you then manually submit the certificate request, retrieve the certificate in a file, and install the certificate on the CA.

Because a certificate is not requested during installation of the subordinate CA, the stand-alone parent CA need not be online when Certification Services is installed. It must, of course, be online when the certificate request is submitted and the certificate is retrieved.

To install the subordinate CA, do the following:

1. Perform Steps 1–10 of the procedure described in the section "Installing a Root CA" with the following exceptions:
   - In the **Certificate Authority Type** dialog box (see Figure 10.2) select either **Enterprise subordinate CA** or **Stand-alone subordinate CA**.
   - In the **CA Identifying Information** dialog box, you will be unable to specify a certificate lifetime in the **Valid for** field.

2. After the **Data Storage Location** (Step 10; Figure 10.5) dialog box, the **CA Certificate Request** dialog box is shown (see Figure 10.7). Select **Save the request to a file**. (This choice can also be used if the parent is an enterprise CA that is currently offline.)

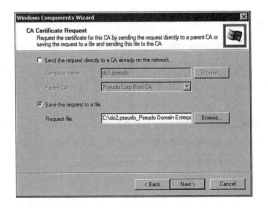

FIGURE 10.7

When the parent is a stand-alone CA, the certificate request must be saved to a file during installation of a child CA.

3. In the **Request file** field, you can accept the filename that is provided by the wizard, enter a path and filename, or browse for an existing file that is to be replaced.

4. After you complete the **CA Certificate Request** dialog box and click **Next**, installation begins. The message box shown in Figure 10.8 reports that CA installation is incomplete and identifies the file that contains the certificate request.

FIGURE 10.8
When the certificate request for a new CA is saved to a file, this message identifies the path and filename of the file.

The CA cannot be made operational until the certificate request is submitted to the parent CA and a certificate is retrieved and installed. To obtain a certificate for the child CA from a parent stand-alone CA, do the following:

1. Submit the certificate request file that was created by the wizard. The procedure for submitting a certificate request from a file is discussed later in the chapter in the section "Requesting Certificates Using PKCS #7 Renewal Request Files and PKCS #10 Certificate Request Files."

2. After the certificate is issued, retrieve it using the procedure discussed in the section "Retrieving a Certificate from a Stand-Alone CA." The certificate cannot be installed on the CA in this step. Choose **Download CA certification path** and save the certificate file, which will have the extension .p7b.

3. On the new CA, open the **Certification Authority** console, which is described in detail in the next section. Right-click the description of the new CA in the object hierarchy. Then choose **All Tasks→Install CA Certificate** from the context menu. Browse for the certificate file and click **Open**. The certificate is imported to the CA's certificate store.

After installation of the certificate, the CA is started. If startup is successful, the red square that was tagging the CA's icon will be replaced with a green check mark.

NOTE

While installing a CA under a stand-alone parent CA, if you select **Send the request directly to a CA already on the network** in the **CA Certificate Request** dialog box, the certificate request is sent to the parent CA, but the certificate cannot be retrieved.

10

PLANNING AND IMPLEMENTING A PUBLIC KEY INFRASTRUCTURE

> Under these circumstances, the certificate request is also saved to a file. As a result, you have two ways to obtain a certificate for the CA:
>
> - Use the procedure just described to submit the certificate request from a file.
> - Have the administrator of the parent CA approve the certificate request and export the certificate to a file on a diskette, as described in the section "Exporting Certificates." Then install the certificate on the new CA as described in Step 3 of the previous procedure.

Managing Certification Authorities

When Certification Services are installed, a CA is running on the server and a **Certification Authority** icon is added to the **Administrative Tools** program group. Use this icon to open the **Certification Authority** console, which is used to manage the CA. (For the sake of brevity, I'm going to call it the CA console from here on.)

With the exception of a very few characteristics, CA functionality is managed by the CA console. Figure 10.9 shows a CA console configured to manage a local and a remote CA. The local CA is a stand-alone root CA, and the remote one (dc2.pseudo) is an enterprise subordinate CA.

Two instances of the Certification Authority snap-in were added to the MMC to create the console in the figure. When you add a **Certification Authority** snap-in to the MMC, you must specify whether it will manage the local computer or a remote computer.

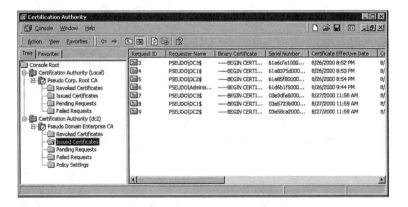

FIGURE 10.9

This Certification Authority console is configured to manage a stand-alone and an enterprise CA.

Each CA icon is tagged with a green check mark or a red square, indicating whether the CA is operational or shut down. The CA will be tagged as stopped if the service has been stopped or if the service cannot be started due to an error or to a bad or missing certificate. The CA must possess a valid certificate before the service can be started.

CA Properties

To open the properties pages for a CA, right-click a CA icon and choose **Properties** from the context menu. Figure 10.10 shows the **General** properties tab.

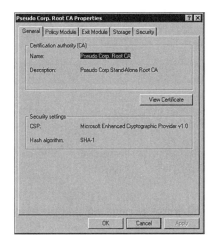

FIGURE 10.10

Certification Authority properties: The General tab.

CA Properties: The General Tab

The **General** tab of the **CA Properties** dialog box reports the name, description, and security algorithms that were specified when the CA was installed. None of these properties can be modified.

Click **View Certificate** to open the **Certificate** pages, which are used to view certificate details, export certificates to files, and modify some certificate properties. A bit later in the chapter, the section "Managing Certificates" delves into the details of certificates and the procedures for exporting them and modifying their properties.

CA Properties: The Policy Module Tab

The **Policy Module** tab is shown in Figure 10.11. The Windows 2000 Certification Services is distributed with a single policy module named `Enterprise and Stand-Alone Policy Module`.

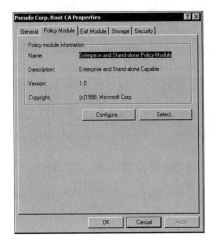

FIGURE 10.11
Certificate properties: The Policy Module tab.

Very little about this policy module can be configured. If you click the **Configure** tab, you can select one of the following settings, which determine how the CA will treat incoming certificate requests:

- **Set the certificate request status to pending. Administrator must explicitly issue the certificate.** This is the default setting for a stand-alone CA, and it is difficult to imagine a situation in which the default should be changed. This choice is not available for enterprise CAs.

- **Always issue the certificate.** This is the default and only choice for enterprise CAs, which can authenticate users submitting certificate requests using Active Directory. While automatic certificate issue can be selected for stand-alone CAs, it is very risky to do so since CAs configured in that manner will automatically issue certificates for all requests without performing any security checks. (In my discussion, I'm going to assume that stand-alone CAs are not configured with this option.)

Although only one policy module is included with Windows 2000 Server, developers can prepare custom policy modules using the Microsoft Platform Software Development Kit (SDK) and either C or Visual Basic, a process that demands programming skills that are outside the scope of this book. See http://msdn.microsoft.com/library/psdk/certsrv/crtsv_about_91pv.htm for more information about developing CA policy modules.

If multiple policy modules are available, click the **Select** button to choose a different one.

CA Properties: The Exit Module Tab

The **Exit Module** tab is shown in Figure 10.12. Exit modules determine the actions performed by a CA after a certificate has been created. The only exit module included with Windows 2000 Server is named `Enterprise and Stand-Alone Policy Module`.

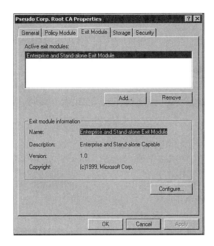

FIGURE 10.12

Certificate properties: The Exit Module tab.

To configure an exit module, select the description in the **Active exit modules** list and click **Configure**. For the `Enterprise and Stand-Alone Policy Module`, two configuration options are available:

- **Allow certificates to be published to Active Directory.** This choice is available only for enterprise CAs and should not be disabled.

- **Allow certificates to be published to the file system.** This choice is available only for stand-alone CAs and should not be disabled.

If certificate publication capability is disabled, certificates will be stored on the CA but will not be stored in a place that the client can directly access. In these cases, it is necessary for a CA administrator to manually export the certificate to a file and deliver the file to the client who must install the certificate on the computer manually.

Custom exit modules can be added to the configuration of a CA. For example, a vendor of smart cards can provide an exit module that publishes certificates to its smart cards. The **Add** and **Remove** buttons can be used to determine the exit modules that are active in the CA's configuration.

10

PLANNING AND
IMPLEMENTING A PUBLIC
KEY INFRASTRUCTURE

CA Properties: The Storage Tab

The **Storage** tab reports the directory locations that were configured when the CA was installed. (See Step 8 in the section "Installing a CA.") The directory locations cannot be changed. To move them, the CA must be removed, data files must be moved to the new locations, and the CA must be reinstalled with the same keys and digital certificate while changing the directory paths. Changes of this nature have the potential to disrupt operation of the CA, and the CA computer should be backed up before attempting the modifications.

CA Properties: The Security Tab

The **Security** tab (see Figure 10.13) defines access control lists that determine the permissions users and groups have with regard to the CA. By default, two types of permissions exist for groups in the same domain as the CA (or for local groups on a server that isn't in a domain):

- The **Authenticated Users** group has permission to Enroll (request certificates) and Read.

- The **Administrators**, **Domain Admins**, and **Enterprise Admins** groups have Read, Enroll, and Write permissions.

FIGURE 10.13

Certificate properties: The Security tab.

Click **Advanced** to open the **Advanced Control Settings** dialog box where permissions are defined on a more granular level. The available permissions, shown in Figure 10.14, are assigned as follows:

- The **Authenticated Users** group has the Enroll, Read, Read configuration, and Read control permissions.

- The **Administrators**, **Domain Admins**, and **Enterprise Admins** groups have all permissions.

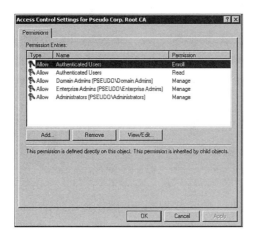

FIGURE 10.14
Advanced Control Settings can be used to configure detailed CA permissions.

If you are configuring a certification hierarchy, you may want to adjust permissions to define administrative users individually for each server. For example, you might set up a **CA Admins** group as the only object that has the `Enroll`, `Approve certificates`, and `Revoke certificates` permissions for root and intermediate CAs, enabling you to strictly limit the users who can authorize issue of a certificate to add a CA to the certification hierarchy.

CA Folders

As Figure 10.9 illustrates, the CA console displays several folders under a CA:

- **Revoked Certificates.** This contains certificates that have been revoked and are no longer recognized as valid by the CA. Revoked certificates are published in Certificate Revocation Lists (CRLs).

- **Issued Certificates.** This folder contains certificates that have been issued by the CA and have not been revoked.

- **Pending Requests.** Certificate requests in this folder have been received by the CA but have neither been approved nor rejected. No certificates will appear in this folder for an enterprise CA because enterprise CAs approve or deny certificate requests automatically. On a stand-alone CA, a CA administrator must approve or deny every request. When an administrator issues a certificate, the certificate is moved to the **Issued Certificates** folder and is published as specified by the exit module. When an administrator rejects a certificate, the certificate is moved to the **Failed Requests** folder and is not published. Certificate requests appear in this folder only for stand-alone CAs that are configured with the **Set the certificate request status to pending** option in the policy module.

- **Failed Requests.** This folder contains certificate requests that failed for any reason, including errors in the request and being denied by the CA's certificate approval authority.
- **Policy Settings.** This folder appears only for enterprise CAs and contains certificate templates that are supported by the CA.

We'll return to these folders from time to time as we discuss the operations they support.

Issuing Certificates and Denying Certificate Requests

When the policy module for a stand-alone CA is configured with the option **Set the certificate request status to pending**, an administrator must manually approve or deny every certificate request. These procedures do not apply to enterprise CAs.

Unapproved certificate requests are held in the **Pending→Certificates** folder of the CA console, shown in Figure 10.15, where they are identified in the **Request Disposition Message** column with the status Taken Under Submission. Before approving or denying a certificate request, the administrator should examine the information that is available for the request as it appears in the Details pane. Two actions can be taken for a certificate request:

- To issue a certificate based on the request, right-click the request and choose **All Task→Issue** from the context menu.
- To deny the certificate request, right-click the request and choose **All Task→Deny** from the context menu.

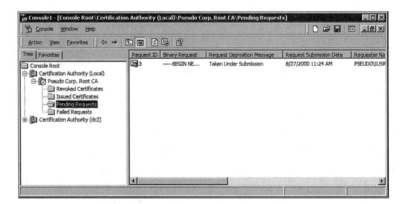

FIGURE 10.15

A certificate request is held in the Pending Requests folder for this stand-alone CA.

The Details pane doesn't display a lot of the information that is included in the certificate request. Especially while you are learning to administer certificates, you will want to examine the certificates after they are issued as described in the section "Certificate Details" appearing a bit later in the chapter.

> **NOTE**
>
> It's even difficult to determine the identity of the user submitting a certificate request. The **Request Common Name** column lists the name of the user requesting the certificate, but this is the name the user entered and is not validated in any way.
>
> All certificate requests sent from the Web Support Pages are identified in the **Requester Name** column with the user name *domain*\IUSR_*servername* where *domain* is the domain of the IIS server and *servername* is the name of the Windows 2000 Server running IIS. IUSR identifies user accounts created to support access to IIS servers. The user email address is the best way to identify the user and should be required on all requests so that you can contact the user and verify his or her identity.
>
> The only way to verify the user who submitted a certificate request is through personal communication or perhaps by secure, signed email.
>
> You cannot view the entire certificate request. For example, you cannot determine the requested certificate purpose or the key length from the information appearing in the **Pending Requests** folder. I am aware of no other means for examining all the pertinent data in a certificate request than to issue the certificate, examine it in the **Issued Certificates** folder, and revoke it if necessary.

Revoking Certificates

From time to time it is necessary to revoke a certificate before it expires. For example, certificates should be revoked for an employee who leaves the company (after any required data are decrypted) or for a notebook computer that is stolen.

To revoke a certificate, right-click the certificate in the **Issued Certificates** folder and choose **All Tasks→Revoke Certificate** from the context menu.

Revoked certificates are moved from the **Issued Certificates** folder to the **Revoked Certificates** folder, where they are tagged with a red X icon. A revoked certificate cannot be re-issued. If a certificate is revoked in error, the client will need to request a new certificate.

Revoked certificates are added to the Certificate Revocation List (CRL), which is published at periodic intervals. To view and modify CRL characteristics, right-click the **Revoked Certificates** folder and choose **Properties** from the context menu. In the **Revoked Certificates Properties** dialog box, you can change the CRL publication schedule, view CRL information, and see a list of certificates in the CRL.

Managing Certificate Templates

You can add and remove templates in the **Policy Settings** folder to tailor the types of certificates an enterprise CA may issue. Suppose that you have a hierarchy consisting entirely of enterprise CAs. You don't want to have the root CA issuing certificates for any other purpose than for validating subordinate CAs. To accomplish that, you simply remove all the certificate templates except Subordinate Certification Authority from the root CA.

Certificate templates can be added and deleted from the **Policy Settings** folder as follows:

- To add a certificate template, right-click **Policy Settings** and choose **New→Certificate to Issue** from the context menu. In the **Select Certificate Template** dialog box, select a certificate template and click **OK** to add the template to the **Policy Settings** folder.

- To remove a certificate template, right-click a template in the **Policy Settings** Details pane and choose **Delete** from the context menu.

Automating Certificate Requests

As explained in Chapter 4, "Active Directory Concepts," Group Policy is a useful method for distributing policy settings to groups of users and computers. With regard to Certification Services, Group Policy is used to configure several PKI-related capabilities:

- Configuring automatic certificate request settings
- Distributing certificates for trusted root CAs
- Establishing certificate trust lists
- Distributing lists of encrypted data recovery agents

NOTE

See the section "Importing Trusted Root CA Certificates" later in this chapter for more information about distributing certificates for trusted root CAs.

Certificate trust lists (CTLs) enable administrators to specify trusted CAs and to restrict the uses that are permitted for certificates from a CA. CTLs are principally used with regard to CAs from outside the organization. Certificate trust lists are defined with the **Certificate Trust List Wizard**, which may be activated from the Group Policy editor. CTLs are not required for the purposes of this book and are not covered. For more information, see the topic "certificate trust lists" in Windows 2000 Help.

Encrypted data recovery agents are empowered to access keys required to recover files that are protected by the Encrypting File System (EFS). EFS is not associated with networking services and is not covered in this chapter. For more information, see the topic "EFS" in Windows 2000 Help.

Of these, automatic certificate request settings is the capability most important to our discussion. If you are implementing a PKI to support secure communication, you almost certainly want to automate requests for a few certificate types.

Once a PKI has been configured, there are a few types of certificates that you may want to be installed on every applicable computer. For example:

- Every Windows 2000 computer should be issued a Computer certificate to be used for identification and authentication.

- Every Windows 2000 domain controller should be issued a Domain Controller certificate.

- If environments using IPSec to implement network security rely on certificates for authentication, every computer should have an IPSec certificate.

- In some instances, certificates must be requested to set up a new service such as an L2TP/IPSec VPN. By automatically installing Enrollment Agent (Computer) certificates, the required certificates are requested as required, without administrative attention.

These certificate types are all issued to computers. To configure automatic certificate issue, you must add a property to the applicable Group Policy as follows:

1. Open the Group Policy object to be configured for editing as described in Chapter 4.

2. Open the following container: **Computer Configuration→Windows Settings→Security Settings→Public Key Policies→Automatic Certificate Request Settings**. Any established automatic certificate request policies will be listed in the Detail pane. Figure 10.16 shows the **Automatic Certificate Request Settings** container.

3. Right-click **Automatic Certificate Request Settings** and choose **New→Automatic Certificate Request** from the context menu to start the **Automatic Certificate Request Setup Wizard**.

4. The **Certificate Template** dialog box, shown in Figure 10.17, lists the types of certificate templates that can be configured for automatic certificate requests. Select a template and click **Next**.

5. The **Certificate Authority** dialog box lists enterprise CAs that are configured to issue the certificate type selected in Step 4. If more than one enterprise CA is listed, you can check any or all of them. The automatic certificate request will be sent only to the first available CA. Selecting multiple enterprise CAs improves responsiveness and fault-tolerance.

6. Click **Next** and review the selected properties before clicking **Finish** to generate the policy.

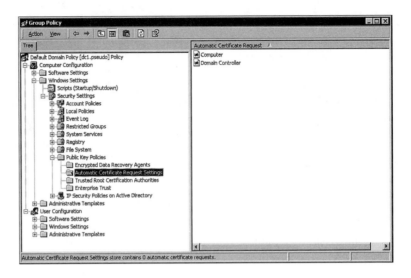

FIGURE 10.16

The Group Policy Automatic Certificate Request container.

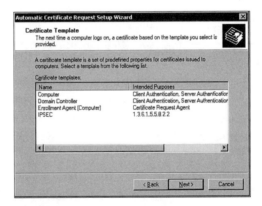

FIGURE 10.17

Select the template to be used in the automatic certificate request.

Only one policy can be defined for each of the four supported certificate templates. If you define a new policy for an existing certificate template, it will replace any existing policy for that template.

Certificates that are requested automatically are also renewed automatically. They can be renewed manually if desired.

Backing Up and Restoring the CA

The certificate database of a CA is very valuable. If the CA's own keys are lost, certificates issued by the CA cannot be validated. If the CA's copies of certificates are lost, clients that lose their certificates will be unable obtain new copies of the certificates and will be unable to decrypt data encrypted with their private keys.

You should perform daily backups of the server on which the CA is running using the Windows 2000 **Backup** located in **Start→Programs→Accessories→System Tools**.

You can also perform backups of the CA private key, certificate, and certificate database.

Backing Up the CA

To back up a CA, open the CA console on the computer where the CA resides and perform this procedure:

1. Right-click the CA in the object tree and choose **All Tasks→Backup CA** in the context menu. This will start the **Certification Authority Backup Wizard**.

2. Proceed to the **Items to be Backed Up** dialog box, shown in Figure 10.18, and complete it as follows:

   - **Private key and CA certificate.** Select this option to back up the CA's own key pair.

   - **Configuration information.** Select this option to back up the CA's configuration information. (I have been unable to activate this field or to learn from Microsoft the conditions under which it is activated.)

   - **Issued certificate log and pending certificate request queue.** Select this option to back up issued certificates and pending certificate requests.

   - **Perform incremental backup.** Select this option if the backup should include only data that changed since the last backup.

   - **Backup to this location.** The CA can be backed up to any local or shared directory and to any file system that is supported by Windows 2000. The directory must be empty.

3. If you checked **Private key and CA certificate** in Step 2, the next dialog box prompts for a password that is used to encrypt the private key. Pick a strong password that is not susceptible to a brute-force attack. (Chapter 9 suggests some criteria for creating strong passwords. See the section "Configuring Password Policy Settings.")

4. On the final page of the wizard, review the backup parameters and click **Finish** to start the backup.

Protect this backup. Consider placing it on removable media and storing the media in a secure location. (Like your top-right desk drawer, under your snacks. <g>)

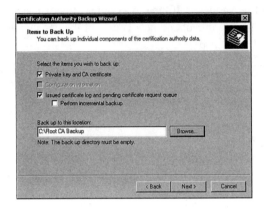

FIGURE 10.18
A CA backup can include any or all of the data listed in this dialog box.

Restoring the CA

A CA can be restored from a backup copy using this procedure:

1. Right-click the CA in the object tree and choose **All Tasks→Restore CA** in the context menu. You will be notified that the CA must be stopped before the restore can proceed. The CA is stopped by the procedure and no intervention is required on your part.

2. After the CA service is stopped, the **Certification Authority Restore Wizard** is started. The first dialog box resembles Figure 10.18, with the same data categories, except that it prompts you to select the items to be restored as well as the directory in which the backup files are located. Complete the dialog box and click **Next**.

3. If you selected **Private key and CA certificate** in Step 2, you are prompted for the password that was used to encrypt the private key. (I hope you didn't forget it, or *you* get to try a brute-force attack.)

4. On the last page of the wizard, verify your choices and click **Finish** to begin the backup. The CA service is restarted after the data are restored.

Requesting Certificates

With the exception of the root CA's own certificate, all certificate requests are initiated by the clients that will use the certificates. Users can request certificates for themselves, their computers, and services running on their computers. Certificates can be requested in several ways:

- The Certificates MMC snap-in, which is also used to manage certificates in local certificate stores, can issue basic certificate requests from Windows 2000 clients.

- The Web Enrollment Support pages allow Windows and non-Windows clients to request certificates in real time or asynchronously by generating PKCS #10 certificate request files. More options are available for Web-based certificate requests than for requests generated with the **Certificates** snap-in.

NOTE

I just lied to you. There's also a command-line utility named certreq that can request certificates using PKCS #10 certificate request files and PKCS #7 certificate renewal files. But certreq cannot generate the PKCS files and is primarily included as a shortcut tool for experienced CA administrators.

Certreq and its companion tools certsrv and certutil are thoroughly described in Windows 2000 Help.

Requesting Certificates with the Certificate Request Wizard

The **Certificate Request Wizard** offers a convenient if limited method of requesting certificates. The wizard is accessed through the **Certificates** snap-in for MMC. Figure 10.19 shows two instances of the **Certificates** snap-in installed in the MMC. When a **Certificates** snap-in is added, it is configured to manage certificates for one of the following:

- **My user account.** A user cannot manage certificates issued to other users.

- **Service account.** In some instances, users must obtain certificates for services running on their computer. A separate instance of the Certificates snap-in must be added for each service that requires certificates.

- **Computer account.** If this option is chosen, **Certificates** can be configured to manage certificates on the local computer on another computer for which the user has the required permissions. Separate instances of the **Certificates** snap-in can be added to support additional computers.

In Figure 10.19, I installed Certificates twice to manage certificates for my user account and the local computer account.

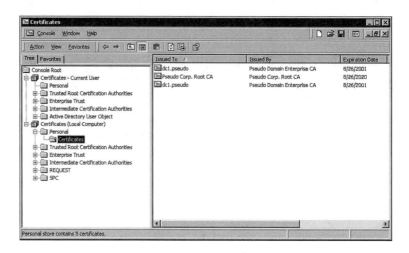

FIGURE 10.19
The Certificates console enables users to request and manage certificates.

The **Certificate Request Wizard** can be used to request certificates from enterprise CAs only. To request a new certificate, do the following:

1. Right-click the **Personal→Certificates** folder and choose **All Task→Request New Certificate** to start the **Certificate Request Wizard**.

2. In the wizard, the **Certificate Template** (see Figure 10.20) dialog box lists the templates available to the requester. A user will see only templates for certificates that can be issued to a user, for example. Select one of the available templates.

   Check **Advanced options** to override default settings for the certificate request.

3. If you checked **Advanced options** in Step 2, the next dialog box is titled **Cryptographic Service Provider**. Select the CSP that you want to generate the key pair.

   Check **Enable strong key protection** to restrict use of the private key. When strong key protection is enabled, a password is assigned to the private key. The password must be entered each time the private key is used.

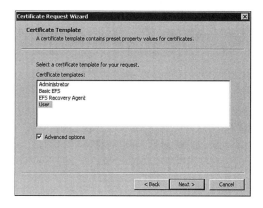

FIGURE 10.20

The Certificates Request Wizard can request template-based certificates from enterprise CAs.

NOTE

In most cases, strong key protection will be enabled for keys issued to users, but not to computers and services. The use of computer and service keys is often performed automatically in the background, and a password requirement would impede operation. However, a user might feel the need to secure a private key that is used to sign critical documents or to perform some other restricted purpose. In such cases, strong key protection provides added assurance that the private key is used only by its owner.

4. If you checked **Advanced options** in Step 2, the next dialog box is titled **Certificate Authority**. If more than one enterprise CA is available, you can select the CA that will be asked to issue the certificate.

5. The next dialog box is titled **Certificate Friendly Name and Description**. Optionally, the following fields can be used to further identify and describe the certificate:

   • **Friendly name**

   • **Description**

6. The next dialog box summarizes the certificate request. Review the settings and return to earlier dialog boxes if it is necessary to make changes. Then click **Finish** to begin creating the keys.

7. If you did not check **Enable strong key protection** in Step 3, go to Step 11.

8. If you checked **Enable strong key protection** in Step 3, the next dialog box is titled **Creating a new RSA exchange key**. The default protection level is medium. To change the security level, click **Set Security Level** to open the dialog box shown in Figure 10.21. The following security settings are available:

- **High.** A password will be assigned to the private key. The system will request your permission and the password when the private key is used. (If you feel the need to protect your private key, this is the only option that greatly enhances security. Even a user who sneaks into your office and uses a computer you left in a logged-in state cannot forge your signature to a document without knowing the private key password.)

- **Medium.** The system will request your permission when the private key is used but a separate password is not created.

- **Low.** No password or permission protection are assigned to the private key. This option cannot be selected here. It is enabled when **Enable strong key protection** is not checked in Step 3. To select this option, you must cancel the certificate request and start again.

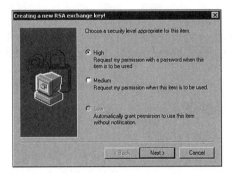

FIGURE 10.21

This dialog box is displayed when strong key protection is requested.

9. If you checked **Enable strong key protection** in Step 3 and **High** in Step 7, the next dialog box accepts the password that will be associated with the private key. Complete the following fields:

- **Password for.** Enter a name or phrase that will be presented when the private key is used. This might be a user's name.

- **Password** and **Confirm password.** Enter the password that is to be assigned.

10. Click **Finish** to return to the **Creating a new RSA exchange key** dialog box. Then click **OK** to continue with the certificate request.

11. The certificate request is complete and is submitted to the CA.

12. Enterprise CAs authenticate certificate requestors through Active Directory. Since you authenticated to AD when you logged in, the certificate request will be approved, barring errors. The CA notifies you of certificate approval with a dialog box that states, `The certificate request was successful`. At this point, you have three options:

    - **Install Certificate.** This choice accepts the certificate and stores it in the client's certificate store.

    - **Cancel.** This option cancels installation of the certificate. However, a valid certificate remains available on the CA. This certificate can be exported from the CA and installed on the client if required, procedures that are described in the section "Managing Certificates."

    - **View Certificate.** This button enables you to examine the certificate prior to installation. Certificate examination is covered in the section "Certificate Details."

After a certificate has been installed, in will be listed in the **Certificates** console in the **Personal→Certificates** folder for the owner of the certificate.

The **Certificate Request Wizard** provides a convenient means of requesting certificates, but many options are unavailable when requesting certificates from Certificates. The primary use of Certificates is to manage certificates after they are requested. We'll be returning to it later in the section "Managing Certificates."

Requesting Certificates with the Web Enrollment Pages

When IIS is configured with a Certificate Server Web site, users can request certificates using a Web browser to access the Web Enrollment Pages. Many choices aren't available when requesting certificates through the **Certificate Request Wizard**. A few capabilities available only through Web-based enrollment are

- Specifying lengths of keys to be generated
- Requesting certificates from stand-alone CAs
- Creating exportable private keys
- Saving certificate requests to PKCS #10 files for later submission
- Submitting requests in PKCS #7 and #10 files
- Requesting certificates for smart cards

Installing the Web Enrollment Pages

If IIS is running on a server on which Certification Services is installed, the Web Enrollment Pages are automatically added to the IIS configuration. To add Web enrollment support to an IIS server running on another computer:

1. Open **Add Remove Programs** in the Control Panel.
2. Select **Add/Remove Windows Components** and check **Certification Services**.
3. Click the **Details** button.
4. Check only the **Certification Services Web Enrollment Support** option.
5. Click **OK, Next**.
6. Enter the following information in the next dialog box:
   - **Computer name.** Enter the domain name of the computer running the CA service, or click the **Browse** button to browse for the computer.
   - **CA.** Select or enter the name of the CA.
7. When the wizard is completed, the Web Enrollment Pages will be added to the IIS configuration and configured for the CA specified in Step 6.

The Web server must be trusted for delegation using this procedure in **Active Directory Users and Computers**:

1. In the object tree, double-click the computer that is to be trusted to open the computer's **Properties** box.
2. On the **General** tab, check **Trust computer for delegation**.
3. Close the **Properties** box and restart the computer to activate the change.

Accessing the Web Enrollment Pages

Some of the Web Enrollment Pages rely on Active Server pages and ActiveX controls and are therefore usable only from Internet Explorer versions 4 and later. Prior to January 2000, exportable versions of IE supported only base cryptography. To use enhanced cryptography, users outside the United States and Canada must obtain versions of IE that support enhanced cryptography.

> **NOTE**
>
> According to Microsoft documentation, Netscape browsers will work with all pages except the **Advanced Certificate Request** page and the **Smart Card Enrollment Station** page. I have not conducted tests to confirm these compatibility statements. Netscape browsers support their own cryptography modules and may not support all the features in the Microsoft CSPs.

To access the Web Enrollment Pages, enter a URL with the following format:

`http://servername/certsrv`

where *servername* is the hostname of the Web server. By default, the Web Enrollment Pages are added to an IIS installation running on the same computer as the CA.

CAUTION

In the URL, `certsrv` must be entered entirely in lowercase. Otherwise you will have trouble checking pending request and receiving certificates.

The Web Support Pages begin with a **Welcome** page that offers these choices:

- **Retrieve the CA certificate or certificate revocation list**
- **Request a certificate**
- **Check a pending certificate**

We will start by exploring the latter two choices.

Requesting Certificates Using Forms

If you choose **Request a certificate** on the **Welcome** page the next page is **Choose Request Type**. This page offers two choices:

- **User certificate request.** This option offers a shortcut method of requesting the types of certificates that are listed. All you need to do is enter identification information. It is possible to request the CSP, but most parameters are predefined. Due to the simplicity of this path, there is no need to follow the steps involved.
- **Advanced request.** This option initiates a certificate request that includes all available options. This is the choice we will take to continue discussion.

After selecting **Advanced request**, the next page is titled **Advanced Certificate Requests**. Three choices are available:

- **Submit a certificate request to this CA using a form.** The certificate request is defined by completing a form, which can be submitted to an online CA or stored in a PKCS #7 or #10 file for later submission.
- **Submit a certificate request using a base64 encoded PKCS #10 file or a renewal request using a base64 encoded PKCS #7 file.** We'll examine this request method in the next section.
- **Request a certificate on behalf of another user.** Smart card certificate requests aren't being considered in this book. (An Enrollment Agent certificate is required to make this type of request.)

10

PLANNING AND
IMPLEMENTING A PUBLIC
KEY INFRASTRUCTURE

If you choose **Submit a certificate request to this CA using a form**, the next page presents the form shown in Figure 10.22. (I've scrolled the form and pasted together two pages to show the whole form at once.) Let's examine the fields in the certificate request form based on the section headers.

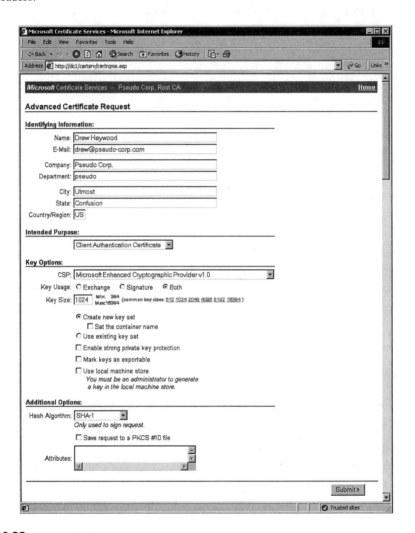

FIGURE 10.22

The Advanced Certificate Request form defines a certificate request in the Web Enrollment Pages.

Identifying Information. The information requested here is self-explanatory. The fields appear only when a certificate request is directed at a stand-alone CA. Enterprise CAs obtain this information from Active Directory. This information is embedded in the certificate.

Intended Purpose. This section appears for certificate requests directed to stand-alone CAs. Many certificate types can be requested, but only these types are identified by name:

- Client authentication
- Email protection
- Server authentication
- Code signing
- Time stamp signing
- IPSec

Additional types of certificates are requested by selecting `Other`. When `Other` is chosen, a new field is added to the form named **O.I.D.** This field accepts an X.509v3 *object identifier*, which is entered in the `Enhanced Key Usage` field of the certificate. The section "Certificate Details" explains how to examine the contents of a certificate.

Object identifiers (OIDs) provide globally unique identifiers for types of certificates. Vendors who need to define certificates specifically for their products can register to use a portion of the object identifiers range. Table 10.3 lists several certificate types that are used on the Microsoft Certification Services, along with their OIDs. It's pretty easy to distinguish standard OIDs from Microsoft's proprietary ones. Microsoft's OIDs all contain the value 311 in the seventh field.

Simply entering an OID in the **O.I.D.** field does not guarantee that a certificate will be created that is the equivalent of a certificate created for the same purpose on an enterprise CA. Several certificate templates add two or more OIDs to the `Enhanced Key Usage` field. For example, a certificate created with the User Signature Only template includes OIDs for Secure E-mail and Client Authentication. When defining certificates with OIDs, you should examine the certificates that are produced and test them to ensure they meet your requirements. More reliable results will be obtained if certificates are requested from an enterprise CA whenever possible.

TABLE 10.3 Sample X.509v3 Object Identifiers

Purposes	Object Identifier
Certificate Trust List Signing	1.3.6.1.4.1.311.10.3.1
Client Authentication	1.3.6.1.5.5.7.3.2
Code Signing	1.3.6.1.5.5.7.3.3
Efs File Recovery	1.3.6.1.4.1.311.10.3.4.1
Encrypting File System	1.3.6.1.4.1.311.10.3.4
Enrollment Agent	1.3.6.1.4.1.311.20.2.1

10

PLANNING AND
IMPLEMENTING A PUBLIC
KEY INFRASTRUCTURE

TABLE 10.3   Continued

Purposes	Object Identifier
IPsec	1.3.6.1.5.5.8.2.2
Secure E-mail	1.3.6.1.5.5.7.3.4
Server Authentication	1.3.6.1.5.5.7.3.1
Smart Card Logon	1.3.6.1.4.1.311.20.2.2

Certificate Template. This section is present only when a certificate is being requested from an enterprise CA. Select the desired template from the drop-down box.

Key Options. This section clearly distinguishes Web-based certificate requests from requests generated by the **Certificate Request Wizard**. Here you can define a variety of key characteristics and security options. The fields in this section are

- **CSP.** Select a cryptographic service provider from the drop-down list. The selection defaults to `Microsoft Base Cryptography Provider v1.0`.
- **Key Usage.** This field offers three choices:
  - **Exchange.** The key is used for symmetric key exchanges only. (This option has nothing to do with the Microsoft Exchange messaging service.)
  - **Signature.** The key is used to create electronic signatures.
  - **Both.** The key may be used for both purposes.
- **Key Size.** Available key sizes depend on the CSP that is selected. Common key sizes can be entered by clicking a value, but keys of any length can be defined manually. Keys as short as 384 bits can be defined by manual entry. As discussed earlier, keys this short provide little security against an attack, and users should be discouraged from defining keys shorter than 1024 bits.

TIP

The Web enrollment pages can be customized if it is desired to enforce policies as to key length, CSPs, and other parameters. Customization requires a developer who has experience with ActiveX controls and Active Server Pages. For more information, search the Microsoft Developer Network Web site (`msdn.Microsoft.com`) for the article "Customizing the Certification Services Web Enrollment Pages."

- **Create new key set.** Select this option to generate a new key pair. Optionally check **Container name** to specify a container for the key pair.

- **Use existing key set.** Select this option to generate a certificate request with a key pair already in use. Optionally check **Container name** to specify a container for the key pair. *Do not generate certificates using keys that are older than their secure lifespan.*

NOTE

The container referred to by the **Create new key set** and **Use existing key set** fields is the container in the user's account certificate store. These certificate stores can be viewed in the **Certificates** console discussed in the section "Managing Certificates" appearing later in the chapter.

By default, certificates are installed in the **Personal** container. Other containers in the user's certificate store may be specified. It is also possible to store certificates in your Active Directory User object container by entering `Active Directory User Object` in the **Container name** field.

- **Enable strong key protection.** Check this box to protect the private key with a password. The functionality of private key passwords is discussed in the earlier section "Requesting Certificates with the Certificate Request Wizard."

- **Mark keys as exportable.** As the section "Managing Certificates" explains, certificates can be exported to files. If the private key is marked as exportable, it can be exported with the certificate. Check this box to tag the private key as exportable. (Exportable private keys increase security risk. A user could export the private key from an unattended computer, for example.)

- **Use local machine store.** By default, issued certificates are stored in the requester's **Personal** certificate store. Administrators can select this option to have the certificate stored in the HKEY_LOCAL_MACHINE subtree of the local system's Registry. Select this option to request and install certificates for the local computer.

Additional Options. This section contains three fields:

- **Hash Algorithm.** This field specifies the hash algorithm used to sign the certificate request. The default hash algorithm is SHA-1, but others can be selected.

- **Save request to a PKCS #10 file.** Check this box to prepare a PKCS #10 certificate request file that can be submitted to the CA at another time. Specify the path and name of the file that is to be created. No file extension is supplied by the application. One

10

choice for a filename extension is `.pub`, which is used when CAs are configured to store certificate requests.

- **Attributes.** This is an advanced field that is beyond the scope of this book and is not required for any of the functions discussed. For more information see PKCS #9.

After completing the form, click **Submit**.

If **Enable strong key protection** was selected, dialog boxes are presented in which the protection characteristics are defined. These dialog boxes are discussed in Steps 8–10 of the procedure in the earlier section "Requesting Certificates with the Certificate Request Wizard."

What happens next depends on whether the request was sent to an enterprise CA or a stand-alone CA. Here are the possibilities:

- **Enterprise CAs** can approve certificate requests and publish certificates automatically. If a certificate is issued, the user sees the prompt **The certificate you requested was issued to you**. The user can receive the certificate by clicking **Install this certificate**.

- **Stand-alone CAs** place incoming certificates in the **Pending** folder, where they remain until approved by an administrator. In this situation, the user sees a **Certificate Pending** page. The user must return later to check on the status of the request and to receive the certificate if it has been issued. The certificate must be retrieved within ten days using the same Web browser that submitted the request. See the section "Retrieving a Certificate from a Stand-Alone CA" for the procedures.

Requesting Certificates Using PKCS #7 Renewal Request Files and PKCS #10 Certificate Request Files

PKCS #7 and #10 files can be used to store a certificate request for later processing. The Web Enrollment Pages can be used to request PKCS #10 files and to submit requests in PKCS #7 and #10 files to a CA. (This isn't just doing things the hard way out of sheer nerdiness. If the issuing CA is offline when you are creating the certificate request, you can save the request and submit it when the CA is available. You can also submit certificate requests created by third parties who don't have browsers that can use the Web Enrollment Pages.)

The Web Enrollment Pages generate a PKCS #10 certificate when the **Save request to a PKCS #10 file** option is checked on the **Advanced Certificate Request** page. Other operations generate PKCS #10 request files as well. For example, when a subordinate CA is configured, a PKCS #10 file is generated in case the automatic procedure fails when creating or publishing the new CA's certificate.

Okay, you've got a PKCS file. So how do you submit it? It's another job for the Web Enrollment Pages. Here's the procedure:

1. On the **Welcome** page select **Request a certificate**.
2. On the **Choose Request Type** page select **Advanced Request**.

3. On the **Advanced Certificate Requests** page select **Submit a certificate request using a base64 encoded PKCS #10 file or a renewal request using a base64 encoded PKCS #7 file**.

4. The **Submit a Saved Request** page is shown in Figure 10.23. To prepare the request, you must obtain the contents of a PKCS #10 or #7 file. This can be done in two ways, described in steps 5a and 5b.

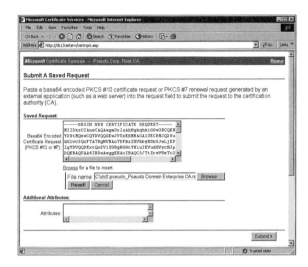

FIGURE 10.23
This form is used to submit a certificate request that is stored in a PKCS #7 or #10 file.

5a. One method is to paste the certificate request into the **Base64 Encoded Certificate Request** scroll box by doing the following:

a. Open the certificate request file in Notepad. Figure 10.24 shows an example of a certificate request opened in Notepad. I'm including the figure so that you can see the full contents of a certificate request file. The comments at the beginning and end of the file are not required and may be absent depending on the process that generated the file.

b. Copy the entire contents of the file into the clipboard. Don't make any changes to the file contents or you will invalidate the request.

c. Paste the clipboard contents into the **Base64 Encoded Certificate Request** scroll box.

FIGURE 10.24

A certificate request file is opened in Notepad so that the contents can be copied and pasted into the Submit a Saved Request page.

5b.   To enter the certificate request by browsing, do the following:

a. Click <u>Browse</u> to open the **File Name** field. Then click the **Browse** button to browse for the file.

b. Double-click the file when it is located. The filename and path will be placed in the **File Name** field.

c. Click the **Read!** button to copy the certificate request to the **Base64 Encoded Certificate Request** scroll box where you can examine the contents.

NOTE

Before you can browse for files as explained in Step 5b.c. you must configure Internet Explorer to trust the Web site. To add the site to IE's trusted sites list, do the following in Internet Explorer:

1. Select **Tools→Internet Options** in the menu bar.

2. In the **Internet Options** dialog box, select the **Security** tab.

3. Select **Trusted Sites** and click **Sites**.

4. Remove the check mark from **Request server verification (https:) for all sites in this zone**. The certsrv Web site does not use Secure HTTP.

5. Enter the URL for the Web server in the field **Add web site to the zone**.

6. Click **Add**. The Web site is added to the **Web sites** list.

6. If the request is being sent to an enterprise CA, you may edit the **Certificate Template** field to change the template that is to be used for the request. This field does not appear for forms being submitted to a stand-alone CA.

7. If any additional attributes are required, enter them in the **Additional Attributes** scroll box. See PKCS #9 for more information about certificate attributes.

8. Click **Submit** when the form is completed.

What happens next depends on whether the request was submitted to a stand-alone or an enterprise CA.

- If the request was submitted to a stand-alone CA, the certificate must be retrieved after it is issued. See the next section "Retrieving a Certificate from a Stand-Alone CA" for the procedures to use.

- If the request was submitted to an enterprise CA, the certificate can be retrieved from the Web Support Pages. However, the certificate must be installed on the client manually.

Certificate requests submitted from a file to an enterprise CA will be approved automatically. When the certificate is issued, a **Certificate Issued** page is displayed. Do the following to retrieve the certificate:

1. On the **Certificate Issued** page select **Base 64 encoded** for certificates to be used on Windows. Select **DER encoded** for non-Windows systems that require that format.

2. Click one of the following options:

   - **Download CA certificate.** This choice downloads only the certificate that was issued to you.

   - **Download CA certification path.** This choice downloads your new certificate along with the certificates of all CAs in the certification path. Use this option for clients that don't already have certificate trust lists for this CA.

3. In the **File Download** dialog box select **Save this file to disk**, select a directory, and either accept the suggested filename (certnew.cer) or provide a different filename. After the file has been received, the certificate(s) it contains must be imported to a certificate store, using the procedure described in the section "Importing Certificates" later in this chapter.

Retrieving a Certificate from a Stand-Alone CA

Unless automatic certificate approval is enabled, as it should almost never be, certificate requests submitted to a stand-alone CA must be approved by an administrator using the procedure described in the section "Issuing Certificates and Denying Certificate Requests" earlier in the chapter. After allowing time for the certificate to be approved the requester can return to the Web site and check on the status of the certificate.

To determine the status of a certificate, follow this procedure:

1. Select **Check a pending certificate** on the **Welcome** page of the Web Enrollment Pages. You must do this from the computer that was used to send the certificate request.

2. The next page is titled **Check On A Pending Certificate Request**, shown in Figure 10.25. Select the request you wish to check on and click **Next**.

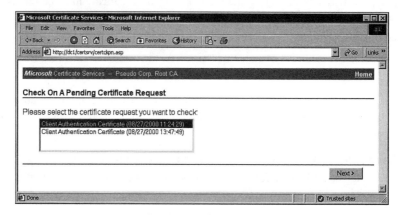

FIGURE 10.25
This page lists all pending requests that match the user and computer.

3a. If the request is still pending, you will see the page shown in Figure 10.26. You must return later to see if the certificate has been issued. Click the **Remove** button to cancel the certificate request.

3b. If the certificate has been issued, the **Certificate Issued** page is displayed. Simply click the **Install this certificate** button to retrieve and install the certificate.

In some situations, automatic certificate installation may be unfeasible or unable to function due to differences in operating systems or to communications difficulties. It is still possible to install the certificate on the client by exporting the certificate in the CA's **Issued Certificates** folder to a file. (In the case of Windows computers certificates are exported to a PKCS #7 file.) This file can be used to install the certificate on the client. The procedures used to export and import certificates are discussed in the section "Managing Certificates," which follows this discussion.

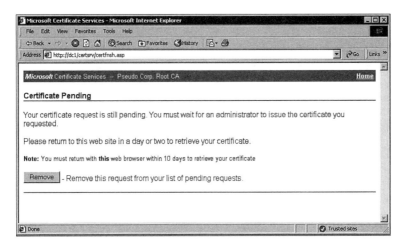

FIGURE 10.26
This page is displayed if a certificate request is held pending attention by an administrator.

Managing Certificates

Certificates issued to users, computers, and services are viewed and managed using the **Certificates** snap-in for the MMC. We encountered the **Certificates** console earlier as the platform used to start the **Certificate Request Wizard**. (See the section "Requesting Certificates with the Certificate Request Wizard.") Now it is time to return to **Certificates** to examine more of its capabilities.

Certificate Stores

Certificate stores are the locations where certificates are stored for use by their owner. Certificate stores are defined in two senses:

- *Physical certificate stores* describe the physical locations where certificates are stored, such as Active Directory (for remotely stored certificates), the Registry (for locally stored certificates), or Group Policy. We seldom have a need to be concerned about certificate stores in terms of their physical storage implementation.
- *Logical certificate stores* organize certificates in terms of their purposes.

Figure 10.27 shows an MMC console configured with three **Certificates** snap-ins, one each for the current user, the local computer, and the local World Wide Web publishing service. Each folder under a **Certificates** container represents a logical certificate store. As you can see, not all logical certificate store types appear for each type of object. By default, physical certificate stores are not shown.

10

PLANNING AND
IMPLEMENTING A PUBLIC
KEY INFRASTRUCTURE

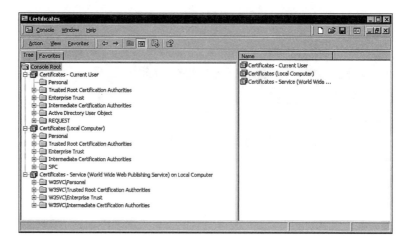

FIGURE 10.27

These Certificates consoles are organized by logical certificate stores.

The following types of logical certificate stores can be examined in the **Certificates** console:

- **Personal.** This store contains certificates issued for the individual use of a user, computer, or service. For example, a user's User certificate appears here. (The Registry is used as the physical store for personal certificates.)

- **Trusted Root Certification Authorities.** This store contains certificates for root CAs that are trusted by the client. Certificates with certification paths to one of these root CAs are trusted by the client. A computer stores only one set of the trusted root CA certificates, which is shared with users, services, and the computer.

- **Enterprise Trust.** Here we find certificate trust lists (CTLs). Certificates that have a certification path to a CTL are trusted for purposes specified in the CTL.

- **Intermediate Certification Authorities.** Certificates in this store are for CAs that are not trusted root CAs (intermediate and subordinate CAs). These certificates are used to validate certification paths. Certificate Revocation Lists (CRLs) are also stored here.

- **Active Directory User Object.** This store appears only for users and contains certificates that are stored in Active Directory.

- **Request.** This store contains pending or rejected certificate requests. It appears in the Certificates hierarchy only after a certificate request has been made for the user, computer, or service.

- **SPC.** Certificates in this store are *software publishers certificates* that are trusted by the computer. Software that has been digitally signed using a certificate in this store are accepted without consulting the user. By default this store is empty. Certificates are added to the store as authorized by the user. For example, when users download digitally signed software using Internet Explorer, they are prompted whether to trust all software from that publisher. If a user decides to trust software from that publisher, the publisher's certificate is added to the SPC store. This store appears in the **Certificates** console for the local computer only.

Enterprise CAs publish certificates, trusted root CA certificates, CTLs, and CRLs to Active Directory. Certificate stores for Active Directory users, computers, and services are automatically populated from Active Directory.

Group Policy provides another means of including trusted root CA certificates and CTLs in the logical certificate stores of Windows 2000 computers.

Consequently, if you examine a logical store container such as **Trusted Root Certification Authorities**, which is selected in Figure 10.27, you will find that it is automatically populated with a wide variety of certificates. Some of these certificates identify root CAs on the Internet that Microsoft has deemed trustworthy and installs automatically on all Windows clients. Other certificates are associated with any root CAs that are created on Windows 2000 Servers that are members of a domain, including stand-alone and enterprise CAs. Thanks to the way CA certificates are distributed automatically, no special steps are configured to establish certificate trusts for Windows 2000 computers operating in the same Active Directory tree.

NOTE

Another way to view trusted root CA certificates that are on your computer is to use **Internet Options,** which can be accessed from the Control Panel or from Internet Explorer by selecting **Tools→Internet Options** in the menu bar.

To view trusted root CA certificates, do the following after starting **Internet Options**:

1. Select the **Content** tab.
2. Click **Certificate**.
3. Select the **Trusted Root Certification Authorities** tab.

Organizing Certificates in the Certificates Console

Logical certificate stores are just one way of organizing certificates in the **Certificates** console. Before moving on, let's look at a method of organizing certificates by purpose. Figure 10.28 shows an MMC console with two instances of the **Certificates** snap-in, both configured to manage the local user. The top instance is organized by logical stores, and the bottom instance is organized by certificate purpose.

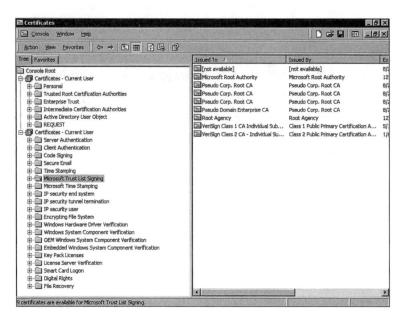

FIGURE 10.28

Two instances of the Certificates snap-in are configured, with the top instance configured to view logical certificate stores and the bottom instance configured to view certificate purposes.

A given certificate will appear on only one logical store. Some certificates have multiple uses, as defined by the object identifiers (OIDs) that are stored in the Extended Key Usage fields of their certificate data structures. When certificates are displayed by purpose, a certificate may be listed under multiple purposes, appearing in any certificate purpose folder that matches one of the OIDs included in the certificate. Some certificates have all purposes enabled, particularly many of the Trusted Root Certification Authorities certificates, and will appear in every purpose folder. As a result, the purpose folders will often be stuffed with large numbers of certificates.

To modify the view for a **Certificates** console, do the following:

1. Select the appropriate **Certificates** object in the object hierarchy.

2. Choose **View→Options** from the menu bar to open the **View Options** dialog box shown in Figure 10.29.

3. Select one of the following view modes:

    - **Certificate purpose**
    - **Logical certificate stores**

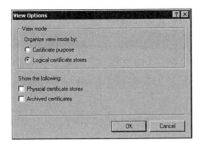

FIGURE 10.29
The View Options dialog box determines the way certificates are organized for Certificates consoles.

4. If **Logical certificates stores** is selected, you can check the **Physical certificate stores** option. When this option is enabled, certificates within a logical store are organized into folders corresponding the physical store for the certificate. Figure 10.30 shows how physical certificates appear in the container hierarchy.

5. Check **Archived certificates** to display certificates that have been archived. Archived certificates are certificates that have been expired or renewed. Unless the **Archived certificates** option is selected, archived certificates are not displayed. It is good practice to retain archived certificates rather than deleting them so that the certificates can be used to verify signatures on documents signed with now-expired or renewed certificates.

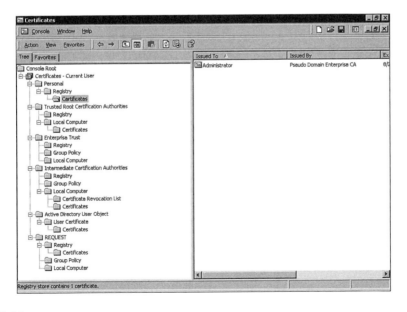

FIGURE 10.30
Physical certificate stores can be displayed by selecting Physical certificate stores in the View Options dialog box.

Examining Certificate Contents

Certificates can be viewed in a number of places, including the **Certificates** and **Certification Authority** consoles. In all instances, when you can see a certificate icon, you can view the detailed parameters within the certificate. Certificates contain the following information:

- **Certificate details** are fields in the X.509v3 certificate structure. Because these fields are protected by a signed message digest, they cannot be modified once the certificate is created.

- **Certificate properties** are certificate attributes that do not appear within the certificate itself, are not protected by the signed message digest, and can therefore be modified by authorized users.

Certificate Details

To display certificate details, open the folder containing the certificate and do one of the following:

- Double-click the certificate description.
- Right-click the certificate description and select **Open** in the context menu.

The certificate shown in Figure 10.31 is issued to a root CA. Note that the **Issued to** and the **Issued by** CAs are the same, a situation we anticipated earlier in the chapter while observing that root CAs are self-certified.

> **NOTE**
>
> The certificates for root CAs are special cases and do not appear in the **Certificates** console. To view the certificate for a root CA, you must do the following in the **Certification Authority** console:
>
> 1. Right-click the CA object in the object tree.
> 2. Choose **Properties** from the context menu.
> 3. Click the **View Certificate** button on the **General** tab of the **CA Properties** dialog box.

The **Details** tab, shown in Figure 10.32, lists detailed information for all certificate properties. This time, I am showing you a certificate issued to the user Administrator, which contains more of the fields that may appear. (To show all the available fields, the figure is a composite of two screens.)

FIGURE 10.31
Certificate details for a root CA: The General tab.

Select a field to view the complete contents of the field. Many fields contain encrypted data and aren't of much interest, but many contain information that administrators will find valuable. Not all fields appear in all types of certificates. Some entries of interest are

- **Issuer.** Identifies the CA that issued the certificate.
- **Subject.** Identifies the user, computer, or service to which the certificate was issued.
- **Key usage.** This field describes cryptography functions that may be performed with the certificate.
- **Public key.** Displays the type and length of the public key. After setting up a new CA, you should check this field on several certificates that it issues to ensure that the characteristics are as required.
- **Enhanced Key Usage.** This field contains OIDs specified for the certificate. Enhanced key uses are also referred to as certificate purposes in other dialog boxes. See the section "Requesting Certificates with the Web Enrollment Pages" for more information about OIDs.
- **Certificate template.** If the certificate was issued by an enterprise CA, this field reports the template on which the certificate is based.
- **Friendly name.** The friendly name that was defined for the certificate. This value is an editable certificate property.

The **Edit Properties** button on the **Details** tab is active only if the certificate is opened in the **Certificates** console. See the next section, "Viewing and Modifying Certificate Properties," for more information on certificate properties.

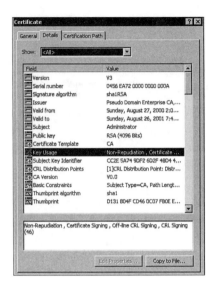

FIGURE 10.32
Certificate details for a user certificate: The Details tab.

The **Copy to File** button starts the **Certificate Export Wizard**, which enables you to export a certificate to a file. We'll return to these procedures later in the section "Exporting Certificates."

The **Certification Path** tab lists the certification trust list that validates this certificate. Figure 10.33 shows the certification path for a domain controller that is certified by a subordinate CA. To view the properties for the certificate owned by another entity, perform one of the following actions:

- Select the certificate description and click **View Certificate** to view the details for the certificate.
- Double-click the certificate description.

If a friendly name has been defined for the certificate, that name appears in the certification path. Otherwise the name of the certificate owner appears.

Viewing and Modifying Certificate Properties

Certificate properties may be viewed in the **Certificates** console. One way to open the certificate **Properties** dialog box is to open the certificate in the **Certificates** console, select the **Details** tab, and click the **Edit Properties** button to open the **Certificate Properties** dialog box shown in Figure 10.34.

FIGURE 10.33

Certificate details for a user certificate: The Certification Path tab.

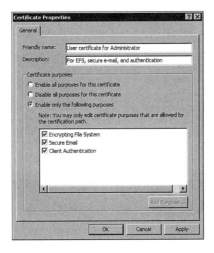

FIGURE 10.34

Properties for a certificate.

Another method of opening the certificate **Properties** dialog box is as follows:

1. Start an instance of **Certificates** for the owner of the certificate.

2. Open the **Personal**→**Certificates** folder.

3. Right-click the certificate description in the Details pane.

4. Choose **Properties** in the context menu to open the **Certificate Properties** window.

10

PLANNING AND
IMPLEMENTING A PUBLIC
KEY INFRASTRUCTURE

The following certificate properties may be modified:

- **Friendly name.** A user-friendly name may be entered for the certificate.
- **Description.** This text field can be used to further describe the certificate.
- **Certificate purposes.** When a certificate is issued, the CA authorizes the certificate to be used for one or more purposes. Purposes can be disabled by the user of the certificate. Purposes can be added, but only to certificates that do not contain any entries in the Enhanced Key Usage field.

It is easy to disable purposes. First select one of the following radio buttons:

- **Enable all purposes for this certificate.** Purposes are enabled as specified when the certificate request was prepared. This is the default setting.
- **Disable all purposes for this certificate.** This choice disables the certificate without deleting it from the client's certificate store.
- **Enable only the following purposes.** With this option, purposes can be enabled or disabled individually.

Adding purposes is beyond the scope of an introductory chapter. Purposes can be added only to a certificate that does not have entries in its Enhanced Key Usage field.

Exporting Certificates

Certificates can be copied to a file, a process that is also called *exporting* the certificate. The export file is a useful way to transport a certificate to another computer, where it can be imported. Exporting can also be used to archive a certificate and the private key associated with the certificate (if exporting was enabled when the private key was created).

> **NOTE**
>
> Certificates, being public, can always be exported. Private keys can be exported only if exporting is explicitly enabled when the key pair is created. Private key exporting is automatically enabled for certificates created using the Basic EFS and EFS Recovery Agent certificate templates. By default, exportable private keys are disabled for all other certificate types.
>
> To request exportable private keys for key pairs of other types, the certificate must be requested using the **Advanced Certificate Request** page in the Web Enrollment Support pages with the **Mark keys as exportable** option selected. The Web Enrollment Support pages are described in the sections "Requesting Certificates" and "Managing Certificates."

Certificates are copied to files using the **Certificate Export Wizard**. To create a certificate export file use this procedure:

1. Start the **Certificate Export Wizard** in one the following ways:
   - Open the details pages for a certificate, as described in the section "Certificate Details" earlier in the chapter. Select the **Details** tab and click **Copy to File**.
   - Right-click a certificate description and choose **All Tasks→Export** from the context menu.

2. The **Export Private Key** dialog box (appearing in Figure 10.35) is displayed only when the wizard is started within the **Certificates** console (the CA console does not have access to client private keys) and only if the private key was made exportable when it was created. Select one of the following choices:
   - **Yes, export the private key.** The private key will exported with the certificate.
   - **No, do not export the private key.** Only the certificate will be exported.

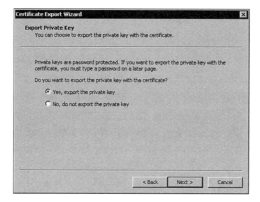

FIGURE 10.35

In some situations, the private key can be exported with the certificate.

3. The next dialog box is **Export File Format,** shown in Figure 10.36. (I've cheated by pasting together portions of two copies of the dialog box so that all the fields are easily viewable in the figure. In practice, however, only selected options are available, as determined by the choice that is made in the **Export Private Key** dialog box.)

When you select **No, do not export the private key** in the **Export Private Key** dialog box, these file formats are available:

- **Cryptographic Message Syntax Standard PKCS #7 Certificates.** PKCS #7 Cryptographic Message Syntax files are employed to transfer certificates to Windows 2000 computers. Optionally, the export file can include all certificates in the certificate trust path. PKCS #7 files have a `.p7b` filename extension.

- **DER encoded binary X.509.** This format is required when exchanging certificates with some non-Windows 2000 computers. These files use a `.cer` filename extension. See `ftp://ftp.rsa.com/pub/pkcs/doc/layman.doc` for more information about this format.

- **Base-64 encoded X.509.** This is another format included for compatibility with some non-Windows 2000 computers. These files have a `.cer` filename extension. See RFC1521 for more information about this format.

When **Yes, export the private key** is selected in the **Export Private Key** dialog box, files are exported using the PKCS #12 Personal Information Exchange format. These files have a `.pfx` filename extension. Three options are available for PKCS #12 exports:

- **Include all certificates in the certificate path if possible.** If all certificates in the path are available, they will be included in the export file.

- **Enable strong protection (requires IE 5.0, NT4.0 SP4 or above).** Strong protection protects the private key with a password that must be entered whenever the private key is used. Strong key protection is a useful precaution when a key pair is transported to an unsecured medium. This option is enabled by default.

- **Delete the private key if the export is successful.** If the purpose of the export is to move the key pair to a different computer, it may be desirable to delete the private key from the current system after an export file has been built successfully.

4. If a PKCS #12 certificate is being created and **Enable strong protection** was selected, the **Password** dialog box requests a password that is used to protect the private key. The exported private key can be used only with this password. This is a very valuable precaution when a private key is being stored on portable media, but only if you select a strong password.

5. The next dialog box is **File to export**. Enter the path and filenames for the certificate export file. The wizard supplies appropriate filename extensions.

6. The final dialog box summarizes the characteristics of the export file that the wizard will create. Review the settings and return to earlier dialog boxes to modify them as necessary. Click **Finish** to create the export file.

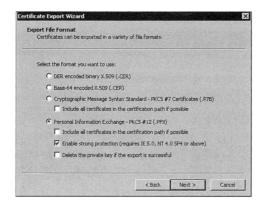

FIGURE 10.36

Certificate file export formats. Available formats depend on the selection made in the Export Private Key dialog box.

If the private key is included in the export, the resulting file is extremely sensitive and valuable. Recall that all data encrypted with the key pair are compromised if the private key becomes available to anyone but the owner of the key pair. The private key should be protected with a password, but the password is susceptible to a brute-force attack. If the export file is lost, it is wise to consider the key pair to be compromised. Revoke the certificate and obtain a new certificate with a new key pair. The need to guard the private key is the reason the default state for most private keys does not permit them to be exported.

Importing Certificates

Certificates, and the associated private keys if included, can be imported from files following the formats described in the previous section. The certificate file may have been created by exporting a certificate, or it may contain a certificate that was issued by a CA. Whatever the situation, the import procedure is the same.

Imports can be started in several places. Some examples are

- In Windows Explorer, right-click a certificate file and click **Install Certificate** for a DER (.cer), Base64 (.cer), or PKCS #7 (.p7b) file. Click **Install PFX** for a PKCS #12 (.pfx) file.

- In the **Certificates** console, right-click a container in the logical certificate store and choose **All Tasks→Import** in the context menu.

- In the **Group Policy** console, right-click **Trusted Root Certificate Authorities** and choose **All Tasks→Import** in the context menu. Only certificates for trusted root CAs can be imported to this container.

Importing Certificates in the Certificates Console

To import a certificate and install it in the owners certificate store, use the **Certificates** console. Here's the procedure:

1. Right-click the certificate store in which the certificate is to be installed. Then choose **All Tasks→Import** in the context menu to start the **Certificate Import Wizard**.

2. In the **File to Import** dialog box, specify the name of the certificate file. Click the **Browse** button to select the file by browsing. The browser assumes a file is a PKCS #12 Personal Information Exchange format with a .pfx extension. If only the certificate was backed up, the file will have a PKCS #7 Cryptographic Message Syntax format and a .p7b filename extension.

3. The next dialog box is **Password**, shown in Figure 10.37. Complete the dialog box as follows:

   - **Password.** Enter the password that was specified when the certificate was exported.

   - **Enable strong private key protection.** Check this box if you want to protect the private key with a password that must be entered each time the private key is used. This option is available only if the private key is included in the certificate file.

   - **Mark the private key as exportable.** Check this box if the private key is to be exportable after it is installed in the target certificate store. This option is available only if the private key is included in the certificate file.

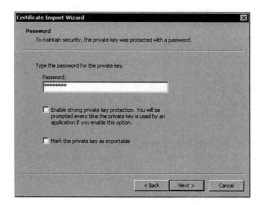

FIGURE 10.37

When a certificate is imported a password must be entered to access the private key if strong protection was enabled when the keys were exported.

4. The next dialog box is titled **Certificate Store**, shown in Figure 10.38. The following options determine which certificate store will receive the certificate:

- **Automatically select the certificate store based on the type of certificate.** Select this option if the **Certificate Import Wizard** should select the destination logical certificate store for the certificate. Although this is not the default choice, it is probably the most appropriate selection in most instances.

- **Place certificates in the following store.** The certificate will be stored in the location specified in the **Certificate Store** field. The default logical certificate store is the store that was right-clicked in Step 1. Click the **Browse** button to open the **Select Certificate Store** dialog box shown in Figure 10.39. In the figure, I've checked **Show physical stores**, expanded the containers, and pasted several copies together so that you can see all the entries. After selecting a certificate store, click **OK** to return to the **Certificate Store** dialog box.

NOTE

In addition to the logical and physical certificate stores that are managed with the **Certificates** console, the **Select Certificate Store** list includes the option `Active Directory User Object`, which uses `User Certificate` as its physical store. When this certificate store is selected, certificates are placed in Active Directory, where they are stored in the User Certificates container in your User container.

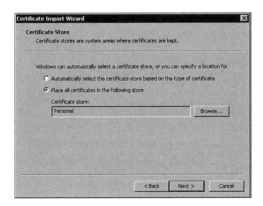

FIGURE 10.38

You can specify the certificate store for an imported certificate or let the certificate be placed in a certificate store based on its function.

FIGURE 10.39
You can browse to select a logical or physical certificate store in which to install an imported certificate.

5. The final dialog box in the **Certificate Import Wizard** summarizes your choices for the certificate import. Review the choices and return to earlier dialog boxes if it is necessary to make changes. Click **Finish** to initiate the certificate import.

Importing Trusted Root CA Certificates

If a trusted root CA is installed on a Windows 2000 Server that is a member of a domain, the root CA's certificate is automatically published to Active Directory. That's how certificates for enterprise CAs and stand-alone CAs (if they are domain members) make their ways into the Trusted Root Certification Authority logical store, which is physically stored on the local computer. This list is stored only once and is shared by all certificate users on the computer.

From time to time, you may want to add the certificate for an external trusted root CA to users' Trusted Root Certification Authority logical stores. While trusted root CA certificates can be imported to the **Trusted Root Certification Authorities** container in the **Certificates** console, that affects certificate users on the local system only.

To make the certificate of a trusted root CA available to many users, the certificate can be added to a Group Policy using this procedure:

1. Open the appropriate Group Policy object.

2. Open the folder **Computer Configuration→Windows Settings→Security Settings→Public Key Policies→Trusted Root Certification Authorities.** (See Figure 10.16.)

3. Right-click **Trusted Root Certification Authorities** and choose **All Tasks→Import** from the context menu.

4. In the **Certificate Import Wizard** specify the certificate file to be imported. In this situation, the certificate can be imported only to the **Trusted Root Certification Authorities** container. Finish the wizard to import the certificate.

All users affected by this Group Policy policy will include this certificate in their **Trusted Root Certification Authorities** stores.

Renewing Certificates

User certificates typically are renewed when half their lifetimes have expired. Depending on the strength of the key, certificates should occasionally be renewed with a new key. Apart from CA certificates, certificates are renewed in the **Certificates** console.

Renewing a Certificate with the Same Key

To renew a certificate with the same key, do the following:

1. Right-click the certificate and choose **All Tasks→Renew Certificate with Same Key**. The **Certificate Renewal Wizard** is started.

2. The first dialog box prompts **Do you want to use default values for the certificate renewal?** Two responses are offered:

   - **Yes, use default values.** With this choice, the certificate renewal request is sent to the same CA that issued the certificate originally.

   - **No, I want to provide my own settings.** With this choice, the next dialog box offers the opportunity to send the certificate renewal request to a different CA.

3. Complete the wizard and click **Finish** to submit the certificate renewal request. If the request is successful, you are notified that the certificate has been issued. Click **Install Certificate** to complete the renewal. The new certificate replaces the existing one in your certificate store.

Renewing a Certificate with a New Key

To renew a certificate with a new key, do the following:

1. Right-click the certificate and choose **All Tasks→Renew Certificate with New Key**. The **Certificate Renewal Wizard** is started.

2. The first dialog box prompts **Do you want to use default values for the certificate renewal?** Two responses are offered:

   - **Yes, use default values.** With this choice, the certificate will be renewed using the same CSP, key length, and CA as were used to create the original certificate. Skip to step 4.

   - **No, I want to provide my own settings.** With this choice, you can modify certain certificate key parameters.

3. If you chose **No, I want to provide my own settings** in Step 2, subsequent dialog boxes enable you to select the following:

- The CSP used to generate the key pair
- Whether strong protection is to be enabled for the private key
- The CA to which the certificate request is to be sent

4. Complete the wizard and click **Finish** to send the certificate renewal request. If the request is successful, you are notified that the certificate has been issued. Click **Install Certificate** to complete the renewal. The new certificate replaces the existing one in your certificate store.

Renewing CA Certificates

The section "Managing Certificate Lifetimes" discusses lifetime and renewal criteria for CA certificates. Because a CA cannot issue a certificate with a lifetime that extends past the expiration of the CA's own certificate, it is essential to renew the CA's certificate while the remaining life of the certificate is greater than the lifetimes of the certificates that the CA issues.

CA certificates are renewed in the **Certification Administrator** console, which must be running on the server with the CA. The procedure is as follows:

1. Right-click the CA object in the object tree and choose **All Tasks→Renew CA Certificate** from the context menu.

2. Certification Services must be stopped for the certificate to be renewed. A dialog box offers you the opportunity to stop the service and continue the renewal process or to leave the service running and cancel the process.

3. If you choose **Yes** in Step 2, the Certification Service is stopped, after which the dialog box in Figure 10.40 is displayed. Select one of the following options:

- **Yes.** Select this option to generate a new key pair. A new key pair should be generated at least once every two times the certificate is renewed.
- **No.** The certificate will be renewed using the key pair used in the current certificate.

If you are renewing a root CA, click **OK** and the certificate is renewed without further input, after which the Certification Service is restarted. Step 4 will not be executed.

4. If you are renewing a subordinate CA, a dialog box prompts for the identity of an online CA that can renew the certificate (see Figure 10.41). The way you proceed depends on whether the parent CA is online or offline.

- If the required CA is online, either enter its name in the **Computer Name** field, or pull down the **Parent CA** field and select the parent CA that will receive the certificate renewal request. Click **OK** to send the request. Install the certificate when the request is approved.

- If the parent CA is offline, click **Cancel**. The certificate renewal request will be stored in a file for later submission as described in the section "Requesting Certificates Using PKCS #7 Renewal Request Files and PKCS #10 Certificate Request Files." The name of the certificate request file is specified in the **CA Certificate Request** dialog box. Click **OK** to generate the certificate request file.

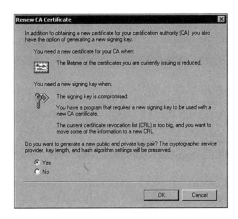

FIGURE 10.40

When renewing a CA's certificate, this dialog box offers the opportunity to generate a new key pair.

FIGURE 10.41

When renewing a subordinate CA's certificate, this dialog box enables you to specify the name of an online parent CA or to send the certificate request to a file for later processing.

Concluding Remarks Regarding Certification Services

As you might conclude from the length of this section, setting up and managing a large-scale PKI can involve a lot of learning, testing, planning, and training of users. It is not something you set up over the weekend. That much labor can be justified if a PKI is a critical component in your organization's security strategy. But what if you only need certificates because you want to configure secure Web servers, IPSec, or L2TP/IPSec tunnels? How can you reduce the investment in time and effort that is needed to get secure IP communication up and running?

Here's a minimalist strategy that will work if your goals are limited to supporting secure network communication:

1. Set up a single, enterprise root CA on a server that has available capacity. For this limited application, a dedicated CA shouldn't be necessary.

2. In the Group Policy for the root domain of your tree, enable all the policies in the **Automatic Certificates Request Settings** container, as explained in the section "Automating Certificate Requests." (You may not need `Enrollment Agent (Computer)` but it does no harm to enable it.)

3. Ensure that the settings are not blocked by another Group Policy. (See the section "Editing Group Policy Object Options" in Chapter 4, "Active Directory Concepts.")

This simple setup is all I used to complete the discussions on IPSec and VPNs that appear in the next chapter.

Now that PKIs have been added to your toolkit, we move on to put certificates to work. There are some situations in which certificates are required and others where they are valuable security enhancements. We'll look at several secure networking technologies including the Secure Sockets Layer, IP security, tunneling, and virtual private networks.

Securing IP Communication

IN THIS CHAPTER

For a variety of reasons, IP was not developed as a secure protocol. The Arpanet, precursor of the Internet, was intended to function primarily as a medium for exchanging non-classified information among vendors, universities, and the Department of Defense. At that time, to secure data communication it was necessary to physically secure the computers and the medium. Often that meant locking everything in a controlled-access building. When data had to be communicated between sites, elaborate anti-intrusion cabling systems were implemented. One early technique was to pressurize the cables so that an air leak would betray any attempt to tap the cable. The DoD was an early adopter of fiber optic cables, then terribly expensive because they were considered harder to tap than copper. Public businesses had to make do with leased telephone lines, satellites, and radio communication with the hope that the media wouldn't be tapped.

Times have changed. The need for security is widespread, but the budgets for secure cable systems just aren't there, even for the Department of Defense, and fixed cable systems just don't provide the flexibility that is needed. Imagine what it would require to run a secure cable to every home so that users could securely send credit card transactions and banking data. If secure cables were the only tools we had, e-commerce would never have gotten off the ground.

What is needed is a way to communicate securely through unsecured media while having a high degree of confidence that even if data are intercepted, they will not be readable. Fortunately, since the late 1960s, digital cryptography has emerged as a viable field. Highly secure algorithms have been developed that can be computed on small computers. We met some of these algorithms in the previous two chapters, so by now you are aware of their characteristics.

You have not seen, however, ways of putting digital cryptography to work to encrypt communications, which is the topic we pick up in this chapter. We are going to look at two methods for securing data exchanged between network devices:

- Packet-based encryption techniques that allow two hosts to establish a secure communication by exchanging packets with encrypted data payloads.

- Secure tunnels that allow all communication between two hosts to be encrypted, enabling the networks to treat an unsecured network as if it were a secure network connection. Because these techniques enable a private network to establish a secure network communication channel through a public network such as the Internet, the secure communication links are referred to as *virtual private networks* (VPNs).

We'll look at VPNs in the section "Configuring IPSec Tunnels and Virtual Private Networks." But first, let's look at two protocols that enable hosts to establish one-to-one secure communication.

The more established of the protocols is the *Secure Sockets Layer* (SSL), which is the mainstay of e-commerce on the World Wide Web. SSL is a strong technology that is likely to be used well into the future. It is valuable enough that the Internet Engineering Task Force (IETF, see Chapter 2, "TCP/IP Protocol Concepts") is developing an Internet standard for the technology. Despite its widespread use, SSL is limited, functioning as a special-purpose solution that cannot be used to encrypt all communication between two endpoints.

Therefore, the IETF is also developing a more general-purpose method of transparently encrypting all IP traffic called IP Security, the IP Security Service, or more often IPSec. As you will see, IPSec is easy to implement and is a very effective means of securing IP communication.

We'll spend a bit of time on SSL, but there isn't much for an administrator to be concerned with. SSL support is built in to most Web servers and browsers, with little configuration required. Management tasks are primarily limited to providing digital certificates and enabling selected Web sites for SSL support.

As an administrator, however, you will need to know how to use and configure IPSec. Consequently, IPSec will receive the greatest emphasis in this chapter.

Secure Sockets Layer/Transport Layer Security

SSL was developed by Netscape Communications as a protocol that uses digital cryptography to secure communication between clients and services. The latest version is SSL version 3.0, issued in 1996. Although Netscape holds the patents for SSL, they have generously made the specifications and source code publicly available. Consequently, SSL has achieved wide acceptance and has grown stronger as a result of public scrutiny.

Transport Layer Security (TLS; RFC2246) is the IETF implementation of SSL, currently on the Internet Standards Track. TLS includes several enhancements to the SSL 3.0 specifications, for example TLS is considered more secure than SSL 3.0, and TLS is generally regarded as the logical successor to SSL 3.0. However, TLS is designed to be downward compatible with SSL, providing a mechanism for shifting down to SSL 3.0 operation when both parties to a communication do not support TLS.

SSL 3.0 and TLS are supported by Internet Information Services v5.0, included with Windows 2000 Server, which attempts to use TLS, falling back to SSL 3.0 if the client does not support TLS. Because SSL and TLS implement the same fundamental technology, you will often see the protocols identified by the combined acronym SSL/TLS. I will follow that practice when appropriate for the remainder of this discussion.

NOTE

Some sources of information about SSL and TLS are

- "Introduction to SSL," available on Netscape's Web site at `http://developer.netscape.com/docs/manuals/security/sslin/contents.htm`.

- "Microsoft Security Advisor Program: Secure Sockets Layer/Transport Layer Security," available at `http://www.microsoft.com/security/tech/ssl/default.asp`.

- "Web Security," an extract from the book *Cryptography and Network Security: Principles and Practice*, by William Stallings, available at `http://www.microsoft.com/TechNet/security/chaptr14.asp`.

- "Transport Layer Security," RFC2246 as developed by the IETF, available at `http://www.ietf.org/ids.by.wg/tls.html`.

SSL and the Internet Protocol Stack

Figure 11.1 illustrates where SSL/TLS fits in the Internet protocol stack. Because SSL/TCP requires a reliable protocol it always operates over TCP. SSL/TLS interfaces with upper-layer applications that are specifically designed to work with it.

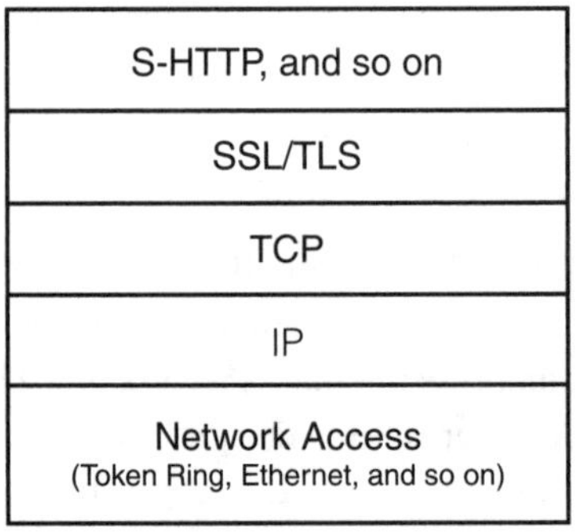

S-HTTP, and so on
SSL/TLS
TCP
IP
Network Access (Token Ring, Ethernet, and so on)

FIGURE 11.1

The Secure Sockets Layer fits between the host-to-host layer protocols and applications.

Notice that the top layer of the SSL/TLS model does not consist of a generic Process/Application layer. Because SSL/TLS replaces the interface that TCP presents to applications, standard TCP applications cannot communicate using SSL/TLS. A separate, secure version of the application must be written to take advantage of SSL/TLS services. The best-known example of an application that uses SSL/TLS is Secure HTTP (HTTPS).

Because they are distinct protocols, standard and secure versions of applications must be configured to use different ports. For example, the well-known port for HTTP is 80, whereas the well-known port for HTTPS is 443. To preserve port numbers and reduce applications, in nearly all cases TLS uses the same port numbers as those established for SSL.

A variety of application layer protocols have been adapted for secure communication over SSL/TLS. Familiar ones are described in Table 11.1. Notice that none of the secure protocols has the status of Internet Standard, even though all are in everyday use. A nearby note expands on the disconnect that exists between the protocol implementation and the standardization processes.

NOTE

Secure protocols are good examples of commercial needs being unwilling to wait for standards to make it through the Internet standards process. Internet standardization sets a high bar, seeking to include all useful features as a result of public input while identifying and correcting weaknesses to the greatest degree possible. In other words, before a technology becomes a standard, it is subjected to a tremendous amount of scrutiny.

Commercial interests that use the Internet often are unwilling to wait for a standard to be finalized. "We need secure HTTP now. Can't wait three years. We'll use whatever's in progress and be ready to upgrade when something better is available." If you look through the RFC index, you will see three sets of documents regarding Secure MIME, versions 1.0 through 3.0, and a fourth set of RFCs is expected in late 2000 after the comment period ends. Before we wonder if vendors aren't getting too far ahead of standards, it's worth reflecting on two things: Where would the Internet be without secure protocols? (As a medium for conducting business it would be dead.) And how many secure protocol breaches have we heard about? (None I'm aware of. While it remains possible to generate denial of service attacks, it's difficult for an attacker to obtain access to encrypted data.) So much work goes into generating a Draft-Standard that it acquires quite a bit of polish even before it hits the Standards Track.

A number of Windows 2000 features are based on standards-in-progress or even on Internet-Drafts. The capability of discovering LDAP services through DNS, a cornerstone of Active Directory, is currently in Internet-Draft form and has yet to enter the Standards Track. DNS service location resource records are described in RFC 2782, currently described as a Proposed Standard. TLS is on the Standards Track, but it isn't an Internet Standard. As long as Microsoft is vigilant for bugs and improvements that emerge during the standards progress, there seems little harm in implementing a protocol before it is classified as a standard.

TABLE 11.1   Select Applications Having SSL/TLS Versions

Application Layer Protocol	RFCS	Secure Protocol Status	Normal Port(s)	Secure Port(s)
Hypertext Transfer Protocol (HTTP/ HTTPS)	RFC2068/ RFC2660	Experimental	80	443
File Transfer Protocol (FTP/FTPS)	RFC959/ RFC2228	Standards Track	20/21	
Internet Message Access Protocol (IMAP/IMAPS)	RFC2060/ RFC2595	Standards Track	143	993
Lightweight Directory Access Protocol (LDAP)	RFC2251/ RFC2829	Standards Track	389	389/ 636

NOTE

As currently defined, LDAP has no mechanism for authenticating clients. When LDAP is implemented over SSL/TLS, authentication can be performed when a session connection is established. The Windows 2000 implementation supports SSL/TLS-based LDAP communication between domain controllers and the LDAP service. To implement this feature is a simple matter of configuring an enterprise CA and ensuring that each domain controller receives a Domain Controller certificate, a task that is easily accomplished by defining Group Policy to enable automatic certificate issue, as described in the section "Automating Certificate Requests" in Chapter 10. When this is done, DCs can communicate with LDAP using either port 389 or 636. See Microsoft Knowledge Base article Q247078 for more information about this feature.

SSL/TLS Functionality

SSL/TLS contributes the following capabilities to TCP/IP communication:

- **Authentication.** Originally (SSL 2.0) SSL permitted clients to authenticate servers. SSL v3.0 and TLS also enable servers to authenticate clients. This capability is required for applications such as online banking.

- **Integrity.** SSL/TLS uses message digests and digital signatures to ensure that data are not modified in transit.

- **Confidentiality.** After an initial handshake, all data above TCP are encrypted using a symmetric cipher.

SSL supports a variety of cryptographic algorithms, and TLS supports a few additional ones. Most of the supported ciphers have been discussed. It is beyond the scope of this book to exhaustively discuss the available ciphers.

SSL/TLS Operation

SSL/TLS makes use of two protocols: a *handshake protocol* to initialize a session and a *record protocol* to exchange data. The details of these protocols are beyond the scope of this book, but it is useful to have a general idea of the way these protocols function.

Before SSL/TLS can exchange data securely, a handshake process must be executed to enable the client and server to agree on ciphers, to authenticate, and to generate keys. When a client attempts to communicate with a secure server, a session must be initialized using the *handshake protocol* as follows:

1. The client sends the server a *hello message* that includes the client's SSL/TLS version number, supported encryption and message digest protocols, supported key lengths, and supported key exchange methods. Included is a *challenge message*, consisting of randomly generated data that the server must include in an authentication response.

2. The server sends the client a *hello message* that includes the server's SSL/TLS version number, mutually supported encryption protocols, message digest protocols, key lengths, and key exchange methods. The message includes a randomly generated challenge to the client and the server's public key certificate. If the server is required to authenticate the client, the message includes a request for the client's certificate.

3. The client attempts to authenticate the server by validating the server's certificate. If the server is authenticated, the client sends a *master key message* to the server, which includes a 384-bit *premaster secret* for the session, encrypted with the server's public key. The premaster secret is based on all data that the client has received from the server to that point.

4. If the server has taken the optional step of requesting authentication of the client, the client sends another message which includes data that are unique to the handshake, digitally signing the message with the client's public key. The encrypted data are sent to the server with the client's certificate.

5. If the server has requested client authentication, the server attempts to authenticate the client by validating the client's certificate. The session is rejected if client authentication fails. If the client is authenticated, the server decrypts the premaster secret using the server's private key and applies an algorithm to generate the 384-bit *master secret.*

6. The client applies the same steps to the premaster secret so that client and server derive the same master secret.

7. The client and server use the master secret to generate *session keys*, symmetric keys that are used to encrypt and decrypt data exchanged throughout the SSL/TLS session.

8. The client sends a message to the server informing the server that all further data will be encrypted with the session key. It then sends a separate, encrypted message informing the server that the client's portion of the handshake is completed.

9. The server sends a message to the client informing the client that all further data will be encrypted with the session key. It then sends a separate, encrypted message informing the client that the server's portion of the handshake is completed.

10. The handshake is now complete and the SSL/TLS session is initiated.

While the session is active all data above TCP are encrypted. Figure 11.2 shows an example of a packet in which the TCP data payload is protected by SSL. I captured this packet while accessing a Web retailer. (No, it doesn't have my Visa number, so don't bother trying to hack it.) Everything past the TCP header is encrypted gibberish. You can't even tell what the application layer protocol is. We can determine that this is an HTTPS packet by the destination port number, 0x01BB or 443 decimal, the well-known port for HTTP over SSL/TLS. (Evidently, Windows 2000 Network Monitor is missing some protocol decodes and is unable to identify HTTPS as the TCP payload protocol.)

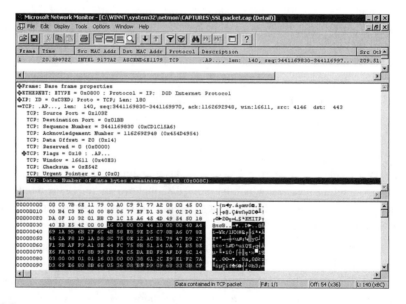

FIGURE 11.2

All data above the TCP layer are encrypted when protected by SSL/TLS.

It's worth noting that SSL/TLS does not protect data at the IP and TCP protocol layers, most significantly the IP addresses of the hosts. Because IP addresses do provide some information about the organization's network structure, there are some situations when everything above the network access layer should be encrypted. That's not the job SSL/TLS is intended to perform. For that level of security we need to look at secure tunneling protocols, the last topic in this chapter.

Distinctions Between SSL Version 3.0 and TLS

In many senses, TLS is SSL version 3.1. TLS strengthens SSL but does not alter SSL's essentials. Most of the differences are technical in nature, made to enhance security or to implement another Internet standard protocol or algorithm. Unless you want to dig into computer code and algorithms, the primary difference from an administrator's viewpoint is that TLS does not support Fortezza key exchange or symmetric encryption methods. Fortezza is a cipher suite used by the U.S. government to protect sensitive but unclassified material.

Enabling Support for SSL/TLS

It is a simple matter to configure a Web site to require SSL/TLS. Before you start, however, you need to decide whether all Web transactions for the server will be protected by SSL/TLS. If a little security is good, more is better, right?

Not necessarily. In most cases, definitely not. The handshaking required to create a Secure HTTP session, encrypting and decrypting data, and closing the session has significantly greater overhead than a comparable HTTP session. If even homepages are encrypted, users may complain about slow response, network traffic will increase, and computers at both ends need to work harder.

Consequently, you should require HTTPS only when there is a need to protect sensitive data. With IIS, you would implement at least two sites on a server: an unsecured HTTP site and a buttoned-down HTTPS site.

I won't be covering IIS management in great detail. In fact, if you aren't experienced with IIS, this information won't accomplish much other than to demonstrate the ease of enabling SSL/TLS support. Only three steps are required:

1. Create the Web site that is to be made secure. Test it and add some content before continuing. My site is named `Secure Web Site`.

2. Obtain a public key certificate for IIS, which includes a wizard for the purpose. (Only one Web server certificate is allowed on a given server. It is shared by all services and Web sites that are configured on the IIS server.)

3. Configure the properties of the Web server with the desired security settings.

Assuming that Step 1 is completed (I'm leaving the really big step up to you), my job is limited to covering Steps 2 and 3.

Obtaining a Public Key Certificate for IIS

Open the Internet Information Services console (for some reason the default name for the icon in **Administrative Tools** is **Internet Services Manager**) and use this procedure to request and install a certificate for IIS:

1. Right-click the Web site and choose **Properties** from the context menu to open the **Web Site Properties** pages.

2. Select the **Directory Security** tab, shown in Figure 11.3. Until a certificate is installed, the **View Certificate** and **Edit** buttons are not activated.

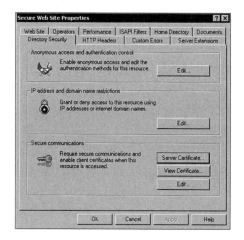

FIGURE 11.3
Web Site Properties: The Directory Security tab.

3. Click the **Server Certificate** button to start the **Web Server Certificate Wizard** (also called the **IIS Certificate Wizard**, depending on which page you are looking at).

4. The **Server Certificate** dialog box offers three choices:

    - **Create a new certificate.** This is the option we will follow. It enables you to specify some certificate parameters and to request and install the certificate.

    - **Assign an existing certificate.** If a suitable certificate is already on the computer, use this option. This choice can be used to install a removed IIS server with an existing key pair.

- **Import a certificate from a Key Manager backup file.** Use this option to import a certificate. (Key Manager is a holdover term from the Windows NT 4 service that performed the same function as Certification Services on Windows 2000.) You will be prompted to enter the name of the backup file. This would be the appropriate choice if you have obtained a certificate from a commercial certification authority.

5. If you chose **Create a new certificate** in Step 4, the next dialog box is titled **Delayed or Immediate Request** and offers two choices:

- **Prepare the request now but send it later.** In most cases, you will use this choice to obtain a certificate from a commercial certification authority. Consult with your certificate vendor for the procedures to use.

- **Send the request immediately to an online certification authority.** Use this choice to send the request to an online enterprise CA on a Windows 2000 Server. This is the choice taken in this example.

6. The **Name and Security Settings** dialog box has the following options:

- **Name.** Specify the name for the new certificate. By default, the certificate name is the same as the name of the Web server that was right-clicked in Step 1. Because this certificate will support all sites on this IIS server, you may wish to choose a more general name.

- **Bit length.** Select or enter a bit length for the key pair. The default length is 512 bits. Per discussion in the previous chapter, public key cryptography authorities now recommend using keys with a minimum length of 1,024 bits. 2,048 bits would not be inappropriate for an e-commerce site. Keep in mind that longer keys will demand more processing by the server and the client. However, these keys are used only during the handshake phase. When data are exchanged a more efficient symmetric cipher is employed.

- **Server Gated Cryptography (SGC) certificate (for export versions only).** This protocol enables financial institutions to use 128-bit cryptography with export versions of Windows 2000 Server. With the relaxation of U.S. cryptography export restrictions, other, preferable cipher suites are now available for users outside the United States.

7. The **Organization Information** dialog box has two fields:

- **Organization.** Enter the name of your organization.

- **Organizational unit.** Select an OU from the pull-down list. This entry is informational only and usually corresponds to the OU of the Windows 2000 Server on which IIS is running.

8. In the **Your Site's Common Name** dialog box, enter the name for the server as it will appear in the certificate. Typically, this is the server's fully-qualified DNS domain name or its NetBIOS name. If this name changes, a new certificate must be obtained for the server.

9. The **Geographic Information** dialog box has three fields that accept entries describing the server's location:

   - **Country/Region**
   - **State/province**
   - **City/locality**

10. In the **Choose a Certification Authority**, select an available enterprise CA to process your request. Only enterprise CAs appear in the drop-down list.

11. After reviewing the parameters for the certificate request on the last page of the wizard, click **Finish** to initiate processing. The certificate will be installed after it is approved.

12. After the certificate is installed, the **Web Site Properties** dialog box is displayed. We'll discuss property settings related to SSL/TLS in the next section.

The **Web Server Certificate Wizard** is used to request, renew, install, and remove certificates used by IIS. When you start the wizard as described in Steps 1 and 2 above, the wizard displays choices that are appropriate depending on whether a certificate is installed or not. To open the wizard at another time, right-click a Web site in the IIS console and choose **Properties** from the context menu.

Configuring Web Site Security Properties for SSL/TLS

In the **Web Site Properties** dialog box, select the **Directory Security** tab to configure properties associated with secure communication. As shown in Figure 11.3, three buttons appear under the **Secure communications** heading:

- **Server Certificate.** This option starts the **Web Server Certificate Wizard,** which can be used at any time to renew, remove, or replace the Web server certificate.

- **View Certificate.** This button opens the **Certificate** dialog box to view certificate properties and to export the certificate. See the section "Examining Certificate Contents" in Chapter 10 for more information.

- **Edit.** This button opens **Secure Communications** dialog box shown in Figure 11.4.

FIGURE 11.4

The Secure Communications dialog box enables certificate-based security support for a Web site.

The **Secure Communications** dialog box can be opened only after a certificate has been installed as described in the previous section. Properties in the **Secure Communications** dialog box are as follows:

- **Require secure channel (SSL).** If you select this option, this Web site will communicate only by using SSL/TLS security. Attempts to open a session by a client that does not support SSL/TLS will be rejected. If this option is not selected, the Web site operates in normal, unsecured mode only.

NOTE

To emphasize a point, if **Require secure channel (SSL)** is enabled, the Web site is an entirely secure site. Secure HTML must be used to access even innocuous Web pages on the site. In general, secure Web sites should be used only for Web communications that must be protected by encryption.

- **Require 128-bit encryption.** When enabled, SSL/TLS sessions require a minimum key length of 128 bits, which in turn requires a client that supports key lengths of 128 bits or greater. This option is active only if **Require secure channel (SSL)** is selected. If Web communications include sensitive data, such as financial transactions or personal information, you should enable 128-bit encryption. The default key length is 40 bits, which is often used on Internet Web servers to support clients that have not been upgraded for 128-bit encryption. (The High Encryption Pack is required to use 128-bit encryption. See Chapter 8, "Supporting Dial-Up Connections with Routing and Remote Access Service" for more information.)

- **Client certificates** offers three choices:
    - **Ignore client certificates.** Certificates will not be used to authenticate clients even if the client presents a certificate to the server.
    - **Accept client certificates.** Client certificates are accepted and, optionally, used to authenticate the client.
    - **Require client certificate.** Select this option to require authentication of the client using the client's certificate. This option is active only if **Require secure channel (SSL)** is enabled.
- **Enable client certificate mapping.** When enabled, client certificate mapping associates a certificate with a user account, enabling administrators to control access to Web resources using user accounts and groups. Click **Edit** under this heading to open the **Account Mappings** dialog box where you can configure one-to-one and many-to-one (many users to one certificate) mappings. You will need a certificate export file for each certificate to be defined. See IIS Help under the topic "Mapping Client Certificates to User Accounts" for more information.
- **Enable certificate trust list.** If this setting is enabled, you can specify an existing file that contains a CTL or click **New** to start the **Certificate Trust List Wizard,** which enables you to create a new CTL. See the note in the section "Automating Certificate Requests" of Chapter 10 for a brief discussion of CTLs.

SSL/TLS security can be balanced with other user access control options. Let's look at an example. Under the **Anonymous access and authentication control** heading on the **Directory Security** tab of **Web Site Properties**, the **Anonymous Access** option enables users to connect to the Web site without password authentication. If the client has a certificate that is recognized by the server, even anonymous users can be authenticated transparently. You can even require client certificates if you want every client to be securely identified.

Conclusions About SSL/TLS

SSL/TLS is the standard method for securing communication with Web servers, and can be used by any application-layer process that is written to the SSL/TLS APIs. Software development tools such as Microsoft Visual C++ and Visual Basic are equipped to create SSL/TLS-aware applications.

The limitations of SSL/TLS are that it does not provide security transparently, which is why applications that aren't SSL/TLS-aware aren't protected, and that it does not protect data at the internet protocol layer and higher. Consequently, Internet researchers are developing a new method of encrypting IP traffic that operates transparently to upper-layer protocols. This more generalized approach to IP data encryption is IPSec, to which we next turn our attention.

The IP Security Service (IPSec)

Unlike SSL/TLS, IPSec (RFC2401) is not a separate Internet protocol but a set of enhancements for IP that enable upper-layer data to be checked for integrity and, if necessary, encrypted. IPSec functions at Layer 3 (the Network layer of the OSI seven-layer model, corresponding to the Internet layer of the Internet model). Consequently IPSec does not add layers to the Internet protocol model and is completely transparent to upper-layer protocols. This isn't to say that SSL/TLS will fall into disuse any time soon, but because IPSec provides a general-purpose answer to TCP/IP security requirements, IPSec represents the future direction of communication security on the Internet.

Besides protocol transparency, IPSec has several useful capabilities. Among them are

- End-to-end security. Only the endpoints (referred to as *peers*) need to be IPSec-aware, and all communications between the endpoints are protected.
- Protection from interception, modification, and optionally from access for all data exchanged by the peers.
- Support for two security protocols enabling administrators to protect data for integrity, authentication, and security as needed.
- Control over the frequency with which keys are changed according to the sensitivity of the data.
- Protection against replay attacks and mitigation of denial-of-service attacks.
- A variety of authentication methods, including public key certificates and shared secrets.

Additionally, on Windows 2000 networks, IPSec uses secure domains as the trust model, supports Kerberos v5 authentication, and can be deployed simply using Group Policy.

Before looking at IPSec implementation issues, we need to examine two topics:

- IPSec security protocols
- Security Associations and key management

IPSec Security Protocols

IPSec supports two security protocols:

- *Authentication header* (AH; RFC2402) protects data integrity and authentication.
- *Encapsulating security payload* (ESP; RFC2406) provides data encryption, integrity, and confidentiality.

Because ESP employs encryption to guard confidentiality, it has greater processing overhead than AH. Consequently, AH is provided as an alternative when message integrity is the primary concern. Because AH provides broader integrity protection than ESP, in some cases both protocols may be employed.

Let's look more closely at the capabilities and datagram structures for AH and ESP.

The Authentication Header Protocol

When AH is employed, the structure of the IP datagram is as shown in Figure 11.5. An AH header is inserted between the original IP header and the TCP header, and use of AH is indicated by a value of 51 in the Protocol field of the IP header. The AH header contains two crucial elements:

- **Security Parameters Index (SPI).** Along with the destination address and security protocol, the SPI identifies the security association used for a given connection. See "Security Associations and Key Management" later in the chapter for more information.

- **Sequence Number.** Each datagram is assigned a 32-bit number that is incremented with each datagram sent. Receivers reject datagrams with sequence numbers that have appeared in earlier datagrams. Consequently, it is impossible for someone to capture a packet and replay it at a later time.

- **Authentication Data.** This field contains the hash checksum that verifies integrity.

Note in Figure 11.5 that the AH signature provides integrity protection for IP and all higher layers.

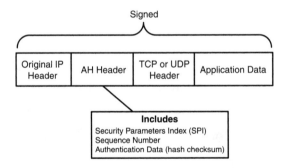

FIGURE 11.5

Datagram structure with the authentication header protocol.

The Encapsulating Security Protocol

All data protected by ESP are encrypted and signed for integrity. Figure 11.6 illustrates the structure of an IP datagram that is protected by ESP. An ESP header and two ESP trailers are added to the packet, providing the following functions:

- **ESP header.** This header contains a security parameters index that has the same function as the SPI in the AH protocol header. It also contains a sequence number to prevent packet replay.

- **ESP trailer.** This trailer provides padding so that the block cipher works with 32-bit blocks, and also contains the protocol ID for the payload, for example TCP or UDP.

- **ESP authentication trailer.** This trailer contains an Integrity Check Value (ICV), a message digest that comprehends the ESP header, payload, and ESP trailer. It also includes a message authentication code that identifies the sender and provides message integrity.

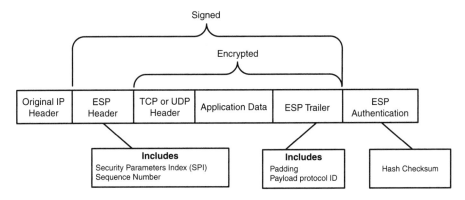

FIGURE 11.6

Datagram structure with the encapsulating security protocol.

Two ESP characteristics should be noted:

- The data and ESP trailer are encrypted.
- The ESP header, data, and ESP trailer are signed. If the integrity of the IP header must be guaranteed, AH can be used in addition to ESP.

NOTE

Security protocols can be nested. For example, ESP can be used to secure a data payload that is already protected by ESP. This might be done when bringing data into a secure site. Routers (perhaps implementing a VPN) would use ESP to ensure that all communications between two sites are secure. A nested ESP or AH payload would provide security between the two communication endpoints.

Security Associations and Key Management

A *security association* (SA) is required for every IPSec connection between peers. If communication flows in both directions between the peers, two SAs are required. Because IPSec communication relies on multiple SAs, it becomes difficult for all communication between the peers to be compromised.

A security association is essentially a communications contract between two peers. The parameters in the SA are negotiated by the peers and define three critical factors:

- An encryption algorithm, usually DES or 3DES
- A message digest algorithm, either SHA and MD5
- A session key, obtained from the Internet Key Exchange

For each SA, there is a unique *security parameter index* (SPI) that enables peers to identify the SA. In instances when a computer such as a server is involved with multiple IPSec connections, the SPI enables the computer to determine the SA that should be used for each connection. The SPI is included in the Security Parameters Index fields that are included in AH or ESP headers.

Of the SA components, only the method of obtaining the key was not discussed earlier in the chapter. To understand how keys are generated, we need to turn our attention to the Internet Key Exchange.

The Internet Key Exchange

The Internet Key Exchange (IKE; RFC2409) has several extremely important responsibilities regarding IPSec:

- Exchange of key material used to generate session keys
- SA negotiation
- Authentication of the communication peers

IKE is a combination of two protocols:

- The Internet Security Association Key Management Protocol (ISAKMP; RFC 2408) defines methods for authenticating peers, creation and management of SAs, key generation, and mitigating threats such as denial of service and replay attacks.
- The OAKLEY Key Determination Protocol (OAKLEY; RFC2412) is used to establish a shared secret that can be used as a key during data exchange.

NOTE

The OAKLEY protocol was developed by the Computer Science department at the University of Arizona. It is not an Internet Standard and RFC2412 is simply informational, providing documentation to the Internet community. This situation is not as unusual as you may think. In many cases developers of protocols want to retain rights to the protocols, perhaps to obtain revenues through licensing. Another example is the Network File System (NFS) developed by Sun Microsystems and the standard protocol for sharing files on UNIX. Sun retains ownership and licensing control of NFS, but the protocol is documented in RFC1094.

Internet Key Exchange Phases

To improve performance, IKE negotiates SAs in two phases. A Phase I (phase one) SA establishes a secure, authenticated channel between peers. The Phase I SA is used to negotiate Phase II SAs on behalf of IPSec. Let's look at these phases to see what they contribute to the IPSec big picture.

IKE Phase I Negotiations

During IKE Phase I, IKE negotiates with computers requesting an IPSec connection to determine the following communication parameters:

- The encryption algorithm: DES or 3DES

- The message digest algorithm: SHA or MD5

- The authentication method: public key certificate, pre-arranged shared secret, or Kerberos v5 (Windows 2000 only). If certificates or shared secrets are used, the computer's identity is protected. If Kerberos is used, the computer identity is unencrypted until the entire identity is encrypted during authentication. IPSec communication cannot be enabled unless both peers are authenticated.

- The Diffie-Hellman (DH) group that will provide the base keying material (the prime numbers that are used to generate keys). The DH group provides the starting point used by the DH algorithm for generating keys during IKE Phase II. Four DH groups are defined, numbered one through four from least to most secure. These DH groups are defined in the OAKLEY protocol specification and are also referred to as OAKLEY groups. OAKLEY also determines key refresh and regeneration parameters.

An IKE Phase I SA must be negotiated at the beginning of every attempt to establish IPSec communication. When attempting to initiate IPSec communication, the following exchange takes place:

1. **Policy negotiation.** The peers agree on secure communication parameters that are used during the remainder of the Phase I negotiation. Parameters are agreed upon as follows:

   a. The initiator transmits a proposal consisting of the security parameters that it considers adequate for the session.

   b. The responder can either accept the initiator's proposal or return a proposal of its own. The responder may require more secure parameters or may be unable to support a parameter in the proposal, in which case the responder creates a proposal and returns it to the initiator.

   c. Proposal exchanges continue until one peer accepts the other peer's proposal.

2. **DH exchange.** DH is used to generate keying material that is shared between the peers. Then the IKE service on each of the peers uses the keying material to generate a *master key*, known only to the peers, which is used to protect communication during the authentication phase.

3. **Authentication.** The peers attempt to authenticate each other. The master key from Step 2 is used, along with the protocols agreed upon in Step 1, to hash and encrypt identity data exchanged during this phase, protecting confidentiality and integrity of the data.

With the IKE Phase I SA established, the peers can proceed to IKE Phase II.

IKE Phase II Negotiations

All Phase II communications are protected by the Phase I SA. The Phase I SA must be generated only once and can be used to protect any number of Phase II negotiations between the peers. (However, Phase I SAs do have lifetime limits and must be regenerated after a prespecified period of time.)

Phase II negotiations are conducted as follows:

1. **Policy negotiation.** The peers agree on security parameters: AH or ESP, 3DES or DES, SHA or MD5. After reaching agreement, two SAs are established, one for each communication direction. An SPI is created for each SA.

2. **Session key material refresh and key generation.** IKE refreshes the Diffie-Hellman key material, after which the peers generate new shared or secret keys for use in authentication and, if ESP is enabled, encryption. If required, a new DH exchange is conducted to generate a new key.

3. The SAs, SPIs, and keys are forwarded to IPSec.

Phase II negotiations must take place for every IPSec connection. Because no two connections have the same SA, compromise of one connection does not jeopardize data in another connection.

> **NOTE**
>
> The keys associated with master and session keys have limited lifetimes. When the keys expire, new SAs must be created.
>
> Phase I SAs are deleted and regenerated by IKE when their lifetimes expire.
>
> Phase II SAs are deleted and regenerated by the IPSec driver.

Key Protection

The effectiveness of IPSec security depends on the DH keying material and the strengths of the master and session keys. Several IPSec capabilities can be used to enhance key strength.

Automatic key regeneration renews keys when their lifetimes expire. As discussed earlier in the chapter, a key should be used for a limited time so that damage is minimized if a key is cracked. Key lifetimes can be specified for master and session keys. When a key's lifetime expires, a new SA is negotiated and the key is refreshed or regenerated. Microsoft recommends that a single key should not be used to protect more than 100 megabytes. Configuration of automatic key regeneration is optional.

Session key refresh limits determine when keys are regenerated (as opposed to being refreshed off existing key material). If the same key material is used too often the shared secret may be compromised. Consequently it is recommended that new key material be generated at intervals that are appropriate to the security requirements. Of course, regenerating key material increases processing overhead.

Perfect Forward Secrecy (PFS) provides the strongest possible key protection. PFS does not permit keys to be refreshed from existing key material. The key must be regenerated using new key material. When PFS is applied to master keys, a new IKE Phase I negotiation is required each time a Phase II negotiation takes place, a process that requires re-authentication and significantly increases processing requirements. If PFS is enabled on either peer, it is in effect for the connection.

Diffie-Hellman Groups determine the lengths of the base prime numbers that provide the keying material for the DH exchange. Windows 2000 supports two DH groups. Group 1 protects 768 bits of keying material. Group 2 protects 1,024 bits of keying material. Larger DH groups provide greater security. The same DH group is used for both Phase I and Phase II SA negotiations.

Windows 2000 IPSec configuration consists of creating IPSec policies in Group Policy and assigning IPSec policies to computers. IPSec policies can get rather complicated once you get past the defaults, so most of our remaining discussion will focus on the management of IPSec policies.

IPSec Policies

Windows 2000 computers obtain their IPSec configuration settings from IPSec policies. These policies can get rather complicated once you get past the defaults, so most of our remaining discussion regarding IPSec will focus on the management of these policies.

Overview of IPSec Policy Assignment

An IPSec policy can be assigned to a Windows 2000 computer in one of three ways:

- Group Policy can be used to assign policies stored in Active Directory to sites, domains, and OUs. Computers in those containers are assigned an IPSec policy based on the priorities of any Group Policy policy assignments that apply to the computer's container.

- Locally-stored IPSec policies can be created on domain-member computers. A local policy can be assigned to a computer only if the computer has not been assigned an IPSec policy through Group Policy.

- Locally-stored IPSec policies can be created on stand-alone computers (non-domain members) and assigned locally.

IPSec policies are managed in two ways: using the **IPSec Security Policy Management** snap-in for the MMC and through the **Group Policy** snap-in.

Figure 11.7 shows an MMC console to which I have added two instances of the **IPSec Security Policy Management** snap-in. (From now on, if you don't mind or even if you do, I'll compress the name to **IPSec** console. It will shorten discussion considerably.) The first instance, selected in the figure, manages IPSec policies on the local machine. The second instance manages IPSec policies for a domain. We'll look at the IPSec console in greater detail a bit later in the section "Managing IPSec Policies."

NOTE

The IPSec console can edit IPSec policies for the local computer, another Active Directory computer, the local computer's domain, or another domain.

Before a policy becomes active it must be assigned. The IPSec console can assign IPSec policies only to the computers that it manages. It cannot assign IPSec policies to Active Directory objects. IPSec policies for sites, domains, and OUs must be assigned using Group Policy.

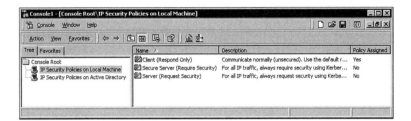

FIGURE 11.7

IPSec policies for computers and domains can be managed in the IPSec Security Policy Management console.

To manage Active Directory Group Policy objects through the **Group Policy** console, open a Group Policy object in the Group Policy console. Then select **Computer Configuration→Windows Settings→Security Settings→IPSec Policies on Active Directory**. A typical result is shown in Figure 11.8.

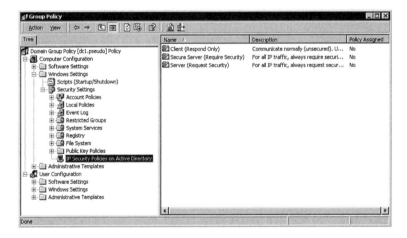

FIGURE 11.8

IPSec policies for Group Policy objects can be created, edited, and assigned to Group Policy objects in the Group Policy console.

At any given time, exactly one IPSec policy can be in effect on a given computer. IPSec policies may be assigned at four levels:

- **Computer.** An individual IPSec policy can be assigned to individual computers using the IPSec console.

- **Site.** An IPSec policy can be assigned to the Group Policy for a site. An IPSec policy assigned to a site overrides any IPSec policy that may be assigned to individual computers at the site.

- **Domain.** An IPSec policy can be assigned to the Group Policy for a domain. An IPSec policy assigned to an OU overrides any IPSec policy that may be assigned to the OU's site or to computers at the site. (Unless the **No Override** option is active for the site Group Policy object.)
- **Organizational Unit.** An IPSec policy can be assigned to the Group Policy for an OU. An IPSec policy assigned to an OU overrides any IPSec policy that may be assigned to the OU's site or parent domain as well as IPSec policies assigned to computers contained by the OU. (Unless the **No Override** option is active for the site or domain Group Policy object.)

Windows 2000 Server includes three default IPSec policies:

- **Client (Respond Only).** The client normally communicates unsecured, but will negotiate secured connections when requested or required to do so. Security is applied only to the protocol and port that is requested by the other computer.
- **Server (Request Security).** This policy is normally applied to servers. The server will request a secure connection but will accept unsecured IP traffic. This policy might be chosen if you prefer to have IP security but still want to support computers that do not have IPSec capability.
- **Secure Server (Require Security).** This policy is normally applied to servers. The server requires secure communication for all IP communication.

These policies are general in nature. They do not specify particular IP addresses, for example. If a server is configured with the `Secure Server (Require Security)` policy, *all* hosts that communicate with the server must do so using IPSec.

In many cases, it is necessary to configure IPSec policies that affect particular computers. If, for example, you want a policy to ensure that all communication between computers Alpha and Beta will be protected, you can configure individual IPSec policy settings that affect communication only between those computers' specific IP addresses.

Because IPSec policy management often branches off into wizards and extra dialog boxes, it's difficult to discuss IPSec policies in a linear fashion. Let's take a high-level look at IPSec policies and then return to particular procedures.

> **NOTE**
>
> So that I don't wind up covering things twice, I'll explain how to create a new IPSec policy after we've examined all the settings that make up a policy. The section "Creating IPSec Policies" appears near the end of our discussion about IPSec policies.

IPSec Policy Elements

An IPSec policy is a fairly complicated thing that is made up of several layers of properties. It's easy to get lost in the layers, so I'm going to stop occasionally to keep you centered. Before we get into details, let's look at the elements of an IPSec policy and see how they relate. Our discussion is illustrated in Figure 11.9.

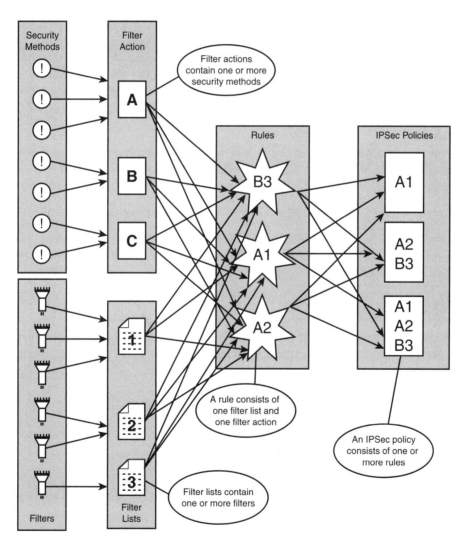

FIGURE 11.9

The elements of IPSec policies and their interrelationships.

IPSec policies and their elements are defined in one of two types of environments:

- In an Active Directory tree, where they are available for use in any site, domain, or OU.
- In a computer, where they are available only locally.

IPSec policies are constructed of five types of elements: filters, filter lists, security methods, filter actions, and security rules. We'll look at each of these elements briefly and see how they contribute to an IPSec policy.

Filters

Filters are the most atomic decision-making elements of IPSec policies. Each filter matches a particular set of conditions; for example, packets sent from a particular subnet to a particular computer.

Filter Lists

Filter lists are bundles consisting of one or more filters. When network conditions match one or more of the filters, the filter list is activated. Thus, a filter list can be activated by a variety of network conditions.

Each filter is defined for a specific filter list. Filters cannot be shared by multiple filter lists.

Filter lists, however, are defined individually, and all filter lists in an environment are available for use in all IPSec policies defined in that environment. Consequently, a given filter list can be incorporated into several IPSec policies.

Security Methods

Security methods match a particular set of IPSec security algorithms and settings, and are used to define proposals during IKE policy negotiations. For example, a security method might specify use of EAP with 3DES encryption and SHA-1 integrity, requiring key regeneration at 100MB or 600-second intervals. In other words, a security method defines one set of security methods with which a computer is willing to establish an IPSec session.

Filter Actions

Filter actions are lists of security methods, ranked in order of preference. When a computer negotiates an IPSec session, it consults its filter actions list and accepts or sends proposals based on the settings defined in the security methods.

Each security method is defined for a specific filter action. Security methods cannot be shared by multiple security actions.

Security actions, however, are defined individually, and all security actions in an environment are available for use in all IPSec policies defined in that environment. Consequently, a given security action can be incorporated into several IPSec policies.

Security Rules

Security rules (usually referred to simply as *rules*) consist of exactly one filter list and one filter action, selected from the filter lists and filter actions that are available in the environment. In addition to the filter list and filter action, a rule specifies authentication methods, network tunnel settings, and connection types that are supported for the rule.

Security rules are defined individually, and all security rules in an environment are available for use in all IPSec policies defined in that environment. Consequently, a given security rule can be incorporated into several IPSec policies.

IPSec Policies and Security Rules

IPSec policies consist of one or more security rules, selected from the security rules that are defined in the environment. At any one time, a computer may be assigned one IPSec policy or none. When the IPSec policy is assigned to the computer, IPSec is active on the computer and monitors network traffic until network traffic matches one of the filters in the policy filter list. When a filter is matched, the filter action for the rule determines the rules that may be used to negotiate an IPSec session.

> **NOTE**
>
> Because filter lists and filter actions are separate objects that are merely referenced by IPSec policies, you can approach IPSec policy creation from two directions:
>
> - You can create a new policy, add a rule, and then define the filter lists and filter actions needed for the rule.
> - You can define the filter lists, filter actions, and security rules first and then incorporate them into policies. See the section "Managing IPSec Filter Lists and Filter Actions" for procedures that enable you to create and edit filter lists and filter actions separately from policies and rules.

IPSec Policy Properties

Now that we've looked at the elements of an IPSec policy, working from filters and security methods to build a policy, we'll look at the details for each element. This time, since this is the way you typically view things, we'll start with IPSec policies and work down to the filters and security methods.

To examine or edit properties of an IPSec policy, right-click the policy in the **IPSec** console or in the **Group Policy** console and choose **Properties** in the context menu. This will open the **IPSec Policy Properties** dialog box with the **Rules** tab selected, as shown in Figure 11.10. The policy in the figure is Secure Server (Require Security) default policy, which is used in the following discussion unless otherwise noted.

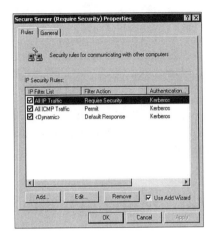

FIGURE 11.10
IPSec Policy Properties: The Rules tab.

While a computer can be assigned only one active IPSec policy at a given time, within that policy rules make it possible to define multiple actions that may be taken in different situations. Each set of IPSec rules is associated with a filter list that determines the type of network traffic to which the rule applies. Depending on the ways rules are defined, the same IPSec policy can have different effects on different computers, or it can have different effects on the same computer in different situations.

IP security rules are listed on the **Rules** tab of the **IPSec Policy Properties** dialog box shown in Figure 11.10. The procedures for adding and editing rules are discussed in a later section titled "Defining IPSec Policy Security Rules."

Figure 11.11 shows the **General** tab of the **IPSec Policy Properties** dialog box. This tab has three editable fields:

- **Name.** This name is purely descriptive and does not determine any IPSec policy properties.

- **Description.** A detailed description of the IPSec policy can be entered here. Since IPSec policies can be complicated, it is useful to provide a detailed description for each, including the action(s) it takes, when those actions are taken, and the protocols to which the policy applies.

- **Check for policy changes every...minutes.** If a domain-based computer is assigned this policy, this setting determines how often it will visit Active Directory to see if there are any updates to the policy.

The **Advanced** button on the **General** tab opens up a dialog box where key exchange settings can be modified. We'll examine those settings in the next section.

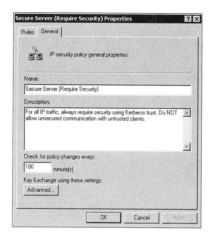

FIGURE 11.11
IPSec Policy Properties: The General tab.

Defining IPSec Policy Key Exchange Settings

Rules are much more complicated than key exchange settings, so let's deal with the shorter topic first. The previous section explained that the **Advanced** button on the **General** tab (see Figure 11.11) of the **IPSec Policy Properties** dialog box is used to access settings related to key exchange. These settings apply to the master key that is generated during IKE Phase I and is used during IKE Phase II to generate session keys.

The **Key Exchange Settings** dialog box is shown in Figure 11.12 and has the following options:

- **Master key Perfect Forward Security.** Selecting this option ensures that a given master key will be used to generate a single session key. Security is greatly enhanced but at a very high cost. Each time the master key is regenerated a new IKE Phase I negotiation is required.

- **Authenticate and generate a new key after every...minutes.** This option specifies the maximum number of minutes the master key may be reused before it must be regenerated. Master key regeneration requires a new IKE Phase I negotiation.

- **Authenticate and generate a new key after every...session.** This option specifies the maximum number of session keys that can be generated before the master key must be regenerated. Master key regeneration requires a new IKE Phase I negotiation.

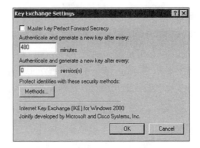

FIGURE 11.12
IPSec Policy Properties: Key exchange settings.

The **Methods** button in the **Key Exchange Settings** dialog box opens the **Key Exchange Security Methods** dialog box shown in Figure 11.13. This dialog box lists security methods that the computer regards as acceptable during IKE key negotiations, ranked by preference. You can add new security methods or edit existing ones.

Each security method consists of three parameters:

- **Integrity Algorithm.** Either SHA1 or MD5 may be specified.
- **Encryption Algorithm.** Either 3DES or DES may be chosen.
- **Diffie-Hellman Group.** Either Low(1) or Medium(2) may be selected. Low(1) protects 768 bits of key material. Medium(2) protects 1,024 bits of key material and therefore provides greater security.

FIGURE 11.13
This example shows security methods for the Secure Server (Require Security) policy.

The policy being illustrated has minimum requirements of DES and MD5. This is actually a fairly casual minimum setting that should be permitted only when the connection carries data of short-term value. In situations requiring greater security, you would be wise to remove the security methods that permit DES encryption.

> **NOTE**
>
> An alternative might be to allow DES but to require key refresh and regeneration at more frequent intervals. That way, if a single DES key is cracked only part of the data are compromised.
>
> In any case, cracking a single DES key only jeopardizes half of the conversation. Recall that a separate SA, and therefore a separate session key, is required for each half of a duplex connection. At present, it would take several days on a state-of-the-art network cluster to crack DES and become privy to the entire data exchange that took place between key refresh events. Unless your data are extremely critical (financial data come to mind), the risk of using DES is not terribly severe.

For the predefined IPSec policies, the security methods listed in the **Key Exchange Security Methods** are ranked starting with the most secure method that is supported. Two reasons why you might want to edit security methods in policies are to raise the minimum security requirement or, in appropriate situations, to grant preference to less strict methods in order to reduce processing overhead.

Defining IPSec Policy Security Rules

An IPSec policy has one or more rules that define different IP security settings for different types of network traffic. Rules enable a single IPSec policy to have multiple actions. Let's look at a simple example of the way rules determine IPSec behavior.

> **NOTE**
>
> We are going to be drilling down through a pretty deep properties hierarchy, so each time we descend, I'm going to include an organizer. In this section, we are at this level in the IPSec policy properties hierarchy:
>
> IPSec policy properties→rules

Suppose that a company has two subnets, 10.1.0.0/16 and 10.2.0.0/16, both of which connect to separate interfaces on a server such the one shown in Figure 11.14. The company requires the following IP security behavior:

- Computers on subnet 10.1.0.0/16 should not communicate with the server using IPSec.

- Computers on subnet 10.2.0.0/16 must always communicate with the server using IPSec.

- Clients on both subnets communicate with the server but clients on one subnet do not communicate with clients on the other subnet. (To keep the example simple, I'm ignoring this possibility, which requires adding more rules to the IPSec policy. I'm also ignoring other servers that might be on the two subnets.)

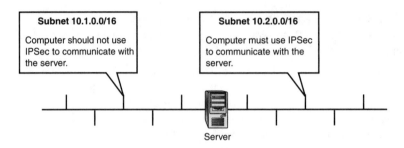

FIGURE 11.14

Computers on subnet 10.1.0.0/16 should not use IPSec. Computers on subnet 10.2.0.0/16 must use IPSec.

The server must behave differently depending on the network with which it is communicating. A computer can be assigned only one IPSec policy, so we need to configure the same IPSec policy to do two things. This is accomplished by creating two rules as follows:

- Rule A matches datagrams with source or destination IP addresses on subnet 10.1.0.0/16. This rule does not require IP security.
- Rule B matches datagrams with source or destination IP addresses on subnet 10.2.0.0/16. This rule requires IP security.

For Rule B to take effect, all computers on subnet 10.2.0.0/16 must be configured with the IPSec policy `Client (Respond Only)` so they will enter into IPSec negotiations when IP security is required by the server. (Actually, any of the default policies would have the desired effect, but it's usually best to let the server's IPSec policy determine the need for security.)

Filters defined in the rules determine the type or types of traffic a rule applies to. Rules are defined on the **Rules** tab of the **IPSec Security Policy** dialog box, shown in Figure 11.10.

Windows 2000 starts with two pre-defined rules:

- `All IP Traffic`. As initially defined, filters in this rule match all IP datagrams. Therefore, this rule defines security settings for all communication over the IP protocol.
- `All ICMP Traffic`. As initially defined, filters in this rule match only ICMP datagrams. Therefore, this rule defines security settings for ICMP only.

A third default rule, named <Dynamic> on the **IPSec Policy Properties** dialog box, can be added when an IPSec policy is defined. The <Dynamic> rule cannot be added or removed after the IPSec policy is created. In an existing policy, it can only be edited or disabled. This rule defines default security settings that are effective when no other rules apply. A `<Dynamic>` rule is included in the `Server (Request Security)` and `Secure Server (Require Security)` policies.

Click **Add** to define a new rule. To modify an existing rule, select the rule and click **Edit**. The dialog boxes used to add or edit a rule differ only in their titles. We'll examine the properties of a rule using the **Edit** option.

Figure 11.15 shows the **Edit Rule Properties** dialog box displayed while editing an existing rule. To see the rule shown, do the following:

1. Open the **Properties** dialog box for the default rule `Secure Server (Require Security)`, shown in Figure 11.10.

2. Select the `All IP Traffic` rule and click **Edit**.

We'll go through the properties tabs one at a time.

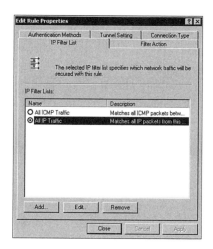

FIGURE 11.15
IPSec Policy Rule Properties: the IP Filter List tab.

IPSec Policy Rule Properties: The IP Filter List Tab

A rule in an IPSec policy can be assigned exactly one *filter list* that specifies the conditions under which the rule is invoked.

NOTE

In this section, we are at this level in the IPSec policy properties hierarchy:

IPSec policy properties→rules→filter lists

A filter list consists of one or more filters that determine the types of network traffic to which the rule applies. At least one filter list must be defined for each IPSec policy rule. The **IP Filter List** tab (see Figure 11.15) displays the filter lists that have been defined for the rule. Only one of these filter lists can be active at a given time. Windows 2000 Server starts with two default filter lists:

- `All ICMP Traffic`. By default, filters in this filter list match only ICMP datagrams.
- `All IP Traffic`. By default, filters in this filter list match only IP datagrams.

> **NOTE**
>
> Remember that a filter list can be used in any rule in the same environment. It doesn't matter that the filter list is being created or edited while working on a particular rule.
>
> A corollary to the above statement is that modifying a filter list affects all rules using that filter list. It is essential not to make changes for the sake of one rule without determining the effects of the changes on other rules.

New filter lists can be added and existing filter lists can be edited using the **Add** and **Edit** buttons on the **IP Filter List** tab. The dialog boxes used to add or edit filter lists are identical apart from their titles.

Filter lists are added or edited in the **IP Filter List** dialog box shown in Figure 11.16. The figure shows the dialog boxes used to edit the `All IP Traffic` filter list. The dialog box has three fields and a check box:

- **Name.** This is the name that appears in the **IP Filter List** tab of the **IP Security Rules Properties** dialog box.
- **Description.** This is the description that appears in the **IP Filter List** tab of the **IP Security Rules Properties** dialog box.
- **Filters.** This list must contain at least one filter, but can contain as many filters as are required.
- **Use Add Wizard.** If this box is checked, clicking the **Add** button starts the **IP Filter Wizard**. If this box is not checked, clicking the **Add** button opens the **Filter Properties** dialog boxes. Both approaches can be used to define a new filter.

A filter list must include one filter but can incorporate many more. Filters in **IP Filters List** can be added, removed, or edited, as discussed in the next section.

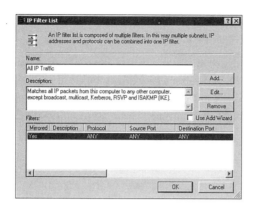

FIGURE 11.16
The IP Filter List tab lists all filters that are included in the filter list. A filter list must include at least one filter.

CAUTION

A lot of confusion can arise due to the names of rules and filter lists. By default, there is a rule named All IP Traffic that incorporates the filter list named All IP Traffic. That alone can make it easy to lose track of what you're working with and how things relate. (Or is it only me?) It is important to remember that this rule and this filter list don't have to be used together. A rule named All IP Traffic could just as easily use a filter list named Some TCP Traffic or Traffic from Joe's computer to Betty's. It wouldn't be a good idea to set things up that way, but it could happen.

Given names such as All IP Traffic, it is also easy to forget that the names are simply labels. They do not determine any of the functional properties of the rule or filter list, and a rule or filter list might do something that has nothing to do with its name. Suppose that you are editing properties for the All IP Traffic rule. A bad mouse click on the **IP Filter List** tab could select the All ICMP Traffic filter list instead of the All IP Traffic filter list. Now you have a rule named All IP Traffic that actually uses filters for ICMP. This sort of error is all too easy to create when defining components of IPSec policies.

So don't pay too much attention to names. The only way to determine how a rule or filter list works is to drill down through the properties. The best help you can provide yourself and other administrators is to create and update detailed descriptions for IPSec policies, rules, filter lists, and filters as they are created and modified.

Defining Filters in Filter Lists A filter is the end of the line so far as nesting is concerned. A filter has properties, but it isn't a container.

Filters can be added using dialog boxes or the **IP Filter Wizard**. The wizard is activated if you check **Use Add Wizard** in the **IP Filters List** dialog box before clicking the **Add** button. The wizard is easy to apply, and I won't go through it here. If you understand the manual-entry dialog boxes discussed in the next section, you'll have no trouble with the wizard.

> **NOTE**
>
> In this section, we are at the following level in the IPSec policy properties hierarchy:
> IPSec policy properties→rules→filter lists→filters
>
> The **Filter Properties** dialog box we're working with in this section is nested pretty deeply. In fact, we've drilled down six levels from the desktop. I want to make sure we're on the same page, so let's review what we did to get here:
>
> 1. We opened the IPSec console or the Group Policy console.
> 2. We selected the **IP Security Policies** container.
> 3. We opened the **Properties** dialog box for the Secure Server (Require Security) IPSec policy.
> 4. In the **IPSec Policy Properties** dialog box, we opened the All IP Traffic rule for editing. (IPSec policies have rules.)
> 5. In the **Edit Rule Properties** dialog box, we opened the All IP Traffic filter list for editing. (IPSec rules have filter lists.)
> 6. In the **IP Filter List** dialog box, we opened the only filter that appears in the **IP Filter List** for editing. (IPSec filter lists have filters.)
>
> That puts us in the **Filter Properties** dialog box.

Figure 11.17 shows the **Addressing** tab for the **Filter Properties** dialog box used to define a filter. This tab has three fields:

- **Source address.** This field specifies the source addresses of datagrams to which the filter applies. Five choices are available for this field. Additional fields may be shown depending on the selection made in here.
  - My IP Address. This selection matches all IP addresses on the local computer and attempts to secure all datagrams that originate from this computer. Do not use this option if the filter should apply only to a specific interface. (This is the selection for the Secure Server (Require Security) policy because it forces the computer to require IP security for all outbound traffic.)

- `Any IP Address`. This selection matches all IP addresses. Select this option to secure all datagrams directed to this computer from any source. (The **Destination address** field can be configured to apply the filter to specific IP addresses on the local computer.)

- `A specific DNS Name`. Choose this option to specify the DNS name of the desired host. The specification matches all IP addresses that are published in DNS for the target host. (This option appears only if Windows 2000 Service Pack 1 is installed.)

- `A specific IP Address`. Select this option to apply security to datagrams sent from a particular local IP address. This option might be used to require IP security for traffic outbound on a particular cable segment. Alternatively, this option might be selected to apply security to all traffic that is inbound from a particular computer. If this option is selected, you must enter an IP address.

- `A specific IP Subnet`. Select this option to apply security to all datagrams originating from a particular subnet. This option might be used to enable IP security for all communication within a department. If this option is selected, you must enter an IP address and subnet mask.

- **Destination address.** This field offers the same options as **Source address**.

- **Mirrored.** If this option is selected, the filter will also match datagrams with the opposite source and destination addresses. Typically, the same rule should apply to both directions of a conversation. This is easily accomplished with mirroring.

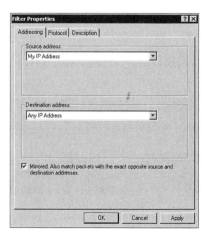

FIGURE 11.17

This dialog box lists properties for a filter appearing in a filter list.

The **Addressing** tab shown in Figure 11.17 is taken from the only filter that appears in the All IP Traffic filter list. The **Source address** value is My IP Address, the **Destination address** value is Any IP Address, and the **Mirrored** box is checked. Consequently, this filter matches any traffic to or from a computer that is configured with the rule. If mirroring was not enabled, the filter would match only traffic that is sent by the computer.

Figure 11.18 shows a more interesting filter that makes use of other address options. In this case, the filter applies to traffic sent from subnet 172.31.56.0 with mask 255.255.255.0 to computer 172.31.56.10. Because mirroring is enabled, traffic both to and from the specified computer is affected. A filter such as this might be used in a rule that requires IP security for all communication between the server 172.31.56.10 and computers on subnet 172.31.56.0/24.

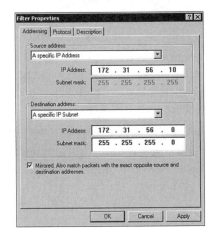

FIGURE 11.18

This filter matches traffic between a specific computer and a specific subnet.

The **Protocol** tab in the **Filter Properties** dialog box is shown in Figure 11.19. This tab has these fields:

- **Select a protocol type.** This field lists a variety of host-to-host layer protocols, including TCP, UDP, ICMP, and several that we haven't mentioned in this book.

    If you select TCP or UDP, the fields are active in the **Set the IP protocol port** box. The protocol ID spin box immediately below **Select a protocol type** is inactive.

    If you select Other, specify a protocol ID in the spin box immediately below **Select a protocol type**.

    If you select Any, the filter matches any and all protocols above the internet layer, in which case the computer will attempt to apply IP security for all upper-layer protocols. This, in fact, is the preferred choice in most cases, including the rule we are examining in the **Secure Server (Require Security)** IPSec policy.

NOTE

In Figure 11.19, I selected Other as the protocol type and then entered 6 as the proto-col ID. As a result, all of the fields on the tab are active for easier examination. 6 is the protocol ID for TCP, but ordinarily you would achieve the same result by selecting TCP as the protocol type.

- If TCP or UDP are selected in **Select a protocol type**, options under **Set the IP protocol port** are active. Application layer processes are identified by port numbers as follows:

    - **From any port.** The filter matches packets sent from any port for the selected protocol (TCP or UDP).

    - **From this port.** The filter matches packets sent from a specific port for the selected protocol (TCP or UDP). A port number must be specified.

    - **To any port.** The filter matches packets sent to any port for the selected protocol (TCP or UDP).

    - **To this port.** The filter matches packets sent to a specific port for the selected protocol (TCP or UDP). A port number must be specified.

If the rule must apply to more than one protocol and Any is not selected in **Select a protocol type**, an individual filter must be added to the filter list for each protocol.

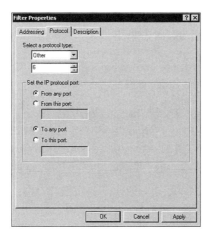

FIGURE 11.19

A filter can match all protocols or a specific protocol.

The **Description** tab in the **Filter Properties** dialog box contains a field where you can enter a description for the filter. Many of the parameters in a filter definition, such as the protocol ID and ports, are specified numerically. It is good practice to use the filter description to document clearly the traffic characteristics that match the filter.

Let's look at an example of a custom filter. Suppose that the Windows 2000 Server 192.168.88.3 is sharing files with UNIX clients using Sun's Network File System (NFS). The files are confidential and should be encrypted on the network. NFS is a UDP protocol that is assigned port 2049. Here are the parameters for a filter that matches those conditions:

- **Addressing** tab
    - **Source Address:** A specific IP address
    - **Source Address→IP address:** 192.168.88.3
    - **Destination Address:** Any IP address
    - **Mirrored:** checked
- **Protocol** tab:
    - **Protocol Type:** UDP
    - **From any port**
    - **To this port:** 2049
- **Description** tab: Matches NFS packets (port 2049) to and from IP address 192.168.88.3.

The filter list containing this rule will fire when a UDP datagram is sent to or from computer 192.168.88.3 to port 2049 from any port on the local computer. **From any port** is selected because clients typically select a local port dynamically when connecting to a remote service, and consequently the local port is not known beforehand. (The filter list takes effect only if it is used by a rule that is used by the IPSec policy that is assigned to computer 192.168.88.3.)

IPSec Policy Rule Properties: The Filter Action Tab

We return to the **IPSec Policy Rule Properties** dialog box, turning our attention to the **Filter Action** tab shown in Figure 11.20. This tab specifies the IPSec settings that are in effect if the rule matches the connection. Only one filter action can be selected for a rule.

NOTE

In this section, we are at the following level in the IPSec policy properties hierarchy:
IPSec policy properties→rules→filter actions

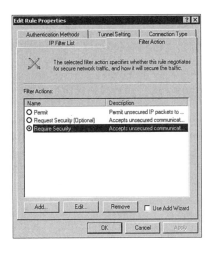

FIGURE 11.20
Filter actions determine the actions that will be taken if a connection matches a filter.

Three default filter actions appear in the list:

- **Permit.** With this option, the computer does not request IP security and permits unsecured connections. No security methods are defined. This action is comparable to the Client (Respond Only) policy, but the default policy is defined in a different way.

- **Request Security (Optional).** With this option, the computer requests IP security but will accept an unsecured connection. This filter action is used in the Server (Request Security) IPSec policy.

- **Require Security.** With this option, the computer will not communicate unless IP security is enabled for the connection. This filter action is used in the Secure Server (Require Security) IPSec policy.

> **NOTE**
>
> Like filter lists, filter actions are not stored as properties of a particular rule. They are stored separately, and may be referenced by all rules that share the same environment.
>
> Thus, as with filter lists, any changes made to filter actions affect all IPSec policies that incorporate those filter actions into their rules.

Defining Filter Actions for an IPSec Rule New filter actions can be added and existing filter actions can be edited. The dialog boxes used to add and edit filter actions are identical except for the names.

Click **Add** to create a new filter action. A **Filter Action Wizard** is available as an alternative way to add filter actions. Enter the wizard by checking **Use Add Wizard** on the **Filter Action** tab before clicking the **Add** button. The wizard is easy to apply, and I won't go through it here. If you understand the manual-entry dialog boxes discussed in the next section, you'll have no trouble with the wizard.

Figure 11.21 shows the dialog box for the `Request Security (Optional)` filter action. The **General** tab contains only **Name** and **Description** fields and requires no discussion. All the fields that define the filter action are on the **Security Methods** tab shown in the figure.

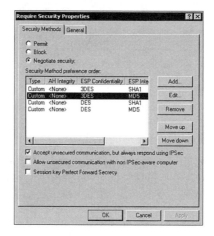

FIGURE 11.21
Security methods determine the actions performed by a filter action.

Three options at the top affect the nature of the security method:

- **Permit.** If **Permit** is selected, no security is requested or required. This option is selected for the `Permit` filter action.

- **Block.** If **Block** is selected, IP traffic is blocked for all connections defined in the filter list. No communication is permitted.

- **Negotiate security.** If **Negotiate security** is selected, the computer will attempt to negotiate IP security for all connections defined in the filter list. This option is selected for the `Request Security (Optional)` and `Require Security` filter actions.

The remaining fields on the tab are active only if **Negotiate security** is selected.

> **NOTE**
>
> We have already seen a **Security Method preference order** list in Figure 11.12 in the section "Defining IPSec Policy Key Exchange Settings." It's easy to forget why two groups of key settings are needed.
>
> Security methods in the **Key Session Security Methods** dialog box (Figure 11.12) affect the creation of the master key during IKE Phase I negotiation.
>
> Security methods in the **IPSec Policy Properties** dialog box (Figure 11.21) affect the creation of the session keys during IKE Phase II negotiations.

The **Security Method preference table** contains one or more security configurations that will be accepted during SA negotiations, ordered with the most preferred security method at the top of the table and the least preferred security method at the bottom. We'll look at the dialog boxes used to add and edit security methods after examining the three check boxes that appear at the bottom of the tab.

- **Accept unsecured communication, but always respond using IPSec.** If this option is selected, the computer will accept unsecured communication from computers matching the filter but will initiate IPSec negotiations with the computer when replying. The other computer must accept IP security or further communication is not permitted. This option is selected for the `Request Security (Optional)` and `Require Security` filter actions.

- **Allow unsecured communication with non IPSec-aware computer.** If the other computer isn't configured to use IPSec, this option permits communication to be established. This option is selected for the `Require Security` filter action.

- **Session Key Perfect Forward Secrecy.** If this option is selected, PFC is applied to the session key only. A new IKE Phase II negotiation is initiated whenever the session key must be refreshed.

Now we'll return to security methods and look at the dialog boxes used to add and edit them. Click **Add** to create a new security method. To modify an existing security method, select it and click **Edit**. The dialog boxes are identical apart from their names. Figure 11.22 shows the **Modify Security Method** dialog box, which has three radio buttons:

- **High (ESP).** Select this button to configure a security method using ESP with default settings. (ESP, no AH, DES, MD5, and keys that do not expire.)

- **Medium (AH).** Select this button to configure a security method that guards integrity but does not encrypt. (AH, no ESP, MD5, and keys that do not expire.)

- **Custom (for expert users).** Select this option and click **Settings** to open the **Custom Security Method Settings** dialog box, where you can define all settings for the security method.

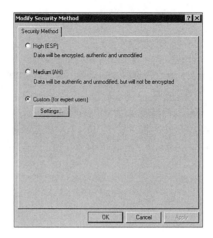

FIGURE 11.22
Start defining security methods in the Modify Security Method dialog box.

Given Microsoft's own warnings in Windows 2000 documentation, neither the **High (ESP)** nor the **Medium (AH)** security methods should be used unless the data being protected are valuable for a short period of time. Because keys never expire with either method, all communications are encrypted with the same key and a compromised key means all data are compromised. Of course, the key regeneration question is moot if connections have short durations because keys are discarded when the connection is terminated. But for long- or continuous-duration connections you should definitely create custom security methods.

Another problem with the predefined security methods is that they do not use the strongest available ciphers. If your data are critical, you will want to use 3DES and SHA1 instead of DES and MD5. (Notice in Figure 11.19 that all of the security methods included with the default IPSec policies are created using the **Custom** option, and that the highest-priority security method uses ESP with 3DES and SHA1.)

Defining Custom Security Methods   A custom security method is about the easiest thing you will need to configure with IPSec, so let's see how it's done. Select **Custom (for expert users)** and click **Settings** to open the **Custom Security Method Settings** dialog box shown in Figure 11.23. In the figure, I selected all the check boxes so that all fields would be active. It would be unusual to enable both AH and ESP.

NOTE

At this point, we are at this level in the IPSec policy properties hierarchy:
IPSec policy properties→rules→filter actions→security methods

The following fields are used to define a custom security method:

- **Data and address integrity without encryption (AH).** If you enable AH, you can select either MD5 or SHA1 in the **Integrity algorithm** pull-down list. By default, AH is disabled.
- **Data integrity and encryption (ESP).** If you enable ESP, you can select <none>, MD5, or SHA1 in the **Integrity algorithm** pull-down list. You can also select <none>, DES, or 3DES in the **Encryption algorithm** field.

  To reduce processing overhead, you can disable the integrity algorithm by selecting <none> for the ESP integrity algorithm if AH is enabled.

  Select <none> as the encryption algorithm if you want to use the ESP format but don't need privacy. (That's the suggestion in Help, although it does not suggest a reason why you would want to do so.)

- **Generate a new key every...Kbytes.** Enable this option to regenerate the session key after it has been used to transmit the amount of data specified. This field is disabled in a new rule but should be enabled in most cases. The default value if the field is enabled is 100 megabytes.

- **Generate a new key every...seconds.** Enable this option to regenerate the session key after it has been used for the period of time that is specified. This field is disabled in a new rule but should be enabled in most cases. The default value if the field is enabled is 3,600 minutes (60 hours).

Consider re-keying more often if DES is being used for encryption.

CAUTION

The default settings for a new rule do not enable re-keying for the session key. Re-keying takes place only if it is enabled for the IKE Phase I key exchange, as specified in the **Key Exchange Settings** dialog box appearing in Figure 11.12. In most cases, re-keying should be enabled for both master and session keys.

IPSec Policy Rule Properties: The Authentication Methods Tab

OK, we're back at the **Edit Rule Properties** dialog box, selecting the **Authentication Methods** tab, shown in Figure 11.24. The **Authentication Method preference order** list displays the Authentication Methods that are permitted for this rule, ranked in order of preference with the preferred entry at the top of the list. By default, only Kerberos is enabled.

You can add new Authentication Methods or edit existing ones. Apart from their names, identical dialog boxes are used to add or edit entries. Figure 11.25 shows the **New Authentication Method Properties** dialog box used to add an entry to the list.

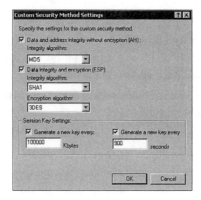

FIGURE 11.23

Security methods consist of security protocols, data integrity and encryption algorithms, and key lifetime specifications.

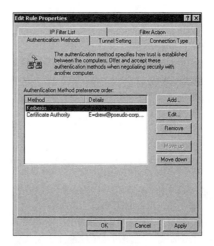

FIGURE 11.24

One or more authentication methods must be specified, ranked from highest to lowest preference.

Three authentication methods can be enabled:

- **Kerberos v5.** This is the Windows 2000 default authentication method.
- **Use a certificate from this certificate authority (CA).** If this method is chosen, an enterprise CA must be specified. Browsing can be used to identify the CA. Automatic IPSec policy assignment can be employed to ensure that each Active Directory computer obtains an IPSec certificate. See the section "Automating Certificate Requests" in Chapter 10.

- **Use this string to protect the key exchange (preshared key).** If you choose this method, you must enter a string of characters that is known to both peers. As with all shared secrets, the problem you will encounter is finding a secure way to share the secret.

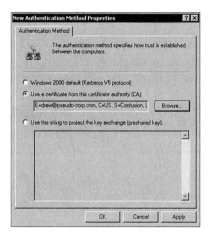

FIGURE 11.25

Kerberos is the default authentication method for Windows 2000 IPSec. Others can be defined.

Which method or methods should you support? Here are some thoughts.

Kerberos v5 authentication is a no-brainer to set up. In fact, it works by default. But it works best for Windows 2000 clients that are in the same Active Directory forest. As we learned in Chapter 4, "Active Directory Concepts," establishing trusts between forests can require a bit of work. It certainly can't be done on an impromptu basis. A security limitation of Kerberos v5 is that the computer name is not encrypted during the early steps in the authentication sequence.

Authentication by certificate requires a public key infrastructure. Windows 2000 clients can obtain IPSec certificates through automatic certificate distribution, so once an enterprise CA is set up and an automatic certificate request is configured for IPSec certificates there isn't much else left to do. Apart from the requirement for at least one CA, certificates aren't difficult to deal with and provide excellent security. You will need to add an entry for each CA that issues certificates you want to trust.

There's no doubt about it. Shared secrets can be difficult to implement. You have to be conscientious about creating a well randomized string of significant length, one that's probably a bear to type, and you need to change the shared secret periodically. Furthermore, you have to share the secret without sharing it with Boris Badenov. One way to distribute shared secrets is to use a secure mail system. If your organization has implemented Secure MIME or another such protocol, you can copy shared secret strings from the **Authentication Method** dialog box and paste them into mail messages. S-MIME would be an effective way to share secrets with users outside your organization. But you need to change the shared secret occasionally, and each time you do you'll regret it. Managing a shared secret that provides security similar to a certificate with a 1,024-bit key would take a bit of work. Given a choice between shared secrets and certificates, I'd lean pretty strongly toward certificates.

IPSec Policy Rule Properties: The Tunnel Settings Tab

The **Tunnel Settings** tab of the **Rule Properties** dialog box can be used to configure IP tunnels between two IP addresses or two IP subnets. Tunneling enhances security, hiding a packet by encapsulating it in another packet. IPSec tunneling encrypts the original packet so that it cannot be viewed as it traverses the network. Tunnel settings provide a simple method of establishing a secure IPSec tunnel between two devices.

Before explaining how to configure an IPSec tunnel, we need to complete discussion of IPSec policies. We'll return to the **Tunnel Settings** tab in the last major section of this chapter, "Configuring IPSec Tunnels and Virtual Private Networks."

IPSec Policy Rule Properties: The Connection Type Tab

The final tab in the **Rule Policy** dialog box is **Connection Type**. If you're ready for a simple tab, this is it. The tab has radio buttons for these three choices:

- **All network connections.** Matches all LAN and remote access connections.
- **Local Area Network (LAN).** Matches only LAN connections. If a Windows 2000 router interfaces to a WAN through a LAN connection to an external router, the router connection matches this selection.
- **Remote Access.** Matches only dial-in connections configured on the computer to which the policy is assigned. Remote access connections do not include direct connections to WANs.

The IPSec rule will apply only to the type of network connection that is selected in the **Connection Type** dialog box.

Managing IPSec Policies

Now that you know what goes into an IPSec policy, it's time to look at the procedures for creating, modifying, and using the policies.

Setting Up the IP Security Policy Management Console

The **IP Security Policy Management** console, which I refer to as the **IPSec** console, is often the most appropriate tool for creating, modifying, and assigning IPSec policies. The console is an MMC snap-in that can be installed in four configurations. When you add an **IP Security Policy Management** snap-in to MMC, the **Select Computer** dialog box is displayed, as shown in Figure 11.26. Select one of the following configurations for the console you are adding:

- **Local computer.** When this option is selected, a console named **IP Security Policies on Local Machine** is added to the MMC.

- **Manage domain policy for this computer's domain.** When this option is selected, a console named **IP Security Policies on Active Directory** is added to the MMC.

- **Manage domain policy for another domain.** When this option is selected, a console named **IP Security Policies on Active Directory** is added to the MMC.

- **Another computer.** If you have administrative permissions on another computer, this configuration can be used to manage the remote computer's IPSec policies. When this option is selected, a console named **IP Security Policies on Local Machine** is added to the MMC.

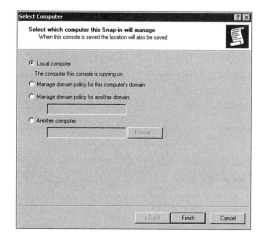

FIGURE 11.26

The IP Security Policy Management can manage IPSec policies in Active Directory domains or on local machines.

Figure 11.7 shows an MMC console that is configured with one **IPSec** snap-in for the local computer and a second snap-in for the computer's domain.

Creating IPSec Policies

New IPSec policies are created with the **IP Security Policy Wizard**. To start the wizard do one of the following:

- In the **IPSec** console (Figure 11.7), right-click the appropriate **IP Security Policies** object in the console object hierarchy and choose **Create IP Security Policy** in the context menu.
- In the **Group Policy** editor (Figure 11.8), right-click the **IP Security Policies on Active Directory** object and choose **Create IP Security Policy** in the context menu.

Complete the **IP Security Policy Wizard** as follows:

1. In the **IP Security Policy Name** dialog box complete these entries:
   - **Name.** Supply a name for the IPSec policy that is active in the Active Directory tree.
   - **Description.** Supply a detailed description of the purpose of the policy, the protocols to which it applies, and any particular details about the rules or filters that are of interest to administrators who may want to use the policy. Although this information is optional, IPSec policies have so many policies distributed on so many dialog boxes and tabs that a good description is essential.
2. In the **Requests for Secure Communication** dialog box, check **Activate the default response rule** if the <Dynamic> rule should be included in the policy.

> **NOTE**
>
> The <Dynamic> rule can be added to an IPsec policy only when the policy is created with the **IP Security Policy Wizard**.

3. In the **Default Response Rule Authentication Method** dialog box, select one of the following:
   - **Kerberos**
   - **Use a certificate from this certificate authority (CA)** and supply the name of a CA.
   - **Use this string to protect the key exchange (preshared key)** and supply the text string that provides authentication.

These options are described in the earlier section "IPSec Policy Rule Properties: The Authentication Methods Tab." Additional authentication methods can be added to the policy after it is defined.

4. In the final dialog box, check **Edit properties** to open the **New IP Security Policy Properties** dialog box, where you can review and edit all properties of the policy.

Modifying IPSec Policies

To modify an existing IPSec policy, right-click the policy description in the **IPSec** console or in the **Group Policy** editor and select one of the following choices in the context menu:

- **Properties** opens the **IPSec Policy Properties** dialog box where all policy properties can be modified.

- **Delete** removes the policy from storage. Remember that a single copy of a given IPSec policy is shared by Group Policy objects throughout Active Directory. When you delete an IPSec policy object you delete it for everybody.

- **Rename** enables you to edit the policy name.

Assigning and Un-Assigning IPSec Policies

The process of activating an IPSec policy in a Group Policy or on a computer is referred to as *assigning the IPSec Policy*. At most one IPSec policy can be assigned to a given Group Policy object or computer.

The process of deactivating an IPSec policy is referred to as *un-assigning the IPSec Policy*.

Assigning Policies for Group Policy Objects

To assign an IPSec policy to a Group Policy object, right-click the IPSec policy name in the **Group Policy** console and choose **Assign** from the context menu. In the Details pane in the **Policy Assigned**, the entry for the IPSec policy will change from No to Yes. If a policy is assigned, it replaces any other policies that may already be assigned.

To un-assign an IPSec policy, follow the same procedure but choose **Un-assign** from the context menu.

Assigning Policies for Computers

IPSec policies may be assigned to computers only if the computer is not affected by an IPSec policy that is assigned via Group Policy.

Two tools can be used to assign IPSec policies to local computers: the **IPSec** console and the **Network and Dial-Up Connections** applet in the **Control Panel**. Administrator permissions are required to change the IPSec policy settings on a computer.

The **IPSec** console is the tool most commonly used for assigning an IPSec policy to a computer. Configure an **IPSec** console for the computer to be managed, right-click the desired IPSec policy, and choose **Assign** from the context menu. The **Policy Assigned** status will change from No to Yes. Figure 11.7 shows the **IPSec** console with the Client (Respond Only) policy assigned to the local computer.

If an IPSec policy is assigned locally but a policy assigned via Group Policy takes precedence, the **Policy Assigned** status will be Assigned, but DS policy is overriding.

To un-assign an IPSec policy, follow the above procedure but choose **Un-assign** from the context menu.

IPSec policies can also be assigned locally as part of the Internet Protocol properties for a computer. Here's the procedure:

1. Open **Network and Dial-Up Connections**, open the Internet Protocol properties for any connection, and choose **Advanced→Options**.

2. On the **Options** dialog box, select **IP security** in the **Optional settings** list and click **Properties** to open the **IP Security** dialog box shown in Figure 11.27.

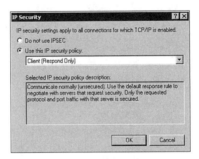

FIGURE 11.27

Local IPSec policies can be assigned using Internet protocol properties.

3. To assign an IPSec policy select **Use this IP security policy** and select a policy from the drop-down list.

   To disable IP security on the computer select **Do not use IPSec**.

Managing IPSec Filter Lists and Filter Actions

When we discussed IPSec filter lists and filter actions in the section "IPSec Policy Rule Properties: The IP Filters List Tab," it was mentioned that IPSec policy filter lists and filter actions are stored separately from IPSec policies so that they can be assigned to multiple policies.

The dialog box shown in Figure 11.28 can be used to manage all the IPSec filter lists and filter actions in an environment. Open the dialog box using one of the following methods:

- Right-click the IPSec console that manages the environment containing the policies and choose **Manage IP filter lists and filter actions** from the context menu.
- Right-click the **IP Security Policies on Active Directory** container in the **Group Policy** console and choose **Manage IP filter lists and filter actions** from the context menu.

FIGURE 11.28
All IPSec filter lists and filter actions can be managed from this dialog box.

The **Manage IP Filter Lists** tab displays all filter lists that are defined in the environment. Filter lists can be added, removed, or edited as described earlier in the section "IPSec Policy Rule Properties: The IP Filters List Tab."

Similarly, the **Manage Filter Actions** tab displays all filter actions that are defined in the environment. Filter actions can be added, removed, or edited as described earlier in the section "IPSec Policy Rule Properties: The Filter Action Tab."

Let me remind you that changing a filter list or a filter action affects all IPSec policies that include the filter list or filter action. It is very possible to break an IPSec policy by modifying or deleting a rule without determining dependencies beforehand.

Exporting and Importing IPSec Policies
As you have seen, IPSec policies can be fairly complex, and if you get an involved policy configured and debugged you may not want to create it again. However, IPSec policies are not shared between IPSec trees or between Active Directory and local machine policy stores, so it takes a bit of work to make policies in one environment available in another.

IPSec policies can be exported from a policy store to a file. They can then be imported to another policy store. Both tasks can be performed using the IPSec console.

You will need to configure IPSec consoles for both environments. For example, to export policies from Active Directory to a computer, you will need to configure IPSec snap-ins for the source and destination environments.

Exporting IPSec Policies

To export IPSec policies from an environment, do the following:

1. Right-click the IPSec console that manages the environment containing the policies and choose **All Tasks→Export Policies** from the context menu.

2. Specify the location and name for the export file. By default, these files have the extension .ipsec.

The same procedure can be performed in the **Group Policy** console to export policies from Active Directory. Right-click the **IP Security Policies on Active Directory** container to initiate the process.

> **NOTE**
>
> Note that this procedure exports *all* policies from the source environment. It is not possible to export select policies.

Importing IPSec Policies

To import IPSec policies to an environment, do the following:

1. Right-click the IPSec console that manages the environment to which the policies are to be imported. Then choose **All Tasks→Import Policies** from the context menu.

2. Browse for the import file and select it.

3. By default, existing policies will not be replaced by imported policies having the same names.

   If all existing IPSec policies should be deleted before importing, check **Delete all existing policy information**.

4. Click **Open** to import the policies.

After the policies are imported, they will appear in the Details pane, where they can be assigned.

The same procedure can be performed in the **Group Policy** console to import policies to Active Directory. Right-click the **IP Security Policies on Active Directory** container to initiate the process.

Restoring the Default IPSec Policies

It may happen that you edit one of the default IPSec policies and wish you hadn't. You can restore the default IPSec policies to their original states by choosing **All Tasks→Restore Default Policies** from the context menu for an IPSec console or for the **IP Security Policies on Active Directory** container in the **Group Policy** console.

Deciding How to Assign IPSec Policies

When you create a new IPSec policy, or modify an existing one, the changes propagate to lower-level containers in the Active Directory hierarchy. (Recall from Chapter 4 that the **Block Policy inheritance** and **No Override** properties for a Group Policy object both result in deviation from the simple rules I'm stating here.) Specifically:

- IPSec policies assigned to a Group Policy for a site apply to all computers in the site and are inherited by all domains at the site.

- IPSec policies assigned to a domain Group Policy override IPSec policies inherited from the site. IPSec policies established for a domain apply to all computers in a domain and are inherited by all OUs in the domain.

- IPSec policies assigned to an OU Group Policy override IPSec policies inherited from the site or the domain. IPSec policies established for an OU apply to all computers in the OU and are inherited by all OUs in the OU.

Here are some corollaries to those rules:

- If you want to assign a default IPSec policy for every computer at a location, create the policy in a site Group Policy object. You will seldom want to assign an IPSec policy at the site level, however, unless it is the `Client (Respond Only)` policy or something similar. It is rare that IP security will be required for an entire site.

- If you want to create a new policy that applies to every computer in a domain, create the policy at the domain level. Depending on the domain architecture of your AD tree, you are more likely to want to assign IPSec policies to domains than to sites.

- OUs are the most useful level for assigning IPSec policies that apply to arbitrary groups of computers within a domain.

Applying IP Security: A Simple Example

Let's look at an exceptionally simple example of IP security that can be set up with almost no work. We'll use default IPSec policies to enable IP security between a client and a server. Figure 11.29 shows the computers and the policies that are assigned.

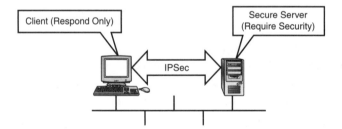

FIGURE 11.29
Default policy assignments establish IP security between these computers.

All that is necessary is to use the **IPSec** console or the **Internet Protocol (TCP/IP) Properties** dialog box to assign IPSec policies as follows:

- Assign the Secure Server (Require Security) policy to the server.
- Assign the Client (Respond Only) policy to the client.

That's it. The computers will instantly negotiate IPSec communication. To see the effect, let's look at two network captures. I made these by starting the client 10.1.0.99 from a cold boot. Figure 11.30 shows the first 29 packets. At a very high level, here's what happens:

1. 10.1.0.99 submits LDAP queries to the DNS server on DC1 to obtain the service location it needs.

2. 10.1.0.99 requests a TCP session with DC1, which is opened.

3. SMB (server message block) packets indicate the initiation of a Microsoft network connection.

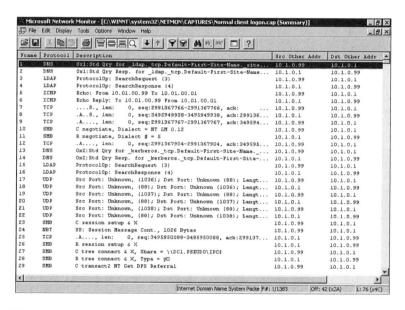

FIGURE 11.30

This trace shows a client starting up without IP security.

Now let's look at what happens when IP security is required by the server. Figure 11.31 shows the startup dialog, which differs significantly from the normal dialog in Figure 11.30.

1. 10.1.0.99 submits an LDAP query to the DNS server on DC1 to obtain the service location it needs.

2. The server refuses to accept the query. It transmits an ISAKMP packet containing an IKE Phase I proposal. Then the server returns an ICMP Destination Unreachable response, informing the client that the requested port is not available.

3. The same exchange is repeated several times until in packet 20 the client responds to the server's IKE Phase I proposal and the SA negotiations begin.

4. After SA negotiations are complete, all subsequent communication is via ESP (the preferred protocol in the Secure Server IPSec policy).

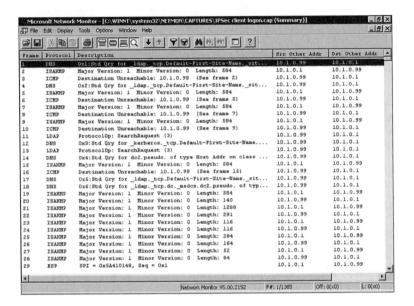

FIGURE 11.31
This trace shows a client starting with a server that requires IP Security.

From that point on, the traffic gets really boring, because everything but ICMP is encapsulated by the ESP protocol. Figure 11.32 shows the decode for a packet that is secured using ESP. Very little information is available above IP. We cannot determine the upper-layer protocol, the port, or anything that reveals the purpose or payload of the packet.

For the sake of comparison, Figure 11.33 shows the details for a secure IP datagram that uses the AH protocol for message integrity. Apart from the insertion of the AH header between IP and TCP there are very few differences from a normal IP datagram. All upper-layer protocol details are visible.

Scaling IPSec

Local IPSec policy assignment is not scalable past a few dozen computers in a fairly simple, stable environment. To support large numbers of Windows 2000 computers that have varying IP security requirements, it is necessary to assign IPSec policies through Group Policy.

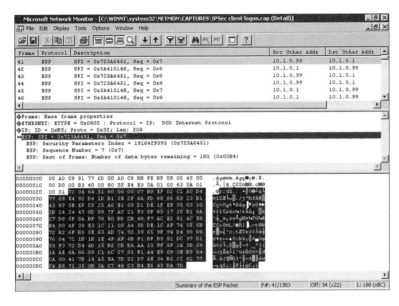

FIGURE 11.32

An example of a packet containing a payload secured by ESP.

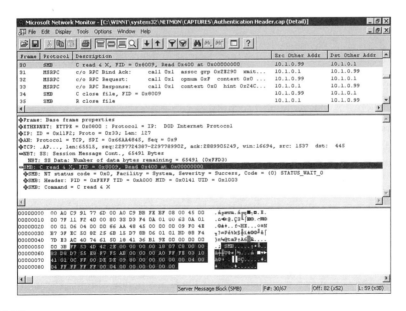

FIGURE 11.33

An example of a packet containing a payload protected by AH.

You can't just barge in, however, because it is likely that different computers will require different IPSec configurations. For example:

- Some clients may be fine with a policy similar to Client (Respond Only).

- Some clients may communicate critical data so that it is necessary for them to use IPSec even when communicating with a server that doesn't require IP security.

- Some servers may require IP security, but do they all? If IP security is required on every server, all your network traffic will be secured. Every computer must negotiate SAs for every computer with which it communicates. More data are transmitted. More encryption and decryption must be performed. In short, universal IP security is enabled, a lot of network bandwidth and processing capability gets eaten up.

- Some Windows 2000 servers may function as endpoints for IPSec tunnels. These servers require special configuration.

In short, you need to determine which IPSec properties should be assigned to which computers, and you then need to figure out how to design domains, OUs, IPSec policies, and Group Policy to achieve the desired results.

How are you planning to use domains? Will you have small domains that follow department boundaries, or large domains that comprehend entire sites or perhaps span sites? If domains parallel departments, you may be able to assign IPSec policies at the domain level. For example:

- HR, the executive offices, and facilities share a domain. There is no need to deploy IP security within the domain. You might assign the Client (Respond Only) policy to the domain Group Policy so that computers in this domain can communicate with computers in other domains that require IP security.

- Research is in a secure facility and has its own domain. The Secure Server (Require Security) could be assigned to the domain Group Policy to ensure that all communications within the domain are secure.

Such simple situations are seldom the rule, however. In most cases, there will be a mixture of requirements. In such situations, the best tools to use are Organizational Units. Let's look at one way a domain could be configured to support multiple IPSec policies. The strategy is illustrated by the **Active Directory Users and Computers** console in Figure 11.34. We'll call the domain pseudo and configure it like this:

- **pseudo.** The domain group policy assigns the IPSec policy Client (Respond Only) so that all computers in the domain will negotiate a secure IP connection if asked to do so. (The **Computers** container is not an OU and can't be assigned a Group Policy. Computers must either be moved to an OU or configured using the Group Policy for the domain.)

- **Domain Controllers.pseudo.** We'll leave servers in this container that don't require secure communication. We'll let servers in this container inherit the `Client (Respond Only)` policy from the domain. If any DCs in other OUs require IP security, these DCs will then be willing to establish an IPSec session in order to exchange domain and service housekeeping information.

- **Secure Clients.pseudo.** If a client computer should require IP security, we'll move it to this OU, which is configured by a Group Policy that assigns the `Secure Server (Require Security)` policy.

- **Secure Servers.pseudo.** If a server or domain controller should require IP security, we'll move it to this OU, which is configured by a Group Policy that assigns the `Secure Server (Require Security)` policy.

- **Tunnel Routers.pseudo.** If the network incorporates IPSec tunnels, the servers that provide the endpoints for the tunnel must be configured with special rules that are activated by special filter lists. (We take up the topic of IPSec tunnels in the section "Configuring IPSec Tunnels and Virtual Private Networks," coming soon to a chapter near you. This one, in fact.) Rather than defining a big IPSec policy that contains these rules but also contains rules for other types of computers, it may be easier to define a separate OU and create a separate IPSec policy just for the routers.

- **No IPSec.pseudo.** Sometimes it's easier to configure a computer with a local IPSec policy. The Group Policy in this OU does not assign an IPSec policy and therefore overrides the domain IPSec policy assignment. This enables computers to be configured locally.

FIGURE 11.34

This trace shows a client starting with a server that requires IP Security.

In the preceding examples, I relied on the default IPSec policies because we already understand their functions. In practice, however, you will likely want to create your own IPSec policies that precisely match your requirements.

Troubleshooting IPSec

The catch with IPSec is that you can't look inside an ESP-encrypted datagram and see if everything is working according to plan. You can use **Network Monitor** to confirm that IPSec is being enabled, but apart from that, packet analysis won't tell you much. And trust me, you won't be able to understand the contents of the ISAKMP datagrams unless you have a love for detail and spend a lot of time with the standards.

For most of us, a simple troubleshooting tool is needed, and one is included in the Windows 2000 Support Tools. We discussed the installation of the Support Tools in Chapter 1.

Included in the tools is the **IP Security Monitor** (`ipsecmon.exe`) shown in Figure 11.35. This utility gives you a high-level view of IPSec operation on the local computer, including the SAs that are active. From the SAs you can determine whether the IPSec configuration you want is in effect. If IP security is being established by the wrong IPSec policy, rule, or filter, you should be able to deduce that from the information shown.

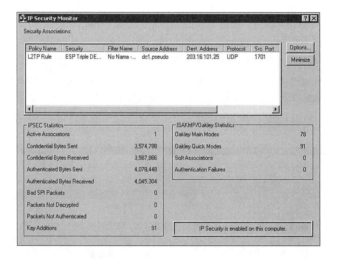

FIGURE 11.35
The IP Security Monitor displays IPSec operation for the local computer.

Some Concluding Remarks Regarding IPSec

The great thing about IPSec is that it is so versatile. The biggest problem with IPSec is that it is so versatile. Depending on the extent to which IPSec will be deployed, there are lots of things that can go wrong. A rule may not fire because of a badly constructed filter in a filter list that detects the wrong conditions. The wrong IPSec policy may be assigned because of an error in Group Policy deployment. Mismatched filter actions may make it impossible for two computers to negotiate security associations. There are lots of ways problems can creep in.

If you can, use local assignment to test the IPSec policies you design before you deploy them in a Group Policy and affect many computers. Use the troubleshooting tools you have to see if IP security is activated as planned. Test the computers to ensure that they are communicating normally.

IPSec should be completely transparent to the computers whose communications it secures. Unfortunately, transparency may mean that you won't be notified if things aren't working. If an administrator changes the Group Policy link for a container, the new Group Policy object may not have been configured with the same IPSec policy. As a result of a Group Policy change, IPSec may be disabled or accidentally enabled in a container. In the first case, you may never hear about it. In the second case the network may grind to a halt. So learn, plan, test, and document as you go along. Don't try to manage IP security by the seat of your pants.

Configuring IPSec Tunnels and Virtual Private Networks

On networks, tunneling is the process of encapsulating a datagram in another datagram. For example, an IPX datagram might be encapsulated in an IP datagram so that IPX data can cross an IP-only network.

Tunneling is a key technology when it is necessary to secure a data stream that must traverse an unsecured network. One tunneling possibility is to encapsulate an IP datagram in an IPSec datagram, which provides a method of encrypting plain IP datagrams so that they can securely cross a public network.

Windows 2000 supports three tunneling methods:

- **IPSec tunneling** provides "vanilla" tunneling that provides security for IP payloads.
- **Point-to-Point Tunneling Protocol** (PPTP; RFC2637) is a tunneling protocol developed jointly by Microsoft and 3Com. PPTP was the standard tunneling protocol for Windows NT 4.0 and is still supported in Windows 2000. While somewhat less secure that L2TP, PPTP has some advantages that we'll discuss.
- **Level Two Tunneling Protocol** (L2TP; RFC2661) is an Internet standards-track protocol that is intended to combine the best features of PPTP and the L2P protocol developed by Cisco Systems. L2TP can be expected to eclipse PPTP for most applications due to its support for IP security and its eventual status as an Internet Standard.

Our goal in the remainder of this chapter is to learn how to build virtual private networks with these protocols. A VPN is a bit more than a tunnel. VPN technology uses security and encapsulation protocols to create a virtual (simulated, not physical) private (secure) network link that to outside devices is indistinguishable from a physical network. Because it is virtual, a VPN works within another network infrastructure and doesn't require its own hardware. Because it is private, a VPN can tunnel data through a public, unsecured network without risk even though the computers exchanging packets do nothing special to secure the data.

Figure 11.36 conceptually illustrates a VPN. A secure tunnel through the Internet enables computers in Seattle and Atlanta to transparently exchange data as though a private network connection existed between the sites. In fact, it could be argued that the VPN is more secure than a leased line because all data in the VPN are encrypted whereas a private network link might be tapped.

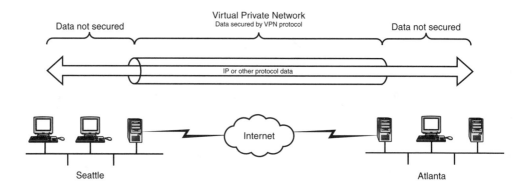

FIGURE 11.36

A VPN provides private line capability for sites communicating through public networks.

When looking at Figure 11.36, it is important to realize that packets are encrypted only between the routers that form the tunnel endpoints. The tunnel does not encrypt packets between the tunnel clients and the tunnel routers. If privacy or integrity must be guaranteed from end-to-end, the endpoints must establish secure communication between themselves, perhaps by enabling IPSec. Unless IPSec is enabled locally, the tunnel endpoints should be configured in network locations where there are no concerns for security. This may mean placing the tunnel endpoints on the routers that connect your local network to the Internet, or placing the endpoints internally on your private network, perhaps in the departments where the data are used. Tunnel endpoints may be located anyplace on the network provided firewalls, if present, are configured to enable tunneled packets to be sent and received.

VPNs also can be configured to enable clients to communicate with servers through a public network. Do you have a traveling workforce that needs to connect remotely to your network?

At one time, your only choices were to have network connections in all the cities where people worked or to support dial-up network access while paying for long-distance telephone calls. As illustrated by Figure 11.37, VPNs provide an alternative. A user who has an Internet dial-up account can connect to the Internet through an ISP and then establish a VPN connection with the home network. Everything's perfectly secure, but long-distance charges are eliminated.

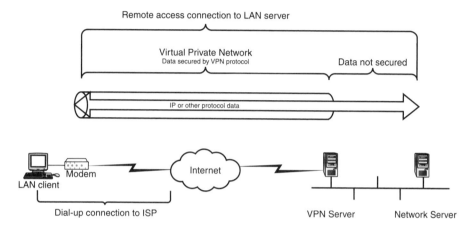

FIGURE 11.37

Remote VPN access enables distant users to communicate with the local network through Internet dial-up connections.

The potential for cost savings is why everybody's doing VPNs. And you can too by adding just a few skills to those you already have. Let's look at the protocol tools that are involved and then move on to implementation procedures.

Protocol Layering and Tunneling Protocols

While I'd prefer to avoid the topic, there's no ignoring the seven-layer OSI network model when discussing tunneling. Tunneling protocols are often discussed in terms of the protocol layers at which they function, where layers are derived from the OSI model, not the Internet protocol model. (It does make a bit of sense. The OSI model is somewhat generic. The Internet model was never intended to describe anything but TCP/IP.)

Figure 11.38 shows the OSI model alongside protocol stacks for TCP/IP, IPX, and NetBEUI (also known as the NetBIOS Frame protocol or NBF). Of these, only IPX is commonly discussed in terms of the OSI seven layers. As we discussed in Chapter 2, TCP/IP has its own model, which doesn't map exactly to OSI layers, and much of the functionality that is described by the OSI model isn't implemented in NetBEUI. I won't discuss the OSI model in detail, or the IPX and NetBEUI protocol stacks for that matter, but I do need to explain how the OSI layers relate to the other protocol stacks.

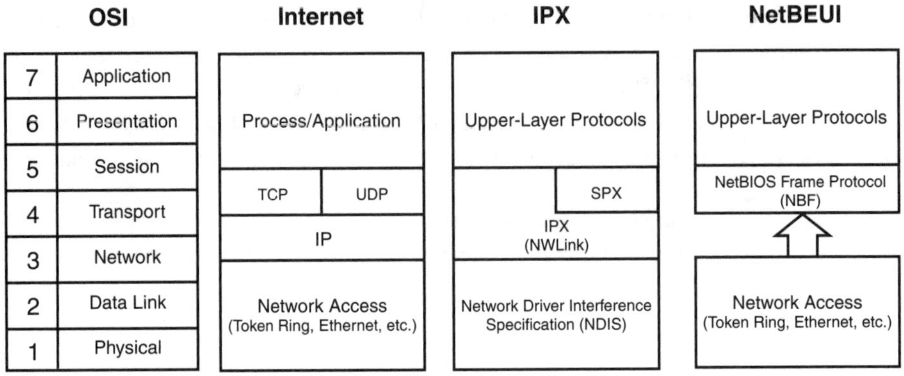

	OSI	Internet	IPX	NetBEUI

7	Application			
6	Presentation	Process/Application	Upper-Layer Protocols	Upper-Layer Protocols
5	Session			
4	Transport	TCP / UDP	SPX	NetBIOS Frame Protocol (NBF)
3	Network	IP	IPX (NWLink)	⇧
2	Data Link	Network Access (Token Ring, Ethernet, etc.)	Network Driver Interference Specification (NDIS)	Network Access (Token Ring, Ethernet, etc.)
1	Physical			

FIGURE 11.38

A comparison of the OSI model with protocol stacks supported by Windows 2000.

The OSI model allocates two layers to network functionality:

- The *physical* layer describes methods used to send and receive data on the network medium.
- The *data link* layer provides physical network addresses for devices and is responsible for formatting, sending, and receiving packets containing data from upper-layer protocols.

Together, the physical and data link layers correspond to the network access layer of the Internet protocol model and to functionality that Microsoft implements with the Network Driver Interface Specification (NDIS). When a protocol is described as a "layer 2 protocol," the reference is to the OSI data link layer and means that the protocol functions just below layer 3.

The *network* layer, layer 3 of the OSI model, roughly corresponds to the internet layer in TCP/IP. It also corresponds to the IPX protocol in the IPX protocol suite. NetBEUI doesn't implement functions ascribed to the network layer because it doesn't implement network addressing or routing. The correspondences I've shown are not exact because the OSI model was originally developed to describe a protocol suite that was to be defined on its own terms. However, it's enough for our discussion to see a rough correspondence between similar layers. When a protocol is described as a "layer 3 protocol," the reference is to the OSI network layer.

Above layer 3, comparisons are difficult to make. TCP combines functions at the transport and session layer. UDP has no session-level functionality. IPX doesn't necessarily implement layer 4 functionality unless the optional SPX protocol is brought into play. NetBEUI provides no functionality that can be associated with layer 4. And none of the protocol suites provide anything that can be unambiguously mapped to the presentation layer. Fortunately, layer 3 is the highest layer we need to concern ourselves with in this discussion.

Recall from discussion in Chapter 2 that a protocol layer is somewhat indifferent to the protocols that operate above it. For example, IP doesn't care about applications at all and supports a variety of host-to-host layer protocols besides TCP and UDP. The ability of protocol layers to accommodate a variety of upper-layer protocols is key with regard to tunneling.

Tunneling protocols are described as layer 2 or layer 3 protocols. A layer 2 tunneling protocol can encapsulate data at OSI layers 3 through 7. A layer 3 protocol can encapsulate data at layers 4 through 7. This is a significant distinction. A layer 2 protocol can (within limits and with proper implementation of the protocol stacks) encapsulate data from any layer 3 protocol. However, a layer 3 protocol can encapsulate data only from layer 4 protocols in a particular protocol suite.

Protocol suites begin to become distinctive at layer 3, but they are pretty similar at the interface between layers 2 and 3, at least within a given vendor's own protocol implementation. TCP/IP and IPX can operate on the same types of networks, for example. Consequently, a single layer 2 protocol can be made capable of encapsulating IP datagrams, IPX datagrams, AppleTalk packets, or NetBEUI frames. PPP is a layer 2 protocol that has those very capabilities.

A layer 3 protocol, however, is operating within a particular protocol stack. A protocol operating in conjunction with IP at the internet layer, such as IPSec, can encapsulate only protocols that function at the host-to-host layer. A layer 3 protocol cannot encapsulate data from a protocol that functions in a different protocol stack.

Clearly, then, layer 2 functionality is a much-desired capability in a tunneling protocol, enabling a single tunnel to transport data from protocols in several protocol stacks. A layer 2 tunneling protocol can, for example, enable IPX datagrams to be encapsulated in IP datagrams so that they can be transported through an IP-only network.

Tunneling Protocols

We need to discuss several protocols in this section. IPSec, PPTP, and L2TP must be covered of course, but we also need to examine the point-to-point protocol (PPP; RFC1661) that we first encountered in Chapter 8, "Supporting Dial-Up Connections with Routing and Remote Access Service." PPP has a variety of capabilities that are relevant to tunneling. By relying on PPP, PPTP and L2TP have access to PPP functionality without needing to implement the capabilities separately. We'll return to IPSec briefly and then move on to PPP. Following that discussion, we can examine PPTP and L2TP.

IPSec

IPSec figures in two of the tunneling methods we will discuss. We have already examined IPSec in some detail but need to add one more observation. IPSec works in conjunction with

IP at the internet protocol layer and consequently functions as a layer 3 protocol. IPSec can encapsulate data units for protocols in the Internet protocol stack, but cannot encapsulate IPX or NetBEUI.

Although IPSec can be configured to operate in tunnel mode, it is not a universal tunneling solution. One clear limitation is that it provides tunneling only for the TCP/IP protocol suite.

The security features of IPSec are formidable, however, so IPSec was selected to provide encryption, integrity, and authentication for the L2TP protocol.

Point-to-Point Protocol

PPP (RFC1661) was developed as a method for encapsulating data in preparation for transport through a WAN. Dozens of RFCs describe enhancements to PPP or adapt PPP to different types of networks. It is safe to say that PPP is a core Internet protocol that provides a rich feature set around which VPN protocols can be built. Both PPTP and L2TP rely on PPP to perform the initial encapsulation of the protocol data that are to be transported through the VPN.

PPP provides a standard method for transporting multi-protocol datagrams over point-to-point links, and is comprised of three main components:

- A method for encapsulating multi-protocol datagrams over a single communication link.
- A method for establishing, configuring, and testing connections, provided by the Link Control Protocol (LCP). LCP troubleshoots link errors, closing links when necessary. Also LCP provides a mechanism whereby a computer can authenticate its peer.
- Methods for establishing and configuring different network-layer protocols (that is, the Internet model's internet layer), provided by a family of Network Control Protocols (NCPs).

The PPP encapsulation format has low overhead, adding eight or nine bytes to the data payload. The primary function of PPP encapsulation is to provide a uniform frame format for transfer through the WAN, regardless of the protocol in the payload. The PPP header contains a *Protocol ID* field that enables the receiver to identify the type of protocol that is in the payload so that it can be forwarded to the correct protocol stack.

The PPP standard does not describe methods for encrypting the PPP payload. Both encryption and compression are optional, but when enabled, Microsoft's PPP implementation uses the Microsoft Point-to-Point Encryption protocol (MPPE), which is based on the RSA RC4 cipher (described in Chapter 9). Base encryption uses 40-bit keys, but the High Encryption Pack (described in Chapter 8) makes 128-bit keys available. MPPE is the only encryption protocol supported for the Microsoft PPP implementation.

Microsoft PPP authentication supports the following authentication protocols: Challenge-Handshake Authentication Protocol (CHAP), Microsoft Challenge-Handshake Authentication Protocol (MS-CHAP) versions 1 and 2, Shiva Password Authentication Protocol (SPAP), Password Authentication Protocol (PAP), and the Extensible Authentication Protocol (EAP). These protocols are described in Chapter 8 in the section "Settings in the Advanced Settings Dialog Box." PPP also supports unauthenticated connections.

Microsoft's PPP implementation also supports payload compression using Microsoft Point-to-Point Compression protocol (MPPC).

Point-to-Point Tunneling Protocol

PPTP encapsulates PPP frames in IP datagrams so that they can be transported through an IP network. Many of the features of Microsoft's PPTP implementation are determined by PPP. Authentication can be provided by Windows or by a RADIUS server, using any of the authentication methods that are supported for PPP. The preferred authentication methods are the Extensible Authentication Protocol (EAP) or MS-CHAP, which must be used to support payload encryption with MPPE.

A PPTP tunnel is formed between a PPTP client, the computer that requests the tunnel, and a PPTP server, the computer that responds to the connection request. PPTP applies four levels of encryption to the data being tunneled. The resulting network packet is shown in Figure 11.39.

1. The IP, IPX, or NetBEUI datagram to be tunneled is encapsulated with a PPP header to create a PPP frame. Data may be encrypted or compressed prior to encapsulation. With PPTP, the optional PPP frame-check sequence trailer is omitted. Packet integrity checking is performed by the data link layer. By itself, the PPP frame is not encapsulated either by TCP or UDP and is not ready to be sent via IP.

2. The PPP frame is encapsulated with a modified GRE header. Generic Routing Encapsulation (GRE; RFC1701,2) is a client of IP and provides a simple, efficient, generic method for encapsulating data to be sent over the IP protocol. The GRE header includes a Tunnel ID that identifies the data stream.

3. The GRE-encapsulated PPP frame is encapsulated in an IP datagram. The source and destination IP addresses in the IP datagram identify the tunnel endpoints.

4. The IP datagram is encapsulated in a data link header and trailer to create a packet that is ready for transport through the network.

Datalink **Header**	IP **Header**	GRE **Header**	PPP **Header**	Encrypted Payload (IP datagram, IPX datagram, NetBEUI frame)	Datalink Trailer

FIGURE 11.39
PPTP encapsulates the payload datagram using PPP, GRE, and IP prior to sending it on the network.

If you are analyzing PPTP tunnel traffic, the packets you see are all addressed to the tunnel endpoints. The IP addresses of the computers that are the original data sender and recipient, as well as such information as the protocol ID, are encrypted in the PPP payload.

> ## CAUTION
>
> Some ISPs utilize GRE locally and filter out GRE packets when they are routed outside the ISP. This practice will also result in blocking PPTP packets. Consult with your ISP if you plan to use PPTP as a VPN protocol.

> ## NOTE
>
> Network Address Translation Firewalls (see Chapter 7) raise special concerns with regard to tunneling protocols. PPTP (and as we shall see, L2TP) do not have a TCP or UDP header above the IP header. Instead, a GRE header is used. Recall that a NAT maps IP addresses, ports, and other protocol parameters between local values and values on the Internet, requiring it to edit upper-layer headers as packets leave the private network and return. The GRE header includes a Tunnel ID that may be edited by the NAT. The NAT included in Windows 2000 RRAS includes a PPTP editor, enabling PPTP to be used to establish tunnels through NAT firewalls.
>
> IPSec traffic, on the other hand, cannot be forwarded by a NAT because NAT editing will damage the payload.

Layer Two Tunneling Protocol

L2TP is the tunneling protocol being developed as the standard VPN protocol for the Internet. L2TP makes use of PPP for payload encapsulation but relies on IPSec for encryption, integrity, and authentication. L2TP security is stronger than PPTP security due to the features contributed by IPSec. Even Microsoft recommends using L2TP when security strength is an important requirement.

Like PPTP, L2TP performs a multi-layered encapsulation of the data payload. Figure 11.40 illustrates the packet that results.

1. The datagram to be tunneled is encapsulated in a PPP header.

2. The PPP frame is encapsulated with an L2TP header.

3. The L2TP frame is encapsulated with a UDP header.

4. The resulting frame is encrypted by IPSec, which adds an ESP header and ESP trailers. Encryption is applied starting with the UDP header and extending through the ESP trailer.

5. The IPSec packet is encapsulated with an IP header. The source and destination IP addresses in the IP header specify the tunnel endpoints.

6. The IP datagram is encapsulated in a data link header and trailer to create a packet that is ready for transport through the network.

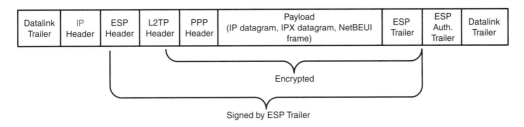

FIGURE 11.40
L2TP encapsulates the payload with PPP, L2TP, IPSec, and IP.

In nearly all cases, IPSec is configured to use ESP, which provides encryption from the UDP header through the ESP trailer. ESP signs the packet from the ESP header to the ESP trailer. AH may be used with ESP if it is desirable to protect the integrity of the IP header. IPSec is seldom configured to use AH alone, which would of course betray the reason for implementing IPSec in the first place.

Because the UDP header is encrypted by IPSec, it is unavailable for modification during packet transit. The resulting packet cannot be forwarded by a NAT firewall because NAT editing will corrupt the encrypted payload. To forward packets for an L2TP tunnel through a NAT it is necessary to allocate addresses on the router that are not subject to NAT processing.

L2TP relies on IPSec for authentication. Because the tunnel must be set up using non-tunneled traffic through an unsecured network, the tunnel endpoints must be configured with computer certificates for use in authentication. The L2TP tunnel cannot be set up using Kerberos as an authentication method.

IPSec Tunneling

Although IPSec tunneling does not have the capabilities of a true VPN, the technique is useful in situations when PPTP and L2TP are not supported.

Let's consider the network shown in Figure 11.41 as an example of IPSec tunneling. We want to protect all data exchanged between private networks 11.1.0.0/16 and 11.2.0.0/16. To achieve this an IPSec tunnel can be established between router interfaces 145.73.28.10 and 203.16.101.25.

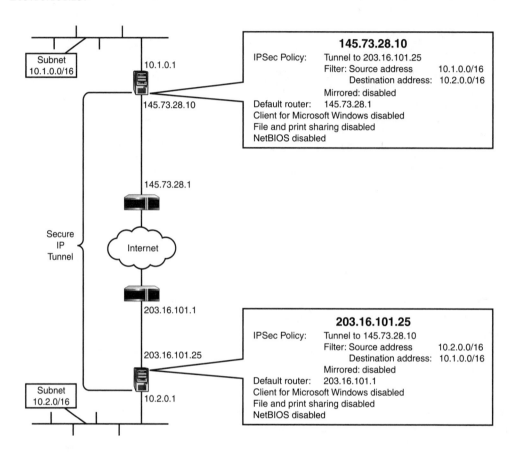

FIGURE 11.41
An IPSec tunnel will be configured between the routers. The figure shows settings that will be used to configure the tunnel.

Configuration of the tunnel consists of two procedures: configuring the routers and configuring the rules that initiate tunneling behavior between the routers. Let's start with router configuration.

Configuring the Routers

If Windows 2000 Servers are used as routers, then RRAS routing must be enabled on both computers. The interfaces 145.73.28.10 and 203.16.101.25 are configured as follows:

- IPSec is enabled using an IPSec policy that contains IPSec tunneling rules. This IPSec policy should be applied only to the routers.

- `Client for Microsoft Networks` and `File and Print Sharing for Microsoft Networks` are disabled on the interface **General** tab of the interface **Properties** pages. These interfaces connect to the external network and should not offer any Microsoft networking services.

- If these are dedicated routers, the Windows Server service should be disabled.

- The default route for 145.73.28.10 is 145.73.28.1. In this instance, the default route is sufficient and static routes are not required.

- The default route for 203.16.101.25 is 203.16.101.1.

- In **Advanced TCP/IP Settings** on the **DNS** tab, **Register this connection's addresses in DNS** is not checked. If this interface appears in DNS, clients may attempt to access the router via its external interface, a situation we would like to avoid.

- In **Advanced TCP/IP Settings** on the **WINS** tab, **Disable NetBIOS over TCP/IP** is checked so that the interfaces won't propagate NetBIOS communication.

Configuring the IPSec Policy Rules

The IPSec policy for the routers must include rules that specify the endpoints for the tunnel and conditions under which tunneling is required. In our earlier discussion, we ignored the **Tunnel Setting** tab of the **Rule Properties** dialog box, and it is time to pick up that discussion. The **Tunnel Setting** tab is shown in Figure 11.42 and has the following options:

- **This rule does not specify an IPSec tunnel.** This is the default setting and disables IPSec tunnel support for the rule.

- **The tunnel endpoint is specified by this IP address.** Select this option to enable tunnel support. You must enter the IP address of the computer that is at the other end of the tunnel.

To enable the IPSec tunnel, we need to define a rule for each router:

- The rule that applies to the router on subnet 10.1.0.0/16 (Rule 1 in later discussion) has the following settings:

  On the **Tunnel Setting** tab, IPSec tunneling is enabled with an endpoint address of 203.16.101.25. (The remote endpoint is the public IP address of the remote router.)

A filter is added to the filter list (see Figure 11.15) with these settings:

- **Source address.** The value is A specific IP Subnet with IP subnet 10.1.0.0 and subnet mask 255.255.0.0.

- **Destination address.** The value is A specific IP Subnet with IP subnet 10.2.0.0 and subnet mask 255.255.0.0.

- **Mirrored** is not checked.

- The rule that applies to the router on subnet 10.2.0.0/16 (Rule 2 in later discussion) has the following settings:

On the **Tunnel Setting** tab, IPSec tunneling is enabled with an endpoint address of 145.73.28.10.

A filter is added to the filter list with these settings:

- **Source address.** The value is A specific IP Subnet with IP subnet 10.2.0.0 and subnet mask 255.255.0.0.

- **Destination address.** The value is A specific IP Subnet, with IP subnet 10.1.0.0 and subnet mask 255.255.0.0.

- **Mirrored** is not checked.

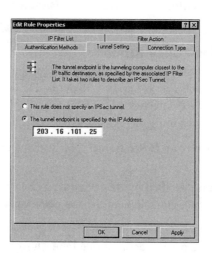

FIGURE 11.42
The Tunnel Setting tab enables IPSec tunneling and specifies the other endpoint of the tunnel.

Other rules in the policy can define different filter lists and filter actions as appropriate for the local network. If IP security is not employed on the local networks, IPSec can be disabled on local computers or the <Dynamic> rule can be used to establish an appropriate default IPSec action.

CAUTION

Mirroring must never be enabled in the filters defined in rules specifying an IP tunnel. If mirroring is enabled, each rule would match both directions of communication. Results would be unpredictable to say the least. A separate rule must be defined for each direction of communication.

Whenever a packet must be sent from subnet 10.1.0.0/16 to subnet 10.2.0.0/16, it matches the filter Rule 1 which takes effect. The router with interface 145.73.28.10 requests an IPSec connection with router 203.16.101.25.

Whenever a packet must be sent from subnet 10.2.0.0/16 to subnet 10.1.0.0/16, it matches the filter in Rule 2 which takes effect. The router with interface 203.16.101.25 requests an IPSec connection with router 145.73.28.10.

In either case, an IPSec tunnel is established between the routers. Traffic through the IPSec tunnel will look very much like IPSec traffic between two computers.

VPN Configuration

RRAS can be used to establish VPN connections using either PPTP or L2TP. VPN connections can be established in two modes:

- Router-to-router, enabling two networks to communicate through a secure link.
- Client-to-RAS, enabling clients to connect to a remote access server through the Internet.

Both types of VPN connections are established as dial-up connections using RAS. In fact, RRAS processes an incoming request to establish a VPN connection in much the same way it processes any dial-in connection to the remote access server.

We're going to configure a VPN based on the network illustrated in Figure 11.41. This time, in addition to configuring router support, we need to create PPTP and L2TP ports as well as dial-out connections that establish the VPN connection. Figure 11.43 shows the network again, this time with settings that are used in RRAS.

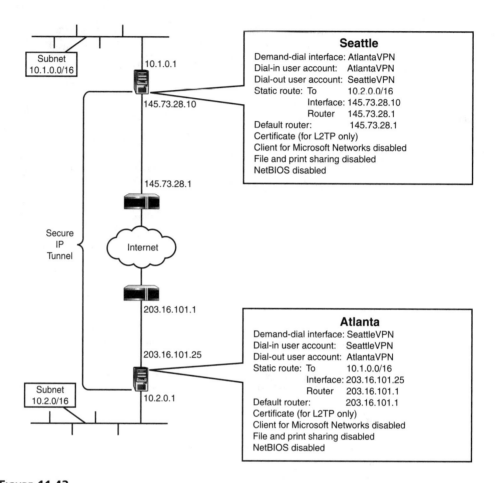

FIGURE 11.43

A VPN will be configured between the routers. The figure shows configuration settings that will be used.

> **NOTE**
>
> You might want to configure RRAS VPN support using the **Virtual private network (VPN server)** option in the **RRAS Server Wizard**. Chapter 7 discusses the wizard in the section "Enabling Routing." Unfortunately, the wizard cannot be re-run unless the existing RRAS configuration is disabled and all current settings are lost. In this chapter, I'm discussing procedures for adding VPN capability to an operating RRAS server. If you're starting from scratch, the wizard ensures you'll have a good initial setup.

CAUTION

If the **RRAS Server Wizard** is used to configure RRAS as a VPN server, the interface that connects to the WAN is configured with input and output filters that block all packet types except for the GRE, PPTP, and L2TP protocols. The remote networks separated by the WAN link will no longer be able to communicate unless a PPTP or L2TP VPN connection is enabled. This may or may not be what you want. If you intend to use the wizard to configure RRAS, first read the section "Configuring Interface Filters."

RRAS Server Properties

To configure RRAS server properties to support VPNs, open the RRAS console, right-click the RRAS server object, and choose **Properties** in the context menu. In Chapter 8, Figures 8.19–8.25 illustrate the contents of the RRAS server properties pages. See the discussion related to those figures for descriptions of the properties and options.

For a VPN server, configure the properties as follows:

- **General** tab. Most changes made to this tab require restarting the RRAS service. This is done automatically when you exit the **RRAS Properties** dialog box. Configure the **General** tab as follows:
  - Check **Router**
  - Check **LAN and demand-dial routing**
  - Check **Remote access server**
- **Security** tab. Settings on this tab apply only to PPTP. In general, select Windows as the authentication and accounting provider. MS-CHAP versions 1 and 2 are the preferred authentication methods. RADIUS is also available as an authentication or accounting provider.
- **IP** tab. Both of the VPN protocols are IP-dependent and IP routing must be enabled even if the tunnel payloads are based on another LAN protocol stack. Configure IP properties like this:
  - Check **Enable IP Routing**.
  - Check **Allow IP-based remote access and demand-dial connections**.
  - Configure **IP address assignment** appropriately depending on whether connections are assigned IP addresses on the local network by DHCP or by having RRAS select addresses from an address pool.

Configuring VPN Ports

The **Ports** container lists PPTP and L2TP virtual ports in addition to hardware ports for devices such as modems. PPTP and L2TP ports are enabled when **Remote access server** is enabled on the RRAS server's **General** properties tab. The only thing you need to configure is the number of ports that are enabled for PPTP and L2TP.

Right-click the **Ports** container and choose **Properties** from the context menu to open the **Ports Properties** dialog box shown in Figure 11.44.

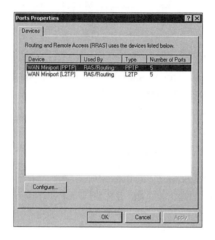

FIGURE 11.44

The Ports Properties dialog box lists the types and numbers of ports that are available on the RRAS server.

A VPN port is used for each router-to-router or remote access (client-to-RAS) connection. RRAS activates ports as needed up to the maximum number you specify. Of course, server hardware and WAN bandwidth determine the number of communication channels that RRAS can profitably support. If RRAS is running on a dedicated computer, you can expect it to support more ports than if RRAS is sharing the computer with other services.

To specify the number of ports, select either **WAN Miniport (PPTP)** or **WAN Miniport (L2TP)** and click **Configure** to open the **Configure Device** dialog box shown in Figure 11.45. Establish port settings as follows:

- Check **Remote access connections (inbound only)** if the port type will support remote access VPN connections.

- Check **Demand-dial routing connections (inbound and outbound)** if the port type will support router-to-router VPN connections.

- Configure **Maximum ports** with the number of VPN ports you want to have available.

FIGURE 11.45
Port settings for a PPTP or L2TP port.

When you configure support by enabling **Remote access server** on the RRAS server's **General** properties tab, the RRAS server is configured with five PPTP ports and five L2TP ports.

If you configure VPN support by setting up RRAS with the **RRAS Configuration Wizard**, the server is configured with 128 PPTP and 128 L2TP ports. In many cases, you will want to reduce the number of ports for either or both protocols.

The **Maximum ports** value cannot be set to 0. To disable PPTP or L2TP entirely, remove the checks from both **Remote access connections (inbound only)** and **Demand-dial routing connections (inbound and outbound)**.

Preparing the Routers for VPN Communication

Before using the **Demand Dial Interface Wizard** to create the VPN interfaces, review the router configurations as follows:

- The default router address must correspond to the IP address of the router at the ISP and should be assigned to the interface that connects to the WAN.

- No routing protocols should be enabled on the interfaces communicating with the Internet. When necessary, static routes must be used to describe explicit routes.

- **Client for Microsoft Networks** and **File and Print Sharing for Microsoft Networks** should be disabled on the interfaces communicating with the Internet.

- Use ping to ensure that the routers can communicate.

Enabling Multicast Support

Several Windows functions make use of multicast messages. To enable RRAS to forward multicast packets through the VPN, you must enable support for IGMP, as described in Chapter 7 in the section "Configuring IP Multicast Routing."

Some of the **RRAS Configuration Wizard** options, including **Virtual private network (VPN server)**, install IGMP support.

Reviewing Demand-Dial Interface and Username Characteristics

Recall from Chapter 8 that demand-dial routing interfaces are used to initiate dial-up connections, whether they go through physical hardware, as with modems, or through virtual dial-in ports, as with demand-dial routing. A VPN routing interface is just a special case of a router-to-router interface.

Also, recall from Chapter 8 that a special convention distinguishes dial-in attempts made by users from dial-in attempts made by routers:

- If the name of the routing interface is different from the username that authenticates the connection, the connection is treated as a user remote access connection. Access to network resources is determined by permissions assigned to the user account.
- If the name of the routing interface is the same as the username that authenticates the connection, the connection is treated as a router-to-router connection. Packets are routed between the WAN and the LAN as necessary.

If we want to enable a remote router to request a connection with a routing interface, we must create a user account with a username that is identical to the name of the routing interface.

Configuring a VPN Routing Interface

Create a VPN routing interface by performing these operations in the **RRAS** console:

1. Right-click the **Routing Interfaces** container and choose **New Demand-dial Interface** to start the **Demand Dial Interface Wizard**.

CAUTION

Do not select **New IP Tunnel** in Step 1. That choice creates an IP tunnel that could be used to route IPX datagrams through an IP-only network, but the tunnel is not a secure VPN connection.

---

2. If a modem is configured, the **Connection Type** dialog box appears first. Select **Connect using virtual private networking (VPN)**.

3. In the **Interface Name** dialog box, specify a name for the interface. I like to name demand-dial routing interfaces according to the destination for the connection. For the sample network, I name the interface on the router in Seattle `AtlantaVPN` and the interface on the router in Atlanta `SeattleVPN`.

4. The **VPN Type** dialog box has three choices:

   - **Automatic selection.** If this option is selected, RRAS first attempts to establish an L2TP connection. If unsuccessful, RRAS sets up a PPTP connection.
   - **Point-to-Point Tunneling Protocol (PPTP).** Make this selection if PPTP should be used exclusively on this connection.
   - **Layer-2 Tunneling Protocol (L2TP).** Make this selection if L2TP should be used exclusively on this connection.

5. In the **Destination Address** dialog box, enter the IP address of the router at the other end of the VPN connection.

6. In the **Protocols and Security** dialog box, check the desired options:

   - **Route IP packets on this interface.** This option configures the VPN to tunnel IP packets. It will be enabled in most cases.
   - **Route IPX packets on this interface.** This option configures the VPN to tunnel IPX packets.
   - **Add a user account so a remote router can dial in.** If the remote router must be able to dial in to establish a connection, an appropriate user account must be created. If the account is not already established, check this option.

7. The **Dial In Credentials** dialog box is used to specify the user account and password that a remote router must supply when authenticating to this connection. This box has the following fields:

   - **User name.** This field is already completed with the name of the interface, as specified in Step 3. (Recall that the interface and user names must be identical for remote router connections.)
   - **Password** and **Confirm password.** Supply the password for the user account.

8. If you checked **Add a user account so a remote router can dial in** in Step 6, the next dialog box is **Dial Out Credentials**. This dialog box defines the credentials used for authentication when this router dials in to a remote router. Complete the fields as follows:

   - **User name.** Enter the name of a user account, which must be identical to the name of the dial-in interface on the remote router.
   - **Domain.** Enter the domain in which the user account is defined.
   - **Password** and **Confirm password.** Supply the password for the user account.

9. Finish the wizard to create the interface.

A demand-dial interface must be defined on the RRAS servers at both ends of the VPN connection. User accounts are required only for routers that accept requests for VPN connections. Figure 11.43 lists the settings I used for my demonstration network.

Configuring Static Routes

As with demand-dial routers, static routes must be configured so that packets sent to the remote network will be directed to the demand-dial interface and initiate a connection. See the section "Static Routes" in Chapter 8 for the procedures.

On the example network, router 10.1.0.1 requires the following static route:

- **Interface:** AtlantaVPN
- **Destination:** 10.2.0.0
- **Network Mask:** 255.255.0.0

Router 10.2.0.1 requires this static route:

- **Interface:** SeattleVPN
- **Destination:** 10.1.0.0
- **Network Mask:** 255.255.0.0

Use this route to initiate demand-dial connections must be enabled for both routers.

Configuring Demand-Dial Interface Properties

To view the properties for a VPN interface, open the **Routing Interface** container, right-click the interface, and choose **Properties** from the context menu. Demand-dial interface properties are covered in Chapter 8 in the section "Configuring RRAS Dial-Up Properties." Here, we'll focus on the distinctions between VPN interfaces and standard dial-out interfaces.

For a VPN, the **General** tab has a single field that specifies the IP address of the router at the remote end of the VPN connection.

The **Options** tab is similar to the example in Figure 8.26. Because it takes several seconds for a VPN connection to be established, the **Persistent connection** option will often be selected for a VPN interface. Windows 2000 housekeeping traffic will usually prevent RRAS from closing the connection even if an idle connection timeout is configured.

The **Security** tab applies only to PPTP connections. This tab is discussed in the section "Settings in the Advanced Settings Dialog Box" in Chapter 8.

The **Networking** tab for a VPN connection (See Figure 11.46) includes a field named **Type of VPN server I am calling**. Three choices are available for this field:

- **Automatic**
- **Point-to-Point Tunneling Protocol (PPTP)**
- **Layer-2 Tunneling Protocol (L2TP)**

If **Automatic** is selected, RRAS will first attempt to establish an L2TP connection. If unsuccessful, RRAS sets up a PPTP connection.

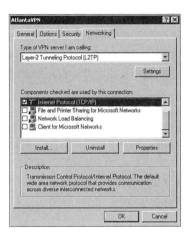

FIGURE 11.46
Networking options for a VPN demand-dial interface.

You can change the protocol used for the connection at any time, although changes will not
take effect until the connection is restarted. To complete the protocol change, disable the
interfaces at both ends, disconnect the connection, enable both interfaces, and restart the
connection.

Enabling a PPTP Connection

PPTP VPNs are stupefyingly easy to get running. Use the **Demand Dial Interface Wizard** to
create the demand-dial connections and user accounts. Then add the required static routes.
Assuming that the routers can communicate through the intervening network, starting the connection is a simple matter of right-clicking one of the demand-dial interfaces in the **Routing
Interfaces** container and choosing **Connect** in the context menu.

If static routes are properly configured, a connection should also be initiated when RRAS
receives packets to be routed from one site to the other.

NOTE

Before starting an L2TP VPN you must install a Computer or Domain Controller certificate on the router. After that, the connection is managed in the same manner as with
PPTP. See the section "Installing Certificates for L2TP" a bit later in the chapter for
more information.

Monitoring a VPN Interface

A VPN interface can be in several states, as indicated by the **Status** and **Connection State** columns in the Details pane for **Routing Interfaces**.

In the **Status** column, the interface is described as follows:

- Enabled. An enabled interface can initiate a connection attempt either on command or in response to a request from a static route. To enable the interface, right-click the interface and choose **Enable** in the context menu.

- Disabled. A disabled interface cannot be used to initiate a connection. To disable the interface, right-click the interface and choose **Disable** in the context menu.

In the **Connection State** column the interface is described as follows:

- Disconnected. The connection is idle but can initiate a connection if it is enabled. To disconnect an active interface, right-click the interface and choose **Disconnect** in the context menu.

- Connecting. The interface is attempting to negotiate a connection.

- Connected. The connection is active. To connect a disconnected interface, right-click the interface and choose **Connect** in the context menu.

- Unreachable. The last attempt to establish a connection was unsuccessful. RAS will not attempt the connection again unless an administrator issues a **Connect** command. Use the **Unreachability reason** in the context menu to determine the reason for the connection failure.

Although only one of the demand-dial interfaces will be connected, each router allocates a port to the connection. Connected ports will be identified as Active in the **Ports** Details pane. There is no easy way to determine which port is associated with a given connection. If you double-click an active port, the **Condition** field in the **Port Status** dialog box identifies the demand-dial interface that requested the connection.

In the report generated by entering the command **IPCONFIG /ALL**, a PPTP interface is identified as a WAN (PPP/SLIP) Interface, which isn't surprising since PPP provides the highest-layer encapsulation of payloads in PPTP and L2TP packets.

Each demand-dial interface that is configured on the RRAS server is assigned an interface identified as a RAS Server (Dial In) Interface, which is assigned an IP address taken from the address pool on the local network. Here is an example:

```
Connection-specific DNS Suffix   . :
Description . . . . . . . . . . . : WAN (PPP/SLIP) Interface
Physical Address. . . . . . . . . : 00-53-45-00-00-00
DHCP Enabled. . . . . . . . . . . : No
```

```
IP Address. . . . . . . . . . . . : 10.2.0.200
Subnet Mask . . . . . . . . . . . : 255.255.255.255
Default Gateway . . . . . . . . . :
DNS Servers . . . . . . . . . . . : 10.1.0.1
```

Each active connection is assigned an interface, which is assigned IP address taken from the address pool on the remote network. Here is a sample:

```
PPP adapter {C19B9648-2984-41C0-9E8D-BA2BC4BEC395}:
    Connection-specific DNS Suffix  . :
    Description . . . . . . . . . . . : WAN (PPP/SLIP) Interface
    Physical Address. . . . . . . . . : 00-53-45-00-00-00
    DHCP Enabled. . . . . . . . . . : No
    IP Address. . . . . . . . . . . : 10.1.0.202
    Subnet Mask . . . . . . . . . . : 255.255.255.255
    Default Gateway . . . . . . . . :
    DNS Servers . . . . . . . . . . : 10.1.0.1
```

Installing Certificates for L2TP

L2TP routers authenticate one another using public key certificates, and before an L2TP VPN can be enabled, each router must be configured with a Computer or Domain Controller certificate issued by a mutually trusted CA. (See the next section for a way to use shared-secret authentication.) The easiest approach is to configure an enterprise root CA, as described in Chapter 9, that will be trusted by all computers in the Active Directory tree. By default, IPSec assumes that both routers will have certificates from the same CA. The problem is obtaining a certificate from a remote site for a Windows 2000 Server that isn't a domain member and cannot therefore request a certificate from an enterprise CA.

Let's assume that you are setting up a new site. You have a Windows 2000 Server at the remote site that will be configured as a VPN router. The server needs to join a domain and obtain a certificate before it can support L2TP. You don't want the server to join the domain using an unsecured Internet connection. Here's a simple approach that solves the problem:

1. Install Windows 2000 Server and configure it to connect to the Internet.

2. Configure a VPN dial-out connection as discussed in the section "Configuring the Client VPN Connection."

3. Dial in to the VPN remote access server. Because a certificate is not installed on the client, a PPTP connection is established, authenticated with an existing username and password. The server is now a remote node on the organization's network.

4. Join the desired domain as a stand-alone server.

5. Request and install a certificate from a CA that is trusted by the RAS server.

6. Disconnect and connect again. This time, an L2TP connection should be established.

Modifying the IPSec VPN Policy

Have you noticed anything missing from our discussion about IPSec as it is used by L2TP? Like the non-mention of any IPSec policies, perhaps? From earlier discussion, we know that IPSec policies are always required by Windows 2000. Is this an exception?

No, an IPSec policy exists, but it is created and maintained automatically without any administrator attention. Ordinarily, this is a real convenience, but occasionally it can be obstructive. For example, the policy requires use of certificates for authentication. Normally, that's a good thing, but what if a router doesn't have a certificate yet? You might want to use pre-shared keys for authentication until a certificate is installed.

The L2TP IPSec policy can be disabled by adding a value entry to the following location in the Registry:

```
HKEY_LOCAL_MACHINE
   \System\
   \CurrentControlSet
   \Services
   \Rasman
   \Parameters
```

Add the value entry ProhibitIpSec of type REG_DWORD. Assign it the value 1 to disable the L2TP IPSec policy. A value of 0 enables the L2TP IPSec policy. The computer must be restarted to activate the change. When the ProhibitIpSec has a value of 1, Windows will check for a local or Active Directory IPSec policy.

Now that you can configure L2TP/IPSec with an administrator-defined IPSec policy, you can freely configure IPSec with a custom IPSec policy.

CAUTION

If the L2TP IPSec policy is disabled and IPSec policy is assigned locally or in Group Policy, Windows attempts the connection without IPSec. It may be useful to create an L2TP tunnel without IPSec when troubleshooting, but during normal operation it is clearly a serious breach of security.

NOTE

The L2TP IPSec policy is described in Microsoft Knowledge Base article Q248750.

The procedure for disabling the L2TP IPSec policy is described in Microsoft Knowledge Base article Q258261.

Both articles are available on http://support.microsoft.com.

Configuring Interface Filters

Microsoft assumes that a RRAS interface that is supporting VPN connections will be dedicated to that purpose. To that end, the **Virtual private network (VPN server)** in the **RRAS Configuration Wizard** automatically installs filters on the interface that block everything except PPTP, L2TP, and GRE packets. If VPN support is configured manually, Microsoft recommends that the same filters be configured manually.

Tables 11.2 and 11.3 summarize the input and output filters that Microsoft recommends and that the **Virtual private network (VPN server)** option configures.

TABLE 11.2 Default Input Filters for VPN Interfaces

Source Address	Source Mask	Dest. Address	Dest. Mask	Protocol	Source Port or Type	Dest. Port or Code
Any	Any	Local Interface	255.255. 255.255	47 (GRE)	Any	Any
Any	Any	Local Interface	255.255. 255.255	TCP	1723 (PPTP)	Any
Any	Any	Local Interface	255.255. 255.255	TCP	Any	1723
Any	Any	Local Interface	255.255. 255.255	UDP	500 (ISAKMP)	500
Any	Any	Local Interface	255.255. 255.255	UDP	1701 (L2TP)	1701

TABLE 11.3 Default Output Filters for VPN Interfaces

Source Address	Source Mask	Dest. Address	Dest. Mask	Protocol	Source Port or Type	Dest. Port or Code
Local Interface	255.255. 255.255	Any	Any	47 (GRE)	Any	Any
Local Interface	255.255. 255.255	Any	Any	TCP	1723 (PPTP)	Any
Local Interface	255.255. 255.255	Any	Any	TCP	Any	1723
Local Interface	255.255. 255.255	Any	Any	UDP	500 (ISAKMP)	500
Local Interface	255.255. 255.255	Any	Any	UDP	1701 (L2TP)	1701

When these filters are in place on the interface that communicates with the Internet, the RRAS server will no longer be able to function as a router to the Internet for standard Internet traffic. If users on the local networks need to communicate with the Internet, a separate router must be configured. Figure 11.47 shows one possible configuration. Clients are configured to use router 10.1.0.1 as a default router. If data must be forwarded to network 10.2.0.0/16 through the VPN, 10.1.0.1 forwards the datagrams to 10.1.0.2.

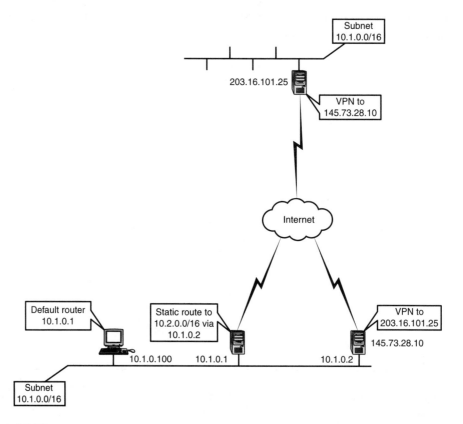

FIGURE 11.47

One option for supporting normal and VPN communication with the Internet.

Large organizations will probably use third-party hardware-based routers for the firewall and VPN support, so the requirement for extra routers is a hardship primarily for small organizations that want to use a VPN to save communication costs with as little extra hardware expenditure as possible.

It is possible to run RRAS Network Address Translation on a server that is also supporting VPN connections. Clearly, there may be performance concerns with such an approach, but the approach remains technically sound. Because static routes direct packets to the VPN interfaces as required, the router's default route can be used to forward Internet packets to a router at the ISP. The NAT provides security for incoming traffic that is not directed to the VPN interface. If a RRAS server is not dedicated to VPN support, the input and output filters recommended by Microsoft should not be enabled.

Supporting Client-to-Server VPN Connections

RAS is ready to support VPN clients as soon as you check **Remote access server** in RRAS **Properties**. All you need to accept client VPN connections is a selection of PPTP and/or L2TP ports and an interface that is accessible from the Internet. After that, there are only a few things to configure, all of which we've looked at before:

- Determine the numbers of PPTP and L2TP ports in **Ports Properties**.
- Configure PPTP authentication methods on the **Security** tab of the RRAS server's **Properties** pages.
- Configure IP address assignment and other IP settings on the **IP** tab of the RRAS server's **Properties** pages.

Windows clients access VPN connections using a variation of a dial-up connection. Capabilities of Windows clients are as follows:

- Windows 2000 clients support VPN connections using PPTP and L2TP.
- Windows NT 4 and Windows 95/98 support PPTP only.

Once RAS is configured to support dial-in VPN connections, it is a simple matter to enable clients to establish a VPN connection through the Internet. Some or all of the following items must be configured to support client VPN access:

- A remote access policy must be created.
- Certificates must be installed on clients that will connect using L2TP.
- A VPN dial-up connection must be configured on the client.

Creating a Remote Access Policy for Client VPN Connections

A user must have permission to dial in to a VPN connection. Permission is a function of the **Remote Access Permission** setting on the **Dial-in** tab of the user's account **Properties** pages, in conjunction with the remote access policy that is used. Methods for allowing and denying user dial-in permissions are covered in Chapter 8 in the section "Dial-In User Authorization Models."

You may want to create an Active Directory group that can be used to distinguish users permitted to establish VPN connections, perhaps a group named **VPN_Users**. This group can be included in a condition for the remote access policy so that only group members are permitted to use VPN remote access. See the section "Remote Access Policies" in Chapter 8 for the procedures used to manage remote access policies. Figures 8.32–8.39 include the dialog boxes used to create the VPN remote access policy.

A remote access policy for VPN users has properties similar to the following:

- **Policy name:** Enter something suitable such as **Allow VPN Access for members of the VPN_Users Group**.
- **Conditions:**
  - If particular group membership is required, add a **Windows-Groups** condition and include the group name or names.
  - Add a **NAS-Port-Type** condition and add Virtual (VPN) to the **Selected Types** list.
  - Add a **Tunnel-Type** condition and add Layer Two Tunneling Protocol and Point-to-Point to the **Selected Types** list. (You can, of course, omit either protocol if you want to support only one type of VPN.)
- **Permissions:** Select Grant remote access permission.

Either delete the policy **Allow access if dial-in permission is enabled**, or ensure that it follows the new VPN policy in the **Remote Access Policies** list.

Installing a Client Certificate

Presumably, the client that will be dialing in is already a member of a domain. If the client does not have a certificate, RAS will establish a PPTP tunnel the first time the client connects. If desired, the client can then request and install a certificate from a CA on the organization's network that is trusted by the RRAS server. After the certificate is installed, RAS will attempt to create an L2TP VPN connection on subsequent connection attempts.

Configuring the Client VPN Connection

To configure a VPN dial-up connection on a Windows 2000 client, do the following:

1. In **Network and Dial-up Connections**, double-click **Make New Connection**.
2. In the **Network Connection Type** dialog box, select **Connect to a private network through the Internet**.
3. In the **Destination Address** dialog box, specify the IP address of the interface for a RRAS server that accepts VPN connections.

4. In the **Connection Availability** dialog box, select one of the following:

- **For all users.** This option enables other users on a local network to share the connection through Network Connection Sharing.

- **Only for myself.** This option prevents users on other computers from sharing the connection.

5. In the **Completing the Network Connection Wizard** dialog box, enter a name for the dial-up connection. Optionally, check **Add a shortcut to my desktop**.

If the remote computer's connection is permanent, for example via DSL or cable modem, the VPN dial-up connection can be invoked immediately.

If the client must dial in to the Internet, a dial-up connection must be started before the VPN connection. Fortunately, there's an easy way to have the VPN connection invoke the dial-up connection automatically.

The **General** tab for a VPN connection's **Properties** dialog box is shown in Figure 11.48. Simply check **Dial another connection first** and specify the name of the dial-up connection in the accompanying field.

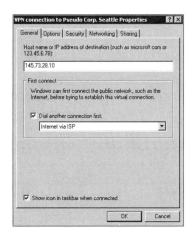

FIGURE 11.48

A VPN connection can start a dial-up connection before the VPN is initialized.

The **Networking** tab for a VPN connection is shown in Figure 11.49. By default, the **Type of VPN server I am calling** field has the value Automatic. Typically, RAS will respond by offering the client an L2TP connection, assuming L2TP ports are available. If a suitable certificate is installed on the client, the L2TP connection is established. Otherwise, RAS attempts to start a PPTP connection.

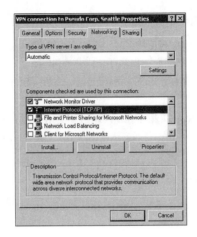

FIGURE 11.49
A VPN client is typically configured for automatic selection of the VPN type.

The **Settings** button on the **Networking** tab accesses the **PPP Settings** dialog box with the following options:

- **Enable LCP extensions** must be checked.
- **Enable software compression** may be checked, in which case hardware compression should be disabled.
- **Negotiate multi-link for single link connections** has no effect in this scenario.

We Finally Can Say Goodbye to RRAS

Virtual Private Networking rounds out our discussion of the Routing and Remote Access Service. It's taken three chapters with a lengthy side discussion of security methods to get through everything, but you now have access to a pretty thorough toolkit for building routing, demand-dial connections, and VPNs.

The next chapter is a sort of catch-all for tools and techniques related to connection management. We'll cover some network management tools, such as Network Monitor and some command-line utilities that haven't yet been addressed. We'll also discuss the simple network management protocol (SNMP) and see how it is supported by Windows 2000.

Managing and Monitoring Connections

IN THIS CHAPTER

We have already discussed several Windows 2000 connection-management tools, most particularly the Network and Dial-Up Connections applet in Chapter 1 and IPCONFIG in Chapter 5. We also examined Network Monitor in several chapters, although discussion to this point has been limited to interpreting network traces. This is a catch-all chapter in which we will examine Network Monitor in greater detail as well as a variety of utilities that assist in managing and troubleshooting network connections.

We'll start by discussing the use of Network Monitor and Performance Monitor, after which we will examine command-line utilities from the Windows 2000 Server CD-ROM and the Windows 2000 Server Resource Kit.

Network Monitor

We have encountered Network Monitor in several places, most particularly in Chapter 2, "TCP/IP Protocol Concepts." While we examined some network traces, we didn't discuss the procedures for using Network Monitor in the first place.

Network Monitor extends your network analysis capability by enabling you to capture network frames for detailed examination. After frames are captured, you can look inside them to perform a thorough analysis of the network's operation.

Network Monitor is equipped with a wide variety of *protocol parsers*, which are modules that examine network frames to decode their contents. The most important ones for the purposes of this book are Ethernet, ARP, IP, TCP, UDP, and a variety of Internet application-layer protocols. Network Monitor also includes parsers for token ring and other network access protocols, IPX, and a variety of other protocols including such Microsoft-specific protocols as Server Message Blocks (SMB).

In this section, we will be focusing on the procedures for using Network Monitor, not on the interpretation of frame contents. See Chapter 2 for more information about the structures of frames carrying IP communication.

NOTE

In most Windows 2000 documentation, Microsoft uses the term *packet* to refer to bundles of data that are transported through a network, and I've followed that lead throughout the book. For some reason, however, when discussing Network Monitor, the term changes to *frame*. The terms are interchangeable, although packet is perhaps a tiny bit more generic than frame. To avoid an occasional silly-sounding sentence, it's easiest for me to follow their lead and employ the term frame when discussing Network Monitor.

Network Monitor and Systems Management Server

As shipped with Windows 2000 Server, Network Monitor has one particularly significant limitation: It can capture only those frames that originate from or are delivered to the computer on which Network Monitor is running, including broadcast and multicast frames that the computer receives or originates. It cannot capture frames that are not sent to or from the server on which it is running.

Microsoft's stated reason for hobbling Network Monitor as it ships with Windows 2000 Server is to prevent unauthorized users from using it to examine network traffic. That explanation seems a bit thin. I'm not sure why a user might go to the expense of obtaining a copy of Windows 2000 Server just to snoop the network when inexpensive analyzers are readily available.

Since several other features of the Windows 2000 Server Network Monitor are unavailable, a more plausible reason for distributing a limited version of Network Monitor is that Microsoft wants to sell you their Systems Management Server (SMS) product. SMS includes a non-crippled version of Network Monitor that can capture all network packets and can obtain network statistics from any Windows computer that is running a Network Monitor Agent, such as the Windows 2000 Network Monitor driver. (*Agents* are proxy programs that collect data and forward them to another computer for analysis.)

Ordinarily, computers on a network are selective and will only receive frames that are addressed to them. As shipped with Windows 2000, Network Monitor is designed to work with standard network adapter cards, which in part accounts for the restriction that Network Monitor can capture only those frames that originate from or are delivered to the computer on which Network Monitor is running.

The SMS Network Monitor captures network traffic in *promiscuous mode*, meaning that it can capture all network data regardless of the destination of the frames. This enables SMS to monitor any computer running a Network Monitor Agent. However, capturing data in promiscuous mode is intense work, and performance will suffer on the computer running SMS. Therefore, monitoring the network with SMS Network Monitor is an activity best reserved for a dedicated network management computer. (On some network types, such as token ring, special network adapters are required to support promiscuous mode. Because the Network Monitor included with Windows 2000 Server does not operate in promiscuous mode, special network adapters are not required.)

SMS has other capabilities as well, including hardware inventory management and software management. Unless you require SMS capabilities other than Network Monitor, however, SMS is neither the most powerful nor the most cost-effective way to analyze network traffic. SMS is not an inexpensive product, particularly because it requires Microsoft SQL Server. Also, Network Monitor's capabilities fall short of those offered by third-party network analyzers, particularly regarding analysis of other vendors' protocols.

Most network administrators will be well served by moderately priced software-based protocol analyzers such as Network Associate's Sniffer Basic or Sniffer Pro (www.sniffer.com), or the EtherPeek and TokenPeek products from Wildframes (www.wildpackets.com). Sniffer Basic (about $1,500 for a two-year license with maintenance) and EtherPeek/TokenPeek ($995 without maintenance) are extremely capable and cost-effective products. Other affordable protocol analyzers include LanExplorer ($799; www.intellimax.com), LANtracer ($995 for single license; www.lantracer.com), and LANSleuth ($649–$949; www.lansleuth.com). All of these products are available via download for trial use. I can only endorse Sniffer (Basic and Pro) and EtherPeek, but any of these products equals or exceeds the capabilities of Network Monitor.

Installing Network Monitor

Network Monitor consists of two components:

- **Network Monitor Driver.** Install this component on computers that will be monitored by a server running SMS. The driver can be installed on Windows 2000 Professional or Windows 2000 Server.

- **Network Monitor Tools.** Install this component on Windows 2000 Server computers that will be used to collect and analyze network frames. Installing the **Network Monitor Tools** component also installs and enables the Network Monitor driver, which captures frames for analysis in Network Monitor.

The Network Monitor driver is installed as a connection component. In the **Properties** dialog box for the desired connection, click **Install**, open **Protocol**, and select **Network Monitor Driver**. The driver requires no configuration. See "Configuring Local Area Network Connections" in Chapter 1 for further discussion of the procedure. Only members of the Administrators group can install this driver.

Use **Add/Remove Programs** in the Control Panel to install **Network Monitor Tools**, which is located under **Add/Remove Windows Components** in the **Management and Monitoring Tools** component category. The Network Monitor driver is installed with Network Monitor Tools and is enabled in the properties of all connections. See "Installing Windows 2000 Components" in Chapter 1 for procedural details.

Network Monitor Security

The Network Monitor agent that is included with Windows 2000 Server can be configured with passwords to restrict access to captured data. Passwords are not required for the Windows 2000 network monitor driver. Only members of the Administrators group can examine data captured by a Network Monitor driver.

Network Monitor detects all copies of the Network Monitor driver that are running on the network and reports the following information about each instance:

- The name of the computer

- The name of the user who is logged in on the computer

- The state of Network Monitor if it is running on the computer, which may be `running`, `capturing`, or `transmitting`, as well as the Network Monitor version number

- The hardware address of the computer's network adapter

CAUTION

Network Monitors detect one another using multicast messaging. If routers do not forward multicast frames, Network Monitor will be unable to detect installations on other networks.

Capturing Network Frames

The Network Monitor Capture window is shown in Figure 12.1, which identifies the toolbar buttons and the panes. The Capture window contains four panes:

- **Graph Pane.** This pane includes bar charts that dynamically display current activity. The five bars in this pane are **% Network Utilization**, **Frames Per Second**, **Bytes Per Second**, **Broadcasts Per Second**, and **Multicasts Per Second**. You can display or hide this pane by clicking the **Toggle Graph Pane** button. (A line in the **% Network Utilization** bar designates the highest utilization encountered during the current capture. The numbers at the right ends of the other bars describe the highest measurements encountered.)

- **Total Statistics.** This pane displays cumulative network statistics. These statistics summarize network traffic in five areas: **Network Statistics**, **Captured Statistics**, **Per Second Statistics**, **Network Card (MAC) Statistics**, and **Network Card (MAC) Error Statistics** (some of which are not visible in the figure). You can display or hide this pane by clicking the **Toggle Total Statistics Pane** button.

- **Session Statistics.** This pane displays statistics about sessions that are currently operating on the network. You can display or hide this pane by clicking the **Toggle Total Session Statistics Pane** button.

- **Station Statistics.** This pane displays statistics about sessions in which this computer is participating. You can display or hide this pane by clicking the **Toggle Total Station Statistics Pane** button.

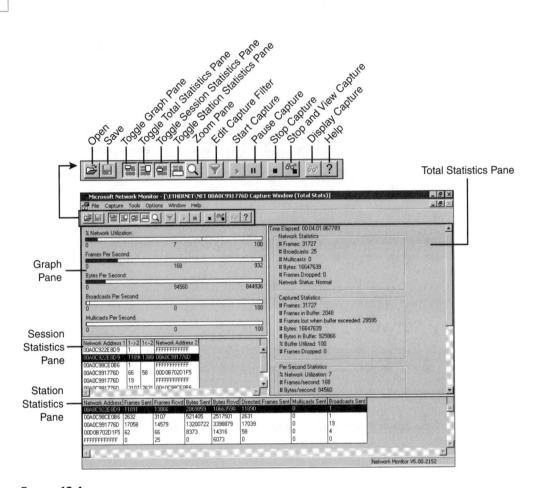

FIGURE 12.1

Elements of the Network Monitor window.

To start capturing frames, use one of the following techniques:

- Select the menu command **Capture→Start**
- Press F10
- Click the **Start Capture** button

To stop capturing frames and remain in the Capture window, do one of the following:

- Select **Capture→Stop**
- Press F11
- Click the **Stop Capture** button

To stop capturing frames and open the Display window, do one of the following:

- Select **Capture→Stop and View**
- Press Shift+F11
- Click the **Stop and View Capture** button

Figure 12.1 was prepared while a capture was taking place. The information in the various panes is updated dynamically while capturing is active.

> **TIP**
>
> The panes in the Capture window can be displayed or hidden by clicking the four toggle buttons in the toolbar. You can focus on the activity in one of the panes. Simply select the pane and click the **Zoom Pane** button in the toolbar. The pane you selected will expand to fill the available space. To return to normal display, click the **Zoom Pane** button again.

Creating an Address Database

When you first capture data in Network Monitor, most devices will be identified by their physical network addresses (such as their Ethernet MAC addresses). The captures shown in Chapter 2, for example, identify computers by MAC or IP addresses.

Because Microsoft network administrators generally prefer to identify computers by their names, Network Monitor includes a feature that identifies the names of computers from which data are captured. In Figure 12.1 most computers are identified by name.

To build the address database, start capturing data on the network and let Network Monitor continue to collect data for an extended period of time. As traffic is generated, computers will be added to the **Session Statistics** and **Station Statistics** panes, identified by their network addresses.

After capturing a large number of frames, stop capturing and switch to the Display window. Then select **Display→Find All Names**. The frames in the capture buffer will be scanned and names that can be identified will be added to the address database. During future capture operations, computers will be identified by name, as shown in Figure 12.2.

Network Address	Frames Sent	Frames Rcvd	Bytes Sent	Bytes Rcvd	Directed Frames Sent	Multicasts Sent	Broadcasts Sent
DC3	19797	22833	5010703	16946184	19796	0	1
DC2	10443	11947	2644086	8676216	10441	0	2
DC1	35033	30423	25756838	7683042	35014	0	19
00D0B702D1F5	190	234	29071	139123	186	0	4
*BROADCAST	0	26	0	6133	0	0	0

FIGURE 12.2

Computers identified by name in Network Monitor.

NOTE

A bit of luck is required to capture frames that include computer names. Each time you capture data, collect names and add them to the database until the list is complete.

You can view the address database, shown in Figure 12.3, by choosing the command **Capture→Addresses** in the Capture window or the command **Display→Addresses** in the Display window. Notice in the figure that a given computer may be represented by multiple entries, associated with different protocols and network types.

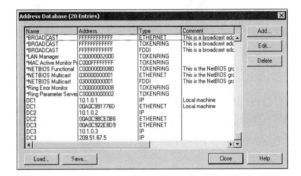

FIGURE 12.3

Viewing the address database.

In the **Address Database** dialog box, you can add, edit, and delete specific entries. You can save the database to a file with an .ADR extension, and load existing address files. The default address database, which is used unless you load another, is saved as DEFAULT.ADR.

Quite a few names are included in the original DEFAULT.ADR file such as Ring Error Monitor for use on token ring networks and NETBIOS Multicast. It is not necessary to remove unused names, and I suggest you make a backup copy of the original DEFAULT.ADR file if you choose to delete some of its original contents.

NOTE

On occasion, you will want to display addresses instead of computer names. Toggle display of computer names by choosing the command **Options→Show Address Names**.

When address names are turned off, Network Monitor's default behavior is to display vendor names instead of the first three bytes of MAC addresses. Display of vendor names can be toggled with the command **Options→Show Vendor Names**.

Selecting the Network to be Monitored

Network Monitor can collect frames from only one network interface at a time. When you start Network Monitor for the first time, you are asked to select the network interface that is to be monitored, which is specified by its MAC address. Use the command **IPCONFIG /ALL** to determine the MAC addresses of a computer's network adapters.

To change the network interface being monitored, select the menu bar command **Capture→Networks** to open the **Select a network** dialog box shown in Figure 12.4. Then select one of the available interfaces and click **OK**.

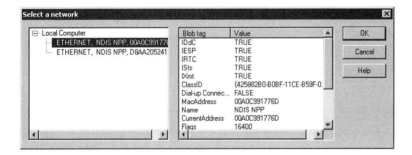

FIGURE 12.4
Selecting the network to be analyzed.

TIP

Start multiple instances of Network Monitor if you want to monitor more than one interface on a multi-homed computer. Doing so may, of course, have a negative impact on performance.

Managing the Capture Buffer

Frames captured by Network Monitor are stored in system memory in a *capture buffer*. Due to their inherent performance limitations, disk storage cannot be used to store frames being captured without the risk of losing frames during the capture process.

To adjust the operating characteristics of the capture buffer, choose **Capture→Buffer Settings** to open the **Capture Buffer Settings** dialog box shown in Figure 12.5. This dialog box has two fields:

- **Buffer Size (MB)** is used to adjust the size of the buffer in one-megabyte intervals.
- **Frame Size (Bytes)** specifies the number of bytes in each frame that are to be buffered starting from the beginning of the frame.

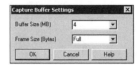

FIGURE 12.5
Configuring the capture buffer.

Adjusting the Capture Buffer Size

Ideally, the capture buffer should reside entirely in RAM. Virtual memory can be used, but frames will probably be lost. Therefore, setting the size of the capture buffer involves compromise. If the buffer is too small, it may not be large enough to capture a reasonable sample of network traffic. If the capture buffer is too large, part of it may be swapped into virtual memory and the efficiency of network data capture will likely be impaired.

When a capture is started, Windows 2000 Server allocates memory to support the entire capture buffer, as designated in the **Capture Buffer Settings** dialog box. When you increase the size of the capture buffer, consult the **Performance** tab of the **Windows Task Manager** (start it by pressing Ctrl+Alt+Delete and clicking the **Task Manager** button) to assess memory usage. Statistics under **Commit Charge (K)** indicate total memory in use, including physical and virtual memory. If **Total Commit Charge** exceeds **Total Physical Memory**, the system must make use of virtual memory to store executing processes and data associated with the processes.

To ensure the best performance for Network Monitor, you should take one or more of the following actions to ensure that **Total Physical Memory** is greater than **Total Commit Charge**:

- Reduce the size of the Network Monitor capture buffer
- Stop unneeded processes
- Install additional RAM

Adjusting the Capture Frame Size

It is often useful to have a protocol analyzer capturing packets on a network segment at all times. For example:

- If a performance problem or network failure occurs, a history of recent frames provides clues to the source of the problem.

- Network statistics can help identify sources of heavy network traffic. Users or computers may be using excessive amounts of bandwidth due to poorly written software, malfunctioning hardware, or misuse, either unintentional or intentional. They can also be used to analyze network patterns such as amounts of broadcast and multicast frames, network traffic load balance, and so forth.

- A protocol analyzer running on a network interface that connects to the Internet can provide valuable information if an intrusion attempt is detected. This information can be used to diagnose the type of the attack and possibly to learn the identity of the network, computer, or even the user originating the attack. This evidence is vital when working with an ISP to shut down the source of an attack or when prosecuting intruders.

12

MANAGING AND MONITORING CONNECTIONS

NOTE

The practice of keeping a protocol analyzer active on each network is particularly important with token ring. If a token ring adapter fails, its nearest downstream neighbor, after realizing it isn't receiving any frames, will transmit a beacon signal to notify management stations of the fault. Captured frames can be used to identify the beaconing computer along with its position in the ring, information that can be used to identify and locate the computer with the failed adapter. A token ring station cannot be inserted into a beaconing ring, so the only way to obtain ring diagnostic information is to have a protocol analysis station operating on the ring before a failure occurs.

When running a protocol analyzer on a permanent basis, you probably want to capture as many recent frames as possible. You probably don't need to retain the entire contents of the frames, however, so you can capture more frames if you limit the capture frame size, perhaps to 200 bytes, so that more frame headers will fit into the capture buffer.

That is the purpose of the **Frame Size (Bytes)** property. By default, the value of this field is Full, indicating that complete frames are to be captured. If you want to capture large numbers of frames carrying IP traffic, you might adjust the capture frame size to 200 so that all headers would be buffered along with the first hundred or so bytes in the data payload.

Avoiding Dropped Frames

When frames are being captured, a significant part of the computer's processing capacity is required to dynamically update the Network Monitor display. When the CPU is busy, frames may be lost. You can reduce CPU loading by placing Network Monitor in dedicated capture mode.

To reduce the processing demands of Network Monitor, choose the command **Capture→ Dedicated Capture Mode**. When capturing is active, the **Dedicated Mode** dialog box is displayed, as shown in Figure 12.6. If capturing is currently stopped, the **Dedicated Mode** dialog box will be displayed when capturing is started.

FIGURE 12.6
Capturing in dedicated mode.

When capturing in dedicated mode, only the number of captured frames is updated in the display. You can stop and pause capturing in the **Dedicated Mode** dialog box. If you choose **Normal Mode**, the Capture window is opened and capturing continues while statistics are updated. If you choose **Stop and View**, capturing will stop and the Display window will be opened.

Using Capture Filters

On a large network, the traffic volume can overwhelm you unless you have a way of focusing on specific types of frames. *Capture filters* enable you to specify which types of frames will be captured, enabling you to capture data from a specific subset of computers or protocols.

> **NOTE**
>
> Capture filters determine which frames will be stored in the capture buffer, however all frames are reported in the performance statistics, regardless of any capture filter that may be in effect.

Structures of Capture Filters

To select, create, or modify a capture filter choose **Capture→Filter** to open the **Capture Filter** dialog box shown in Figure 12.7. Capture filters consist of three sets of criteria that are organized in a decision tree, connected by logical operators. Shown in the figure is the default capture filter, in which all criteria are logically associated by AND operators. Frames will be captured only if they meet all three of the following criteria: SAP/ETYPE, Address Pairs, and Pattern Matches. The capture filter criteria are described in the following sections.

The AND operators that logically relate SAP/ETYPE, Address Pairs, and Pattern Matches conditions cannot be modified. The **OR** and **NOT** buttons in the **Capture Filter** dialog box are active only when defining criteria under the **(Pattern Matches)** heading.

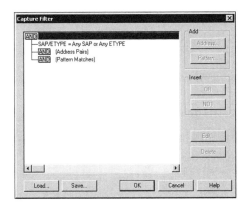

FIGURE 12.7
The default capture filter.

SAP/ETYPE Filters

The frames associated with specific protocols are identified by hexadecimal numbers referred to as SAPs or ETYPEs. By default, Network Monitor captures frames matching all supported protocols, but you can restrict capturing to specific protocols by selecting the SAPs and ETYPEs that will pass through the filter.

ETYPEs (*EtherTypes*) and SAPs (*service access points*) are used to specify the upper-layer protocols that are associated with a frame. We discussed EtherTypes in Chapter 2, where it was mentioned that an EtherType of x800 is associated with the IP protocol. An EtherType of x8137 is associated with NetWare running on an EtherNet II LAN. SAP numbers serve a similar function in Novell's IPX protocol stack.

To establish capture filters for specific SAPs or ETYPES, double-click the **SAP/ETYPE=** line in the Capture Filter dialog box to open the **Capture Filter SAPs and ETYPEs** dialog box shown in Figure 12.8. The capture filter matches frames matching protocols that are specified in the **Enabled Protocols** list, and by default all supported ETYPEs and SAPs are included in this list.

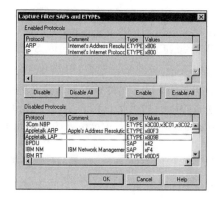

FIGURE 12.8
Filtering SAPs and ETYPEs.

To disable protocols, use the **Disable** or **Disable All** buttons to move protocols to the **Disabled Protocols** list. In Figure 12.8, all protocols have been disabled except for IP and ARP.

To enable disabled protocols, use the **Enable** and **Enable All** buttons to move protocols to the **Enabled Protocols** list.

When you return to the **Capture Filter** dialog box, the enabled protocols are listed following the **SAP/ETYPE=** header.

NOTE

Network Monitor does not provide a direct method of filtering upper-layer protocols. For example, you can't create a capture filter that explicitly says "only capture HTTP packets." To create capture filters of this nature, you must define pattern matches.

Often it is easier to capture all frames for a given internet-layer protocol and to use a display filter to limit the frames that are displayed for analysis. Display filters can be designed for specific upper-layer protocols.

Address Filters

Every frame is associated with a source-destination address pair. By default, frames will be captured for all source-destination address pairs, but you can limit capturing to specific address pairs if desired.

An address pair consists of the following components:

- A source address (or computer name), which can be a MAC address or an IP address
- A destination address (or computer name), which can also be a MAC address or an IP address, although the address type must be the same as the type of the source address
- A direction arrow (--->, <---, or <-->) specifying direction(s) in which traffic should be monitored
- The keyword INCLUDE or EXCLUDE specifies whether frames should or should not be captured for this address pair

Address pairs are established in the **Address Expression** dialog box shown in Figure 12.9. Open this dialog box as follows:

- To edit an existing address pair, select the entry under (Address Pairs) and choose **Edit**, or double-click the entry.
- To create a new address pair, select any line in the (Address Pairs) section and choose **Address** in the **Add** box, or double-click the (Address Pairs) line.

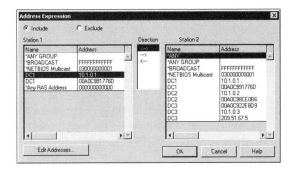

FIGURE 12.9

Filtering on address pairs.

Addresses appearing in the **Address Expression** database are taken from the Address Database. To include a new name or address in an address pair, the name or address must be added to the Address Database. Click **Edit Addresses** to open the **Address Database** dialog box, which is discussed in the section "Creating an Address Database," earlier in the chapter.

You can specify up to three address pairs. Suppose that you wish to display all traffic between the DC1 server and clients, but that you wish to ignore traffic between the DC1 and DC2 servers. The following address pairs establish a filter to accomplish that goal:

```
INCLUDE DC1 <--> ANY
EXCLUDE DC1 <--> DC2
```

Here are some things to remember when specifying address pairs:

- Broadcast and multicast addresses are destination addresses only. They cannot originate frames.

- When multiple address pairs are specified, EXCLUDE statements have priority. If a frame matches an EXCLUDE statement, it will not be captured even though it may also match one or more INCLUDE statements.

- The Windows 2000 Server Network Monitor supports only filters that match frames sent to or from the local server.

Data Pattern Filtering

In some cases, you may wish to filter frames depending whether they include or do not include a specific pattern of bytes. In that case, you must specify one or more entries in the **(Pattern Matches)** section.

To add a pattern criterion to a capture filter, select the **(Pattern Matches)** line and choose **Pattern** in the **Add** box, or double-click **(Pattern Matches)**. This will open the **Pattern Match** dialog box shown in Figure 12.10. Complete the fields as follows:

- **Pattern.** This field defines the sequence of bytes that matches the filter, which can be expressed as a series of hex bytes or as ASCII characters.

- **Hex** and **ASCII.** These radio buttons specify the type of data that is entered in the **Pattern** field.

- **Offset.** The offset specifies the position of the pattern bytes in the frame. The offset can specify the position relative to the beginning of the frame or relative to the end of the topology header. (An offset of 0 specifies the first byte, which is 0 bytes from the beginning of the frame. Therefore, an offset of 19 specifies the 20th byte of the frame.)

- **From Start of Frame.** Select this option if the pattern data can be found in a consistent position with regard to the first byte in the frame.

- **From End of Topology Header.** Specify the offset from the end of the topology header if the topology protocol permits variable length headers, such as Ethernet or token ring MAC frames.

Clearly, to set up filters you must have a thorough understanding of the structures of the frames on your LAN. We have discussed the structures of several frame types in this book, including IP, ICMP, TCP, and UDP. That knowledge, along with some help from Network Monitor, may let you construct the filter you want. Suppose, for example, that you wish to capture only ICMP traffic. ICMP is identified by an IP protocol type of 1, which is placed in the Protocol field of the IP header. If we filter for frames that have the value x01 in the location of the Protocol field we should get only frames with ICMP payloads.

FIGURE 12.10

Entry form for a pattern match filter.

Examination of the IP header reveals that the Protocol field starts on byte 10, resulting in an offset of 9 (x9).

To capture only ICMP packets, define a capture filter with the following properties:

- **Pattern:** 01
- Select **Hex**
- **Offset (in hex):** 9
- Select **From End of Topology Header**

Figure 12.11 shows a **Capture Filter** dialog box that defines a filter using ETYPE, address, and pattern matching criteria.

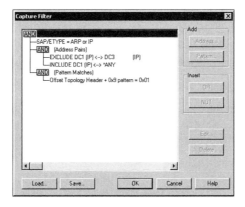

FIGURE 12.11

This capture filter includes ETYPE, address, and pattern matching criteria.

This approach works reliably for fields in IP headers because the first 24 bytes of the IP header have a fixed structure. Also, because IP option fields are seldom used, the offset is fairly reliable for ICMP, TCP, UDP, and other protocols that operate directly above IP. Because variable-length options are used more frequently in TCP, UDP, and other host-to-host protocols, we are less able to take offset values for granted when filtering for upper-layer protocols. In most cases, it is easier to capture packets with little or no filtering and then to use a display filter to reduce the number of packets we need to wade through during analysis.

In any case, capture filtering is useful only when you already know the types of packets you need to examine. If you are diagnosing a network problem of unknown origin, you will more likely capture promiscuously and use display filters as your analysis becomes more focused.

Using Logical Operators

When two or more patterns are entered, you can set up complex filtering criteria using AND, OR, and NOT logical operations. Select the line to receive the logic operator and choose **AND, OR,** or **NOT** in the **Add** box. After you add a logical operator, you can drag the operators and expressions around to construct the logic tree that you require.

The logical operators function as follows:

- An AND branch of the tree will be true if all of the expressions under the AND are true. The AND branch will be false if any of the expressions under the AND are false.
- An OR branch of the tree will be true if any of the expressions under the OR are true. The OR branch will be false if all of the expressions under the OR are false.
- A NOT will be true if the expression under the NOT is false. A NOT will be false if the expression under the NOT is true.

Suppose that you want to capture either TCP or UDP frames exchanged between DC1 and DC3, but wish to exclude frames for ICMP or any other IP protocols. This is easy to accomplish using an OR operator, as shown in Figure 12.12. This filter has the following properties:

- The SAP/ETYPE condition matches only IP packets.
- An address pair condition matches frames traveling in either direction between DC1 and 10.1.0.49.
- A pattern matching condition matches frames with the protocol number x06 (TCP) or x11 (UDP).

Only IP frames are allowed by the first rule, ensuring that that the pattern matching conditions will be applied only to IP packets. Once the packet types are limited to IP, it is a simple matter to establish pattern matching conditions for TCP and UDP based on their protocol numbers. The OR operator ensures that the pattern match is true for either TCP or UDP frames.

To add a logical operator to the pattern matching tree, create at least one pattern matching condition. Select a condition that will be located under the operator you wish to add, after which the **OR** and **NOT** buttons are activated. Click **OR** or **NOT** to add the logical operator to the tree.

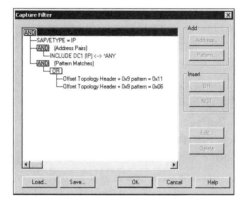

FIGURE 12.12

This capture filter uses logical operators in the pattern matching condition.

> **NOTE**
>
> Pattern matching is the one place in this book where we enter the esoteric realm of boolean algebra. The programmers among you will be comfortable enough, but readers new to boolean logic should be wary when setting up complex filters. It is quite easy to get the logic wrong and to establish filters that misbehave in mysterious ways. If you aren't capturing the frames you want, check the logic in your capture filter.
>
> The Network Monitor capture filtering mechanism is rather limited, and there are filters that simply cannot be implemented. There is no way to design a filter that captures only ARP and ICMP traffic, for example, because filter patterns apply to all packets, not to a specific protocol. Again, display filters are often more useful than capture filters in situations when several protocols must be analyzed.

Saving and Loading Capture Filters

The **Load** and **Save** buttons in the **Capture Filters** dialog box are used to save capture filters and reuse them at a later time. Capture filters are saved in files with the extension .cf.

Using Capture Triggers

On occasion, you may wish to have an action occur when a particular network situation occurs. A *trigger* describes a set of network conditions and an action that takes place when the conditions are met.

To define a capture trigger, choose **Capture→Trigger** to open the **Capture Trigger** dialog box shown in Figure 12.13. The following trigger types can be selected:

- **Nothing.** No triggers are specified. This is the default setting and disables triggers.
- **Pattern Match.** The trigger is initiated when a specified pattern is identified in a captured frame. Specify the pattern in the **Pattern** box in the same manner as you specify a pattern in a capture filter.
- **Buffer Space.** The trigger is initiated when the free buffer space falls below the threshold specified in the **Buffer Space** box.
- **Pattern Match Then Buffer Space.** The trigger is initiated when the pattern specified in the **Pattern** box is identified, followed by a free buffer space that falls below the threshold specified in the **Buffer Space** box.
- **Buffer Space Then Pattern Match.** The trigger is initiated when the free buffer space falls below the threshold specified in the **Buffer Space** box, followed by the detection of a frame that includes the pattern specified in the **Pattern** box.

FIGURE 12.13

Establishing a capture trigger.

CAUTION

Do not combine **Pattern Match Then Buffer Space** with **Buffer Space 100%**. With those options in effect, if the buffer is full when a frame is captured that matches the pattern, Network Monitor begins to count the buffer space when the packet is found, determines that the buffer is full, and overwrites the frame that was captured.

When the trigger occurs, one of three events can take place, as specified in the **Trigger Action** box:

- **Audible Signal Only.** An alarm is sounded, but no other action is taken.

- **Stop Capture.** Capturing will halt when the trigger occurs. This option ensures that the frame that initiated the trigger will remain in the capture buffer.

- **Execute Command Line.** The command specified will be executed when the trigger occurs. Include the path and command to be executed.

TIP

The option of executing a command can be used in a variety of ways. Among the most useful is to execute a script that sends a message to an administrator's alphanumeric pager. The Windows Scripting Host can execute scripts written in Visual Basic Script, VBScript, or Jscript.

Programming of these scripts is, of course, beyond the scope of this book, but Windows 2000 Server includes four help files that serve to introduce you to the technologies. The following files are included on the installation CD-ROM in the folder \VALUEADD\MSFT\XTRADOCS\SCRIPT:

- "Jscript Language Reference" (JSCRIPT5.CHM)
- "Introducing Windows Script Components" (SCPLT.CHM)
- "VBScript Language Reference" (VBSCRIPT5.CHM)
- "Windows Script Host Reference" (WSH.CHM)

Simply copy these files to a convenient location and execute them to view their contents.

Saving Capture Data

After you have stopped capturing data, you can save the contents of the capture buffer for later analysis. Use the **Save** command in the **File** menu to save the capture buffer in a file with a .CAP name extension. Load previously saved data with the **Open** command in the **File** menu.

Examining Captured Data

After frames have been captured, you can examine them in considerable detail. To examine captured frames, do one of the following:

- When capturing is active, click the **Stop and View Capture** toolbar button, choose the **Stop and View** option in the **Capture** menu, or press Shift+F11.

- When capturing is stopped, click the **Display Captured Data** toolbar button, choose **Display Captured Data** in the **Capture** menu, or press F12.

Any of these actions opens the Display window shown in Figure 12.14. The figure identifies the features of the Display window, including the three panes that display captured frames. At first, this window includes one scrolling pane, the Summary pane, which lists all frames currently in the capture buffer. Double-clicking the Summary pane reveals or hides the other two panes.

The capture consists of a single ping event in which DC2 pinged DC1.pseudo by name. (I filtered out everything else so we could ignore all the Windows 2000 housekeeping traffic.) As you can easily determine from the Description column, the sequence begins with a DNS query to determine the IP address of DC1, together with a response from the DNS server. Next, an ARP request and ARP reply establish the physical address of a DNS server. Finally, a series of four ICMP Echo and Echo Reply messages comprise the ping dialog.

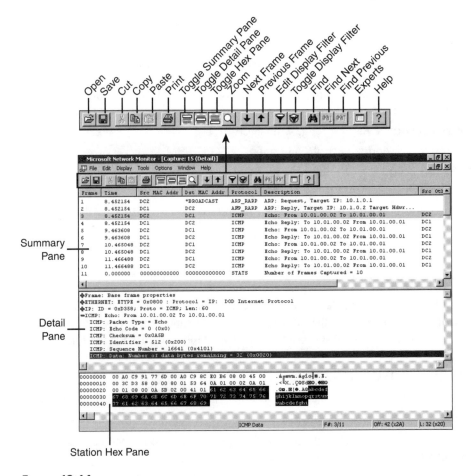

FIGURE 12.14

The Display window showing captured frames.

To examine details for a frame, double-click the frame's description in the Summary pane. In Figure 12.14, an ICMP Echo frame has been opened, revealing two panes in addition to the Summary pane. The panes are as follows:

- **Summary Pane.** This pane includes a one-line summary of each frame in the capture buffer.
- **Detail Pane.** This pane displays the contents of the frame, organized by protocol layer.
- **Hex Pane.** This pane displays the data in the pane in hexadecimal and in ASCII characters. The bytes that are highlighted are associated with the protocol section that is highlighted in the Detail pane.

We examined these panes in some detail in Chapter 2, and I won't repeat information that is presented there. There are a few factoids I'd like to convey to you regarding the Display window, however.

When you select a field in the Detail pane, the legend at the bottom of the window provides some useful information about the field:

- First a brief description of the field is shown.
- `F#`. This box designation specifies the frame's position in the capture buffer. For example, `F# 4/10` designates that this is the fourth of ten frames captured.
- `Off:`. This box specifies the offset of the selected byte from the start of the frame. For example: `Off: 74(x4A)` specifies that the selected byte is offset 74 (decimal) bytes (4A hex) from the first byte of the frame. The first byte of the frame has an offset of 0. (This field is a valuable guide when setting up capture and display filters.)
- `L:`. This box specifies the length of the field in bytes.

The offset and length fields provide information that is useful when defining capture and display filters based on frame contents.

NOTE

In Figure 12.14, I selected the ICMP Data field to highlight the data in the Hex pane. ICMP packets are padded to guarantee a minimum length, and the padding that is used often provides clues to the protocol stack that generated the packet. Windows ping packets, for example, are padded with sequences of letters, as illustrated by the ASCII decodes.

12

MANAGING AND
MONITORING
CONNECTIONS

Display Filters

OK, you've collected a buffer full of frames. On a busy network, the buffer will probably contain lots of frames that don't pertain to the problem you are researching. It would be very useful to have a method of separating the wheat from the chaff so you could focus your attention on just a few without scrolling through the thousands that are available. That problem is easily solved—just design a display filter. Choose **Display→Filter** to open a dialog box where you can design a display filter. Display filters are a bit different from capture filters, so let's take a brief look at the procedure.

Figure 12.15 shows the **Display Filter** dialog box with the default filter, which displays frames for all protocols and computer addresses.

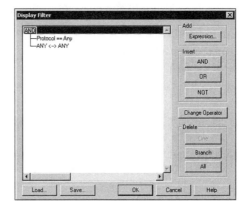

FIGURE 12.15
The default display filter.

Adding Expressions

To add an expression to the display filter, select the line that will precede the new expression and choose **Expression** in the **Add** box to open the **Expression** dialog box shown in Figure 12.16. This dialog box has three tabs, enabling you to enter expressions based on three types of properties: address, protocol, and property. Figure 12.16 shows the **Address** tab.

Address expressions specify the addresses of two computers whose frames are to be captured together with a direction specification. As you select entries for **Station 1**, **Direction**, and **Station 2**, the expression you are constructing is displayed in the Expression box.

The Protocol tab (see Figure 12.17) enables you to enable and disable filters for specific protocols. If a protocol is listed in the **Disabled Properties** list, frames for that protocol will not be displayed. Notice that display filters directly support far more protocols, at more protocol layers, than do capture filters. It is easy, for example, to display all IP frames while suppressing frames for an individual application-layer protocol such as FTP. In Figure 12.17, I've enabled several protocols that might be useful for diagnosing a routing problem.

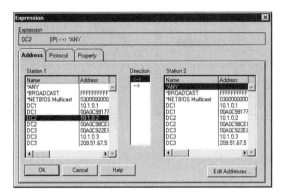

FIGURE 12.16
Constructing an address expression for a display filter.

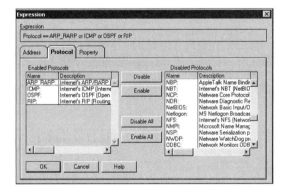

FIGURE 12.17
Constructing a protocol expression for a display filter.

The **Property** tab (see Figure 12.18) is used to construct filters based on data patterns. As you saw, you receive no help when establishing data patterns for capture filters, however, considerable help is available when constructing display filters. Notice how easy it is to establish a property that matches ICMP frames with a message type of 3 (destination unreachable) and a code of 1 (host unreachable).

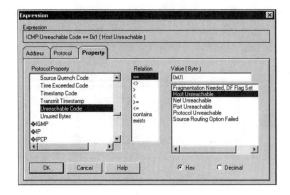

FIGURE 12.18

The Display Filter Property tab.

Each of the protocols in the **Protocol Property** list can be opened to list the data fields in the protocol header. In Figure 12.19, the IP protocol has been expanded to reveal the fields of an IP datagram header. After selecting Destination Address, a list of valid options is revealed in the **Relation** list. And, while I could have manually entered a hex number in the **Value** field, I was able to select one of the predefined options based on the IP addresses that Network Monitor has learned. After selecting DC2, the IP address was entered for me.

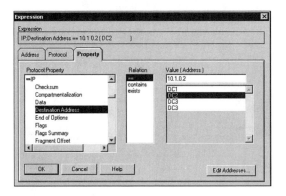

FIGURE 12.19

Constructing a protocol property expression for a display filter.

TIP

It is clearly easier to construct display filters rather than capture filters. You may wish to filter in two stages. So that you don't have unwanted frames cluttering the capture buffer, construct capture filters to limit the general categories of frames that are captured, perhaps sorting by protocol (using SAP or ETYPE filters). Then use display filters to zoom in on the details and isolate specific frames.

Using Logical Operators

You can use AND, OR, and NOT operators to modify the expressions in display filters. To add a logical operator to an expression, select the expression and choose **AND**, **OR**, or **NOT**. The easiest way to organize the structure of the logic tree is to drag expressions and operators around.

> **TIP**
>
> To change a logical operator in a display filter, click the operator icon. The icon will change from AND to OR to NOT with each click.

Monitoring TCP/IP with System Monitor

System Monitor (an updated version of the Windows NT 4.0 Performance Monitor) is a versatile tool that has many uses. It is, therefore, more properly discussed in a general book on Windows 2000 Server administration. This discussion examines the basics of charting statistics in System Monitor, along with some specifics that apply to monitoring TCP/IP objects.

To start System Monitor, select **Performance** in the **Administrative Tools** program group. Then select **System Monitor** in the Performance console object tree. System Monitor starts in chart mode. Figure 12.20 shows System Monitor while monitoring TCP segments sent. It also identifies the buttons in the toolbar.

Before any data are displayed, you need to add one or more chart lines using the following procedure:

1. Click the **Add Counter** button in the toolbar. This opens the **Add Counters** dialog box (see Figure 12.21).

2. Choose **Use local computer counters** to monitor counters on this computer.

   Or

   Choose **Select counters from computer** to monitor counters on another computer that is running the System Monitor console, then specify the UNC name of a computer to be monitored. If desired, you can select a computer from the pull-down list.

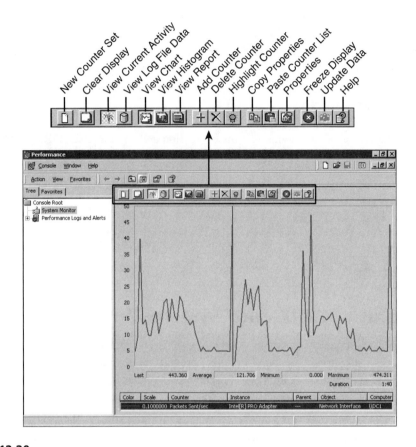

FIGURE 12.20

System Monitor, shown while monitoring TCP segments sent.

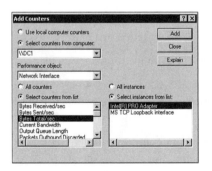

FIGURE 12.21

Specifying parameters for a chart line.

3. In the **Performance object** box, select the object to be monitored. System Monitor includes the following performance objects that relate to monitoring the network, some of which are present only if the associated component is installed:

- DHCP Server
- DNS
- IAS (server and client, authentication and accounting)
- ICMP
- IP
- Network Interface
- RAS (port and total)
- SMTP Server
- TCP
- UDP
- Web Service
- WINS

4. Choose **All counters**, or choose **Select counters from list** to monitor select counters for the performance object.

5. Choose **All instances**, or if the counter you selected has more than one instance (such as two network interface adapters), choose **Select instances from list** if you want to monitor select instances.

6. Choose **Add** to add the line to the chart.

7. Add other lines to the chart as desired.

8. Double-click on the legend for a chart line to edit the line's parameters.

The majority of the available counters should require little explanation. The *Windows 2000 Server Resource Kit* includes an on-disk *Windows 2000 Performance Counters Reference*.

To modify chart properties, right-click anywhere in the chart and choose **Properties** in the context menu. Most properties apply to all chart lines, but individual chart lines can be added, removed, or modified on the **Data** tab.

The Simple Network Management Protocol

A wide variety of activities can fairly be described as "network management." With regard to SNMP, network management means collecting, analyzing, and reporting data about the performance of network components. Data collected by SNMP include performance statistics and other routine reports, as well as alerts that report potential or existing network problems.

SNMP is one of a family of protocols that comprise the Internet network management strategy:

- **SNMP.** The protocol that enables network management stations to communicate with managed devices.
- **MIB.** The *management information base* is the database that stores system management information.
- **SMI.** *Structure and identification of management information* describes how each object looks in the MIB.

Before looking at these protocols, you should understand how an SNMP-based network management system is organized.

Organization of SNMP Management

As Figure 12.22 illustrates, SNMP is organized around two types of devices:

- *Network management stations* serve as central repositories for the collection and analysis of network management data.
- *Managed devices* run an *SNMP agent*, which is a background process that monitors the device and communicates with the network management station. Often, devices that cannot support an SNMP agent can be monitored by a *proxy* device that communicates with the network management station.

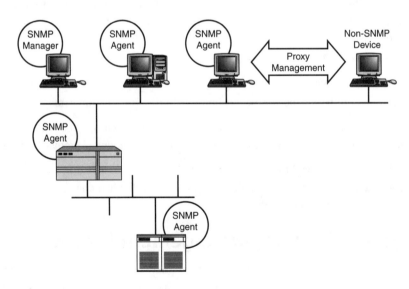

FIGURE 12.22

Organization of an SNMP-managed network.

Information is obtained from managed devices in two ways: polling and interrupts. These methods support different network management goals.

One goal of network management is to maintain a history of network performance that consists of "snapshots" of various characteristics of the network. These snapshots can be used to analyze trends, anticipate future demand, and isolate problems by comparing the current state of the network to prior conditions. The most efficient way to obtain snapshots is to have the management station *poll* managed devices, requesting that they provide the required information. Polling (see Figure 12.23) occurs only at defined intervals, rather than continually, to reduce network traffic. A snapshot of the performance characteristics of a healthy network is called a *baseline*.

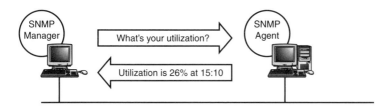

FIGURE 12.23

Polling an agent for information.

Another goal is to quickly notify managers of sudden changes in the network. When operational conditions for a device alter abruptly, waiting for the next poll from the management station is not timely. Managed devices can be configured to send *alerts* (also called *traps*) under predefined conditions. Network managers define thresholds for specific network performance characteristics. When a threshold is exceeded, the agent on a managed device immediately sends a trap to the management station (see Figure 12.24).

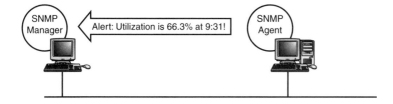

FIGURE 12.24

Network management agent sending a trap.

Essentially, a network management station and an agent can perform the following tasks:

- The network management station can poll agents for network information.
- The network management station can update, add, or remove entries in an agent's database. A router's router tables, for example, might be updated from the management console.
- The network management station can set thresholds for traps.
- The agent on a managed device can send traps to the network management station.

The Management Information Base

An MIB is a set of objects (types of network entities) that are included in the network management database. The MIB specification states the nature of the objects, whereas the SMI describes the appearance of the objects.

Three Internet MIB standards are of general interest:

- **MIB-II (RFC 1213).** The current recommended standard for SNMPv1, defining 10 object groups and 171 objects.
- **SNMPv2-MIB (RFC 1907).** The MIB for SNMP version 2.
- **RMON-MIB (RFC 1757).** The Remote Monitoring MIB is oriented around monitoring network media rather than network devices.

Dozens of other RFCs define MIBs for protocols and types of hardware. Some MIBs are provided by vendors to support unique features of their products.

Experimental MIBs are undergoing trial as they are considered as possible extensions to the MIB standards. MIBs that are proven of value during experimentation can be considered for inclusion in the standard MIB-space.

SNMP Protocol Characteristics

Although SNMPv1 (RFC 1157) was designed for the Internet protocol suite, SNMP is not dependent on the TCP/IP protocols and can operate above a variety of lower-level protocols such as Novell's IPX/SPX. With TCP/IP, SNMP runs over the UDP to reduce network overhead.

SNMP requests are identified by a *community name*, a 32-character, case-sensitive identification that serves somewhat as a password. SNMP implementations may impose limitations on the characters that can appear in community names. Community names serve to identify

SNMP messages but are transmitted as open text and, therefore, are not secure. The three types of community names are as follows:

- **Monitor Community.** This community name grants read access to MIBs and must be included with each MIB query. The default monitor community name is "public."
- **Control Community.** This community name grants read and write access to MIBs.
- **Trap Community.** This community name must accompany trap messages. An SNMP console rejects trap messages that do not match its configured trap community name. The default trap community name is "public."

SNMP entities operate asynchronously. A device need not wait for responses before it can send another message. A response is generated for any message except a trap, but network management stations and managed devices communicate fairly informally.

The current SNMP standard, version 1, can perform four operations:

- **get.** Retrieves a single object from the MIB.
- **get-next.** Traverses tables in the MIB.
- **set.** Manipulates MIB objects.
- **trap.** Reports an alarm.

get, get-next, and set commands originate from the network management station. If a managed device receives the command, a response is generated that is essentially the command message with filled-in blanks.

SNMPv1 has several shortcomings, most particularly in the area of security. SNMP names are sent as clear text, which can be observed by anyone who can observe raw network traffic. SNMPv2 (RFC 1441-1452) is a proposed standard that improves security by encrypting messages. SNMPv2 also improves efficiency, for example, by enabling a management console to retrieve an entire table in one request, rather than record-by-record with get-next.

Network Management Stations

Network management is of little value if the management data is not available for report, analysis, and action. Among the available network management console products are

- Hewlett-Packard OpenView (www.openview.hp.com)
- Sun Microsystems Sun Management Center (www.sun.com/software/sunmanagementcenter/)
- Aprisma (formerly Cabletron) Spectrum (www.aprisma.com)

Functions of the network management station include receiving and responding to traps, maintaining a trap history database, and getting object data from managed devices. More sophisticated—and costly—management consoles provide a graphic interface to the network and can construct a logical picture of the network structure. High-end management consoles generally are costly and require fairly powerful hardware.

> **NOTE**
>
> If you need a less costly SNMP console, visit www.linkanalyst.co.uk and examine their Link Analyst product, which is available for a two-week trial download. Despite its moderate price—around $1,000 depending on the currency conversion rate—Link Analyst does have some glitzy capabilities such as network diagramming and graphic analysis.

Microsoft does not offer a management console comparable to those mentioned above. Several simple utilities are included in the *Windows 2000 Server Resource Kit*. These are rudimentary data collection tools and don't offer the "gee whiz" features of the high-end management consoles. Well, you get what you pay for.

The record-keeping capability of a management console is critical. It enables you to record baseline measurements of the network when it operates normally. These baseline measurements can be used to set thresholds for traps, which alert you to changes in network operation. They also provide a point of comparison that you can use to identify causes of network performance problems.

Configuring SNMP Support on Windows 2000

SNMP support is installed using the **Add/Remove Programs** applet in the Control panel. Under **Add/Remove Windows Components**, install **Simple Network Management Protocol** from the **Management and Monitoring Tools** component group.

Two SNMP services are installed:

- **SNMP Service.** This service includes SNMP agents that collect network information and report it to an SNMP management console.
- **SNMP Trap Service.**

Both services are managed through the **Services** console.

Managing the SNMP Service

To manage the SNMP service, open the **Services** console in the **Administrative Tools** program group or in the **Computer Management** console. Double-click **SNMP Service** in the services list to open the **SNMP Service Properties** dialog box, shown in Figure 12.25. We'll examine the SNMP service properties in the next seven sections.

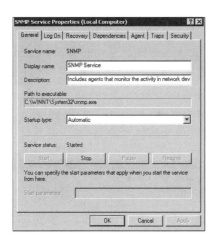

12

FIGURE 12.25
SNMP Service Properties: The General tab.

SNMP Service Properties: The General Tab

The most important functions on the **General** tab have to do with starting and stopping the SNMP service. Similar settings are found on the **General** properties tab for all Windows 2000 services.

- **Startup type.** In this field specify how the service will be started by selecting one of the following options:
    - `Automatic`. The service is started every time Windows 2000 is started.
    - `Manual`. The service must be started manually using the Services console.
    - `Disabled`. The service cannot be started.
- The following buttons can be used to change the state of the service:
    - **Stop.** If the service is started, click this button to stop it.
    - **Start.** If the service is stopped, click this button to start it.

- **Pause.** If the service is started, click this button to pause it. When the service is paused, only members of the Administrators and Server Operators groups can connect with the service.

- **Resume.** If the service is paused, click this button to resume normal operation and enable all authorized users to connect with it.

SNMP Service Properties: The Log On Tab

The **Log On** tab, shown in Figure 12.26, determines how the service will log on to the system. In most cases, services log on using the local System account and do not interact with the desktop. In some cases, it may be desirable to have the service log on using a user account.

Services can also be enabled or disabled for specific hardware profiles. For example, consider a portable computer that connects to the network through a docking station. It would make little sense to start the SNMP service when the computer was undocked.

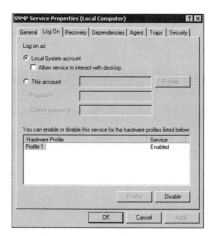

FIGURE 12.26

SNMP Service Properties: The Log On tab.

SNMP Service Properties: The Recovery Tab

The **Recovery** tab, shown in Figure 12.27, determines the steps Windows 2000 is to take should this service fail. A separate action can be defined for the first, second, and subsequent failures. Available actions are

- `Take No Action`. Windows 2000 allows the service to fail without performing any operation in response.

- `Restart the Service`. Windows 2000 attempts to start the service.

- `Run a File`. With this option, Windows 2000 executes a program, script, or batch file that is specified in the **File** field.

- `Reboot the Computer`. This action is seldom warranted except for critical services that are running on dedicated servers. If IIS is the only service running on a computer, a reboot effectively impacts only that service and it makes sense to reboot the server if IIS cannot be restarted. Seldom, however, would it make sense to automatically reboot a computer due to a failure of the SNMP service, which is seldom a critical service.

Other properties on this tab are

- **Reset fail count after.** If a service fails once and the failure does not recur for a significant period of time, it is useful to reset the fail count. Otherwise, three failures in three years could trigger more aggressive failure actions than might normally be warranted.

- **Restart service after.** This field is active only if `Restart the Service` is selected as the action for one of the failure levels. It enables you to configure a delay before restarting the service.

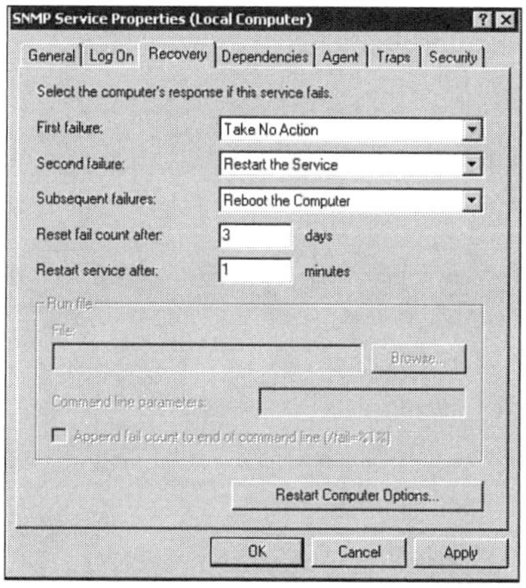

FIGURE 12.27
SNMP Service Properties: The Recovery tab.

SNMP Service Properties: The Dependencies Tab
The **Dependencies** tab lists other services that are required by the service being configured. In the case of the SNMP service, only the Event Log service is required.

SNMP Service Properties: The Agent Tab

The **Agent** tab contains identification, location, and service information that may be requested by an SNMP console. The tab is shown in Figure 12.28 and contains the following fields:

- **Contact.** Specify the name of the person to be contacted for information on this computer. Often this will be a user's email name.

- **Location.** Provide information about the location of this computer. This might be the computer's DNS domain name.

- **Service.** Check the appropriate SNMP service options in the **Service** box. The options are as follows:

    - **Physical.** This computer manages a physical layer TCP/IP device such as a repeater.

    - **Applications.** This computer supports applications that use TCP/IP. This option should be selected for all Windows 2000 computers.

    - **Datalink and subnetwork.** This computer manages a datalink layer device such as a bridge or a subnetwork.

    - **Internet.** This computer manages an internet layer device; that is, it functions as an IP router.

    - **End-to-end.** This computer acts as an IP host. This option should be selected for all Windows 2000 computers.

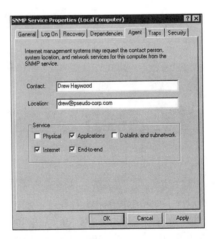

FIGURE 12.28

SNMP Service Properties: The Agent tab.

SNMP Service Properties: The Traps Tab

The SNMP agent can generate trap messages in response to changes such as host system startup, shutdown, or password violation. If this SNMP agent will generate traps, select the **Traps** tab, shown in Figure 12.29. In this tab, use these fields to specify how traps will be generated by this agent:

- **Community name.** Enter the community name that will be included in traps sent by this host. Traps will be accepted only by management stations that are configured with the same community name.

- **Trap destinations.** Add the IP addresses of management stations to which traps will be sent.

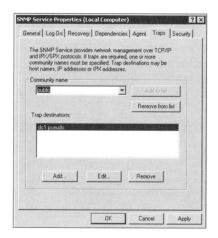

FIGURE 12.29

SNMP Service Properties: The Traps tab.

SNMP Service Properties: The Security Tab

The **Security** tab identifies the community names that are accepted by this host, the host's rights in each community, and the hosts from which this host will accept SNMP packets. The tab is shown in Figure 12.30. Configure fields on the **Security** tab as follows:

- **Send authentication trap.** Check this box to generate traps in the event of authentication failures. This option is enabled by default.

- **Accepted community names.** The agent will identify traps with the community name or names specified here. Only managers that are configured with the same trap community name will receive traps from this agent.

12

Use **Add** to add a community to the list. Each community has the following properties:

- **Community name.** A text string.
- **Rights.** This field specifies the rights this host has when processing SNMP requests with regard to this community. These choices are available:
  - None. This host cannot process any SNMP requests.
  - Notify. This host can send traps to members of the community.
  - Read Only. This host cannot process SNMP set requests.
  - Read Write. This host can process SNMP set requests.
  - Read Create. This host can create new entries in SNMP tables.
- **Accept SNMP packets from any host.** If this option is selected, this host will process SNMP packets from all hosts that use a community name that is specified in **Accepted community names**.
- **Accept SNMP packets from these hosts.** If this option is selected, this host will process SNMP packets only from hosts that are specified in the list. Add the IP address of candidate hosts to the list box.

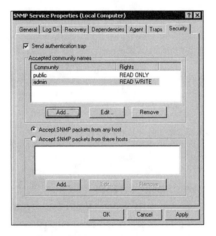

FIGURE 12.30
SNMP Service Properties: The Security tab.

Managing the SNMP Trap Service

To manage the SNMP Trap service, open the **Services** console in the **Administrative Tools** program group or in the **Computer Management** console. Double-click **SNMP Trap Service** in the services list to open the dialog box.

The **SNMP Trap Service Properties** dialog box contains these four tabs: General, Log On, Recovery, and Dependencies. These tabs are essentially identical to the corresponding tabs already examined with regard to the SNMP service and require no discussion. The most likely configuration change you will want to make is to change the **Startup type** on the **General** tab to Automatic.

Troubleshooting Utilities

Microsoft TCP/IP includes several utilities that can be used to troubleshoot the network. Chapter 2 examines **PING** and Chapter 5 examines **IPCONFIG**, but a few useful tools haven't been discussed yet. The tools discussed in this chapter are **ARP**, **TRACERT**, and **NETSTAT**.

ARP

All TCP/IP computers maintain an ARP cache in which are stored the results of recent ARP inquiries. The ARP utility can be used to view and manage the ARP cache. ARP accepts three command options with the following syntaxes, where *ip_address* is an internet IP address, *mac_address* is the physical address of a network interface, and *ip_host_address* is the IP address of the host whose ARP cache is being examined or modified:

```
arp -a ip_address [-N ip_host_address]
arp -d ip_address [ip_host_address]
arp -s ip_address mac_address [ip_host_address]
```

If hosts cannot ping each other, their ARP cache entries could contain incorrect information. To view the ARP cache on a computer, enter the command **arp -a** at a command prompt. The following listing shows the results of an ARP inquiry. If the MAC addresses in the ARP table are incorrect, delete the problematic entries.

```
C:\>arp -a
Interface: 128.1.0.1
  Internet Address      Physical Address      Type
  128.1.1.1             00-00-6e-44-9f-4f      dynamic
  128.1.1.60            00-20-af-8d-62-0e      dynamic
C:\>
```

To restrict ARP to reporting cache entries for a specific IP address, include the address in the command. The following command lists cache entries on the local computer that relate to IP address 128.1.0.60:

```
arp -a 128.1.0.60
```

By default, ARP reports on the cache table for the first network adapter in the computer's configuration. To access other adapters on multihomed hosts you must specify an interface using the -N option (uppercase is required). This command reports cache entries on the second adapter of the host:

```
arp -a -N 128.2.0.1
```

To delete the cache record associated with an IP address, use the -d option. This command removes the entry for host 128.1.0.60 from the cache table for the first network adapter:

```
arp -d 128.1.0.60
```

The cache table for other network adapters can be specified using the -N option.

You can also manually add an entry to the ARP cache. The following example adds a cache entry mapping an IP address to a MAC address:

```
arp -s 128.1.0.60 00-20-af-8d-62-0e
```

As the following listing illustrates, entries added using the **-s** option are regarded as static, in that they are not determined by dynamic ARP inquiries.

```
C:\>arp -a
Interface: 128.1.0.1
  Internet Address      Physical Address      Type
  128.1.1.1             00-00-6e-44-9f-4f      dynamic
  128.1.1.60            00-20-af-8d-62-0e      dynamic
C:\>arp -s 128.1.1.60 00-20-af-8d-62-0e
C:\>arp -a
Interface: 128.1.0.1
  Internet Address      Physical Address      Type
  128.1.1.1             00-00-6e-44-9f-4f      dynamic
  128.1.1.60            00-20-af-8d-62-0e      static
C:\>
```

TRACERT

TRACERT is a route reporting utility that sends ICMP echo requests to an IP address and reports ICMP errors that are returned. Successive attempts are made starting with the Time To Live (TTL) field set to one and incrementing TTL by one with each attempt. Thus, each attempt gets one hop closer to the destination. The result is that TRACERT produces a report that lists all of the routers crossed. Here is an example of a TRACERT report:

```
C:>tracert ftp.microsoft.com
Tracing route to ftp.microsoft.com [198.105.232.1]
over a maximum of 30 hops:
  1    *        *        *       Request timed out.
  2   132 ms   138 ms   144 ms  iq-ind-gw1-en2.iquest.net [198.70.144.10]
  3   176 ms   166 ms   168 ms  border2-hssi1-0.KansasCity.mci.net [204.70.41.5]
  4   316 ms   237 ms   201 ms  core-fddi-1.KansasCity.mci.net [204.70.3.65]
  5   172 ms   176 ms   164 ms  core2-hssi-2.WillowSprings.mci.net [204.70.1.82]
```

```
 6    175 ms    167 ms    167 ms   core1-aip-4.WillowSprings.mci.net [204.70.1.61]
 7    189 ms    188 ms    185 ms   core2-hssi-2.Denver.mci.net [204.70.1.77]
 8    225 ms       *         *     core-hssi-4.Seattle.mci.net [204.70.1.90]
 9       *      224 ms    229 ms   border1-fddi-0.Seattle.mci.net [204.70.2.146]
10    227 ms    220 ms    223 ms   nwnet.Seattle.mci.net [204.70.52.6]
11    239 ms    232 ms    231 ms   seabr1-gw.nwnet.net [192.147.179.5]
12    227 ms    228 ms    229 ms   microsoft-t3-gw.nwnet.net [198.104.192.9]
13    238 ms    236 ms    232 ms   131.107.249.3
14    233 ms    240 ms    237 ms   ftp.microsoft.com  [198.105.232.1]
Trace complete.
```

NETDIAG

NETDIAG is a command-line utility that is included in the Windows 2000 Support Tools, which are described in Chapter 1. NETDIAG performs 24 tests that cover a broad range of network communication processes. Quite a few command-line options can be used with NETDIAG, and I'll let you read about them in the Windows 2000 Support Tools Help file.

Enter the command **NETDIAG** /**HELP** for the command syntax.

For this discussion, I'm simply going to show you what happens when NETDIAG is executed without options. Here is an example of a NETDIAG report:

```
C:>NETDIAG
    Computer Name: DC1
    DNS Host Name: dc1.pseudo
    System info : Windows 2000 Server (Build 2195)
    Processor : x86 Family 6 Model 5 Stepping 2, GenuineIntel
    List of installed hotfixes :
        Q147222


Netcard queries test . . . . . . . : Passed
    [WARNING] The net card 'Intel 8255x-based PCI Ethernet Adapter (10/100)'
➥may not be working.


Per interface results:

    Adapter : Local Area Connection

        Netcard queries test . . . : Failed
        NetCard Status:            DISCONNECTED
            Some tests will be skipped on this interface.

        Host Name. . . . . . . . . : dc1
        Autoconfiguration IP Address : 169.254.176.12
        Subnet Mask. . . . . . . . : 255.255.0.0
```

```
           Default Gateway. . . . . . :
           Dns Servers. . . . . . . . :

      Adapter : 10.1.0.1

           Netcard queries test . . . : Passed

           Host Name. . . . . . . . . : dc1
           IP Address . . . . . . . . : 10.1.0.1
           Subnet Mask. . . . . . . . : 255.255.0.0
           Default Gateway. . . . . . : 10.1.0.3
           NetBIOS over Tcpip . . . . : Disabled
           Dns Servers. . . . . . . . : 10.1.0.1
                                        10.1.0.2

           AutoConfiguration results. . . . . . : Passed

           Default gateway test . . . : Passed

           NetBT name test. . . . . . : Skipped
                NetBT is disabled on this interface. [Test skipped]

           WINS service test. . . . . : Skipped
                NetBT is disabled on this interface.  [Test skipped].

  Global results:

  Domain membership test . . . . . . : Passed

  NetBT transports test. . . . . . . : Passed
       List of NetBt transports currently configured:
           NetBT_Tcpip_{CF04A466-2E40-440B-9415-55B96A856A22}
       1 NetBt transport currently configured.

  Autonet address test . . . . . . . : Passed

  IP loopback ping test. . . . . . . : Passed

  Default gateway test . . . . . . . : Passed

  NetBT name test. . . . . . . . . . : Passed
  [WARNING] You don't have a single interface with the <00> 'WorkStation
  ➥Service', <03> 'Messenger Service', <20> 'WINS' names defined.
```

```
Winsock test . . . . . . . . . . . : Passed

DNS test . . . . . . . . . . . . . : Passed
    PASS - All the DNS entries for DC are registered on DNS server '10.1.0.1'
➥and other DCs also have some of the names registered.
        [WARNING] The DNS entries for this DC cannot be verified right now
➥on DNS server 10.1.0.2, ERROR_TIMEOUT.

Redir and Browser test . . . . . . : Passed
    List of NetBt transports currently bound to the Redir
        NetBT_Tcpip_{CF04A466-2E40-440B-9415-55B96A856A22}
    The redir is bound to 1 NetBt transport.

    List of NetBt transports currently bound to the browser
        NetBT_Tcpip_{CF04A466-2E40-440B-9415-55B96A856A22}
    The browser is bound to 1 NetBt transport.

DC discovery test. . . . . . . . . : Passed

DC list test . . . . . . . . . . . : Passed

Trust relationship test. . . . . . : Skipped

Kerberos test. . . . . . . . . . . : Passed

LDAP test. . . . . . . . . . . . . : Passed

Bindings test. . . . . . . . . . . : Passed

WAN configuration test . . . . . . : Skipped
    No active remote access connections.

Modem diagnostics test . . . . . . : Passed

IP Security test . . . . . . . . . : Passed
    IPSec policy service is active, but no policy is assigned.
```

NETSTAT

The NETSTAT utility reports current TCP/IP connections and protocol statistics. Active Directory computers tend to have a lot of active connections, so I'll just include a portion of a NETSTAT report in the following listing:

C:\>netstat

```
Active Connections
```

```
Proto  Local Address        Foreign Address         State
TCP    dc3:ldap             dc3.pseudo:32350        ESTABLISHED
TCP    dc3:ldap             dc3.pseudo:32377        ESTABLISHED
TCP    dc3:ldap             drew.pseudo:1057        ESTABLISHED
TCP    dc3:ldap             drew.pseudo:1122        TIME_WAIT
TCP    dc3:1026             dc1.pseudo:1610         ESTABLISHED
TCP    dc3:1026             dc3.pseudo:3041         ESTABLISHED
```

NETSTAT reports the following information for each connection:

- `Proto`. The transport prototype with which the connection is established.

- `Local Address`. The name or IP address of the local computer, along with the port number the connection is using.

- `Foreign Address`. The foreign address and the port name or number associated with the connection. Both of the connections shown are NetBIOS resource sharing connections.

- `State`. For TCP connections only, the state of the connection. Possible values are

CLOSED	FIN_WAIT_1	LISTEN	TIMED_WAIT
CLOSE_WAIT	FIN_WAIT_2	SYN_RECEIVED	
ESTABLISHED	LAST_ACK	SYN_SEND	

The syntax of NETSTAT is as follows:

```
netstat [-a] [-e] [-n] [-s] [-p protocol] [-r] [interval]
```

NETSTAT accepts several options that produce enhanced reports:

- `-a`. Displays all connections and listening ports, information not normally reported.

- `-e`. Displays Ethernet statistics. May be combined with the `-s` option.

- `-n`. Displays addresses and ports in numerical rather than name form.

- `-p protocol`. Shows connections for the specified protocol, which may be `tcp` or `udp`. If used with the `-s` option, *protocol* may be `tcp`, `udp`, or `ip`.

- `-r`. Displays routing table data.

- `-s`. Displays statistics separately for each protocol. By default, NETSTAT reports statistics for TCP, UDP, and IP. The `-p` option can be used to display a subset of the three protocols.

- *interval*. Includes an *interval* parameter to have NETSTAT report repeatedly, with *interval* specifying the number of seconds between reports. Press Ctrl+C to stop NETSTAT.

The following listing illustrates use of the -e option:

```
C:\>netstat -e
Interface Statistics
                        Received              Sent
Bytes                    124083             76784
Unicast packets             484               577
Non-unicast packets         195                96
Discards                      0                 0
Errors                        0                 0
Unknown protocols            62
C:\>
```

The -s option reports statistics for the IP, ICMP, TCP, and UDP protocols, as in this example:

```
C:> netstat -s

IP Statistics

  Packets Received                  = 878805
  Received Header Errors            = 0
  Received Address Errors           = 1316
  Datagrams Forwarded               = 0
  Unknown Protocols Received        = 0
  Received Packets Discarded        = 13978
  Received Packets Delivered        = 870498
  Output Requests                   = 846750
  Routing Discards                  = 0
  Discarded Output Packets          = 1740
  Output Packet No Route            = 0
  Reassembly Required               = 0
  Reassembly Successful             = 0
  Reassembly Failures               = 0
  Datagrams Successfully Fragmented = 0
  Datagrams Failing Fragmentation   = 0
  Fragments Created                 = 0

ICMP Statistics

                         Received    Sent
  Messages               12711       21456
  Errors                 0           0
  Destination Unreachable 780        9510
  Time Exceeded          0           0
  Parameter Problems     0           0
  Source Quenches        0           0
  Redirects              0           0
```

12

MANAGING AND
MONITORING
CONNECTIONS

```
Echos                    5859        6087
Echo Replies             6072        5859
Timestamps               0           0
Timestamp Replies        0           0
Address Masks            0           0
Address Mask Replies     0           0

TCP Statistics

  Active Opens                  = 24421
  Passive Opens                 = 23196
  Failed Connection Attempts    = 442
  Reset Connections             = 71
  Current Connections           = 25
  Segments Received             = 804191
  Segments Sent                 = 783219
  Segments Retransmitted        = 946

UDP Statistics

  Datagrams Received    = 42168
  No Ports              = 41242
  Receive Errors        = 0
  Datagrams Sent        = 41124
```

Management. Not Glamorous, but Essential

TCP/IP management is a very complex endeavor and has been the subject of numerous quite substantial books. This and the previous chapters focused on getting you started, but it is quite likely that your network management requirements will go beyond the discussion in this book. You should take the time to examine the various protocol analyzers and SNMP management consoles that are available.

Interoperating with Non-Windows Environments

By Zubair Ahmad

IN THIS CHAPTER

Whether you are planning to migrate to Windows 2000 or simply wish to deploy it in your current environment along with other operating systems, Microsoft has included several services and products in Windows 2000 to make this interoperability easier. UNIX and Novell NetWare have been around for a long time. Businesses that have invested in business applications and services based on these operating systems need to be able to interoperate in a mixed environment, even if they opt to eventually migrate to Windows 2000–based networks. The support for industry standard protocols is noticeable in Windows 2000—protocols such as TCP/IP v4 and v6, Kerberos v5, LDAP v2 and v3, DNS, DHCP, and AppleTalk, to name a few. Compared to Windows NT 4.0, you will find that Windows 2000 is better adapted for interoperating with non-Microsoft networks for two main reasons:

1. Support for industry-wide common standards and protocols
2. A number of services and products offered to integrate Windows 2000 with popular existing network operating systems

Some of the operating systems that Windows 2000 can communicate with are

- HP-UX
- IBM AIX
- Red Hat Linux
- Apple Macintosh
- Novell NetWare
- Sun Solaris

Due to support for LDAP, Windows 2000 can communicate with any LDAP-based services, including Novell NDS, Lotus Notes, Netscape, LDAP-based UNIX directories, and Microsoft's Exchange. In addition, support for database connectivity includes several database platforms such as IBM, Oracle, and Informix.

For performance reasons, it is a good idea to limit the number of protocols to a minimum when you are dealing with multiple protocols. With the addition of each protocol, you need to be mindful of the additional overhead that is associated with it. The effect of the protocol on your network will depend on the type of protocol being used and your network configuration. For example, NetBEUI will have a significant impact in larger environments due to its "chatty" nature but will prove to be very efficient in smaller non-routed networks. When you run services such as GSNW, FPNW, and DSMN (that require IPX/SPX), or services such as File and Print Services for Macintosh (that require AppleTalk), plan your network services carefully to reduce the impact of these additional services.

This chapter will take a closer look at Windows 2000's interoperability tools for UNIX, NetWare, and Macintosh operating systems. Although this book is focused on Windows 2000 network services, for the benefit of readers who have been using Windows NT, we will also mention Windows NT whenever appropriate. Several of the services listed in this chapter also apply to Windows NT.

Interoperating with UNIX

In this section, we will first discuss what Services for UNIX has to offer to a heterogeneous environment that runs a mixture of Windows and UNIX networks. Services for UNIX includes a rather large number of features. We will list all the major features and explain their purpose. There are several requirements that should be met before you begin the installation process. The section on prerequisites includes several tips and gotchas. In addition to the process of installing and removing Services for UNIX, we will examine the password synchronization feature in detail.

Services for UNIX 2.0

Windows 2000 can integrate with UNIX-based operating systems using Services for UNIX 2.0. In my opinion, this is a product that Microsoft should have offered with Windows NT 3.1 in the early '90s. Nonetheless, this valuable service contains several useful integration features, such as a network file system (NFS) server, an NFS client, an NFS gateway, a network information service (NIS) server, an NIS-to-Active Directory migration wizard, a username mapping service, password synchronization, and a personal computer network file system (PCNFS) server. You need to purchase Services for UNIX as an add-on product to Windows 2000.

Services for UNIX offers tools to seamlessly integrate sharing of network resources for end users and the management of administrative tasks for administrators. UNIX and Windows use different directory databases to store network objects, such as users and groups. Furthermore, the rules for storing passwords and user accounts vary considerably. Managing two separate directories is not only time-consuming, it can lead to inconsistencies between the two directories that can either prevent users from properly getting authenticated or deny them access to certain resources. Services for UNIX makes your life easier so the users don't have to remember different account names and passwords to access network resources.

UNIX administrators usually prefer command-line utilities and scripts to manage a UNIX-based network. Windows 2000 administrators primarily use graphical tools to manage their networks, although there are numerous command-line utilities and scripts that are now available to them. With Services for UNIX the administrators can use command-line tools to remotely access a UNIX-based system, centrally manage directory databases on either network, and synchronize passwords for users. The goal for Services for UNIX is to allow users to share data between Windows and UNIX-based networks transparently, regardless of where the users reside. For network administrators, common tools are provided to manage their heterogeneous environments graphically through a Microsoft Management Console (MMC). Scripting tools are also provided to automate repetitive tasks.

Services for UNIX Features

The following is a list of some of the features included in Services for UNIX version 2.0:

Client for NFS

Allows Windows-based clients to access files on UNIX-based NFS servers. Windows clients access UNIX resources transparently as if they were accessing shares on a Windows network.

Server for NFS

Exports Windows folders as NFS file systems so UNIX-based NFS clients can access them.

Gateway for NFS

Acts as a gateway by sharing directories exported by UNIX NFS servers as Windows shares. Windows-based clients can then access these shared directories without installing any NFS client software locally.

Server for NIS

Allows you to administer a UNIX NIS network from a Windows 2000 server by allowing a Windows 2000 domain controller to act as a master NIS server for one or more NIS domains.

Server for PCNFS

Provides PCNFS Daemon services on Windows 2000 so authentication services can be provided for file access to Server for NFS.

Telnet Client

Allows Windows-based computers to use the telnet protocol and connect to a remote computer running Telnet server. You can then either run applications on the Telnet server or administer the remote computer. You can use NTLM authentication for clients provided both computers are running either Windows NT or Windows 2000. NTLM authentication encrypts usernames and passwords.

Telnet Server

Provides terminal sessions to Telnet clients using ANSI, VT-52, VT-100, and VTNT terminals. Both unencrypted (plaintext) and encrypted (NTLM) authentications are supported.

NIS to Active Directory Migration Wizard

This wizard allows you to migrate maps from UNIX-based NIS servers to Active Directory–based servers for NIS. There is a command-line tool called **nis2ad** that performs a similar function. Server for NIS extends the Active Directory Schema during the installation process.

NOTE

You must be logged on as a member of the Schema Admins group before you can install Server for NIS because it extends the Active Directory Schema.

User Name Mapping

Maps UNIX and Windows usernames and groups for Client for NFS, Server for NFS, and Gateway for NFS so that the users can use a single logon to access NFS resources. Usernames and groups do not need to be identical on the two networks before they can be mapped. Username mapping eliminates the need for logging on twice, once to UNIX and then to Windows.

Password Synchronization

Synchronizes UNIX and Windows passwords so users only need to remember one password. Both one-way and two-way password synchronizations are supported. If one-way synchronization is implemented, the UNIX password is synchronized when the Windows password is modified. If two-way synchronization is implemented, changing the password on one system automatically synchronizes the password on the other system.

ActiveState ActivePerl 5.6

Allows you to automate administrative tasks by running Perl scripts natively on Windows 2000.

Services for UNIX Requirements

You can install Services for UNIX on all Windows 2000–based and Windows NT–based computers. However, Windows NT–based computers (servers and workstations) require Service Pack 4 or later. According to Microsoft, the maximum disk space required to install all the components is 60MB (the Services for UNIX Help file claims you need 52MB).

There are several other requirements that you should be aware of. Microsoft documentation states that Services for UNIX requires Internet Explorer 4.01 or later and should not be installed in a folder that has a space in its name. If you use a space when you name the installation folder (for example, UNIX Services), certain UNIX utilities and scripts may fail to run and you may also encounter problems with shortcuts. You must also remove any third-party Telnet servers before installing the Telnet server that comes with Services for UNIX.

If you intend to synchronize domain passwords, Services for UNIX must be installed on a domain controller. If you will be using domain authentication for NFS users, you need to install Server for NFS Authentication on all domain controllers because any domain controller may authenticate the users. If local authentication will be used, install Server for NFS

Authentication on the computer running Server for NFS. If you try to install Client for NFS and gateway for NFS on the same computer, you will be reminded that you can't be a client and a gateway at the same time so you need to choose one or the other.

Services for UNIX supports Terminal Services in Windows 2000 but doesn't support clustering and it doesn't run on Windows 9x. There are a few components that are not supported on Windows NT Workstation and Windows 2000 Professional: Password Synchronization, Server for NIS, Server for NFS Authentication, and Gateway for NFS. If you decide to run some components, such as Server for NFS on Windows NT (SP 4 or later) or Windows 2000 Professional, keep in mind that you are limited to 10 simultaneous inbound connections on these systems. Servers do not have such limitations.

Services for UNIX can interoperate with the following UNIX-based systems:

- Digital Tru64 UNIX 5.0 and later
- HP-UX 10.2 and later
- IBM AIX 4.2 and later
- Red Hat Linux 5.1 and later
- Sun Solaris 2.6 and later

Due to a known bug in the MMC running on Windows NT 4.0 Terminal Server, when you open Help in the Service for UNIX Administration console you may receive an error and the Help index and search tabs may not work. As a workaround, Microsoft suggests you open Help from the Windows Services for UNIX program group. The shortcut is called Help for Services for UNIX.

> **NOTE**
>
> Languages such as Japanese, Chinese, and Korean use a Double-Byte Character Set (DBCS). Services for UNIX doesn't support DBCS for computer names, usernames, hostnames, or domain names. Services for UNIX doesn't support extended-character usernames either.

Installing Services for UNIX

To install Services for UNIX, you should log on as a user who is a member of the Administrators group. You can install Windows Services for UNIX 2.0 from the CD, or as an alternative, copy the files from the CD to the hard disk and then run the setup from the hard disk. The Windows Services for UNIX Setup Wizard guides you through the installation steps. You can choose either a **Standard installation** or **Customized installation** as shown in Figure 13.1.

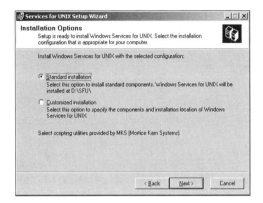

FIGURE 13.1

Installation Options for Services for UNIX.

Depending on the operating system, the Standard installation option installs different components. On a Windows 2000 Professional (or Windows NT 4.0 Workstation), the Standard installation installs Telnet Client, Telnet Server, Client for NFS, and UNIX shell and utilities. On a Windows 2000 server (or Windows NT server), in addition to all the components installed on Windows 2000 Professional, it also installs Server for NFS. On a domain controller, it also installs Server for NFS Authentication. With Customized installation, you get to choose the individual components that you want to install, as shown in Figure 13.2. You can always go back after Services for UNIX is installed and add or remove components as you wish. You do this by going to **Start→Settings→Control Panel→Add/Remove Programs**.

13

INTEROPERATING WITH NON-WINDOWS ENVIRONMENTS

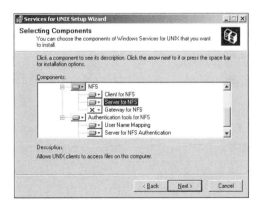

FIGURE 13.2

Customized Installation of Services for UNIX.

Table 13.1 shows a summary of the components that Services for UNIX installs when you opt for a standard installation.

TABLE 13.1   Services for UNIX—Standard Installation

Windows 2000 Professional	Windows 2000 Server	Windows 2000 Domain Controller
Telnet Client	Telnet Client	Telnet Client
Telnet Server	Telnet Server	Telnet Server
Client for NFS	Client for NFS	Client for NFS
UNIX shell & utilities	UNIX shell & utilities	UNIX shell & utilities
	Server for NFS	Server for NFS
		Server for NFS Authentication

If you install Client for NFS, Server for NFS, or Gateway for NFS, the setup wizard will prompt you for a User Name Mapping server, as shown in Figure 13.3. Username mapping lets clients connect to NFS resources with a single logon, both for UNIX and Windows 2000. The usernames do not have to be the same on UNIX and Windows for the name mapping to work.

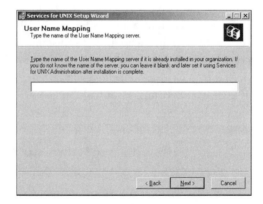

FIGURE 13.3

Specifying a User Name Mapping server.

TIP

It's a good idea to keep a backup of the User Name Mapping database. To back up or restore the database, go to the **Services for UNIX Administration** console, select **User Name Mapping**, and click on the **Map Maintenance** tab. You can back up or restore the database from that screen.

MKS Demoware

Services for UNIX includes a host of migration tools and scripts to make your migration from UNIX to Windows 2000 easier. The free trial version of Mortice Kern Systems (MKS) Toolkit includes about 200 utilities. To install the Demoware, click on **Start→Programs→Windows Services for UNIX→Demoware→Install MKS Demoware from Services for UNIX CD**. When prompted, insert the Services for UNIX CD or provide the path to the source files.

According to the documentation provided with Windows Services for UNIX, the trial version of MKS Demoware is good for 90 days. However, when I installed the trial version of Demoware off of the Microsoft TechNet CD, the dialog box warned me that the trial version is good for 30 days and if I didn't remove the Demoware after 30 days I may lose some functionality of Services for UNIX 2.0 (see Figure 13.4). MKS Toolkit setup prompts you to restart your computer when the setup is complete.

FIGURE 13.4
MKS Demoware dialog box.

13

INTEROPERATING WITH
NON-WINDOWS
ENVIRONMENTS

Password Synchronization

The password synchronization feature provides a mechanism to synchronize Windows domain passwords as well as local passwords for stand-alone computers that are in a workgroup environment. UNIX-based computers can synchronize their passwords on stand-alone computers as well as computers that are members of NIS.

By default, Services for UNIX configures one-way password synchronization where Windows to UNIX passwords are synchronized. You can configure Services for UNIX to support two-way password synchronization by selecting the option **Direction of password synchronization**, as shown in Figure 13.5. Notice the encryption key in the graphic. You can use a different key for encryption as long as you make sure that every UNIX computer that synchronizes passwords with this particular computer has a matching key in the `/etc/sso.conf` file for this computer. For security purposes, it is a good idea to generate a new key for encryption/decryption and update the required entries on the UNIX side. To generate a new key, simply click on **New Key** under **Security configuration**. You will see a new 16-character entry, something like #x@"2&Fj%+50c;1<.

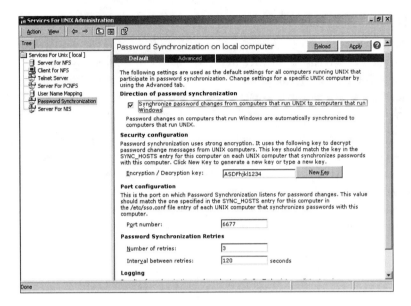

FIGURE 13.5

Password synchronization options.

In order for password synchronization to work, the usernames on both the Windows and UNIX side must be the same—including the case (UNIX names are case sensitive, Windows names are not). In addition, you need to make sure that there are two modules that are installed on UNIX:

1. `Single Sign On Daemon (SSOD)` —Provides Windows-to-UNIX synchronization

2. `Pluggable Authentication Module (PAM_SSO.SO)`—Provides UNIX-to-Windows synchronization

You can configure SSOD (which is available on the Services for UNIX CD) on the UNIX server by configuring the `sso.conf` file on the NIS master server. In the **Services for UNIX Administration** console, shown in Figure 13.5, you can configure several options, including some advanced options for password synchronization. The communication mechanism used for password synchronization between Windows and UNIX computers is TCP/IP sockets. The password synchronization component on the Windows side and the two aforementioned modules on the UNIX side are responsible for encryption, decryption, and synchronization of passwords using triple data encryption standard (triple-DES or 3DES). Triple-DES uses strong encryption keys, making it difficult for hackers to decipher the encrypted packets. Due to the support for a high level of encryption standard like triple-DES, organizations will feel encouraged to implement password synchronization between UNIX and Windows environments.

Services for UNIX comes with several precompiled SSODs. It also includes the source code and make files so even if your version of UNIX is not supported by default, you can do your own compiling on your particular platform. According to Microsoft, the precompiled SSODs included with the Services for UNIX are for the following systems:

- Digital True64 UNIX
- HP-UX 10.3 and later
- IBM AIX 4.3 and later
- Red Hat Linux 5.2 and 6.0
- Sun Solaris 2.6 and later

The PAM_SSO.SO is supported for all the systems listed above except for IBM AIX 4.3 or later.

> **TIP**
>
> You can configure the Windows-to-UNIX password synchronization file (sso.conf) to ignore or force case-sensitive comparisons of usernames. Setting the value of CASE_IGNORE_NAME to 1 ignores comparisons, setting it to 0 (zero) forces comparisons.

Uninstalling Services for UNIX

To uninstall Services for UNIX, go to **Control Panel** and double-click **Add/Remove Programs**. Select **Windows Services for UNIX** from the list of currently installed programs, as shown in Figure 13.6, and then click **Remove**. Select **Remove Services for UNIX** in the **Services for UNIX Wizard**. In the **Services for UNIX** box click **Uninstall**.

FIGURE 13.6

Modifying or uninstalling Services for UNIX.

13

INTEROPERATING WITH NON-WINDOWS ENVIRONMENTS

How Do I Purchase Services for UNIX 2.0?

Windows Services for UNIX version 2.0 is available through retail outlets. The estimated retail price (ERP) is $149.00. It is also available through the MSDN developer program, Microsoft Select, and Microsoft Open Licensing Programs. A limited-time evaluation version is available on the Microsoft TechNet CD. For more information, go to `http://www.microsoft.com/unix/interop/default.asp`.

Interoperating with NetWare

For interoperability with Novell NetWare, Microsoft offers Services for NetWare (SFN) 5.0 as add-on software for Windows 2000. SFN tools are in addition to Gateway Services for NetWare (GSNW), which acts as a gateway to NetWare resources. We will first take a look at GSNW and then SFN.

Gateway Services for NetWare

GSNW allows you to access resources located on a NetWare server. Both Novell Directory Services (NDS) trees and bindery-based servers are supported. GSNW runs only on a Windows 2000 (or Windows NT) server; it doesn't run on Windows 2000 Professional (or Windows NT Workstation). On workstations, you need to run Client Services for NetWare (CSNW). CSNW is a redirector that provides network connectivity to Microsoft clients so they can access resources on a NetWare server. GSNW has all the features of CSNW. In addition to acting as a redirector for Windows server (both NT and 2000), it provides gateway services to Windows clients so they can access resources on NetWare servers without having to install a redirector on the clients.

> **TIP**
>
> While using CSNW, when you run a batch file that makes a call to the command interpreter, start the batch file with **#cmd**, instead of **#command**. For example, if you run a routine in a login script that calls the command interpreter, you should use Windows 2000's command interpreter, **cmd.exe**, instead of the old DOS interpreter, **command.com**.

GSNW service has a limited use because it uses a single account to provide the "pipe" to NetWare. This means that when a Windows server is used as a gateway, only a limited number of users can go through that one account to connect to NetWare resources. How many users? That depends on your network conditions and several other factors. On some networks I have seen consistent problems with even up to ten simultaneous connections. On other networks I have seen dozens of users using one account without any problems. I know of one company that has deployed GSNW successfully for up to 40 users, although they are not all logged in simultaneously. Due to the limitation mentioned earlier, for the most part, GSNW should only be considered a temporary solution and should be used during migration from Novell to Windows 2000.

TIP

Microsoft's client for NetWare doesn't support connecting to NetWare servers using TCP/IP; it only supports IPX/SPX (that is, NWLink). As a workaround, you can use Novell's Client for Windows 2000, which supports TCP/IP. You'll find more on Novell's Client for Windows 2000 later in this chapter in the "Installing MSDSS" section.

The *NWLink IPX/SPX/NetBIOS Compatible Transport Protocol* is required for the operation of services such as GSNW or FPNW. When it comes to configuring NWLink, the concept of frame type and network numbers is important to understand. A *frame type* defines a way that the network card formats the data and places it on the wire. For proper communication between Windows 2000 servers and NetWare servers you should ensure that the frame type matches on Windows 2000 and NetWare servers. The frame types supported by NWLink include 802.2, 802.3, 802.5, and SNAP. You have the option to either configure a frame type automatically or manually. If you configure it automatically and NWLink detects multiple frame types, in addition to 802.2, it defaults to 802.2. If you configure it manually and add multiple frame types, Windows 2000 has the ability to simultaneously use all of them. Whenever you are troubleshooting problems associated with NWLink, it is helpful to verify the frame types.

NWLink uses two types of network numbers for routing: internal and external. This may sound a bit confusing, but Microsoft uses the term *internal network number* to refer to an internal network number and simply *network number* to refer to an external network number. An *internal network number* is a unique 4-byte hexadecimal number on an IPX internetwork that identifies a virtual network inside your Windows 2000 computer. By default, Windows 2000 can automatically detect the internal network number. However, on multihomed computers, manually configuring an internal network number can improve routing between applications because the applications use the virtual network to advertise their location, rather than the physical network. There are certain situations when you must configure a unique internal network number. For example, if your Windows 2000 server is acting as an IPX router or it is running applications that use Service Advertising Protocol (SAP), such as SQL server, you must configure a unique internal network number. Unlike the internal network number, the *network number* is associated with the physical network. All computers on the same network that use a particular frame type must use the same network number. The default network number is

00000000 and you can normally use this default number. However, on a multihomed computer you should assign a network number to each network interface card that is using a given frame type. Windows 2000 Help incorrectly states that the default internal network number is 00000000 and the default network number is automatically detected. Actually, it works the other way around. The internal network number is detected automatically and the network number defaults to 00000000.

To configure a frame type go to **Start→Settings→Network and Dial-up Connections**. Double-click on the network interface card, click on **Properties**, double-click on **NWLink IPX/SPX/NetBIOS Compatible Transport Protocol**, and configure the frame type to either Auto frame type detection, which is the default, or Manual frame type detection. You can also configure the internal network number from the same screen. The option for the external network number is only available when you add a manual frame type. It is referred to as *Network number* in the **Manual Frame Detection** dialog box.

Installing Gateway Services for NetWare

To install GSNW, you need to log on as a member of the Administrators group. GSNW requires NWLink protocol. If NWLink is not installed on your server, GSNW will install it for you. GSNW also installs CSNW for you on the server. In fact, you will notice that during installation the option is now called Gateway (and Client) Services for NetWare. To install GSNW:

1. Go to **Start→Settings→Network and Dial-up Connections**.

2. Right-click on your network interface icon and click **Properties**.

3. On the **General** tab, click **Install**.

4. Select **Client** and click **Add**.

5. Highlight **Gateway (and Client) Services for NetWare** (as shown in Figure 13.7) and click **OK**.

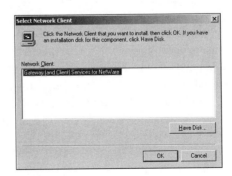

FIGURE 13.7

Installing Gateway Services for NetWare.

You'll need to restart your system to finish the installation process. To verify that the service was installed properly, type `net view /network:nw \\`*`computername`* at the command prompt. You will see a list of NetWare servers if everything was installed properly. After the service is installed, you will find a GSNW icon in Control Panel. You need to configure the services before you can start using it.

Configuring Gateway Services for NetWare

To configure GSNW, go to **Control Panel** and select **GSNW**. In an NDS environment you will configure a Default Tree and Context, otherwise select a **Preferred Server**, as shown in Figure 13.8. You can also configure **Print** and **Login Script** options. To configure the server as a Gateway, click on **Gateway**, click on **Enable Gateway**, enter an account that will be used as a Gateway account, and type in the password. You can then add the shares that point to directories on the NetWare servers so Windows clients can access them through this Windows 2000 server using it as a gateway. There is one thing you must do on the NetWare side as well. Create a NetWare user account (or use an existing account) that will be used as a gateway and make it a member of a group called NTGATEWAY. The account can be named anything but the group must be called NTGATEWAY. Note that this group is created on the NetWare server, not on the Windows 2000 server.

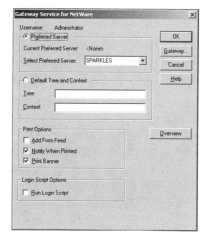

13

FIGURE 13.8

Configuring Gateway Services for NetWare.

Once GSNW has been configured, clients can access shares pointing to NetWare volumes either through My Network Places or at the command prompt. They can also connect to NetWare printers either by using the Add Printer wizard or at the command prompt. Users can change their passwords on both NetWare bindery servers and NDS trees. The access to NetWare resources depends on the permissions assigned to the gateway user account and the NTGATEWAY group on NetWare.

Services for NetWare 5.0

SFN version 5.0 is an add-on product for Windows 2000. It consists of several interoperability components for Novell NetWare environments. These components include

1. File and Print Services for NetWare version 5.0 (FPNW 5.0)
2. File and Print Services for NetWare version 4.0 (FPNW 4.0)
3. Microsoft Directory Synchronization Services (MSDSS)
4. File Migration Utility (FMU)
5. Directory Service Manager for NetWare (DSMN)

FPNW 4.0 and DSMN were also available in the previous versions of SFN. This chapter will primarily focus on Windows 2000 interoperability tools.

File and Print Services for NetWare 5.0

FPNW allows NetWare clients to transparently access file and print resources on a Windows 2000 server. The clients do not require any additional software. The server running FPNW can simultaneously provide file and print services to both Microsoft and NetWare clients.

Is FPNW really NetWare 3.12 Compatible?

The answer to this question depends on who you are talking to. According to Microsoft, the server running FPNW appears to the clients as a NetWare 3.12–compatible file and print server. Novell and Microsoft seem to disagree and Novell has some issues with that. According to the information posted on Novell's Web site, "…FPNW advertises itself as a NetWare 3.12 server but does not emulate a NetWare 3.12 server. It more closely emulates a NetWare 2.2 server." Novell claims that Novell Client for Windows NT doesn't work with Microsoft's FPNW just for that reason. They say, "When the client attaches, it attempts to use features that are available on NetWare 3.12 servers. Since FPNW does not support these features, the client is unable to use FPNW. A fix is available from Microsoft, but Novell testing indicates that the fix still does not provide a complete solution." The quotes are from document #2957853 on Novell's Web site. At the time of writing, the document was last updated on December 5, 2000.

FPNW includes several common utilities that NetWare-enabled clients can use. The list includes utilities to access network resources (map, slist), print resources (capture, endcap), and logon/logoff utilities (attach, chgpass, login, logout, setpass). In addition, the standard Windows 2000 **net user** command-line utility now includes a /fpnw switch. For example, to add a NetWare-enabled user named Chris use the following syntax:

```
net user chris /add /fpnw:yes
```

To disable the account use the switch /fpnw:no.

Installing FPNW 5.0

To install FPNW, right-click **My Network Places**, click on **Properties**, right-click on the network interface card (by default, it is called local area connection) and select **Properties**, click on **Install**, select **Service**, click **Add**, click **Have Disk** and point to the SFN 5.0 CD, or point to the source files on the hard drive. Select **File and Print Services for NetWare**, as shown in Figure 13.9, and click **OK**. Figure 13.10 shows FPNW installation options that you can configure. You need to restart your computer to complete the installation process.

The setup program creates a Supervisor Account for FPNW and makes it a member of the Administrators group. It also creates an FPNW Service Account and prompts you to enter a password for this account. The FPNW server name must be different than the NetBIOS (or computer name) that is used by Windows. Therefore, by default, the FPNW server name is *computername*_**FPNW**. If you decide to change this name later, you will need to restart the FPNW service.

13

INTEROPERATING WITH
NON-WINDOWS
ENVIRONMENTS

TIP

Windows 2000 supports restarting a service with a single click, as opposed to first stopping the service and then starting it again. To restart a service, go to **Administrative Tools**→**Services**, right-click the service, and select **Restart**.

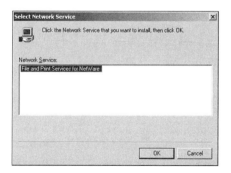

FIGURE 13.9

Installing File and Print Services for NetWare.

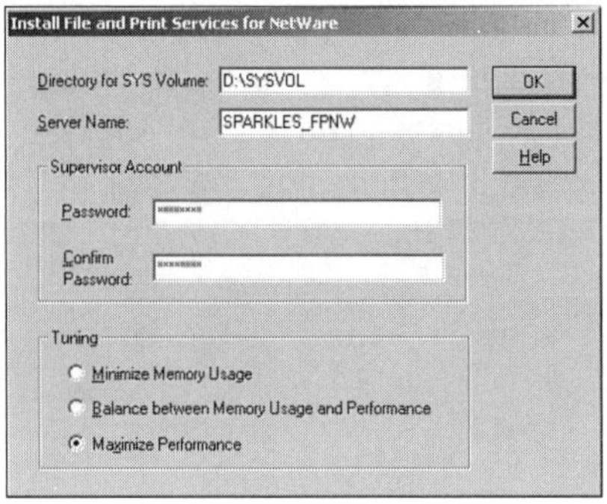

FIGURE 13.10
FPNW installation options.

Configuring FPNW 5.0

To configure FPNW, use the **FPNW** icon in the **Control Panel**. Figure 13.11 shows the main configuration screen for FPNW. Here you can change the FPNW server name and home directory root path, and configure a default print queue. You can also manage users' connections, view information or disconnect users from a shared volume, and manage open files. Specific help on options is available under Help. For more complete information on FPNW and all its features, click on **Overview**.

FIGURE 13.11
Configuring FPNW 5.0.

After FPNW has been configured, you can manage a user's NetWare-compatible login from the Active Directory Users and Computers console. Go to **Start→Programs→Administrative Tools→Active Directory Users and Computers**. Double-click the user's account and select the **NW Compatible** tab, as shown in Figure 13.12. The **Netware compatible password expired** option forces a user to change his or her password the next time he or she logs on from a NetWare client.

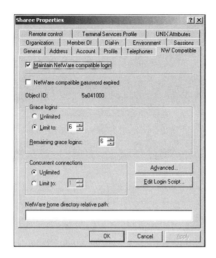

FIGURE 13.12

Maintaining a NetWare-compatible login for a user.

> **TIP**
>
> The Network Providers order determines the order in which the client accesses network resources, as shown in Figure 13.13. You can select the provider and move it up or down to change the order. Depending on your configuration, your system may become painfully slow (especially after you add NetWare or Compatible Network). Simply adjust the order (for example, move Microsoft Windows Network to the top of the order) and you will notice that your system is back to its normal speed.

File and Print Services for NetWare 4.0

FPNW 4.0 offers the same functionality as FPNW 5.0, except for Windows NT 4.0 servers instead of Windows 2000 servers.

Microsoft Directory Synchronization Services

MSDSS allows you to synchronize Active Directory data with Novell's NDS trees and bindery servers. It supports one-way synchronization, where you manage directory resources from Active Directory, and two-way synchronization, where you manage data from either the Windows or Novell side.

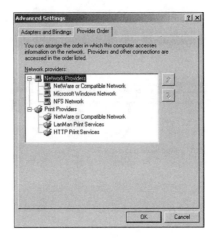

FIGURE 13.13

Adjusting the Network Providers order.

The purpose of MSDSS is to migrate important information from NetWare binderies and NDS to Active Directory. From NDS and binderies, you can migrate objects such as users, groups, and distribution lists. In addition, from NDS, you can also migrate organizations and organizational units (OUs). It is important to note that the permissions on objects are not migrated. Printer objects, application objects, and machine accounts are not migrated. You can use FMU to migrate large volumes of data from NetWare to Windows 2000 while maintaining permissions on objects, as explained in the FMU section.

Installing MSDSS

To install MSDSS you must be logged on as a member of the Schema Admins group because the service extends the schema. By default, only members of the Schema Admins group can modify the schema. Also, you need Novell Client for Windows 2000 before you can install MSDSS on your Windows 2000 server, as Figure 13.14 shows. Novell Client for Windows 2000 is available on Windows 2000 CDs (both Server and Professional) in the \i386\ winntupg\oem\novell folder. Microsoft's Web site has an FAQ that answers questions such as "What is Novell Client for Windows used for?" "What software is shipping with Windows 2000?" and "How do customers benefit from it?" The documentation is available at http://www.microsoft.com/WINDOWS2000/guide/professional/solutions/ netwareinterop.asp.

To install MSDSS, double-click the MSDSS.MSI file in the MSDSS folder on the Services for NetWare CD. The setup wizard will guide you through the installation process. You can select from MSDSS or FPNW from the **Services for NetWare Product Selection** window, as shown in Figure 13.15.

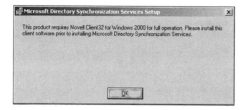

FIGURE 13.14

MSDSS requires Novell Client for Windows 2000.

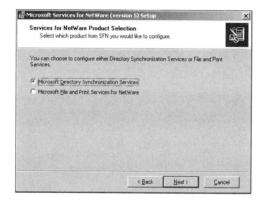

FIGURE 13.15

SFN product selection options.

You can choose either a **Typical** or a **Custom Setup** option. **Custom Setup** lets you customize the installation, as shown in Figure 13.16. As you can see from the screen shot, MSDSS and its subcomponents do not use much disk space.

You will be given a schema update warning, as shown in Figure 13.17. If you recall from our earlier discussion, Server for NIS also requires modification to the schema. Schema modifications are not reversible and must be performed by members of the Schema Admins group.

You will be prompted to restart your computer after the setup process is complete. After the reboot, you will find icons for Directory Synchronization MMC, File Migration Utility, and MSDSS Backup and Restore Utility in **Start→Programs→ Administrative Tools**.

By default, MSDSS backs up the session database every 24 hours at 10:00 p.m. You can modify the schedule by modifying the registry. The Help file explains the procedure and lists all the entries. While the directory synchronization service is running, the session database is locked and can't be backed up. Therefore, MSDSS pauses the synchronization service so the files can be backed up. You can manually back up or restore any time by clicking on **Backup Now** or **Restore Now**, as shown in Figure 13.18.

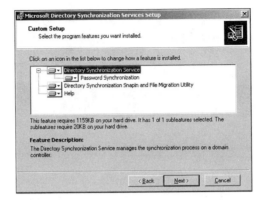

FIGURE 13.16

Custom Setup options.

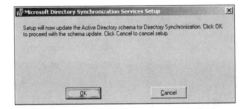

FIGURE 13.17

Schema update warning.

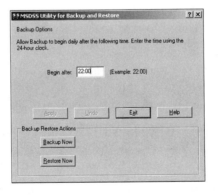

FIGURE 13.18

MSDSS Utility for Backup and Restore.

For more information on deploying MSDSS, you can check out the following white papers on Microsoft's Web site: *MSDSS Deployment: Implementing Synchronization and Migration* at `http://www.microsoft.com/windows2000/library/planning/interop/msdssimp.asp`, and *MSDSS Deployment: Understanding Synchronization and Migration* at `http://www.microsoft.com/windows2000/library/planning/interop/msdssund.asp`.

File Migration Utility

FMU lets you move large volumes of data from Novell NetWare servers to Windows 2000. This is accomplished without compromising directory structure or file permissions associated with that data. FMU is a component of MSDSS and can be installed or removed using the **Custom Setup** option, as shown in Figure 13.16.

FMU supports what are known as one-to-many and many-to-many copying capabilities. You can copy files from one NetWare server to one or many Windows 2000 servers, known as one-to-many capability. Or, you may copy files from several NetWare servers to several Windows 2000 servers, known as many-to-many capability. FMU supports IP as well as IPX and works with most popular NetWare versions. While it is possible for you to use other utilities or mechanisms to copy large amounts of data, the nice thing about using FMU is that it preserves security permissions on objects.

You configure FMU by running a wizard from **Start→Programs→Administrative Tools→File Migration Utility**. The Migration Log Selection in step 1 lets you use an MSDSS migration log that maps NDS users, groups, OUs, and organizations to their corresponding Active Directory objects. The wizard walks you through a total of six different steps, as shown in Figure 13.19. The six steps are described below.

- **Step 1—Mappings:** Here you specify a migration log that contains information about mapping NDS objects to Active Directory objects.
- **Step 2—Security Accounts:** Lets you verify your NetWare connections and NDS context. This step is optional.
- **Step 3—Source and Target:** Allows you to select NDS or Bindery volume that you want to migrate to a Windows 2000 share.
- **Step 4—Log File:** Lets you select a filename for logging events. It also allows you to customize the logging options. This step is optional.
- **Step 5—Scan:** Scanning lets you verify that your source and target objects are valid and that there is enough disk space available on the target drives.
- **Step 6—Migrate:** Once all the other steps are complete, this tab lets you start the actual migration process.

Notice at the bottom of Figure 13.19 that you may complete these steps in any order you wish before starting the migration process in step 6.

13

INTEROPERATING WITH
NON-WINDOWS
ENVIRONMENTS

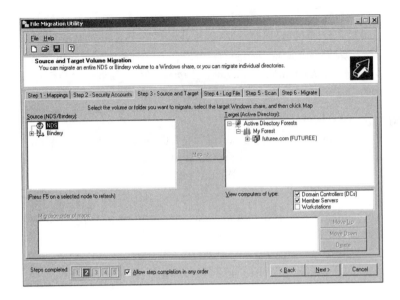

FIGURE 13.19
File Migration Utility wizard.

Directory Service Manager for NetWare

This utility is used to manage NetWare 2.x and 3.x bindery servers from Windows NT 4.0 servers. DSMN allows you to centrally manage NetWare and Windows accounts from one place: Windows NT 4.0 domain controllers. NetWare accounts are copied to Windows NT servers and any changes made to the accounts are propagated back to the NetWare servers.

How Do I Purchase Services for NetWare 5.0?

Services for NetWare version 5.0 is available through Microsoft Authorized Distributors. The estimated retail price is $149.00 with an unlimited client and server license. You can order a limited-time evaluation version online at http://www.microsoft.com/windows2000/guide/ server/solutions/netware.asp. The evaluation version is free but you will have to pay $8.95 plus tax for shipping and handling. The same evaluation version is also available on the Microsoft TechNet CD.

> **NOTE**
>
> All utilities mentioned in this chapter that are used to interoperate with NetWare are installed on Windows 2000–based computers. The only thing that you must do on the NetWare server is create the NTGATEWAY group for configuring GSNW.

Interoperating with Macintosh

What used to be Services for Macintosh in NT 4.0 is now broken down into two separate components:

1. **File Services for Macintosh.** Allows Macintosh users to store files on Windows 2000 servers

2. **Print Services for Macintosh.** Allows Macintosh users to send print jobs to a spooler running on Windows 2000 servers

With support for AppleTalk protocol, Windows 2000 server can also act as an AppleTalk router. Unlike Services for UNIX and Services for NetWare, the support for File and Print Services for Macintosh is integrated in Windows 2000. These services are not provided as add-on products; instead, they are available on the Windows 2000 Server CD. Not to confuse matters, but there is one exception: Print Services for UNIX. These services are included with standard Windows 2000 server so UNIX clients can print to a printer connected to a Windows 2000 server.

File and Print Services for Macintosh

File and print services can be installed independently of each other. To install File and Print Services for Macintosh on your existing Windows 2000 server, use the following steps:

1. Go to **Control Panel**.
2. Double-click on **Add/Remove Programs**.
3. Click on **Add/Remove Windows Components**.
4. From the list of components, select **Other Network File and Print Services**.
5. Click on **Details**.
6. Check the **File** and/or **Print Services for Macintosh** box and click **OK**, as shown in Figure 13.20.
7. Follow the on-screen instructions to finish the installation.

File Services for Macintosh requires an NTFS partition before you can install the service. If the file services and TCP/IP are installed, Apple Filing Protocol (AFP) is automatically installed on your server. If either file or print services are installed, AppleTalk protocol is installed automatically.

After the service has been installed, you can stop or start the service either by using **Administrative Tools**→**Services** or at the command prompt. The instructions to start these services in the Windows Help file are incorrect. Use the following commands to stop or start the services.

13

INTEROPERATING WITH
NON-WINDOWS
ENVIRONMENTS

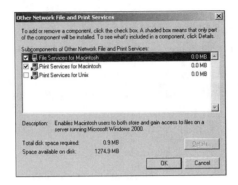

FIGURE 13.20

Installing Services for Macintosh.

For file services:

```
net stop "file server for Macintosh"
net start "file server for Macintosh"
```

For print services:

```
net stop "print server for Macintosh"
net start "print server for Macintosh"
```

> **TIP**
>
> To view all the services that are running on your Windows 2000 server, at the command prompt type **net start** without any parameters. The use of the **|more** parameter is also supported.

Sharing Folders for Macintosh Clients

File Services for Macintosh allows Windows 2000 servers to share folders for Macintosh users. Only members of the Administrators, Server Operators, and Power Users groups can share folders on Windows 2000 servers. This service is not supported on Windows 2000 Professionals or Windows NT Workstations. Macintosh clients must be running the Apple networking protocol to access Macintosh volumes created on Windows 2000 servers.

In Windows NT 4.0, you have several methods available to create SFM volumes. You can use **File Manager, MacFile,** or the **Server** tool. File Manager is not provided with Windows 2000 and SFM volumes can't be created using Explorer in Windows 2000. To manage shared folders, user sessions, and open files, you can use either of the following methods:

1. Go to **Start→Programs→Administrative Tools→Computer Management→System Tools→Shared Folders**, and use the **Shares** folder.

2. Create a custom MMC and add the **Shared Folders** snap-in, as shown in Figure 13.21.

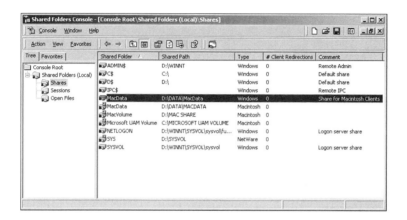

FIGURE 13.21
Managing Macintosh Shares from a Custom Console.

> **NOTE**
>
> Windows 2000 Help incorrectly states that you can use Services and Applications in Computer Management to administer AppleTalk network integration. You won't really find anything for AppleTalk in that area. You need to use the method described below to manage Macintosh volumes. For more details, check out Microsoft's Knowledgebase article Q255958.

To create a share, right-click on **Shares** and select **New File Share**. Figure 13.22 shows that you can create shares for Windows, NetWare, and Macintosh clients. The options available to you depend on the choices you make.

1. If you only select Apple Macintosh, the **Macintosh share name** option is the only option available. Other options are grayed out.

2. If you select only Novell NetWare, the **Share name** option is the only option available. The rest are grayed out.

3. If you select Microsoft Windows, the **Share name** and **Share description** options are available.

FIGURE 13.22
Creating shares for Macintosh users.

For all the options, the **Folder to share** entry must be completed.

The next screen (see Figure 13.23) lets you set share level permissions. By default, everyone has full control permissions at the share level. Keep in mind that these are share level permissions so you should configure file and folder level permissions as well. Notice that the Macintosh and NetWare share icons in Figure 13.21 are a bit different than the Windows share icons.

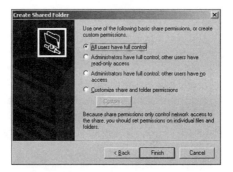

FIGURE 13.23
Setting permissions for Macintosh shares.

To manage a Macintosh volume, simply double-click on the share. You can limit the number of users connecting to the volume and configure a couple of options related to security, as shown in Figure 13.24. The **Security** tab lets you configure NTFS level permissions.

You may have noticed that AppleTalk protocol is available on Windows 2000 Professionals. You cannot use this protocol to share folders or printers for Macintosh clients. As mentioned earlier, for Macintosh file and print sharing you will require a Windows 2000 server. The purpose of AppleTalk protocol on Windows 2000 Professional computers is to provide connectivity to Apple printers. You will see an AppleTalk Printing Device option when you add a new printer port. This refers to Apple network printers available on your network.

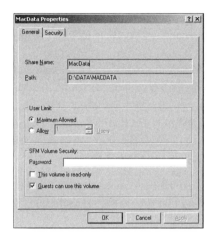

FIGURE 13.24

Managing a Macintosh volume.

Creating Printers for Macintosh Clients

To create a printer for Macintosh clients, go to **Start→Settings→Printers** and double-click on the **Add printer** icon to start the **Add Printer Wizard**. For a printer connected to your Windows 2000 server, select **Local printer**, click **Create a new port** and under **Type** select **AppleTalk Printing Devices**. Select a printer under **AppleTalk zone** and finish the wizard. During setup you can also share the printer with a name that can be up to 32 characters long.

What's in the Name?

When you are reading Microsoft documentation, be aware of the printing terminology that Microsoft uses. A *Printing Device* in Microsoft lingo is the physical hardware that does the printing, for example HP LaserJet 4M. Microsoft defines a *Printer* as "the software interface between the document and the printing device." The term *Printer* refers to the software interface such as Print Manager in older versions of Windows and Printers (located in **Start→Settings**) in Windows 2000. A *Print Queue* is where the documents are waiting to be printed. Microsoft uses this terminology pretty much everywhere—in its Microsoft Official Curriculum (MOC) courses, white papers, and the Windows 2000 Help file.

Windows 2000's Interoperating Solutions

The interoperating solutions that Microsoft offers in Windows 2000 are plenty. These tools include Services for UNIX, Services for NetWare, Gateway Services for NetWare, File and Print Services for Macintosh, and several other utilities covered in this chapter. In addition, Microsoft also provides support for dozens of industry standard protocols such as TCP/IP, Kerberos, LDAP, and DNS. The connectivity tools include solutions for several major non-Windows environments such as UNIX, Novell, and Macintosh. Is there room for improvement? You bet. However, for the most part, the solutions are reliable and do a decent job of integrating Windows 2000 with other operating systems. It seems like Microsoft has taken the task of integration much more seriously in Windows 2000 than it has in the past. The quality and abundance of the products is a testimony to that fact.

Additional Online Resources

There are several resources available online that you may find beneficial. Following is a list of resources on Microsoft's Web site that covers the topics in this chapter in more detail.

- `http://www.microsoft.com/unix/interop/default.asp`

  This is the main page for UNIX interoperability topics. It includes information on Services for UNIX as well as Microsoft Interix 2.2, which is a tool that allows UNIX-based applications and scripts to run on Windows 2000 and Windows NT 4.0.

- `http://www.microsoft.com/TechNet/win2000/sfu.asp`

  An excellent white paper on Microsoft TechNet that covers Services for UNIX 2.0 in great detail.

- `http://www.microsoft.com/windows2000/guide/server/solutions/netware.asp`

  A good overview of Services for NetWare 5.0. It includes descriptions of all the services offered in Services for NetWare 5.0. It also includes information on ordering an evaluation CD online.

- `http://www.microsoft.com/WINDOWS2000/guide/professional/solutions/`
  `netwareinterop.asp`

  A comprehensive document that covers integration of Windows 2000 Professional in a NetWare environment. The focus is on three main areas: Connectivity and Networking, Deployment and Management, and Security. It even includes a valuable FAQ at the end.

- `http://www.microsoft.com/windows2000/library/planning/incremental/`
  `netmigrate.asp`

  This is a NetWare-to-Windows 2000 Server migration planning guide. You can download this 112K document, which is part of Microsoft Windows 2000 technical library.

- `http://www.microsoft.com/windows2000/library/planning/interop/`
  `mdssoverview.asp`

  This document is a technical overview of MSDSS. More specifically, it discusses the
  architecture and technologies of MSDSS, which is part of Services for NetWare 5.0.

- `http://www.microsoft.com/windows2000/library/planning/interop/msdssimp.asp`

  This is a comprehensive deployment planning guide for MSDSS. The focus of this document is on implementing synchronization and migration. You can download this 125K
  document, which is part of Microsoft Windows 2000 technical library.

- `http://www.microsoft.com/windows2000/library/planning/interop/msdssund.asp`

  This white paper is related to the document listed above. It is meant for IT professionals
  and business analysts who may be responsible for architecture, development and design
  of MSDSS. The focus of this document is on understanding synchronization and migration. This is a 108K downloadable white paper.

- `http://www.microsoft.com/mac/default.asp`

  This is the home page for Microsoft products for Macintosh computers. It is called
  MacTopia. Here you will find information on technical support, Mac user groups, downloads, how-to articles, FAQs, and other fun stuff.

INDEX

Other Related Titles

Sams Teach Yourself Network Troubleshooting in 24 Hours
Jonathan Feldman
0-672-31488-6
$19.99 USA/$29.95 CAN

Microsoft Windows 2000 Server Unleashed
Chris Miller; Todd Brown
0-672-31739-7
$49.99 USA/$74.95 CAN

Microsoft Windows 2000 Professional Unleashed
Paul Cassel
0-672-31742-7
$49.99 USA/$74.95 CAN

How to Use Microsoft Windows 2000 Professional
Walter Glenn
0-672-31711-7
$24.99 USA/$37.95 CAN

Sams Teach Yourself Microsoft Windows 2000 Professional in 24 Hours
Dan Gookin
0-672-31701-X
$19.99 USA/$29.95 CAN

Sams Teach Yourself MCSE Networking Essentials in 14 Days
Mark Sportack
0-672-31175-5
$35.00 USA/$49.95 CAN

Sams Teach Yourself TCP/IP Network Administration in 21 Days
Brian Komar
0-672-31250-6
$29.99 USA/$42.95 CAN

Sams Teach Yourself Microsoft Windows 2000 Server in 21 Days
Barry Lewis
0-672-31703-6
$29.99 USA/$44.95 CAN

Peter Norton's Complete Guide to Microsoft Windows 2000 Server
Irfan Chaudhry; Peter Norton; Tom Burke
0-672-31777-X
$29.99 USA/$44.95 CAN

Peter Norton's Complete Guide to Microsoft Windows 2000 Professional
Peter Norton; Richard Mansfield; John Mueller
0-672-31778-8
$39.99 USA/$59.95 CAN

Sams Teach Yourself Networking in 24 Hours, Second Edition
Matt Hayden
0-672-32002-9
$24.99 USA/$37.95 CAN

Sams Teach Yourself Microsoft Windows 2000 Server in 24 Hours
Barrie Sosinsky
0-672-31940-3
$19.99 USA/$29.95 CAN

SAMS

www.samspublishing.com

All prices are subject to change.